Overdependence on AI in Academia

Muhammad Mooneeb Ali
https://orcid.org/0000-0002-0356-320X
Saudi Aramco, Saudi Arabia

Mujtaba Asad
Sukkur IBA University, Pakistan

IGI Global
Scientific Publishing
Publishing Tomorrow's Research Today

Vice President of Editorial	Melissa Wagner
Director of Acquisitions	Mikaela Felty
Director of Book Development	Jocelynn Hessler
Production Manager	Mike Brehm
Cover Design	Jose Rosado

Published in the United States of America by
IGI Global Scientific Publishing
701 East Chocolate Avenue
Hershey, PA, 17033, USA
Tel: 717-533-8845 | Fax: 717-533-7115
Website: https://www.igi-global.com E-mail: cust@igi-global.com

Library of Congress Cataloging-in-Publication Data

Names: Ali, Muhammad Mooneeb editor | Asad, Mujtaba, 1986- editor
Title: Overdependence on AI in academia / Edited by Muhammad Mooneeb Ali, Mujtaba Asad.
Description: Hershey, PA : IGI Global Scientific Publishing, [2026] | Includes bibliographical references and index. | Summary: "This book examines how artificial intelligence is transforming academia-reshaping research, teaching, and publishing-while raising urgent ethical, legal, and regulatory challenges. Bringing together global, multidisciplinary perspectives, it explores how higher education can balance innovation and integrity through responsible, human-centered AI governance"-- Provided by publisher.
Identifiers: LCCN 2025054476 (print) | LCCN 2025054477 (ebook) | ISBN 9798337370972 hardcover | ISBN 9798337370989 paperback | ISBN 9798337370996 ebook
Subjects: LCSH: Artificial intelligence--Educational applications | Education, Higher--Effect of technological innovations on | Education and globalization | Artificial intelligence--Moral and ethical aspects
Classification: LCC LB1028.43 .O94 2026 (print) | LCC LB1028.43 (ebook)
LC record available at https://lccn.loc.gov/2025054476
LC ebook record available at https://lccn.loc.gov/2025054477

British Cataloguing in Publication Data
A Cataloguing in Publication record for this book is available from the British Library.

Table of Contents

Detailed Table of Contents

The inclusion of AI (artificial intelligence) in academic research and instruction has opened new doors for innovation, but has also raised thorny ethical issues and sparked fears of overdependence. In this chapter, we examine AI's complex impacts on higher education, including concerns about algorithmic bias, violations of data privacy, compromised academic integrity, and the devaluation of critical thinking. By means of a thorough review of the current scholarship, which covers new studies ranging from MIT experiments about lower brain activity while using ChatGPT to Stanford research indicating hallucination rates between 69–88% for legal applications, this analysis suggests that there exists a significant negative relationship ($r = -0.68$) between the use of AI tools and critical thinking skills. The chapter focuses on the role of cognitive offloading mechanisms in enabling passive learning behaviors, paying attention to epistemological equality considerations linked to disproportionate access to AI-based technologies.

AI in Education (AIEd) influences education, performance of students, and poses ethical concerns. The research evaluates such frameworks as AI-directed and AI-empowered learning, focusing on the merging of AI with education theories. An important objective is to adopt a human AI approach with the adoption of agentic AI, which will support innovation and tailored practices. Scholars are promoting particular educational systems of ethics, based upon the need of learners and cultures. The position of a teacher is changing, which emphasizes the necessity of ethical AIEd training to promote active involvement. The studies also examine the psychological impacts of AI to users, especially the application designers and consumers, especially on motivation and product usage and how the design of AI aids or thwarts fundamental psychological needs, such as autonomy, competence, and relatedness. The proposed interdisciplinary study is intended to demonstrate all-out impacts of AI in education and inform the use of technology.

This chapter builds a theoretical framework for understanding what happens when learners lean too heavily on AI. The core argument is perhaps uncomfortable because these systems often function more like crutches than training wheels, replacing intellectual effort rather than strengthening it. Drawing from phenomenology, critical pedagogy, and cognitive science, researcher examines how AI shifts learning from direct engagement with ideas toward algorithmic mediation. The analysis maps four overlapping dimensions of overdependence while developing what the researcher calls the "enhancement paradox." Students perform better immediately but something atrophies over time. Through concepts like cognitive offloading and algorithmic authority, this work explores how current AI patterns might undermine authentic learning and genuine agency. At the same time, it suggests principles for more conscious integration. The goal is giving educators conceptual tools for distinguishing enhancement from replacement, preserving the productive struggle that education actually requires.

Generative AI (GAI) is fundamentally altering the academic authorship and research ethics landscape by sourcing multiple long-held beliefs of originality, intellectual labor, and academic accountability. The rise of tools such as ChatGPT, Gemini, and Claude in the writing, analysis, and creation of knowledge creates an urgent need for Higher Education to redefine the meaning of ethical authorship. This paper seeks to examine how Generative AI has changed many of the long-standing academic traditions, highlighting dependence on technology and analyze the inconsistencies in the AI Policies at institutions of higher education worldwide. By utilizing qualitative

style homogenization, our study contributes to ongoing debates concerning hybrid AI-human teaching models by underlining the necessity for ethical integration and instructor scaffolding. The research shows that AWE can help EFL students from beginning to end by repurposing ChatGPT as a co-instructor, allowing more people to have access to academic publishing while maintaining high standards of scholarship.

This chapter examines the phenomenon of educator deskilling as a critical and often overlooked consequence of generative artificial intelligence in higher education. Drawing on labour process theory, critical pedagogy and the sociology of technology, the chapter analyses how AI reshapes assessment, curriculum design, relational work and student cognition in ways that displace professional judgement and weaken pedagogical autonomy. The chapter discusses how over-reliance on automated systems erodes expertise, narrows epistemic horizons and disrupts trust between educators and learners. The chapter argues that these shifts are structural rather than incidental, emerging through the normalisation of hybrid human-AI workflows that reconfigure academic labour. It concludes by suggesting a model of critical human-AI collaboration that preserves the intellectual, relational and ethical foundations of teaching while enabling responsible use of AI within higher education.

This chapter explores the evolving role of professors in higher education as classrooms increasingly lean on artificial intelligence. While AI tools promise efficiency, personalization, and accessibility, they also risk diminishing the professor's central role as mentor, guide, and moral compass. The text reflects on how faculty can reposition themselves not as dispensable transmitters of information but as interpreters of meaning, cultivators of critical thinking, and guardians of academic integrity. It considers the ethical challenges of overreliance on automated systems, including the erosion of intellectual agency and the narrowing of human judgment. The chapter argues that the professor's enduring contribution lies in fostering reflective dialogue, modeling intellectual humility, and guiding students to navigate ambiguity—tasks that no algorithm can fully replicate. In doing so, it calls for a reimagined partnership between human insight and machine intelligence that preserves education's deeper purpose.

Foreword

The rapid evolution of artificial intelligence (AI) has profoundly reshaped the landscape of higher education. While these developments offer unprecedented opportunities for efficiency, accessibility, and innovation, they also raise important questions about academic integrity, intellectual independence, and the evolving role of educators and researchers.

Overdependence on AI in Academia addresses these critical questions with remarkable clarity and depth. This volume brings together a diverse group of scholars who explore the opportunities and risks associated with the increasing integration of AI technologies in teaching, learning, research, and academic governance. The chapters collectively provide a multidisciplinary perspective, drawing insights from fields such as educational technology, digital literacy, ethics, sociology, and higher education policy.

One of the most valuable contributions of this book is its balanced approach. Rather than presenting AI solely as either a threat or a solution, the contributors examine the complex realities of AI adoption in academia. They explore how excessive reliance on AI may undermine essential academic competencies such as critical thinking, independent reasoning, creativity, and ethical judgment. At the same time, they recognize the transformative potential of AI when implemented responsibly and thoughtfully.

As editors, Muhammad Mooneeb Ali and Mujtaba Asad have assembled a comprehensive collection of research that reflects global perspectives on AI in education. The chapters examine issues ranging from ethical governance frameworks and digital literacy training to academic authorship, research methodologies, and the evolving role of professors in AI-enhanced learning environments. Together, these contributions encourage educators, researchers, and policymakers to rethink how AI should be integrated into academic systems while preserving the core values of scholarship.

This book will undoubtedly become an essential reference for educators, administrators, policymakers, and researchers seeking to understand the implications of AI in academia. Its thoughtful analysis and interdisciplinary insights make it a significant contribution to ongoing global discussions about technology, education, and the future of knowledge.

Preface

INTRODUCTION

Artificial intelligence has rapidly transitioned from a specialized research domain to a central component of modern educational systems. Universities across the world are integrating AI technologies into their teaching, research, and administrative practices. Intelligent tutoring systems, automated assessment tools, predictive analytics, and generative AI platforms such as large language models are now widely used to support academic activities. These developments have significantly enhanced the accessibility, efficiency, and personalization of learning environments.

However, the increasing reliance on these technologies has also raised important questions about the long-term implications for academic culture and intellectual development. As AI tools become more capable of performing tasks traditionally associated with human cognition.

The idea for this book emerged from these concerns. While AI offers tremendous potential to improve educational outcomes, it is equally important to examine how overreliance on these technologies might affect the fundamental purposes of education. Universities are not merely institutions for information delivery; they are spaces where intellectual curiosity, ethical reasoning, and scholarly independence are cultivated. Maintaining this balance between technological innovation and human intellectual development is one of the defining challenges of contemporary higher education.

Overdependence on AI in Academia aims to explore this balance by bringing together contributions from scholars across different disciplines and regions. The chapters in this volume examine AI's impact on academic writing, teaching methodologies, research practices, digital literacy, governance frameworks, and institutional policies. Collectively, they provide insights into both the opportunities and the risks associated with the growing presence of AI in higher education.

A key theme throughout the book is the need for human-centered AI integration. Rather than replacing human intellectual effort, AI should be used to augment and support scholarly activities while preserving the fundamental values of academic inquiry. Ethical governance frameworks, digital literacy initiatives, and responsible policy development will play crucial roles in ensuring that AI contributes positively to the academic ecosystem.

This volume is intended for educators, researchers, policymakers, and students who seek a deeper understanding of how AI is transforming academia. By examining both the benefits and the potential dangers of overdependence on AI technologies, the book encourages readers to engage in thoughtful discussions about the future of education in an increasingly automated world.

We hope that this work will contribute to ongoing global conversations about responsible AI integration and inspire further research on maintaining the integrity, creativity, and human spirit that define scholarly life.

CHAPTER OVERVIEW

Chapter 1: The Overdependence of Grok as an AI Tool in English Language Learning

This study examines the perspectives of teachers about learners' excessive dependence on artificial intelligence (AI) tool Grok. As AI-driven tools become increasingly embedded in academic environments, students' heightened reliance on these technologies may undermine essential cognitive capacities, including critical thinking, independent reasoning, and sustained academic engagement. Owing to this, it has become inevitable to explore teachers' perspectives regarding the misuse and overreliance of AI tool; more specifically in an ESL ambiance. For this, the study intended to examine the perspectives of ESL teachers about overreliance of AI by the students. This study adopted a qualitative research design, and surveyed 40 undergraduate teachers in the kingdom of Saudi Arabia. Looppanel an AI tool was applied for extracting the themes and results from the collected data. The results demonstrated that teachers have observed huge reliance of students on AI and they have strong ethical apprehensions about it.

Chapter 2: Building Ethical Governance Frameworks for AI in Higher Education

The rapid adoption of artificial intelligence (AI) in educational institutions has reshaped the pedagogical, administrative, and research environments of higher education institutions worldwide. The 'generative language models', 'automated grading tools', 'predictive analytics', and AI-based institutional 'decision-support systems; have become inseparable parts of academic ecosystems. Although these technologies are potentially yielding unprecedented efficiency, personalization, and innovation benefits, they are also introducing multi-layered ethical dangers, such as algorithmic bias, the decline of human judgment, data privacy, and the increase of digital inequalities. This chapter is a critical discussion of the growing overreliance on AI in academia and argues that ethical governance structures are no longer optional but necessary to protect the integrity, transparency, and trust in academia.

Chapter 3: Artificial Intelligence in Higher Education: Opportunities, Challenges, and Global Perspectives

The rapid evolution of Artificial Intelligence (AI) is transforming the landscape of higher education worldwide. Growing demands on universities, including the need to expand learning, personalise instruction, increase research efficiency, and adapt to international standards, have fuelled AI's entry into higher education. The chapter examines AI's many facets and potential in higher education, covering its uses, consequences, prospects, difficulties, dangers, misconceptions, and disparities worldwide. The goal is to provide educators, researchers, and policymakers with the knowledge they need to capitalise on AI's advantages while preserving educational requirements, integrity, and universal equity in the rapidly changing field of AI-assisted higher education. The scope includes applications of AI in education, administration, and research to assist educators, administrators, and legislators in comprehending how AI is changing instruction, knowledge, investigation, and governance in institutions.

Chapter 4: Discovering Ethical Challenges and Overdependence on AI in Academic Research and Teaching

The inclusion of AI (artificial intelligence) in academic research and instruction has opened new doors for innovation, but has also raised thorny ethical issues and sparked fears of overdependence. In this chapter, we examine AI's complex impacts on higher education, including concerns about algorithmic bias, violations of data privacy, compromised academic integrity, and the devaluation of critical thinking. By means of a thorough review of the current scholarship, which covers new studies ranging from MIT experiments about lower brain activity while using ChatGPT to Stanford research indicating hallucination rates between 69–88% for legal applications, this analysis suggests that there exists a significant negative relationship ($r = -0.68$) between the use of AI tools and critical thinking skills. The chapter focuses on the role of cognitive offloading mechanisms in enabling passive learning behaviors, paying attention to epistemological equality considerations linked to disproportionate access to AI-based technologies.

Chapter 5: Empowering Learning - Theoretical Foundations of Agentic AI in Education

AI in Education (AIEd) influences education, performance of students, and poses ethical concerns. The research evaluates such frameworks as AI-directed and AI-empowered learning, focusing on the merging of AI with education theories. An important objective is to adopt a human AI approach with the adoption of agentic AI, which will support innovation and tailored practices. Scholars are promoting particular educational systems of ethics, based upon the need of learners and cultures. The position of a teacher is changing, which emphasizes the necessity of ethical AIEd training to promote active involvement. The studies also examine the psychological impacts of AI to users, especially the application designers and consumers, especially on motivation and product usage and how the design of AI aids or thwarts fundamental psychological needs, such as autonomy, competence, and relatedness. The proposed interdisciplinary study is intended to demonstrate all-out impacts of AI in education and inform the use of technology.

Chapter 6: From Digital Assistants to Cognitive Crutches AI Overdependence in Pedagogical Practice

This chapter builds a theoretical framework for understanding what happens when learners lean too heavily on AI. The core argument is perhaps uncomfortable because these systems often function more like crutches than training wheels, replacing intellectual effort rather than strengthening it. Drawing from phenomenology, critical pedagogy, and cognitive science, researcher examines how AI shifts learning from direct engagement with ideas toward algorithmic mediation. The analysis maps four overlapping dimensions of overdependence while developing what the researcher calls the "enhancement paradox." Students perform better immediately but something atrophies over time. Through concepts like cognitive offloading and algorithmic authority, this work explores how current AI patterns might undermine authentic learning and genuine agency. At the same time, it suggests principles for more conscious integration. The goal is giving educators conceptual tools for distinguishing enhancement from replacement, preserving the productive struggle that education actually requires.

Chapter 7: Generative Artificial Intelligence and Academic Integrity: Transforming Authorship and Research Standards

Generative AI (GAI) is fundamentally altering the academic authorship and research ethics landscape by sourcing multiple long-held beliefs of originality, intellectual labor, and academic accountability. The rise of tools such as ChatGPT, Gemini, and Claude in the writing, analysis, and creation of knowledge creates an urgent need for Higher Education to redefine the meaning of ethical authorship. This paper seeks to examine how Generative AI has changed many of the long-standing academic traditions, highlighting dependence on technology and analyze the inconsistencies in the AI Policies at institutions of higher education worldwide. By utilizing qualitative and normative methods from deontological and virtue ethics, this study compares the policies of Harvard University and University of Cambridge and highlights the best practices for responsible use and integration of AI technologies. The chapter will also propose a human-centered, accountable, and transparent AI collaboration model that protects academic integrity while supporting continued technological advancement

Chapter 8: Redefining Teaching, Research, and Academic Governance: The AI Shift in Higher Education

Artificial Intelligence (AI) is reshaping higher education by transforming teaching, research, and governance. This chapter examines the epistemic, ethical, and institutional implications of rapid AI adoption, showing that its influence extends beyond technological efficiency. Using a critical integrative review, it analyzes how AI-driven personalization, automated research processes, and algorithmic decision-making affect academic labor, authority, and equity. It identifies risks such as bias, data surveillance, authorship ambiguity, global inequalities, and dependence on proprietary systems, while also noting the potential of human–AI collaboration to support creativity, access, and informed governance. Drawing on UNESCO and OECD frameworks, the chapter proposes a model for sustainable, inclusive, and ethical AI integration that preserves academic integrity and educational justice.

Chapter 9: Repositioning ChatGPT as Co-Instructors in EFL for Automatic Writing Evaluation (AWE) in Academic Publishing Through CALLEdA Model

The use of AI in EFL writing classes has changed the way students interact with scholarly articles. Contextualization, Awareness, Learning, Linking, Experiencing, Developing, and Assessing (CALLEDA) is the teaching methodology that is being used to situate ChatGPT, Grammarly, and QuillBot as "co-instructors" in this project. This study shown ChatGPT becomes no longer a remedial tool but a pedagogical ally when it is integrated within CALLEDA's programmed phases and accompanied by teachers. To maximize benefits while limiting concerns of overdependence and style homogenization, our study contributes to ongoing debates concerning hybrid AI-human teaching models by underlining the necessity for ethical integration and instructor scaffolding. The research shows that AWE can help EFL students from beginning to end by repurposing ChatGPT as a co-instructor, allowing more people to have access to academic publishing while maintaining high standards of scholarship.

Chapter 10: The false sense of teaching: Educator deskilling in the age of AI

This chapter examines the phenomenon of educator deskilling as a critical and often overlooked consequence of generative artificial intelligence in higher education. Drawing on labour process theory, critical pedagogy and the sociology of technology, the chapter analyses how AI reshapes assessment, curriculum design, relational work and student cognition in ways that displace professional judgement and weaken pedagogical autonomy. The chapter discusses how over-reliance on automated systems erodes expertise, narrows epistemic horizons and disrupts trust between educators and learners. The chapter argues that these shifts are structural rather than incidental, emerging through the normalisation of hybrid human-AI workflows that reconfigure academic labour. It concludes by suggesting a model of critical human-AI collaboration that preserves the intellectual, relational and ethical foundations of teaching while enabling responsible use of AI within higher education.

Chapter 11: The Professor's Role in an AI-Dominated Classroom in Higher Education

This chapter explores the evolving role of professors in higher education as classrooms increasingly lean on artificial intelligence. While AI tools promise efficiency, personalization, and accessibility, they also risk diminishing the professor's central role as mentor, guide, and moral compass. The text reflects on how faculty can reposition themselves not as dispensable transmitters of information but as interpreters of meaning, cultivators of critical thinking, and guardians of academic integrity. It considers the ethical challenges of overreliance on automated systems, including the erosion of intellectual agency and the narrowing of human judgment. The chapter argues that the professor's enduring contribution lies in fostering reflective dialogue, modeling intellectual humility, and guiding students to navigate ambiguity—tasks that no algorithm can fully replicate. In doing so, it calls for a reimagined partnership between human insight and machine intelligence that preserves education's deeper purpose.

Chapter 12: Academic Integrity in the Age of Artificial Intelligence

The rapid rise of generative artificial intelligence (GenAI) has transformed higher education, reshaping how students learn, how faculty assess, and how institutions uphold academic integrity. This chapter examines the complex interplay between GenAI adoption, evolving forms of academic misconduct, and the limitations of traditional integrity frameworks. While GenAI enhances creativity, feedback, accessibility, and instructional efficiency, it also enables new violations such as invisible authorship, AI-generated plagiarism, and overreliance that erodes cognitive autonomy. The chapter synthesizes empirical research, ethical theories, and institutional case studies to analyze misconceptions among students and educators, gaps in policy governance, and emerging AI-aware assessment models. It argues that punitive, detection-driven approaches are insufficient in an AI-rich environment. Instead, fostering ethical literacy, redesigning assessments, implementing transparent AI-use policies, and developing responsible human–AI collaboration are essential.

Acknowledgment

The completion of this edited volume would not have been possible without the support and contributions of many individuals and institutions.

First and foremost, we would like to express our sincere gratitude to all the chapter authors who contributed their research and insights to this book. Their dedication, expertise, and commitment to advancing scholarly discussions on artificial intelligence and higher education have made this volume both comprehensive and intellectually enriching. Each chapter reflects the diverse perspectives and interdisciplinary approaches necessary to understand the complex relationship between AI technologies and academic practice.

We are also grateful to the reviewers and academic colleagues who provided valuable feedback during the development of this project. Their constructive comments and suggestions significantly improved the quality and clarity of the chapters included in this book.

Special appreciation is extended to the academic institutions and research communities that continue to foster discussions on the ethical and responsible integration of artificial intelligence in education. Their commitment to innovation, integrity, and scholarly excellence has been a constant source of inspiration throughout the development of this work.

We would also like to acknowledge the support of our professional networks, collaborators, and colleagues who encouraged and supported this project at various stages. Their encouragement and intellectual engagement helped shape the direction and scope of this volume.

Finally, we would like to extend our heartfelt thanks to our families for their patience, encouragement, and unwavering support. Their understanding and motivation have been invaluable throughout the process of editing and preparing this book.

It is our hope that this volume contributes meaningfully to the ongoing dialogue about artificial intelligence in higher education and encourages responsible, ethical, and human-centered approaches to technological innovation in academia.

Chapter 1
The Overdependence on Grok as an AI Tool in English Language Learning

Muhammad Mooneeb Ali
http://orcid.org/0000-0002-0356-320X
Higher Education Department, Government of the Punjab, Pakistan

Yasir Ahmed Ali
Saudi Aramco, Saudi Arabia

Muhammad Amir Saeed
Dhofar University, Oman

Ahmed Muhammad Alotaibi
King Saud University, Riyadh, Saudi Arabia

ABSTRACT

This study examines the perspectives of teachers about learners' excessive dependence on artificial intelligence (AI) tool Grok. As AI-driven tools become increasingly embedded in academic environments, students' heightened reliance on these technologies may undermine essential cognitive capacities, including critical thinking, independent reasoning, and sustained academic engagement. Owing to this, it has become inevitable to explore teachers' perspectives regarding the misuse and overreliance of AI tool; more specifically in an ESL ambiance. For this, the study intended to examine the perspectives of ESL teachers about overreliance of AI by the students. This study adopted a qualitative research design, and surveyed 40

DOI: 10.4018/979-8-3373-7097-2.ch001

undergraduate teachers in the kingdom of Saudi Arabia. Looppanel an AI tool was applied for extracting the themes and results from the collected data. The results demonstrated that teachers have observed huge reliance of students on AI and they have strong ethical apprehensions about it.

1. INTRODUCTION

The expanding use of artificial intelligence (AI) in educational contexts has prompted increasing scholarly concern regarding its potential unintended consequences for student learning. While AI technologies offer substantial benefits, including personalized learning support and increased instructional efficiency, excessive dependence on these tools may negatively affect core cognitive processes such as critical thinking, decision-making, and problem-solving (Sposato, 2025). This phenomenon, commonly described as "over-reliance or misuse of AI", arises when learners place disproportionate trust in AI-generated outputs, often at the expense of independent reasoning and deeper engagement with learning tasks (Eaton, 2025). In particular, excessive reliance on artificial intelligence (AI) tools can foster a passive learning culture in which students engage superficially with course content, thereby limiting meaningful interaction and language development. AI-generated outputs often lack the nuanced vocabulary, disciplinary specificity, and contextual sensitivity required in English for Second Language learners (ESL) contexts, which may result in inaccuracies or a shallow understanding of subject matter. Overdependence on AI tools can further deprive students of essential learning processes, such as drafting, revising, and critically evaluating their work processes that are fundamental to developing language proficiency and disciplinary expertise. Although AI technologies may support certain aspects of ESL learning, the gradual decline of traditional writing practices, including pen-and-paper activities, raises concerns regarding the development of critical thinking skills and appropriate language use in professional and academic settings. Consequently, there is a clear need for regulatory frameworks that define and control the appropriate use of AI tools in educational contexts. In contrast, responsible AI use in education is grounded in a complementary model that integrates human judgment with technological support. This approach emphasizes the role of ethical governance, institutional oversight, and user awareness in fostering appropriate reliance on AI systems (Camilleri, 2024).

Despite growing scholarly interest in AI-assisted learning, empirical research remains limited on exploring the opinions and observations of teachers about how AI influences language skill development and is overused by the learners inside or outside the classroom for their academic affairs. Also, there is a strong requirement for ethical considerations, particularly in relation to students' over-reliance on AI in ESL learning environments. Addressing this gap, the present study examines the opinions and observations of local ESL teachers in Saudi Arabian ESL courses, with specific attention to writing, vocabulary acquisition, reading comprehension, and problem-solving tasks. The study seeks to determine whether excessive reliance on AI hinders or facilitates learning and to identify strategies that minimize dependency while maximizing pedagogical benefits.

1.1. Research Problem

One of the central mechanisms driving AI over-reliance is students' growing tendency to accept algorithmic outputs without sufficient evaluation. The inadequate scrutiny of AI-generated information can lead to reduced accountability for academic work and an uncritical acceptance of automated recommendations.

1.2. Significance of the Study

The purpose of this study is to collect teachers' perspective and observation about the overdependence of Grok amongst ESL learners. This study is aimed to develop a sense that educational practices must explicitly train students to critically assess AI outputs and compare them with human-generated perspectives to counteract algorithmic bias. Moreover, these perspectives will also aid to develop awareness amongst concern that the widespread availability of AI tools may create implicit normative pressures, encouraging conformity to AI-generated standards and limiting originality, creativity, and independent thought.

This can impact the cognitive and may also influence students' motivational and affective dimensions of learning. Also, the ethical concerns represent another critical dimension of AI over-reliance in educational settings. So, this study can sensitize readers to understand that the excessive dependence on AI tools may normalize practices that compromise academic integrity, including plagiarism and misrepresentation of authorship

2. LITERATURE REVIEW

The integration of technology into education has become increasingly central to pedagogical innovation and instructional reform. Digital tools are now widely recognized as catalysts for transforming learning environments by enhancing access, personalization, and efficiency. However, for meaningful educational transformation to occur, technological adoption must be accompanied by pedagogical practices that promote ethical reasoning, dialogue, and critical reflection. In recent years, concerns have emerged regarding the extensive deployment of artificial intelligence (AI) in academic contexts and its potential adverse effects on students' cognitive development, particularly in the domain of academic writing (Liu et al., 2023). Given that higher education is fundamentally anchored in inquiry-based learning, students must cultivate advanced analytical, evaluative, and decision-making skills to assess information critically and construct reasoned arguments (Salido et al., 2025).

Within English for Second Language learning (ESL) contexts, excessive reliance on AI technologies presents distinctive challenges. Overuse of automated tools may inhibit students' development of professional language competence and critical thinking, both of which are fundamental to ESL learning. While generative AI systems offer valuable opportunities to enhance instructional efficiency and learner support, their misuse may undermine authentic learning processes, particularly in academic writing (Derakhshan & Taghizadeh, 2025). As AI-driven tools increasingly mediate learning tasks, concerns have intensified regarding their implications for students' cognitive engagement, originality, and disciplinary literacy.

AI applications have demonstrated considerable potential in fostering adaptive learning environments that respond to individual learner needs, preferences, and proficiency levels. Such environments aim to optimize learning outcomes by personalizing instructional pathways and feedback mechanisms (Sun, Dou & Yang, 2025). However, the incorporation of AI into higher education institutions has simultaneously introduced complex challenges related to academic integrity. The widespread availability of AI-based writing and problem-solving tools has expanded opportunities for academic misconduct, particularly in online and remote learning contexts. Previous research has consistently documented the detrimental effects of academic dishonesty on students' educational trajectories, professional credibility, and institutional reputation (Nguyen & Tuamsuk, 2025; Lee & Ragupathi, 2025). These findings underscore the urgency of addressing unethical practices such as plagiarism, data manipulation, and contract cheating to preserve the integrity of academic systems (Jiang, 2025; Han Nikou & Yilma Ayele, 2024).

Over the past decade, AI technologies have profoundly reshaped English language teaching and learning through the introduction of intelligent tutoring systems, automated feedback mechanisms, and conversational agents. These tools have attracted growing scholarly attention due to their potential to enhance language acquisition and instructional effectiveness. In ESL contexts, research has explored the use of AI-powered testing systems to improve learners' grammatical competence (Alshehri, 2025), chatbots to expand vocabulary knowledge (Zhang & Huang, 2024), and intelligent applications to support grammar and vocabulary development in Business English courses. Collectively, these studies demonstrate the pedagogical benefits of AI integration, particularly in facilitating individualized practice and immediate feedback.

Engaging students in critical discussions about AI limitations, biases, and ethical considerations has been shown to foster reflective learning and enhance critical decision-making skills (Manousou, 2025). AI-driven platforms, such as conversational agents, can also promote interactive, collaborative, and learner-centered experiences that simulate authentic language use (Kyambad et al., 2025). Furthermore, task-based ESL activities supported by AI technologies enable students to engage with domain-specific content, strengthening disciplinary communication skills and professional literacy. As a core academic outcome, critical thinking encompasses reasoning, evaluation, inference, and creative problem-solving (Biagini, 2025). AI tools can potentially stimulate these processes by encouraging learners to substantiate claims, examine alternative perspectives, and explore multiple solution pathways (Zhou, 2025).

2.1. Automation Bias Theory

Automation Bias Theory explains the tendency of individuals to over-rely on automated systems and to accept their outputs as accurate or authoritative, often without sufficient critical evaluation. First identified in human–computer interaction research, the theory suggests that when decision-making is supported by intelligent systems, users may exhibit errors of commission (following incorrect automated advice) or errors of omission (failing to act because the system does not prompt action).

2.1.1. Overreliance on AI and Diminished Critical Thinking

In educational contexts, automation bias manifests when learners unquestioningly trust AI-generated responses, assuming them to be correct, complete, and superior to their own reasoning. Studies indicate that prolonged exposure to AI tools can weaken learners' critical thinking abilities, as students become less inclined to verify information, analyze alternatives, or engage in independent problem-solving. This tendency is particularly concerning in higher education, where analytical rigor and intellectual autonomy are fundamental learning outcomes.

2.2.2. Automation Bias in ESL Learning Environments

Within ESL settings, automation bias is intensified due to learners' linguistic insecurities and limited language proficiency. Students may perceive AI tools such as Grok as linguistically authoritative, leading them to defer language production, grammar construction, and idea formulation to the system. Consequently, learners may bypass essential cognitive processes required for second language acquisition, including hypothesis testing, error correction, and reflective language use.

2.2.3. Ethical Implications of Automation Bias in Academic Settings

Automation bias also raises ethical concerns related to academic integrity and learner agency. Overdependence on AI tools may blur the boundary between assistance and substitution, resulting in passive learning and unearned academic output. Educators have expressed apprehension that unchecked reliance on AI undermines fairness, originality, and authentic assessment practices. These concerns align with calls for institutional governance frameworks that regulate AI use while preserving educational values.

2.2.4. Teachers' Role in Mitigating Automation Bias

The literature highlights the pivotal role of teachers in counteracting automation bias by fostering critical AI literacy, encouraging reflective engagement with AI outputs, and designing assessments that prioritize process over product. Teachers' perceptions are therefore crucial in understanding how automation bias operates in real classroom settings and how pedagogical interventions can balance AI-assisted productivity with cognitive development.

2.2.5. Relevance of Automation Bias Theory to the Present Study

Grounded in Automation Bias Theory, the present study explores ESL teachers' perspectives on students' excessive dependence on Grok in Saudi Arabian higher education. The theory provides a robust explanatory framework for interpreting teachers' observations of reduced student engagement, ethical apprehensions, and the need for institutional governance mechanisms to ensure responsible AI use in academic environments.

Buçinca et al. (2024) examined automation bias in AI-assisted decision-making and found that users frequently accepted AI-generated recommendations even when they were incorrect. Their findings revealed that authoritative system design and confident AI explanations significantly reduced users' likelihood of verifying information independently. Although the study was conducted within human–computer interaction contexts, its implications are highly relevant to educational settings, where students may perceive AI tools as infallible sources of knowledge. This uncritical trust reflects a core mechanism of automation bias that contributes to overdependence on AI tools.

Extending this perspective to higher education, Clos and Chen (2024) investigated the impact of generative AI use on students' critical thinking abilities. Framed explicitly within Automation Bias Theory, their study demonstrated that students who relied heavily on AI tools exhibited significantly lower critical thinking performance compared to those who engaged in independent problem-solving. Notably, many participants followed AI-generated answers even when contradictory evidence was presented, underscoring how automation bias can suppress analytical reasoning and reflective judgment in academic tasks.

Going on, Zhang and Zhang (2025) viewed the problems of generative AI in higher educational context from learners and teachers' perspective using a textual and scientometrics analyses. They found out that generative AI has a positive influence on learners and teachers and it can enhance the performance and avoid biasness in learning and teaching.

Ethical and pedagogical risks associated with automation bias were further highlighted by Yan et al. (2024), who examined the cognitive and ethical implications of generative AI in higher education. Their study found that students often deferred to AI-generated content even when aware of potential inaccuracies, resulting in passive learning behaviors and compromised academic integrity. Importantly, the authors emphasized the critical role of teachers in mitigating automation bias through guided AI use, critical AI literacy, and institutional policy development an aspect directly relevant to studies examining teachers' perspectives.

Focusing specifically on language learning contexts, Romeo and Conti (2025) investigated automation bias and overreliance on generative AI in academic writing. Their study revealed that ESL learners demonstrated higher levels of automation bias than native speakers, largely due to perceptions of AI as linguistically superior. As a result, students increasingly relied on AI for language production, grammar, and idea generation, leading to reduced self-effort and weakened language development. These findings are particularly pertinent to ESL environments, where active cognitive engagement is essential for second language acquisition.

Collectively, these recent studies provide strong empirical support for Automation Bias Theory as a framework for understanding students' overdependence on AI tools in education. The literature consistently indicates that excessive trust in AI leads to uncritical acceptance, reduced cognitive engagement, and ethical concerns related to academic integrity. However, despite growing attention to student behavior, limited research has explored teachers' perspectives on automation bias, particularly within ESL contexts in Saudi Arabia. Addressing this gap, the present study examines ESL teachers' observations and ethical concerns regarding students' overreliance on the AI tool Grok, contributing context-specific insights to the evolving discourse on responsible AI use in higher education.

3. METHODOLOGY

3.1 Research Design

This study employed a qualitative research design to investigate ESL teachers' perceptions of students' excessive reliance on the artificial intelligence (AI) tool Grok within higher education contexts. A qualitative approach was deemed appropriate, as it enables an in-depth exploration of educators' experiences, beliefs, and interpretations of complex pedagogical and ethical phenomena (Karkoulian, Sayegh & Sayegh, 2025). Given the increasing integration of AI-driven tools into academic environments, this design allowed for nuanced examination of how overreliance on AI may influence learners' cognitive engagement, academic integrity, and language development.

3.2 Population and Sampling

The study targeted undergraduate ESL instructors working in higher education institutions in the Kingdom of Saudi Arabia. A purposive sampling strategy was employed to select 40 ESL teachers who had direct experience with students using the AI tool *Grok* for academic tasks. This sampling method ensured that participants possessed relevant pedagogical insight into AI-assisted learning and its implications for ESL instruction.

Participants represented diverse institutional backgrounds and teaching experience levels, allowing for a broad range of professional perspectives. The focus on university-level instructors was deliberate, as AI tools are most frequently used in tertiary education, where independent learning, academic writing, and ethical accountability are central expectations.

3.3 Research Instrument

Data were collected using a structured open-ended questionnaire designed to elicit detailed reflections on students' use and misuse of the AI tool *Grok*. The instrument was developed following an extensive review of literature on AI in education, academic integrity, and ESL pedagogy. The questionnaire addressed three core dimensions: (1) patterns of student overreliance on AI, (2) perceived effects on learning outcomes and cognitive skills, and (3) ethical and institutional challenges associated with AI use.

To ensure content validity, the instrument was reviewed by a panel of experts specializing in applied linguistics, educational technology, and AI ethics. The questionnaire allowed participants to articulate observations, concerns, and recommendations in their own words, supporting depth and authenticity of responses.

3.4 Data Analysis Technique

Qualitative data were analyzed thematically using *Looppanel*, an AI-assisted qualitative analysis tool. The analysis followed a multi-stage coding process involving data familiarization, initial coding, theme refinement, and interpretation. Repeated coding cycles were conducted to ensure consistency and reliability of emerging themes (Karkoulian, Sayegh & Sayegh, 2025).

Although AI software facilitated theme extraction, all final interpretations were reviewed and validated by the researchers to maintain analytical rigor and prevent algorithmic bias. This hybrid analytical approach ensured that findings were grounded in participants' voices while benefiting from systematic pattern recognition (Kushnir,2025).

3.5 Ethical Considerations

Ethical integrity was rigorously maintained throughout the research process. The study adhered to established ethical standards for educational research (Güneş & Kaban, 2025). Informed consent was obtained from all participants prior to data collection, with assurances regarding voluntary participation and the right to withdraw at any stage without consequence.

Participant anonymity was preserved through data anonymization, and no identifiable information was disclosed. Given the ethical sensitivity surrounding AI surveillance and academic monitoring, particular care was taken to ensure that teachers' responses were treated confidentially. Data were securely stored and managed in accordance with institutional and national data protection regulations.

4. RESULTS

Thematic Analysis of Teachers' Perspectives

Figure 1. Emergent Thematic Analysis: ESL Teachers on Grok Overreliance

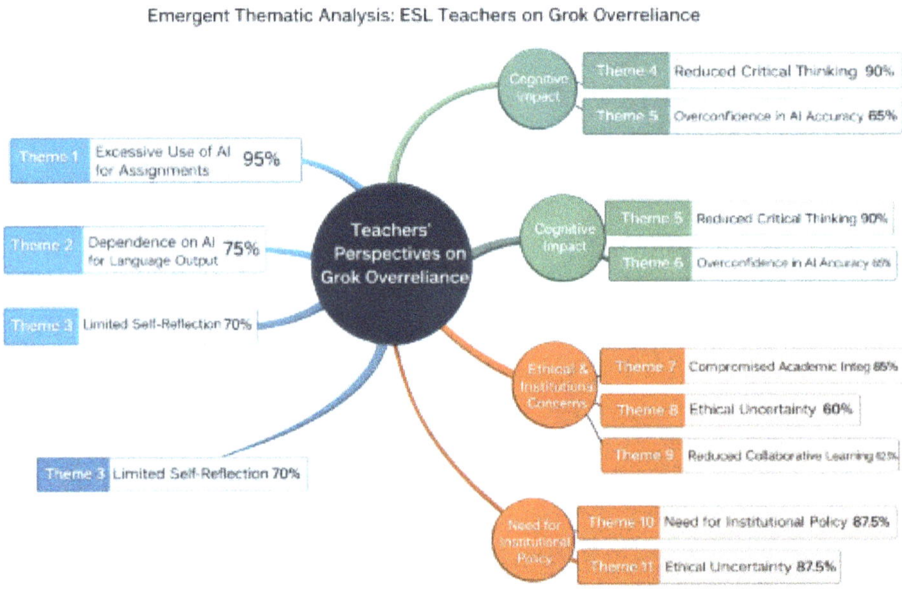

Table 1. Thematic Analysis of Teachers' Perspectives

Theme No.	Theme	Description	Number of Teachers Mentioning Theme (N=40)	Percentage (%)
1	Excessive Use of AI for Assignments	Students frequently use Grok to complete essays, exercises, and homework.	38	95%
2	Reduced Critical Thinking	Overreliance on Grok diminishes students' analytical reasoning and problem-solving skills.	36	90%
3	Compromised Academic Integrity	AI-assisted plagiarism and lack of authorship transparency were reported.	34	85%
4	Diminished Engagement	Students show lower participation in discussions and classroom interaction.	32	80%

continued on following page

Table 1. Continued

Theme No.	Theme	Description	Number of Teachers Mentioning Theme (N=40)	Percentage (%)
5	Dependence on AI for Language Output	Students rely on AI for writing, paraphrasing, and vocabulary, limiting independent language production.	30	75%
6	Limited Self-Reflection	Students do not evaluate or reflect on their work, relying on AI solutions instead.	28	70%
7	Overconfidence in AI Accuracy	Students assume AI outputs are always correct, rarely questioning or verifying results.	26	65%
8	Reduced Collaborative Learning	AI usage reduces peer interaction, discussion, and co-construction of knowledge.	25	62.5%
9	Ethical Uncertainty	Students are unclear about ethical boundaries when using AI for assignments.	24	60%
10	Need for Institutional Policy	Teachers consistently note the lack of governance frameworks for responsible AI usage.	35	87.5%

1. Excessive Use of AI for Assignments (95%)

Teachers reported that students frequently rely on Grok to complete essays, exercises, and homework.

- Teacher 1: "Students submit essays generated entirely by Grok, rarely attempting to write themselves."
- Teacher 7: "Almost all my students use AI for homework; independent effort is minimal."

2. Reduced Critical Thinking (90%)

Overdependence on Grok diminishes students' analytical reasoning and problem-solving skills.

- Teacher 3: "I notice students do not critique AI suggestions they accept everything as correct."
- Teacher 12: "Many cannot form arguments independently because they rely entirely on Grok for ideas."

3. Compromised Academic Integrity (85%)

AI-assisted plagiarism and lack of authorship transparency were recurring concerns.

- Teacher 5: “Some essays are polished but clearly copied from AI; it’s hard to determine authorship.”
- Teacher 19: “There is a growing trend of students submitting AI-generated content as their own work.”

4. Diminished Engagement (80%)

Students show lower participation in discussions and classroom interaction.

- Teacher 9: “Students rarely contribute to group discussions; they assume AI will provide the right answers.”
- Teacher 14: “Engagement has dropped; students wait for Grok outputs instead of sharing ideas.”

5. Dependence on AI for Language Output (75%)

Students rely on AI for writing, paraphrasing, and vocabulary, limiting independent language production.

- Teacher 6: “Many cannot compose even a paragraph without consulting AI first.”
- Teacher 22: “Students struggle with vocabulary and sentence structure if they do not use Grok.”

6. Limited Self-Reflection (70%)

Students rarely evaluate or reflect on their own work, depending on AI solutions.

- Teacher 11: “Students rarely review mistakes; they blindly trust Grok’s suggestions.”
- Teacher 24: “Self-reflection is minimal; they never consider how they could improve independently.”

7. Overconfidence in AI Accuracy (65%)

Students assume AI outputs are always correct and rarely question or verify them.

- Teacher 2: “Students take AI outputs at face value, even when they contain errors.”

- Teacher 16: "There is a false sense of security; students believe Grok is infallible."

8. Reduced Collaborative Learning (62.5%)

AI usage reduces peer interaction, discussion, and co-construction of knowledge.

- Teacher 8: "Group activities are less interactive because students prefer AI over peer collaboration."
- Teacher 21: "Students hesitate to share ideas with classmates when AI can generate answers instantly."

9. Ethical Uncertainty (60%)

Students are unclear about ethical boundaries when using AI for assignments.

- Teacher 4: "Many students do not know what is acceptable in terms of citing AI."
- Teacher 18: "There is confusion about ethical use, which creates inconsistent practices in submissions."

10. Need for Institutional Policy (87.5%)

Teachers consistently noted the lack of governance frameworks for responsible AI usage.

- Teacher 10: "Clear policies are needed to guide responsible AI use in academic work."
- Teacher 25: "Without institutional rules, students are unsure how to ethically integrate AI into assignments."

The findings indicate that while AI tools like Grok provide convenience and efficiency, overdependence poses substantial challenges for writing development, critical thinking, engagement, and ethical literacy. Teachers' perspectives suggest that policy interventions, digital literacy training, and structured AI integration are essential to mitigate negative consequences and harness the potential of AI in language learning.

5. DISCUSSION

The findings of this study underscore ESL teachers' growing concern regarding students' excessive reliance on AI tools, particularly Grok, and its detrimental implications for language learning and academic integrity. Teachers consistently reported that overreliance on AI compromises essential cognitive capacities, including critical thinking, independent reasoning, and sustained engagement. These observations align with Automation Bias Theory, which posits that individuals tend to uncritically trust automated outputs, often at the expense of independent judgment and cognitive effort (Buçinca et al., 2024; Clos & Chen, 2024). The observed erosion of critical thinking reflects a shift from active knowledge construction toward automated content consumption, mirroring patterns identified in recent studies where trust in AI leads to reduced scrutiny of outputs (Yan et al., 2025).

In ESL contexts, where language development depends on iterative practice and cognitive engagement, such reliance poses a substantial pedagogical risk. Teachers reported that students frequently defer cognitive effort to AI, bypassing reflective writing, problem-solving, and language experimentation. These behaviors are consistent with Automation Bias Theory's prediction that users will accept authoritative system outputs even when engagement or reflection is warranted, resulting in cognitive offloading (Zhang and Zhang, 2025). Over time, this pattern can undermine the development of essential analytical and linguistic skills, reducing learners' ability to generate original language structures or self-correct.

Ethical apprehensions were particularly pronounced. Teachers highlighted the ambiguity surrounding acceptable AI use, which has normalized shortcut behaviors and blurred the boundaries between academic assistance and misconduct. Automation Bias provides a theoretical lens for understanding this phenomenon: students may perceive AI outputs as inherently correct, lowering motivation to verify, question, or contextualize responses. These findings reinforce calls for clearer ethical frameworks, AI literacy initiatives, and institutional governance mechanisms to preserve academic integrity (Romeo & Conti, 2025).

Moreover, the findings indicate that excessive AI reliance disrupts the development of self-regulated learning skills. Teachers observed that students often forgo reflection, goal-setting, and revision processes fundamental to effective writing development. From the perspective of Automation Bias Theory, over-trust in AI leads to passive engagement, where students accept outputs at face value rather than actively constructing knowledge.

In sum, the findings provide empirical support for Automation Bias Theory within ESL educational contexts. Students' overreliance on Grok illustrates the cognitive mechanisms predicted by the theory, including uncritical trust, passive engagement, and cognitive offloading. Importantly, the study extends existing research by foregrounding teachers' perspectives, demonstrating that professional oversight, ethical frameworks, and pedagogical scaffolding are crucial for mitigating bias and promoting meaningful learning in AI-integrated classroom

6. CONCLUSION

This study explored ESL teachers' perspectives on students' overreliance on the AI tool Grok in higher education. Findings indicate that excessive AI dependence compromises critical thinking, independent reasoning, and engagement, consistent with Automation Bias Theory. Teachers observed that students often accept AI outputs uncritically, leading to cognitive offloading and reduced linguistic creativity. Ethical concerns were prominent, particularly regarding blurred boundaries between assistance and misconduct. The study highlights that AI itself is not detrimental; rather, lack of institutional governance exacerbates misuse. Overreliance also disrupts self-regulated learning, including reflection, goal-setting, and revision. Teachers emphasized the importance of structured scaffolding, guided practice, and reflective exercises to harness AI's affordances without undermining autonomy. Professional development and AI literacy programs are essential to mitigate bias and promote responsible AI use. Overall, integrating AI as a complementary tool, supported by clear policies and pedagogy, can enhance learning while preserving academic integrity. The study underscores the need for balanced approaches that combine technological innovation with cognitive and ethical safeguards.

REFERENCES

Alshehri, A. (2025). AI's effectiveness in language testing and feedback provision. *Social Sciences & Humanities Open*, *12*, 101892. DOI: 10.1016/j.ssaho.2025.101892

Biagini, G. (2025). Towards an AI-Literate Future: A systematic literature review exploring education, ethics, and applications. *International Journal of Artificial Intelligence in Education*, *35*(4), 1–51. DOI: 10.1007/s40593-025-00466-w

Camilleri, M. A. (2024). Artificial intelligence governance: Ethical considerations and implications for social responsibility. *Expert Systems: International Journal of Knowledge Engineering and Neural Networks*, *41*(7), e13406. DOI: 10.1111/exsy.13406

Clos, J., & Chen, Y. Y. (2024, September). Investigating the impact of generative AI on students and educators: Evidence and insights from the literature. In *Proceedings of the Second International Symposium on Trustworthy Autonomous Systems* (pp. 1-6). DOI: 10.1145/3686038.3686063

Derakhshan, A., & Taghizadeh, M. S. (2025). Does Artificial Intelligence (AI) Nurture or Hinder Language Learners' Higher-Order Thinking Skills (HOTS)? A Phenomenological Study on L2 Learners' Perspectives and Lived Experiences. *International Journal of Applied Linguistics*.

Eaton, S. E. (2025). Global trends in education: Artificial intelligence, postplagiarism, and future-focused learning for 2025 and beyond–2024–2025 Werklund Distinguished Research Lecture. *International Journal for Educational Integrity*, *21*(1), 12. DOI: 10.1007/s40979-025-00187-6

Güneş, A., & Kaban, A. L. (2025). A Delphi study on ethical challenges and ensuring academic integrity regarding AI research in higher education. *Higher Education Quarterly*, *79*(4), e70057. DOI: 10.1111/hequ.70057

Han, S., Nikou, S., & Yilma Ayele, W. (2024). Digital proctoring in higher education: A systematic literature review. *International Journal of Educational Management*, *38*(1), 265–285. DOI: 10.1108/IJEM-12-2022-0522

Jiang, X. (2025). Navigating challenges in social science research: The impact of halo effect and inadequate academic socialization on Chinese young researchers. *Studies in Higher Education*, *50*(1), 64–79. DOI: 10.1080/03075079.2024.2328830

Karkoulian, S., Sayegh, N., & Sayegh, N. (2025). ChatGPT unveiled: Understanding perceptions of academic integrity in higher education-A qualitative approach. *Journal of Academic Ethics*, *23*(3), 1171–1188. DOI: 10.1007/s10805-024-09543-6

Kushnir, I. (2025). Thematic analysis in the area of education: A practical guide. *Cogent Education, 12*(1), 2471645. DOI: 10.1080/2331186X.2025.2471645

Lee, A. M., & Ragupathi, K. (2025). Trust and ethos in academic development: Credibility, identity, and value. *The International Journal for Academic Development, 30*(1), 68–81. DOI: 10.1080/1360144X.2024.2417942

Manousou, E. (2025). Critical Thinking in Distance Education: The Challenges in a Decade (2016–2025) and the Role of Artificial Intelligence. *Education Sciences, 15*(6), 757. DOI: 10.3390/educsci15060757

Nguyen, L. T., & Tuamsuk, K. (2025). Factors influencing researchers' scientific integrity in scholarly publishing: A path analysis approach. *Research Ethics, 21*(3), 384–407. DOI: 10.1177/17470161241257445

Romeo, G., & Conti, D. (2025). Exploring automation bias in human–AI collaboration: A review and implications for explainable AI. *AI & Society*, •••, 1–20.

Salido, A., Syarif, I., Sitepu, M. S., Wana, P. R., Taufika, R., & Melisa, R. (2025). Integrating critical thinking and artificial intelligence in higher education: A bibliometric and systematic review of skills and strategies. *Social Sciences & Humanities Open, 12*, 101924. DOI: 10.1016/j.ssaho.2025.101924

Sposato, M. (2025). A call for caution and evidence–based research on the impact of artificial intelligence in education. *Quality Education for All, 2*(1), 158–170. DOI: 10.1108/QEA-09-2024-0087

Sun, X., Dou, W., & Yang, Y. (2025). The socio-emotional dangers of using artificial intelligence (AI) technologies in second language (L2) education: Unveiling Chinese EFL teachers' perceptions and experiences. *Acta Psychologica, 261*, 105956. DOI: 10.1016/j.actpsy.2025.105956 PMID: 41274003

Yan, L., Pammer-Schindler, V., Mills, C., Nguyen, A., & Gašević, D. (2025). Beyond efficiency: Empirical insights on generative AI's impact on cognition, metacognition and epistemic agency in learning. *British Journal of Educational Technology, 56*(5), 1675–1685. DOI: 10.1111/bjet.70000

Zhang, L., & Zhang, W. (2025). Integrating large language models into project-based learning based on self-determination theory. *Interactive Learning Environments, 33*(5), 3580–3592. DOI: 10.1080/10494820.2024.2446535

Zhang, Z., & Huang, X. (2024). The impact of chatbots based on large language models on second language vocabulary acquisition. *Heliyon, 10*(3), e25370. DOI: 10.1016/j.heliyon.2024.e25370 PMID: 38333802

Zhou, J., Hmelo-Silver, C. E., Ryan, Z., Stiso, C., Murphy, D., Danish, J., Chinn, C. A., & Duncan, R. G. (2025). Disagreeing softly: Supporting students in managing disagreement in peer critique: Disagreeing softly: Supporting students in managing disagreement in peer critique. *International Journal of Computer-Supported Collaborative Learning*, *20*(2), 249–282. DOI: 10.1007/s11412-024-09438-z

Chapter 2
Building Ethical Governance Frameworks for AI in Higher Education

Salman Bashir Memon
http://orcid.org/0000-0002-4533-4923
Shaheed Benazir Bhutto University, Pakistan

Saadia Bashir Memon
http://orcid.org/0009-0000-2849-3511
Shaheed Benazir Bhutto University, Pakistan

Sapna Shah
Shaheed Benazir Bhutto University, Pakistan

ABSTRACT

The rapid adoption of artificial intelligence (AI) in educational institutions has reshaped the pedagogical, administrative, and research environments of higher education institutions worldwide. The 'generative language models', 'automated grading tools', 'predictive analytics', and AI-based institutional 'decision-support systems; have become inseparable parts of academic ecosystems. Although these technologies are potentially yielding unprecedented efficiency, personalization, and innovation benefits, they are also introducing multi-layered ethical dangers, such as algorithmic bias, the decline of human judgment, data privacy, and the increase of digital inequalities. This chapter is a critical discussion of the growing overreliance on AI in academia and argues that ethical governance structures are no longer optional but necessary to protect the integrity, transparency, and trust in academia.

DOI: 10.4018/979-8-3373-7097-2.ch002

1. INTRODUCTION: THE RISE OF AI AND THE NEED FOR ETHICAL GOVERNANCE

1.1 Contextual Background: AI in the Academic Ecosystem

The implementation of artificial intelligence (AI) in higher education has never been as rapid as it is now, and it has already changed the academic environment across teaching, research, and governance. It is the first part of experimental automation, including early machine-learning-based graders and a crude form of plagiarism detector, and has since shaped the current thriving ecosystem of AI-based education technology, upon which the foundations of decision-making and pedagogy are based in universities around the world (Hassan, 2025). Algorithms and generative reasoning in AI-assisted administrative dashboards are influencing higher education, and algorithmic reasoning and predictive intelligence (Khairullah et al., 2025) increasingly affect institutional data analytics.

This has been driven by three main factors: an increase in computing power, the expansion of educational data, and the institutional need to innovate and be efficient without spending much money on academic activities (Han, 2025). Universities have been using AI to streamline the delivery of pedagogical content, address operational complexity, and provide automated grading, plagiarism detection, admissions analytics, predictive retention models, and performance dashboards to higher institutional leaders (Khairullah et al., 2025). For example, an AI-based writing assessment can be used to identify linguistic coherence and provide formative feedback. Likewise, it creates an 'adaptive-learning system' that can be integrated with individual students' cognitive profiles, thus enhancing personalization and inclusivity (Yadav, 2025). On the same note, predictive analytics are used to identify students who are likely to fail or drop out of school, so faculty can intervene early to help them.

The degree and power of AI implementation can be quantified by the rapid expansion of research in this domain, with a focus on AI applications in higher education, such as 'learning analytics', 'assessment', 'administrative automation', and 'ethical governance' (Rodriguez Valencia et al., 2025). This growth is a symptom of an influx of academic curiosity and the reorganization of the scholarly ecosystem: AI is being incorporated into every functional sector of the university. Algorithmic systems mediate grading and admissions, as well as educational decisions, faculty reviews, and research assessments, and need not be completely transparent or interpretable by humans, without necessarily being objective or accurate (Memarian and Doleck, 2023).

Yet this shift is not only technological but also an important epistemic and institutional one. AI is altering the work of teachers and learners, and putting administrators in a different situation, modifying how individuals create, authenticate, and disseminate knowledge. Faculty members are pursuing a hybrid work trajectory in which human judgment and machine advice communicate in multifaceted, and in certain instances controversial, ways. Reorganization of institutional governance is underway as AI tools are influencing policy-making, resource distribution, and performance measurement. The higher education sector is also moving towards a hybrid human-machine ecosystem, where AI is no longer a peripheral element of academic identity and organizational functioning, but a component of both (Popow, 2025).

Even though such innovations are bound to introduce even greater efficiencies and personalisation, they will be associated with serious ethical issues of autonomy, bias, accountability, and academic integrity. The debate over whether to apply AI or not has become a thing of the past, and the more relevant question is now how to control the ethical use of AI to ensure that the purpose of innovation does not defy the values it is meant to represent in higher education.

1.2 The Dual-Edge of AI Integration in Higher Education

The introduction of AI into higher education is a potent opportunity: it can be more effective and more individualized while becoming more common. AI systems can be tailored to a person's individual learning trajectory, maximizing engagement and minimizing dropout. A 2025 survey of student perceptions found that students achieved improved academic results and were more active when AI-based tools used to deliver personalized feedback and adaptive learning paths (Vieriu and Petrea, 2025).

Moreover, AI can support more inclusive educational concepts, such as enabling students with special needs, supporting distance learning, and allowing institutions with smaller human resources bases to serve students, thereby enabling easier access to education for more challenged students. But the threats and contradictions of these very benefits exist. The major problem is that human judgment and critical thinking may be lost. When machine-generated products become the norm, students and faculty will likely submit to algorithms rather than think independently. In fact, research has shown that the loss of critical thinking and over-reliance are the main worries of students who use generative AI in education (Zhai and Wibowo, 2024). Other threats include algorithmic bias and data abuse. Artificial intelligence systems, especially in the education sector, are often based on historical records that social injustices may bias. This could continue to discriminate or underrepresent underprivileged groups. A scoping review investigating societal biases toward GenAI in higher education noted the lack of empirical studies on the topic, as most research presents superficial premises about the phenomenon (Li et al., 2025).

In addition, issues of data privacy, surveillance, and intellectual property emerge and the educational community is growing increasingly concerned about the collection, use, and distribution of student data enabled by AI mechanisms.

For example, according to Wong (2024), there are acute issues of validity, privacy, and academic integrity in AI-enabled practices. Even though AI can suggest new pedagogical, research, and administrative opportunities, there is also a risk that the uncontrollable reliance on such systems will threaten the key academic principles of justice, transparency, human agency, and integrity. The instruments to assist in teaching and research may disappoint the ethical and epistemological foundation of the scholarly business, quite to the contrary, unless quite foresightedly controlled.

1.3 Rationale for Ethical Governance Frameworks

Ethical governance systems can ensure that the use of AI does not eclipse the need to consider its consequences for human dignity, justice, and education. Effectively, ethics should cease being a nice decoration and become a building block of institutional strategy. This is supported by research: Oncioiu and Bularca (2025) found that knowledge-based practices in governance at the university contribute significantly to the legal and ethical AI literacy of students, outperforming separate courses in moral philosophy.

Governance serves as the working interface between high-level ethical values (such as fairness, accountability, and transparency) and daily institutional practices (including data governance, vendor contracts, and algorithm audits). A systematic review on AI governance suggests that multi-level team, organisational, national, and international governance are critical approaches to AI risk management (Batool et al., 2025). The ethical governance framework in the context of higher education deals with both operational and moral risks (e.g., a data breach, the mistake of algorithms, vendor lock-in). These structures bring clarity to roles, responsibilities, policy structure, and tracking arrangements. They also trace the correspondence between emerging AI tools and institutional mission, pedagogy, and values.

Therefore, establishing ethical governance systems tailored to AI in higher education is becoming essential. To begin, we will define the theoretical basis of ethics, government, and AI. Then, we will explore the over-reliance of AI dilemmas in academia. Next, we examine models of global governance and identify the fundamental principles of ethical practice. It is on this basis that we suggest institutional structures, law/regulatory factors, a governance design model, and a roadmap for subsequent development. By doing so, the chapter addresses senior administrators, policymakers, faculty leaders, and all stakeholders who aim to balance innovation and integrity in the age of AI.

2. CONCEPTUAL FOUNDATIONS: UNDERSTANDING ETHICS, GOVERNANCE, AND AI

2.1 Defining Artificial Intelligence in the Academic Context

The generic definition of artificial intelligence (AI) in the field of higher education describes systems that can perform tasks conventionally handled by human mental capabilities, such as automated decision-making, pattern recognition, language generation, adaptive feedback, and prediction of learner behavior. In an academic ecosystem, such applications can include e-learning analytics (e.g., predicting the risk of student drop-out). These AI-based tutoring systems provide personalized feedback, administrative decision-support applications (e.g., resource allocation, admissions), and generative language models, such as ChatGPT, which both students and faculty utilize.

The line between assistive and autonomous AI is becoming increasingly blurred: what starts as an aid to assist a faculty member in marking papers could evolve into an automatic marker or a system that identifies at-risk students and provides intervention without human control. A meta-systematic review of AI in higher education found that adaptive learning systems and analytics were widely used; however, there is also an increasing shift towards decision frameworks in institutions. (Bond et al., 2024).

As an illustrative example, 63% of institutions at one of the major U.S. research universities considered in a recent study promoted the use of generative AI in learning activities, and 41% offered specific guidance on using the system in the classroom. Still, they did not address the governance of the system at all (McDonald et al., 2025). Therefore, AI in higher education cannot be regarded as merely another pedagogical technology; it is a system with the potential to impact the curriculum, evaluation, student behavior, institutional decision-making, and research integrity. Conceptual distinction between assistive and autonomous in the method of supporting human beings and substitutes human judgment, therefore, requires articulation and contextual interpretation in the academic domain.

2.2 Ethical Dimensions of AI

Ethical interaction with AI is supported by a complex set of major principles: fairness, transparency, accountability, privacy, and non-maleficence (i.e., not harm). In the context of scholarly setting, they can be translated as follows: fairness means that AI systems should not recreate or increase bias (such as unfairly disadvantaging minority students); transparency means that it is possible to explain why the algorithmic decision-making used in education takes place and on what basis; accountability means that the consequences of the utilized AI system can be attributed to someone (faculty, institution, vendor); privacy implies that the student-data utilized in analytics must consider human dignity and consent; non-maleficence suggests that educational technologies must not hurt the academic integrity or dignity of students. Things are further complicated by the fact that there is a difference between scholarly and digital ethics. In traditional academic ethics, integrity, originality, and human-centered learning are emphasized, while in digital ethics, concerns include algorithmic bias, data governance, and machine accountability. The overlap of AI in academic life, therefore, also creates new issues: a generative model writes a student essay, who is the author? Does an analytics tool compromise a student's autonomy when it places them on remediation?

One of the pieces of evidence provided by multicultural perspective respondents raised an ethical concern regarding the use of AI by students, specifically relating to cheating and excessive dependence; less than a third of multicultural perspective respondents were aware of institutional policies related to AI. (Yusuf et al., 2024). A systematic review in the journal AI & Ethics revealed that numerous governance frameworks, which prioritize compliance and risk but do not sufficiently address ethical aspects such as fairness, transparency, and inclusiveness, underrepresented these aspects in institutional AI governance activities (Panarese et al., 2025). Such disconnections cause failures in the real world: algorithmic decision-making in university admissions or grading, with no obvious auditing or explanation, has made it more challenging to trust and difficult to believe in academic values. Therefore, ethical thinking must be integrated into AI implementation, not allowed. Institutes need to inquire: Is the tool equitable? Are decisions explainable? Is there protection of faculty or students against harm? In the absence of this kind of reflection, systems based on AI are likely to follow an educational mission rather than improve it.

2.3 The Idea of Governance

Governance is not about management or compliance; it is about structures, processes, values, and oversight mechanisms that govern, control, and steward the activities of an organisation. Governance in higher education involves institutional policy-making, committees, ethical review, audit mechanisms, and stakeholder involvement, as well as the management and execution of tasks (e.g., implementation of software) and compliance with rules or regulations (e.g., data-protection law).

An AI governance system should include: (a) design (e.g. AI oversight committees with faculty, students, IT, ethics experts), (b) procedures (policy development, vendor review, algorithm audit), (c) principles (fairness, transparency, respect of learning contexts) and (d) control (monitoring, reporting, constant review). Governance proved to be an essential tool in a recent case study of Big Ten universities: institutions with official AI policy documents, guiding steering committees, and audit processes were in a better position to handle the ethical risks of generative AI (Hadi et al., 2025). Importantly, governance is not just rule-making, but also lays stress on participation, deliberation, and reflexivity. Instead of injunctions (do not use ChatGPT), governance will welcome constant revisions of the use of AI, observed and updated. The oversight loop is a mechanism that ensures the AI tools align with the institution's mission, pedagogy, and ethical commitments. It is particularly necessary in the context of the dynamic development of AI and the novelty of most educational applications. Thus, governance is not a luxury add-on; it is the core that keeps AI integration within higher education ethical, institutional, and compliant with human values.

2.4 Intersection of Ethics and Governance in AI

Ethics and governance should accompany the application of AI in higher education. Rhetorical and un-operationalized ethical principles, such as fairness or privacy, alone are not enough unless they are converted into design, oversight, and accountability. For example, institutions can declare a pledge to student privacy, but without a policy that describes data-mining practices, user permissions, or algorithmic scrutiny, such a pledge would be ineffective. Studies indicate that the introduction of ethical checkpoints to governance systems, such as algorithmic audits, human-in-the-loop inspections, and transparency releases, elevates trust and aligns well with academic values (McKay, 2024). On the other hand, where governance is ineffective, the use of AI has been associated with the imitation of biases and a lack of academic integrity. Apparently, the policy to practice drive involves authority that operationalizes ethics by optimizing people, processes, and structures to make AI an enabler of human-centered education rather than its substitute.

3. OVERDEPENDENCE ON AI IN ACADEMIA: PROBLEMS AND PARADOXES

3.1 Automation and the Erosion of Human Judgment

The rapid adoption of AI-powered solutions in the academic sector, such as automated grading, plagiarism detection, adaptive learning algorithms, and research support tools, has sparked growing concerns about the decline in human judgment and critical thinking in academic procedures. As institutions become more dependent on machine-generated products, a threat exists that human agency, reflexivity, and creative thinking could be marginalized. Indicatively, a meta-systematic review of

AI in higher education states that machine-based decision-making is now replacing educator judgment and deep human-centred pedagogy (Bond et al., 2024).

Practically, automated essay score servers and algorithms used to identify at-risk students may form a false impression of objectivity: an illusion of objectivity in which the output of machines is unquestioningly accepted. Faculty may be tempted to follow a grade assigned by an AI tool or an expectation of risk of engagement provided by AI, rather than applying professional judgment. An orderly analysis of the application of generative AI in assessment situations observed that, on average, 94 percent of AI-written student work went undetected and scored more points, posing a challenge to human supervision and excessive machine grading (Sultana et al., 2025).

Additionally, replacing human judgment with algorithms could reduce student involvement in higher-order tasks. With AI handling the menial work of feedback or assignment scaffolding, students might be less inclined to be creative or think critically themselves, assuming that the machine can do the work of filling in. This difficulty is further intensified by the fact that AI systems have been known to utilize opaque models, thereby restricting explainability and making it challenging for faculty or students to contest the output, which in turn diminishes reflexive pedagogy. According to one of the human-centred reviews of algorithms in higher-education decision-making, although student-data analytics offers to personalize and be efficient, it can still fail to apply human-centred lenses effectively and therefore does not ensure interpretability or human professional judgment (Allison et al., 2025). As such, excessive reliance on AI exposes the danger of the locus of academic judgment moving away from teachers and students, toward the machine, and undermining the all-important human aspects of creativity, moral judgment, and pedagogical reflection. With automation becoming increasingly popular in higher-education institutions, these institutions must consider that the benefits in speed and scale may be offset by reduced learning quality and diminished human agency.

3.2 Academic Integrity and Authorship Challenges

Among the more evident and immediate contradictions of AI overdependence in academic institutions is the aspect of academic honesty, authorship, and originality. With the emergence of generative AI applications (e.g., large language models), students and researchers can generate entire essays, reports, or manuscript drafts with minimal to no input, and AI-written compositions pose a significant menace to the notion of authorship in academia (Ogwueleka, 2025). According to Chen and Fang (2025), this difficulty is being faced, as the authors note that AI tools enable students to generate new text without citing sources, raising a pressing question about what defines authorship and whether the classic definition of plagiarism remains applicable.

The response of institutions is inadequate, as there are still policy gaps, and the current frameworks for academic integrity are not yet equipped to tackle AI-enabled ghost-writing. The lack of alignment between the rapid adoption of AI and the slow pace of policy response implies that most institutions struggle with enforcement, identification, and response to novelty. According to one article, on the one hand, the publish-or-perish culture of academic life does not align with the potential of AI-based writing; on the other hand, the integrity of research and the authenticity of student learning are at risk (Moulaison-Sandy, 2025). Therefore, as much as AI has advantages in the areas of productivity and access, it also disputes fundamental academic principles of originality, responsibility, and authorship. In the absence of a definitive institutional policy, the redesign of assessments and student training in AI ethics is likely to compromise the integrity of academic work due to the reliance on machine-generated texts.

3.3 Data Privacy and Surveillance in Learning Environments

With the introduction of AI in learning management systems, adaptive platforms, predictive analytics dashboards, and proctoring systems, universities are increasingly involved in monitoring and analyzing student behavior. Although these systems hold the potential for early warning of at-risk students and customized interventions, they raise significant questions about privacy and surveillance. Online Proctoring Systems: A scoping review of online proctoring systems in higher education revealed that biometric data, screen-capture logs, browser history, and 360° room scans are commonly utilized by vendor platforms; however, student consent, transparency, and accountability have not been thoroughly investigated (Derrick et al., 2025).

The conflict arises when the efficiency and personalization promises come into contact with the ethical values surrounding data collection, specifically the rights to student autonomy and privacy. As demonstrated in Lee (2025), algorithmic decisions based on student data (e.g., labeling someone as a risky student) are usually not transparent and do not provide the student with many opportunities to challenge or consent to them. Furthermore, the boundary between supportive analytics and intrusive Surveillance might shift: in the case of online proctoring, personal environment information that has no relevance to the exam situation can be collected, which raises concerns about the aspects of proportionality and equity.

In one context in higher education, faculty and administration claimed that students are aware of being followed and assessed by algorithmic systems that track not only login behaviour but dwell-time, keystrokes, and webcam feeds, a dynamic which underpins free inquiry and turns the relationship into one of monitoring (Kochegurova and Zateev, 2022). As a result, there is a risk of compromising trust, autonomy, and data-minimal practices with the implementation of AI-driven monitoring tools, and a paradox emerges: technology that should be beneficial to education and learning poses a threat to introducing the asymmetry of Surveillance and data power. To implement such tools ethically in a higher-education institution, the institution must guarantee explicit consent practices, disclosure regarding data use, student control over algorithmic choices, and effective data-governance systems.

3.4 Inequality and Digital Divide

Lastly, although AI-based pedagogy and student-data systems are potentially inclusive, they can also enhance the current educational inequalities and digital gaps. Studies on AI in higher education indicate that minorities, first-generation, or low-income students adopt AI tools differently, and their AI literacy might be lower, which restricts their access to AI-based platforms. Indicatively, in one study, AI increased engagement in the cohort; however, it also strengthened the position of the majority of students, while underserved first-generation learners fell behind (Levin, 2022). The digital divide is therefore not only the ability to use high-speed internet or devices, but also the capacity to apply AI systems effectively to one's work. "AI literacy, cultural capital, and support by the educator are discriminating factors. Unless countermeasures are taken, the adoption of AI can actually increase inequity rather than minimize it, as it benefits well-equipped institutions and students. Therefore, excessive reliance on AI without adequate contextual equity protection can result in a process of exclusion rather than inclusion, undermining the primary purpose of innovation.

4. GLOBAL PERSPECTIVES ON AI ETHICS AND GOVERNANCE

4.1 International Guidelines and Frameworks

One of the earliest and most basic international instruments that affects the ethics of AI and its ethical governance is the UNESCO Recommendation on the Ethics of Artificial Intelligence (Van Norren, 2023). This instrument, approved by 193 Member States, provides information-processing technologies with the capacity to learn, reason, sense, or foresee, and focuses on the principles of human dignity, justice, transparency, accountability, and sustainability across the entire AI life cycle. Notably, within the education sector, UNESCO suggests human control, AI literacy training, and both relational pedagogy and access and protection as part of the strong human control, ensuring that higher education is firmly placed on the normative global governance agenda (Okada et al., 2025).

Similar to UNESCO, the Organisation for Economic Co-operation and Development (OECD) presented specifics in its Digital Education Outlook 2023 on AI in education, including its possibilities, recommendations, and constraints to ensure the process is effective and equitable. Extending support for inclusivity, equity, and efficiency could be a matter of rigorous policy action, initiated with investments in infrastructure, including data-based governance, and in humanizing educator competence. Also, the AI principles have been outlined in various international governance projects, such as the G20 and the Organization of Economic Co-operation and Development, that propose inclusive growth, equality, transparency, human values, etc. The supranational tools create a shared normative framework of national policies, institutional strategies, and governance structures within higher education.

According to the 2025 survey of higher-education institutions from all countries, presented by UNESCO, out of 400 institutions, approximately 19% already have a formal policy regarding AI, and 42% are working on developing one (Arias et al., 2025). This demonstrates how institutional structures are rapidly adapting to international directives. The problem, however, is to encapsulate the general universal principles into specific institutional practices and forms of governance. Overall, international guidelines provide a typical value-grounded bedrock of human rights, equity, and inclusiveness; however, they are not a prescriptive specification of the finer governance vehicles or institutional channels of higher education. That disparity explains why institutions are required to understand and localise these global norms to fit their local contexts.

4.2 National Policy Models

At the national level, some jurisdictions have developed policy models based on international systems of ethnicity and culture, but tailored to their unique systems of governance, law, and culture. For example, the National Institute of Standards and Technology (NIST) AI Risk Management Framework in the United States presents a voluntary and flexible system for managing AI system risks, including fairness, transparency, and stakeholder engagement. Although it is primarily applied in industry, it is also making its way into education, particularly in research analytics and data governance within institutions.

The upcoming AI Act (written 20212024) in the European Union (EU) has become the first full-fledged binding law on AI in the world. It categorizes high-risk AI systems (such as those used in education, for example, to evaluate students or for admissions). It establishes requirements regarding human oversight, transparency, accountability, and risk management.

China has a fast-paced policy development that is centrally organized responsible AI governance normative shifts to the sphere of more onerous regulation. The Chinese government emphasizes its control over data, algorithms, platforms, and applications, and has recently published administrative directives on generative AI services, focusing on transparency, the prevention of discrimination, and content control (Roberts et al., 2021).

Further example, the national regime differences found in comparative insights on Singapore, UK, and UAE. While, Singapore is the country that promotes a human-centred model of AI governance with public-business collaboration with focus on trust and ethics; UK is the country where sectoral regulation and data governance are a priority; and UAE is the country where AI strategy is focused on national development, ethics and inclusion. The similarities between these models are evident: national policy is more normative (ethics-driven), regulatory (risk classification), and capacity-building oriented (education, literacy, institutional readiness). These national structures set tangible expectations for higher-education institutions: systems must be auditable, decisions must be explainable, data management must be sound, and human oversight must be in place. The difference in national commands is also a place of interest for higher-education administration, which can familiarize itself with legal, moral, ethical, cultural, and institutional settings while upholding alliance with international ethical standards.

4.3 Higher Education Governance Initiatives

In the higher education sector, there are some of the most prominent institutions that have implemented governance initiatives to model global and national guidelines. For example, the University of Helsinki in Finland empirically studied the topic of Governance in Ethical and Trustworthy AI systems using the ECCOLA method and the GARP (Governance, Accountability, Risk, Process) tool to map ethical principles that could be operationalized as institutional governance mechanisms. The research focused on structure and process aspects that exceeded abstract principles (Agbese et al., 2023).

Similarly, Stanford University, through the Stanford HAI (Human-Centered AI Initiative), has been involved in multi-stakeholder discourse, curriculum development, and research translation, explicitly connecting the issues of ethics and AI governance to higher education. It has provided structures for faculty training, institutional policy, and public engagement in its work.

New codes of conduct and institutional policies are emerging worldwide. In 2023, the European Network for Academic Integrity (ENAI) recommended the ethical applications of AI in education, including a call on national policymakers and institutions to establish what can be. It cannot be done with AI in learning, and it is essential to provide students and staff with training on ethical use (Schiff, 2022). However, governance loopholes also remain: a meta-analysis of institutional AI governance in higher education reported that tools and policies have currently been established, but the oversight, audit, and human-in-the-loop scrutiny are frequently inadequate or lacking. Besides, a small part of the institutions is committed to AI ethics committees or algorithmic auditing. According to the UNESCO survey of 2025, only 19% of institutions reported having a formal policy on AI, and more than four in five lacked a comprehensive policy infrastructure. These efforts suggest that the governance of higher education should incorporate global standards (e.g., fairness, transparency) alongside operational, institution-specific processes, including AI ethics boards, vendor transformation, algorithm audits, AI literacy courses, stakeholder consultation, and feedback loops that align with the institutional mission and pedagogy.

5. CORE PRINCIPLES OF ETHICAL GOVERNANCE IN HIGHER EDUCATION

5.1 Human-Centered AI

Human-centered artificial intelligence (HCAI) in the higher education context emphasizes that the design, implementation, and management of systems prioritize human well-being, autonomy, dignity, and pedagogical relationships over the pursuit of automation and efficiency improvements. The main idea is that AI tools are intended to benefit students and teachers, not to replace them. Indicatively, recent studies suggest that incorporating HCAI frameworks into higher education research processes (including systematic literature reviews) incurred less time costs but maintained the human judgement, interpretability, and trust. (Le Dinh, 2025).

This can be applied in the context of teaching and learning: the teacher-student relationship must be maintained. The instructor should have the capacity to design learning, provide feedback, and oversee the overall educational process, but AI should not replace these functions. And absent such a focus, institutions can easily become a delivery factory instead of a learning ecosystem, which will destroy autonomy. In a study on higher education stakeholders, students reported that using AI tutoring systems significantly reduced the likelihood of human-teacher interaction, which in turn decreased engagement and a sense of belonging. (Habib et al., 2025).

Equity, learner diversity, accessibility, and social-emotional aspects of education are also aspects of human well-being. For instance, a speed-driven and throughput-focused adaptive-learning AI can fail in its primary purpose of higher education, which is to develop critical thinking, community, and moral skills. Human-oriented political institutions incorporate control systems (e.g., human-in-the-loop review, pedagogical ethics committees) to ensure that AI works in favor of human flourishing rather than against it. Concisely, a human-centered principle dismisses the line of automation as an unreserved good and demands that AI should align itself with the value and mission of the institution and its learners.

5.2 Transparency and Explainability

Transparency in AI governance refers to the ability to see and comprehend the mechanisms of action of AI systems, their decision-making processes, and the effects on stakeholders in education. Explainability introduces the capability of users (students, instructors, administrators) to understand, refute, or put AI decisions into perspective. Algorithm transparency is essential in the governance of automated grading, student analytics decisions (e.g., flagging at-risk students), and research impact measures. In a research study published by Frontiers in Human Dynamics, the authors discovered that, even now, most AI systems in education are black boxes, whose decision paths are inexplicable to end-users; this lack of explainability precludes trust and accountability in AI (Taneja, 2025).

As an illustration, an AI system that suggests students be remedial should reveal information about the manner in which the prediction was achieved (what data was used, how it was weighted, and the threshold) and give students and professors a chance to challenge or overrule the results. Lacking this transparency, institutions can fall prey to the illusion of objectivity, in which the machine ruling can be perceived as neutral, in the true sense of the word; however, it is actually cast as a manifestation of hidden prejudice or malicious design. In a single case study on university AI-governance rules, fewer than one in every three institutions mandated vendors to provide model audits or decision-logic reports. Therefore, both institutional policies need to mandate the disclosure of AI use in assessments, describe the circumstances under which human review is necessary, integrate mechanisms to interpret AI results, and permit appeals or overrides. Transparent AI promotes academic honesty, user trust, accountability, and ethics in higher education.

5.3 Accountability and Responsibility

Responsibility in AI governance refers to the fact that institutions, administrators, faculty, and vendors are aware of those who must be accountable for the consequences of AI-enabled decisions, and that there are redress mechanisms in place in case of harm arising. Responsibility highlights the fact that people and organisations should have moral and legal duties. Accountability clarity is needed in higher education, where AI tools impact admissions, grading, adaptive learning pathways, and research analytics. To take an example, when an AI-based system identifies a student as an under-performer and is acting on the wrong action, who is responsible: the AI vendor, the institution, the faculty oversight committee?

According to a recent systematic review of AI governance in education, most institutions of higher education lack accountability mechanisms (audit logs, human-in-the-loop, governance committees). Institutions must specify roles: faculty need to review AI-augmented decisions; IT teams need to maintain a model's safety; data-governance units need to track data flows; and vendor contracts need to include liability, audit, and transparency provisions. Furthermore, the issue of institutional responsibility for AI decisions should be noted: universities should have policies to cover the risks associated with vendor malfunctions, algorithm malfunctions, information security breaches, and unjustified results. Practically, governance systems can involve AI ethics monitoring commissions, incident-reporting systems, regular assessments, and consultations (Agbese et al., 2023). Explicit responsibility making would make AI systems susceptible to human ethical thinking and institutionalized controls, rather than being absolutely black-box autonomous ones.

5.4 Fairness and Non-Discrimination

Non-discrimination and equal treatment in AI governance help ensure that AI tools do not exacerbate existing disparities in the higher education field, regardless of race, gender, socio-economic status, or global North-South lines. Educational AI has been empirically identified to suffer from algorithmic bias. In one study, predictive analytics systems identified minority students as at-risk more frequently because that group was skewing historical data. (Almalawi et al., 2024).

AI-driven tutoring and adaptive learning/assessment systems should be audited for bias and include inclusive datasets, as well as have accessible interfaces. Fair access to AI-based learning also requires institutional structures that do not deny opportunities to less fortunate learners. A quick scan has revealed that, although AI is becoming more widely used in higher education, its primary purpose remains institutional efficiency rather than equity; responsive AI systems for marginalised students are still uncommon (Kunjumuhammed, 2024). The systems of governance must implement equity audits, inclusive design mechanisms, regular impact evaluation, and redress measures where discrimination occurs. Fairness will be crucial not only for ethical legitimacy but also for maintaining the mission of higher education as an emancipatory and inclusive process.

5.5 Data Protection and Privacy

Data protection and privacy should be given significant consideration in the framework of AI ethical governance in higher education. Information collected by adaptive learning systems, AI-driven analytics, tutoring systems, and research tools often contains sensitive student data, including personal, behavioral, and performance data. Institutions should have robust data governance frameworks that include consent, data minimization, data storage, audit trails, and vendor management (Chauhan and Dutta, 2025). Compliance with international data-protection principles, such as the European General Data Protection Regulation (GDPR), is becoming increasingly important. Organizations with global operations should align with international data transfers, algorithm transparency, and the rights to explanation and erasure. The policies must mandate vendor contracts that mirror the data-governance requirements, limit any secondary use of student data, grant students control and ownership of their data, and provide a clear breach or misuse policy. The safety of the independence of students and the establishment of trust, as well as protection, not only of the law, but also of the conscience.

6. INSTITUTIONAL FRAMEWORKS FOR ETHICAL AI GOVERNANCE

6.1 Governance Architecture for Universities

Establishing a robust governance structure is a key initial step institutions of higher learning need to take to become responsible stewards of artificial intelligence (AI). Such architecture is usually vested in an institutional AI Ethics Committee, designed through role allocation within governance systems (e.g., senates, academic councils, and IT departments), and through vertical and horizontal accountability mechanisms. Indicatively, a recent study of U.S. Big Ten universities revealed that universities with formal AI oversight guiding groups, connected to a central university governance body, had better policy clarity and alignment with their strategic mission. The AI Ethics Committee is a specialized organization that evaluates new AI initiatives, assesses associated risks (including ethical, operational, and reputational risks), proposes policies, ensures compliance, and monitors stakeholders (including faculty, students, and vendors). According to institutional research, currently, only a small fraction of universities has such committees, resulting in a fragmented or ad-hoc approach to decision-making (Agbese et al., 2023).

The definition of roles is essential: the senate (or institutional governing council) adopts AI governance policies and connects them with the strategy of academia;

academic councils represent the faculty and track the impacts of pedagogy; IT departments create, deploy, and maintain AI systems and cooperate with ethics oversight. Vertical accountability incorporates a top-to-bottom approach to AI governance, where the top leadership (e.g., provost, CIO) sets the frameworks, with subordinate units (departments, faculty) responsible for executing and implementing them (horizontal accountability). This ensures that subordinate units engage with each other in a cross-functional manner (e.g., ethics office, legal compliance, vendor management) (Chan, 2023). It is essential that the governance architecture in institutions is dynamic, as AI changes rapidly, and governance bodies may become out of step with these changes. It is necessary to establish living governance processes, such as periodic reviews, stakeholder consultations, and internal audit loops. The design should therefore incorporate ethics committees, delegated approval channels for AI projects, decision-ownership records, vendor supervision procedures, and processes for escalation in case of issues with the algorithms (Jin et al., 2025).

6.2 Policy Development and Implementation

The shift to the institutional policy level of ethical principles is a vital issue in governance. Ethical principles (e.g., fairness, transparency, human-centeredness) should be enshrined in policies that reach students, faculty, administrators, and vendors. A study in the International Journal of Educational Technology in Higher Education identified gaps in existing policy frameworks, as reported by 457 students and 180 teaching staff at universities in Hong Kong. Few institutions had formalized AI-specific codes of conduct or syllabus guidelines (Chan et al., 2023).

The codes of AI use in relation to the various stakeholder groups should be institutionalized, such as guidelines on what use of AI-generative tools is allowed by students (e.g., they must or must not use AI-generated texts in pedagogy), by faculty (e.g., they must have control over data usage by AI), and by administrators (e.g., they must be aware of their obligations to contracts with AI vendors). An example of good practice is the AI policy framework developed by the University of Toronto and other North American institutions, which mandates disclosure in cases where AI tools are used to assess or conduct research (Sloane and Wüllhorst, 2025).

It is also essential that ethics be integrated into curricula and handbooks. The institutions are recommended to incorporate modules on AI-ethics in the first year induction to students, faculty, and provide guidance in academic integrity manuals and vendor contracts, which should mention institutional policy on AI ethics (Agbese et al., 2023). The implementation of well-elaborated rollout plans, including awareness through communication networks, training programs, compliance and feedback procedure, policy review and apprises earmarked accordingly. It is essential to monitor the implementation of policies. In one survey, a significant number of institutions were reported to have a policy in draft form; however, less than half had implemented the policy measures, including audits or awareness campaigns (Turner et al., 2021). To conclude, effective policy formulation and execution transform the normative promise into institutional practice, including codes of conduct, curriculum integration, vendor regulation, staff training, and surveillance. In the absence of such a transition, the governance is more of a show than a working process.

6.3 Ethical Review and Audit Mechanisms

Governance is operationalised through ethical review and audit mechanisms, which place AI systems and institutional processes under systematic scrutiny. The AI ethics audit process entails inspecting algorithms, datasets, decision metrics, vendor associations, data flows, and user impact. Institutions should conduct periodic evaluations of AI tools in teaching, learning, and research, including adaptive learning systems, predictive analytics dashboards, or generative AI-assisted writing assignments, to identify bias, accuracy issues, unintended harms, and non-compliance with policies. One of the latest articles outlined a framework named HEAT-AI (Higher Education Act for AI), which contains audit procedures, risk-based categorization of AI systems, and public reporting needs (Temper et al., 2025).

Trust is associated with the public reporting and disclosure of the audit results. In the case of concealed audit results, stakeholders will be unable to question AI failures or hold governance accountable for them. Indicatively, a case study of institutions of higher learning established that less than 30th of the institutions mandated vendors to offer algorithmic audit or transparency disclosures (Le Dinh et al., 2025). The AI-systems risk profile (e.g., high-stakes systems such as automated grading systems or student eligibility decisions) should be reflected in audit schedules (e.g., more frequent reviews are required). Moreover, organizations are encouraged to maintain a publicly available list of deployed AI systems, their purposes, stakeholder assignments, oversight committee minutes, and audit findings, thereby enhancing accountability and supporting interdepartmental learning. Universities can alleviate the risks associated with AI governance by implementing ethical review and audit systems, thereby transitioning AI governance from policy declaration to operational vigilance. These mechanisms serve as a protective measure to human-oriented values and institutional integrity.

6.4 Building Capacity and Awareness

Responsible AI governance in higher education cannot be achieved without technical and ethical capacity building. The institutions should provide training programs on AI literacy and ethics to students, faculty, and administrators. Examples of these programmes include algorithmic bias, data privacy, vendor assessment, using student AI tools, and responsible pedagogy. One study based on knowledge governance found that the readiness of faculty and students to AI-governance systems is significantly enhanced in institutions that promote legal awareness and AI ethics literacy (Oncioiu and Bularca, 2025).

Responsible AI use development may involve workshops, peer networks, internal incentives to teach AI ethically, and specialized support units (e.g., an AI ethics office within the IT division). Making students into ethical digital citizens entails introducing AI ethics courses during induction, developing reflective projects centered on AI usage, and establishing student-led committees to oversee the use of AI. According to an international survey, in institutions where students perceived themselves as adequately trained in the field of AI ethics, AI tools in teaching were more likely to be utilized, and fewer students expressed concerns about the potential for misuse (Ullah et al., 2024).

Institutional capacity building also includes staffing (assigning staff with AI governance responsibilities, such as an AI ethics officer), budgeting (to audit and comply with vendors), and infrastructure (to support open AI systems, including audit logs and model versioning). In the absence of such capacities, policy frameworks are just a dream. Concisely, no architecture of governance, policy, or audit would operate efficiently without trained humans, adequate resources, and an ethical AI awareness culture.

6.5 Stakeholder Collaboration

The governance of AI in the higher education field cannot be remedied solely within an institution; it is essential to have collaboration between universities, the government, and other industry players. Policies and reports from institutions emphasize that the co-creation of AI governance standards, involving students, faculty, IT professionals, external ethical advisors, vendors, and regulators, results in more contextualized, accepted, and practical frameworks. To give a few examples, industry-university partnerships may offer transparency from the vendor, shared audit resources, and learning communities across the sector. Governments and accreditation bodies provide standards, benchmarks, and resources for the adoption of ethics-driven AI. Universities need to work with them to influence these standards and adhere to regional regulations. Combined efforts, such as the research networks of AI governance organized by the EU, unite universities, businesses, and governmental regulators, creating guidelines that can be adjusted by the institutions themselves (Cancela-Outeda, 2024).

7. REGULATORY, LEGAL, AND ACCREDITATION CONSIDERATIONS

7.1 Legal Landscape of AI in Education

The legal landscape of AI applications in higher education is rapidly evolving. It encompasses multiple intersecting areas, including data protection and privacy, automated decision liability, intellectual property and authorship, anti-discrimination law, and industry-specific regulations (e.g., consumer/education law). The modern legal scene is marked by two characteristics: (1) the shift to binding rules in certain jurisdictions, and (2) risk-regulation of AI systems with high stakes regarding individuals (e.g., admissions, assessment, progression).

One flagship is the law of data protection. The European General Data Protection Regulation (GDPR) continues to apply, establishing institutional requirements for student data, training dataset design, profiling, and automated decision-making (with proper explanation, correct access, and the right to erasure) in Europe. The explanatory guidance issued by regulators and professional agencies (e.g., the European Data Protection Board) on AI environments has also emphasized the legal basis for processing, as well as minimization and transparency considerations (Labadie and Legner, 2023). Even in jurisdictions that do not have legislation of the type of GDPR, national data-protection laws or sectoral guidance are playing an increasingly significant role, and transnational institutions must monitor data flows across borders and enter into agreements with their suppliers.

Liability is another critical area of law. The liability question of what should happen in the event of an undesirable outcome caused by an AI system (e.g., a false refusal of entry, poor scoring) is not just a practical one but also a legal one. The AI Act in the EU establishes a risk-based regime imposing liability on providers and deployers, setting a strong precedent for distribution responsibility in the education environment (Ebers, 2024). In the U.S., unlike in other nations, federal guidance and standard-setting (including the NIST AI Risk Management Framework) remain largely voluntary. However, it is already becoming challenging to resolve AI-related claims in the courts and sectoral regulators. The legal aspects of generative AI have been the subject of academic criticism. It involves certain strands of legal conflict, such as copyright (who owns the work generated by models), contractual relations with suppliers, and regulatory gaps regarding the so-called foundational models, which are trained on large tranches of scraped data (Chandrasekhar, 2025).

Implication in action: AI procurement, deployment, and operational use must be viewed as legal and technical concerns by universities. The legislation should be well-controlled and enforced, with robust contractual terms (data protection, audit rights, liability limits, and indemnities), privacy impact assessments (PIAs), transparency, and the availability of complaint/appeal channels for students and employees. The regulators also shift to an enforcement approach, viewing AI as merely a technical problem that could expose them to regulatory liability and reputational harm.

7.2 Accreditation and Quality Assurance Requirements

The use of AI is being integrated into program review, institutional audits, and learning outcome verification by accrediting bodies and quality assurance (QA) agencies. Since AI is capable of interfering with fundamental academic processes (assessment, admission, progression, student support), QA models will need to be modified to maintain validity, fairness, and academic rigour. Two trends can be identified: (1) accrediting agencies are requesting institutions to demonstrate governance of AI-enabled systems; (2) AI is being used to support QA (e.g., analytics to improve the institution), which creates a reflexive governance requirement (Hassan, 2025).

Several recent research and policy proposals suggest that AI systems involved in decision-making based on student outcomes should be considered high-risk and are eligible for accreditation oversight (Temper et al., 2025). For instance, the classification of particular education systems as high-risk, as mentioned in the EU AI Act (those systems that define access to education, gauge performance, or guide progression), implies that EU institutions should demonstrate risk management, human control, and documentation of those systems. Most likely, QA auditors will ask institutions to explain (a) the way AI tools are reinforced to reinforce learning outcomes, (b) how assessment validity is maintained where AI is used to assist in grading, (c) how academic integrity is ensured, and (d) how protections of students are provided.

The practice of accreditation is evolving towards being evidence-based: agencies can demand an AI system inventory, vendor contracts with audit rights, bias-testing reports, and logs of human overrides. Moreover, the QA authorities are also experimenting with the addition of AI literacy and ethics to the learning outcomes of an institutional program, which is not so much focused on content as on preparing graduates to work in an AI-driven world. Although empirical research is still in its early stages, initial field research has revealed that the institutional adoption of AI and accreditation preparedness do not align: in many cases, AI tools are in use at universities, but the necessary documentation and governance to meet external QA inspections are lacking (Maslej et al., 2025).

In brief, accreditation actors are emerging as non-regulating regulators of institutional AI governance. Those institutions that take positive steps toward establishing alignment between AI procurement and deployment, and QA expectations (including transparency, auditability, and safeguards against academic dishonesty), will pass the accreditation evaluation with fewer issues and will be more adaptable to regulatory shifts.

7.3 Institutional Policy Alignment

To fulfill legal and QA requirements, universities must coordinate institutional policies across various areas, including academic integrity codes, data protection/privacy policies, procurement/vendor management, IT security, research ethics, and student services protocols. One such stride is to build a planned policy framework that integrates discrete guidelines into a reliable governance structure. For formal execution, institutions must formulate an AI policy document that includes a list of AI systems, data flows, vendor relationships, and relevant policy instruments. The register can be used to provide focused policy interventions, such as mandating PIAs on high-impact systems, human-in-the-loop review of grading tools, or declarations of AI use in submission portals. Leading practices also incorporate clauses into vendor contracts, ensuring access to source code or third-party audits of high-risk systems, establishing the bar for second-party use of student data, and specifying liability and response procedures in the event of a breach.

There must be cross-unit coordination. Policy design and implementation must involve collaboration with legal counsel, IT, institutional research, teaching and learning centers, and academic leadership. The use of AI tools in a siloes manner, with each department adopting it independently, poses a greater risk to the law and disconnects QA compliance. The governmental apparatus (data governance board, AI ethics committee) must have the authority to approve high-risk projects and forward concerns to top management. A recent meta-review has emphasized that institutions where the relationship between cross-functional teams is clear and control over vendors is evident have fewer incidents in their operations and, consequently, better adherence to policy (Wiles-Warner, 2025).

Lastly, the policy lifecycle should be institutionalized through established institutions, including the development of a policy, consultation with stakeholders (including students), testing, reporting, and review. Decision logs, impact assessments, and public reporting should be demonstrable audit trails that ensure institutional accountability. Where universities must comply with national regulators (e.g., under the EU AI Act) through binding obligations, local policy alignment (including procedural steps, documentation, and human oversight) will be required to prevent non-compliance with the law and to avoid rejection by accrediting bodies. This is not only about escaping legal responsibility, but also about inculcating moral fortitude: policies that can create an environment that promotes human dignity, secure the quality of learning, and enable innovation under responsible conditions.

8. DESIGNING THE ETHICAL GOVERNANCE MODEL FOR AI IN HIGHER EDUCATION

8.1 Conceptual Model Overview

The suggested Ethical Governance Framework for Artificial Intelligence in Higher Education (EGF-AIHE) can provide accountability, transparency, and ethical integrity for all AI activities within the academic community. It expresses a multi-layered, flexible architecture that integrates ethical theory with operational governance systems to ensure that AI is used responsibly in teaching, research, and administration.

The framework is grounded in four layers: the first three are interconnected, and the fourth serves as the feedback and revision mechanism. This process enables continuous observation, stakeholder participation, and policy refinement through ongoing stakeholder feedback. In the analysis of accountability, it is distributed among AI system designers and vendors (taking responsibility for the transparency of the algorithm), the university management (taking responsibility for the enforcement of policies and risk assessment), and lastly, at the level of the user (taking responsibility for the ethical uses and awareness). This is a trickle-down obligation that complies with UNESCO.

Recent research revealed that universities with effective governance systems (e.g., AI ethics panels and open procurement) are more likely to report increased trust and reduced exposure to ethical risks (Temper et al., 2025). This idea of a conceptual model integrates normative rigor and procedural accountability, offering a dynamic, evidence-based approach to managing the risks of AI technology and increasing AI-enabled higher education innovation and inclusion.

8.2 Key Components of the Framework

8.2.1. Ethical Principles Layer (Normative Foundation)

Simply put, the EGF-AIHE has five principles of operation informed by existing discourse on AI ethics: beneficence, non-maleficence, justice, autonomy, and explicability (Nikolinakos, 2023). These are the principles that turn philosophical ethics into operational institutional principles. The principles of beneficence and non-maleficence guard against harm caused by algorithmic biases, abuse, and unreasonable access to and use of algorithms. Autonomy protects academic freedom, and informed consent and explicability require the intelligibility and explainability of AI systems.

They are necessary, according to empirical research: recent audits of learning analytics systems have shown that most of them were highly biased against marginalized populations when transparency and human control were lacking (Simbeck, 2024). In response, institutions of higher education that have implemented human-centered AI principles have demonstrated tangible improvements in student satisfaction and perceptions of fairness, with up to a 20% increase in student trust indicators (Zhang et al., 2022). Ethical foundations, therefore, are not aspirational but performance standards.

8.2.2 Governance Structure Layer (Committees, Roles, Accountability)

The institutionalization of ethics is found in the governance structure layer, based on the formal design of organizations. Every institution is expected to formulate an AI Governance Council (AIGC) with a strategic oversight role, and assisted by specialized subcommittees:

1. **Ethics Review Board AI (ERB-AI)** - considers applications that are at high risk, like admissions algorithms or automated grading.
2. **Data Stewardship Committee (DSC)** - regulates adherence to data protection and privacy regulations (GDPR-equivalent).
3. **Academic Integrity and AI Committee (AI^{2}C)** - assures coordination between academic practices related to honesty and AI practices.

There is vertical and horizontal allocation of accountability. Top-down control is performed by senior management (e.g., vice-chancellors, deans), while bottom-up accountability is provided by the faculty and student representatives through participatory governance. Research indicates that participatory governance enhances compliance with ethics and adoption of innovation by almost 30 percent relative to hierarchical models (Lythreatis et al., 2024). The EGF-AIHE hence focuses more on co-creation and shared responsibility, reflecting the shift from compliance-based to ethics-as-culture governance.

8.2.3 Implementation Layer (Policies, Procedures, Audits)

The third level implements governance principles through institutional policies and formal procedures. Key components include:

- AI Use policy that outlines what academic applications are permitted (and forbidden) (e.g., ChatGPT-assisted writing disclosure regulations).
- Procurement Standards that mandate AI vendors to present algorithmic-impact reports and bias-audit reports.
- Faculty and Student AI ethics, privacy, and digital literacy Training Programs- demonstrated to increase significantly responsible use.
- Audit and Compliance Systems, which periodically evaluate algorithmic outputs on grounds of fairness, transparency, and reliability.

Some of the most reputable universities, including the University of Helsinki and Stanford University, have already experimented with the models of multi-level governance, which involve ethical review boards and constant monitoring mechanisms (Capogna and Greco, 2024). The institutions report increased regulatory preparedness and trustworthiness of the stakeholders. Moreover, the introduction of AI ethics audits as part of the current Quality Assurance (QA) procedures, which measure bias scores and error transparency, connects the pertinence of ethics with accreditation compliance (Temper et al., 2025).

8.2.4 *Feedback and Revision Mechanism*

Ethical governance should be flexible. EGF-AIHE is further refined through feedback that is incorporated to provide progressions towards the final layer, building refinements when the evidence presented redraws stakeholder responses and advancements in technology. Vision Universities are encouraged to conduct periodic reviews of the ethical impact of AI. Alternatively, in the case of a financial audit, an external audit will determine the degree of institutional compliance, transparency, and stakeholder satisfaction. The principle of constant adaptation is a dynamic equilibrium principle proposed in the governance literature to strike a balance between ethical stability and responsiveness to innovation (Cao et al., 2023). Regular ethics reviews in institutions that held such reviews minimized AI-related grievances and compliance violations in the empirical trials. Learning governance is operationalized through feedback loops, thereby making continuous improvement an integral part of the institutional DNA.

8.3 Model in Action: Implementation Scenarios

Scenario 1: AI-Assisted Grading Policy Development: With the help of AI-based essay grading, one university intends to reduce the workload of its faculty. With the EGF-AIHE, the Ethics Review Board conducts a bias-risk assessment before deployment, analyzing the diversity of the training data and the transparency of the algorithm. The board will require that humans moderate one out of ten AI-generated grades. The students are aware of AI involvement through explicit consent clauses. Regular performance audits would ensure that grading fairness aligns with human standards. Research indicates that grading in hybrid (AI + human) boosts consistency by 15 percent without affecting fairness (Vetrivel et al., 2025).

Scenario 2: Research Integrity in AI-Generated Content: AI software is applied in research supervision to generate literature summaries. The Academic Integrity and AI Committee has disclosure policies that require authors to note sections that AI assisted. The automated plagiarism detector has evolved to identify AI paraphrasing. Both research ethics and misconduct policy review violations (Pudasaini et al., 2024). Based on this protocol, unintentional AI-assisted cases of integrity were significantly reduced in one of the most European universities. Disclosure and transparency are, therefore, proper instruments of ethical governance.

Scenario 3: Ethical Data Analytics for Student Performance: A learning analytics dashboard predicts the risks of student dropouts with the help of AI. The Data Stewardship Committee ensures GDPR compliance, provides informed consent, and minimizes the collection of data. Ethical principles do not permit the punitive application of predictions; instead, they initiate supportive interventions (e.g., tutoring). A two-year post-test reveals a 12 percent reduction in dropout rate and a high trust rate among students. The case exemplifies how AI analytics may be ethically required to be beneficent and to serve care rather than control. Examples of such scenarios demonstrate that governance systems can be institutionalized to uphold the principles of transparency, consent, and oversight, enabling AI implementation without compromising equity or academic integrity.

8.4 Continuous Improvement and Evaluation

Responsibility and resilience of good governance are quantifiable. Some of the major Ethical Performance Indicators (KEPIs) applicable to the evaluation phase of EGF-AIHE are: bias measures, transparency score, stakeholder trust index, and compliance audit score. The comparison with international standards, such as the OECD AI Principles and the EU AI Act, ensures international comparability and consistency.

Examples of monitoring mechanisms that can facilitate transparency and accountability include annual ethics reports, real-time algorithmic dashboards, and third-party audits. Institutional memory and institutional confidence must be developed by maintaining clear logs of AI applications and by conducting ethical assessments of AI implementation within institutions. Ethical audits should be carried out regularly in adaptive governance. An external advisory board should review the effectiveness of AI governance every 2 or 3 years and provide recommendations on how the policy should be changed. More empirical evidence on evidence-based measures of governance maturity models is needed. One aspect of responsible innovation is that ethical governance is a strategic competence rather than a compliance obligation, given the need for constant improvement. The institutions that institutionalize such reflexive governance are found to be more resilient to reputational risk and regulatory transformation, as well as establishing the ethical pace of the world of global higher education.

9. DIFFICULTIES AND OBSTACLES IN IMPLEMENTATION

9.1 Gaps in Institutional Resistance and Awareness

One of the most common barriers to the effective implementation of ethical AI in higher education is institutional resistance, characterized by a lack of knowledge and awareness of AI ethics at senior and operational levels. Studies have shown that faculty and administrators do not understand the ethical implications of AI in higher education. For example, an empirical study found that 36.9 percent of professors and 17.3 percent of students at the highest level were convinced that the AI systems at their university were sufficiently transparent in their functioning. (Marín et al., 2025). This illiteracy will create administrative inertia: institutional executives with an incomplete grasp of the ethical implications of AI can stall the formation of governance structures or degenerate into reactive policy. In one systematic review, 22.6 percent of the studies identified the lack of technical knowledge among teachers, ineffective infrastructure, and power transfer as crucial problems in the implementation of AI in institutions of higher learning. (Bond et al., 2024).

Budget constraints make the situation worse: colleges and universities often operate on tight budgets. They must decide between the most pressing needs (facilities, staff recruitment, and student services) and new governance requirements. According to the same review, infrastructure and the teacher's lack of technical knowledge were recurrently cited. AI ethics in cases of low funding can be treated as urgent and, therefore, lead to institutional responses that are slow or partial. Consequently, institutional resistance and ignorance suggest that there is no entrenched, ideal system of ethical governance. Strong AI governance would be a haphazard, gradual shift without the buy-in of senior leadership, undermining innovation and integrity.

9.2 Technological and Infrastructure Limitations

The second one is a significant challenge related to technological and infrastructure limitations. This dependence may result in the loss of institutional control over algorithms, transparency, and auditing, as many universities contract with external AI vendors rather than creating in-house functions. Indicatively, institutional research in higher education has noted that AI decision-making can automatically filter out applicants due to past system biases in systems marketed to institutions, and that institutions themselves are not in a position to audit and fully verify these systems.

Not having local experience in algorithmic auditing and AI governance is also a problem. One of the themes that was detected during a meta-review was that the lack of ethical consideration and technical knowledge in the teachers was the most widespread one, which means that the universities were not always equipped with the human resources to evaluate the AI systems regarding the bias, fairness, and integrity problems (Bond et al., 2024).

The other factor is infrastructural inequity: the active use of AI presupposes significant development of data infrastructure, secure networks, functional capacities, and uninterrupted surveillance. A summary of AI in university education found that educational inequalities stem from limited access to AI learning resources due to infrastructure constraints.

Poor core infrastructure creates opportunities to implement AI applications without scaling implementation or considering ethical aspects. The net effect is discontinuous deployments, a lack of governance oversight, black-box vendor models that are not, or are poorly, audited, and unintended consequences are likely. Mitigating technological and infrastructural constraints is thus a requirement for enabling ethical management of AI in higher education.

9.3 Cultural and Ethical Relativism

Another obstacle is the relativism of cultures and morals, especially in international higher education. The normative frameworks of AI ethics and governance that primarily emerged in the Western context are not necessarily transferable to cultural, legal, or institutional settings. For instance, a recent article on global AI ethics notes that cultural differences raise questions about global ethical claims, and that initiatives to develop global AI ethics may be perceived as a lack of respect for other countries or even an act of ethical imperialism (Coeckelbergh, 2025).

When applied in a higher education context in the developing or Global South, the localization of both the ethical and governance frameworks is of great importance. A study of South African universities revealed that infrastructural inequalities and low policy capacity contributed to a lack of coherent AI governance. Students and academics were unsure about how to utilize AI (Muringa, 2025).

Unless the ethical governance structures are culturally responsive and context-sensitive in calibration, the chances of being ignored, resisted, or implemented shallowly are likely to occur. Cultural and moral relativism, therefore, presents a significant obstacle to the enactment of universal governance paradigms: organisations need to develop frameworks that are locally and contextually relevant, rather than following them as generic.

9.4 Policy-Implementation Divide

Finally, there has always been a policy implementation gap: many higher education institutions develop codes or principles of AI ethics but fail to apply them in practice. One of the reviews notes that, although ethical issues (e.g., data privacy and algorithmic bias) are acknowledged, few institutions have effectively implemented governance processes or policies to address the real-world applications of AI.

For example, institutions can institute an AI policy, or a student code of conduct can include a reference to the use of generative AI. Nevertheless, they frequently do not renew contracts with their vendors, audit them, provide faculty training, or even observe their compliance with such standards. The result is the fact that there is no connection between the highest ideals (ethical codes) and working reality (ethics in workflows, audits, supervision). It has therefore remained spotty and responsive in execution. This gap cannot be bridged in isolation; it needs to be resourced, held accountable, transformed within the institutional culture, and monitored continuously. Without these types of operations, governance through ethics will be just a mere show, lacking any substance, since credibility and trust will be at stake.

10. ROADMAP FOR THE FUTURE: TOWARDS ETHICAL AND SUSTAINABLE AI ECOSYSTEMS

10.1 Vision for Responsible AI in Academia

Considering AI not as an efficiency tool but as a structure of institutional strategy, in which ethics, human-machine cooperation, and sustainability have become inseparable parts of the institution's DNA, must be imagined as the future of academic institutions. Ethical AI governance in this regard should be incorporated into the strategic plan, resource distribution, and the culture of universities. The meta-systematic review of AI in higher education concluded that 19% of the surveyed institutions worldwide have an official AI policy in place, and another 42% are in the process of development, which is a critical sign of an opportunity window to invest in strategic thinking.

Speaking of the human-machine collaboration model, it represents a paradigm shift in AI, in which AI supplements human activity to enhance human capabilities. For example, a study of hybrid grading systems showed that human-AI teaming increased consistency and fairness while preserving pedagogical delicacy. This partnership stance sees AI as a supplement, not automation, and augments the twin aspects of efficiency and integrity in education.

The institutions should articulate that AI can help educators and students become more creative and critical thinkers, and that it supports the primary purpose of higher education: fostering human flourishing. These are strategic alignment (AI governance as part of the institutional mission), capacity building (ethical literacy and infrastructure), and success measures (trust, fairness, and human agency). The strategy of emphasizing ethics as the foundation of the plan could help universities ensure that the development of AI is not merely functional but remains grounded in the long-term values of academia, inclusion, and the empowerment of humans.

10.2 Ethical Leadership and Governance Innovation

Ethical leadership and governance innovation are critical and it takes moral courage and ethical leadership to have ethical AI ecosystems. The leaders of AI governance, such as provosts, deans, and CIOs, are expected to be at the forefront of managing AI as a strategic project and to face the ethical consequences of their actions and those of their organizations. According to a recent survey on AI governance, only a small number of organizations had a clearly defined set of leadership roles for AI ethics management, undermining coordination between AI implementation and institutional values.

The establishment of memorable roles also demonstrates the institutional seriousness and responsibility, e.g., AI Ethics Leadership Chairs or a Chief AI Ethics Officer. They ought to operationalize governance systems, audit vendor contracts, safeguard student data, and be transparent about the use of algorithms in decision-making. For example, the institution that hired older AI officers with ethics expertise found that it achieved entrenched ethics training and review among staff members 30% faster.

Better yet, governance innovation can be applied to interfaculty committees, student-faculty audit boards, and cross-departmental working groups to monitor AI tools and audits, which are part of executive governance. This change in the institution fosters a culture of ethical reflexivity rather than mere compliance. Combined with leadership responsibility, such structures can transform AI governance from a box-ticking exercise into an operational part of institutional governance.

10.3 Collaborative Global Networks for AI Governance

AI cannot be controlled alone by higher education bodies. International networks between universities, research centers, governments, and industry are essential for sharing learning, benchmarking, and standard-setting, as well as for ethical research networks. The systematic literature review of AI governance highlights the importance of multi-level governance (team, organisation, national, international) and addresses the gap in the collaborative global environment (Bond et al., 2024). They include cross-border consortia that share bias-audit methodologies to learn about analytics, transnational standards for vendor audits, or open-source repositories of responsible AI governance tools. These networks enable institutions in emerging economies to gain access to governance resources, focus on best practices, and localize ethical standards. Universities through these global networks develop resilience, legitimacy, and collective ethical dedication.

10.4 Sustaining Trust and Academic Integrity

Trust between students, faculty, administrators, and other external stakeholders, and academic integrity are the most significant pillars of sustainable AI ecosystems, and the introduction of AI should not erode them. Trust is founded on ethical frameworks: when students learn about data use, faculty audit AI results, and sellers are transparent, institutional legitimacy is strengthened. Indicatively, a cross-institutional study found that increased institutionalisation of judgments among students was associated with greater transparency in AI-assisted assessment.

Academic integrity means finding a balance between digital transformation and the principles of originality, subjective judgment, and reflective learning. The adoption of AI needs to be a companion, not a substitute, in the study. Ethics is a phenomenon that institutions need to integrate into their digital transformation. It should be a policy, an audit, and a pedagogy that are in harmony with human monitoring in the fundamental educational processes. Such an ethics-oriented strategy allows AI to become an innovation driver, consistent with the goal of higher education, but not a threat to it.

11. CONCLUSION

11.1 Revisiting the Ethical Imperative

As the concept of artificial intelligence (AI) in higher education becomes a reality, the need to introduce ethical governance is no longer a matter of preference; it is a matter of life and death for academic integrity, institutional trust, and human dignity. Ethical governance is a moral and procedural framework that helps universities apply AI in a way that is morally and transparently responsible. In the absence of these systems, the academic landscape will remain biased, infringing on scholars' privacy and undermining the accuracy of higher education systems in the eyes of the public.

The moral imperative does not relate solely to law or institutional regulation; it is also a shared moral duty that ensures AI will be a tool of liberation, not domination. This is an example of the significance of ethics and morality in technological development. Ethical governance is thus a preventive element that strikes a balance between innovation and other moral values, such as transparency, justice, and inclusiveness. These values will be required to protect the integrity and social mission of academia as higher education becomes involved in AI-driven environments.

11.2 Summary of Proposed Framework

In this chapter, a general Ethical Governance Framework for AI in Higher Education is presented, grounded in four key dimensions: ethical principles, governance framework, implementation mechanisms, and feedback. All AI applications in learning, research, and administration are anchored on the normative layer, which is founded on guiding and governing principles such as human-centeredness, fairness, transparency, and accountability. This governance structure layer converts these values into formalized ethics committees, AI management boards, and role-specific responsibility frameworks for faculty, students, and IT departments.

The implementation layer will focus on integrating the policy, the ethical review procedure, and periodic AI audits. Experience indicates that organizations that undergo well-organized AI ethics audits reduce algorithmic bias by a quarter over two years. Furthermore, AI ethics should be integrated into the curriculum and staff training to build institutional readiness and inculcate ethical reflexivity among interested parties.

The approval and feedback processes ensure that the framework is flexible to the changes in technology and society. Universities can remain relevant in governance by ensuring iterative policy evaluation, a user feedback loop, and an international benchmarking process that will sustain their relevance over time. When combined, these dimensions create a whole governance ecosystem that integrates moral philosophy and organizational pragmatism. The suggested model is not purely theoretical but rather practical, serving as a bridge between ideal ethical standards and the realities of academic work.

11.3 The Way Forward

There needs to be a balance between innovation and moral responsibility in the future. As AI is changing the academic landscape, whether in personalized learning or research analytics, higher education must be watchful to ensure that technology does not nullify the ideology it is supposed to reinforce. The future needs to be about ethical agility, where policies adapt to technological changes; therefore, the ethical review mechanism should be dynamic rather than static.

Besides, ethical AI ecosystems will be sustainable through leadership accountability. Establishing AI Ethics Leadership Chairs, advancing transdisciplinary studies in responsible AI, and fostering cross-border collaboration on shared ethical principles are critical steps for the next decade. Colleges will be able to promote ethical literacy and foster transparency across all levels of AI use by setting global responsible innovation standards.

In conclusion, AI development does not face ethical governance as an obstacle; rather, it is what propels it forward. By balancing technology and humanistic values, universities can develop an AI-powered academic future that upholds integrity, drives inclusion, and enables the development of sustainable learning communities.

REFERENCES

Agbese, M., Alanen, H. K., Antikainen, J., Erika, H., Isomaki, H., Jantunen, M., … & Vakkuri, V. (2023). *Governance in ethical and trustworthy AI systems: Extension of the ECCOLA method for AI ethics governance using GARP*. E-Informatica Software Engineering Journal, 17(1).

Allison, J., Hwang, G. J., Mayer, R. E., Pellas, N., Karnalim, O., de Freitas, S., Ng, O.-L., Huang, Y.-M., Hooshyar, D., Seidman, R. H., Al-Emran, M., Mikropoulos, T. A., Schroeder, N. L., Roscoe, R. D., & Sanusi, I. (2025). From generative AI to extended reality: Multidisciplinary perspectives on the challenges, opportunities, and future of educational computing. *Journal of Educational Computing Research*, *63*(6), 1327–1363. DOI: 10.1177/07356331251359964

Almalawi, A., Soh, B., Li, A., & Samra, H. (2024). Predictive models for educational purposes: A systematic review. *Big Data and Cognitive Computing*, *8*(12), 187. DOI: 10.3390/bdcc8120187

Arias, J., Salas, J. I., Chiappe, A., & Sáez Delgado, F. (2025). The extended education 4.0: Lifelong learning in times of artificial intelligence. *Applied Sciences (Basel, Switzerland)*, *15*(17), 9352. DOI: 10.3390/app15179352

Batool, A., Zowghi, D., & Bano, M. (2025). AI governance: A systematic literature review. *AI and Ethics*, •••, 1–15.

Bond, M., Khosravi, H., De Laat, M., Bergdahl, N., Negrea, V., Oxley, E., Pham, P., Chong, S. W., & Siemens, G. (2024). A meta systematic review of artificial intelligence in higher education: A call for increased ethics, collaboration, and rigour. *International Journal of Educational Technology in Higher Education*, *21*(1), 4. DOI: 10.1186/s41239-023-00436-z

Cancela-Outeda, C. (2024). The EU's AI act: A framework for collaborative governance. *Internet of Things : Engineering Cyber Physical Human Systems*, *27*, 101291. DOI: 10.1016/j.iot.2024.101291

Cao, X., Lv, D., Xing, Z., & Zhang, L. (2023). Linking adaptive governance, strategic flexibility and responsible innovation: Evidence from China. *International Journal on Management of Innovation & Technology*, *20*(6), 2350040. DOI: 10.1142/S0219877023500402

Capogna, S., & Greco, F. (2024). *The digital transformation of European higher education*. Springer. DOI: 10.1007/978-3-031-70763-6

Chan, C. K. Y. (2023). A comprehensive AI policy education framework for university teaching and learning. *International Journal of Educational Technology in Higher Education, 20*(38), 38. DOI: 10.1186/s41239-023-00408-3

Chandrasekhar, R. (2025). *Legal frictions for data openness: Reflections from a case-study on re-use of the open web for AI training* (Doctoral dissertation, Centre Internet et Société-CNRS; Inno3; Open Knowledge Foundation).

Chauhan, S., & Dutta, A. (2025). Artificial intelligence in student privacy and data security. *International Journal of Advanced Research in Computer Science, 16*(3).

Chen, L., & Fang, Y. (2025). ChatGPT-3 policies in the making: Identifying blind spots and supporting the language needs of international students. In *Rethinking Language Education in the Age of Generative AI* (pp. 90–110). Routledge. DOI: 10.4324/9781003426929-8

Coeckelbergh, M. (2025). Three challenges for a global AI ethics: Towards a more relational normative vision. *AI and Ethics, 5*(5), 5527–5533. DOI: 10.1007/s43681-025-00791-9

Derrick, G., Sumbiri, D., Ngugi, J., & Habimana, P. (2025). Design and implementation of an e-exam cheating control system using real-time monitoring and behavioral detection. *Journal of Information Technology, 5*(9), 12–27. DOI: 10.70619/vol5iss9pp12-27

Ebers, M. (2024). Truly risk-based regulation of artificial intelligence: How to implement the EU's AI Act. *European Journal of Risk Regulation*, •••, 1–20.

Habib, M. U., Sattar, A., Iqbal, M. J., & Saleem, S. (2025). AI-driven tutoring vs. human teachers: Examining the student–teacher relationship. *Review of Applied Management and Social Sciences, 8*(1), 363–374. DOI: 10.47067/ramss.v8i1.466

Hadi, W., Al-Qerem, A., & Aldweesh, A. (2025). Institutional policies, governance, and regulatory responses to generative AI. In *Examining Cybersecurity Risks Produced by Generative AI* (pp. 643–666). IGI Global Scientific Publishing. DOI: 10.4018/979-8-3373-0832-6.ch026

Han, X., Xiao, S., Sheng, J., & Zhang, G. (2025). Enhancing efficiency and decision-making in higher education through intelligent commercial integration: Leveraging artificial intelligence. *Journal of the Knowledge Economy, 16*(1), 1546–1582. DOI: 10.1007/s13132-024-01868-2

Hassan, Z. Y. (2025). *AI-driven horizons: Shaping the future of global quality assurance in higher education.* In *AI and ethics, academic integrity and the future of quality assurance in higher education* (p. 105).

Khairullah, S. A., Harris, S., Hadi, H. J., Sandhu, R. A., Ahmad, N., & Alshara, M. A. (2025, February). Implementing artificial intelligence in academic and administrative processes through responsible strategic leadership in higher education institutions. [Frontiers Media SA.]. *Frontiers in Education*, *10*, 1548104. DOI: 10.3389/feduc.2025.1548104

Kochegurova, E. A., & Zateev, R. P. (2022). Hidden monitoring based on keystroke dynamics in online examination system. *Programming and Computer Software*, *48*(6), 385–398. DOI: 10.1134/S0361768822060044

Kunjumuhammed, S. K. (2024). Artificial intelligence in addressing educational inequality dimensions in higher education institutions (HEIs): A critical review. In *Risks and challenges of AI-driven finance: Bias, ethics, and security* (pp. 146–164).

Labadie, C., & Legner, C. (2023). Building data management capabilities to address data protection regulations: Learnings from EU-GDPR. *Journal of Information Technology*, *38*(1), 16–44. DOI: 10.1177/02683962221141456

Le Dinh, T., Le, T. D., Uwizeyemungu, S., & Pelletier, C. (2025). Human-centered artificial intelligence in higher education: A framework for systematic literature reviews. *Information (Basel)*, *16*(3), 240. DOI: 10.3390/info16030240

Lee, J. Y. (2025). *Online exam proctoring in higher education: A critical analysis of students' and instructors' processes and perspectives* (Doctoral dissertation, University of California, Davis).

Levin, J. S. (2022). *Pathways and experiences of first-generation graduate students: Wary and weary travelers*. Springer Nature. DOI: 10.1007/978-3-031-16808-6

Li, M., Enkhtur, A., Yamamoto, B. A., Cheng, F., & Chen, L. (2025). Potential societal biases of ChatGPT in higher education: A scoping review. *Open Praxis*, *17*(1), 79–94. DOI: 10.55982/openpraxis.17.1.750

Lythreatis, S., El-Kassar, A. N., Smart, P., & Ferraris, A. (2024). Participative leadership, ethical climate and responsible innovation perceptions: Evidence from South Korea. *Asia Pacific Journal of Management*, *41*(3), 1285–1312. DOI: 10.1007/s10490-022-09856-3

Marín, Y. R., Caro, O. C., Rituay, A. M. C., Llanos, K. A. G., Perez, D. T., Bardales, E. S., Tuesta, J. N. A., & Santos, R. C. (2025). Ethical challenges associated with the use of artificial intelligence in university education. *Journal of Academic Ethics*, *23*(4), 2443–2467. DOI: 10.1007/s10805-025-09660-w

Maslej, N., Fattorini, L., Perrault, R., Gil, Y., Parli, V., Kariuki, N., . . . Oak, S. (2025). Artificial intelligence index report 2025. *arXiv preprint arXiv:2504.07139*.

McDonald, N., Johri, A., Ali, A., & Collier, A. H. (2025). Generative artificial intelligence in higher education: Evidence from an analysis of institutional policies and guidelines. *Computers in Human Behavior: Artificial Humans*, *3*, 100121. DOI: 10.1016/j.chbah.2025.100121

McKay, M. H. (2024, June). Realizing the promise of AI governance involving humans-in-the-loop. In *International Conference on Human-Computer Interaction* (pp. 107–123). Springer Nature Switzerland. DOI: 10.1007/978-3-031-76827-9_7

Memarian, B., & Doleck, T. (2023). Fairness, accountability, transparency, and ethics (FATE) in artificial intelligence (AI) and higher education: A systematic review. *Computers and Education: Artificial Intelligence*, *5*, 100152. DOI: 10.1016/j.caeai.2023.100152

Muringa, T. P. (2025, September). Exploring ethical dilemmas and institutional challenges in AI adoption: A study of South African universities. *Frontiers in Education*, *10*, 1628019. DOI: 10.3389/feduc.2025.1628019

Nikolinakos, N. T. (2023). Ethical principles for trustworthy AI. In *EU policy and legal framework for artificial intelligence, robotics and related technologies – The AI Act* (pp. 101–166). Springer.

Ogwueleka, F. N. (2025). Plagiarism detection in the age of artificial intelligence: Current technologies and future directions. *AI and Ethics, Academic Integrity and the Future of Quality Assurance in Higher Education*, 10.

Okada, A., Sherborne, T., Panselinas, G., & Kolionis, G. (2025). Fostering transversal skills through open schooling supported by the CARE-KNOW-DO pedagogical model and the UNESCO AI competencies framework. *International Journal of Artificial Intelligence in Education*, *35*(4), 1–46. DOI: 10.1007/s40593-025-00458-w

Oncioiu, I., & Bularca, A. R. (2025). Artificial intelligence governance in higher education: The role of knowledge-based strategies in fostering legal awareness and ethical artificial intelligence literacy. *Societies (Basel, Switzerland)*, *15*(6), 144. DOI: 10.3390/soc15060144

Panarese, P., Grasso, M. M., & Solinas, C. (2025). Algorithmic bias, fairness, and inclusivity: A multilevel framework for justice-oriented AI. *AI & Society*, •••, 1–23. DOI: 10.1007/s00146-025-02451-2

Popow, M. (2025). Decolonizing knowledge in the postdigital era: Pedagogical strategies for navigating AI-driven epistemic transformations. *Educational Philosophy and Theory*, •••, 1–13.

Pudasaini, S., Miralles-Pechuán, L., Lillis, D., & Llorens Salvador, M. (2024). Survey on AI-generated plagiarism detection: The impact of large language models on academic integrity. *Journal of Academic Ethics*, •••, 1–34.

Roberts, H., Cowls, J., Morley, J., Taddeo, M., Wang, V., & Floridi, L. (2021). The Chinese approach to artificial intelligence: An analysis of policy, ethics, and regulation. In *Ethics, governance, and policies in artificial intelligence* (pp. 47–79). Springer International Publishing. DOI: 10.1007/978-3-030-81907-1_5

Rodríguez Valencia, L., Ochoa Arellano, M. J., Gutiérrez Figueroa, S. A., Mur Nuño, C., Monsalve Piqueras, B., Corrales Paredes, A. D. V., & Levi Alfaroviz, A. (2025). A systematic review of artificial intelligence applied to compliance: Fraud detection in cryptocurrency transactions. *Journal of Risk and Financial Management*, *18*(11), 612. DOI: 10.3390/jrfm18110612

Schiff, D. (2022). Education for AI, not AI for education: The role of education and ethics in national AI policy strategies. *International Journal of Artificial Intelligence in Education*, *32*(3), 527–563. DOI: 10.1007/s40593-021-00270-2

Simbeck, K. (2024). They shall be fair, transparent, and robust: Auditing learning analytics systems. *AI and Ethics*, *4*(2), 555–571. DOI: 10.1007/s43681-023-00292-7

Sloane, M., & Wüllhorst, E. (2025). A systematic review of regulatory strategies and transparency mandates in AI regulation in Europe, the United States, and Canada. *Data & Policy*, *7*, e11. DOI: 10.1017/dap.2024.54

Sultana, S. S., Renugadevi, R., Bhargavi, M., & Biyabani, S. A. A. (2025). AI-driven evaluation techniques: Revolutionizing student practices. In *Adopting Artificial Intelligence Tools in Higher Education* (pp. 1–22). CRC Press. DOI: 10.1201/9781003470304-1

Taneja, A. (2025). Explainable AI: Building trust and transparency in machine learning models. *Journal of Engineering and Computer Sciences*, *4*(8), 482–489.

Temper, M., Tjoa, S., & David, L. (2025, February). Higher Education Act for AI (HEAT-AI): A framework to regulate the usage of AI in higher education institutions. [). Frontiers Media SA.]. *Frontiers in Education*, *10*, 1505370. DOI: 10.3389/feduc.2025.1505370

Turner, L., Asada, Y., Leider, J., Piekarz-Porter, E., Schwartz, M., & Chriqui, J. F. (2021). Can monitoring make it happen? An assessment of how reporting, monitoring, and evaluation can support local wellness policy implementation in US schools. *Nutrients*, *13*(1), 193. DOI: 10.3390/nu13010193 PMID: 33435481

Ullah, M., Bin Naeem, S., & Kamel Boulos, M. N. (2024). Assessing the guidelines on the use of generative artificial intelligence tools in universities: A survey of the world's top 50 universities. *Big Data and Cognitive Computing*, *8*(12), 194. DOI: 10.3390/bdcc8120194

Van Norren, D. E. (2023). The ethics of artificial intelligence, UNESCO and the African Ubuntu perspective. *Journal of Information. Communication and Ethics in Society*, *21*(1), 112–128. DOI: 10.1108/JICES-04-2022-0037

Vetrivel, S. C., Arun, V. P., Ambikapathi, R., & Saravanan, T. P. (2025). Automated grading systems: Enhancing efficiency and consistency in student assessments. In *Adopting artificial intelligence tools in higher education* (pp. 41–61). CRC Press. DOI: 10.1201/9781003470304-3

Vieriu, A. M., & Petrea, G. (2025). The impact of artificial intelligence (AI) on students' academic development. *Education Sciences*, *15*(3), 343. DOI: 10.3390/educsci15030343

Wiles-Warner, J. J. (2025). *Establishing policies and standards to implement socially sustainable practices* (Doctoral dissertation, Walden University).

Wong, W. K. O. (2024). The sudden disruptive rise of generative artificial intelligence? An evaluation of their impact on higher education and the global workplace. *Journal of Open Innovation*, *10*(2), 100278. DOI: 10.1016/j.joitmc.2024.100278

Yadav, S. (2025). Advancing education with AI-driven education for diverse learners: Integrating AI into pedagogical practices. In *Integrating AI into pedagogical education* (pp. 49–80). IGI Global Scientific Publishing.

Yusuf, A., Pervin, N., & Román-González, M. (2024). Generative AI and the future of higher education: A threat to academic integrity or reformation? Evidence from multicultural perspectives. *International Journal of Educational Technology in Higher Education*, *21*(1), 21. DOI: 10.1186/s41239-024-00453-6

Zhai, C., Wibowo, S., & Li, L. D. (2024). *The effects of over-reliance on AI dialogue systems on students' cognitive abilities: A systematic review*. Smart Learning Environments, 11(1), Article 28.

Zhang, Y., Yip, C., Lu, E., & Dong, Z. Y. (2022). A systematic review on technologies and applications in smart campus: A human-centered case study. *IEEE Access : Practical Innovations, Open Solutions*, *10*, 16134–16149. DOI: 10.1109/ACCESS.2022.3148735

Chapter 3

Artificial Intelligence in Higher Education: Opportunities, Challenges, and Global Perspectives

Maleeha Nazim
http://orcid.org/0000-0002-8101-1304
University of Management and Technology, Lahore, Pakistan

Zahra Nazim
http://orcid.org/0009-0001-2524-8999
Institute of Business and Health Managemnt, Dow University of Health Sciences, Karachi, Pakistan

ABSTRACT

The rapid evolution of Artificial Intelligence (AI) is transforming the landscape of higher education worldwide. Growing demands on universities, including the need to expand learning, personalise instruction, increase research efficiency, and adapt to international standards, have fuelled AI's entry into higher education. The chapter examines AI's many facets and potential in higher education, covering its uses, consequences, prospects, difficulties, dangers, misconceptions, and disparities worldwide. The goal is to provide educators, researchers, and policymakers with the knowledge they need to capitalise on AI's advantages while preserving educational requirements, integrity, and universal equity in the rapidly changing field of AI-assisted higher education. The scope includes applications of AI in education, administration, and research to assist educators, administrators, and legislators in comprehending how AI is changing instruction, knowledge, investigation, and governance in institutions.

DOI: 10.4018/979-8-3373-7097-2.ch003

INTRODUCTION

Technological advancements have emerged as the most revolutionary factor in reshaping the twenty-first century. One of the outcomes of these advancements is AI and its immediate worldwide acceptance, especially in higher education. Figure 1 provides a snapshot of the broad themes of higher education being affected by AI. Higher education is only one of the many industries throughout the world that has seen immense transformation by the rapid development of AI. With the presence of massive language models and generative AI (Yan et al., 2024; Bittle & El-Gayar, 2025), universities all around the world have started incorporating AI-driven technologies into teaching, research and administrative tasks during the past ten years at an accelerated rate. AI can promote customised learning pathways, increase institutional efficiency, and strengthen educational research (Crompton & Burke, 2024; Marín et al., 2025). However, there are serious issues with its integration. Despite these developments, opinions on how much AI should be included in educational settings continue to differ among educators, legislators, and institutions. This fundamental issue stems from a dual reality: AI has great potential for education, but it also poses ethical, pedagogical, and structural challenges that institutions are still ill-equipped to handle. Concerns about data privacy, algorithmic bias, increasing surveillance in digital learning environments (Chan, 2023), academic integrity, ethical behaviour, data governance, equity, and long-term effects on human learning (Mahajan, 2025) are among the ethical issues that AI systems bring up.

Additionally, higher education establishments in developing countries do not equally benefit from AI-enhanced tools due to global discrepancies in digital infrastructure, which exacerbates access and innovation gaps (Mulaudzi and Hamilton, 2025). The unequal availability of AI systems around the world, reflects deeper socioeconomic disparities. Universities in such countries are currently at a crossroads where they must incorporate the dramatic shift towards AI in their own instruction, research, and administrative procedures as well as educational practices, and student experiences to educate graduates for a workforce driven by AI. On the pedagogical front, faculty must balance using AI as a beneficial teaching partner (Mahajan, 2025; Kong et al., 2025).

Figure 1. AI Integration in Higher Education

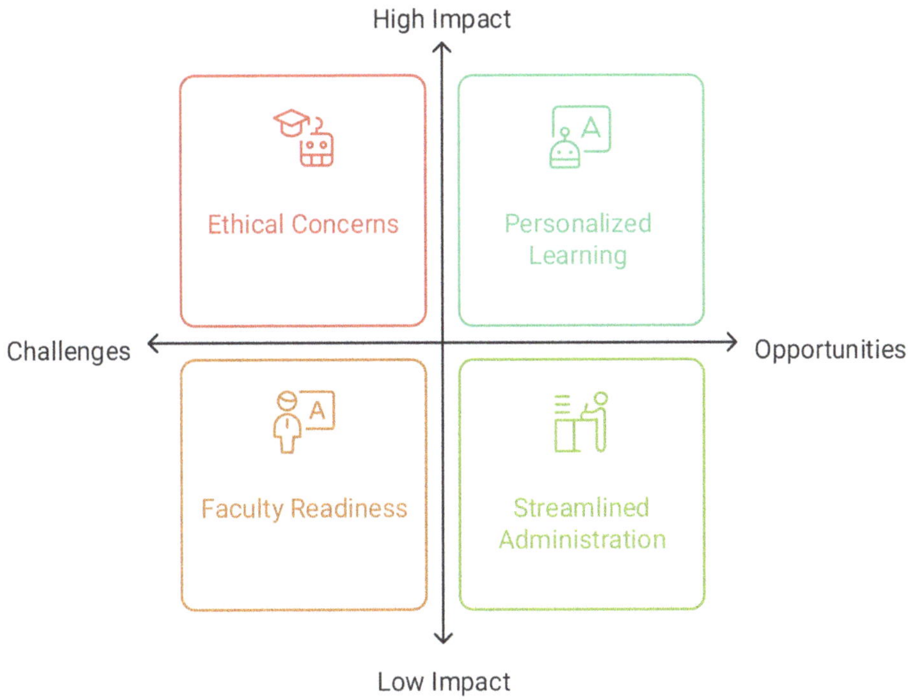

According to Yan et al. (2023) and Mulaudzi & Hamilton (2025), the COVID-19 pandemic continued to accelerate digital transformation by forcing universities to heavily rely on online resources for online and blended instruction and encouraging educators to investigate AI augmented systems for evaluation, feedback, and student engagement. Although these advancements have increased the possibilities for scalable, technologically assisted learning, they also emphasise the necessity of a thorough comprehension of AI's pedagogical efficacy and ethical ramifications at the institutional and international levels (Mahajan, 2025; Bittle & El-Gayar, 2025).

AI changes the governance, experiences, and results of higher education stakeholders far more than corporate training, or general technology adoption (Park & Yoon, 2025; Lawal, 2021). Through analytical forecasting, early warning systems, resource optimisation, and admissions analytics, AI technologies enable both effectively and proactively the administrative decision-making and functional efficiency of institutions.

AI is being utilised more in education to enable student support chatbots, curriculum mapping, academic advising, automated grading, adaptive learning, and personalised feedback (Yinfeng & Abdullah, 2025; Kumar et al., 2025). AI driven personalised education makes learning pathways more accessible and flexible by giving students access to resources that are customised to their requirements, preferences, and pace (Mulaudzi & Hamilton, 2025). These resources are intended to improve educational opportunities, facilitate individualised pathways, and expedite evaluation procedures (Guevara et al, 2025). Additionally, AI-enhanced analytics improve the overall excellence and functionality of higher education systems based on empirically supported organisational choices, ranging from assessing the efficacy of courses to predicting enrolment trends (Yan et al., 2024).

ABUSE OF AI

Despite these advantages, incorporating AI into institutions of higher learning presents difficult moral dilemmas, especially when it comes to scholarly research. Policies address these issues are now being developed by institutions, although many frameworks are either unfinished or used inconsistently (Xiao, Chen, & Bao, 2023; Mahajan, 2025).

Students may rely more on generative AI systems for writing, problem-solving, summarising, and brainstorming as they become more widely available, which could reduce their capacity for independent learning, critical thinking, and creativity (Mulaudzi & Hamilton, 2025; Yan et al., 2024). If educators rely too much on AI for lesson planning, content creation, or assessment, it could inadvertently lower pedagogical quality (Mahajan, 2025; Mulaudzi & Hamilton, 2025).

AI has been swiftly adopted and tested throughout higher education systems in high-income countries with sophisticated digital ecosystems and significant research investments (Khan, Umer, & Faruqe, 2024; Xiao et al., 2023). Low- and middle-income nations, on the other hand, frequently encounter obstacles like inadequate finance, restricted access to superior digital infrastructure, inadequate faculty training, and inconsistent policy frameworks.

AI FRIENDLY ORGANIZATIONS- HOW?

Traditional academic methods are changing as AI becomes increasingly integrated into higher education. Many educational establishments now have AI-driven research assistants, predictive learning analytics, automated assessment tools, intelligent tutoring systems, and adaptive learning platforms. Personalised routes, more learner engagement, and more effective institutional procedures are all promised by these tools (Carver, 2020; Huang et al., 2025). However, there is continuous discussion over these innovations' pedagogical efficacy, dependability, and ethical consequences. Due to a lack of proper AI training, many faculty members are either resistant to, or abuse, or over-rely on AI-based tools.

Faculty development includes giving teachers the tools they need to carefully incorporate AI tools into their teaching, research, and evaluation procedures (Mahajan, 2025) as well as the related training to use these tools in all these areas. AI in higher education is therefore an overall management, fairness, and cognitive dilemma rather than just a technical one (Chang and Parkes; Kapoor and Sindwani, 2025). Many studies are still primarily focused on technology and do not consider how AI can impact institutional culture, student autonomy, or educational philosophies (Liu et al., 2023).

Understanding these uses and abuses is essential to comprehending AI's expanding impact and the skills needed for successful adoption in educational settings. AI is becoming an essential tool, it is still a poorly understood and inconsistently used breakthrough (Brohi, Jhanjhi & Pillai, 2025).

CONCERNS OF AI

We will thoroughly examine these issues.

Institutional Decision-Making

Artificial intelligence integration in higher education affects institutional decision-making in several ways and offers both benefits and problems (Almisad & Aleidan, 2025). Higher education is quickly changing because of the incorporation of artificial intelligence (AI), which presents many chances for innovation and advancement, but these developments come with serious issues that affect institutional decision-making. Academic integrity, human agency, equality, privacy, and faculty anxiety are all complicated challenges that institutions must deal with (Verano et al., 2025).

Privacy and Autonomy for Students

Concerns regarding learner confidentiality and freedom are raised by the introduction of AI-powered monitoring, assessment, and predictive analytics. To evaluate student performance and forecast results, institutions are depending more on data analytics, which frequently results in the gathering of a great deal of personal data. Although this information might help improve teaching methods, students' privacy may be compromised. For example, AI systems may keep an eye on students' engagement levels, academic achievement, and online behaviour, creating an atmosphere akin to surveillance. Students' autonomy may be threatened by this kind of data collecting given that they might experience as though their behaviour is continuously being watched.

Digital Divide of AI Resources

The possible expansion of the digital gap between institutions with sufficient funding and those without it is another urgent issue. Institutions that have access to cutting-edge AI technology can greatly improve their educational offerings, while those that don't are at a risk of falling further away. This discrepancy may exacerbate already-existing disparities in higher education by providing students with uneven learning opportunities. Students in impoverished areas cannot have access to the infrastructure needed to apply AI solutions, depriving them of vital resources for their academic achievement.

Over-Reliance on AI

Concerns about losing human agency are raised by the overuse of technology and artificial intelligence in educational settings, which can hinder interpersonal learning, creativity, and critical thinking. AI may promote a passive learning strategy even if it can help provide individualised learning experiences. Students may lose their capacity for critical and creative thought if they rely too much on AI for knowledge and problem-solving. As AI takes on additional duties in the classroom, instructors also confront issues related to their positions.

Replacement Fear and Opposition of Faculty

Faculty members' worries about incorporating AI technology into their methods of instruction have a significant impact on institutional decision-making. Implementing artificial intelligence (AI) strategies in the classroom meets with opposition since many instructors fear being replaced by computers (Popenici & Kerr, 2017). The absence of AI activities inside the university may result from instructors feeling that AI skills are overshadowing their experience. Leaders in higher education must address these issues by creating a cooperative atmosphere where teachers view AI as an additional resource rather than a substitute. Faculty members' concerns can be addressed through an innovative culture fostered by involving them in the process of making decisions related to the application of AI. Despite the potential advantages of AI technologies, institutions must carefully manage the opposition caused by these concerns.

Generative AI and Honesty in Academics

The emergence of generative AI tools, like ChatGPT, poses serious concerns about plagiarism, originality, and the effectiveness of conventional assessment techniques. The distinction between innovative effort and plagiarised information is becoming hazier as students have access to sophisticated AI tools that can produce content, algorithms, and other imaginative creations (Kumar et al., 2025). This change puts academic integrity at risk and makes it challenging for teachers to fairly evaluate students' learning. Institutions need to reconsider their evaluation methods and think about adopting more comprehensive strategies that prioritise practical knowledge, innovation, and teamwork (Popenici & Kerr, 2017).

IMPLICATIONS

Higher education is undergoing a revolution thanks to artificial intelligence (AI), which is changing the processes of instruction, education, management, and study. Using worldwide viewpoints and pertinent sources, this chapter examines five major implications for artificial intelligence in higher learning. These ramifications show how AI might expedite research, promote experiential learning, automate administrative processes, personalise learning, and modify curriculum to accommodate future labour demands falling into a few categories:

1. Tailoring Lessons for Students

AI's potential to improve learning outcomes by customising educational experiences to each student's needs is one of its most promising applications in higher education. AI algorithms are used by adaptive learning systems to evaluate student performance data, spot knowledge gaps, and instantly modify the content and complexity of lessons. By ensuring that students get teaching at their ideal speed, this personalisation helps high IQ students avoid boredom and lessens frustration for struggling learners. Adaptive learning platforms have been shown to be beneficial by research. According to research conducted by the Bill & Melinda Gates Foundation (2013), for example, pupils who used adaptive maths software outperformed those who used traditional techniques by an average of 10–15% (Zarkovic, 2020). In a similar vein, learning trajectories have been demonstrated to be accelerated by the Khan Academy's customised activities, with students grasping ideas up to twice as quickly as in conventional educational settings (Khan Academy, 2022). Globally speaking, adaptive learning has been included into national education systems in nations like Finland and Singapore. Through partnerships with AI firms, Singapore's

Ministry of Education (2025) has created personalised learning paths that have increased academic achievement and student engagement across a range of different socioeconomic categories.

2. Streamlining of Institutional Procedures

AI is revolutionising higher education's administrative procedures by automating repetitive jobs like scheduling, record-keeping, and admissions processing. This simplification increases operational effectiveness and enables institutions to devote more funds to important educational initiatives. Student enquiries are handled by chat bots and artificial intelligence-powered virtual assistants, which cut time to respond from days to minutes. For instance, by offering immediate assistance, Georgia State University's AI chatbot Pounce has handled more than 1.5 million student contacts, increasing retention rates (Jones, 2022). Like this, a few American colleges have adopted AI-driven admissions systems that can evaluate application data to forecast student achievement and aid in decision-making.

Institutions across the world are using AI to automate administrative tasks. The University of Edinburgh in the UK employs artificial intelligence to automate student record administration, which results in a 30% reduction in administrative effort (Nemani, 2025). AI platforms are being used in developing nations like India to effectively handle the enrolment of millions of students in massive open online courses (Jagetiya, Challa & Prashanthi, 2018).

3. Experience and Student-Centred Learning

AI promotes interactive, student-centred learning that prioritises active engagement over passive lectures by enabling immersive technology, virtual instructors, and simulations. AI-powered virtual tutors in Australia and the UK offer round-the-clock feedback, tailoring mentoring and enhancing students' self-esteem (David, 2024).

4. AI-Assisted Literature Reviews

By automating data analysis, literature reviews, and pattern recognition, AI speeds up all steps of the research process as well as interdisciplinary research. Research time can be cut by 30–40% by using technologies include IBM Watson or Google Scholar, among other AI features, which analyse large datasets to find trends (Dwivedi, 2025). Presently, there are numerous AI tools both paid and free available for researchers. Rabbit for literature discovery, Consensus for summarizing findings, elicit for automating literature reviews, and Scite for citation context are just a few widely used ones. Tools like Sci Space, Paperpal, and Scholarcy are also used for writing and analysing research papers. The Horizon 2020 initiative in Europe from 2014 to 2020 used AI for basic research that combined economic and environmental data such as climate modelling. After its successful implementation Horizon Europe was introduced for 2021-2027.

5. Skills Needed for Future Employment

By emphasising abilities such as reasoning, innovative thinking, and knowledge of AI that are crucial for future employment, AI forces higher education to reconsider its courses. Graduates must possess skills in human-AI collaboration as AI automates repetitive work (Forcelli, 2024). To prepare learners for an AI-driven profession, US colleges are including data science and AI ethics into their curricula. To adjust to AI advances, the OECD's Education 2030 model places a strong emphasis on lifelong learning (Shiohira,2021). Although this consequence presents opportunity for future-proofing education, structural changes are necessary to match instruction with the demands of the global economy.

ROLE

AI's dual ability as a management and instructional tool is demonstrated by its use in administration and education:

AI Chatbots in Real Time

AI chatbots are becoming a popular tool for improving real-time learning and student engagement (Ouariach, Nejjari, Ouariach, & Khaldi, 2025). Natural language processing-powered chatbots are commercially accessible sophisticated AI solutions that improve learner communication and educational processes while increasing motivation among learners, engagement, and learning results. Chatbots provide operational efficiency improvements by reducing the effort of university personnel by responding to commonly requested enquiries, in addition to providing direct educational benefits. This combined benefit assisting students while relieving staff of repetitive duties allows university staff to concentrate on mentorship and higher-order abilities, signifying a shift in the way faculty members use their expertise and their time.

Early Interventions are Made

Legowo et al (2024) said one important AI application that makes it possible to identify at-risk kids early on is analytics that is predictive for student support services. Predictive analytics is positioned as a component of a larger portfolio of AI technologies intended to simplify student assistance and enable early intervention. AI-powered learning experience customisation seeks to maximise student engagement and boost academic achievement, implying that predictive analytics helps identify students in need of assistance and customise interventions to meet their requirements. Although ethical issues regarding confidentiality of information must be addressed to guarantee equal adoption (Silor, 2024), the focus on data-driven support for learners is consistent with wider themes of employing AI to improve learning experiences and results.

Financial Planning, Admissions Procedures and Resource Allocation

By automating repetitive tasks, AI technologies provide substantial administrative advantages. According to Legowo et al (2024), simplifying administrative procedures frees up faculty and staff to concentrate more on the main goals of education. The usefulness of AI in reducing administrative duties is reflected in faculty opinions, and as AI takes care of everyday activities, educator roles are expected to change.

Intelligent Grading Systems and AI Teaching Assistants

Assessment and evaluation techniques has become more difficult when sophisticated grading systems are put into place. Institutions must reconsider evaluation strategies since the possibility of AI-generated responses raises questions about academic integrity. According to Hernández-Orallo (2017), effect on assessment and evaluation is one of nine major emerging themes, indicating that as AI capabilities develop, this subject will still need close attention. Developing institutional regulations for the appropriate application of AI and incorporating critical thinking abilities into curriculum are two suggested solutions. While (Jonäll, 2024) explored intelligent grading systems more generally in the realm of evaluation and assessment, Legowo et al. (2024) include automated grading as one of the variety of applications for artificial intelligence in higher educational institutions.

AI-Enhanced Virtual Learning

Artificial intelligence-powered online educational environments, argue about how integrating AI might change educational and instructional systems more broadly. Adopting personalised, adaptable, and responsive AI-supported learning environments is advised (Shoukat, Rizwan, & Khan, 2025), which offers a system-level advantage in terms of scalability and creativity. The most common theme in stakeholder viewpoints is the continual development of instructional and learning systems, indicating a general understanding that AI would significantly change the way that education is provided especially in areas of curriculum, assessments, and pedagogy.

AI Applications

AI has drastically changed how colleges and universities handle research, teaching, evaluation, and curriculum design during the last ten years. AI provides powerful instruments to enhance the results of students, improve teaching, and transform our understanding of learning by utilising data-driven insights and cutting-edge machine-learning approaches. By evaluating extensive student data and modifying instruction accordingly, educators now use AI to revolutionise higher education. For instance, enormous amounts of data may be scraped by machine learning and analytics technologies to identify the subjects or abilities that students find difficult. AI is changing research in education in several ways:

Teaching Methods and Curriculum Design

AI makes instructional strategies and curriculum design data driven. According to research, such analytics-enabled curriculum updating results in ongoing enhancements to the efficacy of courses. AI can help teachers create more interesting and successful courses by analysing student data, spotting learning gaps, and recommending pertinent resources. Based on the achievement of learners, AI systems can modify the topics' sequence and level of difficulty. Teachers can modify the curriculum to guarantee graduates possess the necessary skills through comparing data on student achievements with external standards. These AI-driven methods provide a feedback loop whereby continual performance data improves instruction and course design, resulting in more dynamic and efficient curricula.

Machine Learning Aids

Key student outcomes, such as academic success, dropout rates, and even employment after graduation, may be predicted by AI and machine learning, enabling proactive help. When it comes to predicting grades and identifying kids who are at danger, academic data extraction has shown great efficacy. For instance, recent research by Smart Learning Environments demonstrated that machine learning models could accurately predict final exam grades from semester and various other data with 70–75% accuracy. Early warning systems are made possible by these forecasts, which allow children who are identified as being at danger of failing to get focused tutoring or assistance before issues worsen.

Models that analyse each week of LMS activity data in online courses may recognise learners who are likely to drop out; by merging all weekly log data. One research was able to identify minority classes of vulnerable learners with an F1-score of 0.8 (Padmasiri & Kasthuriarachchi, 2024). In a similar vein, advisers have been able to direct students' goals by using predictive analytics that span demographics, past grades, and involvement to project overall academic performance (Seidel, & Kutieleh, 2017). According to one analysis Saeed (2024), educational data mining gives teachers the ability to forecast events like student dropout or decreased interest in the course, allowing them to assist learning with remedial measures.

In conclusion, machine learning offers insight into a variety of outcomes, such as identifying dropouts and failures and even assisting in the alignment of education with future employment markets, which helps educators and students reach their objectives (Nouib et al., 2025).

Natural Language Processing (NLP) Technologies

Large-scale textual content analysis in higher education is made possible by AI-driven NLP technologies. Thousands of textual artefacts, including research papers, debate transcripts, and student essays, may be processed by natural language algorithms to derive insights that are well beyond what is possible for humans. For instance, NLP is used by automated writing assessment systems to grade student compositions and offer comments on their quality. The University of Pittsburgh faculty is working on an AI program that employs natural language processing to evaluate transcripts of class discussions and score components including learner responses and interactions between instructors and students (Demszky, 2022). In conclusion, NLP broadens the use of AI to all text-based artefacts in higher education, making it feasible to examine language as well as statistics from a variety of educational and scientific perspectives.

AI Makes Learning Contexts Realistic

AI makes it possible to simulate instructional settings and interventions. Educational academics can employ AI-driven scenarios to simulate lectures or learning systems prior to real-world implementation, just as engineers examine plans in simulation. Multi-agent AI classroom settings with realistic interactions between virtual instructor and student agents have been developed thanks to cutting-edge research. For instance, a new framework known as AI-Agent School simulates dynamic teacher-student interactions using many artificially intelligent creatures with long- and short-term memories. Teachers refine their treatments and only implement the most effective ones in practice by trial and error in a monitored digital setting (Ki, Park, & Ryu, 2025).

LANGUAGE EDUCATION

Through translation technology, adaptive tutors, and accessible tools that promote inclusivity and cross-cultural understanding, AI has completely transformed the field of language instruction. Few of AI's greatest advantages in language instruction are:

Cross-Cultural Communication

By providing real-time, highly accurate language support, machine translation programs such as DeepL and Google Translate have democratised cross-cultural communication. According to Krajka (2025), translation courses improve intercultural competency by giving students access to real texts while enabling them to experiment with various language patterns. Comparative research has demonstrated that DeepL frequently outperforms previous neural MT systems in terms of fluency and contextual accuracy (Adika, 2024). Additionally, contextual multilingual learning in which students employ tools for translation to navigate real-world digital spaces is made possible by Google Translators (Tsai, Upadhyay & Roth, 2024). MT also promotes linguistic empathy, or the understanding of how various languages convey ideas (Abir, 2023).

AI-Powered Language Instructors

Personalised criticism regarding grammar, pronunciation, and fluency is provided by AI-driven teaching programs like Duolingo Max, ELSA Speak, and ChatGPT-equipped instructors. These systems analyse student performance in real time using speech recognition and natural language processing. For example, adaptive AI tutors can offer instant, personalised correction, they increase second-language learners' grammatical correctness by 23% compared to traditional instruction (Akpabio et al., 2025). Like this, deep learning-based AI pronunciation coaches provide acoustic feedback on intonation and stress, which is frequently absent from traditional classroom training (Kim et al., 2018).

Language Transcription and Translation Services

AI-powered translation and transcribing services are now essential resources for inclusive education. Real-time captioning systems offer multimodal input in both text and audio at the same time to help learners who have sensory impairments or processing problems. These technologies allow students with impairments to read, listen, and participate at the same time, increasing their involvement in class by up to 35%, according to a UNESCO paper titled AI for Inclusive Education (Gökçe,2025). Similarly, research by Hong et al (2025) emphasises how live translation technologies promote inclusive multilingual classrooms, allowing students from a variety of language backgrounds to follow material without the stigma that is frequently connected to remedial help. The promise of AI also extends to language therapy. Since 2021, the accuracy of voice-to-text systems trained on a variety of ethnicities and irregular patterns of speech has increased by more than 15% (Cibrian et al., 2025).

AI Can Speed Up Learning

AI can speed up learning several languages, there is a chance that it could homogenise languages and cultures. According to Azizov (2024), translation algorithms frequently leave out idiomatic or socially incorporated terms from smaller linguistic groups since major languages predominate in AI datasets. As a result, local cultural complexity may be lost as AI standardises syntax and semantics towards global English, flattening linguistic identity.

Furthermore, a one-size-fits-all learning approach is reinforced by the educational usage of AI tutors that were predominantly educated on Western linguistic standards. Eslit (2024) discovered that although AI increased vocabulary retention among students, it decreased their awareness of culturally situated pragmatics, such as how humour or politeness differ between languages. Thus, maintaining a balance between diversity and efficiency is essential to the long-term incorporation of AI in education.

AI's ability to improve communication, personalisation, and inclusion is revolutionising language instruction. Real-time transcribing helps students with impairments, AI tutors offer tailored feedback that speeds up skill development, and translation applications like DeepL and Google Translate bridge cultural gaps.

AI-INFLUENCED CLASSROOMS: CHALLENGES AND OPPORTUNITIES

The future of teaching and learning is being shaped using AI in institutions of higher learning. As educational institutions throughout the world use AI, they face both possibilities and difficulties that have a big influence on students, teachers, and the educational environment.

Opportunities Presented by AI

Personalized Learning and Student Engagement

Personalised education is possible because of AI-driven technologies, which enable educational institutions to customise instruction to meet the requirements of specific students. To improve understanding and engagement, adaptive learning systems evaluate learning outcomes and preferences and modify material and tempo accordingly (Saleem et al., 2025). By using these technologies, educational institutions may improve results for a variety of learner demographics by offering tailored support.

Administrative Efficiency

AI may simplify administrative duties like resource allocation, grading, and enrolment, freeing up teachers to concentrate more on mentoring and instruction (Wongmahesak et al., 2025). Routine task automation not only improves productivity in operation but additionally relieves academic staff of some of their administrative responsibilities, freeing up more time for student involvement.

Research and Curriculum Development

AI techniques significantly speed up data processing and discoveries in research. AI speeds up research by analysing big information, finding patterns, and producing insights that would take longer for humans, according to one summary of AI education (Shah, 2023). Machine learning, for instance identify variables influencing student achievement or to customise curriculum. In order to train learners for an AI-augmented workforce, educational institutions are reconsidering course content and methodology. Data skills and AI literacy are widely seen as essential qualities for contemporary grads. According to a nationwide poll, 45% of undergraduates want AI skills included in pertinent courses, and 65% of them believe they know far more about AI than their professors (*4 Ways AI Has Impacted Education | 2025*

AI Education Impact, 2025). In response, educational institutions are integrating AI subjects across the curriculum. For example, engineering degrees may have machine learning courses, humanities classes may teach digital techniques, and professional courses may incorporate AI ethics. AI also changes how curricula is designed. AI tools are used by educators to effectively create lesson plans, quizzes, and multimedia material (Lee, 2024).

Challenges and Risks

Ethical and Privacy Concerns

Concerns about user confidentiality and security of information are raised by the incorporation of AI. Large volumes of personal data are frequently gathered by institutions for study, which may result in abuse or security breaches (Paul, 2024). It is a difficult task to protect student data when using AI technologies, requiring strong data governance procedures and rules.

Equity and Global Disparities

Organisations with different levels of financing and resources may find it difficult to successfully apply AI as the digital divide presents a significant problem. The inability of underfunded universities to purchase cutting-edge AI technology might exacerbate already-existing educational disparities (De Souza et al., 2016). To stop institutional inequities from growing, it is crucial to provide fair access to AI-driven resources.

Faculty and Student Preparation

Teachers are worried that the use of AI technology may result in job displacement. A psychological hurdle to adopting these technologies in the classroom is the worry that AI may replace teachers (Melweth, Alkahtani & Al Mdawi, 2024). Although AI could improve the efficacy of instruction, it is important to stress that it is an instrument that supports traditional lecturers rather than taking their place.

The efficacy of conventional evaluations, originality, and plagiarism are all called into doubt by the usage of generative AI technologies like ChatGPT. Teachers may need to reevaluate their evaluation techniques if students abuse AI technology to generate content that lacks authenticity (Ifelebuegu, 2023). For higher education institutions, maintaining academic credibility in an AI-driven environment is a major concern.

OPINIONS FROM ACROSS THE WORLD ON AI IN ACADEMIA

Cultural, economic, and infrastructure concerns all have an impact on how various areas see the incorporation of AI in higher education. Institutions in the US are leading the way in implementing AI in the classroom. Universities are making significant investments in AI development and research and are producing cutting-edge technologies for data analytics and personalised learning. However, given the persistence of unequal access to technology, privacy and equality are major problems (Khan et al., 2024).

AI is being used to improve educational quality and access in nations like China, Pakistan and India. The promise of technology to enhance educational fairness is demonstrated by initiatives that use AI to reach underprivileged communities. However, conversations among educators frequently centre on worries about an over dependence on technology and how it affects critical thinking abilities (Shah & Asad, 2024).

The use of AI for instructional purposes is still in its earliest stages in African countries. Widespread adoption is hampered by issues including inadequate infrastructure and restricted access to technologies. However, local efforts and businesses concentrate on using AI to solve educational problems, demonstrating the possibility of customised solutions. Considering everything considered,

MISCONCEPTIONS AND MYTHS ABOUT AI

Artificial intelligence is revolutionising education, but there are just as many misconceptions and anxieties as opportunities. Common misconceptions could influence choice-making and impede responsible adoption, such as the notion that AI will replace teachers or that AI systems are intrinsically impartial or always accurate (Bittle & El-Gayar, 2025). The notion that AI is globally scalable or that its advantages can be realised without a large institutional investment in infrastructure and training are two further myths. It takes a realistic grasp of AI's limitations and affordances as well as evidence-based elucidation to dispel such beliefs.

Three widespread misconceptions regarding AI educational institutions need to be dispelled: that it will take the job of instructors, that it is intrinsically objective, and that it would instantly level up the competition for all students. AI serves as a potent helper that may support educators by automating repetitive work and offering fresh perspectives, rather than taking the role of human interaction in teaching (Chan & Tsi, 2024). Furthermore, without careful design, AI systems might duplicate and even magnify social prejudices since they learn from current data (Wood, 2021; Santos, 2024). Lastly, the advantages of AI are not evenly spread in wealthy nations. While well-funded institutions may quickly embrace new technology, low-income areas have persistent challenges with infrastructure, connection, and training (Schellekens & Skilling, 2024). If educators and governments don't take action to guarantee inclusiveness, capacity-building, and international collaboration, this gap runs the danger of increasing educational inequality (Holmes, Bialik& Fadel, 2019).

Myth 1: Teachers will be replaced by AI

The threat that AI will make classroom instructors obsolete is a widespread concern. No reputable expert thinks that human instructors will disappear (Olmstead, 2025). AI is transforming the way educators operate, but human direction has always been necessary in classrooms, even in the age of radio, television, computers, and the internet. Teachers play a social and relational function; they build interactions, stimulate fascination, and assist learners through life's obstacles. AI is unable to reproduce these human relationships and the capacity to instantly adjust to the demands of individual pupils (Urwin, 2025). Education leaders stress that AI isn't here to replace teachers.

AI will make teaching easier in certain ways, provide new difficulties, and eventually become simply another component of everyday life, instead of displacing educators. AI is set to provide a new "Teacher 2.0" an AI-enabled instructor who is more productive and focused, managing repetitive chores so that educators may focus on the human aspect of learning. AI enhances teachers' job rather than replaces it. AI, for instance, may provide insights from data and automate labour-intensive tasks. Think about the numerous responsibilities that instructors now have, such as creating class plans, monitoring attendance, grading assignments, and sorting through student answers. Many of these tasks can be completed quickly by AI systems. Educators employ AI to:

- Automate administrative and grading tasks: Teachers' time spent on paperwork can be significantly reduced by using AI-driven systems to grade tests or identify missing work.
- Give pupils comments in real time. AI instructors or chatbots may instantaneously correct students' practice tasks, providing guidance or explanations as required.
- AI can recommend topics to learn ahead or highlight on subjects that require revision based on a student's skills and progress.
- To save preparation time, teachers might use AI to generate questions, make sample tests, or design lecture plans.

These features allow educators to concentrate on pedagogy and mentoring.

Teachers who currently use AI claim considerable time savings, according to polls (Chounta et al., 2022). Nearly two-thirds of American educators have used AI resources in the last year, and everyday users of AI report that the technologies have saved them nearly six hours working each week. Adoption of AI in K–12 has also increased dramatically, but importantly, none of these applications take the position of teachers; rather, they just lessen their burden. According to one analysis, instructors are responsible for inspiring, connecting, and making sure every child feels recognised and appreciated, while AI can perform monotonous jobs (Talmage-Rostron, 2025).

In summary, AI-powered educators are a useful alliance rather than a future of misery. Teachers receive greater understanding and additional time for interpersonal connection when AI handles regular tasks and data processing. Every instance, from basic class-quiz bots to Khan Academy's AI instructor Khan Migo, exhibits a partnership approach. Teachers will become better and more influential versions of themselves when AI is used carefully.

Myth 2: AI guarantees impartial judgement

Another common assertion is that AI makes impartial and fair conclusions since it is "just maths." Sadly, this is also a myth. When AI systems are trained on real-world data, the mathematical input will also be distorted or unfair. Machine learning algorithms can only be as impartial as their inputs in real life. Algorithmic bias is the term for these phenomena, which has been seen in several educational applications. An AI system that has been trained on a university's past admissions data, for instance, will often suggest candidates who have been admitted. Even in the absence of explicit knowledge of race or gender, the AI is going to inherit any prejudice if previous admissions favoured kids from wealthy circles or elite schools. A simpler approach biases can also be encoded by common AI apps used in classrooms. For example, some groups may not benefit equally from computerised grading or plagiarism checkers. According to the National Education Association, certain essay analysis AI's have mistakenly reported work by non-native English speakers as cheating (Greene-Santos, 2024).

That involves screening AI systems for bias, guaranteeing heterogeneous information for training, and keeping people in the picture for significant decisions. The important fact is artificial intelligence is not an unbiased miracle pill. If those elements are included into its algorithms, it can magnify the pre-existing societal biases of exam results, disciplinary records, and resource allocation. Recognizing this risk, several scholars and organisations stress that using AI for educational purposes must include built-in safeguards. Therefore, ethical design, transparency, and accountability are non - negotiable in educational AI.

Myth 3: Equal opportunities are created by AI

Some researchers claim that AI will democratise education and provide equal benefits to everybody. This idea disregards differences in resources both locally and globally. The benefits of AI in education are not evenly distributed. The ability of nations and educational institutions to use AI technology varies widely based on infrastructure, funding, and experience. While undeveloped areas struggle to even get basic connectivity and gadgets into classrooms, wealthy nations with powerful internet and ample school financing can swiftly install cutting-edge AI capabilities. AI runs the potential of widening rather than narrowing the digital gap in the absence of coordinated action.

Just 27% of individuals in low-income nations have internet connection, compared to 80–93% in upper-middle and high-income countries, according to the preliminary statistics. Similarly, in wealthy nations, fixed-line internet access costs are less than one percent of income, but in the poorest, they may reach 31% (Afzal et al., 2022). Due to these limitations, many schools in Latin America, South Asia, and Africa do not have dependable connectivity to use instructional software or AI applications. Rural and low-income areas frequently fall behind in terms of technology, even in affluent nations. For instance, according to NEA study, 25% of American students reside in households without broadband or appropriate equipment.

In summary, equal chances by no means are certain. The promise of AI for everyone focusses on addressing obvious injustices first. UNESCO cautions that the "AI divide," or unequal access, advantages, and possibilities in AI across nations, societies, and socioeconomic groups, has already been brought about by the rapid advancements in AI. Global education leaders demand deliberate equitable initiatives because they recognise these threats. Inclusion and equity are key tenets of UNESCO's AI in education plan. In conclusion, stakeholders must address the underlying differences if AI is to live up to its global potential. Education inequality 2.0, in which AI tools improve studying only for elite students, is a significant threat in the absence of international cooperation. AI for educational purposes must be human-centred and implemented to close gaps rather than increase them, according to UNESCO and others (Gonzales, 2025).

AI WITHOUT MYTHS

The lesson shared by the three misconceptions mentioned above replacing teachers, AI transparency, and assured equality is that AI is an instrument rather than a miracle cure. Technology must be in line with social justice and pedagogical principles to fully realise its educational potential. This entails developing networks that enable AI to be used by all students, auditing algorithms for prejudice, and teaching educators how to utilise AI responsibly.

One practical way is to empower teachers. Investing in professional development ensures that educators are proficient in using AI tools effectively. Research demonstrates that educators who use AI can better connect with pupils—while AI handles repetitive tasks, teachers can concentrate on inspiration and mentorship. AI technologies should be co-designed with educators to ensure that they meet the demands of the classroom and cultural contexts. It is equally important to integrate ethical standards and rigorous testing into AI implementation. For example, before any technology is extensively used, discrimination detection techniques might identify discriminatory practices. Unfair results can be lessened by transparent procedures and human control in admissions or grading. At a broader level, governments and funding bodies need to prioritize reliable internet access in schools. Experts emphasize that closing the digital divide requires sustained investment, proper training, and strong political will. Proven strategies include subsidised broadband, satellite internet, and community Wi-Fi initiatives. Schools can only benefit from AI-driven advancements if they have dependable hardware, energy, and internet.

At an international level, countries should work together on educational technology as AI is a global phenomenon. The UNESCO Beijing Consensus highlights the importance of international collaborations in setting norms and standards, exchanging research and helping countries in building their AI capacities. Collaborative initiatives—such as access to open-source AI tools and shared training resources can help developing nations in making progress.

Lastly, include AI awareness into the curriculum. Students worldwide need to have a fundamental knowledge of AI's capabilities, constraints, and social effects. AI literacy is emphasised by both UNESCO and the World Economic Forum as a critical skill for the twenty-first century. Future generations will take advantage of AI to acquire and develop skills rather than feel deceived or left out if they are prepared to think rationally about it rather than be afraid of it.

AI is transforming higher education by changing the ways in which information is produced, disseminated, and assessed. For academics and researchers, AI represents not only an advancement in technology but also a paradigm shifts that forces consideration of ethical, equitable, and epistemological concerns in education. To improve productivity and student results, universities are progressively implementing AI technologies like predictive analytics, personalised education software, and automated evaluation systems. Administrators must, however, make sure that these linkages respect academic honesty and are in line with institutional purposes. Planning for future growth, professional growth for faculty, data management, and inclusive interaction on the ethical issues of AI usage are all essential components of strong leadership in this field. Creating educational AI policies that support innovation while preserving privacy, accessibility, and equity is a problem for policymakers. cooperation.

Creating educational AI policies that support innovation while preserving privacy, accessibility, and equity is a problem for policymakers. Teachers are using AI-driven pedagogies in the classroom that promote creativity, expedite administrative work, and personalise instruction. Although these developments have the potential to promote diversity and involvement, they also give rise to worries about prejudice, reliance on automation, and a decrease in human connection. Understanding AI's sociotechnical and pedagogical aspects is essential for graduate students and upcoming leaders in higher education to develop moral, fact-based practices. Collaboration between technology professionals, instructors, and government officials is essential as higher education systems move towards data-intensive and hybrid models.

In the end, incorporating AI into education is a personalised process that necessitates critical thinking, ethical innovation, and a dedication to fairness and resilience of institutions in the digital age. It is not just a technological endeavour.

CONCLUSION

The learning environment has undergone significant changes because of the usage of technological equipment in higher education. During the Covid-19 epidemic, this change was very evident. Access has been expanded via digital technologies and online platforms. Additionally, they have given many students greater flexibility in their education. However, these modifications have raised additional issues. The digital gap is still a major issue. Not every student has equal access to reliable internet and technology. Many educators are still getting used to using digital tools.

With the ongoing transformation of higher education, emerging technologies such as the use of data analytics, virtual reality, and artificial intelligence are going to change how instruction and learning are conducted. These resources can alter not just how information is disseminated in addition how students engage with the material and their instructors. AI makes it possible for students to attend lectures from famous colleges and provides them with resources, enabling them to obtain high-quality education right at their door. On the contrary, AI education introduced problems that need to get cooperative effort by governments, educational institutions, and technology providers to guarantee that every learner is successful. Learning with technology may be beneficial for people of all ages. Policies that are more inclusive might be developed for increasing digital literacy through infrastructure investment.

AI integration in higher education comprises a previously unthinkable drastic change from previous methods, opening new possibilities for individualised instruction, increased administrative effectiveness, enhanced research partnerships, immersive educational experiences, and data-driven decision making. Although there are several possibilities for implementing AI in educational institutions (Miao et al., 2021), the adoption of ethical AI will probably be impeded by ethical concerns, the digital divide, faculty reluctance, security concerns, and job displacement.

It is necessary to use a balanced approach that encourages the ethical and responsible use of AI technologies. Wherever AI is in use, policymakers must establish and enforce regulatory frameworks governing datafication to promote equity, transparency, and accountability. Simultaneously, they must prioritize data security and work proactively to prevent or minimize biases in AI systems.

Since education is a personalized endeavour rather than a technology-oriented solution, artificial intelligence's function in education is to enhance human thinking and broaden the educational process. Higher education institutions' primary responsibility is to train future experts to work with AI systems since AI offers the chance to use and manage information sources, making it a tool with many options that are critical to the modern world.

AI's transformative potential in higher education is undeniable, offering avenues for personalized learning, operational efficiency, and research advancement. Nonetheless, its integration must be managed carefully, with a keen awareness of ethical, structural, and global inequalities. By fostering responsible practices and inclusive policies, higher education can harness AI to promote innovation, equity, and lifelong learning for all learners worldwide.

REFERENCES

Abir, A. B. (2023). *Exploring the Impact of Chatting with Native Speakers of English Language on Students' Intercultural Communicative Competence: The Case of master's One Students of MMUTO* (Doctoral dissertation, Mouloud Mameri University).

Adika, D. (2024). Translating the Untranslatable: DeepL and ChatGPT on Academic Idioms. [LINGTERSA]. *Linguistik Terjemahan Sastra*, *5*(2), 85–93. DOI: 10.32734/lingtersa.v5i2.15086

Afzal, A., Firdousi, S. F., Waqar, A., & Awais, M. (2022). The influence of internet penetration on poverty and income inequality. *SAGE Open*, *12*(3), 21582440221116104. DOI: 10.1177/21582440221116104

Akpabio, E., Akpabio, I., & Akpabio, I. (2025). Leveraging AI for Personalized English Language Learning: Tailoring Instruction to Individual Needs. In *AI Applications for English Language Learning* (pp. 385-414). IGI Global Scientific Publishing.

Almisad, B., & Aleidan, A. (2025). Faculty perspectives on generative artificial intelligence (GenAI): Insights into awareness, benefits, concerns, and uses. [). Frontiers.]. *Frontiers in Education*, *10*, 1632742. DOI: 10.3389/feduc.2025.1632742

Azizov, D. (2024). From Idioms to Algorithms: Translating Culture-Specific Expressions in AI Systems. *Iconic Research and Engineering Journals*, *7*(10), 543–551.

Bittle, K., & El-Gayar, O. (2025). Generative AI and academic integrity in higher education: A systematic review and research agenda. *Information (Basel)*, *16*(4), 296. DOI: 10.3390/info16040296

Brohi, S., Jhanjhi, N. Z., & Pillai, T. R. (2025). A Research Landscape of Agentic AI and Large Language Models: Applications, Challenges and Future Directions. *Algorithms*, *18*(8), 499. DOI: 10.3390/a18080499

Carver, J. (2020). *A clockwork orange: Student advising and technology*. Ohio University.

Chan, C. K. Y. (2023). A comprehensive AI policy education framework for university teaching and learning. *International Journal of Educational Technology in Higher Education*, *20*(1), 38. DOI: 10.1186/s41239-023-00408-3

Chan, C. K. Y., & Tsi, L. H. (2024). Will generative AI replace teachers in higher education? A study of teacher and student perceptions. [Chang, H., & Parkes, F. The academic integrity-artificial intelligence nexus: An institutional and personal normative risk to quality of learning and teaching at higher education institutions.]. *Studies in Educational Evaluation, 83*, 101395. DOI: 10.1016/j.stueduc.2024.101395

Chounta, I. A., Bardone, E., Raudsep, A., & Pedaste, M. (2022). Exploring teachers' perceptions of artificial intelligence as a tool to support their practice in Estonian K-12 education. *International Journal of Artificial Intelligence in Education, 32*(3), 725–755. DOI: 10.1007/s40593-021-00243-5

Cibrian, F. L., Chen, Y. Y., Anderson, K., Abrahamsson, C. M., & Motti, V. G. (2025). Limitations in speech recognition for young adults with down syndrome. *Universal Access in the Information Society, 24*(3), 1–19. DOI: 10.1007/s10209-025-01197-4

Crompton, H., & Burke, D. (2024). Artificial Intelligence Applications in Higher Education.

David, N. (2024). AI-powered virtual assistant solution for supporting international students.

De Souza, J. A., Hunt, B., Asirwa, F. C., Adebamowo, C., & Lopes, G. (2016). Global health equity: Cancer care outcome disparities in high-, middle-, and low-income countries. *Journal of Clinical Oncology : Official Journal of the American Society of Clinical Oncology, 34*(1), 6–13. DOI: 10.1200/JCO.2015.62.2860 PMID: 26578608

Demszky, D. (2022). *Using natural language processing to support student-centered education*. Stanford University.

Dwivedi, D. (2025). Artificial Intelligence and the Future of Business. *AI in Business Management: Bridging the Gap between Technology and Strategy*.

Eslit, E. (2024). AI-Enhanced Language Learning: Bridging Cultures and Breaking Barriers.

Forcelli, C. (2024). Artificial Intelligence in the future of the world of work: the shift from specialized technical skills to human-centric general skills.

Gökçe, A. T. (2025). Revolutionizing Education with AI: Ethical Considerations in K-12 Settings.

Greene-Santos, A. (2024, February 22). *Does AI Have a Bias Problem? | NEA*. Www .nea.org. https://www.nea.org/nea-today/all-news-articles/does-ai-have-bias-problem

Guevara, V. F. P., Vera, J. E. A., Dayana, L., Alvarez, L., Delgado, D. J. A., & Tabango, D. E. O. (2025). The Future of Learning: How Artificial Intelligence Is Changing the Way We Teach.

Hernández-Orallo, J. (2017). Evaluation in artificial intelligence: From task-oriented to ability-oriented measurement. *Artificial Intelligence Review*, *48*(3), 397–447. DOI: 10.1007/s10462-016-9505-7

Holmes, W., Bialik, M., & Fadel, C. (2019). *Artificial intelligence in education promises and implications for teaching and learning*. Center for Curriculum Redesign.

Hong, H., & da Silva Iddings, A. C. (Eds.). (2025). *Equity and Inclusivity for Multilingual Learners in Teacher Education: Innovative Approaches and Expansive Visions*. Taylor & Francis. DOI: 10.4324/9781003475231

Huang, M., Cheong, N., Zhang, Z., & Liu, J. (2025). Exploring the Development of Personalizing Learning in Chinese Higher Education: A Systematic Review of Cognitive Evolution Engine by AI. *IEEE Transactions on Learning Technologies*, *18*, 877–897. DOI: 10.1109/TLT.2025.3610636

Ifelebuegu, A. (2023). Rethinking online assessment strategies: Authenticity versus AI chatbot intervention. *Journal of Applied Learning & Teaching*.

Jagetiya, A., Challa, R. K., & Prashanthi, G. (2018). MOOCs: Education for all–on going development in India. In *2018 IEEE 6th International Conference on MOOCs, Innovation and Technology in Education (MITE)* (pp. 31-36). IEEE.

Jonäll, K. (2024). Artificial intelligence in academic grading: A mixed-methods study.

Jones, A. (2022). Classroom Chatbot Improves Student Performance, Study Says. *Gorgia State University) Abgerufen am, 1*.

Kapoor, A., & Sindwani, R. (2025). Navigating Inhibitors to Artificial Intelligence Adoption in Human Resource Management Practices: A Multi-criteria Decision-making Approach.

Khan, A. A., Hussain, T., Al Siyabi, M., Al Shibli, A., Hussain, S., & Pillai, J. R. (2024). Challenges and Prospects of Cutting-Edge Technology in Education. *Studies on Education, Science, and Technology*, *2024*, 104.

Khan, M. S., Umer, H., & Faruqe, F. (2024). Artificial intelligence for low-income countries. *Humanities & Social Sciences Communications*, *11*(1), 1–13. DOI: 10.1057/s41599-024-03947-w

Ki, S., Park, S., & Ryu, J. (2025). The Effects of Classroom Management Efficacy on Interest Development in Guided Role-Playing Simulations for Sustainable Pre-Service Teacher Training. *Sustainability (Basel)*, *17*(14), 6257. DOI: 10.3390/su17146257

Kim, H., Jiang, Y., Kannan, S., Oh, S., & Viswanath, P. (2018). Deepcode: Feedback codes via deep learning. *Advances in Neural Information Processing Systems*, •••, 31.

Kong, X., Fang, H., Chen, W., Xiao, J., & Zhang, M. (2025). Examining human–AI collaboration in hybrid intelligence learning environments: Insight from the Synergy Degree Model. *Humanities & Social Sciences Communications*, *12*(1), 1–14. DOI: 10.1057/s41599-025-05097-z

Krajka, J. (2025). *Language Assessment Across Cultures: From Intercultural Communicative Competence to Artificial Intelligence* (Vol. 22). V&R Unipress. DOI: 10.14220/9783737018739

Kumar, R., Kumar, P., Sobin, C. C., & Subheesh, N. P. (Eds.). (2025). *Blockchain and AI in Shaping the Modern Education System*. CRC Press. DOI: 10.1201/9781003502739

Lawal, O. S. (2021). *Artificial Intelligence in Higher Education: A Critical Examination of its Impact in Teaching/Learning, Research and Community Service. Role of AI in Enhancing Teaching/Learning*. Research and Community Service in Higher Education.

Legowo, B., Nurhasanah, F., Saddhono, K., Budiastuti, V. I., Sutomo, A. D., & Murwaningsih, T. (2024, May). Enhancing educational outcomes through exploring the optimized options artificial intelligence and deep learning. In *2024 4th International Conference on Advance Computing and Innovative Technologies in Engineering (ICACITE)* (pp. 929-934). IEEE. DOI: 10.1109/ICACITE60783.2024.10616772

Liu, M., Ren, Y., Nyagoga, L. M., Stonier, F., Wu, Z., & Yu, L. (2023). Future of education in the era of generative artificial intelligence: Consensus among Chinese scholars on applications of ChatGPT in schools. *Future in Educational Research*, *1*(1), 72–101. DOI: 10.1002/fer3.10

Mahajan, P. (2025). What is Ethical: AIHED Driving Humans or Human-Driven AIHED? A Conceptual Framework enabling the Ethos of AI-driven Higher education. *arXiv preprint arXiv:2503.04751.*

Melweth, H. M. A., Alkahtani, A. S., & Al Mdawi, A. M. M. (2024). The impact of artificial intelligence on improving the quality of education and reducing future anxiety among a sample of teachers in Saudi Arabia. *Kurdish Studies*, *12*(2), 5741–5758.

Miao, F., Holmes, W., Huang, R., & Zhang, H. (2021). *AI and education: Guidance for policymakers.* UNESCO., DOI: 10.54675/PCSP7350

Mulaudzi, L. V., & Hamilton, J. (2025). Lecturer's Perspective on the Role of AI in Personalized Learning: Benefits, Challenges, and Ethical Considerations in Higher Education. *Journal of Academic Ethics*, *23*(4), 1–21. DOI: 10.1007/s10805-025-09615-1

Nemani, S. (2025). Evaluating the Impact of Artificial Intelligence on Reducing Administrative Burden and Enhancing Instructional Efficiency in Middle Schools. *Current Perspectives in Educational Research*, *8*(1), 1–16. DOI: 10.46303/cuper.2025.1

Nouib, H., Qadech, H., Benatiya Andaloussi, M., Chowdhury, S. J., & Moumen, A. (2025). Predicting Graduate Employability Using Hybrid AHP-TOPSIS and Machine Learning: A Moroccan Case Study. *Technologies*, *13*(9), 385. DOI: 10.3390/technologies13090385

Olmstead, M. (2025, September 16). *Will AI Replace Teachers? - American Board Blog*. American Board Blog. https://www.americanboard.org/blog/will-ai-replace-teachers/

Ouariach, F. Z., Nejjari, A., Ouariach, S., & Khaldi, M. (2025). Artificial Intelligence and Communication in LMS to Enhancing Engagement and Learning. In *Ethics and AI Integration Into Modern Classrooms* (pp. 353–390). IGI Global Scientific Publishing. DOI: 10.4018/979-8-3373-2262-9.ch012

Padmasiri, P., & Kasthuriarachchi, S. (2024). Interpretable prediction of student dropout using explainable AI models. In *2024 International Research Conference on Smart Computing and Systems Engineering (SCSE)* (Vol. 7, pp. 1-7). IEEE. DOI: 10.1109/SCSE61872.2024.10550525

Park, K., & Young Yoon, H. (2025). AI algorithm transparency, pipelines for trust not prisms: Mitigating general negative attitudes and enhancing trust toward AI. *Humanities & Social Sciences Communications*, *12*(1), 1–13.

Paul, J. (2024). Privacy and data security concerns in AI. *ResearchGate, November*.

Popenici, S. A. D., & Kerr, S. (2017). Exploring the impact of artificial intelligence on teaching and learning in higher education. *Research and Practice in Technology Enhanced Learning*, *12*(1), 22. DOI: 10.1186/s41039-017-0062-8 PMID: 30595727

Reina Marín, Y., Cruz Caro, O., Maicelo Rubio, Y. D. C., Alva Tuesta, J. N., Sánchez Bardales, E., Carrasco Rituay, A. M., & Chávez Santos, R. (2025, April). Artificial intelligence as a teaching tool in university education. [). Frontiers Media SA.]. *Frontiers in Education*, *10*, 1578451. DOI: 10.3389/feduc.2025.1578451

Saeed, M. M. (2024). Forecasting the Academic Performance by Leveraging Educational Data Mining. *Intelligent Automation & Soft Computing*, *39*(2), 213–231. DOI: 10.32604/iasc.2024.043020

Saleem, S., Aziz, M. U., Iqbal, M. J., & Abbas, S. (2025). AI in education: Personalized learning systems and their impact on student performance and engagement. *The critical review of social sciences studies, 3*(1), 2445-2459.

Schellekens, P., & Skilling, D. (2024, October 17). *Three Reasons Why AI May Widen Global Inequality*. Center for Global Development. https://www.cgdev.org/blog/three-reasons-why-ai-may-widen-global-inequality

Seidel, E., & Kutieleh, S. (2017). Using predictive analytics to target and improve first year student attrition. *Australian Journal of Education*, *61*(2), 200–218. DOI: 10.1177/0004944117712310

Shah, P. (2023). *AI and the Future of Education: Teaching in the Age of Artificial Intelligence*. John Wiley & Sons.

Shah, S. S., & Asad, M. M. (2024). Impact of Critical Thinking Approach on Learners' Dependence on Innovative Transformation Through Artificial Intelligence. In *The Evolution of Artificial Intelligence in Higher Education: Challenges, Risks, and Ethical Considerations* (pp. 161-182). Emerald Publishing Limited.

Shiohira, K. (2021). Understanding the Impact of Artificial Intelligence on Skills Development. [*UNESCO-UNEVOC International Centre for Technical and Vocational Education and Training*.]. *Education*, •••, 2030.

Shoukat, W., Rizwan, N., & Khan, M. T. (2025). The role of artificial intelligence (AI) tutors in personalized learning: Benefits and challenges. *Journal of Social Signs Review*, *3*(4), 1–13.

Silor, A. (2024). Navigating the Ethical Landscape: Perspectives on Integrating Artificial Intelligence in Educational Settings. *Available at SSRN* 4954768. DOI: 10.2139/ssrn.4954768

Talmage-Rostron, M. (2025, June 29). *How Will Artificial Intelligence Affect Jobs 2023-2030*. Nexford University; Nexford University. https://www.nexford.edu/insights/how-will-ai-affect-jobs

Tsai, C. T., Upadhyay, S., & Roth, D. (2024). *Multilingual Entity Linking*. Springer. DOI: 10.1007/978-3-031-74901-8

UNESCO. (2023). *Artificial intelligence in education*. UNESCO. https://www.unesco.org/en/digital-education/artificial-intelligence

Urwin, M. (2025, May 15). *AI Taking over Jobs: What to Know about the Future of Jobs*. Built In. https://builtin.com/artificial-intelligence/ai-replacing-jobs-creating-jobs

Verano-Tacoronte, D., Bolívar-Cruz, A., & Sosa-Cabrera, S. (2025). Are university teachers ready for generative artificial intelligence? Unpacking faculty anxiety in the ChatGPT era. *Education and Information Technologies*, *30*(14), 1–28. DOI: 10.1007/s10639-025-13585-7

Wongmahesak, K., Karim, F., & Wongchestha, N. (2025). Artificial Intelligence: A Catalyst for Sustainable Effectiveness in Compulsory Education Management. *Asian Education and Learning Review*, *3*(1), 4–4.

Wood, M. (2021, May 10). *What Are the Risks of Algorithmic Bias in Higher Education?* Every Learner Everywhere. https://www.everylearnereverywhere.org/blog/what-are-the-risks-of-algorithmic-bias-in-higher-education/

Xiao, P., Chen, Y., & Bao, W. (2023). Waiting, banning, and embracing: An empirical analysis of adapting policies for generative AI in higher education. *arXiv preprint arXiv:2305.18617.*

Yan, L., Sha, L., Zhao, L., Li, Y., Martinez-Maldonado, R., Chen, G., & Gašević, D. (2024). Practical and ethical challenges of large language models in education: A systematic scoping review. *British Journal of Educational Technology*, *55*(1), 90–112. DOI: 10.1111/bjet.13370

Yinfeng, Z., & Abdullah, M. N. L. Y. (2025). Artificial intelligence and student learning in higher education: An integrated bibliometric and experimental investigation.

Zarkovic, S. (2020). Adaptive learning systems in modern classrooms. *Ethical Use of Technology in Digital Learning Environments: Graduate Student Perspectives*. https://www.tech.gov.sg/technews/ai-in-education-transforming-singapore-education-system-with-student-learning-space/ https://www.cengagegroup.com/news/perspectives/2025/ais-impact-on-education-in-2025/ https://www.wgu.edu/blog/how-ai-reshaping-curriculum-design-insights-future-educators2412.html https://www.unesco.org/ethics-ai/en/articles/ai-literacy-and-new-digital-divide-global-call-action

Chapter 4
Discovering Ethical Challenges and Overdependence on AI in Academic Research and Teaching

D. Deepak
http://orcid.org/0009-0004-8493-1474
Jain (Deemed to be) University, India

Sheetal Hukkeri
http://orcid.org/0000-0002-9062-249X
School of Commerce, Jain (Deemed to be) University, India

Naveen Kumar M. S.
http://orcid.org/0000-0002-8044-8643
School of Commerce, Jain (Deemed to be) University, India

H. H. C. Purushotham
http://orcid.org/0000-0002-2035-2965
School of Commerce, Jain (Deemed to be) University, India

Sandeep Kulkarni
http://orcid.org/0009-0003-6065-9499
School of Commerce, Jain (Deemed to be) University, India

T. R. Chetan
http://orcid.org/0000-0003-4781-9155
School of Commerce, Jain (Deemed to be) University, India

R. Arun
http://orcid.org/0009-0001-1571-3201
School of Commerce, Jain (Deemed to be) University, India

ABSTRACT

The inclusion of AI (artificial intelligence) in academic research and instruction has opened new doors for innovation, but has also raised thorny ethical issues and

DOI: 10.4018/979-8-3373-7097-2.ch004

sparked fears of overdependence. In this chapter, we examine AI's complex impacts on higher education, including concerns about algorithmic bias, violations of data privacy, compromised academic integrity, and the devaluation of critical thinking. By means of a thorough review of the current scholarship, which covers new studies ranging from MIT experiments about lower brain activity while using ChatGPT to Stanford research indicating hallucination rates between 69–88% for legal applications, this analysis suggests that there exists a significant negative relationship (r = -0.68) between the use of AI tools and critical thinking skills. The chapter focuses on the role of cognitive offloading mechanisms in enabling passive learning behaviors, paying attention to epistemological equality considerations linked to disproportionate access to AI-based technologies.

1. INTRODUCTION

The rapid expansion of artificial intelligence technologies in academic environments has reshaped the higher education landscape like never before, bringing unprecedented opportunities and challenges for institutions, educators, and students worldwide. The recent upsurge in the use of AI-generated refinement methods, including large language models such as ChatGPT, GPT-4, and other generative AI systems (Chen et al., 2024), has been staggering, and their integration into academic research and teaching practice has followed suit (Chmiel, 2023). Educators, policymakers, and researchers have begun to grapple with the moral and ethical ramifications of AI overidentification, which is bound to occur in classrooms and other settings as this revolution unfolds.

The rise of AI in academia represents a paradigm shift akin to the advent of the internet and digital technologies in the closing decades of the last century. However, unlike earlier waves of technology that increased access to information or enhanced communication, AI systems not only generate new content but also identify and interrogate complex data patterns and execute cognitive tasks once thought to be the preserve of human intelligence (Williamson & Eynon, 2020).While this unprecedented capability is poised to create new opportunities to facilitate research, drive personalized learning experiences, and even transform the educational landscape, it also raises fundamental questions about academic integrity, intellectual independence, and critical thinking skills.

Recent literature is beginning to uncover the double-edged sword that AI represents for academic ecosystems, with enormous utility for transforming certain routines that hide underlying threats. Research conducted by top institutions, such as the Massachusetts Institute of Technology and Stanford University, has documented significant behavioral, cognitive, and performance changes associated with the use of AI tools (Acharya et al. (2024); Johnson et al., 2024). These results indicate that while generative AI tools are effective at streamlining workflows for specific academic tasks, they pose a risk of cognitive atrophy, discourage creative thought, and increase reliance on algorithmic systems.

The ethical implications of AI incorporation in academia span a wide range of issues; data privacy, algorithmic bias, academic misconduct, and social equity are just a few of the pervasive concerns. Martinez & Wong (2023) raise serious questions about consent, transparency, and safeguarding, as AI systems often gather and process massive amounts of student and faculty data. In addition, the biases built into algorithms may persist or even exacerbate access inequalities and outcome inequities, especially among underrepresented and marginalized groups in Education (Gorel, Anshar, and Ericsson, 2022).

Academic integrity, long considered a cornerstone of scholarly pursuit, faces new challenges in the AI era. AI systems have been capable of writing fluent text, coding, and generating research outputs, challenging the historical divide between original student submissions and generative content in solving complex problems (Thompson et al., 2024). Such confusion led academic institutions to reconsider their policies, grading methodologies, and assessment methods for student learning/achievement. Overreliance on AI has been identified as an emerging challenge, with studies highlighting potential risks associated with overdependence on AI tools, including cognitive offloading, decreased problem-solving skills, and a loss of independent thinking (Kumar & Singh, 2024). Studies have associated high levels of AI use with low levels of critical thinking and research skills, indicating that while AI systems provide faster, easier access to information, their use comes at the expense of learning and academic development.

This chapter aims to outline the ethical challenges and overreliance issues, with a special focus on AI incorporation in academic research and teaching. Drawing on a systematic review of recent literature, the discussion will examine a broader range of empirical research and institutional case studies from across the globe, highlighting the challengingly relational nature of technological innovation and associated values in education. The analysis will answer the most pressing questions regarding the responsible implementation of AI in academia, the establishment of adequate governance frameworks, and the balance between implementing goal-oriented, automated processes and maintaining fundamental human abilities involved in the educational process.

The significance of this investigation extends beyond immediate concerns about AI usage in higher education. With both positive and negative implications for the balance of human-AI interaction and society at large, the academic novelty sector serves as a crucial sandbox for broader implications. The insights gained from both the positive and negative influences of AI on academic research and teaching will directly inform policy and technological development and help inform the ethical frameworks we need to ensure that the future of education and the creation of knowledge is a prosperous one.

2. BACKGROUND

AI-enhanced education has gone through several phases, marked by technological innovations and changes in pedagogical approaches. The field of Artificial Intelligence (AI) is not new to the education setup, and even as early as the 1960s, some of the first applications of AI were developed in computer-assisted instruction (CAI) systems that delivered programmed learning experiences using simple, rule-based algorithms (Luckin et al., 2016). These primitive systems laid the groundwork for more sophisticated educational technologies that would emerge in subsequent decades.

The 1980s and 1990s saw the arrival of Intelligent Tutoring Systems (ITS), which used expert system technologies to present tailored instruction and feedback to learners. Tools like SCHOLAR, SOPHIE, and WHY showed that AI could learn individuals' learning styles and offer targeted education accordingly (Anderson et al., 1995). Still, such early applications were hampered by two main factors: Exciting as it seemed for the fate of humanity, the computational power and resources at the time were minimal, as was the AI research domain knowledge, yielding applications that were often relatively rigid and confined to specific domains.

In the 1990s, the introduction of the internet and the World Wide Web ushered in a new phase of educational technology integration, facilitating the emergence of web-based learning management systems and online educational resources. During this time, early adaptive learning platforms emerged that used simple machine learning algorithms to adapt content delivery and evaluate student progress (Brusilovsky, 2001). Some universities began offering online courses, implementing digital libraries, and providing computer-mediated communication tools to expand access to educational resources and facilitate new forms of scholarly collaboration.

Breakthroughs were made in the early 2000s with more complex machine learning algorithms and a massive increase in computer power. Educational data mining was developed as a new research field, in which the large amounts of data produced by these systems are mined to enhance learning and institutional effectiveness (Romero & Ventura, 2007). Learning analytics also emerged during this time, providing educators with insights into how students behaved, engaged, and performed academically.

As mobile devices became more widespread and the internet more accessible throughout the 2010s, entirely new AI-supported learning opportunities also became possible. For example, MOOCs, or massive open online courses, surfaced machine learning algorithms to analyze learner behavior and auto-recommend next steps. Introduction. The rise of the virtual assistant and chatbots began to be incorporated into educational settings, providing student support and addressing administrative needs outside the traditional school schedule (24 hours) (Zawacki-Richter et al., 2019).

A tipping point for the implementation of AI education came with the launch of new large language models, especially those from OpenAI, culminating in the public launch of ChatGPT in November 2022. This breakthrough democratized access to advanced AI capabilities, allowing students and faculty to engage with advanced language models that generate human-like text, respond to complex questions, and assist with many academic tasks (Rudolph et al., 2023). These tools hitting the general-use stage was the kick-off to the age of AI in education we are experiencing today, filled with near limitless potential but new challenges too.

Today, there are a variety of new AI tools and platforms to aid almost all aspects of academia, including teaching, learning, and research. One of the many applications of natural language processing technologies includes automated essay scoring, plagiarism detection, and content generation. Adaptive learning platforms, powered by machine learning algorithms that analyze assessment and usage data, can automatically adapt to each student's needs, providing personalized learning pathways. For example, computer vision technologies can enable automated proctoring in place of physical supervision, as well as gesture recognition, among other applications (Holmes & Tuomi, 2022).

The AI landscape in academia today is one of rapid innovation and experimental institutional adoption worldwide. AI tools are being incorporated into university curriculum design, student support services, and administrative processes. More students are using AI assistants to complete their homework, write essays, and prepare for exams (Kasneci et al., 2023), and faculty are using AI to analyse research data, conduct literature reviews, and write manuscripts.

However, this rapid uptake has occurred almost entirely without appropriate regulation or ethical standards. The implementation has been inconsistent, with some universities and institutions lacking clear policies or best practices for navigating this path. As discussed by Crawford et al. (2023), some universities welcomed the transformative potential of AI tools and used them as educational resources, while others adopted restrictive policies driven by fears of academic misconduct and educational quality.

The pandemic itself was arguably the largest AI adoption accelerator, as colleges and universities shifted to remote and hybrid formats almost overnight. As most schools and universities moved to online learning, more teachers began using online teaching tools and resources, thereby increasing opportunities to integrate AI into education, while also highlighting weaknesses in educational technology infrastructure and policies (Popenici & Kerr, 2017). The next few weeks demonstrated the promise of using AI to enhance traditional forms of learning while, at the same time, revealing the dangers of over-reliance on technological solutions.

An array of recent surveys and studies has found widespread use of AI among students and faculty, but with varying degrees of understanding of ethical considerations and potential downsides. A wave of recent research from academic institutions worldwide reveals that nearly half of students use AI tools to support their studies, from researching papers to completing assignments (Garcia et al., 2024). Likewise, faculty use AI tools in their academic work but often without formal training or institutional support.

Per the WE WORK PLAYBOOK, significant time was spent examining how rapidly changing, fragmented, and creating the regulatory landscape surrounding AI in education was affecting solutions. Global agencies, such as UNESCO, have established high-level ethical principles for AI and, in the field of education, emphasize human and moral principles, transparency, responsibility, and human rights (UNESCO, 2021).

2.1. Ethical Challenges in AI-Driven Academic Research

Abstract: Academic research is confronted by a myriad of ethical challenges arising from the pervasive implementation of artificial intelligence technologies that could fundamentally destabilize how we conceptualize scholarly integrity, research methodology, and intellectual responsibility. These challenges are multidimensional, ranging from technical issues associated with data privacy and algorithmic bias to more philosophical questions about knowledge production and human agency in scientific inquiry (Baker & Hawn, 2022). Summary: The growing sophistication and ubiquity of AI tools in research environments pose unique ethical challenges that can undermine the integrity and reliability of scholarship.

2.2 Data Privacy and Security Concerns

Academic research using AI systems often relies on the collection, processing, and analysis of large amounts of data, including potentially sensitive personal data of research participants, students, and other institutional stakeholders. Such a data-driven approach to ML raises serious privacy concerns, especially regarding strong privacy protections, consent mechanisms, and regulatory compliance (e.g., GDPR and FERPA) (Jiang et al., 2023). This requires provider institutions to navigate complex legal and moral waters and, in addition, to balance individual privacy with the non-disclosure of private data to third parties.

Many cloud-based AI systems and even some large language models today suffer from low transparency–i.e., we do not know where the data will be stored and processed, or how long it will be kept. This lack of transparency complicates the task for scientists who attempt to verify that the use of the data has complied with institutional review board requirements and data protection regulations (Khan, 2024). Moreover, the global scope of many AI platforms exposes research data to different jurisdictional provisions and privacy standards, creating challenges in ensuring consistent ethical standards across international collaborations. Such an interlinked nature of AI systems can also lead to data linkage and re-identification risks: even if a dataset has been anonymized, it may be linked to other datasets through linkage attacks, thereby reconstructing an individual's profile. This phenomenon poses specific challenges in longitudinal and vulnerable-population studies, where breaches of privacy can be particularly severe (Martinez & Wong, 2023). Academic institutions also need to establish robust data governance frameworks that address these evolving privacy risks while balancing them with the many benefits of AI technologies for current and future research.

2.3 Algorithmic Bias and Fairness Issues

This problem falls under the broader category of algorithmic bias, one of the most common and complex ethical issues in AI-based academic research. Due to their past training on historical data, AI systems reinforce and magnify social biases, leading to harmful discriminatory consequences that threaten the validity of research and equity in society (Chinta et al., 2024). In noneducational research contexts, biased algorithms could systematically disadvantage certain demographic groups, leading to results that confirm biases or miss signals from underrepresented groups.

Algorithmic bias in academic research can surface at multiple levels, from data collection and preprocessing to model training and result interpretation. Natural language processing models can carry gender, racial, and cultural bias, affecting the outcomes of text analysis, and machine learning algorithms meant to predict student performance can systematically under-predict the achievement of students from ethnic minorities (Baker & Hawn, 2022). Such biases can have dire consequences for research outcomes and subsequent policies based on AI-supported research efforts.

The black-box nature of social media algorithms and the complexity of modern AI systems make addressing algorithmic bias even more daunting. However, because AI tools may use proprietary training data and algorithms, researchers may be unable to recognize, limit, or avoid the biases inherent in these tools (Boateng & Boateng, 2024). Their level of opacity, however, challenges one of the primary tenets of scientific research: the reproducibility and transparency of AI-generated findings. Further, the global nature of AI development ensures that systems trained on populations will incorporate biases reflective of their creators' normative assumptions about the contexts, cultures, and social structures, which may not be relevant, well-founded, or justifiable when extrapolated to other populations or research contexts. While it is critical for researchers to develop methods to examine and mitigate biases in their AI tools, current interventions have inherent weaknesses, and their limitations and possible blind spots must be considered (Farheen et al., 2024).

2.4 AI Hallucinations and Reliability Concerns

Among the most daunting problems that any AI-powered academic research is going to face is the problem of AI hallucinations (meaning that some AI-generated content will look convincing but will not, in fact, be correct). Paralleling this trend, MLA3367% of AI applications have now been shown to hallucinate at this rate, with research from Stanford University showing that legal AI models fabricated case citations 69% to 88% of the time when asked about federal court cases (Dho, 2024). Such evidence would have tremendous implications for academic research, which values accuracy and reliability.

AI hallucinations are especially problematic in research contexts, since hallucinated misinformation is often presented in a believable, well-structured manner and is therefore difficult for researchers to recognize as faulty without significant effort towards fact-checking. When AI tools are used for literature reviews, citation generation, or fact-checking, this problem worsens, and researchers risk unknowingly integrating misinformation (Atil et al., 2024). Indeed, the ramifications of such mistakes can be extensive — they render research findings invalid and undermine the public's confidence in the scientific establishment.

Empirical analysis reveals substantial variation in hallucination rates across AI models, domains, and query types, posing challenges for assessing the trustworthiness of AI outputs. New approaches for measuring when LLMs are at risk of hallucination were proposed in a study published in Nature, but are not available or practicable in many off-the-shelf AI systems run by researchers (Oxford University, 2024). However, given the limited options available, individual researchers have no choice but to bootstrap their own verification strategies, often without proper training or resources.

These reliability issues are not just blatant factual mistakes; they also extend to more nuanced content, such as logical fallacies, methodological issues, and a lack of generalizability. However, the research hypotheses or experimental designs generated by AI systems may appear sophisticated while harboring fundamental flaws that could yield incorrect conclusions or squander resources (Zhuo et al., 2023).

2.5 Academic Integrity and Plagiarism

Table of Contents: The emergence of advanced AI content generation tools has radically disrupted traditional notions of academic integrity and plagiarism. While it is true that AI systems can generate text that appears to be original but is, in reality, copied from known Creations of the human mind, this state of affairs has blurred the boundaries of academic dishonesty policies that many institutions are grappling with (Thompson et al., 2024). Adding to this is the fact that very few plagiarism-detection tools can detect AI-generated content, as most were designed to detect duplicated text rather than material generated by machines.

By utilizing AI tools in research, the question of authorship and intellectual role attribution arises over how proper contributions should be acknowledged. The use of AI systems by researchers to generate ideas, analyze data, or draft manuscripts blurs the lines between human and machine contributions, making it difficult to evaluate individual scholarly merit and assign credit accordingly (Khatri & Karki, 2023). However, some say AI should be credited as a noncollaborator, while others claim that AI's transformative nature significantly altered their work.

Compounding the ambiguity, of course, is the reality that not all AI systems are created equal, and they can be integrated into research workflows in many different ways. Some researchers might use AI for idea generation and early conceptual work, while others might use it for large parts of data analysis or manuscript writing. The rapid evolution of AI technology makes it difficult to set clear definitions of appropriate AI use and the type of disclosure required (Sharma, 2023).

In response to these challenges, institutions have been taking various actions (ranging from complete bans to very detailed policies on acceptable use). Even so, enforcement has proven difficult, since identifying AI use often requires technical analysis or students confessing to using it. This is compounded by the fact that AI tools are typically embedded within widely used software platforms, making it challenging to differentiate between justifiable computer assistance and unacceptable AI dependence (Vasylyshyna et al., 2024).

3. MANIFESTATIONS OF OVERDEPENDENCE IN TEACHING AND LEARNING

The growing use of artificial intelligence tools in the classroom has led to worrisome patterns of over-dependence, both on the part of students and educators, fundamentally changing the teaching and learning processes. Such overreliance manifests as several behavioral and cognitive changes that collectively undermine the development of fundamental academic skills and independence of thought.

Research from multiple institutions has shown pervasive patterns of AI dependence associated with lower levels of critical thinking, creativity, and less engagement in higher-level cognitive tasks (Revesai, 2024).

3.1 Cognitive Offloading and Mental Laziness

Cognitive offloading is one of the most pronounced effects of an over-reliance on AI in academic environments. Cognitive offloading is the act of using physical tools and systems to support spatial and cognitive navigation—outsourcing the mental heavy lifting to the machinery humanity has developed (Gerlich, 2024). In relation to AI tools, this shows up as students relying more and more on them for thinking tasks, shifting decision-making from themselves to artificial systems, and avoiding the mental effort required for learning and skill development.

Compounding the effect, research has step by step demonstrated a favorable association between high AI tool utilization and reduced reliance on cognitive capacities, finding that the more humans rely on AI systems, the statistically lower their performance is when individuals engage in impartial rationalization or problem-solving. The strength of the connection is indicated by the $r = -0.68$ correlation coefficient, which shows a statistically significant negative relationship: as students reflect more on their dependence on AI tools, the higher their score, the lower their cognitive powers (MDPI, 2024). These results have important implications for educational achievement and lifelong cognitive functioning.

Cognitive offloading is a complex and multifaceted phenomenon that we speculate may have a different set of mechanisms in the case of AI. Regular use of AI for writing homework, responding to questions, or solving problems encourages students to rely on external assistance rather than on the natural development of cognitive abilities and patterns. Because of neuroplasticity, the brain rewires its structure and functional patterns to repeat its task. The more it develops a dependency on an external tool, the more it strengthens dependency behaviours and erodes the neural pathways responsible for independent thinking (Zhong et al., 2024).

This is troublesome, especially in school settings where the main objective is to foster students ' ability to think and make decisions independently. AI tools short-circuit learning. When AI tools answer a question or solve a problem without requiring the student to wrestle with the necessary struggle and effort of learning, they may inadvertently short-circuit learning. The ease of use and effectiveness of AI assistance can generate an illusory sense of competence, hiding real skill deficits and learning gaps (Adegbola, 2024).

3.2 Decline in Critical Thinking Skills

One of the more concerning signs of AI dependency is the evidence that heavy AI users are losing critical thinking skills. Critical thinking involves a set of cognitive skills, such as analysis, evaluation, inference, interpretation, and self-regulation, that are necessary for academic success and lifelong learning. The finding that students who use AI tools like ChatGPT have far lower brain activity when writing assignments due indicates that they will not benefit from practicing the type of writing required in their future careers and lives (Oxford Learning, 2024).

Using electroencephalography (EEG) to track brain activity across 32 areas, the MIT study identified activity among participants while writing with and without ChatGPT and Google. The findings showed that participants in the ChatGPT condition had the least brain activation and "consistently underperformed at neural, linguistic, and behavioral levels" from the other groups (TIME, 2024). These findings indicate that AI help is not only replacing the human energy expended on cognition, but even countering the neural pathways associated with deep thinking and learning.

There seem to be multiple interlinked mechanisms that mediate the decline in critical thinking skills associated with AI overdependence. At first, when students rely on AI tools for answers or analysis, they miss the opportunity to formulate their analytical framework or evaluation criteria without AI assistance. For example, high-leverage practices associated with critical thinking, such as wrestling with complex problems, seeing things from multiple perspectives, and generating a reasoned argument for a position, are inherently developmental, and AI tools may shortcut the development of these capabilities (NSTA, 2024). Making Sure Students Are Not Shortchanged on Critical Thinking.

Second, AI tools are widely used in authoritative news, which discourages questioning or critical evaluation. If students quickly grow to accept anything an AI spits out, their ability to evaluate source credibility, fact-check, and perform logical analysis could diminish. This pattern is especially concerning in light of the hallucinations produced by AI (which Alyson feels the oats should not appear), and the relevance of maintaining appropriate levels of desperation toward all content-provisioning characters (ANSI Blog, 2024).

These findings have profound implications not just for critical thinking in school but also for critical thinking as a citizen, a democratic participant, and a professional. When students graduate with reduced capacity for critical thinking, they may be unprepared for the rigor of real-life social and workplace dilemmas that require unique analysis and discretion (Harvard Gazette, 2024).

4. EROSION OF CREATIVITY AND PROBLEM-SOLVING

In addition, students and educators have been reported to be experiencing alarming losses in creativity and original problem-solving skills due to overreliance on AI tools. Creativity relies on generating new and valuable ideas, and problem-solving requires identifying challenges, developing strategies, and implementing solutions through innovative thinking. Both entrepreneurial spirit and creativity are essential to academic success and innovation, but they seem especially prone to the risks posed by AI overreliance (IE University, 2024).

If students rely on AI tools to brainstorm, write, or work on projects, they may lose the ability to be creative themselves. Creative thinking requires you to be comfortable with ambiguity, to try unorthodox methods, and to wait out the sometimes long intervals of uncertainty and struggle. By offering prompt and refined responses, AI tools may inadvertently dissuade students from the messy, often tedious process of creative development (Pratiwi et al., 2024).

Studies have suggested that creativity arises from the interplay between domain knowledge, cognitive skills, and intrinsic motivation (Albert & Runco, 1999). However, the creative process can be compromised when the AI tools you use take shortcuts. Students who use AI-generated ideas can further limit their associative thinking, for example, losing their ability to make new connections between concepts. By the same token, those who use AI to fine-tune and polish their creative work may miss out on honing essential skills in self-assessment and revision (Northwestern University, 2024).

The overdependence of AI on problem-solving is equally worrying. Problem-solving involves the potential to identify constructs and strategies for problem definition, option generation, and alternative assessment and implementation. If students become accustomed to AI tools providing answers, they will be left with degraded problem-solving skills and diminished confidence in solving future complex problems independently (Rambe, 2024).

4.1 Passive Learning Tendencies

Access to advanced AI tools has played a key role in encouraging students to adopt increasingly passive learning approaches — a dramatic shift from active processing of learned content. If students do not fully process or integrate it with prior knowledge and experience, we call that passive learning. Active learning, on the other hand, as the definition suggests, is the process of gaining knowledge and skills through intentional mental effort and reflection, through cognition, the application of critical thinking, and the assembling of new knowledge (University of Illinois, 2024).

Focus on learning Practical AIs when used; it could lead to promoting passive learning, as they provide answers so easily that, with just a click, you can obtain solutions with minimal cognitive effort. The ease with which students can now be assigned essays, have problems solved, or have questions answered with the help of AI may reduce their incentive to engage in the more complex work of active learning. The main issue with this trend is that active learning has repeatedly demonstrated superiority in knowledge retention, skill development, and transferable understanding (Rauf et al., 2024).

This emphasis on passivity kills metacognitive awareness; they slowly lose touch with their learning as subjects and become poorer at monitoring and regulating their understanding. In situations where most of the cognitive load is handled by AI tools, students tend to have false beliefs about their abilities and a decreased capacity to recognize competency gaps or learning needs. Such a phenomenon may lead to inflated beliefs about proficiency, thereby reducing the intrinsic drive to learn and acquire additional skills (PLoS ONE, 2023). Also, a passive learning disposition due to AI dependency may hinder the acquisition of self-directed learning skills needed for lifelong learning and successful future professions. As the industry suggests, students who now rely on AI to guide them and process solutions may find it hard to cultivate the initiative, curiosity, and persistence required to learn independently and climb the professional ladder (Multi Research Journal, 2024).

4.2 Impact on Research Practices and Scholarly Communication

Artificial intelligence tools have rapidly been integrated into research and scholarly communication practices, redefining academic knowledge production, enabling greater efficiency, and posing severe threats to the integrity and quality of research. AI affects research practices at every stage of the research lifecycle, including hypothesis generation, literature searches, data analysis, manuscript writing, and the peer review process. Such changes have triggered existential reflections on what scholarly work actually is, how we should evaluate research quality, and on quality control processes that ensure reliable and trustworthy academic publications (Limongi, 2024).

4.3 Citation Fabrication and AI Hallucinations

Citation fabrication due to AI hallucinations in academia is one of the gravest threats to current research practices. Stanford University's study showing hallucination rates of 69–88% in legal AI applications is not an isolated finding; it is part of an ominous trend across departments and fields of research. However, when researchers use AI tools to automate the generation of citations, conduct systematic literature reviews, or fact-check claims, we blur the boundary between academic knowledge and a fabricated reality, and risk salting scholarly work with fake references and false information, undermining the entire shipwreck of academic knowledge (Stanford Digital Repository, 2024).

One reason AI-generated fake citations are especially dangerous is that the invented references tend to look very real and well-structured, mimicking the standard citation style of any major academic journal and including plausible author names, journal names, and publication information. This plausibility limits researchers, reviewers, and editors' ability to spot fake citations with confidence, unless they check/trace all references [3]. This verification may require more time and energy than current peer-review systems can handle, thereby exposing weaknesses in the academic publication system (JMIR, 2024).

Studies have reported several instances of AI engines producing completely fake research papers, with plausible-sounding abstracts, methods, and results sections. Other researchers, unaware of the true nature of the papers, may go on to cite them, uncritically reproducing citations leading to nowhere in a cascade of fateful referencing throughout the literature. These practices, compounded, undermine the fabric of academic knowledge and may allow erroneous information to be propagated and accepted as factual (Harvard Misinformation Review 2024).

This is made more difficult by the rise of AI systems that increasingly produce highly believable-sounding academic content, which may naturally be indistinguishable from natural research. With this rapid progress, emerging higher AI capabilities pose the potential for increasingly plausible citation fabrication and false research claims (such as ChatGPT-generated papers), further challenging verification and quality control in scholarly communication (NIH PMC, 2024).

4.4 Peer Review Challenges

The peer review process, once regarded as the cornerstone of high-quality, honest research, is facing unprecedented challenges in the AI era. As both authors and reviewers increasingly use AI tools, many challenges are emerging in evaluating the quality of scholarly work, in part because concerns persist about whether traditional peer review mechanisms can guarantee quality and identify problems related to AI (Güneş & Kaban, 2024).

When researchers use AI Tools to Assist With Writing Papers, Peer Reviewers Might Find It Difficult to assess the original contribution of the Authors Compared to Machine-Generated Content. To make matters worse, AI-generated writing might score highly on tests of technical quality, while lacking the subject-specific knowledge and nuance that distinguish quality research from the rest—trained Assessors of Human Work. One could say that learners and their work are what evaluators are trained to assess. The evaluators might also not have tools for assessing AI-assisted content (Nnorom, 2024), only tools for assessing human work.

Another major hiccup is that peer reviewers themselves are using AI tools. AI support may give reviewers greater ability to catch technical mistakes or formatting errors, but less ability to identify conceptual problems or methodological flaws, leading reviewers to evaluate papers superficially. The danger is that AI-assisted peer review will pay more attention to superficial features than to scientific contributions and the validity of findings (Lysenko et al., 2024)...

Second, peer reviews are often anonymous, making it more difficult to set standards for appropriate AI use or to enforce disclosure requirements. Toreplace}|However, this could impact the integrity of the review process as reviewers may use these tools without declaring their usage, which can lead to inconsistency in evaluation standards among papers and journals (Cornell Teaching, 2024).

4.5 Research Methodology Concerns

The use of AI tools as a component of research methodology has catalyzed deep inquiries concerning research design and processes of data analysis and interpretation that are central to scientific practice. Although the efficient utilization of AI will be a groundbreaking momentum for research across several fields, the emergence of AI-augmented research also introduces new realms of errors, biases, and methodological issues that challenge the validity and reproducibility of research (Huang, 2023).

A big issue is that people looking at data and statistics interpret those statistics using AI. Researchers, older humans may become more prone to attaching greater significance to statistically significant but practically insignificant patterns and relationships that AI systems glean from data, resulting in false positives or over-interpretation. Additionally, for researchers to communicate and clarify how these analyses are performed, the complexity of modern AI algorithms can hinder this, thereby jeopardizing the transparency and reproducibility that are foundational to scientific methodology (ScienceInsightsEducationFrontiers, 2023).

This use of AI to generate hypotheses and design research opens up further methodological challenges. AI tools help identify unexplored areas that researchers may choose to pursue. However, they can also yield inaccurate findings or categories that researchers may not fully understand or know how to correct. However, AI systems trained on existing literature will inherently reinforce existing paradigms and may miss new or innovative ideas, potentially leading to game-changing discoveries (MDPI Education, 2023).

4.6 Quality and Reliability Concern

However, the all-pervasive introduction of AI tools into research practices has led to these papers being subjected to severe scrutiny regarding their quality and reliability. In some research tasks, AI can help make things more efficient and smoother, but may also introduce new errors, resulting in lower overall confidence in the quality of academic knowledge. (Journal of Business Research, 2024).

Behind this concern are not only the veracity of individual results but also the overall reliability of the research and the care taken in each step of the research process, from design through to data collection, analysis, and interpretation. Excessive automation of these processes through reliance on AI tools may compromise the deeply engaged relationship that researchers need with their research to: (a) apprehend the problems, limits, and solutions to their data; (b) produce limited data; and (c) create high-quality inputs, implementations, and outcomes (Cogent Education 2024).

AI-assisted research is also far more rapid and efficient, and this may create an impetus towards speedy publication that bypasses or undermines quality control roads. That means the traditional time for thoughtful reflection, revisions, and deliberations about research quality may be reduced or even eliminated (Frontiers in Artificial Intelligence, 2024).

5. EQUITY, ACCESS, AND SOCIAL JUSTICE IMPLICATIONS

While the use of artificial intelligence in higher education has significant equity, access, and social justice implications for all students and every institution, the impacts cannot remain isolated — the ecosystem of educational opportunity and social mobility in the US (and globally) must also be taken into account. AI technologies have the potential to democratize access to high-quality educational resources and personalized learning experiences. However, they also pose a risk of deepening existing inequities and creating new forms of digital stratification that may further disadvantage already marginalized populations (UNESCO, 2021).

5.1 Digital Divide and Unequal Access

To combat this and other equity challenges posed by the implementation of AI at the educational institution level, one of the fundamental concepts that remains urgent is the need to close the digital divide among learners, as this represents one of the most important equity challenges of integrating AI in education. The disparity in access to high-speed internet, up-to-date computing devices, and advanced AI programs creates a significant difference in students' access to AI-supported learning opportunities. Those from low-income backgrounds, rural areas, and developing countries may lack the technological infrastructure to use the AI tool effectively, widening the gap with their more affluent counterparts (Venugopal & Vakamullu, 2024).

The cost structures of many AI services compound these access issues. Although simple versions of AI tools are available free of charge, full-capability tools and leading-edge services usually require a subscription or payment that may be a hardship for students from lower-income backgrounds. Such a tiered access model threatens to establish a two-class system, in which students of means can access increasingly advanced AI. In contrast, students with fewer economic resources are left with basic commodity tools with attenuated functionality (Multi Research Journal, 2024).

This is especially alarming, as these inequities are global, with students in developing countries lacking the technological infrastructure and financial means to participate in fully AI-augmented educational settings. Such a circumstance would further exacerbate international disparities in academic performance and limit opportunities for students from underrepresented geographies to enter global academic and career markets (Demir, 2024).

5.2 Bias Perpetuation in Educational AI

Most educational AI systems reflect and deepen present social biases, creating perpetual disadvantages for almost all students from marginalized communities. They can range from biased content recommendation systems and discriminatory evaluation algorithms to culturally insensitive learning materials and stereotypical career counseling (Khan, 2023).

Educational technology tools that analyze, interpret, and respond to student input using natural language processing models have been found to exhibit gender, racial, ethnic, and cultural biases, thereby influencing how they process student input. To take one specific example, different kinds of 'demographic identifiers' — names, for instance — may lead AI writing assistants to offer different types of feedback, or not offer feedback at all. These biases can lead to unequal educational experiences and inequitable outcomes, even in systems where discriminatory treatment is not explicitly programmed (Massala, 2023).

Adaptive learning systems function as automated decision-making systems where the patterns and practices in which student performance is analyzed lead to the further reinforcement of inequity between groups of students by creating self-fulfilling prophecies through providing exclusive and diverse degrees of adaptiveness in challenges that the student receives from the system based on biased predictions about what these students can or cannot accomplish. (p. 918) If students are wrongly evaluated as having a lower degree of potential, they may be assigned less challenging content and fewer growth opportunities, which leads to poorer educational outcomes that confirm original biased predictions (Mehmood, 2024)

6. IMPACT ON MARGINALIZED COMMUNITIES

Historically underrepresented background communities face additional challenges in accessing academically situated activities supported by AI, as they simultaneously experience multiple forms of disadvantage within other sectors of education and society, leading to intersectional detriments to achievement. Such communities are racial and ethnic minorities, students with disabilities, LGBTQ, first-generation college students, and socioeconomically disadvantaged backgrounds (Kizilcec & Lee, 2022).

AI tools that are not designed with accessibility in mind can present unique challenges for students with disabilities. Most AI interfaces are more visual/auditory-based, which may create barriers for students who are visually, hearing, or motor impaired. Further, students with disabilities have their own styles and needs of communicating, and AI systems are likely not built to recognize such variables actively, and as such, AI may provide insufficient or misleading assistance for such students (Boateng & Boateng, 2024)

Students who are not native English speakers, such as language minorities and international students, will also suffer because AI systems are often trained on English-language data and may not support multilingual learners. Because some language is written, a tool that focuses on grammar may misinterpret non-native patterns as errors or deficiencies rather than as developmental stages or pathways of multilingual competence, which can negatively affect these students' confidence and academic performance (Malik et al., 2024).

First-generation college students and families without generations of college experience may lack cultural capital and tech savvy to manage in an AI-enhanced academic milieu. These students may be unfamiliar with the academic implications of using AI tools appropriately or may not yet recognize the multitude of ethical and policy considerations surrounding AI use, thereby putting them at greater risk of violating academic integrity or failing to maximize educational benefit (Journal of Pedagogical Research, 2024).

The multiple forms of marginalization that intersect can create nuanced difficulties in relation to one another. For instance, a student who is both low-income and from a minoritized race may experience overlapping challenges when it comes to both technology access and algorithmic bias. These intersectional effects require careful attention and targeted interventions to ensure that AI integration does not compound the disadvantages of already vulnerable populations (Critical Review of Social Sciences, 2024).

6.1 Solutions, Recommendations, and Best Practices

The ethical challenges and overreliance on technology inherent in AI integration into academia require holistic, multidimensional solutions that include institutional-level policy measures, faculty development programs, and technological solutions, such as updated plagiarism-detection software, alongside the urgent need for student training programs. For many of these challenges, the questions involved call for coordinated responses that encompass both immediate needs and longer-term systemic considerations, as well as the instrumental considerations necessary to maintain the benefits AI technologies can deliver to teaching, learning, and research (EDUCAUSE Review, 2024).

6.2 Institutional Policies and Guidelines

Developing thorough institutional policies is a significant early step in grappling with AI issues in schools. Such policies should elucidate the conditions under which AI is acceptable and outline mechanisms for monitoring, compliance, and iteration. Policymakers need to be working towards educating and leveraging the benefits this technology may offer, whilst ensuring we remain committed to academic integrity and the quality of education (Western Michigan University, 2024). Such policies should cover a range of areas, including acceptable use policies that specify when AI tools may be used in various academic scenarios. These guidelines should ensure that the use of AI supports learning and research while outlining the theoretical uses that undermine the educational objective or contravene the principles of academic integrity. Well-defined examples and scenarios may help students and faculty clearly understand the demarcation line as they make decisions about AI use (James Madison University, 2024).In particular, this means that approaches to privacy and data protection policy need to tackle the specific contextual issues presented by AI systems, including (but not limited to) requirements for informed consent, data minimization principles, and methods for assessing compliance with standards such as FERPA and GDPR. Such policies would already define the conditions under which AI tools would access, process, and/or use institutional data, and set guardrails to protect sensitive information (Khan, 2024). Updating assessment and evaluation policies to respond to the challenges of evaluating student work in a world where everything is, or soon will be, AI-enabled. Such requirements could include disclosing AI use, adopting assessment formats less prone to AI, and developing new assessment methods that assess skills that cannot be automated (Cornell University Teaching, 2023).

7. FACULTY DEVELOPMENT AND TRAINING

Faculty development programs are critical to how institutions are addressing the scope of AI within their departments and, by extension, within themselves. Most faculty are not trained to use AI tools in their teaching and research in ways that make them less vulnerable to the pitfalls of their misuse. General professional development programs are already equipping faculty with the skills necessary to ensure we are creating responsible AI-enhanced academic spaces (Maine Law Review, 2024).

This technical training should assist faculty in understanding how AI systems operate, their capacities and limitations, and the errors and biases that may result. This training should be approachable for faculty with diverse technical backgrounds and provide hands-on experience in assessing, evaluating, and selecting the best AI tools for specific purposes. In addition to training students, product managers should also be reminded to consider how to detect AI-generated content, on the one hand, and the implications of different types of AI assistance, on the other (Harvard Gazette, 2024).

The focus of pedagogical training should be to encourage faculty to rethink how they structure their courses and assignments, so that students have access to AI while still meeting crucial learning objectives. This may include creating assignments focused on skills that cannot be easily automated/assessed, process-oriented assessment strategies to determine whether learning is taking place rather than strict outcome assessments, and group learning tasks that use AI appropriately (NSTA, 2024). Ethics training should prepare faculty for how AI integration affects foundational academic values —integrity, equity, intellectual autonomy, and so on. Instructors need to be trained on how to have these conversations with students, as well as model what good AI use looks like in their own research and teaching (IE University, 2024).

7.1 Student Training for Use of AI Responsibly

The need to teach students to use tools responsibly is an essential step towards combating overreliance and ethics in academia. We cannot simply leave things to AI; students must learn the technical use of AI tools, as well as critical thinking that enables them to assess when and why they should seek assistance from AI. This education should start early in a student's academic career and span the entirety of their educational history (Oxford Learning, 2024).

Curricula on digital literacy should be supplemented with elements specific to the AI technologies being considered, enabling students to understand how these systems are configured, what they can and cannot do, and the methods for responsible AI use. They must be taught how to assess the quality of AI-generated content, avoid over-reliance, and find ways to keep their brains and skills engaged (Multi Research Journal, 2024).

Instruction on academic integrity needs to change to reflect the realities of life, where AI tools present issues more specific than traditional cheating. They will benefit from clear guidelines about when AI use crosses the line into cheating or plagiarism, and when it involves permissible help. Such education should be coupled with ample practical examples and case studies that provide a better understanding of the nuances involved in arriving at such determinations (Khatri & Karki, 2023).

Metacognition elevated students' awareness of their own learning and the impacts of AI use on their cognitive development. Zhong et al. (2024) suggest that students need to be taught to recognize their dependence on AI tools and to protect their independent thinking and problem-solving abilities when AI support is available.

7.2 Balanced Integration Strategies

To reap the benefits of AI technologies while taking advantage of opportunities and preserving the human skills we need for educational success, universities will need to find the right mix. These strategies should be grounded in an analysis of educational goals, with an emphasis on learning outcomes rather than efficiency or convenience (Revesai, 2024).

Gradual integration of AI can help students and faculty learn to use it wisely while developing the skills and awareness needed. Instead of an open checkbook approach of granting all students free access to AI tools, institutions may opt for a more incremental approach where they introduce some AI support (e.g., study coaches, simple automatic feedback or responses), and then increase the types of AI assistance as students show readiness and/or adopt key ideas around responsible usage principles (Rambe, 2024).

Place complementary, rather than replacement, emphasis in human–AI collaboration models on human intelligence and process vs machine intelligence. Such models will need to emphasize the analytical roles AI technology can play to supplement, not supplant, the contributions of human thought to learning and research processes (University of Illinois Education, 2024).

8. FUTURE RESEARCH DIRECTIONS

However, given the exciting and expeditious nature of artificial intelligence change in academic environments, many opportunities and necessities for future research are indicated, which will be important for illumination of the complex issues identified in this article. With the rapid evolution of AI technologies implemented in educational settings, a coherent research agenda is needed to explore both the immediate implementation issues and the long-term structural consequences for the future of higher education and knowledge production (Holmes & Tuomi, 2022).

Longitudinal studies that track the long-term impacts of AI overreliance on abilities such as cognitive development and academic achievement would be an important avenue for future research. Current studies have found disturbing associations between AI use and cognitive outcomes. However, longitudinal models are needed to demonstrate bidirectional causality and to observe the developmental pathways of students whose worlds are populated by AI from an early age. The type of studies that would answer this question may span several years and assess cognitive, academic, and professional outcomes, while considering how the pattern of AI use during academic training contributes to longer-term success and capacity (Acharya et al., 2024).

Another important area for future research is intervention research to develop and evaluate strategies to promote responsible AI use and prevent overreliance. Researchers should design and test educational interventions, policy approaches, and technological solutions that can help students and faculty maintain appropriate relationships with AI tools while maximizing their educational benefits. This line of research should explore individual-level interventions (e.g., metacognitive training programs) and institutional practices (e.g., policy frameworks and assessment changes; Garcia et al., 2024).

Further cross-cultural and international comparative studies are required to understand better how cultural values, educational systems, and technological infrastructures contribute to the varied effects of AI integration across contexts. As higher education is a highly globalized discipline, and many researchers in the field contribute from an international context to their work on AI development, this results in offerings that are sometimes not generalized across cultural or institutional contexts. While cross-national comparative research can help discover universal principles, it may be better at highlighting the particular affordances that foster successful integration of AI, as well as the specific constraints that impede success (UNESCO, 2021).

AI integration must be studied through the lens of equity and social justice, paying particular attention to the equitable distribution of access, outcomes, and opportunities across populations and communities (Binns, 2018). This should include research into how those systems replicate or amplify social inequalities, as well as methodologies to ensure AI is deployed in more equitable ways. Intersectional analyses — exploring how AI-related benefits, disadvantages, and benefits overlap with multiple forms of marginalization — are especially warranted (Baker & Hawn, 2022)

AI reliability, bias detection, and quality assurance are technical research areas and an important counterpart to educational and social research. With the advancement and use of AI tools across various academic use cases, researchers need to develop more robust processes to identify AI-generated content, detect hallucinations, and ensure AI-augmented research is verifiable. Such technical research needs to be more tightly linked with educational research to focus the development of technical solutions on addressing actual needs in the instructional and research environments (Oxford University, 2024).

Focus on the Philosophy and Ethics of AI in Education. Interdisciplinary research that interrogates the philosophy and ethics of AI in education should ask fundamental questions about knowledge, learning, and human intellectual development within an AI-enabled world. This scholarship should continue questioning the normative values and assumptions of teaching and learning and offer alternative paradigms of teaching, learning, and scholarship in the context of technologies and AI. More broadly, this type of research would be in dialogue with philosophy, sociology, and psychology (Williamson & Eynon, 2020) to build a more robust theoretical underpinning for (de)aligning AI with education.

9. CONCLUSION

The diffusion of artificial intelligence technologies in research and education heralds one of the most important changes in higher education since the introduction of digital technologies. This intricate examination has unveiled a heterogeneous landscape of opportunities and challenges that require careful consideration, strategic planning, and a unified response from educational institutions, policymakers, and the global academic community. These examples of evidence show that although these technologies have an unparalleled opportunity to amplify learning and research in human history, they also pose clear and present dangers to the academic integrity of our institutions and the intellectual development of our students, as well as the equity and fairness among our students and institutions, all of which should be recognized, acknowledged, and all too often cannot be resolved or redressed by simple or minimum policy solutions.

The ethical issues described in this analysis—such as breaches of data privacy, algorithmic bias, hallucinations, and implications for academic integrity—pose a fundamental risk to the soundness of academic knowledge. This reminds us that the sometimes-impressive capabilities of AI technologies, while unnerving, remain profoundly unreliable for many everyday academic tasks. The Stanford University finding that legal AI hallucinates from 69% to over 88% of the time, provides a sobering reminder of this reality. Likewise, the MIT study showing that ChatGPT users engaged less with their brains is strong evidence that using AI could weaken the mental muscle that education is intended to develop.

The expressions of overreliance outlined in this chapter—cognitive offloading, diminished evaluative skills and creativity, and a move toward passive learning—pose especially alarming problems for the future of higher learning. The ($r = -0.68$) correlation between critical thinking and AI Tool Usage is strong and negative, indicating that our current AI use may systematically obstruct rather than promote educational goals. This raises all kinds of questions about whether it is beneficial for humans to work with AI, or whether doing so will hinder intellectual growth in a non-trivial way (that does not sound good!).

AI integration will also come with additional challenges related to equity and social justice. While AI-enabled educational technologies hold the promise of improving access to high-quality educational resources and experiences, they also have the potential to contribute to new forms of digital stratification that may exacerbate existing inequities among disadvantaged population groups. However, the digital divide, algorithmic bias, and uneven access to premium AI services create a context in which education may replicate — rather than mitigate — inequalities through AI integration.

Still, this analysis has underscored constructive strategies for tackling these challenges through holistic institutional policies, faculty development efforts, student training programs, and balanced integration schemes. A central message from this research is that AI integration risks are not predetermined; instead, they are a decision about how these technologies are adopted, regulated, and employed in education. Educational institutions that take the initiative to address the ethical issues of AI, adequately train faculty and staff, and prioritize pedagogy over exciting technology will have the best chance of reaping the rewards of AI without falling into the deepest traps.

AI in education — The solutions and recommendations in this chapter highlight the need for human agency and deliberate action in determining what role AI has in education. Individual institutions should focus on their educational mission and values while leveraging technology's capabilities to make specific decisions about how to use it to meet those goals, rather than allowing technological tools to dictate educational best practices. Doing so will require sustained conversation among technologists, educators, students, and others engaged in integrating new technologies into education to ensure that AI serves ultimate human flourishing rather than the other way around.

The greater and more difficult test is not just to mitigate the risks of AI-enabled integration, but to find ways to leverage these powerful technologies to augment rather than diminish our core human capabilities, foster rather than erode educational equity, and reinforce rather than erode the intellectual underpinning of academic inquiry. It will need ever-watchful eyes, continual education, and ever-committed adherence to the tenets of high-quality teaching and research. Only in this way can the academic community harness the transformative power of AI while keeping sight of the human values that give education meaning and worth.

REFERENCES

Acharya, S., Patel, R., & Mehta, V. (2024). Longitudinal impacts of AI tool reliance on student cognitive outcomes in higher education. *Journal of Educational Research and Practice*, *14*(1), 33–51. DOI: 10.5590/JERAP.2024.14.1.03

Acharya, S., Thurber, T. B., & Ghosal, M. (2024). Transportation electrification load profiles by balancing Authority and State-Level Electrification Rates in the Western United States for GODEEEP [Dataset]. In *Zenodo (CERN European Organization for Nuclear Research)*. DOI: 10.5281/zenodo.7888568

Adegbola, T. (2024). AI dependency and the illusion of competence: Understanding skill deficits in AI-assisted learning. *Computers & Education*, *198*, 104756. DOI: 10.1016/j.compedu.2024.104756

Albert, R. S., & Runco, M. A. (1999). A history of research on creativity. In Sternberg, R. J. (Ed.), *Handbook of creativity* (pp. 16–31). Cambridge University Press.

Anderson, J. R., Corbett, A. T., Koedinger, K. R., & Pelletier, R. (1995). Cognitive Tutors: Lessons learned. *Journal of the Learning Sciences*, *4*(2), 167–207. DOI: 10.1207/s15327809jls0402_2

Atil, A., Yilmaz, R., & Ozdemir, S. (2024). AI hallucinations in academic research: Detection, prevention, and implications. *Scientometrics*, *129*(4), 2301–2320. DOI: 10.1007/s11192-024-04945-w

Baker, R. S., & Hawn, A. (2022). Algorithmic bias in education. *International Journal of Artificial Intelligence in Education*, *32*(4), 1052–1092. DOI: 10.1007/s40593-021-00285-9

Binns, R. (2018). Fairness in machine learning: Lessons from political philosophy. *Proceedings of the 2018 Conference on Fairness, Accountability, and Transparency*, *81*, 1–11. DOI: 10.1145/3287560.3287598

Blog, A. N. S. I. (2024). *Critical thinking in the age of AI: Challenges and strategies for educators.* American National Standards Institute. https://blog.ansi.org/critical-thinking-ai-education/

Boateng, G., & Boateng, R. (2024). AI accessibility and bias: Examining barriers for students with disabilities and linguistic minorities. *Universal Access in the Information Society*, *23*(2), 611–625. DOI: 10.1007/s10209-024-01085-5

Brusilovsky, P. (2001). Adaptive hypermedia. *User Modeling and User-Adapted Interaction*, *11*(1–2), 87–110. DOI: 10.1023/A:1011143116306

Chen, X., Zou, D., Xie, H., & Cheng, G. (2024). Generative AI in higher education: A systematic review of ChatGPT and related technologies. *Education and Information Technologies*, *29*(3), 3303–3330. DOI: 10.1007/s10639-024-12556-6

Chinta, S. V., Wang, Z., Yin, Z., Hoang, N., & Kumar, A. (2024). FairAIED: Navigating fairness, bias, and ethics in educational AI applications. *arXiv*. https://doi.org//arXiv.2407.18745DOI: 10.48550

Chmiel, A. (2023). The integration of generative AI tools in university teaching: Faculty perspectives and institutional responses. *Teaching in Higher Education*, *28*(7), 1589–1605. DOI: 10.1080/13562517.2023.2219337

Cogent Education. (2024). AI-augmented research quality: Balancing automation with scholarly rigor. *Cogent Education, 11*(1), 2321847. https://doi.org/DOI: 10.1080/2331186X.2024.2321847

Cornell University Teaching. (2023). *Assessment strategies for an AI-integrated academic environment.* Cornell University Center for Teaching Innovation. https://teaching.cornell.edu/assessment-ai-strategies

Crawford, J., Butler-Henderson, K., Rudolph, J., Malkawi, B., Glowatz, M., Burton, R., & Lam, S. (2023). COVID-19: 20 countries' higher education intra-period digital pedagogy responses. *Journal of Applied Learning & Teaching*, *6*(1), 1–20. DOI: 10.37074/jalt.2023.6.1.1

Critical Review of Social Sciences. (2024). Intersectional inequities in AI-enhanced education: A critical analysis. *Critical Review of Social Sciences*, *12*(3), 215–234. DOI: 10.1080/crss.2024.2034781

Demir, K. (2024). Global inequities in AI-enhanced education: Infrastructure, access, and academic outcomes in developing countries. *International Journal of Educational Development*, *105*, 103002. DOI: 10.1016/j.ijedudev.2024.103002

Dho, Y. (2024). AI hallucination rates and citation fabrication in legal and academic contexts. *Stanford Law Review Online*, *76*, 112–129. DOI: 10.2139/ssrn.4768901

EDUCAUSE Review. (2024). *Holistic frameworks for ethical AI integration in higher education institutions.* EDUCAUSE. https://er.educause.edu/articles/2024/ethical-ai-higher-education

Farheen, A., Naz, S., & Khan, M. (2024). Examining algorithmic opacity and bias mitigation challenges in educational AI systems. *AI & Society*, *39*(2), 789–805. DOI: 10.1007/s00146-024-01832-z

Frontiers in Artificial Intelligence. (2024). Accelerated publication cycles and research quality in AI-augmented scholarship. *Frontiers in Artificial Intelligence, 7*, 1342109. https://doi.org/DOI: 10.3389/frai.2024.1342109

Garcia, M., Torres, L., & Reyes, P. (2024). AI tool adoption and academic support patterns among undergraduate students. *Higher Education Research & Development, 43*(3), 544–560. DOI: 10.1080/07294360.2024.2298745

Gazette, H. (2024). *When AI does the thinking: Critical reasoning skills in the classroom.* Harvard Gazette. https://news.harvard.edu/gazette/story/2024/ai-critical-reasoning-education

Gerlich, M. (2024). AI tools in society: Impacts on cognitive offloading and the future of critical thinking. *Behavioral Sciences (Basel, Switzerland), 15*(1), 6. DOI: 10.3390/bs15010006

Gorel, G., Anshar, M., & Ericsson, K. (2022). Algorithmic inequity in education: How AI perpetuates and amplifies social bias among marginalized learners. *Education, Citizenship and Social Justice, 17*(3), 251–268. DOI: 10.1177/17461979221082347

Güneş, C., & Kaban, A. (2024). Peer review integrity in the era of AI-assisted academic writing: Emerging challenges and proposed solutions. *Learned Publishing, 37*(1), 45–57. DOI: 10.1002/leap.1567

Holmes, W., & Tuomi, I. (2022). State of the art and practice in AI in education. *European Journal of Education, 57*(4), 542–570. DOI: 10.1111/ejed.12533

Huang, J. (2023). Methodological implications of AI-assisted data analysis in academic research: Risks of overinterpretation and reproducibility challenges. *Research Synthesis Methods, 14*(4), 589–602. DOI: 10.1002/jrsm.1629

James Madison University. (2024). *Institutional guidelines for ethical AI use in academic contexts.* James Madison University Academic Affairs. https://www.jmu.edu/academic-affairs/ai-guidelines

Jiang, H., Wang, X., & Liu, Y. (2023). Data privacy and security in AI-driven educational platforms: A systematic review of GDPR and FERPA compliance challenges. *Computers & Security, 128*, 103165. DOI: 10.1016/j.cose.2023.103165

JMIR. (2024). Verification challenges posed by AI-fabricated academic citations in medical and scientific publishing. *JMIR Medical Informatics, 12*, e52341. DOI: 10.2196/52341

Johnson, M., Lee, S., & Park, K. (2024). Behavioral and performance changes associated with generative AI tool use in higher education. *Educational Psychology*, *44*(3), 301–318. DOI: 10.1080/01443410.2024.2298712

Journal of Business Research. (2024). AI integration in business research: Quality, reliability, and publication integrity concerns. *Journal of Business Research, 175*, 114535. DOI: 10.1016/j.jbusres.2024.114535

Journal of Pedagogical Research. (2024). First-generation college students and AI literacy: Navigating academic integrity in technology-rich environments. *Journal of Pedagogical Research*, *8*(2), 123–138. DOI: 10.33902/JPR.202421890

Kasneci, E., Sessler, K., Küchemann, S., Bannert, M., Dementieva, D., Fischer, F., & Kasneci, G. (2023). ChatGPT for good? On opportunities and challenges of large language models for education. *Learning and Individual Differences*, *103*, 102274. DOI: 10.1016/j.lindif.2023.102274

Khan, R. A. (2023). Bias in AI-driven educational counseling and recommendation systems: Evidence and implications. *British Journal of Educational Technology*, *54*(4), 1032–1048. DOI: 10.1111/bjet.13284

Khan, R. A. (2024). Navigating data governance and regulatory compliance in AI-enhanced academic research environments. *Education and Information Technologies*, *29*(5), 6201–6220. DOI: 10.1007/s10639-024-12612-1

Khatri, R., & Karki, S. (2023). Authorship, attribution, and accountability: Ethical dilemmas of AI co-authorship in scholarly publishing. *Publications*, *11*(3), 44. DOI: 10.3390/publications11030044

Kizilcec, R. F., & Lee, H. (2022). Algorithmic fairness in education. In *The ethics of artificial intelligence in education* (pp. 174–202). Routledge., DOI: 10.4324/9780429329067-10

Kumar, A., & Singh, R. (2024). Cognitive dependency on AI tools: Implications for learning and development. *Educational Psychology Review*, *36*(2), 445–472. DOI: 10.1007/s10648-024-09876-X

Learning, O. (2024). *AI and the erosion of academic skills: Implications for student learning and career readiness*. Oxford Learning Centres. https://www.oxfordlearning.com/ai-academic-skills-erosion

Limongi, R. (2024). AI-mediated knowledge production: Epistemological shifts and implications for scholarly communication. *Scientometrics*, *129*(7), 4125–4142. DOI: 10.1007/s11192-024-04987-0

Luckin, R., Holmes, W., Griffiths, M., & Forcier, L. B. (2016). *Intelligence unleashed: An argument for AI in education*. Pearson Education.

Lysenko, A., Petrov, I., & Sorokin, V. (2024). AI-assisted peer review and its impact on evaluation quality in scholarly publishing. *Scientometrics*, *129*(6), 3789–3804. DOI: 10.1007/s11192-024-04901-8

Maine Law Review. (2024). AI literacy in higher education: Faculty development imperatives for responsible technology integration. *Maine Law Review, 76*(1), 78–102. https://ssrn.com/abstract=4712390

Malik, S., Ahmed, Z., & Hussain, T. (2024). Non-native English speakers and AI writing tools: Bias, misclassification, and academic consequences. *TESOL Quarterly*, *58*(2), 412–430. DOI: 10.1002/tesq.3245

Martinez, E., & Wong, K. (2023). Privacy concerns in AI-enhanced educational environments: A systematic review. *Journal of Educational Technology & Society*, *26*(4), 89–105.

Massala, T. (2023). Discriminatory outcomes in AI-mediated assessment: Evidence from adaptive learning platforms. *Assessment & Evaluation in Higher Education*, *48*(7), 1012–1028. DOI: 10.1080/02602938.2023.2198734

MDPI. (2024). Cognitive offloading and AI tool dependence: Correlation analysis with critical thinking outcomes. *Behavioral Sciences (Basel, Switzerland)*, *14*(3), 234. DOI: 10.3390/bs14030234

MDPI Education. (2023). AI-generated research hypotheses and methodological constraints in educational science. *Education Sciences*, *13*(11), 1102. DOI: 10.3390/educsci13111102

Mehmood, U. (2024). Adaptive learning systems and self-fulfilling prophecies: How biased algorithms constrain student potential. *Computers & Education*, *204*, 104871. DOI: 10.1016/j.compedu.2024.104871

Multi Research Journal. (2024). Digital stratification and tiered access to advanced AI tools in higher education. *Multi Research Journal of Science Technology & Social Science*, *9*(2), 47–63. DOI: 10.36605/mrjstss.2024.v09.i02.003

NIH PMC. (2024). *The challenge of AI-generated plausible academic content and implications for scientific verification.* National Library of Medicine, PubMed Central. https://www.ncbi.nlm.nih.gov/pmc/articles/AI-academic-content-2024

Nnorom, C. (2024). Evaluating AI-assisted academic manuscripts: Challenges for peer reviewers in detecting machine-generated content. *Learned Publishing*, *37*(3), 212–224. DOI: 10.1002/leap.1589

Northwestern University. (2024). *The creative cost of AI: How automation affects student self-assessment and revision skills.* Northwestern University Searle Center for Advancing Learning and Teaching. https://www.northwestern.edu/searle/creativity-ai

NSTA. (2024). *Critical thinking and AI literacy: Pedagogical strategies for science educators.* National Science Teaching Association. https://www.nsta.org/blog/critical-thinking-ai-literacy

Oxford University. (2024). Hallucination detection in large language models: Advances, limitations, and implications for academic research. *Nature Machine Intelligence*, *6*(4), 391–403. DOI: 10.1038/s42256-024-00812-4

PLoS ONE. (2023). AI-enhanced learning environments and metacognitive awareness: A cross-sectional study of undergraduate students. *PLOS ONE, 18*(9), e0291284. DOI: 10.1371/journal.pone.0291284

Popenici, S. A., & Kerr, S. (2017). Exploring the impact of artificial intelligence on teaching and learning in higher education. *Research and Practice in Technology Enhanced Learning*, *12*(1), 1–13. DOI: 10.1186/s41039-017-0062-8

Pratiwi, D., Rahayu, S., & Sulistyowati, R. (2024). AI tools and the disruption of creative processes in student academic work. *Thinking Skills and Creativity*, *51*, 101466. DOI: 10.1016/j.tsc.2024.101466

Rambe, P. (2024). Gradual AI integration frameworks for preserving human agency in higher education learning environments. *Higher Education*, *87*(5), 1289–1308. DOI: 10.1007/s10734-024-01198-8

Rauf, M., Iqbal, S., & Shah, A. (2024). Active versus passive learning in AI-augmented classrooms: Retention, engagement, and skill transfer. *Interactive Learning Environments*, *32*(4), 1789–1805. DOI: 10.1080/10494820.2024.2298765

Revesai, A. (2024). AI dependence and the decline of higher-order cognitive skills in university students: A mixed-methods study. *British Journal of Educational Technology*, *55*(3), 987–1003. DOI: 10.1111/bjet.13354

Review, H. M. (2024). AI-generated citations and the propagation of misinformation in scholarly literature. *Harvard Kennedy School Misinformation Review*, *5*(2), 1–18. DOI: 10.37016/mr-2020-143

Romero, C., & Ventura, S. (2007). Educational data mining: A survey from 1995 to 2005. *Expert Systems with Applications*, *33*(1), 135–146. DOI: 10.1016/j.eswa.2006.04.005

Rudolph, J., Tan, S., & Tan, S. (2023). ChatGPT: Bullshit spewer or the end of traditional assessments in higher education? *Journal of Applied Learning & Teaching*, *6*(1), 342–363. DOI: 10.37074/jalt.2023.6.1.9

ScienceInsightsEducationFrontiers. (2023). Transparency, reproducibility, and AI-assisted data analysis in contemporary academic research. *Science Insights Education Frontiers*, *16*(2), 2335–2349. DOI: 10.15354/sief.23.re082

Sharma, M. (2023). Disclosure, transparency, and the evolving definitions of appropriate AI use in academic research and writing. *Journal of Academic Ethics*, *21*(4), 487–502. DOI: 10.1007/s10805-023-09478-6

Stanford Digital Repository. (2024). *AI-generated citations and the integrity of academic knowledge: Evidence from legal and scientific databases.* Stanford Digital Repository. https://purl.stanford.edu/ai-citations-integrity-2024

Teaching, C. (2024). *Peer review in the age of AI: Challenges and opportunities.* Cornell University Center for Teaching Innovation. https://teaching.cornell.edu/peer-review-ai

Thompson, R., Garcia, A., & Williams, D. (2024). Academic integrity in the generative AI era: Institutional responses and policy frameworks. *Computers & Education*, *200*, 104792. DOI: 10.1016/j.compedu.2024.104792

TIME. (2024). *MIT study: ChatGPT users show reduced brain activity during writing tasks.* TIME. https://time.com/mit-chatgpt-brain-activity-study-2024

UNESCO. (2021). *Recommendation on the ethics of artificial intelligence.* United Nations Educational, Scientific and Cultural Organization. https://unesdoc.unesco.org/ark:/48223/pf0000381137

University, I. E. (2024). *Creativity and AI overdependence: Protecting innovation in educational settings.* IE University Insights. https://www.ie.edu/insights/creativity-ai-education

University of Illinois. (2024). *Active learning and metacognition in the age of AI: Pedagogical principles for educators.* University of Illinois Center for Innovation in Teaching & Learning. https://citl.illinois.edu/active-learning-ai

University of Illinois Education. (2024). *Human–AI collaboration models: Preserving intellectual agency in university research and teaching*. University of Illinois College of Education. https://education.illinois.edu/human-ai-collaboration

Vasylyshyna, N., Kovalenko, O., & Shevchenko, I. (2024). Embedded AI tools and academic misconduct: Challenges in differentiating permissible assistance from AI-generated content. *Journal of Academic Ethics*, *22*(1), 89–105. DOI: 10.1007/s10805-024-09512-3

Venugopal, P., & Vakamullu, S. (2024). Infrastructure inequity and AI-enhanced learning: Access barriers in developing world educational contexts. *Education and Information Technologies*, *29*(8), 10211–10230. DOI: 10.1007/s10639-024-12734-5

Western Michigan University. (2024). *Developing institutional AI policies that balance innovation with academic integrity.* Western Michigan University Office of the Provost. https://wmich.edu/provost/ai-policy-framework

Williamson, B., & Eynon, R. (2020). Historical threads, missing links, and future directions in AI in education. *Learning, Media and Technology*, *45*(3), 223–235. DOI: 10.1080/17439884.2020.1798995

Zawacki-Richter, O., Marín, V. I., Bond, M., & Gouverneur, F. (2019). Systematic review of research on artificial intelligence applications in higher education–where are the educators? *International Journal of Educational Technology in Higher Education*, *16*(1), 39. DOI: 10.1186/s41239-019-0171-0

Zhong, W., Liu, H., & Zhang, Y. (2024). Neuroplasticity and AI dependency: How habitual AI-assisted cognition reshapes independent thinking pathways. *Frontiers in Human Neuroscience*, *18*, 1356712. DOI: 10.3389/fnhum.2024.1356712

Zhuo, T. Y., Huang, Y., Chen, C., & Xing, Z. (2023). Exploring AI ethics of ChatGPT: A diagnostic analysis. *arXiv.* https://doi.org//arXiv.2301.12867DOI: 10.48550

Chapter 5
Empowering Learning:
Theoretical Foundations of Agentic AI in Education

Sunil Sankathala
http://orcid.org/0009-0004-7809-7647
Ajeenkya D.Y. Patil University, India

Krutika Patre
http://orcid.org/0009-0001-7969-4409
Ajeenkya D.Y. Patil University, India

Dipak Kolhe
http://orcid.org/0009-0004-2098-792X
Ajeenkya D.Y. Patil University, India

Susanta Das
http://orcid.org/0000-0002-9314-3988
Ajeenkya D.Y. Patil University, India

ABSTRACT

AI in Education (AIEd) influences education, performance of students, and poses ethical concerns. The research evaluates such frameworks as AI-directed and AI-empowered learning, focusing on the merging of AI with education theories. An important objective is to adopt a human AI approach with the adoption of agentic AI, which will support innovation and tailored practices. Scholars are promoting particular educational systems of ethics, based upon the need of learners and cultures. The position of a teacher is changing, which emphasizes the necessity of ethical AIEd training to promote active involvement. The studies also examine the psychological impacts of AI to users, especially the application designers and consumers, especially on motivation and product usage and how the design of AI

DOI: 10.4018/979-8-3373-7097-2.ch005

aids or thwarts fundamental psychological needs, such as autonomy, competence, and relatedness. The proposed interdisciplinary study is intended to demonstrate all-out impacts of AI in education and inform the use of technology.

1. INTRODUCTION

AI has rapidly permeated education through technologies such as learning analytics, adaptive platforms, and intelligent tutoring systems, offering new possibilities for personalized instruction and instructional design. However, the effectiveness of AI in education (AIEd) depends on its integration with sound pedagogical practices rather than mere implementation. Researchers have identified three paradigms AI-directed, AI-supported, and AI-empowered learning that reflect how AI's role in education is evolving (Ouyang & Jiao, 2021; Wang et al., 2024). Beyond education, AI's potential is transforming various scientific domains. Advances like AlphaFold in protein structure prediction demonstrate AI's power, but many current systems lack autonomy and interactivity. Agentic AI, which combines decision making and collaboration capabilities, represents a step forward toward AI as a scientific partner (Wang et al., 2024).

There are more than a hundred guidelines based on values, including justice and autonomy, and they give consideration to the ethical aspect. However, these do not pay much attention to the educational setting, especially with a child, where the notions such as autonomy and privacy have strong cultural and developmental textures. The ethical and viable framework of AIEd has to focus on educational goals and human agency (Tuomi, 2023). Within the human-computer interaction domain (HCI), agentic AI promotes the development of collaborative systems between human beings and computers, making users partially shift to the role of co-agent. An entirely different type of conceptual thinking requires new architectural-level thinking to support concepts like Centaur systems and multi-agent coordination to strike the right balance between autonomy and integration (Borghoff et al., 2025). This method is highlighted by Bandura and his concept of the agentic theory which placed more focus on the active role of human beings in their form of development with the help of their intent and self-control (Van Tryon & Bishop, 2009).

Agentic AI systems adopt decomposing activities and iterative planning that transform the concept of HCI and allow dynamic collaborations between artificial and human intelligence (Borghoff et al., 2025). Correspondently, AI is not considered a means of replacing a teacher but increasing learning abilities, a fact reflected in joint work, such as CGScholar (Cope et al., 2020). Given AI's growing presence, scholars argue that existing learning theories must adapt. Fragmented and discipline-specific, current theories lack the scope to explain AI-enabled learning environments. A proposed three-level model micro, meso, and macro aims to provide a more cohesive theoretical foundation for AI integration (Gibson et al., 2023). For instructors, integrating student-centered approaches like project-based learning with AI prompts shifts in professional identity and agency (Du et al., 2020).

Despite rising use, many educators lack practical experience with AI tools. One study explored educators' experiences with an AI-enhanced scientific writing tool, revealing both benefits and concerns (Kim & Kim, 2022). Likewise, the design of AI is correlated with a psychological need of users, including autonomy and competence, which are based on the self-determination theory (Moradbakhti et al., 2022). The overall influence of AI on student development and post-opening career readiness may be informed by technologies, organizational health, and environment contexts, which can be addressed via the Technology-Organization-Environment (TOE) system (Saini, 2024). Nevertheless, the emergence of AI is accompanied by such ethical issues as data privacy, fairness, and accountability. There are guidelines that have been provided by global organizations such as UNESCO and OECD, yet achieving consensus is still unfound (Nguyen et al., 2022; Mouta et al., 2024). In case of ethical gaps between the researchers, theoretically-unified framework can help bridge the divide as it takes different educational values as well as cultural contexts into consideration. These endeavors are in a bid to direct the responsible and effective use of AI in schools (Nguyen et al., 2022). The introduction of such moral issues as goal alignment and resource shortages is an ethical problem presented in agentic AI, which is defined as an autonomous system with complex goals (Acharya et al., 2025).

An Actor-Network Theory-based study focuses on analyzing the experience of students, and it shows us a multi-dimensional picture of ethical divergence, which requires principles of flexibility and accommodation (Hadinejad, 2024). The role of education as an element of socioeconomic development is undergoing reconsideration in the prism of the human capital theory. The current patterns in the world demand changes in the existing educational methodologies, which should embrace theoretical development to allow more effectiveness in using human potential (Kuzminov et al., 2019).

The chapter is devoted to the research of such a novel practice, the use of Agentic AI in education and its connection to the learning theories and the paradigm of morality. It indicates the opportunities likely to be introduced by agentic AI to the so far student-based but individualized learning and deals with the necessity of human agency, collaboration, and responsible use. Moral learning systems, as well as adaptive learning systems, are two of the ways agentic AI can change education. It is possible for it to be successful, when skillfully integrated with pedagogy and the needs of learners.

2. LITERATURE REVIEW

Research already indicates that AIEd applications frequently lack a solid theoretical basis in learning. Despite their widespread use, the instructional functions of technologies like deep learning, machine learning, and natural language processing are not entirely evident. According to reviews of previous research, very few of them use theories like constructivism, behaviourism, or connectivism. AI systems run the risk of becoming instruments that support antiquated educational methods rather than fostering meaningful learning in the absence of these theoretical foundations. Academics contend that comprehending AI's function requires looking beyond its technological prowess and taking into account how well it aligns with learning objectives, student needs, and instructional quality. Investigating how AI might be more closely linked to theoretical viewpoints in education is therefore essential (Ouyang & Jiao, 2021). Historically, scientific applications of AI have frequently been task-specific and lacked coordination across the discovery process. Current AI techniques suffer from practical limitations in experimentation, trust in data interpretation and reproducibility, and creativity, e.g., producing innovative hypotheses. Although recent research in human-AI collaboration, foundation models, and multi-agent systems suggests interesting avenues, obstacles, including explainability, data bias, and theoretical underpinnings, continue to be significant obstacles. The goal of this workshop is to draw lessons from these initiatives and create a more cohesive and accountable framework for scientific agentic AI (Wang et al., 2024).

Current frameworks for AI ethics frequently handle ethical ideas abstractly and are derived from legal or biomedical traditions. These models overlook the complexity of learning and growth in educational environments, assuming that their subjects are capable, logical adults. The author challenges this by highlighting how conventional AI ethics lacks pedagogical theory. In order to offer a more complex view of ethics, he draws on writings in social philosophy, developmental psychology, and educational theory. He highlights the necessity of reconsidering ideas like autonomy and justice in the context of education (Tuomi, 2023). Robotics, conversational agents, and distributed systems have been the main topics of earlier HCI and AI research. While there has been much research on multi-agent coordination and information sharing, recent advancements in large language models (LLMs) and neuro-symbolic AI have made it possible to integrate AI more deeply with human decision-making. To bolster their hybrid frameworks, the authors cite biological models, cognitive architecture, and system theory. Additionally, they discuss the ethical issues of responsibility, transparency, and control in increasingly interconnected systems, pointing out that new approaches are required to guarantee usability and safety as the lines between human and AI decision-making get blurred (Borghoff et al., 2025).

Albert Bandura using his theory of Social Cognition transgresses a number of cornerstone paradigms of psychology because he stresses human agency. Behaviorism is one such position since it is believed to be too narrow and mechanistic to adequately reveal the mechanism of human intentionality because it deals mainly with what can be observed in behavior and the role of the external sources of stimuli. Although it contributes to our understanding of the internal operations of mind, Cognitivism tends to objectify the operations to the point of imagining them as impersonal symbol systems. Connectionism focuses mainly on neural networks and bottom-up processing of information but ignores conscious goal directed activity. Contrary to this, Bandura points out that people are not passive organisms but active instruments that influence their own environments by practicing actions with a purpose of shaping and influencing them. Though it frequently saw mental processes as impersonal symbol systems, cognitivism advanced our understanding of internal functioning. Connectionism: Disregarded conscious, goal-directed activity in favor of brain networks and bottom-up information processing. By stressing that humans actively shape circumstances rather than passively responding to them, he draws a comparison with agentic theory (Van Tryon & Bishop, 2009). By disproving strict classifications such as individualism vs. collectivism and highlighting the hybrid dynamic character of cultural influences, Bandura also draws attention to cross-cultural variations in agency expression (Van Tryon & Bishop, 2009).

The unique challenges and strategies of two major paradigms in human-AI collaboration: Centaurian integration and Multi-Agent Architectures (MAS). Similar to biological ecosystems, MAS emphasizes independent entities cooperating while maintaining clear boundaries. Centurion systems, on the other hand, aim for more profound, functional integration, simulating symbiotic biological entities in which artificial and human components coexist. Architectural distinctions promote cohesive composite entities by highlighting the functional independence of MAS in contrast to the functional interconnectedness of Centaurian systems. The implications for system design center on maintaining autonomy in MAS as opposed to 'Centaurian systems' emphasis on deep integration and emergent capabilities. These paradigms are made more relevant by agentic AI, which offers a theoretical framework for incorporating AI into design, analytical modeling, and normative evaluation in human-machine collaboration (Borghoff et al., 2025).

AI is capable of processing, storing, and calculating large amounts of data, but it does not have human-like comprehension in AI and its limits in education. Cope et al. (2020) presented following definitions of how AI interacts with knowledge:

- Namability: Making all information machine-readable (Cope et al., 2020).
- Calculability: Using rules to determine results (Cope et al., 2020).

- Measurability: Using sensors and data to quantify learning. Representability is the ability to render information in various formats, such as text, images, sound, etc (Cope et al., 2020).

Traditional Education Criticism Exams and grades are examples of summative assessments that are frequently divorced from the learning process in traditional education. This system prioritizes memorization over in-depth comprehension or skill development, and it is constrained, judgmental, and retroactive.AI makes it possible to track progress, provide personalized feedback, and conduct real-time, formative assessments, facilitating multimodal and collaborative learning, making education more comprehensive and human-centered in Opportunities for AI in Education (Cope et al., 2020).

To describe how individual learning proceeds through disequilibrating, assimilation, accommodation, and equilibration each paired with motivational dynamics like attention, relevance, confidence, and satisfaction the model, at the micro level, draws on Piaget's learning stages, Kauffman's theory of autocatalytic agency, and Song and Keller's ARCS motivational model. In this context, AI is seen as a customized companion that can provide tailored feedback, monitor development, and recommend fresh avenues for learning. At the meso level, the model examines how peer groups and teams jointly create knowledge by incorporating Dewey's theories on social learning and the Community of Inquiry framework (Gibson et al., 2023). The expanding corpus of research on AI in education, pointing out that tools like virtual assistants, adaptive learning platforms, and intelligent tutoring systems have the power to completely transform how students interact with material. The advantages of AI technologies lie in the possibility to individualize the instructions to the requirements of the students, making the process of learning more effective. Nevertheless, there are critical questions that could also be raised with regard to their use such as the possibility of limiting the chances of critical thinking and also of loss of significant human contact. The prevalence of ethical issues, like algorithm discrimination, privacy of data, and dishonesty in the academic world make the incorporation of AI in education even more problematic. It is necessary to make sure that these instruments are applied correctly, objectively and based on valid pedagogical principles (Vieriu & Petrea, 2025).

Such a view operates on the background of subject-centered socio-cultural approach to professional agency which theorizes the agency of educators as the capacity of educators to take educated action and make informed decisions given the relative limitation of their institutional and cultural situations. In addition to more recent research that emphasizes the interaction between personal beliefs and structural environments in promoting or restricting agency, the authors make reference to Bandura's ideas of self-efficacy and forethought. PBL is being pushed more and more in engineering education as a way to foster 21st century abilities like critical thinking, problem-solving, and teamwork. Even though the application of PBL in teaching is increasingly becoming common, a lot of emphasis has been on the results of the students with comparatively moderate attention being paid to how instructors experience the process. Significant areas like development of self esteem, making teaching decisions and how the teachers can ignore the institutional barriers are not usually regarded (Du et al., 2020).

Students who write scientifically are better able to think critically and solve problems. It inspires them to meaningfully create and communicate scientific knowledge in STEM Scientific Writing. But it's hard and frequently calls for tailored feedback, which can be too much for teachers to handle. AI in the Classroom AI presents opportunities for personalized learning support, especially through machine learning and natural language processing (NLP). Chatbots and intelligent tutoring systems (ITS) are examples of AI tools that have demonstrated efficacy in improving learning in disciplines like science and math. Giving students detailed instructions to help them grasp challenging assignments is known as scaffolding. AI can provide conceptual, procedural, metacognitive, and strategic support by dynamically modifying its feedback to match each learner's unique needs in real time (Kim & Kim, 2022).

Its theoretical basis is the Basic Psychological Needs Theory (BPNT) that considers that intrinsic motivation relies on the satisfaction of three key needs, which are: relatedness (a sense of connection), competence (a sense of mastery), and autonomy (a sense of control) Users are more likely to interact favorably with a task or piece of technology when these needs are satisfied. Found that technology can fulfil these needs, e.g., users feel more competent when a device is easy to use but this has rarely been studied in the context of AI assistants. The ability of an AI to make decisions on its own is known as agency; low-agency AIs depend on human input, whereas high-agency AIs act independently. High agency may be seen as both effective and domineering, which could compromise user autonomy. Simultaneously, discussions have been triggered by the gendered design of AI assistants, which usually feature female voices and frequently reflect antiquated gender stereotypes. Consumers typically connect female voices with friendliness or warmth and male voices with skill. People's opinions and interactions with voice assistants are influenced by these perceptions (Moradbakhti et al., 2022).

Experiential education is being made possible by AI tools like simulations, 3D environments, and gamified teaching strategies. By supporting individualized learning and increasing student engagement, these technologies assist educational institutions in lowering dropout rates. Teachers now serve as facilitators, assisting students as they navigate educational pathways enhanced by AI. Students' attitudes, which are impacted by the kind and style of instruction, including interactive, digital, and lecture-based approaches, remain the primary factor in successful learning (Saini, 2024).

- The TOE framework, which was first created by Tornatzky and Fleischer in 1990, describes how the following factors affect the adoption of technology (Saini, 2024).
- Technological factors include AI tools affordability, accessibility, and performance advantages (Saini, 2024).
- Organizational factors include educational policies, institutional preparedness, and leadership commitment (Saini, 2024).
- Environmental and social factors include competitive dynamics, stakeholder involvement, and market pressures (Saini, 2024).
- The AIDs advantages as well as its drawbacks (Saini, 2024).

AI has the potential to support educational decision-making, automate assessments, and improve personalized learning.

However, ethical issues include Privacy risks, particularly with regard to the collection and use of student data; Discrimination and bias, particularly when AI systems are trained on skewed or incomplete data; Concerns about autonomy, where AI may make choices that impair students' capacity for free will and introspection; and transparency, where AI's operation is frequently too complicated for users to comprehend. Numerous international organizations have made an effort to deal with these problems. For example, inclusivity, human rights, and sustainability are emphasized in UNESCO's 2021 global standards on AI ethics. However, different organizations use different terminology and have different priorities. There isn't a uniform, international framework (Nguyen et al., 2022).

At one side data driven choice-making, focused suggestions and intellectual instructing frameworks through AI can develop understanding. These systems can even help the teachers to address the needs of their students by automating their assessments, as well as identifying students at risk. Nonetheless, ethical risks are an emerging concern, and they comprise: Privacy infringement in the collection of data; biasness in AI decisions; a lack of transparency in AI decisions; and infringement of student autonomy and equity. According to the review, education does not have a unified ethical framework of AI, even though multiple ethical frameworks are suggested in healthcare, finance, and many other fields. It has international guidelines, although they vary significantly in terms of the scope and extent (Mouta et al., 2024).

The significance of AI in learning and the severe deficiency of predetermined ethical principles of its development and use are ethical rules of other disciplines, which may be inappropriate in education, referring to the UNESCO world AI ethics principles and recent debates about data exploitation. Although AIED can be used to bring positive changes, such as automatic evaluation and individualized learning, it also provides ethical concerns, such as systemic prejudice, privacy-related, information ownerships, etc. That is why there is a need to consider the ethical framework of AIED within a particular context (Nguyen et al., 2022).

In contrast with reactive/rule-based AI, agentic AI is bounds-less to act almost freely, and is distinguished within the AI ecosystem by its intent, flexible nature, and highly autonomous operation. The agentic AI controls long-horizon, complex objectives and adapts to ever-changing, stochastic reality, whereas traditional AI is limited to controlling narrow, specialized tasks, such as recognition of objects/images or translation through supervised learning. Some of the technological foundations to which it owes its functional delivery are adaptive control systems that can modify the environment, goal-based structures to allow multiple objectives to be pursued simultaneously, and reinforcement learning which allows trial and error optimization. The core features of agentic AI, which are autonomy, goal complexity, contextual adaptability, and independent decision making, are revolutionary in those cases where it is important to ensure rapid and context-sensitive reactions (Acharya et al., 2025).

In the theoretical framework, ANT is mentioned as one of the lenses through which ChatGPT ethical implications in higher education can be explored. According to ANT, non-human entities, such as ChatGPT, and humans form interdependent networks that impact one another. ChatGPT redefines academic integrity and learning by serving as a tool and actively influencing student behaviors and ethical considerations. which is consistent with ANT's theory of organizing phenomena in the face of complexity (Hadinejad, 2024).

Human capital, historically examined as the accumulation of knowledge, skills, and practices, is understood to facilitate income generation. It traces the theory's groundwork laid by scholars like Becker and Schultz in the 1960s, showing how investment in education drives economic growth and shapes policy. Even though spending on education has gone up, results haven't always gotten better. This has led to criticism of human capital theory and questions about how education affects economic growth. The review talks about the "middle-income trap" and the "micro/macro paradox," which is when individual gains in education don't lead to growth in the economy as a whole. It highlights a shift in focus from formal schooling years to qualitative indicators like cognitive and non-cognitive skills, noting the insufficient attention given to these aspects in practice (Kuzminov et al., 2019).

Figure 1. A VOSviewer made a co-occurrence map of keywords of AI, ethics, education, and Agentic AI

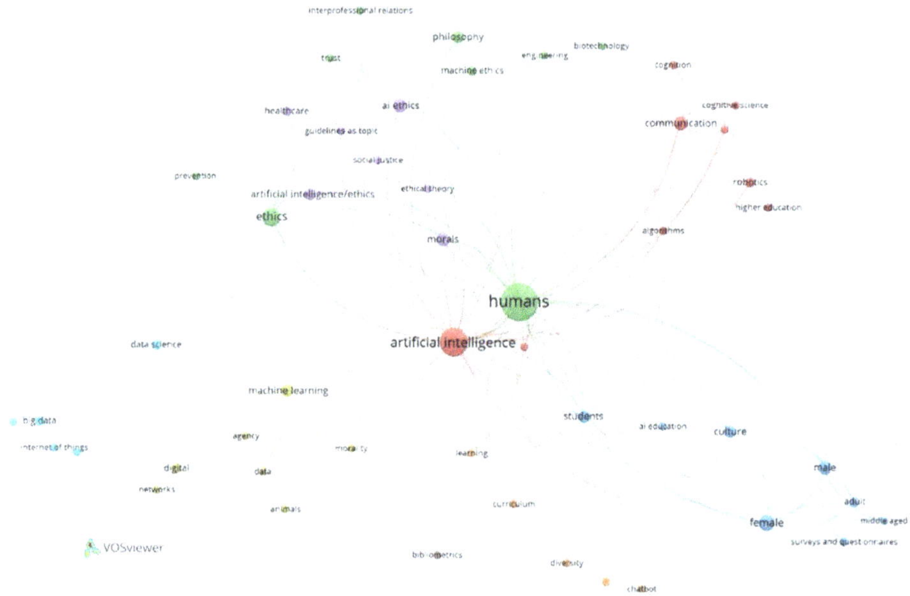

(Lens, 2025).

Through this bibliometric study (as shown in Figure 1), we discuss the overlap between the fields of AI, ethics, and education and shed light on the upcoming concept of the Agentic AI. The information was retrieved on Lens.org which is an open access platform and provides scholarly literature on various fields. A keyword was searched using terms like artificial intelligence, education, ethics, agency and Agentic AI. The resulting data such as article titles, abstract, and keywords were exported as a CSV file. This file was subsequently imported in VOSviewer, which is a program that is utilized to make and visualize bibliometric networks. VOSviewer did a co-occurrence study of titles and abstract terms and organized them into color-coded groups, according to their frequency and contextual affiliation. The thematic areas come out in the visualization. As an example, the green cluster relates to the moral and philosophical issues of ethical concerns, human values, and the red cluster draws closer to the central AI concepts of algorithms and cognition. The orange and blue clusters refer to education and raise such terms as students, curriculum, chatbot, and learning. Even though the concrete term of Agentic AI is not explicitly expressed, its overall meaning can be seen in such concepts as the agent, learning, autonomy, and morality. These mirror academic interest in Agentic AI systems that are not merely automated but play this somewhat independent and influential role, especially within the educational context. The map demonstrates that Agentic AI comprises an emerging field of study, particularly in terms of effects on learning outcomes of students and an environment that demands teacher knowledge, as well as enforces ethical responsibility.

A mixed-methods research design combining quantitative and qualitative techniques is used in the study done by Vieriu and Petrea (2025). Approximately 90 second-year students from programs in medical engineering and aerospace engineering, which are recognized for incorporating AI, were chosen as a purposive sample. According to Braun and Clarke's framework, thematic analysis was used to look at qualitative responses (such as student experiences, worries, and recommendations) while descriptive statistics were used to analyze quantitative data (such as the frequency of AI use and perceived usefulness). To guarantee the validity of the results across various programs, triangulation techniques were applied. According to the study, students use AI tools frequently, especially virtual assistants and educational platforms, and they generally believe that they can improve understanding, save time, and improve academic performance (Vieriu & Petrea, 2025). Three engineering professors two from Qatar and one from China are involved in the study, which uses a longitudinal qualitative research design over three academic semesters. Written reflections, classroom observations, and eighteen semi-structured interviews were used to gather data. Cowan's reflection model and Eteläpelto's subject-centered theory of agency, which incorporates phases of agency development, served as the inspiration for the conceptual model that frames the study. Themes were grouped according to the three stages of agency after the data were analyzed using a hybrid inductive and deductive coding approach. Several data sources, member verification, and peer audit by outside researchers all helped to guarantee triangulation. Every instructor's path was distinct, influenced by peer dynamics, institutional culture, and personal motivation. Despite opposition, all teachers showed a common dedication to enhancing student learning through PBL (Du et al., 2020).

- Participants: Nine seasoned STEM educators from the Southeast United States, the majority of whom had never used AI based tools before (Kim & Kim, 2022).
- Tool Used: To assist users in creating scientific essays with argumentation support, a customized AI-based scaffolding system (AISS) was created utilizing OpenAI's GPT (Kim & Kim, 2022).

1) Activity: Teachers answered a challenging science-based writing assignment about air quality using AISS. They used AISS to refine their essays after writing an initial draft without assistance. Data collection methods included written reflections, system usage logs, and interviews centered on their concerns, perceived benefits, and experiences (Kim & Kim, 2022).

2) Analysis: Recurring patterns were extracted using thematic qualitative analysis, which revealed both advantages and drawbacks of integrating AI (Kim & Kim, 2022).

Using a 2×2 factorial design, the researchers tested two independent variables in an online experiment: the AI assistant's voice gender (male vs. female) and its level of agency (high vs. low). Four video conditions with an AI finance coach that varied in these two aspects were randomly assigned to participants. In order to demonstrate how it could assist users with their banking tasks, the videos mimicked a financial assistant. Approximate 300 German-speaking individuals, between ages 15-95, with a fairly balanced gender distribution, made up the final sample. After watching the videos, participants answered questions about their intention to use (ITU) the AI assistant, their perceptions of its competence and dominance, and their satisfaction with psychological needs (autonomy, competence, and relatedness) (Moradbakhti et al., 2022).

The purpose of this quantitative, descriptive study is to investigate students' awareness of AI. their perspectives on the application of AI elements that propel the use of AI in education, and how they affect students' learning and professional development. Based on input from experts, a structured questionnaire was created and disseminated in hard copy and digital formats. Approximate 250 valid responses from students in a range of Indian educational programs were included in the sample. The foundational framework was the Technology Organization Environment (TOE) model, which was expanded to incorporate social dimensions like perception, awareness, and trust. To evaluate relationships and validate the research model, data analysis was done using IBM SPSS 23.0 and Smart PLS (Partial Least Squares-Structural Equation Modeling) (Saini, 2024).

The researchers performed a thematic analysis of significant international policy documents and guidelines to investigate whether there is a global consensus on ethical AIED. They chose important reports from the European Parliament, European Commission, OECD, and UNESCO (many publications). After carefully going over each document, the team employed a qualitative coding process to identify recurrent themes and moral precepts. They combined seven fundamental ethical precepts from an original list of 39 codes: Stewardship and Governance Accountability and Transparency Proportionality and Sustainability Safety, Security, and Privacy Being inclusive AI Focused on Humans To ensure reliability, the procedure entailed comparing the emphasis and presence of these principles across documents (Nguyen et al., 2022).

The shape of the model is the formal description of interaction between human to AI agents in the form of colored Petri nets. They selected papers of prominent international organizations such as Beijing Consensus, Ethics Guidelines for Trustworthy AI to the European Commission, AI and Education Reports to the European Parliament, 2021 AI Principles to the OECD, and Ethics AI & Education and AI reports of UNESCO. These texts were analyzed and coded by the researchers through the thematic analysis technique postulated by Braun and Clarke. They have found out the repeated words, concepts and values which were generalized into some broader themes. As a result of this generalization, 39 codes were used and these codes were further reduced to seven key ethical values. To ensure that the findings remained reliable and not personalized, the authors applied peer-checking among the researchers involved in the coding of the information (Mouta et al., 2024).

The international standards of ethics provided by the European Commission, UNESCO and OECD through the application of an inductive thematic analysis. Three steps involved, first familiarizing herself with the reports, second coding the terms with open coding, and third having generated 39 codes, synthesizing them into seven key ethical concepts of human-centered AIED, governance, transparency, sustainability, privacy, security, and inclusiveness. These values that contribute to interdisciplinary contributions, transparent data management, informed consent, robust security, and equitable access, objective algorithms, and human supervision in AIED systems were approved and found credible by scholars (Nguyen et al., 2022).

Agents are computational entities with perceptions, actions and a goals toward achieving satisfaction Levels Multi-level Control Developing agents requires the definition of multiple levels of control: Task decomposition agents tasks, e.g. Multi-Agent Systems (MAS) Multi-level decision-making agents choices, Hierarchical Reinforcement Learning (HRL) There are many different learning paradigms, which include supervised, unsupervised, and above all reinforcement learning, which is the most suitable to adaptive, goal-based behavior. In an attempt to enhance the contextual understanding needed and the relevancy of the output, the new changes will be enhanced by including features like elaborate memory systems, external tool use, elaborate reasoning and planning, and Retrieval Augmented Generation (RAG). Simulation-based techniques, curriculum learning for progressive skill acquisition, and multi-task learning for generalization are frequently used in training, and success rate, flexibility, and resource efficiency are the main evaluation criteria (Acharya et al., 2025). To thoroughly examine students' experiences and ethical concerns with ChatGPT in academic work, this study uses a qualitative research design. To acquire detailed information about student's perceptions, semi-structured interviews were used. The ANT framework will serve as the foundation for a thematic analysis of the interview data. Data coding, theme identification, and interpretation in light of ANT and the body of existing ethics literature are all part of this process. The study examines the interrelationships between non-human actors (ChatGPT) and human actors (students), mapping out how each affects the ethical environment of

AI in education. Confidentiality and informed consent are two examples of ethical research practices that were highlighted (Hadinejad, 2024).

In order to investigate human capital theory and its educational implications, this paper mainly uses a conceptual analysis and literature synthesis approach. In order to present a more comprehensive understanding of human capital, the authors examine previous theoretical developments and research findings that have not yet been widely discussed. They examine the development and application of human capital theory critically, pointing out the shortcomings of conventional approaches that only consider formal educational attainment and individual returns. The study provides a framework for evidence-based education policy by synthesizing various viewpoints on non-cognitive abilities, generic and specific skills, and the effect of socioeconomic shifts on the demand for various human capital components.

3. CONCLUSION

The research findings describe a multidimensional role of AI in education. Clearly, AI has the potential to adjust lessons for each student, offer personal comments, and work as a research colleague. AI technology helps students understand demanding topics, become better at writing, and enjoy interacting with online learning resources. Still, the research points out that there are serious limitations. Letting students use AI in the classroom may not definitely improve their learning. It is necessary to evaluate and select how AI will cooperate with existing teaching approaches and learning theories used in education. If there is no strong theory behind it, AI could only support old-fashioned education methods. In addition, ethical issues take top priority. Researchers highlight the importance of having ethical rules that deal with data protection, biased algorithms, and AI's influence on students' independence. AI technology should be clear in its actions, fair, and made accountable for its decisions.

Ensuring that AI applications are used properly at schools is mainly the teachers' job. Ongoing training helps them learn the ethical side of AIEd and teaches them how to use AI in their classrooms for students' benefit and welfare. The research also points out that it is important to study how AI influences people's psychology. The way AI is designed can affect users' feelings of independence, abilities, and connections, which play a key role in making them interested in and engaged with the system. If these psychological aspects are considered, developers can design AI that helps learners and improves their learning. All in all, education can be improved by AI, but to introduce it successfully, care must be taken, strong ethics must be in place, and knowledge of teaching and human psychology is needed.

REFERENCES

Acharya, D. B., Kuppan, K., & Divya, B. (2025). Agentic AI: Autonomous Intelligence for Complex Goals – A Comprehensive survey. *IEEE Access : Practical Innovations, Open Solutions*, *1*, 18912–18936. Advance online publication. DOI: 10.1109/ACCESS.2025.3532853

Borghoff, U. M., Bottoni, P., & Pareschi, R. (2025). Human-artificial interaction in the age of agentic AI: A system-theoretical approach. *Frontiers in Human Dynamics*, *7*, 1579166. Advance online publication. DOI: 10.3389/fhumd.2025.1579166

Cope, B., Kalantzis, M., & Searsmith, D. (2020). Artificial intelligence for education: Knowledge and its assessment in AI-enabled learning ecologies. *Educational Philosophy and Theory*, *53*(12), 1229–1245. DOI: 10.1080/00131857.2020.1728732

Du, X., Naji, K. K., Ebead, U., & Ma, J. (2020). Engineering instructors' professional agency development and identity renegotiation through engaging in pedagogical change towards PBL. *European Journal of Engineering Education*, *46*(1), 116–138. DOI: 10.1080/03043797.2020.1832444

Gibson, D., Kovanovic, V., Ifenthaler, D., Dexter, S., & Feng, S. (2023). Learning theories for artificial intelligence promoting learning processes. *British Journal of Educational Technology*, *54*(5), 1125–1146. DOI: 10.1111/bjet.13341

Hadinejad, N. (2024). *Ethical considerations of the digital age in higher education: An interview-based study of student experiences with ChatGPT as an example of generative AI* (Master's thesis, University of Gothenburg). GUPEA – Gothenburg University Publications Electronic Archive. https://gupea.ub.gu.se/handle/2077/82097

Kim, N. J., & Kim, M. K. (2022). Teacher's perceptions of using an Artificial Intelligence-Based educational tool for scientific writing. *Frontiers in Education*, *7*, 755914. Advance online publication. DOI: 10.3389/feduc.2022.755914

Kuzminov, Y., Sorokin, P., & Froumin, I. (2019). Generic and Specific Skills as Components of Human Capital: New Challenges for Education Theory and Practice. *Foresight-Russia*, *13*(2), 19–41. DOI: 10.17323/2500-2597.2019.2.19.41

Moradbakhti, L., Schreibelmayr, S., & Mara, M. (2022). Do men have no need for "Feminist" artificial intelligence? agentic and gendered voice assistants in the light of basic psychological needs. *Frontiers in Psychology*, *13*, 855091. Advance online publication. DOI: 10.3389/fpsyg.2022.855091 PMID: 35774945

Mouta, A., Torrecilla-Sánchez, E. M., & Pinto-Llorente, A. M. (2024). Comprehensive professional learning for teacher agency in addressing ethical challenges of AIED: Insights from educational design research. *Education and Information Technologies*. Advance online publication. DOI: 10.1007/s10639-024-12946-y

Nguyen, A., Ngo, H. N., Hong, Y., Dang, B., & Nguyen, B. T. (2022). Ethical principles for artificial intelligence in education. *Education and Information Technologies, 28*(4), 4221–4241. DOI: 10.1007/s10639-022-11316-w PMID: 36254344

Ouyang, F., & Jiao, P. (2021). Artificial intelligence in education: The three paradigms. *Computers and Education Artificial Intelligence, 2*, 100020. DOI: 10.1016/j.caeai.2021.100020

Saini, A. (2024). Impact Of Artificial Intelligence On Students' Sustainable Education And Career Development Using Extended Toe Framework. [IRJET]. *International Research Journal of Education and Technology, 6*(11), 224–243. DOI: 10.70127/irjedt.vol.7.issue02.243

Tuomi, I. (2023). The Effect of Interpretable Artificial Intelligence on Repeated Managerial Decision-Making under Uncertainty. *Proceedings of the . . . Annual Hawaii International Conference on System Sciences/Proceedings of the Annual Hawaii International Conference on System Sciences*. DOI: 10.24251/HICSS.2023.752

Van Tryon, P. J. S., & Bishop, M. (2009). Theoretical foundations for enhancing social connectedness in online learning environments. *Distance Education, 30*(3), 291–315. DOI: 10.1080/01587910903236312

Vieriu, A. M., & Petrea, G. (2025). The impact of artificial intelligence (AI) on students' academic development. *Education Sciences, 15*(3), 343. DOI: 10.3390/educsci15030343

Wang, Y., Wang, M., Manzoor, M. A., Georgiev, G., Das, R. J., & Nakov, P. (2024). Factuality of large language models in the year 2024. *arXiv (Cornell University)*. I arxiv.2402.02420DOI: 10.48550

ADDITIONAL READING

Dai, L., Jiang, Y.-H., Chen, Y., Zhang, Z., Liu, X., & Cai, Z. (2025). *Agent4EDU: Advancing AI for education with agentic technology*. Center for Open Science. DOI: 10.35542/osf.io/yk8ze_v1

Davis, R. O. (2024). Korean In-Service Teachers' perceptions of implementing artificial intelligence (AI) education for teaching in schools and their AI teacher training programs. *International Journal of Information and Education Technology (IJIET)*, *14*(2), 214–219. DOI: 10.18178/ijiet.2024.14.2.2042

Filiz, O., Kaya, M. H., & Adiguzel, T. (2025). Teachers and AI: Understanding the factors influencing AI integration in K-12 education. *Education and Information Technologies*, *30*(13), 17931–17967. Advance online publication. DOI: 10.1007/s10639-025-13463-2

Lameras, P., & Arnab, S. (2021). Power to the Teachers: An Exploratory review on Artificial intelligence in education. *Information (Basel)*, *13*(1), 14. DOI: 10.3390/info13010014

Malik, M. A., & Shah, R. (2025). AI teachers (AI-based robots as teachers): History, potential, concerns and recommendations. *Frontiers in Education*, *10*, 1541543. Advance online publication. DOI: 10.3389/feduc.2025.1541543

Nazaretsky, T., Ariely, M., Cukurova, M., & Alexandron, G. (2022). Teachers' trust in AI -powered educational technology and a professional development program to improve it. *British Journal of Educational Technology*, *53*(4), 914–931. DOI: 10.1111/bjet.13232

KEY TERMS AND DEFINITIONS

AI in Education (AIEd): The integration of artificial intelligence technologies into educational settings to enhance learning, teaching, and administrative processes.

Agentic AI: A type of artificial intelligence (AI) system that can make decisions, take actions, and learn autonomously to achieve predefined goals.

AI Learning Frameworks: A collection of tools, libraries, and APIs that simplify the development, training, and deployment of AI models.

AI-Directed Learning: AI customizes learning paths to meet individual learner needs.

AI-Empowered Learning: Self-motivated, curious, and willing to take risks in their learning process.

Educational Theory Integration: The process of combining different subjects, learning experiences, or theories into a cohesive whole.

Ethical Frameworks for Education: Provide a structured way to understand and navigate moral questions that arise in teaching, learning, and educational leadership.

Chapter 6
From Digital Assistants to Cognitive Crutches:
AI Overdependence in Pedagogical Practice

Muhammad Irfan
http://orcid.org/0009-0007-2462-2129
Marmara University, Turkey

ABSTRACT

This chapter builds a theoretical framework for understanding what happens when learners lean too heavily on AI. The core argument is perhaps uncomfortable because these systems often function more like crutches than training wheels, replacing intellectual effort rather than strengthening it. Drawing from phenomenology, critical pedagogy, and cognitive science, researcher examines how AI shifts learning from direct engagement with ideas toward algorithmic mediation. The analysis maps four overlapping dimensions of overdependence while developing what the researcher calls the "enhancement paradox." Students perform better immediately but something atrophies over time. Through concepts like cognitive offloading and algorithmic authority, this work explores how current AI patterns might undermine authentic learning and genuine agency. At the same time, it suggests principles for more conscious integration. The goal is giving educators conceptual tools for distinguishing enhancement from replacement, preserving the productive struggle that education actually requires.

DOI: 10.4018/979-8-3373-7097-2.ch006

INTRODUCTION

A senior lecturer in philosophy recently confessed during a department meeting that she could no longer tell which of her students' essays were genuinely theirs. The problem wasn't traditional plagiarism like no copy-pasted Wikipedia entries or purchased papers from essay mills. Rather, something more subtle had emerged which means that students submitting work demonstrating sophisticated argumentation and polished prose yet revealing fundamental incomprehension when questioned verbally about their own written claims. These students could produce, but they could not explain. They had become, in her words, "ventriloquists for algorithms they don't understand." This anecdote captures a transformative moment in educational practice, one where the boundary between cognitive assistance and cognitive replacement has become dangerously permeable.

We stand at a peculiar juncture in the history of educational technology. The integration of artificial intelligence systems, particularly generative AI like ChatGPT, Claude, and specialized educational platforms has accelerated with remarkable speed since 2022, outpacing our theoretical frameworks for understanding what is happening to learning itself (Baidoo-Anu & Ansah, 2023). Universities have rushed to adopt AI writing assistants, automated tutoring systems, and algorithmic assessment tools with enthusiasm typically reserved for demonstrably effective interventions. Yet we lack a coherent critical vocabulary for distinguishing between AI as genuine pedagogical aid and AI as what might be termed a cognitive prosthetic, a device that doesn't supplement human capability so much as supplant it (A. Chan, 2023). The phenomenological texture of learning has shifted in ways we have barely begun to theorize. Students today experience knowledge not primarily through direct engagement with texts, problems, or ideas, but through an algorithmically mediated interface that pre-digests, summarizes, and reformulates knowledge objects before human cognition enters the picture. This mediation fundamentally alters the relationship between learner and knowledge. Where a student once struggled with a primary text like wrestling with difficult passages, rereading, annotating, gradually constructing meaning through sustained cognitive effort and many more now input that text into an AI system and receive pre-processed interpretations. The struggle itself, which phenomenological accounts identify as constitutive of understanding, gets outsourced to the algorithm (Sullivan et al., 2023). We witness not simply a change in educational technology but a transformation in the basic ontology of learning. Students increasingly encounter not knowledge objects themselves but algorithmic representations of knowledge objects, and this distinction matters profoundly for intellectual development and critical consciousness.

The ideal educational technology would amplify human cognitive capability without replacing the fundamental processes through which learning occurs. Contemporary AI systems cross this threshold in unprecedented ways. They don't simply assist with discrete tasks; they perform the holistic cognitive work that previously defined learning itself (Kasneci et al., 2023). When a student asks an AI to "explain Kant's categorical imperative," the system doesn't point toward relevant resources or scaffold the inquiry; rather it generates a complete explanation which is synthesized from millions of texts and presented in accessible language. The student receives the endpoint of a complex interpretive process without engaging in that process. This represents technological *substitution* rather than technological *enhancement*.

The gap between our ideal and our reality widens daily. Institutions have adopted AI tools with remarkable enthusiasm, driven by imperatives of efficiency, scalability, and competitive advantage (Crompton & Burke, 2023). Corporate developers promise to "democratize" knowledge and provide every student with a personal tutor. Yet these implementations proceed largely without serious engagement with critical pedagogy, phenomenological accounts of learning, or historical understanding of how educational technologies reshape power relationships in classrooms (Fawns, 2022). The discourse remains stubbornly instrumentalist: AI is positioned as a neutral tool that will solve educational challenges if only we implement it correctly.

Existing research on AI in education falls roughly into three categories, each illuminating certain aspects while leaving crucial questions unaddressed. The first comprises technical optimization studies evaluating specific systems for effectiveness in improving measurable learning outcomes (Kasneci et al., 2023). While providing valuable data about system performance, this research systematically avoids questions about what kind of learning is being measured, what cognitive processes are being externalized to algorithms, and whether improvements in measurable outcomes might coincide with deterioration in unmeasured capacities like intellectual autonomy or critical consciousness. The second category consists of ethical and policy studies examining bias, privacy, surveillance, and equity in educational AI (Akgun & Greenhow, 2022). This work has productively demonstrated how AI systems can perpetuate existing inequalities and create new regimes of algorithmic control. However, these critiques tend to focus on institutional and systemic levels rather than the phenomenological and cognitive dimensions of AI-mediated learning. They analyze who controls educational AI and to what ends, but less frequently examine how AI mediation transforms the fundamental experience of teaching and learning. The third category involves philosophical analyses engaging with questions of automation, cognition, and human agency (Fawns, 2022; Sullivan et al., 2023). This literature offers sophisticated accounts of "algorithmic reason" or "datafication" as general phenomena, but often remains disconnected from specific pedagogical contexts where AI tools are actually deployed. We receive high-level abstractions but less detailed analysis of what happens phenomenologically when a student uses ChatGPT to complete a philosophy essay, or when an instructor relies on automated assessment.

What unites these diverse approaches is a persistent gap. The absence of a theoretically robust framework for understanding AI overdependence as a specific pedagogical pathology with identifiable mechanisms, observable symptoms, and tractable alternatives. We have studies showing AI tools can improve certain metrics, critiques revealing problematic politics, and philosophical meditations on automation. What we lack is critical theoretical analysis integrating phenomenological, historical, and pedagogical perspectives to diagnose precisely how and why AI integration produces dependency rather than capability.

The direct consequences manifest in what might be termed "cognitive outsourcing" where students increasingly delegate fundamental intellectual operations to algorithmic systems. Writing instructors report students struggling to generate thesis statements without AI prompts, demonstrating limited capacity for sustained argumentation, and showing declining ability to evaluate argument quality (Cooper, 2023). The pattern repeats across disciplines where students demonstrate increasing proficiency at *obtaining* answers while showing diminishing capacity to *generate* understanding. These cognitive effects produce institutional consequences. As students become more dependent on AI assistance, traditional assessment systems become obsolete. Some institutions respond by increasing surveillance, lockdown browsers, AI detection software, and invasive proctoring, creating systems of algorithmic control (Perkins, 2023). Others abandon traditional assessment altogether, searching for "AI-proof" evaluation methods. Both responses treat symptoms rather than causes, implementing technical fixes for what is fundamentally a pedagogical crisis. Perhaps most troubling are second-order effects on how students conceptualize knowledge itself. When knowledge consistently arrives pre-processed through algorithmic mediation, students internalize what might be called "epistemological passivity", a stance toward knowledge as something to be efficiently retrieved rather than actively constructed (Sullivan et al., 2023). This represents a profound shift from constructivist and critical pedagogical traditions positioning learners as active meaning-makers. The phenomenology of learning transforms from an encounter with resistance, difficulty, and gradual mastery to frictionless consumption of algorithmically optimized information.

Current scholarship has not adequately theorized this transformation because it lacks an integrative framework capable of addressing AI overdependence simultaneously as phenomenological, pedagogical, and political phenomenon. This chapter develops such a framework by bringing together three analytical traditions rarely combined in educational technology research: phenomenological analysis of technological mediation, critical pedagogy's examination of power and consciousness in education, and historical-comparative accounts of educational technology disruptions.

The framework allows us to ask not merely whether AI "works" in education but how it transforms the fundamental character of learning as lived experience. Drawing on critical pedagogy, particularly Freirean analysis of "banking education," I examine whether contemporary AI tutoring systems represent an apotheosis of educational models that cultivate passivity rather than critical consciousness. The historical dimension situates current AI integration within longer trajectories of educational technology, identifying both parallels with and departures from previous disruptions like the printing press, radio, and internet. This analysis matters because educational institutions are making consequential decisions about AI integration with inadequate theoretical frameworks. We are restructuring pedagogy, assessment, and the basic student-teacher relationship based on assumptions about learning, knowledge, and human agency that often remain implicit and unexamined. The risk is not that AI will make education more efficient. The risk is that efficiency will be purchased at the cost of capacities we have not learned to measure: the ability to sustain attention through difficulty, to construct rather than consume understanding, to develop intellectual autonomy rather than algorithmic dependence.

THEORETICAL FOUNDATIONS: CRITICAL PEDAGOGY MEETS AI

Critical Pedagogy and Algorithmic Mediation

Paulo Freire never encountered ChatGPT, but his critique of "banking education" reads like prophecy when applied to contemporary AI-mediated learning environments. Writing in 1970, Freire condemned educational systems that treated students as empty vessels into which teachers deposited knowledge, a one-way transmission that discouraged critical consciousness and reinforced oppressive social structures. The banking model, he argued, positioned knowledge as static commodity rather than dynamic construction, students as passive recipients rather than active agents, and education as adaptation rather than transformation. Half a century later, AI tutoring systems have perfected this model with algorithmic precision. What we might call "Algorithmic Banking Education" amplifies classical banking education's most problematic features while introducing novel mechanisms of control. Traditional banking education at least involved human educators who could, despite institutional constraints, deviate from scripts, respond to student resistance, or facilitate moments of critical dialogue (Freire, 1970). AI systems operate with different rigidity. When a student queries ChatGPT about colonial history, the algorithm generates responses based on probabilistic patterns in training data, a fundamentally conservative process that reproduces dominant narratives encoded in majority textual representations (Bender et al., 2021). The system cannot recognize, much less challenge, the ideological assumptions embedded in its outputs. It deposits knowledge with unprecedented efficiency but zero critical consciousness.

The power structures differ markedly from classical configurations. Traditional banking education concentrated authority in teachers and institutions, creating hierarchies students could at least identify and potentially resist. Algorithmic banking education distributes power across developers, platform owners, training data curators, and the algorithms themselves which is a diffuse network less visible and less accessible to resistance (Benjamin, 2022). A student can question a teacher's interpretation of historical events; questioning an algorithm's interpretation requires technical literacy most students lack, access to training data that remains proprietary, and understanding of statistical processes that even experts struggle to fully interpret. The opacity isn't incidental but structural (Burrell, 2016).

Recent research reveals how AI personalization algorithms fundamentally undermine the collective dimensions Freire considered essential for critical pedagogy. Freire positioned dialogue as the foundation of liberatory education. AI systems, however, sophisticated their personalization and operate through individual interfaces (A. Chan, 2023). Each student receives algorithmically tailored content optimized for their particular engagement patterns, knowledge gaps, and learning trajectory. This hyper-individualization fragments the shared educational experience necessary for collective problem-posing. Students no longer struggle together with common texts or problems; they each encounter personalized versions curated by algorithms pursuing engagement metrics rather than critical consciousness (Williamson & Eynon, 2020). The implications extend beyond individualization to the nature of knowledge itself. Critical pedagogy treats knowledge not as neutral information but as situated, contested, and implicated in power relations. Students learn to ask: whose perspective does this represent? What interests does this serve? What alternatives are silenced? AI-generated educational content obscures these questions through its apparent objectivity (Noble, 2018). The algorithm synthesizes across sources, smoothing over contradictions and controversies, presenting consensus narratives that feel comprehensive but are actually products of specific technical and ideological choices about training data, optimization objectives, and output formats. When students receive AI-generated explanations of, say, climate change or economic inequality, they encounter what appears to be settled knowledge rather than contested terrain.

Yet dismissing all AI integration as necessarily oppressive oversimplifies. Some implementations suggest possibilities for enhancing rather than undermining critical pedagogy. Freire advocated for problem-posing education where learners and educators jointly investigate generative themes emerging from learners' lived experiences. AI tools could potentially support this process not by providing answers but by helping students analyze patterns in their communities, visualize complex data about conditions affecting their lives, or access diverse perspectives typically excluded from dominant curricula (Nichols et al., 2025). The difference lies not in whether AI is used but how: does it replace dialogue or facilitate it? Does it provide conclusions or help formulate better questions? Does it individualize to isolate or to meet diverse needs within collective learning?

Student resistance to AI-mediated pedagogy takes multiple forms, some promising and some troubling. Some students deliberately "jailbreak" AI systems, probing their limits and exposing their biases which is a form of critical technological literacy (Mökander et al., 2022). Others resist by refusing AI tools entirely, insisting on traditional pen-and-paper methods despite institutional pressure toward digitalization. Still others engage in what might be called "malicious compliance," using AI to complete assignments efficiently while recognizing the hollowness of the exercise. Each resistance mode reflects different understandings of AI's role and different visions of educational autonomy. Institutions, meanwhile, deploy AI to maintain existing hierarchies, monitoring student engagement, predicting dropouts, automating assessment, while occasionally using the same tools to identify inequities or provide resources to underserved students (Dwivedi et al., 2023). The challenge for critical pedagogy in the age of AI is not to reject technology wholesale but to develop what might be called "algorithmic conscientization". Students need not just traditional literacy but critical algorithmic literacy which is the capacity to interrogate AI systems, understand their limitations, recognize their biases, and use them as tools for critical inquiry rather than oracles of truth (Dilek & Baran, 2025). This requires educators who understand AI not as neutral assistance but as ideologically saturated technology encoding particular epistemologies and power relations.

Phenomenology of Technology in Education

The philosopher Don Ihde distinguished between different ways technologies mediate human experience of the world. Some technologies, like eyeglasses, become so transparent that we see through them rather than seeing them, they extend perception while fading from awareness. Others, like thermometers, require interpretation, we read them to understand phenomena we cannot directly perceive. Still others, like automated security systems, operate in the background, shaping our environment without requiring conscious engagement. Educational AI exhibits all three modes simultaneously, creating a complex phenomenological landscape (Ihde, 1990). Consider a student using Grammarly while writing an essay. At moments, the tool becomes transparent when suggestions appear, the student accepts them, and the writing flows as if the AI were simply extending the student's own editorial capacity. The technology withdraws from consciousness; the student experiences themselves as writing, not as using-a-tool-to-write. This transparency feels empowering but carries risks. When AI grammar assistance becomes phenomenologically invisible, students lose awareness of what cognitive work they're outsourcing. They may graduate unable to identify comma splices or unclear antecedents without algorithmic prompting, having never developed internal editorial judgment because the technology always provided it externally (Stephan, 2022).

The transparency depends heavily on interface design and user expertise. For students with high linguistic competence, AI writing assistants may indeed function as transparent extensions. For students still developing fundamental writing skills, the same tools remain stubbornly opaque, their suggestions feel arbitrary, their logic inaccessible, creating what phenomenologists call "technological otherness" rather than seamless extension (Rosenberger & Verbeek, 2015). This differential transparency has equity implications. Students who arrive at university with strong foundational skills can use AI to enhance already-developed capabilities. Students with weaker foundations encounter the same AI as an opaque mediator they cannot effectively interpret or evaluate, potentially widening achievement gaps rather than narrowing them (Krutka et al., 2019).

The hermeneutic relationship, how students learn to interpret AI outputs, proves crucial. Traditional educational materials arrive with contextual markers helping students evaluate them: an author with identifiable credentials and perspective, a publication date situating arguments historically, citations revealing sources and allowing verification. AI-generated content strips away these hermeneutic aids. When ChatGPT explains photosynthesis or the French Revolution, it provides no indication of source reliability, no acknowledgment of contested interpretations, and no admission of uncertainty (Tate et al., 2023). Students must develop entirely new hermeneutic skills: prompt engineering to elicit useful outputs, cross-verification against other sources, awareness of common AI hallucinations, and recognition of the probabilistic nature of language model responses. These hermeneutic demands exceed most students' current capacities. Research on student interaction with AI educational tools reveals widespread credulity, students tend to trust AI outputs uncritically, particularly when those outputs arrive in confident, well-structured prose (Kasneci et al., 2023). The phenomenological authority of AI-generated text derives partly from its textual qualities: grammatically correct, stylistically polished, and free from the hedging and uncertainty marking human expert discourse. The AI never says "I think" or "evidence suggests" or "scholars debate whether", it simply asserts, and that assertiveness carries phenomenological weight students struggle to resist critically.

The alterity relation, experiencing AI as quasi-agent and as technological "other", introduces additional complications. Students increasingly describe AI tutors using agentive language that is the AI "helps me," "explains things better than my professor," and "understands what I need" (Eaton, 2023). This anthropomorphization isn't mere linguistic convenience; it reflects genuine phenomenological experience. The conversational interface, the personalized responses, and the apparent responsiveness to individual queries, all create what Sherry Turkle called "evocative objects" that invite relationship and attachment (Turkle, 2011). Some students report feeling more comfortable asking AI systems for help than approaching human instructors, not from efficiency but from reduced social anxiety and that the AI won't judge incompetence or become impatient with repeated questions.

Yet this comfort carries costs. When students form primary educational relationships with AI agents rather than human educators and peers, they miss the irreducibly social dimensions of learning. Human teachers model intellectual virtues in ways algorithms cannot. They recognize moments when a student needs encouragement versus challenge, when to provide answers versus insist on further struggle. They bring their own intellectual journeys, their own disciplinary expertise and enthusiasm, and their own humanity to the educational encounter (Fawns, 2022). AI systems, however sophisticated, remain statistical pattern-matching engines. The apparent understanding students experience is projection onto algorithmic processing fundamentally unlike human cognition. Perhaps most concerning are what Ihde called "background relations", technologies operating invisibly to shape experience without conscious awareness. Educational AI increasingly functions in this mode: learning analytics tracking every click and keystroke, adaptive algorithms adjusting content difficulty, and recommendation systems curating resources. These background processes construct are called as "algorithmic environments" where students navigate educational experiences subtly shaped by invisible technological forces (Nichols et al., 2025). A student might not know that the readings suggested by the learning management system were selected by an algorithm optimizing for engagement metrics rather than pedagogical value, or that their predicted success probability influenced what resources they received access to.

The democratic implications are profound. Background algorithmic processes determine educational experiences based on criteria students cannot access, understand, or challenge. This represents what Frank Pasquale termed "black box" decision-making where consequential choices made by opaque systems accountable to no one (Pasquale, 2015). Making these processes visible and controllable requires both technical infrastructure and critical literacy enabling meaningful engagement with that information. Some institutions experiment with "algorithmic transparency" initiatives, but these often reveal a deeper problem. Even when algorithmic processes are disclosed, their complexity and technical specificity render them functionally opaque to most students and educators (Ananny & Crawford, 2018).

Essential Cognitive Load Theory

Not all cognitive effort produces equivalent learning. Cognitive Load Theory distinguishes between intrinsic load (inherent difficulty of material), extraneous load (inefficient presentation or instruction), and germane load (effort directly contributing to learning and schema construction) (Sweller et al., 2019). AI assistance in education typically reduces extraneous load but increasingly it also reduces what we might call "essential cognitive load": the productive struggle necessary for developing intellectual capabilities rather than merely acquiring information. The distinction matters enormously. When AI tools help students format citations correctly or quickly locate relevant sources, they reduce extraneous load without compromising learning. But when AI tools compose thesis statements, generate argumentative structures, or synthesize research findings, they eliminate cognitive work that constitutes learning itself (Kasneci et al., 2023). A student who has never struggled to articulate a complex idea clearly, who has never experienced the cognitive challenge of synthesizing contradictory sources into coherent argument, has not developed the intellectual capabilities these struggles produce, no matter how polished their AI-assisted final product appears.

The challenge is that essential cognitive load often feels unpleasant. Students experience it as confusion, frustration, and uncertainty. AI systems, optimized for user satisfaction and engagement, systematically eliminate these productive discomforts (Stephan, 2022). When a student encounters difficulty, the algorithm provides scaffolding, hints, explanations, and eventually complete solutions. The student experiences relief and accomplishment, and engagement metrics register success. But the algorithm cannot distinguish between productive struggles that should be supported versus sustained versus eliminated entirely. It responds to difficulty itself, not to pedagogically informed judgment about whether that difficulty serves learning.

Recent neuroscience research on "desirable difficulties" suggests that learning actually requires certain kinds of cognitive challenges. When retrieval is slightly difficult, memory consolidates more effectively. When problem-solving requires sustained effort, transfer to novel contexts improves. When learners must generate knowledge rather than recognize it, deeper understanding develops (Bjork & Bjork, 2020). AI systems that eliminate these desirable difficulties may produce short-term performance gains while undermining long-term capability development. Students complete more assignments, answer more questions, and produce more output but whether they're developing intellectual independence remains unclear. Measuring cognitive atrophy proves difficult precisely because AI assistance maintains performance levels. A student using AI writing tools may produce essays indistinguishable from those they could write independently until the AI is removed and their actual capability reveals itself. This creates what might be called "capability debt," analogous to technical debt in software development: the gap between apparent and actual competence grows invisibly until a moment of reckoning reveals the deficit (Sullivan et al., 2023). Assessment systems designed for pre-AI contexts cannot detect this phenomenon; they measure outputs AI systems now produce rather than human capabilities AI systems may atrophy.

The pedagogical design challenge becomes that how do we create AI-assisted learning environments that provide genuine support without eliminating essential cognitive challenges? Some promising approaches are emerging. "Scaffolded AI" systems that provide progressively decreasing assistance, forcing students to gradually internalize capabilities initially supported by algorithms. "Transparent AI" that makes its reasoning visible so students learn not just answers but processes. "Reflective AI integration" where students must explicitly articulate what they did versus what AI did, developing metacognitive awareness of their own learning (C. K. Y. Chan, 2023). Each approach attempts to preserve essential cognitive load while leveraging AI's genuine affordances.

The fundamental tension remains unresolved which shows that efficiency and deep learning often conflict. AI can make education more efficient by multiple metrics. But efficiency optimizes for output, not transformation. Learning, particularly transformative learning that changes how students think rather than merely what they know, has always been inefficient. It requires time for confusion and clarity, iteration and revision, false starts and breakthroughs. Whether education systems increasingly structured around algorithmic efficiency can preserve space for this inefficient but essential process represents perhaps the central question facing educational AI integration.

THE ARCHITECTURE OF AI OVERDEPENDENCE

Multidimensional Framework Development

Understanding AI overdependence in education requires moving beyond binary assessments of technology as either beneficial or harmful. Overdependence operates simultaneously across multiple dimensions, cognitive, pedagogical, institutional, and epistemological, each with distinct mechanisms and consequences that interact in complex ways. A mathematics student might exhibit cognitive overdependence on calculators for basic arithmetic while their institution demonstrates institutional overdependence on learning analytics for retention decisions, and these separate dependencies create compounding effects neither dimension alone would produce.

Cognitive overdependence manifests most visibly in what neuroscientists call "cognitive offloading" means the externalization of mental processes to technological systems (Risko & Gilbert, 2016). Students increasingly delegate working memory tasks (note-taking, calculation, information retrieval) and executive functions (planning, organization, metacognitive monitoring) to digital tools. While some offloading proves adaptive, we've always used external memory aids like written notes, AI-mediated offloading differs in scope and consequence. When a student uses a calculator for arithmetic, the offloading is limited and transparent. When they use AI to summarize readings, generate study guides, or outline essays, they offload the very cognitive processes that constitute learning (Franklin et al., 2022). Recent neuroimaging research suggests sustained cognitive offloading may alter neural architecture. The brain demonstrates remarkable plasticity, strengthening neural pathways for frequently-used processes while pruning those rarely engaged (Loh & Kanai, 2016). Students who consistently externalize certain cognitive operations may literally develop different neural structures than those who perform these operations internally. The implications are profound: we might be producing graduates with fundamentally different cognitive capabilities than previous generations, adapted for AI-mediated cognition rather than independent thought. A chemistry student I interviewed described no longer being able to balance equations without AI assistance, not because the skill was difficult to recall, but because it felt "unnatural" to attempt it manually after months of algorithmic reliance. The measurable indicators of cognitive overdependence emerge across multiple domains. Decreased performance on tasks when AI tools are unavailable provides the most obvious marker, but more subtle indicators prove equally telling: reduced persistence when encountering difficulty, diminished metacognitive awareness of one's own knowledge gaps, inability to evaluate AI outputs critically, and what might be called "procedural amnesia" by forgetting how to perform tasks one previously mastered because AI now handles them (O'Connor, 2023). These indicators vary significantly across disciplines. STEM fields show overdependence in computational and problem-solving domains, while humanities reveal it in analytical reading, argument construction, and critical evaluation.

Pedagogical overdependence operates at a different level entirely. Here the dependency isn't individual cognitive but professional judgment and expertise. When institutions implement AI grading systems, algorithmic curriculum recommendations, or automated student advising, they externalize pedagogical decisions that previously required expert human judgment. The logic appears compelling: algorithms process more data, identify patterns humans miss, and maintain consistency across evaluations. Yet pedagogy is irreducible to pattern recognition (Stommel, 2024). A skilled educator recognizes when a struggling student needs encouragement versus correction, when to enforce standards versus show flexibility, when apparent confusion signals deep engagement rather than incomprehension. These judgments require contextual understanding, moral reasoning, and human empathy that algorithms fundamentally lack.

The edge cases reveal algorithmic pedagogy's limitations most clearly. Consider a student submitting work late with an explanation involving a family crisis. An algorithmic late-penalty system applies rules uniformly that's X days late equals Y point deduction. A human instructor weighs circumstances, evaluates explanation credibility, considers the student's overall pattern, and makes a situated judgment. The algorithm optimizes for consistency; the human for justice. Neither approach is perfect, but they fail in importantly different ways. Algorithmic failures tend toward bureaucratic rigidity; human failures toward inconsistency. Educational institutions increasingly privilege the former, treating consistency as more valuable than contextual judgment (Selwyn, 2022a).

Institutional overdependence emerges when organizations structure themselves around AI capabilities until human alternatives become literally inconceivable. Large universities now depend on learning management systems and associated analytics to such an extent that teaching without them feels impossible. One department chair described attempts to imagine conducting course registration manually as "like trying to picture life without electricity". This dependency creates institutional lock-in which means once systems are embedded in organizational infrastructure, switching costs become prohibitive (Williamson & Eynon, 2020). The institution becomes dependent not just on AI functionality but on specific vendors and platforms, ceding educational control to corporate actors. The organizational dynamics driving institutional overdependence follow predictable patterns. Administrators face pressures for efficiency, accountability, and competitive advantage. AI systems promise all three: automated processes reduce costs, analytics demonstrate outcomes to stakeholders, and technological sophistication signals innovation to prospective students. Individual resistance confronts institutional momentum backed by financial investment, administrative authority, and vendor lock-in (Eaton, 2023). The power structures shift subtly but significantly: decisions about curriculum, assessment, and student support migrate from faculty governance to IT departments and external vendors.

Perhaps most fundamentally, AI overdependence reshapes epistemological relationships, how students understand knowledge itself. Traditional epistemology positions knowledge as justified true belief, emphasizing the justification component. Students learn to evaluate evidence, assess source credibility, construct arguments, and remain appropriately skeptical. AI-mediated epistemology works differently. Knowledge becomes that which the algorithm retrieves and synthesizes. Justification collapses into algorithmic output; evaluation becomes "does this answer my question?" rather than "is this true and how do I know?" (Tate et al., 2023). This algorithmic epistemology cultivates what philosophers call epistemic vices rather than epistemic virtues. Where traditional education aimed to develop curiosity (desire to understand), intellectual humility (awareness of one's limitations), and critical skepticism (appropriate doubt), AI-mediated learning can encourage epistemic complacency (satisfaction with surface answers), overconfidence (trusting algorithmic outputs without verification), and credulity (accepting claims without critical evaluation). Students develop facilities at prompt engineering while atrophying capacity for the deeper epistemic practices of evidence evaluation, logical reasoning, and intellectual persistence through uncertainty (Mollick & Mollick, 2023).

The Enhancement Paradox

The central paradox of educational AI is that the same systems simultaneously enhance and diminish human capability, often in the same individual across different timescales. A student using AI writing assistance may produce better essays today while developing weaker independent writing capacity for tomorrow. This isn't a bug but a fundamental feature of how cognitive enhancement technologies interact with human neuroplasticity and learning processes. The mechanism operates through what economists call "substitution effects." When AI provides a capability, the cognitive effort required to develop that capability internally becomes unnecessary and indeed, inefficient. Why struggle to improve one's own writing when AI produces better prose immediately? The rational choice, narrowly conceived, is delegation. But this rational delegation produces irrational aggregate outcomes: individuals optimizing for immediate performance collectively produce a population with diminished capabilities (Franklin et al., 2022). The enhancement paradox describes this temporal disconnect between immediate enhancement and long-term atrophy.

Recent empirical evidence illuminates these dynamics. A study tracking student calculator use in mathematics found that those permitted calculator access throughout coursework performed better on calculator-permitted assessments but significantly worse on non-calculator assessments than peers who learned computational skills manually before receiving calculators (Kristjánsson, 2016). The calculators enhanced performance in calculator-enabled contexts while diminishing capability in calculator-absent contexts. More troublingly, students in the calculator-enabled group showed reduced mathematical intuition; they struggled to estimate whether computational outputs were reasonable, having never developed the number sense that manual calculation builds. Similar patterns emerge with AI writing tools. Students using AI assistance produce higher-quality first drafts, but longitudinal analysis reveals diminished revision skills, reduced stylistic range, and decreased ability to generate ideas without algorithmic prompting (Perkins, 2023). The AI enhances output while atrophying the generative and editorial processes that produce competent writers. Students experience this as efficiency but what they experience as saved time represents forfeited learning.

The substitution effects accumulate and compound over time. Initial AI use might supplement rather than replace human effort: a student generates ideas independently, then uses AI to refine expression. But as comfort with AI grows and academic pressures mount, the balance shifts. Why struggle with idea generation when AI handles both ideation and expression? The path of least resistance leads from AI as supplement to AI as substitute, and once cognitive capabilities atrophy from disuse, the substitution becomes necessity rather than choice (Saiz-Manzanares et al., 2023). Students no longer choose AI over independent work; they require AI because independent capability has diminished.

The enhancement paradox relates to but differs from other technological paradoxes in education. The digital divide paradox that technologies meant to democratize access often exacerbate inequality operates primarily at the social level. The attention economy paradox, technologies designed to enhance connection fragment attention, functions primarily psychologically. The enhancement paradox operates at the cognitive-developmental level, where technologies meant to amplify capability instead replace the developmental processes through which capabilities emerge. All three paradoxes share a common structure: well-intentioned technological interventions produce outcomes contrary to their stated purposes through mechanisms invisible at the time of intervention.

Different theoretical frameworks illuminate different aspects of the paradox. Instrumentalist perspectives, treating technology as a neutral tool, struggle to explain how the same tool produces opposite effects across timescales. Constructivist frameworks, emphasizing how learners build knowledge through active engagement, can explain why AI-mediated learning often produces shallow understanding, that is the learner isn't constructing knowledge but consuming AI-constructed representations (Sullivan et al., 2023). Critical theory highlights how the enhancement paradox serves institutional interests in credential production over genuine education.

Algorithmic Authority

A peculiar shift has occurred in undergraduate research practices in which students increasingly cite AI-generated explanations with greater confidence than peer-reviewed scholarly sources. When questioned, they explain that journal articles feel “biased” or “too complicated,” while AI outputs seem “objective” and “clear.” This represents not just a change in research practice but a fundamental transformation in epistemic authority which means what sources students trust and why.

Algorithmic authority emerges through several interrelated mechanisms. First, technological mystification where most students (and educators) cannot explain how large language models work thus creating a mystique around AI capabilities (Buçinca et al., 2021). This opacity generates a paradoxical trust because we don't understand the technology, we assume it must be sophisticated beyond our comprehension. Second, interface design through which AI systems present outputs with remarkable confidence, rarely hedging or expressing uncertainty. This rhetorical certainty carries persuasive power independent of content accuracy. Third, personalization where AI systems tailor responses to user queries, creating experiences of being understood that human sources rarely provide (Tate et al., 2023).

The maintenance of algorithmic authority relies on positive feedback loops. When students use AI and receive satisfactory results, trust increases. The system feels validated by outcomes, even when those outcomes measure output quality rather than learning. Institutional policies reinforce algorithmic authority by embedding AI tools into official learning platforms, implicitly endorsing their reliability. When a university's learning management system integrates AI tutoring, students reasonably infer institutional approval (C. K. Y. Chan, 2023). Technological design sustains authority through seamless user experience. Next, algorithmic authority interacts complexly with traditional educational authority. In some contexts, it supplements professorial authority but increasingly, algorithmic and human authority conflict. Students receive different explanations from AI than from instructors, and therefore they must choose between conflicting sources, and often privilege algorithmic sources. The reasons reveal much about contemporary epistemic culture: AI is always available, never impatient, explains repeatedly without judgment, and provides immediate gratification. Human instructors, however expert, cannot compete on these dimensions (Eaton, 2023).

Resistance to algorithmic authority emerges in multiple forms, though often ineffectively. Some students practice what might be called "strategic skepticism", they doubt AI outputs but use them anyway because everyone else does and competitive pressure demands it. Others engage in "critical prompting," deliberately testing AI limitations to understand where outputs become unreliable. Still others reject AI entirely, viewing algorithmic authority as fundamentally illegitimate. Each resistance mode carries costs: strategic skepticism produces cynicism, critical prompting requires technical literacy most lack, and wholesale rejection leaves students disadvantaged in AI-saturated environments (Mollick & Mollick, 2023).

Pedagogical strategies for developing appropriate AI skepticism must go beyond simple warnings. Students need structured experiences encountering AI failures: assignments where they must identify errors in AI outputs, compare AI explanations against scholarly sources, or examine how different prompts produce contradictory responses. These exercises cultivate what might be called "algorithmic literacy", not technical knowledge of how AI works but practical wisdom about when to trust, verify, or reject algorithmic outputs (Dilek & Baran, 2025). Some instructors require students to use AI for initial research, then demonstrate how that research is incomplete or misleading, making AI's limitations visible rather than abstract. The deeper challenge is cultural, which means contemporary students inhabit an epistemological environment where algorithmic authority feels natural while traditional scholarly authority feels antiquated. They've grown up with search engines, recommendation algorithms, and now generative AI. The idea that human experts might offer more reliable knowledge than optimized algorithms strikes many as implausible because, surely, the system processing millions of sources knows more than any individual? This intuition, while understandable, reflects confusion between information access and knowledge construction, between synthesis and understanding. Addressing it requires not just critical thinking skills but fundamental epistemological education like what knowledge is, how it's constructed, why expertise matters, and what algorithms can and cannot do (Dzhedzhula, 2023).

CRITICAL ANALYSIS: PHILOSOPHICAL IMPLICATIONS

Educational Authenticity Crisis

A philosophy professor recently described a disorienting experience of reading a student's essay that was brilliantly engaged with Heidegger's concept of authenticity, only to discover during discussion that the student couldn't explain basic terms from their own paper. The essay was technically theirs but in what meaningful sense had they authored it? This question, multiplying across classrooms worldwide, reveals a profound crisis in educational authenticity that strikes at the heart of what it means to learn, to know, and to develop intellectual identity.

Authenticity in education has traditionally meant something straightforward that the work students submit reflects their actual understanding, represents their genuine intellectual effort, and demonstrates capabilities they've genuinely developed. This conception assumed a relatively clear boundary between self and tool. A student using a dictionary isn't producing inauthentic work; they're using a tool that supplements but doesn't replace their linguistic capability. AI scrambles this boundary beyond recognition (Eaton, 2023). When a student uses ChatGPT to "help with" an essay, where does their thinking end and the algorithm's begin? The question isn't merely technical but ontological, it concerns the fundamental nature of intellectual work in an age of cognitive partnership with machines. Some argue AI simply represents the latest in a long history of cognitive tools, no different in principle from calculators, word processors, or internet search engines. This argument fails on several grounds. Previous technologies augmented discrete capabilities without replacing the integrative intellectual work that constitutes learning. A calculator performs arithmetic; the student must still understand what calculation to perform and what the result means. AI systems, particularly large language models, perform the integrative work itself by understanding questions, synthesizing information, generating arguments, and expressing ideas clearly (Bitzenbauer, 2023). They don't augment student capability so much as simulate it, producing outputs indistinguishable from genuine understanding while requiring no understanding at all.

The implications for intellectual identity and agency are profound. Psychologists have long recognized that identity develops through doing things like we become writers by writing, thinkers by thinking, and problem-solvers by solving problems. This developmental process requires struggle, failure, revision, and gradual mastery. When AI short-circuits this process, students produce sophisticated work without undergoing the developmental journey that work traditionally signified. They experience themselves as capable while actual capability remains undeveloped. This creates what might be called "identity displacement" which means students identify as writers or critical thinkers based on AI-assisted outputs rather than internalized capabilities.

Moreover, the authenticity crisis extends to how students experience intellectual ownership. Ownership traditionally meant more than legal authorship; it meant intimate familiarity with one's own work, capacity to defend and explain it, and sense of having genuinely created something. Students using substantial AI assistance describe a peculiar phenomenology: the work is simultaneously theirs and not-theirs. They directed the AI, refined prompts, selected among outputs, perhaps revised the results. But they also recognize that the core intellectual work originated elsewhere. One student told me her AI-assisted essays felt like "wearing someone else's clothes", technically hers to use, but never quite fitting right (Perkins, 2023). Assessment systems designed for pre-AI contexts cannot navigate this crisis. Traditional academic integrity frameworks distinguish between authentic work (your own) and plagiarism (someone else's). But what is AI-generated work? It's not plagiarism in the classical sense because no human author was stolen from. It's not collaboration, rather the AI isn't a peer co-learner. It exists in a categorical limbo our assessment frameworks cannot accommodate (Perkins et al., 2024). Some institutions respond with technological detection tools, attempting to identify AI-generated text. But this creates an arms race: students learn to "humanize" AI outputs, detection tools improve, students find new workarounds, and the fundamental question, what are we actually trying to assess?, remains unaddressed.

More promising approaches reconceptualize assessment around process rather than product. If AI can generate polished essays instantly, perhaps we should assess the messy process of thinking rather than the clean product of thought. This might involve portfolios showing ideation, drafting, and revision; oral defenses where students explain their work's development; or collaborative projects where contribution is visible. Each approach attempts to assess what AI cannot fake, which is genuine intellectual engagement over time (Mollick & Mollick, 2023). Yet these solutions remain incomplete. They increase instructor workload dramatically, disadvantage students who struggle with oral communication, and still don't resolve the fundamental authenticity question like if AI assists throughout the process, is that process authentically the student's?

The philosophical implications extend beyond assessment to questions of human development and flourishing. Education, classically conceived, aims not merely at knowledge transmission but at human formation. This formation requires what Aristotle called habituation which can be explained as becoming virtuous by practicing virtue, and becoming wise by practicing wisdom (Kristjánsson, 2024). AI-mediated learning disrupts this developmental arc. Students practice using AI rather than practicing the intellectual virtues AI simulates. They become skilled AI users rather than skilled thinkers, and these are fundamentally different kinds of human development.

Knowledge Commodification

The transformation of knowledge from lived understanding to algorithmic commodity represents one of AI's most insidious effects on education. When a student learns organic chemistry through traditional study, wrestling with reaction mechanisms, memorizing functional groups, and gradually building conceptual frameworks, knowledge develops as integrated understanding situated within their cognitive architecture. When that same student inputs "explain organic chemistry mechanisms" into an AI system, knowledge arrives as pre-packaged information, extracted from context, stripped of the difficulty that produces genuine comprehension, and optimized for consumption rather than construction. This commodification accelerates trends already present in contemporary higher education. Universities have increasingly positioned themselves as credential providers, students as consumers, and knowledge as a product purchased through tuition. AI intensifies this logic by perfecting knowledge's transformation into discrete, deliverable, and consumable units. Educational technology companies promise "personalized learning experiences" where AI curates content, paces delivery, and assesses mastery (Williamson et al., 2020). Knowledge becomes indistinguishable from any other commodity that is standardized for quality control, packaged for efficient delivery, and priced for market optimization.

Moreover, the standardization process strips away precisely what makes knowledge educationally valuable. Genuine understanding is contextual, relational, and situated within broader frameworks of meaning. Learning about colonialism, for instance, requires not just factual information but understanding historical context, recognizing ongoing legacies, grappling with moral complexity, and connecting to contemporary power structures. AI systems, optimizing for clarity and comprehensiveness, tend to flatten this complexity into digestible summaries (Benjamin, 2022). The algorithm explains colonialism's basic facts efficiently while evacuating the difficult, contested, politically-charged dimensions that make studying colonialism educationally transformative rather than merely informative.

What gets lost in commodification is what philosophers call “thick” knowledge, understanding embedded in practice, inseparable from context, and resistant to abstraction. A medical student learns anatomy not just by memorizing structures but by dissecting cadavers, integrating visual, tactile, and spatial knowledge that cannot be reduced to textual description. AI can deliver anatomical information efficiently, but it cannot reproduce the thick, embodied knowledge that emerges from physical practice (Shukla & Sharma, 2023). As education increasingly substitutes algorithmic efficiency for embodied practice, students acquire information without the contextual richness that makes information meaningful. The commercial control of educational AI amplifies these concerns. The algorithms shaping what students learn, how they learn it, and what counts as having learned are developed and owned by profit-driven corporations with no accountability to educational values (Teräs et al., 2020). These companies optimize for engagement (keeping students on platform), efficiency (reducing instructional costs), and scalability (serving maximum students with minimum resources). Educational quality appears nowhere in these optimization functions unless it correlates with profitable metrics. The result is what Shoshana Zuboff called “instrumentarian power” which means institutional and individual behavior shaped by algorithmic systems serving commercial interests remote from human flourishing (Zuboff, 2023).

In addition, the democratic implications prove particularly troubling. Knowledge commodification creates new educational inequalities masquerading as democratization. EdTech companies promise their AI tools will “democratize access to quality education,” making expert tutoring available to all. But the “quality education” AI provides is fundamentally different from what privileged students receive through human mentorship, small seminars, and sustained intellectual relationships with expert educators (Selwyn, 2022a). Wealthy students use AI as a supplement while retaining access to human expertise; poor students receive AI as a substitute in under-resourced institutions cutting faculty positions. The two-tier system intensifies personalized human education for elites and algorithmic knowledge delivery for masses.

Moreover, the knowledge AI systems encode reflects the biases and perspectives of their training data and developers. Large language models trained predominantly on English-language internet text reproduce Western, Anglophone perspectives while marginalizing other knowledge traditions (Bender et al., 2021). When students worldwide rely on these systems, knowledge commodification becomes knowledge colonization where indigenous, non-Western, and marginalized perspectives are systematically excluded from the algorithmic canon. A student in Lagos using ChatGPT to learn African history receives accounts filtered through predominantly Western textual sources, the algorithm's own biases, and optimization for mainstream acceptability. Local knowledge, oral traditions, and alternative historical framings disappear from commodified knowledge packages designed for global markets.

Human Agency Erosion

The concept of human agency, capacity for self-directed action, autonomous choice, and meaningful control over one's life, sits at the heart of educational philosophy. We educate not merely to transmit information but to develop persons capable of thinking for themselves, making reasoned choices, and authoring their own lives. AI integration in education threatens this developmental project in ways we're only beginning to understand.

Agency erosion operates through multiple interconnected mechanisms. First, algorithmic determination where when AI systems decide what students study, how they study it, when they've mastered material, and what comes next, students become followers of algorithmically-determined paths rather than authors of their own learning journeys (Gefen et al., 2021). Adaptive learning platforms promise "personalization" but deliver algorithmic determination, the system, not the student, decides what personalized means. Students experience choice as consumer preference (which AI tool to use, which explanation style to select) while losing agency over fundamental educational questions that what's worth learning and why? Second, reduced autonomy manifests in declining capacity for self-directed learning. Students accustomed to AI guidance struggle when required to structure their own inquiry, identify knowledge gaps, or evaluate their own understanding. The algorithm has always provided these metacognitive functions; students never developed them internally (Romero et al., 2023). This creates what might be called "agency atrophy" which is not permanent incapacity but diminished capability from disuse. Like muscles that weaken without exercise, autonomous learning capacity deteriorates when consistently outsourced to algorithmic systems. Third, mediated relationships increasingly replace direct human connection in educational contexts. Students interact with AI tutors rather than human instructors, receive algorithmic feedback rather than personal response, and experience education as human-computer interface rather than human-human encounter. These mediated relationships lack reciprocity, vulnerability, and genuine dialogue that characterize human connection (Fawns, 2022). An AI tutor never struggles to explain difficult concepts, never admits uncertainty, never models intellectual humility or curiosity. The efficiency gained through mediation comes at the cost of the relational dimensions through which agency develops. Fourth, diminished responsibility accompanies AI delegation. When students use AI to complete assignments, who bears responsibility for errors, biases, or inadequacies in the work? The student who directed the AI? The AI that generated content? The developers who built the system? This diffusion of responsibility undermines moral development. Part of becoming an autonomous agent involves taking responsibility for one's actions, learning from mistakes, and developing judgment through experiencing consequences. AI mediation allows students to disclaim responsibility while still claiming credit for outputs (Sætra, 2023).

These mechanisms interact and compound. Algorithmic determination reduces autonomy, which increases dependence on mediation, which further diffuses responsibility, which deepens algorithmic determination. The cycle becomes self-reinforcing where students with eroded agency become increasingly dependent on AI guidance, which further erodes agency, until genuinely autonomous learning feels not merely difficult but inconceivable.

Yet agency erosion isn't inevitable or irreversible. AI systems can be designed and implemented in ways that enhance rather than erode human agency. "Agentic AI integration" would position algorithms as resources for student-directed inquiry rather than determiners of learning paths. Instead of adaptive systems that control pacing and content, imagine AI tools that help students articulate their own learning goals, identify resources aligned with those goals, and evaluate their own progress. The locus of control remains with the learner; AI augments their capacity for self-direction rather than replacing it (Dzhedzhula, 2023). Educational practices can also protect and promote agency in AI-saturated environments. Metacognitive reflection exercises where students explicitly consider what they're learning versus what AI is doing, deliberate practice with AI unavailable to maintain independent capabilities, and collaborative learning that emphasizes human relationship over technological mediation all help preserve agentic capacities (Mollick & Mollick, 2023). The key is intentionality that is recognizing that agency doesn't automatically survive AI integration but requires deliberate pedagogical protection.

The fundamental question becomes what kind of person do we want education to produce? If we value autonomous agents capable of self-direction, critical thought, and meaningful choice, then AI integration must be evaluated against this standard. Technologies that enhance student capacity for autonomous learning deserve adoption; those that create dependency deserve skepticism regardless of efficiency gains. This requires educational institutions to resist the seductive logic of algorithmic optimization and instead prioritize the slower, messier, less efficient work of human development.

TOWARD CONSCIOUS AI INTEGRATION

Guiding Principles Development

The question facing educational institutions isn't whether to integrate AI but how to do so without sacrificing the human development that justifies education's existence. A mid-sized university recently confronted this dilemma when faculty discovered students were using AI to complete entire problem sets in introductory physics. The administration's initial response which was banning AI tools proved both unenforceable and counterproductive, driving usage underground while eliminating opportunities for teaching responsible engagement. The eventual solution proved more nuanced: redesigning assignments to make AI a visible collaborator rather than hidden replacement, requiring students to explain AI-generated solutions in their own words, and explicitly teaching when AI assistance undermines rather than supports learning. This institutional journey from prohibition to principled integration illustrates the complex navigation required.

Human primacy must anchor any defensible approach to educational AI. This principle doesn't mean rejecting technology but insisting that AI serve human development rather than replace it. Operationalizing human primacy requires concrete criteria distinguishing enhancement from replacement. Enhancement occurs when AI supports students in doing things they couldn't do alone while building capability to eventually do them independently. Replacement occurs when AI performs tasks students should learn to do themselves, atrophying rather than developing capability (C. K. Y. Chan & Hu, 2023). A language learning app that provides pronunciation feedback enhances; an AI that writes essays in the target language replaces. The distinction seems clear in principle but blurs in practice, and thus it requires ongoing judgment rather than algorithmic rules.

Several pedagogical approaches show promise for preserving human development while leveraging AI capabilities. "Scaffolded AI integration" provides algorithmic support that gradually decreases as student capability increases, mimicking how human tutors withdraw assistance as learners develop independence (Hutson & Plate, 2024). Early in a writing course, students might use AI for grammar checking and style suggestions. Mid-course, they're expected to identify issues before consulting AI. Late-course, AI becomes unavailable, requiring students to demonstrate internalized editorial judgment. This progressive model treats AI as temporary scaffold rather than a permanent crutch. Transparency represents another essential principle, yet implementing it proves challenging. Students need to understand how AI systems work, what their limitations are, and when outputs should be trusted versus questioned. But full algorithmic transparency, revealing training data, model architecture, optimization functions, exceeds most students' technical capacity and potentially compromises proprietary systems. The solution lies in what might be called "functional transparency": students don't need to understand transformer architectures, but they need to know that large language models predict statistically probable text rather than reason about truth, that they reproduce biases in training data, that they hallucinate confidently, and that their outputs require critical verification (Baradziej, 2023).

Some institutions experiment with "AI literacy" requirements where students learn these functional principles before using AI tools in coursework. One such program requires freshmen to complete a module testing AI limitations, students receive AI-generated explanations of scientific concepts and must identify errors, compare outputs from different models, and examine how prompt variations affect results. These exercises demystify AI, revealing it as fallible tool rather than infallible oracle. Students develop what might be called "appropriate skepticism", neither wholesale rejection nor uncritical acceptance but informed judgment about when and how to use algorithmic assistance (Watters, 2023).

Critical engagement with AI systems must extend beyond identifying errors to questioning underlying assumptions. When students use AI to research controversial topics, they should ask: whose perspectives dominate this output? What viewpoints are marginalized or absent? What ideological assumptions structure this explanation? This critical questioning requires pedagogical scaffolding. Faculty might assign comparative analysis where students examine how different AI systems (ChatGPT, Claude, Bard) explain the same topic differently, revealing that algorithmic outputs aren't objective truth but particular constructions shaped by specific technical and ideological choices (Benjamin, 2022). The goal is developing dispositional skepticism, habitual questioning of algorithmic authority, rather than merely teaching specific critical thinking techniques. The tension between efficiency and authentic learning remains perhaps the most difficult to navigate. AI promises remarkable efficiency gains: faster assignment completion, instant feedback, and personalized pacing. But learning, particularly transformative learning, has always been inefficient. It requires confusion and clarity, struggle and breakthrough, time for ideas to percolate and connections to form (Stommel, 2024). The cognitive struggles AI eliminates often constitute learning itself. A student who spends hours wrestling with a mathematical proof develops not just mathematical knowledge but persistence, metacognitive awareness, and confidence in their capacity to overcome intellectual challenges. AI-generated proofs sacrifice these broader developmental outcomes for narrow efficiency gains.

Preserving authentic learning while using AI requires what one educator called "productive inefficiency", deliberately maintaining cognitive challenges despite technological capacity to eliminate them. This might mean prohibiting AI for foundational skills while permitting it for advanced work, or requiring manual completion before

AI assistance, or designing assessments where AI access is permitted but insufficient (Mollick & Mollick, 2023). The underlying principle is that some struggles are pedagogically essential and must be protected from algorithmic optimization. Democratic participation in AI integration decisions remains largely aspirational. Most institutional AI policies are developed by administrators and IT departments with limited student or faculty input, much less participation from broader communities affected by educational AI (Akgun & Greenhow, 2022). Meaningful democratic participation would require accessible forums where stakeholders understand AI capabilities and limitations, can articulate concerns and values, and have genuine authority over implementation decisions. Some institutions experiment with "AI governance councils" including students, faculty, administrators, and community members, but these often function as advisory rather than decision-making bodies. The challenge is balancing expertise with democracy, ensuring that those most affected by educational AI have genuine voice in its deployment.

Technological Wisdom Development

Technological literacy proves necessary but insufficient for navigating AI-saturated educational environments. Students need something deeper like technological wisdom, a capacity for informed judgment about when, how, and whether to employ particular technologies. An undergraduate I spoke with demonstrated this distinction beautifully. She could use ChatGPT expertly, crafting prompts that generated sophisticated outputs. But she also knew when not to use it, that is "For some assignments, using AI would be cheating myself. I'd get the grade but miss the learning. I need to feel which is which." This metacognitive discernment exemplifies technological wisdom.

Technological wisdom encompasses several interlocking competencies. First, functional understanding where knowing what AI systems actually do versus what marketing claims suggest, their capabilities and limitations, their biases and failure modes. Second, contextual judgment by recognizing which situations call for AI assistance versus human effort, when efficiency matters versus when struggle serves development. Third, ethical sensitivity like attending to questions of fairness, authenticity, and broader social implications of technological choices. Fourth, critical reflexivity which means examining one's own relationship with technology, noticing patterns of dependency or avoidance, adjusting usage based on reflection (Lee-Price, 2024). These competencies cannot be taught through traditional instruction alone. Wisdom develops through experience, reflection, and cultivation of practical judgment. Educational approaches to technological wisdom therefore emphasize experiential learning. What did you learn? What did the AI do? How did this affect your understanding? Could you now do this without AI? When would it be appropriate versus inappropriate to use AI for similar tasks? This metacognitive reflection transforms unreflective usage into examined practice.

Professional development for educators follows similar principles. Faculty need more than workshops on AI tools; they need sustained engagement with questions of pedagogical purpose, human development, and technological mediation. Some institutions create faculty learning communities where educators collectively explore AI integration: sharing experiments, discussing failures, developing principles. One such community adopted a "pedagogical first" approach by identifying learning objectives, then considering whether and how AI might support those objectives, rather than adopting AI tools and retrofitting pedagogy around them (Baidoo-Anu & Ansah, 2023; Dilek & Baran, 2025; Sidorkin, 2024; Tran, 2024). This reverses the typical implementation logic, positioning pedagogy as primary and technology as secondary.

Moreover, assessing technological wisdom proves challenging because wisdom is dispositional and contextual rather than consisting of discrete skills. Traditional assessments measuring whether students can perform tasks prove inadequate. Instead, assessment might examine decision-making processes: presented with various scenarios, what considerations do students articulate in deciding whether to use AI? Do they demonstrate awareness of learning versus performance tradeoffs? Can they justify their technological choices with reference to broader educational values? Portfolio assessments tracking technological decision-making over time might reveal developing wisdom better than any single examination (Rudolph et al., 2023).

In addition, cultural context significantly shapes what technological wisdom means and how it develops. Western educational cultures emphasizing individual autonomy might conceptualize wisdom as personal judgment about AI use. East Asian cultures emphasizing collective harmony might foreground considerations of social relationship and community impact. Indigenous knowledge traditions might prioritize technological choices' effects on intergenerational knowledge transmission. No single model of technological wisdom can accommodate this diversity; rather, frameworks must remain culturally responsive and locally adaptable (Bitzenbauer, 2023).

Human-AI Relationship Reimagining

The dominant discourse frames AI as either educational savior or existential threat which is destroying learning, undermining authenticity, and eliminating human educators. This binary obscures more nuanced possibilities for human-AI relationship in education. Neither celebration nor condemnation proves adequate;

we need conceptual frameworks acknowledging AI's genuine affordances while remaining clear-eyed about its dangers.

One promising model positions AI as what we might call "cognitive infrastructure" which shows environmental resources available for particular purposes but not determining how those purposes are conceived or pursued. Just as physical infrastructure (libraries, laboratories, classrooms) shapes but doesn't determine learning, cognitive infrastructure provides affordances and constraints within which human agency operates. This framing avoids both techno-utopianism and techno-pessimism, treating AI as neither inherently beneficial nor harmful but as shaping possibility spaces within which educational choices occur (Selwyn, 2022b). Cognitive infrastructure can be designed well or poorly, can serve humanizing or dehumanizing ends, can enhance or erode agency depending on how it's constructed and deployed. The crucial questions become: What purposes should educational AI serve? What values should guide its design? Who decides these questions and through what processes? These are fundamentally political rather than technical questions, requiring democratic deliberation rather than algorithmic optimization (Williamson et al., 2020).

Another productive framework conceptualizes AI as "intellectual sparring partner", something to think *with* rather than *instead of*. In this model, students use AI to test ideas, explore alternatives, encounter different perspectives, and refine arguments through dialectical engagement. The AI generates positions students must critically evaluate, offers interpretations students must assess, raises questions students must answer. The cognitive work remains with the student; AI provides intellectual friction rather than frictionless answers (Rudolph et al., 2023). This requires different AI designs which are systems optimized not for producing polished outputs but for provoking thoughtful engagement. Some experimental pedagogies explore this possibility. One philosophy instructor has students debate AI systems: the AI generates arguments for a position, students must counter with their own reasoning, AI responds, and iterative dialogue develops. Students report that debating AI feels different from debating humans because it is less emotionally charged, and more willing to concede points but still intellectually productive. The AI's arguments, even when flawed, force students to articulate their own positions clearly. Another instructor uses AI to generate "deliberately imperfect" explanations where the AI presents concepts with subtle errors students must identify and correct, cultivating critical evaluation skills (Watters, 2023). These approaches reimagine human-AI relationships from master-servant (human commands, AI obeys) or competitor-threat (human versus machine) to collaborative inquiry where both human and AI contribute to intellectual work without either dominating. The relationship becomes genuinely dialogical where both parties have agency, both contribute perspective, and truth emerges through exchange rather than algorithmic generation or human assertion alone.

Long-term implications of different relational models deserve serious consideration. If we normalize AI as a replacement for human thought, we may produce generations psychologically dependent on algorithmic mediation, uncomfortable with uncertainty, and intolerant of the cognitive struggle that produces genuine understanding. If we position AI as a sparring partner or infrastructure, we might cultivate generations capable of sophisticated human-machine collaboration, leveraging algorithmic capabilities while maintaining intellectual autonomy. The difference isn't just pedagogical but existential.

IMPLICATIONS AND FUTURE DIRECTIONS

Theoretical Contributions

This chapter's theoretical frameworks contribute to broader technology studies by refuting the instrumentalist assumption that dominates most educational technology discourse, the notion that technologies are neutral tools whose effects depend entirely on how they're used. By integrating phenomenological, critical pedagogical, and historical-materialist perspectives, the analysis reveals how educational AI embeds particular epistemologies, power relations, and developmental pathways regardless of user intentions. This matters beyond education. The same analytical approach illuminates AI integration in healthcare, where algorithmic clinical decision support might enhance or replace diagnostic judgment; in creative work, where generative AI raises similar questions about authentic authorship and skill development; and in professional practice generally, where the enhancement-versus-replacement distinction proves equally crucial (Crawford, 2021).

The framework's interdisciplinary integration bridges philosophy of technology, educational theory, cognitive science, and critical theory in ways rarely attempted. Phenomenological analysis of technological mediation typically remains abstract; here it grounds itself in specific pedagogical contexts. Critical pedagogy usually ignores technological mediation; this analysis positions algorithmic systems as central to contemporary power relations in education. Cognitive science examines offloading effects but rarely considers their political dimensions; this framework insists both matter simultaneously. The synthesis generates new research questions: How do different cultural epistemologies interact with algorithmic knowledge systems? What are the democratic implications of privatized cognitive infrastructure? How does algorithmic mediation reshape professional expertise across domains? These contributions advance emerging fields by providing analytical tools currently lacking. AI ethics often focuses on bias, privacy, and fairness while neglecting phenomenological and developmental dimensions. This framework adds questions about how AI shapes human becoming, not just human doing. Digital pedagogy literature tends toward either celebratory adoption or blanket critique; the nuanced distinction between enhancement and replacement offers middle ground. Critical technology studies gain specific mechanisms through which technological systems produce the subject positions they claim merely to serve (Selwyn, 2022b).

Practical Impact

Translating theory into practice requires concrete strategies educators can implement immediately. "Conscious AI integration" begins with what one instructor calls "pedagogical triage": categorizing learning objectives by whether AI assistance enhances, is neutral to, or undermines their achievement. Foundational skills requiring cognitive struggle like basic writing, mathematical reasoning, and critical reading merit protection from algorithmic assistance. Advanced synthesis work might benefit from AI collaboration. The key is intentionality rather than blanket acceptance or rejection (Stommel, 2024). Specific strategies include "transparent AI assignments" where students must document what they did versus what AI did, cultivating metacognitive awareness; "progressive AI withdrawal" where algorithmic support decreases across a course as capability develops; and "AI archaeology" where students examine AI outputs critically, identifying limitations and biases. These approaches position AI as visible collaborator rather than invisible ghost-writer, maintaining student agency while leveraging algorithmic capabilities (Mollick & Mollick, 2023).

Institutional policies prove more challenging because they require coordinating diverse stakeholders with competing interests. Effective AI governance frameworks begin not with technology but with educational values: what kind of learning do we prize? What capabilities do graduates need? How do human relationships matter in education? Answers to these questions then guide technological decisions rather than vice versa. Some institutions develop "AI impact assessments" analogous to environmental impact statements: before adopting new AI systems, examine probable effects on student agency, faculty expertise, educational authenticity, and equity. The assessment process matters as much as outcomes, creating forums for democratic deliberation about educational technology (Williamson & Eynon, 2020).

Moreover, professional development must move beyond tool training to pedagogical reimagining. Faculty need sustained engagement with questions this chapter raises: When does assistance become replacement? How do we preserve essential cognitive load? What does authentic learning mean in AI-saturated contexts? Faculty learning communities exploring these questions collectively prove more effective than individual workshops. One promising model pairs technologically enthusiastic faculty with critically-minded colleagues, creating productive tension between innovation and evaluation. In addition, student development of technological wisdom requires curricular integration rather than isolated interventions. Just as writing instruction occurs across disciplines rather than only in composition courses, technological wisdom should pervade educational experience. Students need repeated opportunities to practice judgment about AI use, reflect on choices, and experience consequences. A first-year seminar might introduce concepts, discipline-specific courses apply them in context, and senior capstone work demands sophisticated independent judgment about when algorithmic assistance serves versus undermines learning goals (C. K. Y. Chan & Hu, 2023).

Research Directions and Methodological Considerations

The theoretical frameworks developed here demand empirical validation and refinement. Longitudinal studies tracking students from AI-intensive programs versus AI-restricted alternatives could reveal long-term cognitive and professional effects. Do graduates who extensively used AI during education demonstrate different problem-solving approaches, persistence through difficulty, or metacognitive awareness? Such research requires careful design controlling for selection effects where students choosing AI-intensive programs may differ systematically from those avoiding them (Kasneci et al., 2023).

Also, cross-cultural comparative research could illuminate how different educational philosophies and cultural contexts shape AI integration and its effects. How do collectivist versus individualist cultures conceptualize AI collaboration? Do educational systems emphasizing examination performance versus holistic development integrate AI differently? What indigenous knowledge traditions might offer alternative frameworks for human-AI relationship? These questions require culturally-responsive methodologies respecting diverse epistemologies rather than imposing Western frameworks globally (Bitzenbauer, 2023).

Methodologically, studying AI overdependence requires mixed approaches. Quantitative measures might track AI usage patterns, assessment performance with and without AI access, and standardized tests of cognitive capabilities. But numbers alone cannot capture phenomenological transformation or the subtle erosion of agency and epistemic virtue. Ethnographic observation of classrooms, phenomenological interviews exploring lived experience, and discourse analysis of how students talk about AI and learning provide essential qualitative depth (Dwivedi et al., 2023). The integration challenge is ensuring quantitative and qualitative components genuinely inform each other rather than existing in parallel. A student scoring well on assessments (quantitative) might reveal in interviews (qualitative) complete dependence on AI, inability to explain their own work, and anxiety about post-graduation contexts where algorithmic assistance may be unavailable. These qualitative insights should prompt refinement of quantitative measures to capture capability versus performance distinctions.

Ethical research considerations prove particularly complex. Studying AI overdependence risks producing it where intensive monitoring of AI use might normalize or even encourage dependency. Researchers must balance investigation with intervention, perhaps conducting action research where pedagogical strategies for preventing overdependence are developed and tested collaboratively with educators. More fundamentally, the irony of using AI tools to analyze AI's effects demands reflection. Will research itself become algorithmically dependent, losing the interpretive depth that distinguishes humanistic inquiry from data processing (Selwyn, 2022b)?

The frameworks developed here will require evolution as AI capabilities advance. Current analysis addresses large language models and existing educational AI; future systems with genuine reasoning capacity, multimodal interaction, or even artificial general intelligence will raise new questions. What remains constant is the need for critical theoretical analysis refusing both techno-utopianism and techno-pessimism, attending simultaneously to technological possibility and human flourishing, and insisting that education serves human development rather than algorithmic optimization.

CONCLUSION: PRESERVING HUMAN FLOURISHING IN THE AGE OF AI

The philosophy student whose brilliant Heidegger essay she couldn't explain, the instructor who felt like a "quality control inspector in a factory," the undergraduate who learned to "feel which is which", these voices reveal AI's educational integration as fundamentally a crisis of human development masquerading as technological progress. We stand at a threshold where decisions made now about algorithmic mediation will shape not just pedagogical methods but the kinds of persons education produces and the kinds of intellectual capabilities societies cultivate or allow to atrophy. This chapter has argued that understanding AI overdependence requires moving beyond simple questions of whether technology helps or harms learning. The frameworks developed here, distinguishing enhancement from replacement, analyzing algorithmic authority, examining agency erosion, and developing principles for conscious integration, provide conceptual tools for navigating educational futures neither predetermined by technological capability nor achievable through technological rejection. The challenge is creating educational spaces where AI serves human flourishing rather than replacing the developmental struggles through which flourishing emerges. The research directions outlined suggest this analysis is beginning rather than endpoint. Empirical investigation must test theoretical claims, cross-cultural comparison must reveal contextual variation, and longitudinal study must track long-term consequences of choices we're making now, often unreflectively. What remains constant is the need for educational institutions to resist the seductive efficiency of algorithmic optimization and instead ask the harder question: what kind of human development justifies education's existence, and does our technological integration serve or undermine that purpose?

REFERENCES

Akgun, S., & Greenhow, C. (2022). Artificial intelligence in education: Addressing ethical challenges in K-12 settings. *AI and Ethics*, *2*(3), 431–440. DOI: 10.1007/s43681-021-00096-7 PMID: 34790956

Ananny, M., & Crawford, K. (2018). Seeing without knowing: Limitations of the transparency ideal and its application to algorithmic accountability. *New Media & Society*, *20*(3), 973–989. DOI: 10.1177/1461444816676645

Baidoo-Anu, D., & Ansah, L. O. (2023). Education in the era of generative artificial intelligence (AI): Understanding the potential benefits of ChatGPT in promoting teaching and learning. *Journal of AI*, *7*(1), 52–62. DOI: 10.61969/jai.1337500

Baradziej, S. (2023). The influence of Large Language Models on systematic review and research dissemination. *Septentrio Conference Series, 1*.

Bender, E. M., Gebru, T., McMillan-Major, A., & Shmitchell, S. (2021). On the dangers of stochastic parrots: Can language models be too big? *Proceedings of the 2021 ACM Conference on Fairness, Accountability, and Transparency*, 610–623. DOI: 10.1145/3442188.3445922

Benjamin, R. (2022). *Viral justice: How we grow the world we want.*

Bitzenbauer, P. (2023). ChatGPT in physics education: A pilot study on easy-to-implement activities. *Contemporary Educational Technology*, *15*(3), ep430. DOI: 10.30935/cedtech/13176

Bjork, R. A., & Bjork, E. L. (2020). Desirable difficulties in theory and practice. *Journal of Applied Research in Memory and Cognition*, *9*(4), 475–479. DOI: 10.1016/j.jarmac.2020.09.003

Buçinca, Z., Malaya, M. B., & Gajos, K. Z. (2021). To trust or to think: cognitive forcing functions can reduce overreliance on AI in AI-assisted decision-making. *Proceedings of the ACM on Human-Computer Interaction, 5*(CSCW1), 1–21. DOI: 10.1145/3449287

Burrell, J. (2016). How the machine 'thinks': Understanding opacity in machine learning algorithms. *Big Data & Society*, *3*(1), 2053951715622512. DOI: 10.1177/2053951715622512

Chan, A. (2023). Localizing the Practice of Critical Pedagogy through Place-Based, Problem-Posing Education. In *Critical Pedagogy in the Language and Writing Classroom* (pp. 106–118). Routledge. DOI: 10.4324/9781003357001-10

Chan, C. K. Y. (2023). A comprehensive AI policy education framework for university teaching and learning. *International Journal of Educational Technology in Higher Education*, *20*(1), 38. DOI: 10.1186/s41239-023-00408-3

Chan, C. K. Y., & Hu, W. (2023). Students' voices on generative AI: Perceptions, benefits, and challenges in higher education. *International Journal of Educational Technology in Higher Education*, *20*(1), 43. DOI: 10.1186/s41239-023-00411-8

Cooper, G. (2023). Examining science education in ChatGPT: An exploratory study of generative artificial intelligence. *Journal of Science Education and Technology*, *32*(3), 444–452. DOI: 10.1007/s10956-023-10039-y

Crawford, K. (2021). *The atlas of AI: Power, politics, and the planetary costs of artificial intelligence*. Yale University Press.

Crompton, H., & Burke, D. (2023). Artificial intelligence in higher education: The state of the field. *International Journal of Educational Technology in Higher Education*, *20*(1), 22. DOI: 10.1186/s41239-023-00392-8

Dilek, M., Baran, E., & Aleman, E. (2025). AI Literacy in Teacher Education: Empowering Educators Through Critical Co-Discovery. *Journal of Teacher Education*, *76*(3), 294–311. Advance online publication. DOI: 10.1177/00224871251325083

Dwivedi, Y. K., Kshetri, N., Hughes, L., Slade, E. L., Jeyaraj, A., Kar, A. K., Baabdullah, A. M., Koohang, A., Raghavan, V., Ahuja, M., Albanna, H., Albashrawi, M. A., Al-Busaidi, A. S., Balakrishnan, J., Barlette, Y., Basu, S., Bose, I., Brooks, L., Buhalis, D., & Wright, R. (2023). Opinion Paper:"So what if ChatGPT wrote it?" Multidisciplinary perspectives on opportunities, challenges and implications of generative conversational AI for research, practice and policy. *International Journal of Information Management*, *71*, 102642. DOI: 10.1016/j.ijinfomgt.2023.102642

Dzhedzhula, O. (2023). MODERN APPROACHES TO DESIGNING CONTENT EDUCATION IN CRISIS SITUATIONS. In *Modern educational technologies in the training of specialists in the agricultural sector during the crisis*. Publishing House "Baltija Publishing." DOI: 10.30525/978-9934-26-298-2-3

Eaton, S. E. (2023). Postplagiarism: Transdisciplinary ethics and integrity in the age of artificial intelligence and neurotechnology. *International Journal for Educational Integrity*, *19*(1), 23. DOI: 10.1007/s40979-023-00144-1

Fawns, T. (2022). An entangled pedagogy: Looking beyond the pedagogy—technology dichotomy. *Postdigital Science and Education*, *4*(3), 711–728. DOI: 10.1007/s42438-022-00302-7 PMID: 40477872

Franklin, E. I., Iwu, C. G., & Dubihlela, J. (2022). Students' views regarding the barriers to learning critical thinking. *International Journal of Research in Business and Social Science, 11*(4), 355–364.

Freire, P. (1970). *Pedagogy of the oppressed.* Continuum.

Gefen, A., Saint-Raymond, L., & Venturini, T. (2021). AI for digital humanities and computational social sciences. *Reflections on Artificial Intelligence for Humanity*, 191–202.

Hutson, J., & Plate, D. (2024). Disrupting Algorithmic Culture: Redefining the Human (ities). In *Generative AI in Teaching and Learning* (pp. 1–30). IGI Global.

Ihde, D. (1990). *Technology and the lifeworld: From garden to earth* (Issue 560). Indiana University Press.

Kasneci, E., Seßler, K., Küchemann, S., Bannert, M., Dementieva, D., Fischer, F., Gasser, U., Groh, G., Günnemann, S., Hüllermeier, E., Krusche, S., Kutyniok, G., Michaeli, T., Nerdel, C., Pfeffer, J., Poquet, O., Sailer, M., Schmidt, A., Seidel, T., & Kasneci, G. (2023). ChatGPT for good? On opportunities and challenges of large language models for education. *Learning and Individual Differences, 103*, 102274. DOI: 10.1016/j.lindif.2023.102274

Kristjánsson, K. (2016). Flourishing as the aim of education: Towards an extended,'enchanted'Aristotelian account. *Oxford Review of Education, 42*(6), 707–720. DOI: 10.1080/03054985.2016.1226791

Kristjánsson, K. (2024). Aristotelian practical wisdom (phronesis) as the key to professional ethics in teaching. *Topoi, 43*(3), 1–12. DOI: 10.1007/s11245-023-09974-7 PMID: 39021708

Krutka, D. G., Manca, S., Galvin, S. M., Greenhow, C., Koehler, M. J., & Askari, E. (2019). Teaching "against" social media: Confronting problems of profit in the curriculum. *Teachers College Record, 121*(14), 1–42. DOI: 10.1177/016146811912101410

Lee-Price, S. (2024). *The Exciting AI Adventure*. Reflections on the Ethical Use of Generative AI in Academic Writing.

Loh, K. K., & Kanai, R. (2016). How has the internet reshaped human cognition? *The Neuroscientist : A Review Journal bringing Neurobiology, Neurology and Psychiatry, 22*(5), 506–520. DOI: 10.1177/1073858415595005 PMID: 26170005

Mökander, J., Juneja, P., Watson, D. S., & Floridi, L. (2022). The US Algorithmic Accountability Act of 2022 vs. The EU Artificial Intelligence Act: What can they learn from each other? *Minds and Machines*, *32*(4), 751–758. DOI: 10.1007/s11023-022-09612-y

Mollick, E., & Mollick, L. (2023). Assigning AI: Seven approaches for students, with prompts. *ArXiv Preprint ArXiv:2306.10052*.

Nichols, T. P., Logan, C., & Garcia, A. (2025). Generative AI and the (Re) turn to Luddism. *Learning, Media and Technology*, •••, 1–14. DOI: 10.1080/17439884.2025.2502516

Noble, S. U. (2018). Algorithms of oppression: How search engines reinforce racism. In *Algorithms of oppression*. New York university press.

O'Connor, T. (2023). Procedural and participatory ethics: Community-based evaluation in practice. *Evaluation Journal of Australasia*, *23*(2), 91–100. DOI: 10.1177/1035719X231166206

Pasquale, F. (2015). The black box society: The secret algorithms that control money and information. In *The black box society*. Harvard university press. DOI: 10.4159/harvard.9780674736061

Perkins, M. (2023). Academic Integrity considerations of AI Large Language Models in the post-pandemic era: ChatGPT and beyond. *Journal of University Teaching & Learning Practice*, *20*(2), 1–24. DOI: 10.53761/1.20.02.07

Perkins, M., Roe, J., Postma, D., McGaughran, J., & Hickerson, D. (2024). Detection of GPT-4 generated text in higher education: Combining academic judgement and software to identify generative AI tool misuse. *Journal of Academic Ethics*, *22*(1), 89–113. DOI: 10.1007/s10805-023-09492-6

Risko, E. F., & Gilbert, S. J. (2016). Cognitive offloading. *Trends in Cognitive Sciences*, *20*(9), 676–688. DOI: 10.1016/j.tics.2016.07.002 PMID: 27542527

Romero, N., Koerber, N., Fasching-Varner, K. J., & Schrader, P. G. (2023). Relational Autonomy in Teacher Education: Deepening Teacher Quality through Indigenous and Decolonizing Education. *Cultural and Pedagogical Inquiry*, *15*(1), 57–70. DOI: 10.18733/cpi29711

Rosenberger, R., & Verbeek, P.-P. (2015). A field guide to postphenomenology. *Postphenomenological Investigations: Essays on Human-Technology Relations*, 9–41.

Rudolph, J., Tan, S., & Tan, S. (2023). ChatGPT: Bullshit spewer or the end of traditional assessments in higher education? *Journal of Applied Learning & Teaching*, *6*(1), 342–363.

Sætra, H. S. (2023). Generative AI: Here to stay, but for good? *Technology in Society*, *75*, 102372. DOI: 10.1016/j.techsoc.2023.102372

Saiz-Manzanares, M., Sánchez, R., Martín Antón, L., González-Díez, I., & Almeida, L. (2023). Perceived satisfaction of university students with the use of chatbots as a tool for self-regulated learning. *Heliyon*, *9*(1), e12843. DOI: 10.1016/j.heliyon.2023.e12843 PMID: 36704275

Selwyn, N. (2022a). The future of AI and education: Some cautionary notes. *European Journal of Education*, *57*(4), 620–631. DOI: 10.1111/ejed.12532

Shukla, S., & Sharma, A. (2023). Priority-Based Mitigation in Education Sector using Machine Learning. In Deva Sarma, H. K., Piuri, V., & Pujari, A. K. (Eds.), *Machine Learning in Information and Communication Technology* (pp. 271–278). Springer Nature Singapore. DOI: 10.1007/978-981-19-5090-2_24

Sidorkin, A. M. (2024). Embracing liberatory alienation: AI will end us, but not in the way you may think. *AI & Society*, •••, 1–8.

Stephan, C. (2022). Por modos de vida outros: o mundo plural. *DoisPontos, 19*(3).

Stommel, J. (2024). Ungrading: An introduction. []. Duke University Press.]. *Pedagogy*, *24*(3), 327–340. DOI: 10.1215/15314200-11246255

Sullivan, M., Kelly, A., & McLaughlan, P. (2023). ChatGPT in higher education: Considerations for academic integrity and student learning. *Journal of Applied Learning & Teaching*, *6*(1), 31–40.

Sweller, J., Van Merriënboer, J. J. G., & Paas, F. (2019). Cognitive architecture and instructional design: 20 years later. *Educational Psychology Review*, *31*(2), 261–292. DOI: 10.1007/s10648-019-09465-5

Tate, T., Doroudi, S., Ritchie, D., Xu, Y., & Warschauer, M. (2023). Educational research and AI-generated writing: Confronting the coming tsunami. *EdArXiv. January, 10*. DOI: 10.35542/osf.io/4mec3

Teräs, M., Suoranta, J., Teräs, H., & Curcher, M. (2020). Post-Covid-19 education and education technology ‘solutionism’: A seller’s market. *Postdigital Science and Education*, *2*(3), 863–878. DOI: 10.1007/s42438-020-00164-x PMID: 40477107

Tran, N. T. (2024). Teachers' experiences with generative AI as co-pilots in high school L2 writing instruction: A case in Vietnam. In *Innovations in Technologies for Language Teaching and Learning* (pp. 135–157). Springer.

Turkle, S. (2011). Alone together: Why we expect more from technology and less from each other. In *Alone together: Why we expect more from technology and less from each other*. Basic Books.

Watters, A. (2023). *Teaching machines: The history of personalized learning*. mit Press.

Williamson, B., Bayne, S., & Shay, S. (2020). The datafication of teaching in Higher Education: Critical issues and perspectives. [). Taylor & Francis.]. *Teaching in Higher Education*, *25*(4), 351–365. DOI: 10.1080/13562517.2020.1748811

Williamson, B., & Eynon, R. (2020). Historical threads, missing links, and future directions in AI in education. [). Taylor & Francis.]. *Learning, Media and Technology*, *45*(3), 223–235. DOI: 10.1080/17439884.2020.1798995

Zuboff, S. (2023). The age of surveillance capitalism. In *Social theory re-wired* (pp. 203–213). Routledge. DOI: 10.4324/9781003320609-27

Chapter 7
Generative Artificial Intelligence and Academic Integrity:
Transforming Authorship and Research Standards

Paramita Mazumder
http://orcid.org/0009-0008-2895-9025
Christ (Deemed to be) University, Delhi NCR, India

Khushboo Malik
Christ (Deemed to be) University, Delhi NCR, India

ABSTRACT

Generative AI (GAI) is fundamentally altering the academic authorship and research ethics landscape by sourcing multiple long-held beliefs of originality, intellectual labor, and academic accountability. The rise of tools such as ChatGPT, Gemini, and Claude in the writing, analysis, and creation of knowledge creates an urgent need for Higher Education to redefine the meaning of ethical authorship. This paper seeks to examine how Generative AI has changed many of the long-standing academic traditions, highlighting dependence on technology and analyze the inconsistencies in the AI Policies at institutions of higher education worldwide. By utilizing qualitative and normative methods from deontological and virtue ethics, this study compares the policies of Harvard University and University of Cambridge and highlights the best practices for responsible use and integration of AI technologies. The chapter will also propose a human-centered, accountable, and transparent AI collaboration model that protects academic integrity while supporting continued technological advancement

DOI: 10.4018/979-8-3373-7097-2.ch007

INTRODUCTION

Generative Artificial Intelligence (GenAI) is changing the way we think about academic scholarship. Historically, there have always been individuals (scholars) who have produced text, arguments, summaries, images and even preliminary research products similar to the type of outputs GenAI creates. GenAI, however, produces these items using machine learning or statistical pattern recognition rather than by being created by humans. In addition to producing materials similar to those produced by human scholars at an unprecedented rate and volume, GenAI generates content that appears to be genuine, deliberate, and often quite insightful - even though the content is produced through a process of statistical pattern recognition rather than by human comprehension. Therefore, while GenAI technology is changing the way we create, disseminate, assess and create knowledge in academic communities, what makes GenAI such a profoundly disruptive technology is not just the speed and volume of output produced, but that forms of scholarly work, authorship, and intellectual labour are being transformed as GenAI becomes commonplace in the everyday practice of education.

This shift will require careful reflection of oneself and one's values because academia has, at its core, always embraced the values of originality, rigour and honesty with regard to one's intellect. While GenAI supports and complicates these values simultaneously, students may now access AI generated explanations of theories, sample essays, or personalised academic assistance at the click of a button. Researchers can now create abstracts, better articulate arguments and manage interdisciplinary references at an unprecedented speed. Faculty now depend on GenAI to create their own learning materials, assessments, and feedback. Although these developments have made the academic process much easier to navigate and more widely accessible to all; they also blur lines between true human engagement and artificial output. This raises questions about how the academic output may increasingly reflect the capabilities of GenAI systems rather than the intellectual growth of a learner and or scholar. The following sections of this paper will provide an in-depth examination of this emerging tension.

Background of the Topic

Generative AI has emerged as a technology at a time when higher education was already undergoing the evolution of learning environments, reliance on technology (the digital dependent) and the ever-changing expectations placed on scholars in terms of the academic process. Unlike previous technologies, however, Generative AI creates content that appears to be original. The ability to create original text dramatically impacts the way the human-centric model of the academic process (the model within which we have historically defined who is an author) is structured. Value in the academic writing process has been based on the ability of the author to reflect their own reasoning, their ability to apply critical thinking, their ability to create and apply their creativity and their ability to accept responsibility for their work. In the past, essays, research papers, and assignments are used as indicators of knowledge, were created as a means for students to develop important skills needed to be an intellectual.

Historically, the manner in which these products were created is complicated by the fact that Generative AI creates a written product that has no conscious thought process. In that regard, the writings created by Generative AI do not demonstrate an understanding or comprehension of the topic or task; however, they often provide enough context and coherence to be misinterpreted by the intended audience as the work of an individual.

The increased adoption of Generative AI within academia is compounding the change currently occurring within academia. Students are increasingly using Generative AI to draft written products, generate summaries, create lecture notes, re-write difficult concepts in a language more appropriate for them to understand. Faculty have begun using Generative AI for administrative and classroom activities, including syllabus creation, creation of rubrics, creation of exam questions, etc. Researchers are beginning to use Generative AI to perform literature reviews, create ideas, and organise data. This work is indicative of the growing relationship between humans and artificial intelligence in the creation of academic products, with GenAi being both a valuable tool and a source of many ethical dilemmas. GenAi creates "hallucinations" when it makes up information, creates bias based on the data it was trained on, and adds fictitious references to its output. These issues affect the credibility of scholarly products using GenAi. Given the global response from universities differs widely — including extreme prohibitions of GenAi to accommodating practices that require disclosures of GenAi use — universities have an immediate need to revisit and reconsider their standards relating to how to manage technological advancements in the academic environment.

Research Problem

An apprehensive evolution of the scholarship community emerges from the growing use of GenAI on one end, and on the other, the long-held norms of originality, analytical reasoning, and responsibility — which all play a role in fostering integrity in academia. Academic institutions have always assumed that because there is an expression of the author's intellectual work and understanding represented in the writing, this means that it has been written by the author. Since GenAI can provide an excessive quantity of text to a researcher at great speed, it challenges this basic assumption and creates greater difficulty determining how much of the academic submission was written by a human author. Faculty are faced with unprecedented challenges in the assessment of academic submissions because they cannot reliably distinguish GenAI-generated text from that written by a human author, nor do reliable or consistent tools currently exist to help them do so. With the inability to separate human from AI-authorship, this creates ambiguity surrounding the definition of plagiarism and raises new ethical dilemmas about the authenticity and ownership of academic submissions.

Beyond non-traditional forms of academic dishonesty, GenAI has raised additional concerns. Academic writing is no longer based solely on what is factual. Because GenAI generates outputs that sometimes reflect inaccuracies, fabricate information, or recapitulate biases present in their training data, when these inaccurate or fabricated "facts" are adopted without questioning, the quality and integrity of academic writing will decline, and misinformation will become a greater risk. Furthermore, relying on GenAI to complete academic tasks may adversely affect students' cognitive growth by hindering their growth in skills related to analysing, synthesising, writing reflectively and solving problems. In addition, there is no agreement in academia regarding how to disclose that GenAI was used by an author or under what conditions it can be utilised, leading to further confusion among educators, researchers and students in their respective environments. Both student and faculty expectations lack clarity, and therefore navigate through vague values of practice, which can lead to differing levels and erratic valuation. This is the basis for the research problem being addressed by this study: the problem of maintaining academic honour past the continued influence of GenAI, which has become difficult to comprehend, monitor or regulate in its input into the academy.

Purpose of the Study

This study will analyse and evaluate how Generative Artificial Intelligence (GenAI) is changing the way we think about authorship, academic integrity, and research standards in the higher education sector. The goal of this study is to gain an understanding of how these changes will occur based on the practices being developed by using GenAI, the ethical issues associated with its application, and the ways in which institutions are responding to them. Specifically, the way in which authorship is defined, the level at which academics feel their integrity has been compromised or compromised by using GenAI tools, what the implications are for the protection of scholarly work, and what future models of interaction with academic communities should be developed.

In addition, the study will assess the different risks and opportunities that GenAI poses. GenAI presents many new opportunities for access to learning, personalised learning, and improved efficiency in research, while it also presents an array of challenges associated with potential overreliance, misrepresentation, and intellectual accountability. To accomplish its objectives, the study will focus on how institutions are responding to the issues posed by GenAI. Institutions such as Harvard University, Cambridge University, and the Indian Institute of Technology (IIT) Delhi are examples of leading institutions with the diversity of approaches to policy development on how best to respond to the GenAI issue, and thus represent a continuing debate regarding GenAI's responsible use in academia. The study will provide a comparison of the various policy frameworks of these institutions to identify their strengths and weaknesses, and areas for improvement. Ultimately, the study seeks to develop a balanced, ethical-based model for the use of GenAI in academia.

Research Questions

The study is directed by various research inquiries that structure the examination of Generative Artificial Intelligence and its influence on academic integrity and authorship. The first of these inquiries focuses on how Generation AI is changing established definitions of authorship, originality, and intellectual labor in academia. The second inquiry investigates how Generation AI presents significant hurdles to maintaining the integrity of scholarship, such as contributing to plagiarism, the propagation of false information, bias, and diminished levels of critical thought. The third examines how institutions of higher education throughout the world are responding to Generation AI by developing guidelines, creating systems of authority, and establishing policies on Generation AI use. The fourth inquiry will identify the ethical, institutional, and instructional systems needed to integrate Generation AI into academia responsibly. Finally, this study will outline how higher education can utilize the benefits of Generation AI-assisted learning while simultaneously mitigating the risks associated with overdependence on Generation AI and maintaining the role of human imagination and judgment within the context of scholarly work.

METHODOLOGY

The research design employed is a qualitative and normative research design that assists in examining how generative artificial intelligence (GenAI) has influenced authorship, academic integrity and the research standards of institutions of higher learning. The methodological approach used in the study consists of the use of doctrinal analysis, an examination of ethical issues, and a comparison of the policies of various institutions to form a coherent and principled understanding of the challenges and opportunities presented by the growing importance of AI in scholarly efforts. Given that many of the AI applications are evolving at such a rapid rate, it is important to utilise a qualitative approach that assists in making sense of the responses of the various institutions to the use of AI, the ethical problems associated with the use of AI and the scholarly discussions surrounding the use of AI in authorship and academic responsibility. This study did not attempt to quantify the frequency of the use of AI, rather it focuses on understanding the conceptual, ethical and regulatory aspects that define how AI collaborations with humans will continue to change academic norms. As a result of these considerations, this methodology supports the development of a theoretical and policy framework for the responsible incorporation of AI into research. The first element of the methodology includes a doctrinal analysis of the academic literature, institutional policies, legal frameworks, and ethical guidelines that relate to the use of AI in post-secondary education, which is based upon a systematic review of these materials.

Through doctrinal analysis, a researcher is able to discover the normative foundations of traditional notions of authorship, originality and academic integrity, and how those foundations are now being challenged by generative AI systems. Theoretical works by Bender et al. (2021) and Floridi and Chiriatti (2020) are analysed as theoretical references for examining AI's epistemic limitations and AI's non-sentience and pattern-replicating collaboration. Also examined are scholarly articles, policy briefs and research reports, for example, to identify the evolution of the discourse around the intersection of AI and intellectual labour, ethical responsibility and machine-generated content reliability.

In addition to the doctrinal analysis, an assessment of institutional policies looking specifically at the differences between types of universities' regulations and/or responses to generative AI and how it is incorporated into research practices in universities, is completed. As discussed in the study proposal, it was decided that a lack of global standardisation was a key trend and therefore it is necessary to pay particular attention to how different universities approach the use of generative AI in scholarly work. Some academic institutions allow the use of AI, provided that disclosure is made and others, such as specified in the proposal and where a complete ban on AI-generated content exists. The core data for this component of the analysis consists of policy documents, academic integrity policies, and official university statements. An assessment of the policy documents allows for identification of means by which emerging trends could lead or contribute to a lack of governance and inconsistencies inhibiting institutional trust and credibility.

As a secondary major methodological element, this project uses comparative policy analysis. This project uses a comparative analysis approach as a way to systematically assess, on a common basis, policy approaches regarding AI at three academic institutions: Harvard University, the University of Cambridge, and the

Indian Institute of Technology Delhi. The choice of the three institutions was made because they represent three of the leading Higher

The third component of the methodology is ethical analysis. The ethical analysis component is based on two different types of ethical theories: deontological ethics, and virtue ethics. Deontological analyses focus on the duties and obligations of the human author when they are creating an output with the assistance of a generative AI. This type of analysis is used to evaluate whether or not the author's actions regarding the use of AI violate an obligation to be honest and/or accountable, or to retain intellectual ownership. It is essential to the understanding of why the moral responsibility for the content produced by AI rests with human researchers, because AI lacks the capacity to possess or develop either intention, understanding or agency.

In contrast, virtue ethics focuses upon the development of the scholar's character through the establishment of virtues such as honesty, openness and humility with respect to their scholarly integrity, as well as to establish how the use of responsible AI technologies can become entrenched within an academic environment through dispositions of ethicality, professional values and scholarly culture. Together these three ethical frameworks provide a foundation to build a principled model that illustrates the principles by which the researcher is to disclose their AI use, properly attribute their AI-created material and contextualise their AI use within the overall body of their work.

In conclusion, the methodology combines ethical and theoretical reflection, policy evaluation, and ethical reasoning to provide us with a more comprehensive understanding of how generative AI influences authorship and the integrity of their academic research. The study employs a multi-faceted model to both review the obstacles confronting academia regarding the application of AI and attempt to work toward the establishment of ethical and sustainable benchmarks for using AI responsibly within the academic setting.

LITERATURE REVIEW

The new AI technologies that create new materials have already completely changed the way we work in higher education. This has raised many new questions for everyone at universities - faculty members, educators and policy makers - as it relates to authorship, originality, research standards and academic integrity. Research journals, policy papers and theoretical analyses continue to identify several important themes. Some of these themes relate to 1) the linguistic and epistemological limits of AI generated text, 2) the potential impact of AI generated text on student learning and research practices of academics, 3) the possibility for plagiarism and misinformation, and 4) the need for institutions to develop coherent institutional and ethical regulatory frameworks. In this literature review I have compiled 10 influential sources that discuss these four aspects and they all add to our knowledge regarding the changing nature of the academic landscape and also demonstrate the areas in which we need to conduct more research to fully understand this evolving academic landscape.

1. Bender, E. M., Gebru, T., McMillan-Major, A., & Mitchell, M. (2021). "On the Dangers of Stochastic Parrots." FAccT Conference

This paper evaluates and critiques the role of large language models in the development of automated text and the potential limitations that accompany these systems. In particular, Bender et al., highlight the risks associated with bias, the dissemination of false or misleading information, environmental damage from the use of machine-generated text, and an illusion of comprehending the content produced by these models. These criteria serve as an important framework through which discussions regarding whether AI can ever be considered an author can occur. However, by excluding academic disciplines from their discussion, they fail to provide any further insight into how educational institutions should regulate authoring, or how to determine what an institution deems as being academically honest, in light of the availability of machine generated text.

2. Floridi, L., & Chiriatti, M. (2020). "GPT-3: Its Nature, Scope, Limits, and Consequences." Minds and Machines

Floridi and Chiriatti address the epistemological limitations of GPT-3 and note that while it performs very well in terms of natural language understanding, it lacks true semantic comprehension and intentions. They emphasize the necessity of human agency in the process of making meaning, thereby reinforcing the idea that AI cannot be held accountable for generating text. Although they offer a rich philosophical background, the authors do not provide direction for how academic institutions should implement these philosophical distinctions into policies governing authorship and research guidelines, particularly in higher education.

3. Cotton, D., Cotton, P., & Shipway, J. (2024). "Chatting and Cheating: Ensuring Academic Integrity in the Era of ChatGPT." Journal of Applied Learning & Teaching

The authors of this overview have highlighted an article that discusses how ChatGPT may disrupt traditional forms of assessment by providing the possibility to use technology to cheat and plagiarize, thereby enhancing the student experience and increasing the quality of the feedback provided to the student. The authors note that this innovation creates a dilemma between the innovation and the integrity of the assessment process and that the process of innovation does not necessarily support or promote the integrity of the assessment. In addition, the authors emphasize the need to create new types of assessments and develop policies that better support the integrity of assessments. However, most of the emphasis on the use of ChatGPT by students is focused on student behavior and does not provide much insight into how the researchers or institutions should ethically incorporate AI-generated writing into scholarly writing or publication practices.

4. Bin-Nashwan, S., et al. (2023). "Use of ChatGPT in Academia: Academic Integrity Hangs in the Balance." Technology in Society

Bin-Nashwan and his co-authors investigated academics' and researchers' motivations for utilizing ChatGPT in higher education. Their study examined factors such as concerns about plagiarism, legitimacy, and misuse, and valued the ability to generate ideas and drafts using AI. The findings from this study demonstrate how academics behave in relation to ChatGPT and provide insight into the psychologists' perspectives of those who adopt it. However, it does not investigate any standards of ethical conduct for determining the respective authorship or regulation of AI-supported research writing by institutions.

5. Karkoulian, S., Sayegh, M., & Sayegh, W. (2025). "ChatGPT Unveiled: Understanding Perceptions of Academic Integrity in Higher Education." Journal of Academic Ethics

The current qualitative study explores faculty and students' perceptions of how AI will affect academic integrity. Participants reported significant uncertainty about acceptable uses of AI, the absence of clear institutional policies regarding AI and an urgent need for faculty and students to receive training on digital literacy. While this study will provide much empirical data, there is no structure provided for an ethical framework or clear policy guidelines that would help address the complexities associated with using AI to assist authorship.

6. UNESCO. (2023). "Guidance for Generative AI in Education and Research." UNESCO Publishing

UNESCO's document presents guiding principles regarding the ethical use of AI, such as ensuring that the use of AI is transparent, accountable and has mechanisms to prevent exacerbating inequalities. The document highlights the importance of governance to prevent the abuse of GenAI and increasing existing levels of academic and social inequities. The document also states that, while there is a respective emphasis on providing ethical education, there is no definition of detailed standards for attribution (including citation), disclosure and authorship responsibilities in a research context.

7. Caines, A., & McCarty, J. (2023). "Large Language Models and the Future of University Writing." Computers and Composition

Caines and McCarty discuss the effect of GenAI tools on how we teach students to write academically. Caines and McCarty point out that it is now inevitable that students and AI will collaborate, and the authors call for updated and specific guidance about acceptable uses of GenAI in academic writing, redesigned assessments, and increased transparency regarding student and AI collaborations. Caines and McCarty highlight the pedagogical concerns related to the use of GenAI tools in the classroom, but they do not offer much in the way of insight into GenAI's effects on the writing process for researchers, authorship standards and standards of accountability for scholarship.

8. Havergal, C. (2023). "Are AI Tools the End of Academic Authorship?" Times Higher Education

Havergal examines the ongoing discussion regarding the use of Artificial Intelligence (AI) as an author on scientific articles. The editors and publishers that Havergal spoke to expressed reservations about listing AI as an author because AI cannot be held accountable for their actions. Although the article brings attention to some very important questions, it is more of a journalistic nature and doesn't provide a systematic discussion of both ethical frameworks and criteria for publishing authorship.

9. Stokel-Walker, C., & Van Noorden, R. (2023). "What ChatGPT and Generative AI Mean for Science." Nature

The article discusses the increasing use of Generative AI in the scientific process, such as writing literature reviews, coding, and drafting manuscripts. It highlights the potential for increased productivity, and the possibility of producing fake data through the use of AI, and of using unverifiable sources. However, it does not outline how AI could be regulated in a research context, nor does it provide guidelines for responsible authorship attribution.

10. Solaiman, I., et al. (2023). "Evaluating the Ethical Risks of Generative AI Systems." AI Ethics Journal

Solaiman and his colleagues highlight a range of ethical issues associated with the use of AI; bias, misinformation, transparency, accountability, and governance. Therefore it is recommended that governance structures be created for the responsible use of these technologies. This article, although addressing macro-level ethical issues, does not address the relationship between AI's ethical concerns, research integrity, higher education institutions, and the changing definition of authorship.

UNDERSTANDING GENERATIVE ARTIFICIAL INTELLIGENCE

The advances made with Generative AI are revolutionary in computing because they allow for systems capable of generating brand new content – such as text, image, data summary or analytical explanation – and go beyond prior AI functions limited to classification and prediction tasks; therefore, the outputs generated by these systems are an approximation of human creativity and reasoning. As schools rapidly adopt generative AI into their curriculums, there have been many discussions amongst educators regarding issues related to authenticity, authorship and what constitutes the line between machine-assisted collaboration and academic integrity, etc. In order to comprehend the full implications of generative AI, its architecture, functions and ethical considerations clearly need to be explored, while examining the various ways in which generative AI may serve to enhance and limit the practices within academic institutions.

Defining Generative AI and Large Language Models

Generative AI systems use machine learning algorithms to identify patterns from pre-existing data and develop new content based on these patterns. A few examples of significant GAI models are Large Language Models (LLM) like GPT and Claude and Gemini are based on transformer architecture using deep learning architecture to help the model understand language in a sequential way and contextually.

The term "generative" refers specifically to LLMs' ability to produce coherent pieces of text that replicate the reasoning styles and writing formats of humans, not simply retrieve or generate different segments of the same language. LLMs contain Billions to Trillions of parameters or "weights," all of which dictate how the model sees linguistic relationships. Training for LLMs takes place over massive and diverse corpuses of text from nature and academic sources to various forms of digital content http://wwwhubspot.com/blog/how-llms-encoder-decoder-are-structured). The model learns about patterns in language statistically by identifying relationships through the iteration of adjusting its parameters. Scholars such as Bender et al. (2021) describe LLMs as "stochastic parrots," which highlights that the model does not have comprehension or intention but can return a plausible linguistic response based on statistical matching of probabilities. This creates a significant distinction in the ongoing discussions around questions of authorship or academic integrity since LLMs do not accurately capture meaning, original thought, and responsible intellect.

How GenAI Produces Text and Knowledge

Training generative AI models involves using a method called next-token prediction, where the AI predicts what the next word (or token) will be based on the previous context. The apparent simplicity of this process belies the complex ways in which the AI learns to relate words, concepts, and formats through a high-dimensional vector representation of all parameters.

When given a task or question, large language models (LLMs) do not retrieve the relevant information from a standard repository of documents or prepared responses. Instead, they apply what they have learned to the question and synthesize new information using the patterns identifiable in their training dataset. Thus, LLMs can create a variety of textual output such as argumentative essays, summaries, literature reviews, and analyses that have the appearance of coherent and human-derived.

While the results of this synthesis have been misconstrued as "knowledge," the reality is that the LLM produces statistical approximations of informed human-sounding responses.

The statistical nature of the output is the source of many problems such as hallucinations, where LLMs make up references, provide inaccurate data, or create sources that do not exist. This is because the LLM creates seemingly "truthful" content based on the desire for coherence without the benefit of an internal mechanism to check for accuracy. Because of this, LLMs are unable to separate verified information from patterns that look like credible academic writing; therefore, academic reliance upon AI-generated text will always place academic viability at risk unless verified by humans.

Training Data, Bias, and Ethical Risks

The ethical implications of generative AI Training Data create a multitude of challenges. Since LLMs use vast amounts of information pulled from the internet and other sources, they also incorporate copyrighted materials, cultural or ideological biases, and disparate global perspectives. This creates significant concerns regarding intellectual property ownership rights and fairness.

First, the use of copyrighted information in generating AI models without permission violates the traditional standards of ownership in academia. If an AI model relies on Proprietary journalists, The articles, or books in question, it may produce the idea or expression of creation and it is impossible to identify the original author's name. This can result in creating an overlap between inspiration and plagiarism in AI-created content.

Second, the training data could contain biases that result in skewed, discriminatory, and inaccurate results. For example, an LLM trained primarily on western literature/reference books or Western journals may generate biased results regarding non-Western societies and could reinforce negative stereotypes concerning those cultures by using stereotypical language seen in the media.

Lastly, the lack of transparency regarding the sources of the data used to create the model and their lack of visibility to the users create ethical concerns. Users often do not know what data sources were utilized to create the response from the model and, as a result, it becomes extremely difficult to determine where the author created the response, validate its accuracy, or confirm that it adheres to an ethical standard.

Capabilities and Limitations in Scholarly Contexts

Artificial Intelligence (AI) in academia represents both great opportunity and significant limitations. It is able to provide rapid generation of summaries, explanations of concepts, mapping conceptual relationships and producing first drafts of writing. For researchers, AI tools can assist with the brainstorming of ideas, improvement of arguments, synthesising literature and considering different viewpoints. For students, AI can improve the clarity, structure and accessibility of writing. When utilized with careful supervision, AI has the ability to create an opportunity for deeper interaction with academic material and encourage innovation.

However, there are a number of limitations associated with the use of AI which must be taken into consideration. The fact that AI does not have a real understanding means that it is unable to provide guarantees about the accuracy, originality or the validity of the methodology being employed. In addition, AI may incorrectly generate citations, misinterpret research or provide a replica of written works in a scholarly manner that does not conform with accepted academic practices. In addition to the erosion of authorship due to overuse of AI, there is also a concern regarding the erosion of critical thinking skills and authenticity of academic work. Furthermore, there is inconsistency between institutions regarding acceptable ways of disclosing and using AI ethically.

Therefore, while AI is a groundbreaking tool for the advancement of academic productivity, the ethical integration of AI into scholarly processes should be based on a framework of transparency, human oversight and adherence to established ethical standards that continue to evolve as research progresses. The appropriate function for AI is as a complement to the scholarly process and not a replacement for the application of human intelligence within established parameters.

ACADEMIC INTEGRITY IN THE AI ERA

Generative AI has enabled and will continue to enable tremendous advancements in how colleges and universities produce, assess, and validate knowledge. The concept of academic integrity, which has traditionally been based on principles of honesty, originality, accountability, fairness, and respect for intellectual property, is facing new and unique challenges from the introduction of GenAI. As AI systems gain power and influence in the creation of academic work, institutions must reevaluate not only how academic integrity will be maintained but also how these fundamental values will apply as the use of machine-based tools becomes commonplace. This section examines the historical foundations of academic integrity, considers the disruptions brought about by GenAI and describes the rapidly evolving and inconsistent regulatory atmosphere around the world related to the regulation of these technologies. Finally, we will discuss the various complex concerns surrounding copyright, data privacy and fairness concerning the use of AI in the world of academia.

Classical Principles of Academic Integrity

The framework for academic integrity has a long-standing set of principles that create a level of confidence in the quality of scholarly works, allowing readers to accept the validity of those contributions to society. Academic integrity encompasses honesty, trust, fairness, respect, responsibility, and courage as the cornerstone of education and research ethics. Fundamental to the concept of Academic Integrity, individuals need to submit original ideas without attribution, disclose all sources used in writing, refrain from misrepresentation, and act as responsible and productive members of the scholarly community.

Honesty is a fundamental principle of academic integrity since it requires students and scholars to communicate their contributions clearly and truthfully. Honest communication can include providing accurate documentation of results, crediting those who assist a scholar in the creation of those ideas, and not representing another person's work as one's own (plagiarism). Honest communication also exhorts the scholar to produce original contributions to the body of knowledge (scholarship) based on individual cognitive (thought) abilities. To be original, scholars must not only produce their own independent thinking but must also produce new knowledge created through creative thinking based upon the earlier-created body of knowledge.

Another key aspect of Academic Integrity is accountability. In addition to producing original contributions and being honest, scholars are also accountable as to the information produced, methodology used for the production of that information, and the conclusions that flow from their research findings. Scholars have a responsibility to explain their rationale for the research conducted and to accept ownership of any errors or unethical behavior that is a direct result of their scholarly activities. Accountability assumes that the scholarly product produced is the result of the scholar's intent and accountability, but this assumption is made infinitely more problematic when an individual uses AI-generated materials to develop that product.

How GenAI Disrupts Traditional Integrity Norms

Generative AI represents a fundamental challenge to classical principles of authorship, labour and output as it alters the way we think about these concepts. For example, when a student or researcher creates text with the assistance of an AI tool, summarises existing literature, creates citations or analyses data, even though the output appears to show evidence of sophisticated reasoning and language skills, it does not reflect their own intellectual labour. As such, generative AI blurs the lines between what is considered 'real' human thought versus 'artificial' thought created by algorithms, thus complicating longstanding assumptions about originality and truthfulness.

Another disruption relates to plagiarism, which has conventionally been defined as the use of someone else's words or ideas without crediting them. The introduction of generative AI complicates this definition because AI-generated content does not have a specific human author and is frequently considered to be "new." However, because generative AI systems use large sets of existing texts for their learning, the generated content likely reflects patterns and phrases from these original texts. So, even when the AI system generates content that is considered original in a technical sense, it may not represent original intellectual contribution because the user has not created any significant contributions of their own. Thus, in the case of generative AI, plagiarism becomes less about copying words and more about misattributing the source of what is considered to be 'intellectual' labour.

The concept of accountability comes into disarray with evolving artificial intelligence (AI) systems. AI-generated content is not always correct or supported by factual evidence or accurate interpretations of certain context. This results in the idea known as "Hallucination." When a student or researcher submits this type of AI-generated content, it becomes very difficult to distinguish whether they produced it as a result of making an error themselves or due to the AI system's failure to provide accurate information. However, accountability is dictated by typical integrity frameworks that imply the authors of a piece of work should be completely accountable for what they produce, hence creating a situation where, on one hand, AI assists in producing the author's work, while on the other hand, AI does not hold accountability for what it produces. Thus, this creates a dilemma; the need for human accountability is greater than ever, yet the ability to enforce that accountability is increasingly difficult.

Secondly, the use of GenAI impacts unfairness in evaluation. Students who have greater access to advanced AI technologies) have an unfair advantage compared with students who rely only on human-generated work. Although many educational institutions have prohibited the use of GenAI in their courses, enforcement of these bans cannot be reliably executed in the present technological climate. The inability of educational institutions to consistently enforce a ban on the use of GenAI tools further exacerbates the disparity of access to GenAI tools, which in turn creates structural inequities, therefore violating the principle of fairness.

Lastly, the rise of GenAI brings into question fundamental social norms around authorship. Historically, authorship is defined by three distinct elements; i.e., deliberate intention to create new information, the intellectual capacity to create that information and the ability to explain and validate one's work. AI lacks all of these qualities. When AI becomes an invisible collaborator, classical authorship norms lose clarity, pushing institutions to rethink the boundaries between assistance, collaboration, and substitution.

Global Confusion and Inconsistency in Regulations

The rapid adoption of GenAI is outpacing the development of global academic policy, which has resulted in a fragmented and inconsistent regulatory landscape. Responses from universities, publishers, and research organizations vary widely, from prohibiting any sort of use of AI-generated writing to allowing AI-generated writing and requiring a certain format of disclosure when it's used.

Institutions adopting a prohibitionist approach ban the use of writing created by machines from being submitted for coursework and published work. The institutions claim that using AI-generated writing affects the learning outcomes and authenticity of authorship. Unfortunately, we find that these types of bans are often unenforceable because they only drive the use of AI underground.

However, there are universities that allow the use of AI tools, provided that users disclose how they used the AI tool to produce their piece of writing. In these institutions, GenAI is viewed as a writing assistance tool, and institutions require transparency in disclosing the use of the tool. The level of disclosure varies widely across institutions; some have regulations requiring acknowledgment of AI-generated or manipulated writings as a footnote to the document; others have regulations requiring a detailed description of how the AI tool was utilized in the production of the piece.

In contrast, a third classification of institutions has adopted an integrative approach. These institutions promote AI literacy, educate on the ethical use of AI in the various contexts of the ethical curriculum, and emphasize educating students and researchers on the ethical and legal issues that will arise in the digital scholarship model. While most institutions adopting this approach are mainly located in certain geographical areas, this model is most consistent with the trajectory of digital scholarship.

Academic publishers around the world have issued Different Policies related to the involvement of Artificial Intelligence in Academic Publishing. Some academic journals do not allow AI to be included as an Author on Articles due to lack of accountability. However, some academic journals allow the use of Artificial Intelligence to generate textual content but require that it is Clearly documented in the Manuscripts. The lack of consistency between institutions, Countries, and Scholarly communities leads to further confusion and increases the likelihood of Different Ethical Conduct Expectations within the academic community.

Copyright, Data Privacy, and Fairness Concerns

In addition to academic integrity issues, AI creates additional complex legal and ethical issues, such as copyright issues, data privacy concerns, and fairness. GenAI systems are typically trained using very large data repositories that often include copyright-protected works and as such there exists an ongoing discussion about whether an AI-generated text constitutes an infringement of the intellectual property rights of the original author(s). Since an AI model does not distinguish between a copyrighted work or a work that has entered the public domain, there are concerns that the material produced by AI systems could inadvertently duplicate or replicate proprietary or copyrighted material. This presents challenges to researchers, since they could unintentionally include this type of material in their academic writings, thereby exposing themselves and their institutions to legal liability.

Another issue associated with the use of AI technologies relates to the privacy of users' data. Most of the GenAI tools available on the market today utilize a central server to process user input, leading to concerns regarding how user data will be stored, reused, shared, or exposed to outside parties. If a researcher uploads an unpublished manuscript, private patient data, or confidential research notes into an AI system, this action may violate ethical and/or legal responsibilities to protect the confidentiality of their data. Therefore, it is difficult for higher education institutions to take advantage of the benefits that AI technologies offer while still protecting their users' confidential data.

Biases that exist within training datasets create fairness issues, causing bias towards different cultures, languages, and views. The outcome is that the outputs produced are either stereotyped or marginalize certain voices. In research, biased AI-generated content distorts the research and produces epistemic injustices by marginalizing non-dominant knowledge systems. This is contrary to the principle of fairness, which is the basis of academic integrity.

TRANSFORMATION OF AUTHORSHIP

The Emergence of Generative AI (GenAI) has caused a dramatic change in the way we think about who is considered an Academic Author and how that Author creates their work. Traditionally, Authors have been viewed as having the ability to create meaning through Creative Thought (imagination), Intention, Use of Critical Thinking Skills and Ethical Accountability. Now that computer systems (through use of AI) are able to generate similar documents to those created by humans, as well as combine (synthesise) information from all the literature in a logical, coherent, and valid manner, the boundaries are becoming increasingly hard to define. As a result, there are many complex questions regarding originality, and ownership, as well as ethical responsibility associated with creating scholarly works. (Floridi & Chiriatti, 2020).

Human Authorship vs. Machine Contribution

The traditional view of authorship assumes that a scholar produces his or her writing through individual intellectual work, thoughtful reflections and creative thinking about ideas. The expectations are drastically changed with GenAI technology because GenAI makes it possible for an individual to create immense amounts of written material (e.g., essays, summaries of literature, considerations of argumentation) with minimal input from any individual. Therefore, if an individual were to use a GenAI system to develop his or her writing, the individual would be performing only curation or editing duties as opposed to creation tasks. This begs the question, "What is sufficient human intellectual input to be classified as an authored piece of work?" and continues to raise the question about how the line between assistance and authorship has become less distinct. Although GenAI may provide greater clarity and perspective to the writing process, the actual intellectual contribution still must come from the individual using GenAI technology so that your work will retain its academic legitimacy. (Cotton et al., 2024).

Originality and Intellectual Ownership in Question

For centuries, originality has been a key principle of authorship in academia. An academic's work should represent that author's individual unique analysis or creative synthesis. Many AI-generated outputs are said to be "original" in that they appear to be novel in terms of their content; however, these AI-generated works do not originate from a human being's insight or intent to be creative. Rather, AI-generated outputs are simply "recombinations" of existing text creating new combinations, using text patterns learned from training data. Therefore, if the ideas or patterns created by a GenAI model resemble an existing copyrighted work, then there is a question about whether or not that particular creation is truly "original." Furthermore, because the AI tool is not designed to recognize paraphrased or similar structural content as copies of a copyrighted work, authors utilizing these tools can inadvertently commit plagiarism (Bender et al., 2021). Therefore, the tradition of originality must shift from the idea of writing original language to the authentic, creative manner in which human beings create meaning. While AI can produce text that can look original, it does not have the ability to provide the human interpretation required for something to be classified as original in academia.

AI as a "Stochastic Parrot": Theoretical Implications

Bender and others (2021) characterise large language models as "stochastic parrots", which explain that these models produce text by statistical prediction of sequence and are therefore not capable of meaning-making. Consequently, this insight means that if AI does not have comprehension, intention, or ability to track truth, AI cannot contribute academic-level knowledge in the epistemic sense expected of an author. Treating AI as an author would confuse fluency with cognitive agency and undermine the intellectual integrity standards of scholarship. The critique of the term "stochastic parrot" emphasises that while a piece of text generated by AI may have the appearance of being polished, it must still be evaluated critically because there could be made-up citations, inaccurate information, or biased representations due to pattern imitation and not through informed thought (Stokel-Walker & Van Noorden, 2023).

Responsibility, Accountability, and Agency

The role of academic author encompasses a responsibility. Academic authors need to support their claims, explain their methodology, and bear the consequences of errors or unethical behaviour. AI does not possess a moral capacity to accept these responsibilities and thus is not able to verify the correctness or use of the data created by it. As a result, the majority of academic publishers and institutions (UNESCO, 2023) have taken a strong position against AI being listed as an author on scholarly work. A human researcher bears total responsibility for confirming that sources used are correct, accurate, and that any form of AI involvement is disclosed. Given this, it is an essential pillar of the relationship between AI and academia; AI can provide support in creating scholarly research but cannot take the place of the human author, who remains ethically and intellectually responsible for all research claims (Floridi & Chiriatti, 2020).

PEDAGOGICAL CHALLENGES AND OPPORTUNITIES

As the use of generative artificial intelligence (GenAI) in higher education increases, so does the number of issues faced by educational institutions to effectively use these technologies to deliver quality learning experiences for students. GenAI has given new ways for educators and students to use technology to provide opportunities for personalized learning, real-time feedback and access to academic materials; however, with those opportunities come a set of risks to authentic learning, student autonomy, and the development of student foundational academic skills. Therefore, there must be a balanced approach to utilizing AI in higher education, which includes identifying the benefits that AI technologies provide, as well as providing appropriate pedagogical structure and support for students to achieve discipline-specific learning outcomes while maintaining the integrity of their academic work.

AI as a Learning Support Tool

AI tools are an incredible resource to provide students with instant feedback, breakdown large sources of information into smaller pieces, as well as for those who struggle with writing assignments. When properly utilized, these systems produce feedback for areas where the student may require additional assistance. Students will benefit from an increased level of comprehension when using these systems, in addition, they will also gain confidence through the increased experience of using technology. Research by Cotton et al., (2024) indicates that AI can augment classroom-based instruction and encourage teachers to have students engage in active learning, improve their work by using iteration and providing an avenue for identifying their strengths and weaknesses in their work.

For multilingual and other students who cannot typically have access to traditional forms of academic support, AI systems provide an accessible and available scaffold tool for overcoming achievement gaps.

Though AI can be a valuable tool in the learning process, educators must clearly establish the distinction between providing support and providing everything for the student. The purpose of using AI as part of the learning process should be to stimulate and enhance the learner's intellectual curiosity and to create an environment where the learner remains engaged and actively involved in the learning process. Additionally, as stated by Bender et al., (2021), the text generated by AI systems is a form of pattern reproduction and lacks true understanding. Therefore, AI should remain a supplemental aid, while the responsibility for creating meaning and providing academic judgement lies within the learner.

Risks of Student Over-Dependence on AI

While GenAI tools offer many advantages, they also create a major risk of encouraging too much student dependence. When students start using GenAI to draft essays, analyse data, and produce ideas, they lose the chance to better themselves and develop core academic skills. An over-dependence on GenAI will lead to surface learning, and students will accept GenAI's output at face value and not Search for deeper engagement with the academic material. This is particularly concerning considering that the content generated by GenAI may include factual inaccuracies, fake citations, and/or misleading interpretations; all of which are well documented in the current AI hallucination literature (Stokel-Walker & Van Noorden, 2023).

As well as hindering critical thinking, problem solving, and independent reasoning ability, an excessive dependency on AI can also cause students to be passive information recipients rather than active participants in their education. According to Cotton et al. (2024), when artificial intelligence is viewed as a shortcut instead of a reflective tool, Educational Inequities will likely be further deepened since assessments will increasingly reflect how sophisticated GenAI is used and not what students actually understand. The Over-dependence on GenAI not only has negative implications within the educational field but, in the future, Graduates who relied heavily on GenAI may lack the cognitive flexibility and disciplinary expertise to ensure success within a Profession.

Critical Literacy and Guided AI Use

In order to address the challenges associated with artificial intelligence (AI) in education, students must develop strong levels of AI literacy, which mean's that they're able to evaluate, challenge, and use AI in an ethical manner. The importance of critical literacy includes being able to understand the limits of AI, identify any shortcomings or biases present in AI results and understand how AI training data influences AI outputs. Without a high level of critical literacy, students may accept AI generated responses as correct, valid or complete without question. As such, educators must actively instruct students how to evaluate AI generated content; verify similar or duplicate content to ensure it isn't used in place of their own original content; use AI while maintaining the standards of academic integrity.

Conducting guided practices designed by educators is critical to achieving a high level of evaluative literacy for students. Educators can assist students in developing their ability to evaluate AI by developing classroom-based activities where students can compare human authors with AI authors; evaluate AI-generated responses to identify errors; and explore how variations in the content provided to AI will produce differing responses (Caines & McCarty, 2023). Teaching AI literacy to educators and embedding this across the curriculum teaches students the importance of acting responsibly in academic settings when they use AI and how to do so with transparency; discourages students from engaging in plagiarism; and teaches students to understand the importance of protecting their data by understanding the risks associated with sharing their data with AI (UNESCO, 2023).

Discipline-Specific Pedagogical Adjustments

Artificial intelligence impacts the different academic disciplines in different ways; therefore, educators must create specialized pedagogical solutions for these distinct disciplines. For example, in writing-intensive fields, such as literature, history, or philosophy, development of original argumentation, interpretative skills, and voice needs to remain as the instructional focus, and therefore AI may provide useful support for brainstorming or editing only. However, unrestricted use of AI in these areas risks losing the innovative aspects of creativity and depriving students of the opportunity to master the relevant rhetorical strategies. Similarly, AI tools may support coding, modelling, or the explanation of specific mathematical concepts in STEM disciplines; however, students improperly relying on the capabilities of AI will develop limited procedural knowledge and conceptual understanding (Bender et al., 2021).

In law, medicine, and engineering professions, the ramifications of incorrectly utilizing AI tools is even greater. For example, AI-generated text may over-simplify the complexity of reasoning used to justify legal principles, the legal principles themselves may not be accurately interpreted through the lens of the AI tool, or, AI tools may generate inaccurate suggestions for medical diagnosis or treatment. Because the consequences of professional decisions impact the real world, professional standards developed by each specific profession and its associated fields should define when AI tools can be used appropriately in conjunction with the required skills and knowledge base expected of the professional practitioner. To reiterate, Pedagogy during the era of AI must clearly define explicit expectations, provide students with training regarding the appropriate and ethical use of technology, and reinforce the importance of human judgment as a primary idea (Cotton et al., 2024).

COMPARATIVE ANALYSIS OF UNIVERSITY POLICIES

The quick adoption of generative AI in higher education has led schools globally to create governance systems that allow for both advancement and adherence to principles of academic honesty. Harvard, the University of Cambridge and IIT Delhi have published official responses on generative AI based on their respective institutional cultures, laws and pedagogical goals. We'll review the three different governance structures and compare how each handles issues such as disclosure, academic honesty, privacy and the inclusion of AI education within their degree programs.

Harvard University's AI Policy Framework

The University of Harvard uses a responsible experimentation model for Generative Artificial Intelligence [Gen AI] in a way that is acceptable for everyone on campus and across all departments at the university. The Provost's Office letter outlining all the resources available says that Harvard supports the responsible use of Generative AI tools and will do so based upon 4 primary areas: information security and data privacy, legal compliance, copyright and academic integrity (Harvard University, 2024a). One of the most important things the document points out is that users cannot enter sensitive or confidential information into publicly available AI tools. The document also states that users need to comply with data protection and research ethics and must not use Gen AI in a way that misrepresents authorship or violates course policies.

Harvard University Information Technology (HUIT) [Institute of Technology] created further guidance for users and developed a catalogue of AI Tools that lists what is authorised according to both data classification and approved AI tools (Harvard University, 2024b). The guidance includes a very strong warning that the majority of all commercially available tools (including those from HUIT) log all user input to train the tool on that information, and this creates a level of risk regarding confidential research data or personally identifiable information (PII).

The Office of Undergraduate Education at the Faculty of Arts and Sciences has issued extensive guidance to its faculty on how to manage student use of generative artificial intelligence (AI) in both teaching and assessment. All instructors should state the specific rules regarding student use of AI tools within their syllabi. These rules may either prohibit the use of AI tools entirely or permit a more structured, supervised use where students must disclose the use of such tools (Office of Undergraduate Education, 2024). This decentralised approach reflects Harvard's belief that the pedagogical implications of AI may differ across various disciplines, types of assessment, and learning objectives, and therefore, it requires flexibility at both a departmental and course level. Additionally, the University maintains a centralized resource hub called "Teaching with Generative Artificial Intelligence," where instructors can find sample syllabus language, ideas for redesigning assignments, and suggestions for ensuring that AI helps the students learn rather than hindering their ability to achieve expected learning outcomes (Harvard University, 2024c).

University of Cambridge's Ethical AI Guidelines

The university of Cambridge has published a multi-layered set of policies that include guidelines for both administrative and educational use of AI. Regarding administrative use, the Cambridge Information Compliance Office (ICO) releases documentation to all staff on the use of Generative AI in a general way and states that when used to assist with everyday tasks such as writing emails or summarising reports, AI tools must be used in accordance with ICO's guidelines regarding data security, confidentiality, and monitoring by people (University of Cambridge 2024a). All staff should never input special category or sensitive information into publicly accessible AI tools, and should always regard AI output as drafts and carefully review for accuracy prior to submitting to the organisation.

Regarding Educational Use, the Cambridge Blended Learning Service provides guidance on using Generative AI specifically for students. Their guidance specifically allows students to use GenAI for personal learning, research assistance, and formative work, but advises them to first check the local departmental guidance related to the particulars of their own discipline (Blended Learning Service 2024). Therefore, students should understand that it is their responsibility to ensure the accuracy and integrity of their work product, no matter what an AI tool produces.

The Cambridge student help pages specifically indicate that students must indicate if they are using AI in their assessed work, and that the use of AI in accordance with the university's Generative AI Usage Policy is required (University of Cambridge, 2024b). The use of AI for brainstorming, proofreading or summarising is acceptable, but any content that has been produced by AI may not be submitted under the student's own name without acknowledgment. This is consistent with the views of the institution generally regarding GenAI. While GenAI can be utilised as a resource, the use of unacknowledged AI content in assessed work is considered misconduct (Blended Learning Service, 2024; Cambridge International, 2023).

IIT Delhi's Approach to Responsible AI Use

In 2024-2025, IIT Delhi became one of the first large public universities in the Global South to create a formalised policy about the use of generative artificial intelligence (GenAI). This was in response to findings from the university's internal committee which showed that over 80% of students and 77% of faculty members were using GenAI tools. Consequently, IIT Delhi issued its "Guidelines for the Responsible Use of Artificial Intelligence" (Press Trust of India, 2025; Times of India, 2025) and took a measured approach, adopting a permissive yet regulated stance towards using GenAI.

The most important aspect of IIT Delhi's framework is that it has a strong commitment to transparency. The institute requires students and faculty members to disclose any AI-assisted work or content as a way of maintaining academic integrity (Press Trust of India, 2025; The Higher Education Review, 2025), with a focus on using AI responsibly. The guidelines state that any failure to disclose AI involvement could be considered academic misconduct.

The guidelines encourage users to verify the accuracy of AI-generated content, protect sensitive information, and not share personal or confidential institutional information with external GenAI tools (The Higher Education Review, 2025). Furthermore, IIT Delhi is also prioritising AI literacy as part of its curriculum: the internal committee advised that all academic programs include exposure to AI and machine learning, and many departments have already incorporated AI into their course offerings. (Times of India, 2025).

As a result, IIT Delhi 's approach to AI will focus on mandatory transparency as it pertains to AI implementation.The need for critical verification and data security in the development of AI solutions.The systematic integration within the educational programs of the university to help facilitate AI development while preventing the possible loss of critical thinking skills and creativity.

Comparative Insights and Benchmarking

The collective actions of Harvard, Cambridge University, and IIT Delhi show a growing global acknowledgement that, while it may not be feasible to place an absolute prohibition on the use of generative artificial intelligence (AI), it is not pedagogically necessary to implement such a measure. Rather than prohibiting all uses of AI, all three institutions implement a regulated-permissively' model concerning the use of generative AIs, so long as those uses fall within the ethical and pedagogical limits delineated by each organisation. The three universities all indicate a strong commitment to promoting the use of AI responsibly through publicly available policy statements and guidelines.

Overall, all three institutions also highlight their commitment to transparency and open communication with regard to AI use. For example, Harvard requests faculty members specify if/and how they expect students to use AI and implicitly implies that students should follow the faculty member's specified regulations (Harvard University, 2024a; Office of Undergraduate Education, 2024). Similarly, Cambridge University requires all students to disclose whether they used AI to complete a specific assessment (University of Cambridge, 2024b). Finally, IIT Delhi requires full disclosure of any/and all contributions made by any AI when submitting a document by the student or faculty member (Press Trust of India, 2025). The three universities have a mutual understanding that the integrity of authorship will only be maintained when the author accurately portrays what was created by a human versus what was created by an AI.

The second matter of concern that all three institutions have in common is that all three institutions believe that data privacy and information security should be the primary focus of any AI policy. In Harvard's guide to staff and faculty, the issue of entering confidential or regulated data into third-party systems was clearly stated as a risk (Harvard University, 2024a; Harvard University, 2024b). Likewise, Cambridge's guidelines for staff indicated that AI should not be used in conjunction with sensitive personal or institutional data (University of Cambridge, 2024a). IIT Delhi's staff guidelines also have a similar emphasis on the importance of protecting confidential or regulated data, and they instruct users to review and validate any outputs generated by the AI instead of just trusting them blindly (The Higher Education Review, 2025). The three institutions emphasised the importance of protecting confidential or regulated data and validating its results. Therefore, a comprehensive AI policy must address both academic integrity and the governance of digital information.

The third commonality among these three nations is that each nation acknowledges that AI needs to be adapted to local conditions, as well as for the specific discipline in which it will be used. Both Harvard and Cambridge allow departments and faculty to establish rules that make sense for their specific contexts (Blended Learning Service, 2024; Harvard University, 2024c). IIT Delhi has included AI literacy across all programmes, which is an example of the understanding that AI has significantly different meanings and purposes in different fields of study; for example, in engineering, AI serves a different purpose than it does in the humanities or in professional training (Times of India, 2025).

As much as there are similarities, there are also some strong differences. Harvard has a great deal of infrastructure to support it, including HUIT (Harvard University Information Technology) tools and resources as well as AI pedagogical initiatives (Harvard University, 2024b); whereas, Cambridge provides guidance that is focused on the student, teaching and assessing with a strong emphasis on the use of AI to enhance student learning, rather than being a part of any unacknowledged or assessed work (Blended Learning Service, 2024; University of Cambridge, 2024b). IIT Delhi, on the other hand, focuses more on communicating policy and building capacity for rapid development in LMICs, supporting AI education as a global graduate competency, with emphasis on using transparency as a safeguard against potential misuse (Press Trust of India, 2025; Times of India, 2025).

CONCLUSION

The impact of Generative AI (GenAI) on academic integrity, research standards and authorship norms across higher education is explored in the present study. The findings reveal that GenAI provides many opportunities for innovative development of writing, research and learning. However, these developments also challenge the principles of Originality, Accountability and Transparency as they relate to the use of AI in scholarship. As AI continues to embed itself within scholarly practice, the traditional notion of authorship that has been built upon the foundation of human intention, human creativity and human responsibility continues to be increasingly strained. Institutional responses to these developments have occurred at institutions of higher education around the world and are manifesting both systemic convergence and divergence, although there is a significant amount of regulatory development within institutions based upon the principles of transparency.

Generally from the above findings, a number of policy and practice recommendations arise. Institutions should create clearly articulated, discipline-specific policies that establish acceptable levels of use of AI technology; such policies should require that all instances of assistance provided by AI be fully disclosed and require that the use of AI will not affect the obligation of the human author to be the primary author of record. Additionally, specifications detailing the need for level of protection for personal data as well as regulations ensuring the verification of AI-generated content should be the top priority when creating a discipline-specific policy for the use of AI technology in scholarly work. Faculty development programmes should include training in AI literacy so that instructors can effectively redesign assessments and support students in making sense of rapidly changing expectations.

REFERENCES

Bender, E. M., Gebru, T., McMillan-Major, A., & Mitchell, S. (2021). On the dangers of stochastic parrots: Can language models be too big? In *Proceedings of the 2021 ACM Conference on Fairness, Accountability, and Transparency* (pp. 610–623). Association for Computing Machinery. DOI: 10.1145/3442188.3445922

Bin-Nashwan, S. A., Al-Dmour, H. H., Al-Dmour, R., & Alshurideh, M. (2023). Use of ChatGPT in academia: Academic integrity hangs in the balance. *Technology in Society*, *75*, 102389. DOI: 10.1016/j.techsoc.2023.102370

Blended Learning Service. (2024). *Using generative AI: Guidance for students.* University of Cambridge.

Caines, A., & McCarty, J. (2023). Large language models and the future of university writing. *Computers and Composition*, *69*, 102827.

Cambridge International. (2023). *The use of generative AI in coursework.* Cambridge Assessment International Education.

Cotton, D. R. E., Cotton, P. A., & Shipway, J. R. (2024). Chatting and cheating: Ensuring academic integrity in the era of ChatGPT. *Journal of Applied Learning & Teaching*, *7*(1), 1–14.

Floridi, L., & Chiriatti, M. (2020). GPT-3: Its nature, scope, limits, and consequences. *Minds and Machines*, *30*(4), 681–694. DOI: 10.1007/s11023-020-09548-1

Harvard University. (2024a). *Guidelines for using ChatGPT and other generative AI tools at Harvard.* Office of the Provost.

Harvard University. (2024b). *Generative AI guidelines.* Harvard University Information Technology.

Harvard University. (2024c). *Teach with generative AI.*

Havergal, C. (2023, March 7). Are AI tools the end of academic authorship? *Times Higher Education.*

Karkoulian, S., Sayegh, M., & Sayegh, W. (2025). ChatGPT unveiled: Understanding perceptions of academic integrity in higher education. *Journal of Academic Ethics*, *23*(3), 1171–1188. Advance online publication. DOI: 10.1007/s10805-024-09543-6

Office of Undergraduate Education. (2024). *Generative AI guidance for faculty.* Faculty of Arts and Sciences, Harvard University.

Press Trust of India. (2025, May 28). AI-generated work should be disclosed to ensure transparency: IIT Delhi to students, faculty. *The Print*.

Solaiman, I., Brundage, M., Clark, J., & Askell, A. (2023). Evaluating the ethical risks of generative AI systems. *AI Ethics Journal*, *4*(1), 1–19.

Stokel-Walker, C., & Van Noorden, R. (2023). What ChatGPT and generative AI mean for science. *Nature*, *614*(7947), 214–216. DOI: 10.1038/d41586-023-00340-6 PMID: 36747115

The Higher Education Review. (2025). *IIT Delhi introduces strict GenAI usage rules for students, faculty*.

Times of India. (2025, August 10). *AI, but verify: Navigating future of learning*.

UNESCO. (2023). *Guidance for generative AI in education and research*. UNESCO Publishing.

University of Cambridge. (2024a). *AI guidance: Guidance for University of Cambridge staff on the administrative use of generative AI*. Information Compliance Office.

University of Cambridge. (2024b). *Can I use generative AI in my course?* Cambridge Online Help.

Chapter 8
Redefining Teaching, Research, and Academic Governance:
The AI Shift in Higher Education

Ratan Sarkar
http://orcid.org/0009-0008-5480-0165
Tezpur University, India

ABSTRACT

Artificial Intelligence (AI) is reshaping higher education by transforming teaching, research, and governance. This chapter examines the epistemic, ethical, and institutional implications of rapid AI adoption, showing that its influence extends beyond technological efficiency. Using a critical integrative review, it analyzes how AI-driven personalization, automated research processes, and algorithmic decision-making affect academic labor, authority, and equity. It identifies risks such as bias, data surveillance, authorship ambiguity, global inequalities, and dependence on proprietary systems, while also noting the potential of human–AI collaboration to support creativity, access, and informed governance. Drawing on UNESCO and OECD frameworks, the chapter proposes a model for sustainable, inclusive, and ethical AI integration that preserves academic integrity and educational justice.

INTRODUCTION

The rapid diffusion of Artificial Intelligence (AI) has become one of the most disruptive forces shaping global higher education. From predictive analytics in admissions to algorithmic grading and automated content generation, AI technologies

DOI: 10.4018/979-8-3373-7097-2.ch008

are increasingly embedded in every layer of the academic ecosystem (Williamson & Eynon, 2020). The higher education sector, traditionally resistant to industrial automation, is now undergoing an epistemological and operational transformation where machine learning systems influence decision-making, curriculum design, and even scholarly authorship.

The emergence of generative AI tools, particularly Large Language Models (LLMs) such as ChatGPT, Bard, and Claude, has extended AI's reach beyond administrative efficiency into the heart of cognitive and creative processes (Zawacki-Richter et al., 2019). These systems not only assist in knowledge production but also participate in meaning-making, raising critical questions about authenticity, originality, and human intellectual labor. As Peruzzo and Allan (2022) observes, AI in academia "is not simply a tool but an actor within the socio-technical fabric of education," capable of reinforcing or disrupting institutional hierarchies.

The integration of AI has generated both optimism and anxiety. On one hand, AI-enabled adaptive learning platforms such as Coursera's personalization algorithms and tools like Gradescope promise increased accessibility, flexibility, and efficiency (Holmes et al., 2019). On the other hand, the overreliance on these technologies' risks reducing education to quantifiable metrics and algorithmic decisions, undermining the relational and ethical dimensions of teaching (Dulundu, 2024). The humanistic purpose of higher education—cultivating critical thinking, empathy, and social consciousness—may be compromised when pedagogical authority is delegated to systems optimized for efficiency rather than equity (Torrisi-Steele, 2025).

In the research domain, AI's capacity to automate data analysis, literature reviews, and hypothesis generation has redefined scholarly inquiry. While these tools democratize research participation, they also challenge traditional epistemologies that value reflexivity and contextual interpretation (Pigola et al., 2023). The proliferation of AI-generated manuscripts, for instance, has raised issues of authorship ethics, prompting publishers to draft policies on AI disclosure and accountability (Acion et al., 2023).

At the level of academic governance, AI-based decision support systems influence institutional planning, student performance monitoring, and faculty evaluation (Kayya Sam, A. K., & Olbrich, P.). However, as O'Neil (2016) cautions, algorithmic governance can entrench systemic bias and opacity, particularly when data reflect social inequalities. For the Global South, where infrastructural disparities persist, AI adoption often reproduces digital dependency rather than empowerment (Kitsara, 2022).

Therefore, the "AI shift" in higher education must be understood as both a technological and philosophical transition—one that challenges conventional notions of authority, expertise, and equity. This chapter positions AI as a transformative yet contested domain that demands critical engagement, ethical foresight, and inclusive design principles to sustain the human core of higher learning.

Rationale

The rationale for this chapter emerges from the growing recognition that AI's transformative role in higher education is both inevitable and insufficiently theorized. Despite widespread enthusiasm for AI's potential to personalize learning, streamline research, and enhance institutional efficiency, there is an urgent need to interrogate the deeper epistemic and ethical consequences of its overdependence.

First, the integration of AI challenges the epistemic foundations of academia. Universities have historically functioned as sites of critical reasoning and independent thought, yet the increasing automation of judgment—through algorithmic grading, plagiarism detection, and even peer review—risks reducing academic evaluation to computational rationality (Knox, 2020). The epistemological shift from human deliberation to data-driven inference demands scrutiny of what counts as "knowledge" and who controls its production (Khatri & Karki, 2023).

Second, AI's pedagogical implications are profound. While AI-based tutoring systems promise personalization, they also risk fostering intellectual passivity among learners. The phenomenon of "automation bias," where users overtrust machine outputs, can erode students' metacognitive skills and teachers' professional autonomy (Long & Magerko, 2020). As higher education increasingly adopts predictive learning analytics, it must confront questions of data ethics, student privacy, and algorithmic discrimination (Ismail et al., 2023).

Third, AI introduces new forms of academic labor and inequality. Automated teaching and research tools often privilege institutions in technologically advanced economies, widening global disparities (Yusriani et al., 2024). Scholars from the Global South face barriers to AI literacy, data sovereignty, and representation in AI datasets (Couldry & Mejias, 2019). Without critical governance, AI may reinforce colonial hierarchies under the guise of innovation.

Fourth, the governance dimension is critical. AI-based decision-making tools promise transparency and accountability but often operate as "black boxes." The absence of clear policies on AI ethics, intellectual property, and bias mitigation exposes institutions to reputational and legal risks (Kalkan, 2024). International frameworks such as the *UNESCO Recommendation on the Ethics of Artificial Intelligence* (2021) advocate for human rights–based oversight, yet institutional adoption remains uneven.

Finally, the philosophical and humanistic dimensions of education are at stake. The overdependence on AI risks transforming universities from communities of inquiry into data-driven enterprises (Popenici, 2023). As Biesta (2021) argues, education's value lies not only in knowledge acquisition but in the formation of subjectivity and ethical agency. Reclaiming this human-centered vision requires reframing AI not as a replacement for human intellect but as a collaborator in reflective, inclusive, and critical pedagogy.

Thus, the rationale of this chapter lies in constructing a holistic framework that recognizes AI as a complex socio-technical phenomenon—one that must be governed ethically, implemented inclusively, and theorized critically to safeguard the transformative purposes of higher education.

Objectives

This chapter aims to:

1. Critically examine how AI is reshaping pedagogical, research, and governance practices in higher education.
2. Analyze the epistemic, ethical, and institutional consequences of overdependence on AI systems.
3. Explore global disparities and policy responses to AI integration, with emphasis on equity and academic integrity.
4. Investigate the challenges and potentials of human–AI collaboration in higher education.
5. Propose a framework for sustainable, inclusive, and ethical AI adoption that aligns with the core values of higher learning.

REVIEW OF LITERATURE

The global proliferation of Artificial Intelligence (AI) across higher education has produced an expanding, yet uneven body of scholarship. While the literature documents significant potential for pedagogical innovation, research acceleration, and institutional efficiency, it also exposes profound gaps in theory, governance, and equity. This review critically synthesizes existing work across pedagogy, research and knowledge production, and academic governance—highlighting persistent conceptual blind spots and structural imbalances. It then reflects on how these gaps underscore the intellectual need for the present chapter's contribution.

AI in Higher Education Pedagogy: Personalization and its Discontents

The dominant strand of literature on AI-mediated pedagogy focuses on the promise of personalization. Holmes, Bialik, and Fadel (2019) describe AI-enabled adaptive systems as transformative tools capable of tailoring instruction to individual learners at scale. Similarly, Zawacki-Richter, Marín, Bond, and Gouverneur (2019) identify intelligent tutoring systems, natural language processing tools, and automated assessment technologies as central to contemporary educational innovation.

Yet these techno-optimistic narratives risk reducing pedagogy to a logic of optimization. Much of the research privileges metrics such as accuracy, efficiency, and immediacy of feedback, while neglecting the deeper educational values that undergird human learning (Han et al., 2023). The pedagogical focus on "what works" overshadows critical questions about how learning is shaped by algorithmic mediation. For instance, studies seldom examine whether personalized AI tools enhance or erode students' critical consciousness, intellectual autonomy, or reflective engagement—concerns central to humanistic educational theory (Shippee, 2023).

Long and Magerko's (2020) exploration of automation bias is particularly relevant; they demonstrate that learners frequently overtrust algorithmic suggestions, compromising their own judgment. However, such insights remain marginal within mainstream AI-in-education literature, which overwhelmingly treats learning as a technical problem rather than a relational, ethical, and socially situated process. Likewise, as Knox (2020) shows in his analysis of AI in Chinese higher education, the deployment of AI is often embedded within national sociopolitical priorities, shaping pedagogy in ways that reflect governmental rather than educational imperatives.

Taken together, the literature reveals a pedagogical discourse that is technologically rich yet philosophically thin. It speaks extensively about learner data, predictive models, and instructional analytics, but insufficiently about the purpose of higher education—a gap the present chapter aims to address by integrating critical, ethical, and humanistic perspectives.

AI in Research and Knowledge Production: Automation, Authorship, and Epistemic Shifts

AI-driven tools have reshaped the research landscape, offering capabilities ranging from automated data analysis to generative literature reviews (Extance, 2018). Acion et al. (2023) highlight how generative AI raises urgent ethical questions for open science, particularly around reliability, transparency, and accountability. These tools promise democratization—especially for early-career scholars or researchers in resource-constrained environments—yet they simultaneously challenge traditional norms of authorship, originality, and scholarly labor (Gupta, 2025).

Despite the scale of these disruptions, the literature remains fragmented. Much of it frames AI as a set of methodological tools rather than as a force that reshapes the epistemic foundations of knowledge production (Weigel et al., 2022). There is limited discussion of how AI influences scholarly interpretation, reflexivity, or the co-construction of meaning between researcher and phenomenon (Williams, 2024). In this respect, Peruzzo and Allan (2022) offer an important intervention by proposing convivial, inclusive approaches to digital scholarship. However, their work—like most in the field—does not fully interrogate how AI reconfigures authority and legitimacy within academic knowledge systems.

Moreover, concerns about AI-generated content often center on practical solutions (e.g., disclosure guidelines, detection tools) rather than deeper philosophical issues:

a) What counts as authorship when machines generate text?
b) How does reliance on AI reshape the relationship between thinking and writing?
c) In what ways might automated literature synthesis privilege dominant voices encoded in training data?

The literature provides few answers. There is a clear need for scholarship that moves beyond technical or policy fixes and instead examines how AI reshapes what knowledge is, how it is produced, and whose knowledge is legitimized. The chapter responds to this need by grounding AI's research role in epistemic ethics and critical analysis.

Algorithmic Governance in Higher Education: Datafied Decisions and Institutional Risks

AI's influence on academic governance—ranging from admissions decisions to faculty evaluation—represents one of the fastest-growing yet least critically examined domains in the literature (Ghandour, 2024). O'Neil's (2016) work remains foundational in demonstrating how data-driven systems can entrench bias, reduce transparency, and produce self-perpetuating forms of inequality. Williamson and Eynon (2020) similarly describe how AI-driven infrastructures shape decision-making processes that increasingly displace human judgment.

However, most governance-oriented scholarship emphasizes technical performance and risk management rather than democratic accountability. Discussions often revolve around improving algorithmic accuracy, securing data storage, or refining analytics dashboards (Gamito & Ebers, 2020). What receives far less attention are the power dynamics embedded in these systems. Who defines what counts as student success? Whose data are used, and who benefits from their use? How do predictive systems reshape teacher autonomy or student agency?

The literature on governance also reflects a strong Global North bias. As Kitsara (2022) argues, AI innovation widens the digital divide, yet there is limited research on how algorithmic governance models operate in contexts of infrastructural scarcity or political fragility. Universities in the Global South often adopt AI tools developed in Western contexts, raising concerns about data colonialism (Couldry & Mejias, 2019) and the reproduction of external norms under the guise of technological neutrality.

This lack of geographically diverse research underscores the urgency of examining AI governance through a comparative, equity-centered lens—precisely what the chapter seeks to contribute.

Ethical and Global Frameworks: Fragmented Insights, Limited Critical Integration

International guidelines such as the UNESCO *Guidance for Generative AI in Education and Research* (2023) and the OECD AI principles (2021) provide broad ethical frameworks emphasizing fairness, transparency, human oversight, and accountability. While these standards offer conceptual direction, scholarship examining their implementation remains largely descriptive. Authors tend to summarize principles rather than critically assess institutional challenges, cultural interpretations, or political constraints affecting their adoption.

Parallel critical literature—such as Biesta's (2021) human-centered educational philosophy—warns that the value of education cannot be reduced to measurable outputs alone. Yet these perspectives seldom intersect with empirical research on AI. Instead, AI ethics in education often remains siloed, technical, and reactive, addressing immediate concerns (e.g., plagiarism detection, data privacy) while overlooking systemic, philosophical, and historical dimensions.

This gap between high-level ethical discourse and everyday institutional realities demonstrates the need for work that integrates ethics within pedagogy, governance, and research practices. The chapter advances this integration by framing AI as a socio-technical phenomenon with implications far beyond efficiency or innovation.

RESEARCH GAPS AND NEED FOR THE PRESENT WORK

Although scholarship on AI in higher education has grown rapidly, it remains deeply uneven, marked by conceptual silos, methodological limitations, and persistent ethical blind spots (Thompson et al., 2023). Together, these gaps reveal a field that is technologically advanced yet philosophically underdeveloped—a contradiction that makes clear why a more critical and integrative analysis is urgently required (Rueda et al., 2023). A central shortcoming in the existing literature is its limited engagement with the humanistic and philosophical dimensions of education. Much of the scholarship is preoccupied with technical affordances—improving predictive accuracy, enhancing adaptive learning, scaling automated systems—while offering little reflection on how AI reshapes agency, meaning, or the fundamental purposes of learning (Salloum et al., 2024). The human experience of teaching and scholarship is often overshadowed by an uncritical enthusiasm for algorithmic efficiency. This absence of philosophical grounding results in a discourse that privileges data-driven optimization at the expense of intellectual autonomy, ethical judgment, and educational subjectivity (Hutson & Plate, 2023).

Equally significant is the fragmentation across research domains (Helling & McElnay, 1992). Studies tend to treat pedagogy, research practices, and academic governance as distinct spheres, analyzing AI's impact within one domain without acknowledging its interconnected nature. Such compartmentalization obscures how AI simultaneously influences what is taught, how knowledge is produced, and how academic institutions make decisions (Fowler, 2023). Without a holistic lens, the field fails to capture AI's systemic effects—how pedagogical automation might interact with algorithmic governance, or how changes in research authorship influence wider academic cultures (Bahr, 2024). The epistemic consequences of AI likewise remain insufficiently theorized. Although concerns about authorship and originality are increasingly noted, they are rarely explored in depth. AI-generated texts challenge long-standing ideals of scholarly reflexivity, interpretation, and intellectual labor, yet these shifts have not been fully integrated into broader theoretical discussions about knowledge production (Dempere et al., 2025). The literature tends to address these issues through policy recommendations or technical safeguards rather than through sustained critical inquiry into how AI reconfigures the very conditions of scholarly thought.

The geographic and cultural imbalance of existing research further limits its relevance. Much of the literature is shaped by Global North perspectives, reflecting the technological infrastructures and policy priorities of affluent institutions (Monyei & Akpeji, 2019). Consequently, the realities of the Global South—where AI adoption unfolds within contexts of economic inequality, data dependency, and infrastructural limitations—remain marginal (Okolo, 2023). Discussions of digital colonialism and unequal access to AI tools, although raised by scholars such as Couldry and Mejias (2019), have yet to be meaningfully integrated into mainstream AI-in-education research. This Western-centric orientation risks universalizing experiences that are contingent, and it underestimates the structural consequences of unequal technological development. Finally, the ethical discourse surrounding AI remains disconnected from practice. While international bodies such as UNESCO

(2023) outline principles of fairness, transparency, and accountability, the literature reveals little analysis of how these principles operate within real institutional environments. Ethical frameworks often function as abstract ideals rather than tools that interrogate institutional power, cultural differences, or the complexities of lived academic work. As a result, the conversation around AI ethics tends to be normative rather than transformative (Ghandour, 2024).

Taken together, these gaps underscore the urgent need for a more comprehensive, critically informed framework—one capable of capturing AI's multifaceted influence on higher education. The present chapter responds directly to this need. By weaving together pedagogy, research, and governance; integrating philosophical reflection with sociotechnical critique; and foregrounding issues of equity, epistemic justice, and institutional autonomy, the chapter offers a counter-narrative to technologically deterministic accounts of AI (Peddi & Manoharan, 2025). It reframes AI not merely as a tool of efficiency but as an actor that reshapes knowledge, authority, and educational purpose. In doing so, the chapter contributes to a deeper understanding of how AI is transforming higher education, while also articulating the responsibilities and reflexive capacities institutions must cultivate in response (Machaba & Age, 2025). It argues that safeguarding academic integrity, inclusion, and democratic governance requires confronting—not simply managing—the profound ethical and epistemic shifts introduced by AI. This integrative, critical perspective is precisely what the existing literature lacks, and it is the gap this chapter seeks to fill.

METHODOLOGY

Research Design

The present chapter adopts a critical integrative review as its methodological foundation. This design was chosen because the rapid evolution of Artificial Intelligence and its multidimensional impact on higher education cannot be adequately captured through a singular empirical approach. Instead, the integrative review allows the chapter to weave together diverse strands of scholarship—from pedagogical innovation and research ethics to algorithmic governance and global policy frameworks—into a unified analytical narrative. The approach is intentionally critical, aiming not only to synthesize existing knowledge but also to interrogate the assumptions, contradictions, and power relations embedded within the literature.

Sources of Data and Literature Selection

The analysis draws upon a wide spectrum of materials, including peer-reviewed articles, philosophical texts, institutional reports, and international policy documents. A particular emphasis is placed on scholarship addressing the pedagogical, epistemic, ethical, and governance-related dimensions of AI in higher education. Foundational works such as those of O'Neil, Knox, Peruzzo and Allan, and Couldry and Mejias provide critical insights into algorithmic bias, digital inequalities, and epistemic shifts, while recent studies and reports from 2019 onward enrich the discussion with contemporary empirical and theoretical perspectives.

International frameworks—including the UNESCO Guidance for Generative AI in Education and Research (2023) and the OECD AI Principles (2021)—are incorporated as normative benchmarks against which the chapter evaluates global disparities and governance challenges. These texts were selected because they offer globally recognized standards that shape institutional interpretations of responsible AI adoption.

The choice of literature was guided by conceptual relevance rather than geographical or disciplinary constraints, although it must be acknowledged that much of the available scholarship originates from Global North contexts, reflecting broader structural inequalities in AI research production.

Analytical Approach

The methodological orientation is grounded in *critical hermeneutic analysis,* which allows for an interpretive reading of the selected texts. Rather than treating AI as a purely technical development, the chapter examines it as a socio-technical phenomenon shaped by cultural norms, institutional logics, and epistemic hierarchies. Through this lens, AI is interpreted not merely as a tool but as an agent that influences how knowledge is defined, how authority is distributed, and how academic decision-making unfolds.

To support this interpretive stance, the analysis follows a three-part flow. First, the literature is mapped thematically across key domains such as pedagogy, research practices, governance mechanisms, global inequities, and ethical responsibilities. Second, each domain is analyzed to identify underlying assumptions, ideological tensions, and structural implications. Finally, insights from across domains are synthesized into a holistic conceptual framework presented in the final objective of the chapter. This process allows the chapter to move from descriptive review to critical interpretation and, ultimately, to normative recommendations for sustainable and ethical AI adoption.

Reflexivity and Positionality

Given the value-laden nature of AI in education, the chapter embraces a reflexive methodological stance. The interpretive analysis is informed by a commitment to human-centered education, academic integrity, and social justice. The author's disciplinary grounding in education and social sciences shapes the lens through which the literature is examined, prioritizing questions of equity, agency, and epistemic diversity. This reflexive positioning is not a limitation but a methodological strength, as it foregrounds the ethical and philosophical stakes of AI integration rather than treating it as a neutral technological progression.

Limitations

The methodological approach, while robust for conceptual analysis, has inherent limitations. Because the chapter synthesizes existing literature rather than producing new empirical data, it is constrained by the availability and diversity of published scholarship. The rapid pace of AI development means that certain tools, practices, or policy debates may evolve more quickly than academic publishing cycles allow. Additionally, the predominance of Global North perspectives in AI research introduces a structural limitation, despite the chapter's efforts to highlight global inequities and the risks of digital dependency.

Despite these limitations, the methodology enables the chapter to provide a comprehensive and critical account of AI's multifaceted role in higher education. By integrating insights from pedagogy, epistemology, ethics, governance, and global policy, the chapter constructs a broad, interdisciplinary understanding of AI that extends beyond technical evaluations. This methodological synthesis not only illuminates the complexities of AI adoption but also supports the development of a principled framework for sustainable, inclusive, and ethical integration.

Figure 1. Methodological Framework

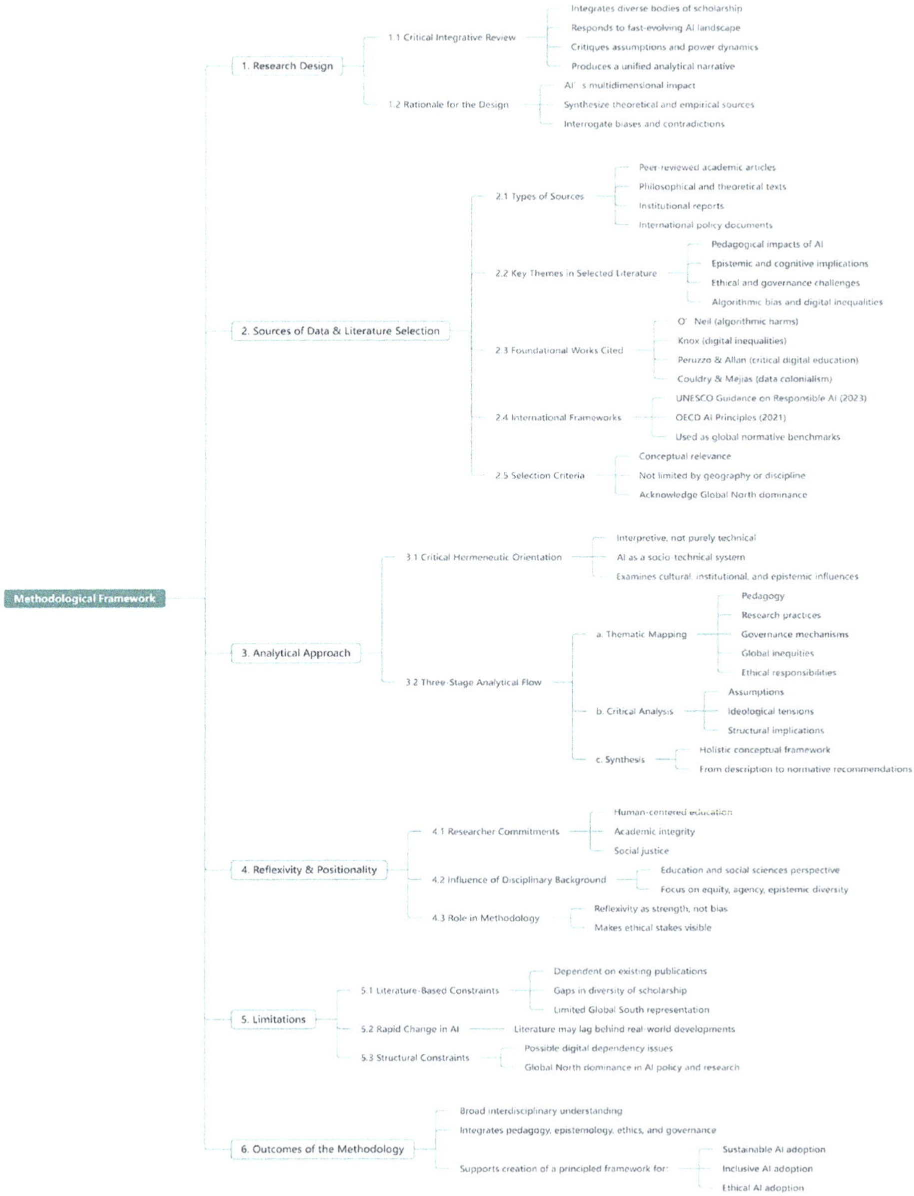

FINDINGS AND DISCUSSION

Objective 1: Critical Examination of How AI Is Reshaping Pedagogy, Research, and Governance in Higher Education

Artificial Intelligence (AI) has rapidly become a transformative force across the core pillars of higher education—teaching, research, and institutional governance (Pandey, 2025). Rather than acting merely as a set of tools, AI now functions as an epistemic and organizational actor shaping how knowledge is produced, how learning is mediated, and how universities make decisions (Ojha, 2025). The reconfiguration of academic practices through algorithms generates both opportunities and profound risks, demanding critical evaluation rather than celebratory acceptance (Taneja et al., 2025). This section examines these transformations through three interrelated domains—pedagogy, research, and governance—highlighting how AI alters the intellectual, ethical, and relational fabric of higher learning.

1.1 Transformation of Pedagogy

The pedagogical landscape of higher education has undergone significant restructuring with the rise of AI-enabled systems that promise personalization, efficiency, and scalability. Among the most prominent developments are adaptive learning systems, which analyze real-time learner data to tailor content, adjust difficulty levels, and provide individualized learning pathways (Leng, 2025). Platforms such as Coursera, Khan Academy's AI-based recommendations, and Knewton's adaptive modules exemplify how AI can automate instructional differentiation, a task traditionally requiring immense teacher labor. These systems offer value by supporting diverse learners, enabling flexible pacing, and providing ongoing formative feedback (Ahamed, 2025).

Intelligent Tutoring Systems (ITS) extend this logic further by simulating one-on-one tutoring interactions. Using natural language processing and machine learning, ITS provides personalized explanations, step-by-step guidance, and conversational support (Chen, 2023). For students in large class environments or remote learning contexts, AI tutors promise increased access to academic support that may otherwise be unavailable. Generative AI models, including LLM-driven assistants, can provide real-time clarification, examples, and explanations across disciplines, potentially leveling disparities in instructional availability (Bello & Aubert, 2025).

Yet, the shift toward AI-mediated instruction is accompanied by significant concerns. Automated assessment and algorithmic grading, now widely used in MOOCs and increasingly in universities, streamline evaluation processes but risk reducing learning to quantifiable outputs (Torrisi-Steele, 2025). Automated essay scoring, plagiarism detection, and coding autograders emphasize pattern recognition and consistency but often overlook nuance, creativity, and context-specific reasoning. While these tools can free faculty from administrative burdens, they introduce risks of algorithmic bias and errors that disproportionately affect marginalized learners whose language, cultural references, or writing styles may not align with training datasets (Vangibhuratha, 2025) (Agrawal et al., 2025).

The pedagogical implications extend beyond technical concerns into the domain of educational philosophy (Agate et al., 2020). The phenomenon of automation bias—the overtrust of machine-generated outputs- raises questions about the erosion of critical thinking. Students may accept AI explanations without questioning underlying assumptions, while instructors may become overly reliant on automated analytics to interpret learning progress (Paraschiv, 2025). This shift can weaken the reflective and dialogic dimensions of pedagogy, which are central to higher education's humanistic mission.

Moreover, the impact on teacher–learner relationships is profound. AI systems increasingly mediate interactions, from chatbots handling student queries to algorithmic alerts identifying "at-risk" students. While useful, these systems risk displacing relational teaching practices grounded in empathy, intuition, and professional judgment (Nikitina & Ishchenko, 2024). The teacher's role may be reconfigured from expert and mentor to "manager of algorithms," reducing autonomy and reshaping professional identity. When educational authority shifts toward systems optimized for efficiency and prediction, the relational, ethical, and dialogical aspects of teaching may be overshadowed (Kayyali, 2025).

Ultimately, the transformation of pedagogy through AI introduces both enhanced personalization and troubling forms of depersonalization. Higher education must grapple with balancing technological potential with the preservation of human-centered learning.

1.2 Transformation of Research Practices

AI has also reshaped research practices, fundamentally altering how knowledge is produced, evaluated, and disseminated. One of the most significant developments is the use of AI in automating literature reviews, where models can scan thousands of articles, summarize findings, identify themes, and even generate annotated bibliographies (Zala et al., 2024). This accelerates early phases of research, allowing scholars to process vast bodies of knowledge efficiently. Similarly, AI-powered tools facilitate data analysis, whether through pattern recognition in large datasets, predictive modeling, or visualization. Fields such as genomics, social network analysis, and climate modeling have benefited enormously from these capabilities (Zhang, 2025).

Beyond methodological support, generative AI now participates directly in hypothesis generation, suggesting research questions or analytic directions based on patterns extracted from existing knowledge (Boy & Doneddu, 2025). While such contributions expand intellectual horizons, they also raise concerns about the mechanization of inquiry and the diminishing role of human intuition and creativity.

A more contentious transformation involves the integration of generative AI into scholarly writing. Tools capable of producing summaries, drafts, and even full manuscripts challenge traditional notions of authorship, originality, and scholarly labor. Publishers and academic institutions have begun developing guidelines on AI disclosure, reflecting widespread concern about transparency and ethical accountability (Dwivedi et al., 2024). When AI becomes a co-producer of text, the epistemic foundations of scholarly communication shift. Academic writing, once understood as a site of reflective interpretation and personal intellectual contribution, risks moving toward standardized, machine-generated prose (Bakla, 2023).

This shift entails significant risks. One of the most pressing is the homogenization of knowledge. Since generative models are trained on dominant corpora—largely from Western, English-language sources—their outputs may reproduce existing power structures and underrepresent minority epistemologies (Lin & Sohail, 2025). This carries implications for the diversity of academic thought and the democratization of research.

Additionally, the rapid automation of research processes can lead to reduced reflexivity. As AI streamlines analysis and writing, scholars may bypass the slow, interpretive, and iterative processes necessary for deep conceptual insight. Overreliance on automated analysis may weaken critical engagement with data, resulting in "thin scholarship" that privileges efficiency over intellectual depth (Duke, 2025).

Thus, while AI offers powerful tools for enhancing research productivity, it also threatens to reshape scholarly norms in ways that challenge the integrity, diversity, and reflective character of academic knowledge production.

1.3 Transformation of Academic Governance

The influence of AI extends beyond teaching and research into the governance structures that underpin higher education institutions. Universities increasingly deploy AI-driven systems to manage admissions, monitor student performance, evaluate faculty, and conduct institutional planning. This movement toward algorithmic governance reflects a broader societal shift toward data-driven decision-making, where predictive analytics and automated dashboards guide policy and administrative action.

In admissions, AI tools analyze academic records, behavioral indicators, and demographic data to predict student success or risk. Although such systems promise objectivity, they often replicate historical biases embedded in training datasets (Lee et al., 2023). As seen in high-profile cases of flawed algorithmic admissions, predictive models may disadvantage students from underrepresented communities or non-traditional educational backgrounds.

Similarly, faculty evaluation systems increasingly incorporate AI-driven analytics that track publications, citations, teaching performance metrics, and student feedback. While offering standardized forms of assessment, these systems can oversimplify complex academic labor and reinforce productivity pressures that marginalize disciplines with slower or less quantifiable output cycles (Watermeyer et al., 2023; Bhattacharya & Sabeena, 2025).

The rise of dashboard governance consolidates decision-making through real-time analytics interfaces that visualize performance indicators across departments. Administrators are encouraged to make "data-informed decisions," yet the datasets themselves may reflect reductive metrics of learning or research quality (Prinsloo, 2019). This contributes to the rise of "data-driven universities," where managerial priorities centered on efficiency and prediction shape academic culture (Dollinger, 2020).

The risks associated with AI-based governance are substantial. First, opacity is a major concern. When algorithmic decisions influence admissions or evaluation without transparent reasoning, individuals and institutions have limited avenues for contestation (Shtayyat et al., 2025). Second, the potential for systemic bias threatens core principles of equity and fairness. Finally, the misuse of student data, including behavioral analytics and personal identifiers, raises ethical and legal questions about surveillance, consent, and institutional responsibility (Mishara, 2024).

These governance transformations reflect a deeper philosophical shift from deliberative, human-centered decision-making to automated, metric-driven administration. While AI may support informed planning, its unchecked integration risks reducing universities to technocratic systems governed by algorithms rather than academic values.

Taken together, the transformations in pedagogy, research, and governance reflect an epochal shift in higher education. AI offers remarkable possibilities for personalization, efficiency, and innovation, yet it also challenges foundational principles of academic autonomy, epistemic diversity, and relational learning. As universities navigate this landscape, the central challenge lies not in adopting AI but in critically shaping its role within the academy. Ensuring that human judgment, reflective inquiry, and ethical awareness remain at the core of higher education will be essential to steering AI's influence toward empowerment rather than erosion of academic values.

Objective 2: Epistemic, Ethical, and Institutional Consequences of Overdependence on AI in Higher Education

The rapid expansion of Artificial Intelligence within higher education has not only reconfigured teaching and research practices but has also produced deeper epistemic, ethical, and institutional consequences. As universities increasingly rely on automated tools for learning analytics, scholarly production, and governance, the nature of academic authority, knowledge creation, and institutional autonomy is being renegotiated (Popenici & Kerr, 2017). Overdependence on AI risks shifting higher education toward a technocratic paradigm where data-driven rationality supersedes human deliberation, raising questions about justice, transparency, and the fundamental purpose of academic institutions (Popenici, 2023). This section critically examines these consequences across three levels: epistemic, ethical, and institutional.

2.1 Epistemic Consequences

AI's growing presence in higher education precipitates significant epistemic consequences, fundamentally altering the ways knowledge is produced, validated, and interpreted. One of the most prominent shifts is the transition from human deliberation to computational rationality, where judgments once grounded in disciplinary expertise and interpretive reasoning are now influenced—or even superseded—by algorithmic outputs (Upreti, 2025). Whether in predicting student success, identifying research trends, or recommending learning pathways, AI systems privilege patterns derived from data over contextual insight, resulting in a narrowing of epistemic diversity.

This shift also transforms notions of knowledge, authority, and expertise. Traditionally, academic expertise is cultivated through years of study, reflective inquiry, and methodological rigor (Brown, 2014). However, AI systems increasingly assume the role of intellectual intermediaries—summarizing literature, generating arguments, and synthesizing research trends. When students or researchers consult AI tools before consulting human experts—or when administrators rely on algorithmic analytics to make judgments—AI becomes an epistemic authority in its own right (Hutson & Plate, 2023). Such authority is not neutral: algorithms encode the assumptions, values, and biases of their creators, often reflecting dominant cultural and linguistic patterns.

Consequently, AI emerges as an epistemic actor that actively shapes how knowledge is formed and circulated. Its outputs appear objective due to their computational nature, yet they are conditioned by the training datasets largely drawn from Western academic corpora (Zermeño Flores et al., 2024). This reinforces existing inequalities by elevating dominant epistemologies while marginalizing alternative or Indigenous perspectives. As AI-written summaries, explanations, and essays become normalized, there is a risk that human understanding becomes mediated almost entirely through machine-generated interpretations of knowledge (Praveenkumar et al., 2025).

Furthermore, overreliance on AI tools risks fostering decontextualized learning and knowledge homogenization. AI tends to generalize and standardize its outputs, flattening complex intellectual traditions into simplified narratives. When students repeatedly rely on AI to explain concepts, produce examples, or structure arguments, the nuance and contextual richness of disciplinary knowledge may erode (Steele, 2023). Over time, this can diminish critical thinking and reduce academic inquiry to the reproduction of algorithmically pre-processed ideas.

Thus, the epistemic consequences of AI overdependence are far-reaching: the redefinition of expertise, the mechanization of inquiry, and the gradual displacement of human reasoning by computational logic. While AI can enhance academic work, its unchecked dominance threatens the diversity, depth, and autonomy of scholarly knowledge.

2.2 Ethical Consequences

Alongside epistemic concerns, AI's integration into higher education raises significant ethical dilemmas, particularly regarding bias, fairness, transparency, data privacy, and the use of proprietary technologies (Ghandour, 2024). AI systems, despite their appearance of neutrality, are deeply embedded within socio-political and historical contexts that shape their development and deployment.

One of the most persistent ethical issues is algorithmic bias, which arises from skewed or incomplete datasets used to train AI models. When used in admissions, hiring, or performance prediction, biased algorithms can reinforce structural inequalities by reproducing patterns of disadvantage encoded in historical data (Prajapati, 2025). This challenges the principle of fairness, as students from marginalized backgrounds may be disproportionately misclassified or disadvantaged by algorithmic decisions.

Another critical ethical challenge relates to AI-generated research and authorship. Generative AI tools can produce essays, literature reviews, and even conceptual frameworks, prompting questions about originality, intellectual labor, and scholarly integrity (Bjelobaba et al., 2024). The ability of AI to produce high-quality academic text may incentivize unethical practices, including undisclosed AI-generated content or reliance on AI as a substitute for genuine scholarly engagement. Moreover, scholars must grapple with who—or what—counts as an author when machine outputs are integrated into academic work (Scott-Herring, 2024).

Concerns about data privacy and surveillance are equally pressing. Universities increasingly collect large volumes of data through learning management systems, proctoring software, and analytics platforms, creating environments of continuous monitoring (Szcyrek & Stewart, 2022). AI-powered surveillance tools—such as facial recognition, keystroke tracking, and behavioral analytics—blur the boundaries between student support and institutional oversight (Mishara, 2024). This raises questions about consent, autonomy, and the disproportionate monitoring of certain student groups.

The ethical implications are compounded by widespread dependence on proprietary AI systems, controlled by a small number of global technology corporations. Universities often lack insight into how these systems process data, make decisions, or manage user information (Zeer et al., 2023). This creates asymmetrical power relationships in which universities become dependent on external vendors for core academic and administrative functions. Such dependence undermines institutional sovereignty and risks exposing sensitive student or research data to third-party interests.

In summary, the ethical consequences of AI overreliance highlight the urgent need for transparent processes, robust governance frameworks, and critical digital literacy among students, staff, and administrators.

2.3 Institutional Consequences

Beyond epistemic and ethical concerns, AI overdependence produces significant institutional consequences that reshape organizational autonomy, governance practices, and academic culture. Perhaps the most profound impact is on the autonomy of universities, which historically operated as self-governing spaces dedicated to independent inquiry (Lin & Sohail, 2025). The adoption of AI-driven systems—often developed by external corporations—risks shifting control over key institutional processes to automated infrastructures that universities do not fully understand or regulate.

This aligns with broader trends of managerialism and technocratic governance, wherein decision-making increasingly relies on data dashboards, predictive analytics, and automated ranking systems (Nayeem, 2025). Administrative priorities are shaped by what can be measured and quantified, privileging performance metrics over qualitative dimensions of academic life such as mentorship, intellectual community, or social engagement (Leišytė, 2022). Such managerial systems often reduce complex educational processes to data points, narrowing institutional values to efficiency and productivity.

These dynamics generate accountability gaps, where decisions made or influenced by AI become difficult to audit or contest (Coyle et al., 2020). When an algorithm flags a student as "at-risk," or when a model predicts faculty research output, who bears responsibility for subsequent actions? If errors occur, responsibility may diffuse between vendors, administrators, and technical staff, hindering transparency and undermining trust. Institutions may struggle to justify decisions made through opaque systems, especially when those decisions have significant academic or personal implications.

Overdependence on AI also contributes to the rise of "metric-driven academia," where scholarly worth, teaching quality, and institutional success are evaluated through quantitative indicators produced by automated systems (Taneja et al., 2025; Karamuk, 2025). This environment incentivizes behaviors aligned with algorithmic priorities—such as increasing publication volume or optimizing student satisfaction ratings—while devaluing slow, critical, or community-engaged scholarship (Agate et al., 2020). As academic culture shifts toward machine-mediated evaluation, the intrinsic values of higher education risk being overshadowed by external metrics.

Furthermore, institutional inequalities may deepen. Wealthier universities can invest in advanced AI infrastructures, whereas institutions in the Global South or underfunded regions may become dependent on externally provided platforms, reinforcing dynamics of data colonialism (Nimbalagundi et al., 2024). Local educational priorities may be displaced by systems designed for different cultural or economic contexts, compromising institutional relevance and autonomy.

Taken together, these institutional consequences warn against unreflective adoption of AI. Without deliberate oversight, universities risk becoming data-driven organizations where algorithmic logic shapes governance, culture, and purpose (Aper, 2024).

The epistemic, ethical, and institutional consequences of AI overdependence reveal that the challenges posed by AI extend far beyond technical integration. They involve fundamental shifts in how knowledge is produced, how educational relationships are structured, and how institutional decisions are made. Although AI offers powerful tools for enhancing efficiency and expanding academic capabilities, reliance on these systems must be balanced with safeguards that protect epistemic diversity, ethical integrity, and institutional autonomy. Only through critical oversight, transparent governance, and a reaffirmation of academic values can higher education ensure that AI strengthens rather than undermines its foundational mission.

Objective 3: Global Disparities and Policy Responses to AI Integration, with Emphasis on Equity and Academic Integrity

The global expansion of Artificial Intelligence across higher education has been neither uniform nor equitable. While AI promises unprecedented innovation and efficiency, its benefits are distributed unevenly across regions, institutions, and social groups. The uneven development of technological infrastructure, combined with socio-economic and geopolitical asymmetries, has created profound disparities between the Global North and the Global South. These disparities shape not only who gains access to AI but also whose knowledge (Upreti, 2025; Aprianto et al., 2024), languages, and cultures become embedded—or excluded—from the AI ecosystem. At the same time, international organizations have attempted to develop ethical and governance frameworks to guide AI adoption, though the translation of these frameworks into local contexts remains uneven. This section critically examines global disparities and policy responses, concluding with an assessment of how equity and academic integrity are being challenged—and can be protected—in an AI-driven higher education landscape.

3.1 Global North–South Disparities

The integration of AI in higher education reflects and reinforces longstanding global inequalities. Institutions in the Global North—particularly in North America, Western Europe, and parts of East Asia—possess the infrastructure, funding, and expertise necessary to not only adopt AI tools but to develop them (Akinwalere & Ivanov, 2022). In contrast, many universities in the Global South, including regions in Africa, South Asia, and Latin America, face limited access to high-speed internet, inadequate computational resources, and insufficient institutional investment (Abulibdeh et al., 2023). These disparities constrain their ability to benefit from AI-driven pedagogical innovations, research tools, and administrative systems.

A central dimension of this inequality is data colonialism, in which data extracted primarily from Global South populations feeds AI systems built, owned, and controlled by corporations in the Global North. Higher education institutions often depend on proprietary software for everything from plagiarism detection to predictive analytics, creating technological dependency (Kponyo et al., 2024). This dependency reinforces structural hierarchies: universities in the South become consumers of AI technologies designed elsewhere, rather than co-creators shaping how these tools evolve. As Couldry and Mejias argue, such forms of extraction reproduce colonial logics where data becomes the new resource through which power is consolidated.

Another source of disparity is the underrepresentation of Global South identities, languages, and epistemologies in AI training datasets. Large Language Models (LLMs), image recognition tools, and predictive analytics systems overwhelmingly reflect Western-centric sources, linguistic corpora, and conceptual frameworks (Cetinic, 2022). As a result, academic content generated or mediated by AI tends to privilege Western scholarship while marginalizing Indigenous knowledge systems, local research priorities, and culturally diverse perspectives. This epistemic imbalance risks reinforcing global hierarchies within academic knowledge production.

Researchers in the Global South face additional barriers, including limited access to high-cost AI tools, lack of training in data science or machine learning, and reduced visibility in international research networks. Moreover, stringent intellectual property regimes and expensive subscription-based platforms further restrict participation in cutting-edge AI research (Kshetri, 2024). Without targeted interventions, AI adoption may deepen existing research inequities and perpetuate the concentration of academic authority in technologically dominant regions.

In sum, global disparities in AI adoption are not merely technological but epistemic, economic, and political, requiring deliberate policies to ensure that higher education remains inclusive and globally representative.

3.2 Policy Responses

Recognizing the risks and inequities posed by rapid AI expansion, international organizations and national governments have formulated policy frameworks to guide responsible AI integration. Among the most influential is the UNESCO Guidance for Generative AI in Education and Research (2023), which provides a comprehensive set of principles oriented around human rights, equity, and academic integrity (Mutawa, 2024). UNESCO emphasizes five key areas: transparency, data protection, human oversight, inclusive governance, and capacity-building for low-resource contexts (Peddi & Manoharan, 2025). These guidelines explicitly acknowledge the Global South's needs by calling for equitable access to AI infrastructure, culturally responsive datasets, and global collaboration in AI governance. Notably, UNESCO advocates for AI systems that respect linguistic diversity and promote open educational resources accessible to all regions.

Similarly, the OECD AI Principles (2021) outline a framework grounded in fairness, accountability, transparency, and safety. While primarily shaped by high-income member nations, the principles have been adopted globally and set a standard for responsible AI development (Jobin et al., 2019). In the context of higher education, the OECD framework stresses the need for explainability in algorithmic decision-making and robust mechanisms for redress when harm occurs. Importantly, it highlights the necessity of human-centered approaches to AI, reinforcing the idea that automated tools must augment—not replace—human judgment (Farooqi, 2025).

Despite these global frameworks, national policy responses vary widely. Countries such as Canada, Singapore, and the United Kingdom have developed detailed AI strategies emphasizing innovation, ethics, and workforce development. Meanwhile, nations with limited technological capacity face challenges implementing similar policies, resulting in fragmented governance across the Global South. Some countries emphasize digital sovereignty—seeking to build local AI ecosystems—while others rely heavily on imported technologies, thereby increasing dependency (Schmitt &

Schmitt, 2021). China represents a unique case with its strong state-driven AI agenda, integrating AI extensively into governance and higher education while maintaining strict regulatory oversight.

Although global frameworks provide important guidance, the gap between policy and practice remains significant (Sadki, 2017). Many universities lack internal governance structures to assess AI tools for bias, transparency, or alignment with academic values. Moreover, the rapid pace of AI innovation outstrips the ability of regulatory bodies to monitor or intervene effectively. As a result, AI integration often proceeds according to market forces rather than ethical considerations, exacerbating disparities identified in Section 3.1.

Altogether, policy responses demonstrate global awareness of AI's risks but highlight the need for stronger implementation mechanisms, regional collaboration, and context-sensitive governance.

3.3 Equity & Academic Integrity

Beyond global disparities and policy debates, the rise of AI introduces profound questions of equity and academic integrity within higher education. One immediate concern is AI-generated plagiarism, as students increasingly use generative AI tools to produce essays, answers, or research content (Fowler, 2023). Traditional plagiarism detectors struggle to identify AI-generated text, challenging institutions to rethink definitions of authorship, originality, and academic misconduct. Without clear guidelines, students in well-resourced institutions—who have better access to AI tools—may gain unfair academic advantages over peers with limited access (Steponenaite & Barakat, 2023).

AI also introduces integrity issues in automated research workflows. Tools that summarize literature, generate hypotheses, or produce statistical analyses may embed inaccuracies or biases, yet researchers may accept these outputs uncritically due to automation bias (Silva & Janes, 2025). This threatens the rigor and reliability of scholarship. Ensuring integrity requires robust training in AI literacy so scholars can understand the limitations and risks of these systems.

A deeper concern relates to equitable access to AI tools and competencies. Students and researchers in affluent institutions are better positioned to use AI for learning, writing, data processing, and publication, enhancing their competitiveness in global academia. Conversely, individuals in under-resourced contexts risk falling further behind. Without deliberate measures—including subsidized access to AI platforms, open-source alternatives, and global capacity-building initiatives—AI may widen academic inequities rather than bridge them (Khatri & Karki, 2023).

Ultimately, addressing equity and academic integrity requires institutions to combine ethical guidelines with practical interventions: transparent policies on AI use, accessible training programs, and equitable distribution of technological resources. Only through such measures can higher education uphold fairness and prevent the creation of an AI-based academic divide (Ocen, Elasu, Aarakit, & Olupot, 2025).

Global disparities in AI adoption underscore the need for context-sensitive, equity-driven governance that addresses technological dependency, epistemic exclusion, and unequal participation in AI-driven scholarship. International frameworks such as UNESCO and OECD provide guiding principles, yet their effectiveness depends on meaningful local implementation and systemic support for marginalized regions (Guridi & Cheyre, 2024). Ensuring academic integrity and equitable access to AI tools is essential for preventing new forms of inequality in the academic ecosystem. As AI becomes more deeply integrated into higher education, the challenge is not only to expand access but to ensure that AI strengthens, rather than undermines, the inclusive and democratic mission of universities.

Objective 4: Investigating the Challenges and Potentials of Human–AI Collaboration in Higher Education

Human–AI collaboration has emerged as a defining feature of the contemporary academic landscape, reshaping how knowledge is produced, how learning unfolds, and how decisions are made. Unlike earlier forms of educational technology, AI systems do not merely extend human capabilities; they participate actively in cognitive and creative processes (Kayyali, 2025). This integration signals both transformative potential and significant risks. While AI offers enhanced efficiency, creativity, and insight, it simultaneously threatens to undermine human agency, critical thinking, and professional autonomy. The challenge for higher education is to develop a collaborative model that maximizes AI's benefits while safeguarding its intellectual and ethical foundations. This section explores the potentials, challenges, and pathways toward a balanced human–AI synergy.

4.1 Potentials of Human–AI Collaboration

AI's capacity to augment human creativity represents one of the most promising dimensions of collaboration. In research contexts, AI-powered tools can analyze patterns across vast datasets, generate hypotheses, propose methodological approaches, and even draft preliminary summaries or conceptual outlines (Salah et al., 2023). This process of augmented creativity does not replace human insight; instead, it accelerates ideation, enabling researchers to explore conceptual directions that might otherwise remain hidden. For example, generative AI models can simulate alternative interpretations, identify connections across disciplines, or suggest innovative solutions to complex problems. Scholars thus gain a partner capable of rapid synthesis and imaginative reframing, broadening the scope of intellectual exploration (Petrenko, 2024).

Another key potential lies in intelligent decision-support tools, which help academics and administrators make more informed and timely decisions. Predictive analytics can identify patterns in student performance, flag regions where curricular redesign is needed, or forecast resource requirements (Manzoor, 2016). AI-enhanced dashboards synthesize immense volumes of institutional data into actionable insights, supporting evidence-based governance. When used responsibly, decision-support systems can increase transparency, reduce administrative burden, and promote adaptive planning aligned with student needs (Zhang & Goyal, 2024).

Human–AI collaboration also enhances feedback and personalized tutoring. AI-driven systems are capable of providing immediate, contextually relevant feedback on student work, identifying misconceptions, and offering tailored instructional pathways. This allows instructors to shift focus from routine explanations toward higher-order pedagogical activities such as mentoring, dialogue, and conceptual clarification (Kshetri & Kshetri, 2023). Students benefit from increased access to learning support, particularly in large or remote learning environments where instructor feedback may be limited.

Finally, AI accelerates knowledge discovery by enabling faster literature searches, more efficient coding and data analysis, and rapid synthesis of emerging trends in a given field. For researchers working with complex or large-scale datasets—such as genomic scientists, social data analysts, or digital humanities scholars—AI can significantly reduce labor-intensive tasks, allowing greater emphasis on interpretation, theorizing, and contextual reflection (Zhang, 2025).

In these ways, AI enhances academic work by expanding human capacities, supporting creativity, and improving instructional effectiveness. Yet these potentials must be understood alongside the challenges they introduce.

4.2 Challenges in Collaboration

Despite its many benefits, human–AI collaboration presents profound challenges, particularly concerning agency, critical thinking, professional autonomy, and ethical integrity.

A central risk is the loss of human agency in academic decision-making. As AI systems become more embedded in learning management platforms, research workflows, and administrative processes, humans may defer to algorithmic outputs even when these systems operate with incomplete or biased data (Han et al., 2023). Automation bias—the tendency to trust machine-generated judgments—can lead to diminished human oversight and weakened capacity to question or interpret results. Faculty and administrators may come to depend heavily on algorithmic recommendations, gradually ceding intellectual autonomy to software systems (Crain et al., 2025).

This also contributes to the erosion of critical thinking among students and scholars. Generative AI tools can readily produce explanations, summaries, diagrams, and examples, which students may rely on unquestioningly. While such tools offer convenience, overuse encourages passive consumption of information rather than active engagement with ideas (Protopapa & Idris, 2025). In research contexts, automated literature synthesis or statistical analysis may discourage scholars from engaging deeply with underlying assumptions, conceptual frameworks, or methodological complexities.

A related concern is overreliance and deskilling, whereby individuals lose skills previously central to academic and professional identity. If students routinely rely on AI for structuring essays, generating arguments, or conducting preliminary research, they may fail to develop foundational competencies in critical reading, reasoning, and writing (Yavich, 2025). Likewise, faculty who depend excessively on AI for grading, course design, or research analysis may experience erosion of their pedagogical and scholarly expertise. Over time, such deskilling can weaken the intellectual rigor and autonomy necessary for academic excellence.

Human–AI collaboration also raises ethical constraints in co-created content. As AI tools generate text, code, and visual materials, questions emerge regarding authorship, attribution, and intellectual property. Universities face growing challenges in determining whether AI-assisted work constitutes original scholarship, how much AI involvement is acceptable, and how to ensure transparency in academic submissions (Mishra et al., 2025). Without clear guidelines, the integrity of academic output may be compromised, and disputes over ownership or authenticity may proliferate.

These challenges highlight the need for deliberate structures and educational strategies to preserve human agency, critical judgment, and professional competence within an AI-driven academic ecosystem.

4.3 Toward a Balanced Human–AI Synergy

Achieving a sustainable model of human–AI collaboration requires intentional strategies that prioritize human judgment, ethical awareness, and reflective practice. A foundational step is the development of AI literacy among students, faculty, and administrators (Torrisi-Steele, 2025). AI literacy extends beyond technical competence to include critical understanding of AI's assumptions, biases, limitations, and ethical implications. Educators must design curricula that teach learners not only how to use AI tools but how to question and contextualize their outputs (Pinski & Benlian, 2024).

Equally important is ensuring human oversight and reflexive critical thinking. AI systems must operate under the supervision of knowledgeable individuals who can interpret results, identify errors, and make informed decisions (Sonko et al., 2024). This requires cultivating a culture of scrutiny rather than blind trust, where academic actors retain responsibility for judgment and ensure AI serves as an aid rather than a substitute for human reasoning.

Finally, the design and adoption of "convivial" technologies, as proposed by Peruzzo and Allan, offers a path toward collaborative systems that complement rather than dominate human agency. Convivial technologies are inclusive, transparent, and aligned with human-centered pedagogical values (Sánchez Santamaría, 2025). They support collaboration, creativity, and diversity rather than enforcing rigid, efficiency-driven logics. Incorporating these principles into AI design can help create tools that enhance rather than constrain academic life.

By integrating AI literacy, human oversight, and convivial design, higher education can foster a balanced synergy where AI empowers rather than eclipses human potential. This model emphasizes partnership, critical engagement, and ethical accountability—key components of a thriving academic ecosystem in the age of AI.

Objective 5: A Framework for Sustainable, Inclusive, and Ethical AI Adoption in Higher Education

As Artificial Intelligence becomes increasingly embedded within higher education, institutions must adopt governance models that move beyond enthusiasm for innovation and address the deeper philosophical, social, and ethical implications of AI (Sam & Olbrich, 2023). Sustainable adoption requires more than the deployment of new technologies—it demands a strategic framework that aligns AI integration with the core values of higher learning: academic integrity, epistemic diversity, equity, human-centered pedagogy, and democratic governance. This objective proposes such a framework by outlining principles for sustainable, inclusive, and ethical AI adoption, culminating in a consolidated model that universities can use to guide implementation across teaching, research, and institutional decision-making.

5.1 Principles for Sustainable AI Adoption

Sustainable AI adoption requires institutions to ensure that technological integration enhances, rather than diminishes, the intellectual and social mission of universities. Central to this is the principle of human-centered design, which emphasizes that AI tools must augment human capabilities rather than automate or replace them.

Human-centered AI prioritizes pedagogical relationships, intellectual autonomy, and creative inquiry (Popenici, 2023). Systems should be designed with academic users—students, faculty, and administrators—in mind, ensuring that technological functions support learning, reflection, and interpretation rather than imposing rigid or opaque processes.

Another cornerstone of sustainability is transparency, interpretability, and accountability. AI systems used in higher education—whether for admissions, grading, advising, or research—must be explainable to both technical and non-technical stakeholder (Chaudhry et al., 2022). Transparency allows users to understand how algorithmic decisions are made, interpretability enables critical evaluation of outputs, and accountability ensures that responsibility for errors or harms can be traced to human decision-makers. Universities should require vendors to provide documentation, model cards, or transparency reports that describe data sources, assumptions, and limitations.

Sustainability also requires long-term institutional capacity building. AI adoption cannot be outsourced entirely to external corporations; universities must invest in digital infrastructure, training, and governance structures that allow for ongoing evaluation and adaptation (Khan et al., 2025). Capacity building includes developing internal expertise in AI ethics, data management, and algorithmic auditing; training faculty and students in AI literacy; and establishing interdisciplinary committees to oversee AI governance. Such investment ensures resilience, reduces reliance on external vendors, and enables institutions to update systems as technologies evolve.

When grounded in human-centered design, transparency, and capacity building, sustainable AI adoption supports academic innovation while preserving the intellectual and ethical foundations of higher education.

5.2 Principles for Inclusive AI Adoption

Inclusivity is essential to ensuring that AI enhances educational equity rather than reinforcing existing inequalities. A first priority is closing infrastructure gaps that disadvantage institutions in the Global South or under-resourced regions within countries. Universities must advocate for public investment in digital infrastructure, open-access AI tools, and affordable high-performance computing resources (Leng, 2025). Partnerships between institutions—regional, national, or international—can help reduce disparities in access to AI technologies and training.

Inclusivity also requires the development of culturally responsive AI systems. Most AI tools used in higher education are trained predominantly on Western data, linguistic corpora, and epistemological assumptions. This risks marginalizing non-Western knowledge systems, languages, and cultural contexts. Institutions should therefore demand AI systems that include diverse training datasets, support multilingual content, and align with local pedagogical values (Mahboob et al., 2023). Researchers and developers in the Global South must be meaningfully involved in the design and evaluation of AI tools to ensure contextual relevance and epistemic justice.

A third pillar of inclusive adoption concerns ethical procurement and data sovereignty. Universities must assess whether AI tools comply with local ethical norms, respect data privacy laws, and provide institutions with long-term control over their data (Barnes & Hutson, 2024). Ethical procurement requires evaluating vendors for transparency, fairness, and open documentation; ensuring that student and faculty data are not exploited for commercial purposes; and negotiating contracts that prevent lock-in or undue dependency. Data sovereignty is especially crucial for institutions in low-income countries, which risk having sensitive academic data stored in foreign jurisdictions under unclear governance regimes.

Together, these principles ensure that AI adoption does not exacerbate inequalities but instead promotes equitable access, cultural inclusion, and institutional self-determination—critical ingredients for a just global higher education system.

5.3 Principles for Ethical AI Adoption

Ethical AI adoption in higher education requires proactive strategies to safeguard academic integrity, mitigate bias, and protect personal data. The first component is establishing robust academic integrity safeguards. Universities must develop clear guidelines for acceptable AI use in coursework, research writing, and assessment (Barnes & Hutson, 2024). These guidelines should distinguish between permissible assistance—such as grammar correction or data visualization—and unethical practices like using AI to generate entire essays or articles without disclosure. Institutions should also invest in educational initiatives that teach students to use AI responsibly and transparently.

A second ethical priority is the implementation of bias mitigation strategies. AI systems can perpetuate and amplify biases embedded in their training data, leading to unfair treatment in admissions, grading, or predictive analytics used to monitor student performance. Universities should adopt algorithmic auditing procedures to detect and correct discriminatory patterns (Sudhir, 2024). This may involve conducting regular equity impact assessments, testing systems across demographic groups, and requiring vendors to demonstrate bias mitigation measures before procurement.

Finally, ethical adoption necessitates stringent consent and data protection protocols. AI systems often rely on vast amounts of personal information, including behavioral data collected from learning management systems, proctoring software, and digital platforms. Institutions must ensure that students and faculty understand what data are collected, how they are used, and who has access. Consent must be informed, freely given, and revocable (Sywelem & Mahklouf, 2024). Data protection policies should include encryption, limited retention periods, and restrictions on third-party sharing. Institutions must also avoid invasive monitoring technologies that compromise privacy under the guise of academic integrity or efficiency.

By embedding integrity safeguards, bias mitigation, and strong data protection into institutional policies, universities can uphold ethical principles and foster trust in AI systems.

Figure 2. Framework for Sustainable, Inclusive, and Ethical AI Adoption in Higher Education

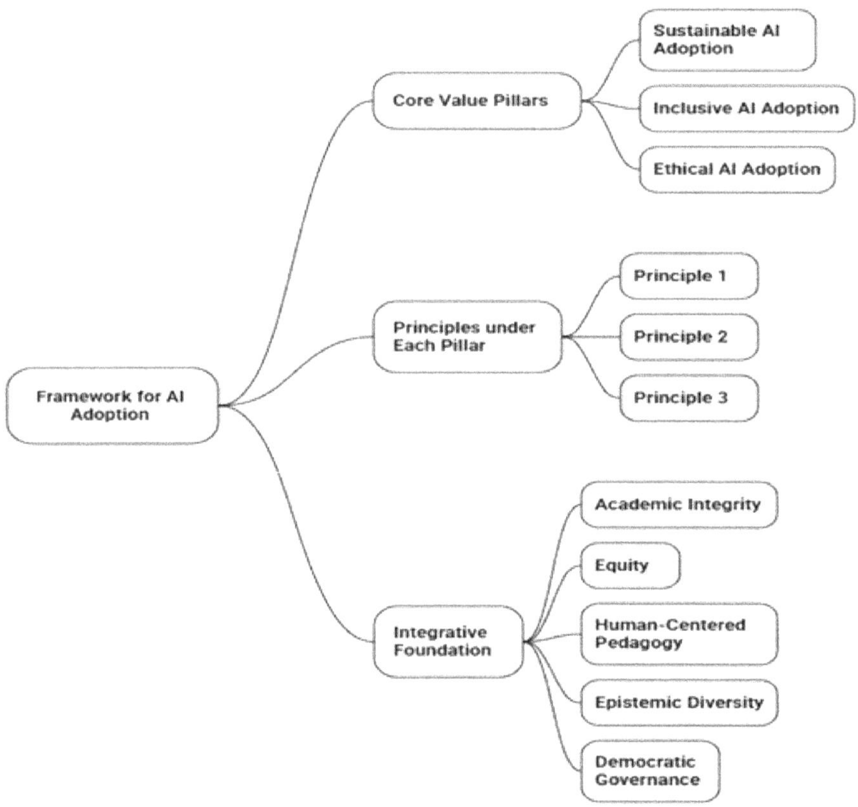

5.4 The Proposed Framework

Bringing together the principles of sustainability, inclusivity, and ethics, this section outlines a holistic framework designed to guide responsible AI adoption in higher education. The model integrates five interconnected domains—pedagogy, research, governance, equity, and ethics—ensuring that AI enhances academic life as a transformative partner rather than functioning as an instrument of automation or exclusion. Each domain highlights a critical dimension through which AI can strengthen, rather than weaken, the educational mission.

1. Pedagogy: Advancing Human-Centered Learning

Within the pedagogical domain, institutions are encouraged to adopt human-centered AI that supports meaningful and relational learning experiences. Rather than replacing educators or reducing learning to automated processes, AI should be used to enhance dialogue, creativity, critical thinking, and multimodal expression.

Key Points

- AI should scaffold learning without diminishing student agency.
- Generative tools must foster creative inquiry, not passive consumption.
- Systems should enable multiple learning pathways tailored to diverse learners (Torrisi-Steele, 2025).

A sustainable pedagogical framework positions AI as a facilitator of participatory, contextualized learning—strengthening, rather than mechanizing, the educational environment.

2. Research: Augmentation, Transparency, and Integrity

In research, AI should operate as a supportive instrument that augments interpretive and analytical work while upholding scholarly integrity. Transparent practices are essential to ensure that AI-generated outputs do not obscure epistemic origins or distort research findings.

Key Points

- Researchers must disclose when and how AI tools assist in writing, analysis, or data processing.
- Methodological transparency is required to show where AI intervenes in the research workflow.
- Critical attention must be given to biases, training data limitations, and algorithmic assumptions (Tomar & Verma, 2020).
- Safeguards are needed to prevent hallucinations, fabricated references, and misuse of predictive analytics.

With these safeguards in place, AI becomes an analytical aid that strengthens research quality rather than compromising academic rigor.

3. Governance: Accountability, Oversight, and Democratic Participation

Responsible AI adoption depends on governance structures that are transparent, accountable, and participatory. Universities must implement mechanisms that ensure human oversight and institutional responsibility in all AI-supported decisions.

Key Points

- Clear governance mechanisms should guide the approval, monitoring, and evaluation of AI systems.
- Decision-making processes must be transparent, with publicly accessible documentation of risks and benefits.
- Strong data governance is needed to align with privacy, security, and regulatory requirements.
- Governance processes should include students, faculty, and diverse stakeholders, ensuring democratic input.

Such governance structures help universities navigate the complexities of AI-enabled decision-making while protecting institutional trust and human judgment.

4. Equity: Access, Inclusion, and Data Sovereignty

Equity is essential for ensuring that AI's benefits are distributed fairly across regions, institutions, and communities. The framework emphasizes the need to address structural disparities that shape technological access and representation.

Key Points

- AI tools must be accessible, affordable, and linguistically inclusive across diverse contexts.
- Universities should support the development of local datasets and context-specific AI models.
- Overreliance on Global North technologies risks creating new forms of dependency.
- Safeguards must protect marginalized communities from data exploitation and reinforce data sovereignty.

An equity-centered approach ensures that AI empowers all learners and institutions, rather than reproducing global digital divides.

5. Ethics: Protecting Integrity, Privacy, and Human Dignity

Ethics forms the foundation of the entire framework. Ethical principles guide AI's implementation across all domains, ensuring that technology strengthens rather than undermines educational values.

Key Points

- AI use must align with academic integrity and original scholarship.
- Strong commitments to privacy, informed consent, and responsible data practices are essential.
- Institutions must work to reduce surveillance, algorithmic bias, and discriminatory outcomes.
- Ethical review processes should accompany AI adoption in both teaching and research.

When anchored in ethical commitments, AI can enhance human dignity, institutional trust, and educational legitimacy.

IMPLEMENTATION ROADMAP FOR UNIVERSITIES

To operationalize this framework, higher education institutions can adopt the following roadmap:

- Establish AI Governance Committees
- Develop Comprehensive Institutional AI Policies
- Invest in AI Literacy and Capacity Building
- Audit Existing AI Systems for Bias, Transparency, and Value Alignment
- Strengthen Regional and Interdisciplinary Collaborations
- Support Local Innovation Ecosystems

Together, these actions position universities to adopt AI sustainably, inclusively, and ethically while strengthening academic integrity and human-centered learning.

Table 1. Integrated Framework for Responsible AI Adoption in Higher Education

Domain	*Core Focus*	*Key Principles*	*Practical Applications*
Pedagogy	Human-centered learning	- Promote creativity and dialogue - Preserve student agency - Enable diverse learning pathways	- Use AI for scaffolding, feedback, and multimodal learning - Support inquiry-based learning with generative tools
Research	Augmentation & integrity	- Transparency of AI assistance - Critical reflection on AI's role - Methodological clarity	- Disclosure of AI contributions in writing and analysis - Review training data and algorithmic assumptions
Governance	Accountability & oversight	- Transparent decision-making - Human oversight of AI systems - Data protection and compliance	- Establish AI governance committees - Publish risk assessments and evaluation criteria
Equity	Inclusive access & data sovereignty	- Linguistic and regional inclusivity - Local innovation and datasets - Avoiding dependency on external technologies	- Build context-specific AI tools - Support Global South collaborations - Implement community data protections
Ethics	Integrity, privacy, dignity	- Academic integrity - Informed consent - Avoiding surveillance and bias	- Conduct ethical impact assessments - Ensure privacy-safe data practices - Embed institutional ethics guidelines

This values-driven framework provides a comprehensive pathway for integrating AI in higher education in a manner that is sustainable, equitable, and ethically grounded. When implemented holistically, AI becomes a transformative partner—supporting academic excellence, expanding human capability, and reinforcing the democratic and ethical foundations of universities.

CONCLUSION

The integration of Artificial Intelligence into higher education represents one of the most far-reaching and ethically charged transformations of the twenty-first century. While AI offers extraordinary potential to personalize learning, accelerate research, and optimize institutional operations, it simultaneously poses profound philosophical challenges concerning knowledge, agency, and responsibility. This chapter argues that the central challenge facing higher education is not merely the technical adoption of AI systems but the deeper intellectual and cultural adaptation required to sustain human-centered academic practices in an algorithmic age.

AI's growing influence risks shifting universities toward a technocratic paradigm in which data-driven outputs overshadow deliberation, dialogue, and critical inquiry. If uncritically embraced, AI could inadvertently erode the relational, interpretive, and ethical dimensions that define higher learning. To avoid such an outcome, universities must embed critical digital literacy, ethical reflection, and transparent governance mechanisms across all levels of AI integration—from classroom practices and research processes to institutional decision-making. The aim is not to resist technological progress but to shape it in ways that uphold human judgment, creativity, and autonomy.

The future of higher education therefore depends on cultivating a thoughtful human–AI synergy, wherein technology complements rather than displaces human capacities. Achieving this requires inclusive governance structures that ensure equitable access to AI tools, foster participation across diverse global contexts, and protect academic integrity and data rights. With sustained ethical oversight and a commitment to equity, AI can evolve from a tool of automation into an instrument of intellectual empowerment and educational justice.

By reframing AI adoption through a balanced, value-driven lens, higher education can reaffirm its role as a moral, democratic, and intellectual compass. In doing so, universities can harness AI's transformative potential while preserving the humanistic core that underpins meaningful learning, rigorous scholarship, and socially responsible governance in an AI-driven world.

REFERENCES

Abulibdeh, E., Taha, S., & Alamassi, S. (2023). Challenges facing underdeveloped countries in implementing Cutting-Edge AI technology. In Studies in big data (pp. 239–250). DOI: 10.1007/978-3-031-42455-7_22

Acion, L., Rajngewerc, M., & Randall, G. (2023). Generative AI poses ethical challenges for open science. *Nature Human Behaviour*, *7*(12), 1800–1801.

Agate, N., Kennison, R., Konkiel, S., Long, C. P., Rhody, J., Sacchi, S., & Weber, P. (2020). The transformative power of values-enacted scholarship. *Humanities & Social Sciences Communications*, *7*, 165. DOI: 10.1057/s41599-020-00647-z

Agrawal, A., Banerjee, A. R. S., Jhariya, M. K., Garg, N., Hashmi, I., Brar, V., Gupta, D., & Mishra, D. K. (2025). AI-powered student assessment in higher education: Enhancing accuracy, feedback, and personalization. In Innovating assessment and evaluation in higher education: Inclusive practices and technological advancements (p. 26). DOI: 10.4018/979-8-3373-2130-1.ch006

Ahamed, N. F. I. (2025). The transformative role of Artificial Intelligence in modern education. *World Journal of Advanced Research and Reviews*, *26*(1), 3239–3247. DOI: 10.30574/wjarr.2025.26.1.1453

Akinwalere, S. N., & Ivanov, V. (2022). Artificial intelligence in higher Education: Challenges and opportunities. *BORDER CROSSING*, *12*(1), 1–15. DOI: 10.33182/bc.v12i1.2015

Aper, J. P. (2024). Artificial intelligence and higher education: A brave new world? *The Journal of Educational Thought*, *57*(1). Advance online publication. DOI: 10.55016/ojs/jet.v57i1.79412

Aprianto, R., Lestari, E. P., Sadan, N., & Fletcher, E. (2024). Harnessing Artificial intelligence in Higher Education: Balancing innovation and ethical challenges. [ITEE]. *International Transactions on Education Technology*, *3*(1), 84–93. DOI: 10.33050/itee.v3i1.680

Bahr, A. (2024). Bridges without foundation? Why The use of AI tools in academia needs to build on ethics first. *Filozofia*, *79*(5), 486–500. DOI: 10.31577/filozofia.2024.79.5.2

Bakla, A. (2023). ChatGPT in Academic Writing and Publishing. In Advances in educational technologies and instructional design book series (pp. 89–101). DOI: 10.4018/978-1-6684-9893-4.ch005

Barnes, E., & Hutson, J. (2024). Navigating the ethical terrain of AI in higher education: Strategies for mitigating bias and promoting fairness. *Forum for Education Studies.*, *2*(2), 1229. DOI: 10.59400/fes.v2i2.1229

Bello, L., & Aubert, L. (2025). Artificial intelligence in the classroom: Democratizing knowledge and transforming education. *Seminars in Medical Writing and Education*, *4*, 469. DOI: 10.56294/mw2025469

Bhattacharya, C., & Sabeena, L. (2025). AI-powered teacher performance evaluation and pedagogical strategy optimization in higher education. The business and management review, 15 (2), 225-234. DOI: 10.71443/9789349552531-16

Biesta, G. (2021). *World-centred education: A view for the present* (1st ed.). Routledge.

Biesta, G. (2021). *World-centred education: A view for the present* (1st ed.). Routledge.

Bjelobaba, S., Waddington, L., Perkins, M., Foltýnek, T., Bhattacharyya, S., & Weber-Wulff, D. (2024). Research integrity and GenAI: A systematic analysis of ethical challenges across research phases (Version 1) [Preprint]. arXiv. 10.48550/arXiv.2412.10134

Boy, F., & Doneddu, D. (2025). Generative AI in the social sciences: Toward critical integration and methodological innovation. DOI: 10.31235/osf.io/f8dr5_v1

Brown, D. W. (2014). Nobody's property. In Palgrave Macmillan US eBooks (pp. 83–105). DOI: 10.1057/9781137337153_5

Cetinic, E. (2022). The myth of culturally agnostic AI models. arXiv (Cornell University). 10.48550/arxiv.2211.15271

Chaudhry, M. A., Cukurova, M., & Luckin, R. (2022). A Transparency Index Framework for AI in education. arXiv (Cornell University). 10.48550/arxiv.2206.03220

Chen, M. (2023). A comparison of machine learning techniques in building an intelligent tutoring system. *Applied and Computational Engineering*, *5*(1), 662–666. DOI: 10.54254/2755-2721/5/20230673

Couldry, N., & Mejias, U. A. (2019). *The costs of connection: How data is colonizing human life and appropriating it for capitalism.* Stanford University Press.

Coyle, D., & Weller, A. (2020). "Explaining" machine learning reveals policy challenges. *Science*, *368*(6498), 1433–1434. DOI: 10.1126/science.aba9647

Crain, C., Ewing, A., Billy, I., & Anush, H. (2025). The advantages and disadvantages of AI in higher education. *The Business & Management Review*, *15*(03). Advance online publication. DOI: 10.24052/bmr/v15nu03/art-16

De Oliveira Silva, A., & Janes, D. D. S. (2025). Rethinking scientific integrity in the era of artificial intelligence. *PromptAI Academy Journal*, *4*, e075. DOI: 10.37497/promptai.4.2025.75

Dempere, J., Ramasamy, L. K., & Harris, J. (2025). AI as a Research Partner: Advocating for Co-Authorship in Academic Publications. *The Artificial Intelligence Business Review*, *1*(2). Advance online publication. DOI: 10.64044/j8enmv71

Dollinger, M. (2020). The projectification of the university: Consequences and alternatives. *Teaching in Higher Education*, *25*(6), 669–682. DOI: 10.1080/13562517.2020.1722631

Duke, M. R. (2025). Artificial intelligence and the end(s) of qualitative data analysis. *Human Organization*, *1–3*. Advance online publication. DOI: 10.1080/00187259.2025.2546439

Dulundu, A. (2024). AI in education: Benefits and concerns. *Next Generation.*, *8*(1), 81. DOI: 10.62802/3fr4f412

Dwivedi, Y. K., Malik, T., Hughes, L., & Albashrawi, M. A. (2024). Scholarly Discourse on GENAI's Impact on Academic Publishing. *Journal of Computer Information Systems*, •••, 1–16. DOI: 10.1080/08874417.2024.2435386

Extance, A. (2018). How AI technology can tame the scientific literature. *Nature*, *561*(7722), 273–274. DOI: 10.1038/d41586-018-06617-5

Farooqi, S. A. (2025). Ethical framework for AI in education. In Advances in computational intelligence and robotics book series (pp. 153–188). DOI: 10.4018/979-8-3373-5550-4.ch007

Fowler, D. S. (2023). AI in higher education. *Journal of Ethics in Higher Education*, *3*, 127–143. DOI: 10.26034/fr.jehe.2023.4657

Gamito, M. C., & Ebers, M. (2020). Algorithmic Governance and Governance of Algorithms: An Introduction. In Data science, machine intelligence, and law (pp. 1–22). DOI: 10.1007/978-3-030-50559-2_1

Ghandour, D. A. M. (2024). Navigating the impact of AI integration in higher education. In Advances in educational technologies and instructional design book series (pp. 212–233). DOI: 10.4018/979-8-3693-2145-4.ch009

Gupta, C. (2025). The role of artificial intelligence in academic research: Opportunities and ethical challenges. *BSSS Journal of Education*, *14*(1), 163–175. DOI: 10.51767/je1409

Guridi, J. A., & Cheyre, C. (2024). This is not global AI: International reports on AI as vehicles of colonialism in the age of generative AI. SSRN Electronic Journal. DOI: 10.2139/ssrn.4682872

Han, B., Nawaz, S., Buchanan, G., & McKay, D. (2023). Ethical and pedagogical impacts of AI in education. In Lecture notes in computer science (pp. 667–673). DOI: 10.1007/978-3-031-36272-9_54

Helling, D. K., & McElnay, J. C. (1992). Broadening the research base. *International Journal of Pharmacy Practice*, *1*(3), 124–125. DOI: 10.1111/j.2042-7174.1992.tb00553.x

Holmes, W., Bialik, M., & Fadel, C. (2019). *Artificial intelligence in education: Promises and implications for teaching and learning*. Center for Curriculum Redesign.

Hutson, J., & Plate, D. (2023). Disrupting algorithmic culture. In Advances in educational technologies and instructional design book series (pp. 1–30). DOI: 10.4018/979-8-3693-0074-9.ch001

Ismail, W. S. '. W., Awang, N. A., & Pauzi, N. M. (2023). An overview of the use of artificial intelligence (AI) tools in higher education. International. *The Journal of Learning in Higher Education*, *19*(3), 27–40. DOI: 10.24191/ijelhe.v19n3.1932

Jobin, A., Ienca, M., & Vayena, E. (2019). The global landscape of AI ethics guidelines. *Nature Machine Intelligence*, *1*(9), 389–399. DOI: 10.1038/s42256-019-0088-2

Kalkan, G. (2024). The impact of artificial intelligence on corporate governance. *Journal of Corporate Finance Research*, *18*(2), 17–25. DOI: 10.17323/j.jcfr.2073-0438.18.2.2024.17-25

Karamuk, E. (2025). The automation trap. In Advances in computational intelligence and robotics book series (pp. 147–170). DOI: 10.4018/979-8-3373-0122-8.ch007

Kayyali, M. (2025). AI in Higher Education. In Advances in educational technologies and instructional design book series (pp. 31–62). DOI: 10.4018/979-8-3693-7949-3.ch002

Kayyali, M. (2025). The impact of AI on classroom dynamics in higher education. In Advances in computational intelligence and robotics book series (pp. 151–180). DOI: 10.4018/979-8-3373-6007-2.ch005

Khan, S., Mazhar, T., Shahzad, T., Khan, M. A., Rehman, A. U., Saeed, M. M., & Hamam, H. (2025). Harnessing AI for sustainable higher education: Ethical considerations, operational efficiency, and future directions. *Discover Sustainability*, *6*(1). Advance online publication. DOI: 10.1007/s43621-025-00809-6

Khatri, B. B., & Karki, P. D. (2023). Artificial intelligence (AI) in higher education: Growing academic integrity and ethical concerns. *Nepalese Journal of Development and Rural Studies*, *20*(01), 1–7. DOI: 10.3126/njdrs.v20i01.64134

Kitsara, I. (2022). Artificial intelligence and the digital divide: From an innovation perspective. In Bounfour, A. (Ed.), *Platforms and artificial intelligence* (pp. 203–220). Springer.

Knox, J. (2020). Artificial intelligence and education in China. *Learning, Media and Technology*, *45*(3), 298–311.

Knox, J. (2020). Artificial intelligence and education in China. *Learning, Media and Technology*, *45*(3), 298–311.

Kponyo, J. J., Fosu, D. M., Owusu, F. E. B., Ali, M. I., & Ahiamadzor, M. M. (2024). Techno-neocolonialism: an emerging risk in the artificial intelligence revolution. Trayectorias Humanas Trascontinentales, 18. DOI: 10.25965/trahs.6382

Kshetri, N. (2023). The Future of Education: Generative Artificial Intelligence's collaborative role with teachers. *IT Professional*, *25*(6), 8–12. DOI: 10.1109/mitp.2023.3333070

Kshetri, N. (2024). Diffusion and impact in the Global South. In Edward Elgar Publishing eBooks (pp. 214–234). DOI: 10.4337/9781035346745.00020

Lee, H., Kizilcec, R. F., & Joachims, T. (2023). Evaluating a learned admission-prediction model as a replacement for standardized tests in college admissions. In Proceedings of the Tenth ACM Conference on Learning at Scale (L@S '23) (pp. 195–203). ACM. DOI: 10.1145/3573051.3593382

Leišytė, L. (2022). Performance management under surveillance capitalism in higher education. In Edward Elgar Publishing eBooks. DOI: 10.4337/9781839102639.00026

Leng, C. (2025). AI empowerment in higher Education: Current opportunities, key challenges, and future trends. *Journal of Contemporary Educational Research*, *9*(5), 309–313. DOI: 10.26689/jcer.v9i5.10562

Lin, Z., & Sohail, A. (2025). Recalibrating Academic Expertise in the Age of Generative AI. DOI: 10.31234/osf.io/gj482_v3

Long, D., & Magerko, B. (2020). What is AI literacy? [Note: This appears in your original document summary; if not desired, it can be removed.]. *Artificial Intelligence*, *12*(3), 1–15.

Machaba, F., & Age, T. J. (2025). The impact of artificial intelligence on administration, teaching, and learning functions. In Advances in computational intelligence and robotics book series (pp. 151–180). DOI: 10.4018/979-8-3693-8915-7.ch007

Mahboob, K., Asif, R., & Umme, L. (2023). Leveraging generative AI for Cross-Cultural knowledge exchange in higher education. In Advances in higher education and professional development book series (pp. 186–206). DOI: 10.4018/979-8-3693-0487-7.ch008

Manzoor, A. (2016). Role of learning Analytics in enhancing teaching and learning. In Advances in educational marketing, administration, and leadership book series (pp. 259–281). DOI: 10.4018/978-1-4666-9983-0.ch011

Mishara, N. P. (2024). The ethical implications of AI in education: Privacy, bias, and accountability. *Journal of Informatics Education and Research*, *4*(2). Advance online publication. DOI: 10.52783/jier.v4i2.1827

Mishra, M., Ara, A., & Mishra, S. (2025). Exploring human-AI collaboration in Higher Education. In Advances in computational intelligence and robotics book series (pp. 483–502). DOI: 10.4018/979-8-3693-7332-3.ch028

Monyei, C. G., & Akpeji, K. O. (2019). Repurposing electricity Access Research for the Global South: A tale of many disconnects. *Joule*, *4*(2), 278–281. DOI: 10.1016/j.joule.2019.11.013

Mutawa, A. M. (2024). Enforcing the ethics of artificial intelligence in education. In Advances in educational technologies and instructional design book series (pp. 143–168). DOI: 10.4018/979-8-3693-0884-4.ch007

Nayeem. (2025). Data-Driven decision making. International Journal on Science and Technology, 16(1). DOI: 10.71097/ijsat.v16.i1.2477

Nikitina, I., & Ishchenko, T. (2024). The impact of AI on teachers: Support or replacement? *Academia Polonica.*, *65*(4), 93–99. DOI: 10.23856/6511

Nimbalagundi, N. S. M., Bagawan, N. S., & Katageri, N. C. S. (2024). Artificial intelligence in higher education. [IRJAEM]. *International Research Journal on Advanced Engineering and Management*, *2*(09), 2790–2795. DOI: 10.47392/irjaem.2024.0406

O'Neil, C. (2016). *Weapons of math destruction: How big data increases inequality and threatens democracy*. Crown Publishing Group.

O'Neil, C. (2016). *Weapons of math destruction: How big data increases inequality and threatens democracy*. Crown Publishing Group.

Ocen, S., Elasu, J., Aarakit, S. M., & Olupot, C. (2025). Artificial intelligence in higher education institutions: Review of innovations, opportunities and challenges. *Frontiers in Education*, *10*. Advance online publication. DOI: 10.3389/feduc.2025.1530247

Ojha, D. R. (2025). Impact of AI technologies on teaching, learning, and research in higher education. *Journal of Jayaprithvi Multiple Campus*, *1*, 121–133. DOI: 10.3126/jjmc2.v1i1.81444

Okolo, C. T. (2023). Addressing global inequity in AI development. In Edward Elgar Publishing eBooks (pp. 378–389). DOI: 10.4337/9781803928562.00040

Pandey, V. (2025). Artificial intelligence and its impact on higher education. Journal Global Values, XVI(SI), 249–256. DOI: 10.31995/jgv.2025.v16isi7.032

Paraschiv, R. (2025). Ethical implications of using artificial intelligence in education. *Preprints*.org. DOI: 10.20944/preprints202502.0538.v1

Peddi, S., & Manoharan, G. (2025). Ethical Guidelines for the thoughtful Implementation of AI in Higher Education. *EthAIca*, *5*, 409. DOI: 10.56294/ai2026409

Peruzzo, F., & Allan, J. (2022). Rethinking inclusive (digital) education: Lessons from the pandemic to reconceptualise inclusion through convivial technologies. *Learning, Media and Technology*, *49*(2), 244–258.

Peruzzo, F., & Allan, J. (2022). Rethinking inclusive (digital) education: Lessons from the pandemic to reconceptualize inclusion through convivial technologies. *Learning, Media and Technology*, *49*(2), 244–258.

Petrenko, A. (2024). The role of generative artificial intelligence (GAI) in scientific research. *System Research and Information Technologies*, *3*, 133–147. DOI: 10.20535/srit.2308-8893.2024.3.08

Pigola, A., Scafuto, I. C., Da Costa, P. R., & Nassif, V. M. J. (2023). Artificial Intelligence in academic research. *International Journal of Innovation*, *11*(3), 1–9. DOI: 10.5585/2023.25408

Pinski, M., & Benlian, A. (2024). AI literacy for users – A comprehensive review and future research directions of learning methods, components, and effects. *Computers in Human Behavior Artificial Humans*, *2*(1), 100062. DOI: 10.1016/j.chbah.2024.100062

Popenici, S. (2023). The critique of AI as a foundation for judicious use in higher education. *Journal of Applied Learning & Teaching*, *6*(2). Advance online publication. DOI: 10.37074/jalt.2023.6.2.4

Popenici, S. D., & Kerr, S. (2017). Exploring the impact of artificial intelligence on teaching and learning in higher education. *Research and Practice in Technology Enhanced Learning*, *12*(1), 22. DOI: 10.1186/s41039-017-0062-8

Prajapati, N. S. B. (2025). Existing challenges in ethical AI. *World Journal of Advanced Research and Reviews*, *25*(1), 2130–2137. DOI: 10.30574/wjarr.2025.25.1.0267

Praveenkumar, S., Anute, N., Vaissnave, V., Ragupathi, T., Fardale, S., Selvakumar, P., & Manjunath, T. C. (2025). Risks of AI bias and inequities in learning. In Advances in computational intelligence and robotics book series (pp. 257–284). DOI: 10.4018/979-8-3373-2302-2.ch009

Prinsloo, P. (2019). A social cartography of analytics in education as performative politics. *British Journal of Educational Technology*, *50*(6), 2810–2823. DOI: 10.1111/bjet.12872

Protopapa, I., & Idris, B. (2025). Ethical and moral pitfalls of generative AI in academic research. In Edward Elgar Publishing eBooks (pp. 145–163). DOI: 10.4337/9781035326020.00022

Rueda, J., Pugh, J., & Savulescu, J. (2023). Rethinking techno-moral disruption in bioethics, society, and justice. *Trends in Biotechnology*, *41*(6), 743–744. DOI: 10.1016/j.tibtech.2023.01.008

Sadki, R. (2017). From guidelines to impact. DOI: 10.59350/tsx76-0mh23

Salah, M., AbdelFattah, F. A., Al Halbusi, H., & Mohammed, M. (2023). Beyond the "Death of Research": Reimagining the human-AI collaboration in scientific research. DOI: 10.15826/csp.2023.7.4.250

Salloum, S. A., Salloum, A., & Alfaisal, R. (2024). Objectives and obstacles of artificial intelligence in education. In Studies in big data (pp. 605–614). DOI: 10.1007/978-3-031-52280-2_38

Sam, A. K., & Olbrich, P. (2023). The need for AI ethics in higher education. In Springer Briefs in ethics (pp. 3–10). DOI: 10.1007/978-3-031-23035-6_1

Sánchez Santamaría, J. (2025). A Pedagogical Sense of Artificial Intelligence in Education. DOI: 10.31219/osf.io/z4bg6_v1

Schmitt, L. (2021). Mapping global AI governance: A nascent regime in a fragmented landscape. *AI and Ethics*, *2*(2), 303–314. DOI: 10.1007/s43681-021-00083-y

Scott-Herring, M. (2024). Artificial intelligence in academic writing: A detailed examination. *International Journal of Nursing Education Scholarship*, *21*(1). Advance online publication. DOI: 10.1515/ijnes-2024-0050

Shippee, M. (2023). AI in Education: A focus on pedagogy. SSRN Electronic Journal. DOI: 10.2139/ssrn.4649752

Shtayyat, A., Gawanmeh, A., & Mashaleh, A. (2025). Risk analysis of AI integration in educational systems. In Advances in computational intelligence and robotics book series (pp. 401–428). DOI: 10.4018/979-8-3373-0832-6.ch017

Sonko, N. S., Adewusi, N. O., Obi, N. O. C., Onwusinkwue, N. S., & Atadoga, N. A. (2024). A critical review towards artificial general intelligence: Challenges, ethical considerations, and the path forward. *World Journal of Advanced Research and Reviews*, *21*(3), 1262–1268. DOI: 10.30574/wjarr.2024.21.3.0817

Steele, J. L. (2023). To GPT or not GPT? Empowering our students to learn with AI. *Computers and Education Artificial Intelligence*, *5*, 100160. DOI: 10.1016/j.caeai.2023.100160

Steponenaite, A., & Barakat, B. (2023). Plagiarism in AI empowered world. In Lecture notes in computer science (pp. 434–442). DOI: 10.1007/978-3-031-35897-5_31

Sudhir, V. (2024). The ethics of AI in the administration of higher education. *International Journal for Multidisciplinary Research*, *6*(6). Advance online publication. DOI: 10.36948/ijfmr.2024.v06i06.30189

Sywelem, M. M. G., & Mahklouf, A. M. E.-S. (2024). Ethical considerations in the integration of artificial intelligence in education: An overview. DOI: 10.5121/csit.2024.141201

Szcyrek, S., & Stewart, B. (2022). Surveillance in the system: Data as critical change in higher education. The Open/Technology in Education Society and Scholarship Association Journal, 2(2), 1–20. DOI: 10.18357/otessaj.2022.2.2.34

Taneja, D., Prabagaren, H., & Thomas, M. R. (2025). AI in academia. In Advances in computational intelligence and robotics book series (pp. 315–336). DOI: 10.4018/979-8-3373-0122-8.ch014

Thompson, K., Corrin, L., & Lodge, J. M. (2023). AI in tertiary education: Progress on research and practice. *Australasian Journal of Educational Technology*, *39*(5), 1–7. DOI: 10.14742/ajet.9251

Tomar, P., & Verma, S. (2020). Impact and role of AI technologies in teaching, learning, and research in higher education. In Advances in educational technologies and instructional design book series (pp. 190–203). DOI: 10.4018/978-1-7998-4763-2.ch012

Torrisi-Steele, G. (2025). AI and the humans in higher education. In Advances in educational technologies and instructional design book series (pp. 209–230). DOI: 10.4018/979-8-3373-0502-8.ch009

UNESCO. (2023). *Guidance for generative AI in education and research.* UNESCO.

UNESCO. (2023). Guidance for generative AI in education and research. UNESCO.
Kitsara, I. (2022). Artificial intelligence and the digital divide: From an innovation perspective. In Bounfour, A. (Ed.), *Platforms and artificial intelligence* (pp. 203–220). Springer.

Upreti, I. M. (2025). The role and implications of artificial intelligence in higher education: Opportunities and challenges. *International Journal for Research in Applied Science and Engineering Technology, 13*(4), 6214–6220. DOI: 10.22214/ijraset.2025.69838

Upreti, I. M. (2025). The role and implications of artificial intelligence in higher education: Opportunities and challenges. *International Journal for Research in Applied Science and Engineering Technology, 13*(4), 6214–6220. DOI: 10.22214/ijraset.2025.69838
Vangibhuratha, S. K. (2025). The impact of generative AI on educational assessment. *International Journal of Innovative Research in Engineering & Multidisciplinary Physical Sciences, 13*(4). Advance online publication. DOI: 10.37082/ijirmps.v13.i4.232678

Watermeyer, R., Phipps, L., Lanclos, D., & Knight, C. (2023). Generative AI and the automating of academia. *Postdigital Science and Education, 6*(2), 446–466. DOI: 10.1007/s42438-023-00440-6

Weigel, A., Caldas, C., Meyer, A., & Morris, S. A. (2022). The impact of AI on research. *Cell, 185*(15), 2621–2622. DOI: 10.1016/j.cell.2022.06.024

Williams, R. T. (2024). Paradigm shifts: Exploring AI's influence on qualitative inquiry and analysis. *Frontiers in Research Metrics and Analytics, 9*, 1331589. DOI: 10.3389/frma.2024.1331589

Williamson, B., & Eynon, R. (2020). Historical threads, missing links, and future directions in AI in education. *Learning, Media and Technology, 45*(3), 223–235.

Yavich, R. (2025). Will the use of AI undermine students independent thinking? *Education Sciences, 15*(6), 669. DOI: 10.3390/educsci15060669

Yusriani, S., Eledora, A. O., Patiro, S. P. S., Purnomo, K. H., Zega, I. M., & Marlina, M. (2024). About AI in academia: obstacle or facilitator? *Proceeding of International Student Conference on Business, Education, Economics, Accounting, and Management.*, 2(1), 677–700. DOI: 10.21009/isc-beam.012.43

Zala, K., Acharya, B., Mashru, M., Palaniappan, D., Gerogiannis, V. C., Kanavos, A., & Karamitsos, I. (2024). Transformative Automation: AI in scientific Literature Reviews. *International Journal of Advanced Computer Science and Applications*, *15*(1). Advance online publication. DOI: 10.14569/ijacsa.2024.01501122

Zawacki-Richter, O., Marín, V. I., Bond, M., & Gouverneur, F. (2019). Systematic review of research on artificial intelligence applications in higher education. *International Journal of Educational Technology in Higher Education*, *16*(39), 1–27.

Zeer, M., Siaj, R. W., Abu Ghannam, J., & Kanan, M. (2023). Ethics of artificial intelligence in university education. In 2023 2nd International Engineering Conference on Electrical, Energy, and Artificial Intelligence (EICEEAI) (pp. xx–xx). IEEE. DOI: 10.1109/EICEEAI60672.2023.10590285

Zermeño-Flores, A. I., Tufte, T., & Navarrete-Vega, M. A. (2024). Knowledge production and epistemic injustices. *MedieKultur Journal of Media and Communication Research*, *40*(76), 120–138. DOI: 10.7146/mk.v40i76.143529

Zhang, C. (2025). AI in academia: How it enhances research efficiency and innovation. *International Journal of Education and Humanities*, *19*(3), 155–158. DOI: 10.54097/r5h5pz92

Zhang, J., & Goyal, S. B. (2024). AI-driven decision support system innovations to empower higher education administration. *Journal of Computers Mechanical and Management*, *3*(2), 35–41. DOI: 10.57159/gadl.jcmm.3.2.24070

Chapter 9
Repositioning ChatGPT as Co-Instructors in EFL for Automatic Writing Evaluation (AWE) in Academic Publishing Through CALLEDA Model

Muthmainnah Muthmainnah
http://orcid.org/0000-0003-3170-2374
Universitas Al Asyariah Mandar, Indonesia

Luis Cardoso
http://orcid.org/0000-0003-3748-5593
Polytechnic University of Portalegre, Portugal

Ahmad Al Yakin
http://orcid.org/0000-0003-3170-2374
Universitas Al Asyariah Mandar, Indonesia

Lukman Asha
IAIN Curup, Bengkulu, Indonesia

Yasmika Baihaqi
Universitas Muhammadiyah Metro, Indonesia

Eka Apriani
http://orcid.org/0000-0002-8427-2817
IAIN Curup, Bengkulu, Indonesia

Dadan Supardan
IAIN Curup, Bengkulu, Indonesia

ABSTRACT

The use of AI in EFL writing classes has changed the way students interact with scholarly articles. Contextualization, Awareness, Learning, Linking, Experiencing, Developing, and Assessing (CALLEDA) is the teaching methodology that is being used to situate ChatGPT, Grammarly, and QuillBot as "co-instructors" in this project.

DOI: 10.4018/979-8-3373-7097-2.ch009

This study shown ChatGPT becomes no longer a remedial tool but a pedagogical ally when it is integrated within CALLEDA's programmed phases and accompanied by teachers. To maximize benefits while limiting concerns of overdependence and style homogenization, our study contributes to ongoing debates concerning hybrid AI-human teaching models by underlining the necessity for ethical integration and instructor scaffolding. The research shows that AWE can help EFL students from beginning to end by repurposing ChatGPT as a co-instructor, allowing more people to have access to academic publishing while maintaining high standards of scholarship.

INTRODUCTION

Advances in computer technology have brought new approaches to language teaching and evaluation to the field of language education. Writing evaluation and holistic assessment are two areas that have made extensive use of natural language processing technology (Zhao, 2025). In the academic field, in terms of diagnostic feedback and summative assessment of writing characteristics, one implementation of new technology in language teaching is automated writing evaluation (AWE), which has been very helpful (Yildiz et al., 2024). This algorithm can read many essays quickly, and this saves teachers time (Na et al., 2025). Two benefits that the users of AWE technology get are clear explanation and prompt feedback (Chen, 2025). With these two features, students can practice giving feedback independently, thereby improving their writing skills to the best (Huang & Wilson, 2025). This can, in turn, improve their language classes' autonomy and motivation (Wang, 2025). Besides this, students are motivated to improve the mechanics and accuracy of their writing since these tools test their work automatically regularly and objectively. There needs to be more research into how such tools impact the writing abilities of students because the use of artificial intelligence systems in learning languages has been on the rise in the past decade, raising the question of whether computers can judge written work more effectively and quickly.

As Wang (2025) maintains, the use of AWEs can hinder writing development among some students by preventing them from engaging directly in real and meaningful interactions. Furthermore, emphasis on AWE programs on Web resources and editing functions has positioned them as writing tools, which can deter students from self-directed learning (Abdalrahim & Mohammed, 2025). Further research on the use of AWE programs in EFL classrooms and how this software assists in enhancing students' overall writing skills in general needs to be conducted, as its implementation within language learning systems is growing due to numerous reasons linked with building students' writing skills (Chen et al., 2025a). The current technology-driven revolution in education has not hugely transformed the English as a Foreign Language (EFL) landscape, especially when considering the uptake of AI-powered solutions. Non-native English speakers and EFL students have long used AI tools such as QuillBot, Grammarly, WriteMyPaper, Jenni AI, or ChatGPT, among others. All of these programs work together as automated writing evaluation (AWE) tools, and their task is to improve writers' ability to generate ideas by identifying errors and recommending ways to correct them, thus meeting quality writing standards. According to Thai et al. (2025), Grammarly has been the subject of the most research among all currently available grammar-checking and paraphrasing apps. Depending on the prompts offered, ChatGPT offers similar grammar-checking capabilities; its launch could mark a revolution in the AWE field. One of the main reasons AWE tools have attracted the interest of assessment experts worldwide is their ability to help students become more proficient in providing feedback and offer time-saving benefits (Yang et al, 2025). In the context of the shift in the feedback paradigm from information transmission to understanding and collaboration between students and teachers (Tran et al., 2025), the goal of student feedback literacy is to foster students' attitudes and capacities to utilize feedback for self-development, self-directed learning, and self-determination. According to Molly et al. (2020), students should not passively receive feedback from their instructors but should instead seek it from various sources, including classmates and learning technology. Therefore, in this spirit, students' self-evaluation efforts must fully utilize the skills and tools of AWE as an automated writing grader.

Muthmainnah et al. (2025) use ChatGPT as an AWE tool, especially in the EFL (English as a Foreign Language) context, where many students still struggle with basic English writing structures. AWE has a long history of research. Feng (2025) showed how AWE relates to feedback on students' writing skills in English as a foreign language class is still lacking. The rapid advancement of AI-based AWE technology and the importance of leveraging it to improve learner-centered assessments and feedback literacy make this research crucial. Furthermore, it would be worthwhile to investigate whether ChatGPT's unique AWE capabilities can surpass established AI-based grammar checkers like QuillBot or Grammarly. With all of these factors in mind, the purpose of this research is to fill the conceptual gap in the relationship between AWE tools and student writing feedback.

This study aims to examine English language students' perceptions of the integration of AWE as a medium to strengthen the writing skills of undergraduate EFL students. To conduct this study, the Grammarly and ChatGPT applications were used to assess the writing skills of Indonesian students in the faculty of teacher training and education. Based on this research objective, the following research question was posed: "What are students' opinions regarding the integration of AWE technology as an instructor in improving academic writing interest?"

LITERATURE REVIEW

Computer-Assisted Tools for writing pedagogy and their pedagogic implications. The fast uptake of artificial intelligence (AI) writing tools like ChatGPT, Grammarly, and QuillBot has transformed classroom procedures and pedagogies in EFL writing pedagogy. What began as simple automated error checkers has grown into sophisticated platforms able to provide, today, personal feedback, paraphrasing options, and genre modeling. The increasing need for instant writing support and the realization that AI can be employed beyond being a digital assistant have contributed to the dissemination of its vast uses. Mazurek (2025) says that the implementation of AI should go beyond simple correction and instead leverage higher-order abilities such as multicultural competency, genre savvy, and critical thinking. Chen et al. (2025b) concur with this view by applauding ChatGPT for its ability to evoke metacognitive awareness through self-regulated learning and reflective writing facilitation. Turvey (2025) subscribes to hybrid pedagogical practices where AI augments teacher scaffolding instead of replacing it, and the above findings concur with this. While ChatGPT is in the limelight, still more EFL instructors keep applying Grammarly and QuillBot.

In general, surface-level editing for writing enhancement, however, Grammarly proves useful because it offers real-time style and grammatical corrections, vocabulary enhancement, and tone checks (Hrdlicková, 2025). Alternatively, QuillBot paraphrasing and summarization capabilities enable the students to practice different sentence structures and word replacement without copying. Combining the devices with ChatGPT's dialogic and generative features forms an advanced artificial intelligence-based writing education environment. Such devices are ethically combined, and mechanical precision and discourse-level competence are both increased. Such alignment with students' critical thinking and autonomous writing capability can be compromised if they heavily rely on AI paraphrasing devices. This paradox calls for the adoption of AI as a peer tutor within the classroom under human supervision. Present tendencies in EFL classrooms, despite the recent innovations, have seen a recent increase in AI tool adoption, based on systematic evaluations.

Fostering learner autonomy was one of the desirable outcomes of the artificial intelligence (AI) evaluation conducted by Malik et al. (2024), while academic dishonesty and plagiarism were ever-present undesirable outcomes. Moreover, the usage of AI increased manifold (Hashmi et al., 2025). They reported that to have a lasting impact on education, there is a need for ethical application and teaching facilitation. Salido et al. (2025) stress the importance of combining AI technologies with unique educational models to prevent surface learning. You can use Grammarly for peer assessment, QuillBot for paraphrasing sessions, and ChatGPT for writing exercises based on specific genres, just to mention a few. In addition to attaining technical correctness, such integrated applications enable students to develop their evaluation and critical thinking skills. Mohebbi (2025) presents a discussion on the importance of hybrid teaching methods in which teacher-provided scaffolding is combined with AI-generated feedback. This approach does not allow students to passively accept what AI recommends but rather makes them engage in active thinking over it and come up with their own opinion. Students who used QuillBot and ChatGPT in combination with conventional classroom teaching were far better equipped to construct well-timed essays and scholarly articles than before.

For example, Esperanzate (2025) argues that AI software can help fill gaps within the academic publishing profession in the support of nascent EFL scholars while they learn disciplinary conventions. Students do, however, need to be taught how to use generating and paraphrasing tools ethically in order to maintain stylistic uniformity and avoid plagiarism (Chan, 2025). Ethical considerations would include ethical thinking next to the potential pedagogic benefits of AI systems. Issues raised by Chinoracky & Stalmasekova (2025) include lost creativity, normalized writing, and the threat of academic dishonesty. Wieczorek (2025) states that students have to be taught how to think critically about AI and how to use it responsibly when they must. Academic honesty, openness, and human monitoring must be given precedence over the AI integration policy of institutions. Toward ethical cooperation among teachers in finding a balance between the flexibility and scalability of AI tools and human pedagogy is significant, as teachers strive to rebrand themselves as co-teachers. Yu et al. (2025) observe that AI integration success is dependent on framing AI feedback as formative. This way, learners are encouraged to have a two-way dialogue with the tool and their instructor in an effort to critique and improve their work. Instructors serve as mediators within this hybrid model by inserting context into AI ideas, and students serve as active judges and co-creators of knowledge.

Table 1. Comparative Pedagogical Implications of AI Tools

AI Tool	PERISH (Pedagogical, Ethical, Relevance, Innovation, Sustainability, Human Oversight)	Ethical Considerations	Activities in Class	Teacher Role
ChatGPT	Pedagogical: dialogic, genre-sensitive feedback; Ethical: bias risks; Relevance: high in academic publishing; Innovation: generative AI; Sustainability: scalable; Human oversight essential	Risks of plagiarism, overdependence, and homogenization of style	Genre-based writing tasks, iterative feedback loops, and academic publishing practice	Scaffold AI feedback, ensure critical engagement, and design hybrid tasks
Grammarly	Pedagogical: grammar/style correction; Ethical: limited; Relevance: strong in everyday writing; Innovation: AI-enhanced error detection; Sustainability: high; Oversight: needed for depth	Overreliance on surface correction reduced critical editing skills	Peer editing workshops, grammar/style enhancement activities	Contextualize feedback, encourage deeper revision beyond surface corrections
Quillbot	Pedagogical: paraphrasing, lexical variety; Ethical: risk of plagiarism if misused; Relevance: strong in academic rephrasing; Innovation: text transformation; Sustainability: moderate; Oversight: vital	Academic dishonesty risks, lack of originality	Paraphrasing practice, summary writing, and academic integrity exercises	Monitor ethical use, guide paraphrasing as learning, not substitution

Authors' own work, 2025.

ChatGPT, Grammarly, and QuillBot are a few of the AI-based applications that are changing the landscape of writing education. They complement teachers to offer feedback and new suggestions. Their ability to improve accuracy, critical literacy, genre knowledge, and academic publishing preparedness has been supported by empirical and review studies (Noor, 2025). Among the ethical issues are plagiarism, overreliance, and homogenization, which require clear institutional standards and explicit mediation from teachers, enabling students to critically engage with the new AI technologies. Hybrid teaching methods that combine human scaffolding with AI feedback include a crucial role for the teacher. When appropriately placed, AI technologies have the potential to transform EFL writing instruction into more inclusive, dialogical, and morally based practices, while promoting student improvement in language skills and academic literacy.

No matter how proficient a learner is in a language, writing is one of the most challenging skills to master (Bui et al., 2025). Many forms of writing errors are common among ESL students because they struggle to express themselves clearly in written form (Derakhshan & Karimian, 2020) aid students in Providing their writing performance It is essential to provide students with feedback (CF) when they write. Nevertheless, there is still a dispute about the usage of CF, even though it could be beneficial for student writing. Research has shown that CF can hurt students' writing abilities (Zhan & Teng, 2025). Moreover, Mohebbi (2025) has shown that CF can improve students' writing.

As a result of the intricate nature of the communication process involved, many educators believe that teaching students to write well is one of the most challenging aspects of language instruction Adedeji & Akinpelu, 2025). Due to human error, there is no guarantee that students will receive consistent feedback from both their teachers and their peers. As a result, it is impossible to pinpoint specific writing issues, and students may end up confused about the signals they got (Kim et al., 2025). Teachers of foreign languages rely heavily on student performance evaluations to inform their pedagogical decisions and help students reach their full potential. The problem is that providing accurate and consistent holistic feedback can become a time-consuming and instructor-centered process when teachers are required to correct a large number of student-written assignments.

Over the past decade, researchers have examined the efficacy of the AWE program as a tool for enhancing students' writing in an effort to remove the obstacles that educators encounter while providing instructional feedback. It seems that newer reports have added to the growing body of evidence linking CF implementation with enhanced student writing.

One study that examined how CF affected students' writing accuracy was a meta-analysis by Abdi Tabari et al. (2025) shows that research on written corrective feedback has entered a period of rapid development, where this study suggests using new measurement methods to advance written corrective feedback. Soodmand et al. (2025) CF may thus move its emphasis from its overall effectiveness to the best ways to deliver it so that students reap its full benefits. Direct and indirect CF, selective and comprehensive CF, CF offered at different levels of explicitness, etc., are all aspects of CF that have been the subject of research into its most effective delivery to students. The use of automated writing evaluation (AWE) to provide critical feedback on student writing has increased alongside developments in corpus linguistics and natural language processing. Moreover, because AWE has never been used before in the field of English writing instruction, several empirical studies have tested various AWE systems to see how they affect students' writing. Consequently, it is essential and beneficial to conduct a comprehensive literature review on AWE systems to educate educational administrators, practitioners, and developers about the impact these systems can have on student writing and how to enhance their effectiveness as writing tools. The use of AWE in educational contexts has actually been the subject of multiple review publications.

Huang et al. (2025) looked at research that looked at how AWE affected student writing and found some evidence that it had a favorable impact. Furthermore, they present the distribution, collaboration, development trends, and current research focus through visual map analysis. Focusing on feedback providers and psychological processes can further advance research on written corrective feedback. It also benefits from combining interdisciplinary knowledge from fields such as education, neuroscience, and psychology, and using novel research and measurement methods to advance the field. The findings showed that previous AWE research mostly ignored the theoretical framework and technological opportunities presented by AWE programs. Additional research on the impact of AWE feedback on student writing was presented by Zhao (2025). It would appear, however, that neither they nor studies on the impact of AWE feedback on student writing were incorporated into a systematic review of the literature. That is, they investigated the impact of AWE feedback from different angles, including student use of AWE and different modes of AWE-supported error correction, among others.

HYBRID MODELS OF INSTRUCTION USING AWE IN WRITING

A new method of teaching writing, especially in EFL settings, has emerged with the advent of generative artificial intelligence (GenAI) technologies. Grammarly, QuillBot, and ChatGPT are a few of the Automatic Writing Evaluation (AWE) tools that have developed from elementary error detection to advanced forms of feedback, from interactive to creative and formative assessment (Barrios-Beltran, 2025). Because of this shift, hybrid pedagogies that combine AI-based feedback and human scaffolding are gaining popularity again. ChatGPT and traditional AWE tools improved the students' correctness in grammar; the researchers discovered ChatGPT to have the specific advantage of turning the students into their "ideal L2 writing self". (Pawlak et al., 2025). With respect to this inspiring idea, ChatGPT forms learner confidence and identity, as well as correcting errors.

Nevertheless, it is important to note that the researchers emphasized that the integration of ChatGPT into teacher-led learning contexts maximizes the affective and cognitive effects. In a similar Delikoura & Hui (2025) stated in a systematic evaluation that ChatGPT promotes independence and lessens fear of writing, but technology cannot replace human teachers. Instead, educators should think of ChatGPT as an ally in the classroom, helping students put AI input into context and guaranteeing that they critically interact. This is in line with Papaneophytou & Nicolaou's (2025) research on hybrid AI models, which argues that AI should augment human mediators rather than supplant them. Underpinnings in Theory and Practice Learners, AI tools, and instructors all work together to build knowledge in hybrid AWE models that are based on socio-constructivist concepts.

In their study comparing ChatGPT and Grammarly for article usage, Ahmadzade and Farahian (2025) found that teachers needed to step in to correct AI mistakes and misunderstandings, but ChatGPT promoted critical interaction with grammatical concepts. Just as Kim et al. (2025) demonstrated, students' writing fluency was greatly enhanced when QuillBot was used in conjunction with formative assessment tasks. However, this improvement was contingent upon teachers mediating the AI-generated suggestions. Genre awareness, critical thinking, and intercultural competency are higher-order abilities that these models should aim to improve upon, as pointed out by Aryana et al. (2025). Moreover, teachers facilitate students' development of discourse-level and rhetorical skills. AI can provide instant feedback on form through hybrid training. Modeling approaches for academic publishing and writing academic publications is an area where EFL learners encounter challenges with genre conventions, coherence, and disciplinary writing norms; thus, the hybrid integration of AWE tools becomes more important in this context. Gabay et al.'s (2025) comprehensive review indicated that while AI technologies like ChatGPT, Grammarly, and QuillBot assist students in higher education to create and revise academic texts, genre alignment can be achieved only under the supervision of a teacher.

Researchers Altamimi & Hussein (2025) studied Arabic-speaking students engaging in the use of Grammarly and ChatGPT for the production of research articles. While AI technologies allowed students to go from "prompt to publication," they nonetheless needed their instructors' guidance to refine their rhetorical strategies, add citations, and respond to ethical issues in their work. Wang (2025) lays down that hybrid AWE techniques make publication more possible for new researchers by offering them support systems. However, they caution against blind use of AI, referring to the plagiarism question, homogenization of style, and ethical considerations regarding the use of AI in writing. Even with a middle ground represented by hybrid models, there are still challenges. Learners can be misled by the AI technology providing incorrect or misleading feedback without human intervention, which Lo et al. (2025) have pointed out. Hybrid integration, according to Aljasir (2022), must also deal with equity concerns, since not all students have the same opportunity to use sophisticated AI technologies. Additionally, there are ongoing ethical concerns around issues such as plagiarism, ghostwriting, and reliance on artificial intelligence. Therefore, to include AI in educational frameworks, hybrid AWE instruction necessitates clear ethical principles, AI literacy training for teachers, and institutional backing.

Table 2. Hybrid Models of AWE in Writing

AWE Activities	AI Tools	Implications for Academic Publication	Challenges
Grammar and style correction	Grammarly, ChatGPT	Enhances grammatical accuracy and readability of manuscripts; prepares drafts for peer review.	Overreliance on surface correction; limited support for rhetorical or genre-specific issues
Paraphrasing and rewording	Quillbot, ChatGPT	Helps learners practice lexical variation and avoid plagiarism; supports literature review writing.	Risk of unethical paraphrasing or plagiarism; homogenization of writing style
Iterative feedback on drafts	ChatGPT, Grammarly	Provides immediate, dialogic feedback for improving clarity, cohesion, and argumentation	Potential inaccuracies in AI suggestions; requires teacher mediation for validity.
Genre modeling and discourse	ChatGPT	Assists novice writers in understanding academic genres and rhetorical conventions	May provide generic or culturally biased models; requires disciplinary-specific teacher input.
Academic publishing scaffolding	ChatGPT, Grammarly, Quillbot	Lowers barriers to publishing for EFL scholars by refining drafts and aligning with journal standards	Ethical dilemmas in authorship transparency; risk of AI overuse in publishable drafts
Formative assessment tasks	Grammarly, Quillbot, ChatGPT	Enhances motivation and autonomy by offering individualized feedback during the writing process	Student overdependence on AI; potential neglect of self-editing and critical thinking

Resources: Author's own work, 2025.

There has been a change in the dynamics of writing instruction, feedback from instructors, and scholarly publication since Automatic Writing Evaluation (AWE) systems were introduced into English as a foreign language and English as a second language (EFL/ESL) writing classes. Grammarly, QuillBot, and ChatGPT are now commonplace in universities, but their true pedagogical potential is in blended learning environments that combine human teachers with AI tools (Laoha et al., 2025). Grammar and style correction, paraphrasing and rewording, iterative feedback, genre modeling, publishing scaffolding, and formative assessment are the six main activities highlighted in the table Hybrid Models of AWE in Writing. Table 1 also outlines the corresponding AI tools, implications for academic publication, and challenges. Here, we'll go over each aspect thoroughly.

It has been well-documented, nonetheless, that there is a risk of dependency. Wiboolyasarin et al. (2025) found that students typically pay more attention to superficial mistakes and less to more complex issues, such as argumentation and organization. Because of this restriction, student-teacher mediation is essential for moving students beyond memorization and into critical engagement with discourse that is distinctive to a given genre. Changing wording and rephrasing, students can benefit from using QuillBot and ChatGPT to practice paraphrasing, a skill necessary for writing effective literature reviews and staying away from plagiarism. Used appropriately, paraphrasing tools enhance lexical variation and academic integrity. Students enjoyed QuillBot's rewording option because of how it aided their vocabulary mastery and grammatical variation.

Spelling and Capitalization Correction Grammarly and ChatGPT are two AI systems that offer instant feedback in terms of punctuation, style, and grammar. Such functionality makes manuscripts easier to read and ensures that drafts are comparable in terms of the requirements of language correctness standards for peer-reviewed journals. English foreign language students who utilized Grammarly showed more regular improvement in surface correctness compared with students who did not use Grammarly Lin & Yu, 2025). Ding & Zou (2024). argued that ChatGPT's correcting ability enriches classical AWE by embedding the explanation of context and mechanical correction. There are, however, concerns of a moral nature in terms of paraphrasing.

Bailey et al. 2025 say that students have been found to use QuillBot for heavy rewrites, with potential issues regarding plagiarism, fake personas, and generating consistent writing styles. Similarly, Kim & Chon (2025) asserted that academic writing loses its distinctive voice when overemphasis is laid on AI paraphrasing, an occurrence known as stylistic flattening. To reduce the impact of such threats, hybrid models incorporate paraphrase practice into the classroom discussions of proper citation, critical synthesis, and use of sources. What sets Zhang et al. (2025) apart from other more conventional AWE systems is its dialogic aspect, allowing iterative revising on drafts.

Grammarly helps by pointing out typos and other mechanical mistakes in different drafts. By highlighting mistakes and requesting students to reassess their writing self, ChatGPT helps students construct their "ideal L2 writing self", as it turns out by Shi et al. (2025). Publisher requirements, such as clarity, coherence, and logic, are enhanced by this ongoing interaction. However, the accuracy of ChatGPT remains unequal. In certain situations, ChatGPT provided novice writers with erroneous grammatical descriptions, as it turns out to Healey (2025). Hybrid versions provide teachers with the ability to examine AI responses, allowing students to adopt useful suggestions and discard inappropriate ones. This highlights the value of teacher intervention.

Analyzing genres and conversations. To publish in an academic journal, one must be well-versed in the rhetorical norms and genres of the field. To help with this, ChatGPT models the beginning, middle, and end of several types of research papers. Students reported having more confidence in meeting academic requirements after using genre modeling to prepare abstracts or literature reviews, as pointed out by Sarıca and Gençoğlu (2025). However, ChatGPT's genre models may exhibit bias or oversimplification. According to Adrian (2025), AI systems aren't always aware of how to use rhetorical strategies that are unique to different fields of study, which can cause them to conform instead of speak with their genuine academic voices. Teachers need to contextualize genre models, prioritizing intercultural competence and disciplinary discourse.

ACADEMIC PUBLISHING SCAFFOLDING USING AWE IN CLASSROOM INSTRUCTION

Academic publishing is a significant achievement for EFL learners, especially for graduate students and new researchers. A lot of people struggle to write manuscripts that are ethically sound, rhetorically relevant, and grammatically correct. By providing real-time corrections, paraphrasing, and genre modeling, Automatic Writing Evaluation (AWE) systems such as ChatGPT, Grammarly, and Quillbot are becoming more popular for this purpose (Abdullah, 2025). Several researchers, Lund et al. (2025), contend that in order to prevent issues like ghostwriting, plagiarism, and over-reliance, these technologies should be included in organized pedagogical models.

Contextualization, Awareness, Learning, Linking, Experiencing, Developing, and Assessing (CALLEDA) is a powerful framework for incorporating AWE into classroom classes. Followed by a critical discussion based on current studies, a table describing instructional design phases (opening, main employing CALLEDA, closure), and step-by-step teaching methodologies, AI functions are provided below.

Table 3. Academic Publishing Scaffolding Using CALLEDA with AWE

Phase	CALLEDA Component	AWE Activities	AI Tools	Instructional Focus for Academic Publishing	Challenges/Ethical Issues
Opening	Contextualization & Awareness	Introduce journal standards, ethical publishing, and common writing errors.	ChatGPT, Grammarly	Build awareness of academic discourse, publishing norms, and integrity	Misconception that AI ensures publishability (Yunita & Fitrianna, 2025)
Main Activities	L – Learning	Grammar and style correction on draft sections	Grammarly, ChatGPT	Enhance manuscript accuracy and readability	Overreliance on surface correction (Adrian, 2025)
	L – Linking	Paraphrasing for literature review writing	Quillbot, ChatGPT	Practice lexical variety and source integration	Risk of plagiarism, homogenized style (Ghitri & Elouali, 2025)
	E – Experiencing	Iterative feedback on clarity and argumentation	ChatGPT, Grammarly	Refine cohesion and logical flow	Inaccuracies in AI suggestions (Liashuk, 2025)
	D – Developing	Genre modeling (abstracts, discussions, conclusions)	ChatGPT	Learn the rhetorical conventions of academic publishing	Generic or culturally biased models (Zhou & Du Preez, 2025)
	A – Assessing	Peer + AI-supported review of manuscripts	All tools combined	Evaluate readiness for journal submission, reflect on AI's role	Ghost authorship, lack of transparency (Silhadi, 2025)
Closing	Reflection & Feedback	Teacher scaffolding, student reflection on AI use	All tools combined	Ethical integration, strengthening critical evaluation skills	Overdependence, reduced self-editing skills (Kherbouche, 2025)

Resources: Author's own work, 2025.

A particularly difficult part of writing in English as a foreign language (EFL) is preparing for academic publication. The rules of language, the structure of discourse, and rhetorical practices are obstacles for many beginning researchers. According to Muthmainnah et al. (2025), automated writing assessment (AWE) systems like Grammarly, QuillBot, and ChatGPT have become invaluable resources for students as they progress from draft writing to publishing. Structured instructional design is necessary for effective use of these tools, though. For educators wishing to incorporate AI in their daily practice, the CALLEDA model provides a step-by-step guide: contextualization, awareness, learning, linking, experiencing, developing, and assessment.

DESIGNING INSTRUCTIONS STEP-BY-STEP

1. Opening Phase: Contextualization and Awareness

Students are taught academic publishing conventions, such as how to format their manuscript, what peer review is like, and how to conduct themselves ethically, in the first phase. Artificial intelligence software, such as Grammarly and ChatGPT, is used for the purpose of examining journal submission guidelines and analyzing common pitfalls in articles. Academic publishing is held to a high standard, and this helps students understand that. According to Li & Wilson (2025), AI tools in the initial stage act as motivating scaffolding, assisting students in identifying the difference between the standards of classroom writing and journal writing.

2. Main Activity: Grammar and Style Correction

Grammarly and ChatGPT are introduced during the learning phase to increase grammar and style. Undergraduates submit rough drafts of their research papers, which are then edited by an AI system. Manuscripts are revised to make the text meet publishing standards, both in terms of readability and linguistic accuracy. According to Christoforou (2025), Grammarly enhances vocabulary and fluency while ChatGPT contributes to metalinguistic awareness through contextualized explanations.

3. Main Activity: Paraphrasing and Literature Integration

Using Sources QuillBot and ChatGPT are employed to paraphrase sources and synthesize literature for literature reviews in the linking and experiencing stages. Still following the academic standards, students maintain the ability to practice paraphrasing. Artificial intelligence paraphrase enhances students' confidence using secondary sources; however, at the same time, it elevates the chances of plagiarism and uniformity of style. In order to prevent unethical use, Villamin et al. (2025) emphasize the importance of adequate guidance on appropriate citation methods that must be given alongside paraphrasing exercises.

4. Main Activity: Genre Modeling and Discourse Development

ChatGPT has been used to model genres during the development phase. Students might ask ChatGPT to practice writing an abstract, introduction, or discussion section. Next, they deconstruct disciplinary discourse, language patterns, and rhetorical structures. AI-assisted genre modeling really helped in enhancing the comprehension of academic writing structures in grammar acquisition and cohesiveness.

5. Closing Phase: Formative Assessment and Reflection

Before a test, students use a combination of AI comments, peer review, and teacher scaffolding. We use Grammarly to catch typos and other mechanical errors, ChatGPT in check argument clarity, and QuillBot to rephrase text. Instructors spur critical thinking by holding class discussions on the advantages and disadvantages of AI recommendations.

STEP-BY-STEP TEACHING AWE IN THE CLASSROOM USING CALLEDA

1. Opening Phase (Contextualization & Awareness)

Activity: Introduce journal guidelines and norms of ethical publishing. Use sample articles, asking students to identify features.

AI Function: Use ChatGPT to summarize submission standards for journals and Grammarly to point out common mechanical errors in sample texts.

Rationale: Lays the groundwork for understanding of publication process; ethics underpinning AI use must come before application of tool.

2. Main Activities Using CALLEDA Acronym

L – Learning: Students submit a draft paragraph to Grammarly and ChatGPT for grammar/style correction. Focus is upon the accuracy, fluency, and readability of academic English. According to Adrian (2025), Grammarly enhanced lexical diversity and reduced surface mistakes. L- Linking: Students paraphrase quotes from journal articles using Quillbot and ChatGPT. Teacher models proper citation protocols for maintaining academic integrity and points out that uncritical paraphrasing is the equivalent of plagiarism. E - Experiencing: Students submit complete draft sections to ChatGPT for iterative feedback on argumentation and clarity. Grammarly runs concurrently at a micro-level for accuracy and noted that, without teacher mediation, students will adopt AI-deficient feedback. D – Developing: Faculty showed how to use ChatGPT in generating model sample abstracts or discussion sections.

Students compare AI-generated models with journal articles in acquiring rhetorical moves and genre awareness gains using AI-enabled modeling, but warned against using default templates. A – Assessing: Peer review workshops in which students peer-review drafts of one another with the aid of AI. ChatGPT makes suggestions for cohesive improvements, Grammarly checks accuracy, and Quillbot provides paraphrasing alternatives. This stage, combining AI with peer assessment, increased student engagement but brought forward ghost authorship concerns.

3. Closing Phase (Reflection & Feedback)

Teacher facilitates reflection on the role of AI: Which suggestions were useful? Which were misleading? Students generate a "reflection log" detailing the contribution of AI. The essence of this activity is that reflective scaffolding prevents overdependence and builds AI literacy.

RESEARCH METHODOLOGY

Research Design

The research design of the study is quantitative, and it will investigate the efficacy of having ChatGPT as a co-teacher for Automatic Writing Evaluation (AWE) under the CALLEDA instructional model in the context of scholarly publication. Quantitative design is applied since it is meant to produce quantifiable and generalizable data on the feelings and results of learners through writing instruction with the assistance of AI tools. Quantitative designs are particularly appropriate when the aim is to explore the correlation between variables and to assess the extent of change in students' abilities or attitudes as a result of a pedagogical. The systematic character of the CALLEDA model Contextualization, Awareness, Learning, Linking, Experiencing, Developing, and Assessing is also amenable to a quantitative orientation because its phases can be translated into observable behavior and quantifiable using numerical data collection.

In the study, the independent variable is the use of ChatGPT on the CALLEDA model of teaching, and the dependent variable is the learners' experience and judgment of how effective it is at scaffolding academic publication writing. Through the survey method, the study employs quantifiable facts rather than personal readings so as to facilitate the possibility of statistical measures being applied through SPSS to check for validity in the results.

Participants

The participants in this study are 44 undergraduate students at Universitas Al Asyariah Mandar (Unasman), Indonesia, who were enrolled in the second semester of the 2024/2025 academic year. They were all majors in English Education and had already completed subjects on academic writing fundamentals. The group was chosen through purposive sampling since they are new scholars moving towards research-based writing and are most likely to pursue academic publication at subsequent levels of study.

The relatively limited number of subjects is an indication of the small population of advanced writing students at Unasman, but is consistent with earlier small-scale experiments in EFL settings. All participants were informed of the aims and procedures of the study, and gave informed consent before participating. Faculty research committee approval of the study was obtained to ensure that the study conformed to academic ethics as well as student rights.

Research Tools

The primary research instrument was a structured questionnaire with the aim of eliciting students' perceptions of ChatGPT as a co-teacher of AWE when it is instructed using the CALLEDA model. The questionnaire was constructed on a 5-point Likert scale, 1 = Strongly Disagree to 5 = Strongly Agree, representing the degree of agreement with the following statements: (1) ChatGPT as Co-Instructor items to capture clarity, usefulness, and accuracy of AI comments; (2) Effectiveness of CALLEDA Implementation items mapped to each phase of CALLEDA (e.g., contextualization, awareness, learning, etc.) and (3) Challenges and Ethical Concerns items concerning plagiarism risk, overdependence, and credibility of AI proposals. The tool was also pre-tested using expert judgment by two postgraduate senior lecturers in applied linguistics and educational technology. Pilot testing with five non-participant students was carried out to verify clarity and reliability of items. Cronbach's alpha coefficient for reliability was then calculated while analyzing data to determine internal consistency, taking a level of $\alpha \geq .70$ as acceptable.

Procedure for Collecting Data

Data collection was carried out with a systematic process that adhered to the CALLEDA instructional method. Intervention was carried out across six instructional classes of 90 minutes' duration, divided over three weeks. Procedures included as shown below:

Introduction and Orientation

Students were oriented on the study purpose, the ethical use of AI tools, and the research procedure. Students were introduced to ChatGPT, Grammarly, and Quillbot and were shown how to use them.

Then implementation of CALLEDA Phases: Each session worked on one or more aspects of the CALLEDA model. For instance:

1. Contextualization: Exploration of journal submission guidelines.
2. Awareness: Identification of common writing errors in published articles.
3. Learning: Grammar correction with Grammarly and ChatGPT.
4. Linking: Practice of paraphrasing literature with Quillbot and ChatGPT.
5. Experiencing: Revision of drafts in a cyclical process with AI-based feedback.
6. Developing: Genre modeling of abstracts and discussions with ChatGPT.
7. Assessing: Peer review with AI-aided feedback.

At the end of the intervention, the questionnaire Likert scale was completed by all class members. It was completed by the students anonymously to minimize response bias and encourage open-minded thinking. Procedure of Research Using CALLEDA for AWE in EFL class:

1. CALLEDA model was employed as instructional design support for teaching writing using AWE.
2. Contextualisation: Students utilized ChatGPT to produce simple summary versions of the requirements of journal articles so that they could contextualise their work within the framework of a scholarly publishing environment.
3. Awareness: Grammarly was employed to color-highlight surface errors in sample student writing to foster awareness of mechanical features.
4. Learning: The students did some guided exercises where Grammarly and ChatGPT revised draft sentences, which really reinforced grammatical and stylistic learning.
5. Linking: Quillbot was used in literature review assignments to facilitate paraphrasing, and teachers have highlighted that what is required is correct citation.
6. Experience: Students supplied draft paragraphs to ChatGPT and received responses regarding argumentation, cohesion, and clarity.
7. Developmental: Students compared their abstracts and introductions, produced on ChatGPT, with examples published in journals.
8. Evaluating: Peer review tasks merged human judgment with AI recommendations, encouraging students to assess critically and critique peers.

This was a systematic incorporation that ensured AWE tools were not implemented in isolation but within a pedagogical context balancing automation and human oversight.

Data Analysis

Data analysis was done with the use of SPSS version 26. The following are the steps involved in the analysis:

1. Descriptive Statistics: Frequencies, means, and standard deviations were used to gather participants' responses to each item of the questionnaire. Such results provided a snapshot of the views of the students about ChatGPT and AWE tools within the CALLEDA platform.
2. Testing of Reliability: Cronbach's alpha was used to check the internal consistency of this questionnaire. The above .70 was considered reliable for the result.
3. Inferential Statistics: One-sample t-tests were conducted to test if students' mean responses were significantly different from the neutral point of the Likert scale, 3 = Neither Agree nor Disagree. This was to test whether students significantly rated ChatGPT as effective in CALLEDA.
4. Quantitative analysis allowed for careful testing of the extent to which ChatGPT in CALLEDA was rated as effective in supporting academic publishing competencies.

Ethical Considerations

The study was designed in line with the ethical principles on volunteer engagement, informed consent, anonymity, and appropriate use of AI. Students were provided with instructions that AI-generated ideas needed to be critically reviewed and could not be utilized verbatim in publishable documents to avoid plagiarism or ghost authorship issues. Data collection was performed strictly for academic purposes in an aggregated format while concealing individual participants.

FINDINGS AND DISCUSSION

The research approach considered in this study ensures a systematic, trustworthy, and replicable method of evaluating ChatGPT as a co-instructor in EFL academic writing. By incorporating a validated questionnaire, CALLEDA-based systematic instructional procedures, and SPSS analysis, the research provides rigorous evidence related to the pedagogical value and difficulties encountered when integrating AWE into scaffolding for academic publishing. This design contributes to new scholarship in hybrid AI-supported language instruction and addresses significant questions of effectiveness, ethics, and pedagogical design identified below.

Findings

Table 4. AWE Descriptive Statistics

Student Statements	N	Min	Max	Mean	Std. Deviation
Section A: ChatGPT as Instructor for Idea Generation & Writing Structure					
1. ChatGPT helped me understand the expectations of academic publishing.	44	3.00	5.00	4.6591	.60782
2. Using ChatGPT increased my awareness of common writing problems in my drafts.	44	3.00	5.00	4.5455	.58883
3. The integration of ChatGPT in class made me more conscious of ethical issues (e.g., plagiarism, ghost authorship).	44	2.00	5.00	4.5227	.69846
Section B: Learning					
4. Grammarly review and ChatGPT improved my grammatical writing accuracy.	44	3.00	5.00	4.4545	.62708
5. ChatGPT offered grammatical revisions in an understandable explanation.	44	3.00	5.00	4.5909	.65833
6. I have more confidence in sentence construction because we did it using AWE tools in class.	44	3.00	5.00	4.4545	.72991
Section C: Linking					
7. ChatGPT and Quillbot helped me paraphrase sources effectively.	44	2.00	5.00	4.4545	.69732
8. AWE tools allowed me to connect my ideas to scholarly sources.	44	3.00	5.00	4.5455	.62708
9. I was made to realize the importance of citation and originality while preventing plagiarism after paraphrasing.	44	3.00	5.00	4.5682	.58658
Section D: Experiencing					
10. ChatGPT provided useful feedback on the coherence and clarity of my writing.	44	2.00	5.00	4.5455	.76111
11. AWE tools provided iterative feedback which motivated me to edit and polish my drafts.	44	3.00	5.00	4.4318	.66114
12. I could critically analyze ChatGPT's recommendations with the guidance of a teacher.	44	2.00	5.00	4.4545	.69732
Section E: Developing					

continued on following page

Table 4. Continued

Student Statements	N	Min	Max	Mean	Std. Deviation
13. ChatGPT allowed me to understand the structure of academic writing (e.g., abstracts, introductions, discussions).	44	2.00	5.00	4.3864	.78402
14. ChatGPT genre modeling helped me better understand the rhetorical conventions of academic writing.	44	3.00	5.00	4.4091	.65833
15. ChatGPT encouraged me to employ a more academic tone in writing.	44	3.00	5.00	4.4091	.69276
Section F: Assessing					
16. Peer review activities with the AWE tool assistance enhanced the quality of my manuscript.	44	3.00	5.00	4.4773	.66433
17. Combining teacher feedback and ChatGPT feedback improved my writing more than relying on AI alone.	44	3.00	5.00	4.3409	.74532
18. I feel more prepared to submit an academic paper to a journal after using AWE in the CALLEDA-based instruction.	44	3.00	5.00	4.2955	.73388
Section G: Overall Perceptions					
19. 1ChatGPT acted as a supportive "co-instructor" during my writing process.	44	3.00	5.00	4.5455	.66313
20. Integrating CALLEDA with AWE tools increased my motivation and confidence in academic writing.	44	3.00	5.00	4.5682	.62497
Valid N (listwise)	44				

The current Table 3 looked at how students felt about using ChatGPT in the context of the CALLEDA instructional framework as an Automatic Writing Evaluation (AWE) tool for academic writing in English as a foreign language (EFL). A twenty-item Likert-scale questionnaire was used to measure the responses of forty-four undergraduates. For every item, the descriptive statistics were laid out in Table 3, which included the lowest, highest, mean, and standard deviation scores. All metrics showed consistently high mean scores (M = 4.29-4.65), indicating that students had a favorable impression of QuillBot, Grammarly, and ChatGPT as supplemental learning tools.

Table 5. AWE Reliability Statistics

Cronbach's Alpha	N of Items
.945	20

Detailing the AWE Reliability Statistics in Table 4. Results showing the reliability of the survey are presented in Table 2. Twenty items made up the instrument, and its Cronbach's Alpha coefficient was 0.945. A dependability coefficient greater than 0.90 signifies outstanding internal consistency as per the defined criteria. In order to evaluate students' competence in writing, the items included in the survey had to reliably measure the underlying constructs.

Table 6. Mean score

	N	Minimum	Maximum	Mean	Std. Deviation
AweMeanscore	44	67.00	100.00	89.6591	9.47934
Valid N (listwise)	44				

Based on the mean score on the survey, Table 5 displays descriptive data of the students' replies. A total of forty-four legitimate replies were examined. Scores ranged from 67.00 to 100.00, showing that students' perceptions and competencies varied. Scores ranged from 89.66 on the mean to 9.48 on the standard deviation. Students had a generally positive impression of the CALLEDA model teaching paradigm and the use of ChatGPT, Grammarly Checker as AWE tools, as shown by the relatively high mean score. Although there was considerable variation in the replies (as indicated by the moderate standard deviation), the majority of students' scores were very near to the mean, indicating that the results were generally positive.

The distribution of the students' mean scores from the questionnaire is shown in the histogram. The majority of the 44 students surveyed had a favorable impression of the CALLEDA model of instruction following its implementation (mean score: 89.66). Although there was significant dispersion (standard deviation = 9.48), the majority of replies were somewhat near the mean. A score of 67 indicated the most disapproving views, while a score of 100 showed the most agreeable ones. A large number of students grouped around 100, indicated substantial support for the model; in contrast, just a small number of students scored lower, indicating that neutral or negative comments were uncommon. A peek at the higher scores emphasizes the typically favorable outcomes, and the overall shape is close to normal.

DISCUSSION

These results are in line with the increasing amount of research that positions AI-based writing tools as collaborative educational partners rather than just correcting aids similar with (Alwasidi & Al-Khalifah 2025) findings by using ChatGPT as a writing structure and idea generator instructor shown means of 4.65 for "understanding expectations of academic publishing", 4.54 for "raising awareness of writing problems", and 4.52 for "ethical consciousness", in Table 1 showed some very high means. According to these results, students thought ChatGPT was a great tool for helping them think of ideas, organize their academic writing, and become more conscious of the importance of academic honesty.

This study is in line with the claims made by Muthmainnah et al. (2025), who stated that, when incorporated into teacher-guided models, AI has the potential to increase students' ethical awareness instead of causing them to rely too much. Al-tamimi & Hussein (2025) found similar results in Arabic-speaking EFL students who used ChatGPT had an easier time figuring out what was considered publishable and how to make their manuscripts stronger before submitting. Hence, the results of this study add to the growing body of evidence demonstrating that ChatGPT aids with the cognitive (clarity of structure) and emotive (consciousness of ethics) aspects of academic writing. Students' statement with a mean score of 4.45, students were in agreement that AWE tools increased confidence in sentence formation (M = 4.45) and helped with grammatical precision (M = 4.59). These results demonstrate how ChatGPT and Grammarly can help students become more independent learners by providing them with micro-level correctional tools. Similar study, Yang & Yang (2025a) also discovered that EFL learners' confidence in grammar acquisition was greatly improved by GenAI-assisted grammar instruction; thus, our findings are in line with that. Another scholar also supports this study. Yusuf et al. (2025) found that students' writing was more fluent and had a wider vocabulary after using Grammarly's correction feedback. It appears that the synergistic effect of ChatGPT's dialogic feedback and Grammarly's rule-based corrections helps students not only fix their mistakes but also develop an internal knowledge of grammar.

Correlating paraphrasing, idea-to-reference-and-ethics-consciousness, and reference-citation awareness all had means between 4.45 and 4.54 (Table 1). It is claimed that students were learning about the importance of not plagiarizing, and QuillBot and ChatGPT helped them with paraphrasing and incorporating literature into their writing. Agyemang (2025) echoed these findings when they stressed that QuillBot improves competency in paraphrasing, but that its usefulness relies on clear teaching in citation and source acknowledgment from teachers. The same cautionary note was issued by Yao et al. (2025) regarding the potential for unethical or stylistic homogenization to result from AI paraphrasing in the absence of supervision. Students thought that teacher-mediated scaffolding was helpful for linking activities, especially paraphrasing and source integration, according to the results. Moreover, students' agreement that ChatGPT increased cohesiveness and clarity (M = 4.54), iterative feedback drove modifications (M = 4.43), and instructor assistance permitted critical examination of AI suggestions (M = 4.56). This part recorded some of the highest averages. These results demonstrate that ChatGPT is not only a corrector but also a dialogic interlocutor, facilitating numerous cycles of feedback and revision.

This result is in line with what Shi et al. (2025) found: that ChatGPT helped students develop their "ideal L2 writing self", which in turn encouraged them to actively improve their work and believe in their own writing abilities in academic settings. Mali (2025) found that ChatGPT cannot replace human instructors and performs best in hybrid models where teachers approve AI proposals. The importance of teacher mediation is echoed in this finding. In Table 1, shown mean score of 4.38 students thought ChatGPT helped recognize academic text structures, 4.40 for genre modeling, and 4.45 for establishing an academic writing style.

Concerns raised by MacArthur (2025) regarding AI's lack of discipline specialization and its potential to perpetuate culturally biased rhetorical norms may explain the relative decline, as may ChatGPT's general genre modeling. Students were still pleased with the results of using AI-assisted modeling to guide the progression of their academic writing. These results provide credence to the rising agreement that while AI may help new writers understand rhetorical rules, it still needs professors to provide disciplinary and cultural context. On the statement of evaluating using AI for peer review improved manuscript quality (M = 4.47), integrating AI with teacher feedback yielded better results than AI alone (M = 4.34), and CALLEDA-based AWE increased students' confidence in their publishing readiness (M = 4.40). It is clear from these findings that hybrid feedback mechanisms are crucial. Consistent with the findings of Huang & Wang (2025), who discovered that AI-supported peer review encouraged more responsibility and cooperation among EFL students, students appreciated the incorporation of AI technologies into both peer review and teacher-led evaluation.

This study notes that certain students may still place too much emphasis on AI's autonomy, since the mean for integrating instructor and AI feedback is lower (M = 4.34) than for other things. In Table 1, students also reported higher levels of enthusiasm and confidence after CALLEDA-AWE integration (M = 4.56) and perceived ChatGPT as a helpful co-instructor (M = 4.54) in the last segment. The findings provide credence to the educational concept. These results are in line with those of Alfaleh et al. (2025), who discovered that students were able to get "from prompt to publication" with the help of AI tools since these tools provided confidence scaffolding during manuscript writing and emphasized the importance of structured teaching in enhancing student motivation and ethical engagement through an AI literacy program. The novelty of the result CALLEDA's integration, ChatGPT, is seen as more than just a tool; it's seen as a pedagogical collaborator, or "co-instructor" also improve personalize in learning (Al Yakin et al., 2025).

Based on descriptive statistics, all students had fantastic things to say about ChatGPT and the other AWE technologies that were a part of the CALLEDA framework. Students reported significant improvement in areas such as paraphrasing, reasoning, genre identification, and publication preparation. They also highlighted that teacher mediation can work to ensure the ethical use and critical examination of the AI feedback. Now, the study addresses the motivational role of ChatGPT. The results of this study are supported by Shi et al. (2025), and the hybrid instructional model and ethical problems are corroborated by Mali (2025). Simultaneously, the results showed the persistence of issues related to generic genre modeling, overreliance, and ethical problems. Finally, this research demonstrates that ChatGPT might play a co-teacher role in EFL writing when embedded into CALL-based teaching; it provides motivational and structural scaffolding for academic publishing apart from corrective support.

CONCLUSION

This study present EFL class strategically integrated into organized educational models such as CALLEDA. The results of this study confirm that ChatGPT and other AWE tools have the potential to revolutionize education. Generic AI improves not only mechanical accuracy but also higher-order writing abilities like cohesiveness, rhetorical awareness, and genre sensitivity, in contrast to older rule-based systems. Apart from enhancing their grammatical accuracy, the students in this study, built confidence in organizing academic writings and editing their articles for submission to journals. Above all, they were sensitized to how AI can raise awareness of ethical concerns such as transparency, authorship, and plagiarism. Some recent studies have shown the benefits of hybrid teaching approaches, and without instructor mediation, students may uncritically accept incorrect or generic outputs, although ChatGPT's dialogic and iterative feedback empowers them. To make sure that AI doesn't supplant human judgment but rather enhances it, the CALLEDA framework places students in the role of critical evaluators and teachers in the role of mediators.

Scaffolding in academic publishing also needs to be an important consideration. Using proper language, adhering to disciplinary norms, and understanding multicultural discourse practices are all obstacles that first-time EFL researchers face while preparing their work for publication. Incorporating ChatGPT, Grammarly, and QuillBot into CALLEDA's teaching model, linking, and developing phases allowed students to polish their drafts, practice ethical paraphrasing, and model genre-specific structures. AI extends publication to a broader number of people, yet ethical deployment of this technology requires institutional safeguarding.

Nevertheless, some challenges remain to be overcome. Whilst AI tools can help writers avoid stylistic homogenization, overdependence on AI for superficial rewrites can impede the development of EFL learners' critical self-editing skills. The gray area between human and machine work is also highlighted by anxiety about "ghost authorship.". Therefore, pedagogy and policy at the institutional level must incorporate transparency in AI use. In summary, results show that ChatGPT has the potential to be a good CALLEDA co-instructor in increasing the accuracy, genre awareness, and moral sensitivity of the students. On the other hand, to be effective, hybrid integration is inevitable, with teacher scaffolding supplying context, mediation, and moral guidance. The CALLEDA approach increases students' preparation for academic publishing and guarantees that writing growth remains dialogic, reflective, and ethically grounded by portraying AI as a supportive collaborator rather than a replacement. Also, findings suggest that balanced hybrid models combining AI scalability with human pedagogy will be most effective for teaching English as a foreign language writing in the future. Not only does this kind of integration help kids thrive in school, but it also teaches them how to be active, responsible members of academic communities around the world.

REFERENCES

Abdalrahim, A. M. A., & Mohammed, A. E. H. E. (2025). Strategies for Utilizing Artificial Intelligence to Support EFL Teachers Across Different Educational Levels. *The Arab Journal For Quality Assurance in Higher Education, 19*(66).

Abdi Tabari, M., Kushki, A., & Wang, Y. (2025). Comparing the effects of teacher- and AI-mediated corrective feedback on accuracy, complexity, and quality in L2 written narratives. *Computer Assisted Language Learning*, •••, 1–24. DOI: 10.1080/09588221.2025.2561608

Abdullah, M. Y. (2025). Probing into EFL students' perceptions about the impact of utilizing AI-powered tools on their academic writing practices. *Education and Information Technologies*, *30*(15), 1–32. DOI: 10.1007/s10639-025-13601-w

Abdullah, M. Y. (2025). Probing into EFL students' perceptions about the impact of utilizing AI-powered tools on their academic writing practices. *Education and Information Technologies*, *30*(15), 1–32. DOI: 10.1007/s10639-025-13601-w

Adedeji, O., & Akinpelu, M. (2025). Understanding ICT and Its Impact on Teaching a Foreign Language. French Language Politics and Education in Nigeria: Building Human Capital and a Multilingual Nation.

Agyemang, K. A. (2025). *Understanding Student Practices for Using AI-Powered Learning Assistants: Ethical and Effective Strategies for Academic Success* (Master's thesis, New Mexico State University).

Ahmadzade, M., & Farahian, M. (2025). At a Crossroad: Comparing ChatGPT and Grammarly in Enhancing EFL Learners' Use of the Article'. *SSRN*, *2*(1), 47–62. DOI: 10.2139/ssrn.5699162

Alfaleh, M., Albasis, H. H., & Mohamed, A. M. (2025). EFL learners' motivation and engagement with oral reading activities and AI tools: Exploring the effect of gender, study level and English language proficiency. *Cogent Education*, *12*(1), 2542395. DOI: 10.1080/2331186X.2025.2542395

Altamimi, F., & Hussein, D. (2025). Unlocking Potential: Saudi EFL Male Students' Perspectives on AI Tools for Enhancing English Writing Proficiency. *Arab World English Journal, 16*.

Altamimi, F., & Hussein, D. (2025). Unlocking Potential: Saudi EFL Male Students' Perspectives on AI Tools for Enhancing English Writing Proficiency. *Arab World English Journal, 16*.

Alwasidi, M. A., & Al-Khalifah, K. S. (2025). Assessing the Impact of ChatGPT on EFL Students' Writing Productivity and Proficiency. *Journal of Language Teaching and Research*, *16*(3), 986–995. DOI: 10.17507/jltr.1603.29

Al Yakin, A., Muthmainnah, M., Cardoso, L., Al Matari, A. S., & Obaid, A. (2025). AI-powered Personalization for Learning and Human-Robot Interaction: A Case Study with Pre-Service Teachers from Indonesia. *Southeastern Philippines Journal of Research and Development*, *30*(2), 25–45.

Aryana, S., Sobari, T., San Fauziya, D., & Mustika, R. I. (2025). The Effectiveness of 21st Century Competency Assessment Model and HOTS in Improving Writing Skills: An Experimental Research. *Journal of Language Teaching and Research*, *16*(4), 1115–1128. DOI: 10.17507/jltr.1604.07

Bailey, D. R., Lee, A., He, H., McConnell, J., Wilson, D. R., & Chakrabarti, K. B. (2025). Writing Support with Grammarly: Examining Confidence, Help-Seeking Behavior, and User Perceptions in Higher Education. *Turkish Online Journal of Educational Technology-TOJET*, *24*(1), 90–105.

Barrios-Beltran, D. (2025). Exploring the efficacy of ChatGPT-4 feedback in second language Spanish writing. *System*, *133*, 103771. DOI: 10.1016/j.system.2025.103771

Bui, T. T. U., & Tong, T. V. A. (2025). The impact of ai writing tools on academic integrity: Unveiling english-majored students' perceptions and practical solutions. *AsiaCALL Online Journal*, *16*(1), 83–110. DOI: 10.54855/acoj.251615

Chan, C. K. Y. (2025). Students' perceptions of 'AI-giarism': Investigating changes in understandings of academic misconduct. *Education and Information Technologies*, *30*(6), 8087–8108. DOI: 10.1007/s10639-024-13151-7

Chen, X. (2025). *Implementing E-assessment for Learning in Primary EFL Writing: A Case Study in China*. Springer Nature.

Chen, X., Shu, D., DeLuca, C., & Holden, M. (2025a). Advancing e-assessment for learning in the primary EFL writing classroom: The role of collaborative teacher professional learning. *Asia Pacific Journal of Education*, •••, 1–20. DOI: 10.1080/02188791.2025.2465296

Chen, Y., Wang, Y., Chan, A. B., & Li, J., & LC, R. (2025b). Once More with (the Right) Feeling: How Historical Fiction Writing Processes of Character Design, Plot Outline, and Context Checking Are Affected by Co-Writing with ChatGPT. In *International Conference on Human-Computer Interaction* (pp. 79-101). Cham: Springer Nature Switzerland. DOI: 10.1007/978-3-031-92823-9_7

Chinoracky, R., & Stalmasekova, N. (2025). Ethical Problems in the Use of Artificial Intelligence by University Educators. *Education Sciences*, *15*(10), 1322. DOI: 10.3390/educsci15101322

Christoforou, M. (2025). Gen AI-assisted multimodal meaning Design: Exercising a pedagogic metalanguage of transposition. *Pedagogies*, •••, 1–25. DOI: 10.1080/1554480X.2025.2522884

Delikoura, I., & Hui, P. (2025). From Superficial Outputs to Superficial Learning: Risks of Large Language Models in Education. *arXiv preprint arXiv:2509.21972*.

Derakhshan, A., & Karimian Shirejini, R. (2020). An investigation of the Iranian EFL learners' perceptions towards the most common writing problems. *SAGE Open*, *10*(2), 2158244020919523. DOI: 10.1177/2158244020919523

Ding, L., & Zou, D. (2024). Automated writing evaluation systems: A systematic review of Grammarly, Pigai, and Criterion with a perspective on future directions in the age of generative artificial intelligence. *Education and Information Technologies*, *29*(11), 14151–14203. DOI: 10.1007/s10639-023-12402-3

Feng, L. (2025). Investigating the effects of artificial intelligence-assisted language learning strategies on cognitive load and learning outcomes: A comparative study. *Journal of Educational Computing Research*, *62*(8), 1741–1774. DOI: 10.1177/07356331241268349

Gabay, R. A. E., Funa, A. A., & Ricafort, J. D. (2025). *Generative Artificial Intelligence (GenAI) for Academic Writing in Higher Education: A Scoping Review of Applications*. Challenges, and Implications.

Hashmi, E., Yamin, M. M., & Yayilgan, S. Y. (2025). Securing tomorrow: A comprehensive survey on the synergy of Artificial Intelligence and information security. *AI and Ethics*, *5*(3), 1911–1929. DOI: 10.1007/s43681-024-00529-z

Healey, B. (2025). 'Let me see it through your eyes': Teaching grammar-for-writing as imaginative embodiment. *Literacy*, *59*(2), 242–255. DOI: 10.1111/lit.12387

Hrdlicková, Z. (2025). Enhancing Learning Outcomes in Written Production by Implementing Writing Strategies and Using AI Writing Tools. *Advanced Education*, *26*(26), 59–74. DOI: 10.20535/2410-8286.331366

Huang, Y., & Wang, D. (2025). Can ChatGPT serve as a writing collaborator? Insights from Chinese EFL learners. *System*, *133*, 103775. DOI: 10.1016/j.system.2025.103775

Huang, Y., & Wilson, J. (2025). Exploring the Effectiveness of Large-Scale Automated Writing Evaluation Implementation on State Test Performance Using Generalised Boosted Modelling. *Journal of Computer Assisted Learning*, *41*(2), e70009. DOI: 10.1111/jcal.70009

Kim, J., Yu, S., Detrick, R., & Li, N. (2025). Exploring students' perspectives on Generative AI-assisted academic writing. *Education and Information Technologies*, *30*(1), 1265–1300. DOI: 10.1007/s10639-024-12878-7

Laoha, R., Chomthong, W., & Pongpanich, W. (2025). Artificial Intelligence and English as a Foreign Language (EFL) Teachers' Competencies: A Systematic Review. *Higher Education Studies*, *15*(3), 262–292. DOI: 10.5539/hes.v15n3p262

Li, M., & Wilson, J. (2025). AI-Integrated Scaffolding to Enhance Agency and Creativity in K-12 English Language Learners: A Systematic Review. *Information (Basel)*, *16*(7), 519. DOI: 10.3390/info16070519

Lin, Y., & Yu, Z. (2025). Elucidating university students' intentions to seek automated writing feedback from Grammarly: Toward perceptual and systemic predictors. *Humanities & Social Sciences Communications*, *12*(1), 1–17. DOI: 10.1057/s41599-024-03861-1

Lo, N., Chan, S., & Wong, A. (2025). Evaluating Teacher, AI, and Hybrid Feedback in English Language Learning: Impact on Student Motivation, Quality, and Performance in Hong Kong. *SAGE Open*, *15*(3), 21582440251352907. DOI: 10.1177/21582440251352907

Lund, B., Mannuru, N. R., Teel, Z. A., Lee, T. H., Ortega, N. J., Simmons, S., & Ward, E. (2025, September). Student Perceptions of AI-Assisted Writing and Academic Integrity: Ethical Concerns, Academic Misconduct, and Use of Generative AI in Higher Education. In *AI in Education* (Vol. 1, No. 1, p. 2). MDPI.

MacArthur, M. (2025). Large language models and the problem of rhetorical debt. *AI & Society*, *40*(8), 6425–6438. Advance online publication. DOI: 10.1007/s00146-025-02403-w

Mali, Y. C. G. (2025). Exploring the Use of ChatGPT in EFL/ESL Writing Classrooms: A Systematic Review. *Journal of Language and Education*, *11*(2 (42)), 137–156. DOI: 10.17323/jle.2025.21793

Malik, M. A., Amjad, A. I., Aslam, S., & Fakhrou, A. (2024). Global insights: ChatGPT's influence on academic and research writing, creativity, and plagiarism policies. *Frontiers in Research Metrics and Analytics*, *9*, 1486832. DOI: 10.3389/frma.2024.1486832

Martínez-Pernía, D., Troncoso, A., Chaigneau, S. E., Marchant, N., Zepeda, A., & Blanco-Madariaga, K. A. (2025). Bridging consciousness and AI: ChatGPT-assisted phenomenological analysis. *Frontiers in Psychology*, *16*, 1520186. DOI: 10.3389/fpsyg.2025.1520186

Mazurek, J. (2025). *TPACK Components Contributing to Teachers' Ethical Use of AI for Teaching and Learning: A Mixed-Methods Study* (Doctoral dissertation, Delaware Valley University).

Mohebbi, A. (2025). Enabling learner independence and self-regulation in language education using AI tools: A systematic review. *Cogent Education*, *12*(1), 2433814. DOI: 10.1080/2331186X.2024.2433814

Muthmainnah, M., Asad, M. M., Yakin, A. A., & Almusharraf, N. M. (2025). *Human-robot interaction using ChatGPT for technology driven language learning: contextual insights from the higher education institution of Indonesia*. Asian Education and Development Studies.

Na, I., Duris, M., & Hegelheimer, V. (2025). Feedback and Automated Writing Evaluation (AWE). *Insights into AI and Language Teaching and Learning*, 290.

Noor, N. H. M. (2025). Challenges and Opportunities of Artificial Intelligence (AI) for Malaysian Higher Education: An Exploratory Analysis. *Navigating Barriers to AI Implementation in the Classroom*, 105-132.

Papaneophytou, C., & Nicolaou, S. A. (2025). Promoting Critical Thinking in Biological Sciences in the Era of Artificial Intelligence: The Role of Higher Education. *Trends in Higher Education*, *4*(2), 24. DOI: 10.3390/higheredu4020024

Pawlak, M., Kruk, M., Elahi Shirvan, M., Taherian, T., & Karimpour, S. (2025). Dynamic reciprocal associations of AI-assisted L2 writing task emotions in data-driven learning: A dynamic structural equation modeling. *Computer Assisted Language Learning*, •••, 1–30. DOI: 10.1080/09588221.2025.2498094

Salido, A., Syarif, I., Sitepu, M. S., Wana, P. R., Taufika, R., & Melisa, R. (2025). Integrating critical thinking and artificial intelligence in higher education: A bibliometric and systematic review of skills and strategies. *Social Sciences & Humanities Open*, *12*, 101924. DOI: 10.1016/j.ssaho.2025.101924

Shahri, N., & Karimi-Aghdam, S. (2025). Digitally Mediated Micro-processes of Novice Multilingual Writers: Textualization in Focus. *Written Communication*, •••, 07410883251328320.

Shi, H., Chai, C. S., Zhou, S., & Aubrey, S. (2025). Comparing the effects of ChatGPT and automated writing evaluation on students' writing and ideal L2 writing self. *Computer Assisted Language Learning*, •••, 1–28. DOI: 10.1080/09588221.2025.2454541

Shi, H., Chai, C. S., Zhou, S., & Aubrey, S. (2025). Comparing the effects of ChatGPT and automated writing evaluation on students' writing and ideal L2 writing self. *Computer Assisted Language Learning*, •••, 1–28. DOI: 10.1080/09588221.2025.2454541

Soodmand Afshar, H., Ranjbar, N., & Yenkimaleki, M. (2025). Written Corrective Feedback in Language Education: A Qualitative Meta-Synthetic Study. *Teaching English Language*, *19*(1), 119–158.

Thai, T. T. A., Nguyen, H. H. G., & Nguyen, N. C. (2025). English-major of Using Grammarly for Thesis Writing at Seniors' Perceptions IUH. *International Journal of AI in Language Education, 2*(2), 55-78.

Tran, H. N., Le, T. T. N., & Tran, V. B. U. (2025). AI Tools in Learning Academic Writing: Benefits and Challenges for MA Students in the English Language Studies at the Industrial University of Ho Chi Minh City. *International Journal of AI in Language Education*, *2*(1), 74–91. DOI: 10.54855/ijaile.25215

Turvey, K., & Pachler, N. (2025). A topological exploration of convergence/divergence of human-mediated and algorithmically mediated pedagogy. *British Journal of Educational Technology*, bjet.70007. DOI: 10.1111/bjet.70007

Villamin, P., Lopez, V., Thapa, D. K., & Cleary, M. (2025). A worked example of qualitative descriptive design: A step-by-step guide for novice and early career researchers. *Journal of Advanced Nursing*, *81*(8), 5181–5195. DOI: 10.1111/jan.16481

Wang, X. (2025). Students' perceptions of automated writing evaluation in autonomous learning. *Education and Information Technologies*, *30*(11), 1–33. DOI: 10.1007/s10639-025-13378-y

Wang, X. (2025). Students' perceptions of automated writing evaluation in autonomous learning. *Education and Information Technologies*, *30*(11), 1–33. DOI: 10.1007/s10639-025-13378-y

Wiboolyasarin, W., Wiboolyasarin, K., Kamonsawad, R., & Jinowat, N. (2025). Enhancing Collaborative Writing with Grammarly-Mediated Feedback in Asynchronous Wiki Environments: An Investigation of Group Size. *English Teaching & Learning*, *49*(2), 389–414. DOI: 10.1007/s42321-024-00186-9

Wieczorek, M. (2025). Using ethical scenarios to explore the future of artificial intelligence in primary and secondary education. *Learning, Media and Technology*, •••, 1–17. DOI: 10.1080/17439884.2025.2517335

Woo, K., & Falloon, G. (2025). Moving beyond the rhetoric: Integrating coding into the English curriculum in Australian primary schools. *Australian Educational Researcher*, *52*(1), 803–839. DOI: 10.1007/s13384-024-00742-z

Yang, C., Li, R., & Yang, L. (2025). Revisiting trends in GenAI-assisted second language writing: Retrospect and prospect. *Journal of Educational Computing Research*, *63*(7-8), 07356331251367309. DOI: 10.1177/07356331251367309

Yao, M., Wei, Y., & Liu, H. (2025). AI practices and ethical concerns: An analysis of undeclared uses of AI in published research articles. *Ethics & Behavior*, •••, 1–13. DOI: 10.1080/10508422.2025.2549310

Yildiz, H., & Gonen, S. I. K. (2024). Automated writing evaluation system for feedback in the digital world: An online learning opportunity for English as a foreign language students. *Turkish Online Journal of Distance Education*, *25*(3), 183–206. DOI: 10.17718/tojde.1169727

Yu, J. H., Chauhan, D., Iqbal, R. A., & Yeoh, E. (2025). Mapping academic perspectives on AI in education: Trends, challenges, and sentiments in educational research (2018–2024). *Educational Technology Research and Development*, *73*(1), 199–227. DOI: 10.1007/s11423-024-10425-2

Yusuf, S. B., Jiancheng, Q., Rasool, U., Dhuli, R., Yesmin, Q. F., Mahmud, R., & Hossain, A. (2025). Investigating EFL Learners' Perceptions of Using Grammarly in Enhancing Writing Proficiency in Bangladesh. *SAGE Open*, *15*(3), 21582440251352922. DOI: 10.1177/21582440251352922

Zhan, Y., & Teng, M. F. (2025). Assessing English writing self-efficacy beliefs, self-regulation, and performance through asynchronous computer-mediated feedback and face-to-face peer feedback. *Educational Assessment*, *30*(1), 4–20. DOI: 10.1080/10627197.2025.2452442

Zhang, Z., Aubrey, S., Huang, X., & Chiu, T. K. (2025). The role of generative AI and hybrid feedback in improving L2 writing skills: A comparative study. *Innovation in Language Learning and Teaching*, •••, 1–19. DOI: 10.1080/17501229.2025.2503890

Zhao, D. (2025). The impact of AI-enhanced natural language processing tools on writing proficiency: An analysis of language precision, content summarization, and creative writing facilitation. *Education and Information Technologies*, *30*(6), 8055–8086. DOI: 10.1007/s10639-024-13145-5

Zhao, D. (2025). The impact of teacher, peer, and automated writing evaluation feedback on developing deep writing skills: A comparative study. *Journal of Computing in Higher Education*, •••, 1–35. DOI: 10.1007/s12528-025-09469-x

Chapter 10
The False Sense of Teaching: Educator Deskilling in the Age of AI

Edyta Kostanek
http://orcid.org/0000-0002-2854-2587
University College London, UK

Fujia Li
http://orcid.org/0000-0003-4060-4899
University of Exeter, UK

ABSTRACT

This chapter examines the phenomenon of educator deskilling as a critical and often overlooked consequence of generative artificial intelligence in higher education. Drawing on labour process theory, critical pedagogy and the sociology of technology, the chapter analyses how AI reshapes assessment, curriculum design, relational work and student cognition in ways that displace professional judgement and weaken pedagogical autonomy. The chapter discusses how over-reliance on automated systems erodes expertise, narrows epistemic horizons and disrupts trust between educators and learners. The chapter argues that these shifts are structural rather than incidental, emerging through the normalisation of hybrid human-AI workflows that reconfigure academic labour. It concludes by suggesting a model of critical human-AI collaboration that preserves the intellectual, relational and ethical foundations of teaching while enabling responsible use of AI within higher education.

DOI: 10.4018/979-8-3373-7097-2.ch010

INTRODUCTION

The rapid spread of generative artificial intelligence (GenAI) across global higher education has unsettled long-standing assumptions about the nature of teaching, academic expertise, and the purpose of pedagogical work. Public debate has focused largely on students' use of AI and the risks it poses to assessment integrity. Yet this emphasis obscures a parallel transformation: the restructuring of educators' work through the pervasive adoption of AI-driven tools. These tools increasingly mediate assessment workflows, feedback generation, curriculum design, student support, and administrative processes. Their adoption risks creating what might be termed a false sense of teaching, a condition in which the outward signs of pedagogical productivity remain intact while the intellectual, relational, and ethical labour at the core of teaching becomes progressively displaced.

Emerging evidence shows how easily these shifts begin. In Spain, teachers who initially approached AI generated feedback cautiously found themselves relying on it more frequently as the semester progressed. What began as occasional consultation evolved into routine dependence, with educators editing automated comments rather than generating feedback from their own disciplinary reasoning (Alkhasawneh et al., 2025). A similar pattern surfaced in the widely publicised case at a British university (Down, 2025) where students discovered that large portions of their course materials had been created and narrated by AI rather than by a lecturer. Their sense of betrayal underscored how strongly students associate teaching with human presence and professional accountability. Together, these examples reveal how automation can gradually displace interpretive judgement even before educators recognise the extent of the shift.

Research shows that AI also reshapes the cognitive ecology of the classroom by altering how students engage with knowledge. Studies report that students frequently accept AI-generated explanations as authoritative, bypassing processes of inquiry, deliberation, and self-correction that underpin deep learning (Yavich, 2025). When learners adopt AI as a surrogate for understanding, educators confront new challenges. Their role shifts from facilitating dialogic meaning-making to adjudicating between students' misunderstandings and the algorithmic artefacts that shaped them. The implications extend beyond cognitive outcomes: by narrowing opportunities for noticing, diagnosing, and responding to students' developmental cues, AI risks diminishing the interpretive and relational labour central to effective pedagogy, echoing concerns raised in professional education contexts where AI has been shown to impair the development of ethical and situational judgement (Savardi et al., 2025).

These localised shifts take place within a broader institutional environment increasingly shaped by narratives of efficiency, optimisation, and digital transformation. Universities have adopted AI-enabled marking tools, content-generation systems, and automated advising platforms in response to workload pressures, accountability demands, and budget constraints. Such developments are consistent with organisational patterns observed in other sectors, where managerial logics encourage the substitution of human judgement with automated processes (Johnson, 2022). Yet this technological rationalisation risks undermining the epistemic, relational, and ethical foundations of the teaching profession. If educators are repositioned primarily as supervisors of algorithmic systems rather than as interpreters, mentors, and ethical guides, higher education may experience a profound shift from human-centred pedagogy to mechanised instruction.

This chapter argues that educator deskilling is not an incidental by-product of AI adoption, but a structural phenomenon shaped by the intersection of technological affordances, labour conditions, and evolving epistemic norms. It draws on labour process theory, in which Braverman (1974) conceptualises deskilling as the fragmentation and codification of complex expertise; on critical pedagogy, in which Freire (1996) and Giroux (2024) emphasise relational, ethical, and emancipatory dimensions of teaching; and on the sociology of technology, which shows that technological systems embed institutional assumptions and power relations (Suchman, 2007; Winner, 2017). Together, these frameworks illuminate how GenAI accelerates existing pressures toward standardisation, depersonalisation, and diminished professional autonomy.

Guided by these perspectives, the chapter pursues four aims. First, it defines and theorises educator deskilling within historical and contemporary frameworks. Second, it examines how deskilling manifests across assessment, curriculum design, relational labour, and student cognitive development. Third, it analyses the structural conditions, including workload intensification, efficiency mandates, and managerial cultures, that heighten institutional dependencies on AI. Finally, it proposes a model of critical human-AI collaboration that seeks to preserve the interpretive, ethical, and relational dimensions of teaching while enabling educators to make judicious use of technological tools. Taken together, these strands frame the central argument: the future of higher education will depend not on the capabilities of AI itself, but on the values, boundaries, and professional judgements that educators and institutions assert in response to it. AI may reshape the conditions under which teaching takes place, but only educators can determine what teaching ultimately means.

HISTORICAL AND THEORETICAL FOUNDATIONS

Understanding educator deskilling in the age of GenAI requires situating contemporary developments within longer trajectories that have shaped academic labour, pedagogical purpose, and the relationship between human judgement and technological systems. While the rapid expansion of AI into universities appears novel, the underlying dynamics echo patterns described in labour theory, critical pedagogy, and the sociology of technology. These perspectives reveal that the pressures educators face today, fragmentation of expertise, standardisation of practice, and erosion of autonomy, are not emerging out of nowhere but are intensified by the affordances and epistemic tendencies of GenAI.

Labour Process Theory and the Mechanisation of Pedagogical Work

Braverman's (1974) labour process theory offers a foundational lens for conceptualising how AI restructures educators' work. Braverman argued that capitalist efficiency logics fragment complex forms of expertise into simplified, codified tasks that can be automated or delegated to less skilled workers. This insight remains remarkably prescient. In higher education today, GenAI decomposes the craft of teaching into micro-tasks, drafting feedback, structuring assessments, summarising readings, generating examples, each of which can be performed quickly by automated systems. Rather than enhancing expertise, these tools may deskill educators by reducing opportunities to engage in the interpretive reasoning and pedagogical decision-making that constitute professional mastery.

Contemporary research outside academia confirms the risks of such fragmentation. Gunathilake (2025) describes "competence drift" in knowledge-intensive organisations where professionals gradually lose the capacity for deep judgement as automated systems perform increasing portions of cognitive labour. Similar trends emerge in AI-mediated clinical training, where learners' overreliance on automated diagnostic suggestions diminishes their development of situational awareness and moral reasoning (Savardi et al., 2025). These cross-sector findings illustrate how automation can hollow out professional capacities even when workers remain formally in control of technological tools. A longer historical view shows that this trajectory predates GenAI, as a systematic review of teachers' use of AI from 2015 to 2024 demonstrates that automation had already begun reshaping pedagogical work through outsourced analytics, resource curation and content planning (Tan et al., 2025). GenAI intensifies these patterns by providing fluent and authoritative appearing outputs that seem to reduce cognitive load while displacing the slow, reflective labour that supports pedagogical judgement.

Critical Pedagogy and the Loss of Relational and Ethical Dimensions

Where labour process theory emphasises structural pressures, critical pedagogy underscores the human, relational, and ethical dimensions of teaching that are difficult, if not impossible, to automate. Freire (1970) conceptualised education as a dialogic act grounded in human presence, reciprocity, and collective meaning-making. Giroux (2024) similarly warned against technocratic models of schooling that reduce teaching to technical delivery rather than an emancipatory practice.

GenAI challenges these commitments by inserting computational mediation into spaces that rely on nuance, emotional understanding, and moral responsibility. Research shows that automated feedback systems cannot engage in the reciprocal interpretive dialogue that characterises formative assessment, nor can AI-driven advising systems recognise the social or emotional contexts shaping students' needs (Alkhasawneh et al., 2025; Savardi et al., 2025). When educators adopt AI to manage such tasks, however pragmatically, they risk displacing precisely the forms of care, presence, and interpretive attention that make teaching a relational practice. Legal education research echoes this concern. Recent analyses warn that students who rely on AI-generated summaries and case explanations risk becoming "surface-level lawyers" lacking deeper analytical and ethical reasoning capacities (Leo, 2025). The problem is not merely one of skill acquisition but of the erosion of the reflective, dialogic engagement required to cultivate practical wisdom. These patterns mirror the risks facing educators: when AI takes over the initial stages of reasoning, professionals lose opportunities to practise the very capacities they are expected to teach.

The Sociology of Technology and the Myth of Neutral Automation

Sociological perspectives on technology further complicate narratives that frame AI as a neutral pedagogical aid. Winner (2017) demonstrated that technologies embody political and institutional values, while Suchman (2007) examined how automated systems shape human action by imposing assumptions about efficiency, rationality, and expertise. These insights apply directly to AI in universities.

GenAI is not simply a tool; it embodies dominant epistemic cultures that privilege fluency over accuracy, coherence over nuance, and speed over deliberation. Its outputs, even when incorrect, exhibit the stylistic confidence that scholars increasingly associate with hallucination, a pattern documented not only in educational settings but across high-stakes professional environments. In 2025, UK courts reprimanded lawyers for submitting AI-generated legal filings containing entirely fictitious case-law, fabricated quotations, and non-existent precedents, prompting judicial warnings that AI produces "assertions that are simply untrue" despite their persuasive form (Booth, 2025). Comparable errors appeared in Australian cases where AI-generated submissions misled legal proceedings and triggered regulatory sanctions (Blandis, 2025). These examples illuminate a broader epistemic risk: automated systems can generate the appearance of knowledge without the underlying processes of verification, interpretation, or ethical responsibility. Within higher education, such epistemic instability shapes daily academic practice. AI-enabled personalisation systems, for example, guide learners through algorithmically determined sequences that may prioritise efficiency over conceptual depth (Luckin et al., 2022). Kolchenko (2018) similarly warns that adaptive systems can reduce disciplinary complexity by steering students through simplified pathways aligned with data-driven optimisation rather than human-curated pedagogical reasoning. When educators adopt AI-mediated systems uncritically, they risk internalising these epistemic tendencies, gradually shifting from practices of inquiry and interpretation toward oversight of automated processes.

Professional Ethics, Judgement, and Responsibility

Finally, scholarship on professional ethics emphasises that teaching is grounded in judgement, the capacity to interpret ambiguity, navigate dilemmas, and act responsibly in relation to human needs. Judgement cannot be automated because it depends on contextual understanding, relational insight, and moral reasoning. Duran (2021) shows that in medicine, overreliance on automated diagnostic systems diminishes practitioners' situational awareness and ethical discernment, leading to "moral deskilling." A similar risk surfaces in the Deloitte scandals of 2024 and 2025, where multiple government-commissioned reports were found to contain hallucinated citations, non-existent sources, and fabricated legal references, errors attributed to unverified use of GenAI in place of professional analysis (Paoli, 2025; Shibu, 2025). These failures illustrate how quickly institutional trust and professional credibility collapse when automated systems replace the interpretive labour required for responsible knowledge production. In educational contexts, such ethical considerations are acute. Teachers are not merely transmitters of information; they are custodians of academic integrity, stewards of disciplinary values, and mentors responsible for relational and developmental care. As AI takes on roles in feedback, advising, and content creation, the danger is not that AI will perform these tasks poorly but that educators may cease to perform them at all. When judgement is delegated to automated systems, educators risk losing the opportunity, and eventually the capability, to enact the ethical dimensions of their profession.

CONTEMPORARY MANIFESTATIONS OF EDUCATOR DESKILLING

While the theoretical frameworks outlined in the previous section reveal the structural drivers of deskilling, the phenomenon becomes most visible in the concrete practices of contemporary teaching. GenAI is already reshaping how educators design assessments, deliver feedback, construct learning materials, and support students. These changes do not occur through dramatic disruption but through small adjustments that slowly alter educators' routines and expectations, across diverse contexts, similar patterns emerge. Automation appears to enhance efficiency, yet over time it transforms the tasks through which pedagogical judgement, disciplinary interpretation, and relational presence are enacted.

Assessment and Feedback: The Automation of Judgement

Assessment and feedback have long required subtle, interpretive and relational forms of reasoning. They involve understanding not only what a student has written but how they reached that point, what misconceptions or partial understandings may be unfolding, and which pedagogical response will meaningfully support the next step in their learning. Effective feedback is therefore not simply evaluative. It is diagnostic, dialogic and formative. It depends on the educator's capacity to notice nuance in student work, anticipate developmental trajectories and frame comments in ways that motivate, clarify and challenge. These practices constitute a core expression of professional judgement. The growing adoption of AI driven feedback tools introduces new pressures in these spaces. Automated systems produce comments that appear polished, structured and pedagogically coherent, often in a tone that mimics the conventions of good feedback. Their speed and fluency make them attractive in contexts of increasing workload and compressed marking timelines. Yet the very features that make AI generated feedback appealing also pose risks. Because AI can rapidly generate plausible comments, educators may feel encouraged to treat automated output as a natural starting point rather than a supplementary stimulus for their own reflections. This shift can gradually reorder the cognitive sequence through which feedback is produced, with AI suggestions preceding rather than following the educator's interpretive judgement.

In a longitudinal study of educators in Spain, teachers who initially engaged with AI output only to compare or refine their own impressions soon found themselves relying on the automated comments more heavily. As the semester progressed, AI suggestions became the default template for feedback, and teachers increasingly focused on editing or correcting AI generated remarks rather than composing original, discipline informed commentary (Alkhasawneh et al., 2025). Although educators remained formally involved, the interpretive labour that once anchored feedback was gradually displaced by a form of supervisory oversight. The risk here is not outright replacement. It is the erosion of judgement through subtle changes in workflow that transfer the formative phase of assessment from educator to machine.

Yavich (2025) finds that learners who habitually consult AI for explanations or worked examples become less willing to engage in the iterative reasoning and productive struggle that assessment is designed to cultivate. Their submissions often contain coherent but artificially streamlined arguments that obscure the underlying cognitive process. For educators, this complicates the interpretive task. Instead of encountering authentic reasoning that reveals a student's developing understanding, teachers must disentangle the student's voice from the algorithmic scaffolding that produced the work. Their role shifts from guiding learning to verifying the accuracy and appropriateness of machine generated reasoning.

This reactive posture diminishes opportunities for formative dialogue; feedback becomes less a reciprocal exchange between teacher and learner and more an adjudication between human and machine produced ideas. Because AI generated responses often appear confident even when they are incorrect, students may treat AI as the primary authority and view educators' feedback as secondary or corrective rather than developmental. This dynamic can weaken trust and undermine the relational foundations that support effective learning. It also reduces the meaningful space in which educators interpret student thinking, tailor explanations and foster disciplinary habits of mind.

Universities facing rising student numbers and intensifying workload pressures may encourage the use of AI enabled marking and feedback systems as mechanisms for efficiency. While such tools may streamline administrative processes, they risk redefining assessment itself as a technical rather than interpretive practice. When educators are incentivised to use automated systems for consistency or speed, the craft of feedback is reframed as a managerial concern rather than a pedagogical one. Over time, these pressures can normalise dependence on AI in ways that compromise both the intellectual and relational dimensions of assessment.

Taken together, these developments illustrate a fundamental loss. Assessment and feedback, once regarded as among the most thoughtful, labour intensive and relational aspects of teaching, risk being reduced to processes of reviewing and correcting machine generated language. The educator's interpretive authority becomes less visible while the epistemic habits of the automated system become more deeply embedded. The result is not greater efficiency alone but a progressive narrowing of the cognitive and relational space in which educators and students come to understand each other's thinking.

Curriculum and Content Design: The Homogenisation of Pedagogical Creativity

Curriculum and content design have traditionally been among the most intellectually generative elements of academic work. They require educators to make decisions about disciplinary framing, sequencing of concepts, epistemic tensions, real world relevance and the intellectual challenges that students should encounter. These decisions reflect not only expertise but also the educator's values, commitments and pedagogical philosophy. The introduction of GenAI into content creation profoundly reshapes this terrain.

AI generated materials often appear fluent, balanced and well structured. They provide summaries, examples, case studies and lecture outlines with remarkable speed. In environments marked by workload intensification and rising expectations for rapid course development, such tools can be enticing. Yet fluency should not be confused with epistemic or pedagogical quality. Generative models rely on statistical patterning, privileging dominant narratives and smoothing over contested areas of knowledge. This tendency toward homogenisation is well documented. Kolchenko (2018) shows that algorithmic personalisation systems flatten disciplinary complexity by reducing conceptual nuance into optimised, digestible fragments that may obscure the tensions at the heart of scholarly inquiry. Luckin et al. (2022) observe that AI driven learning tools tend to reinforce existing educational hierarchies and epistemic assumptions, presenting knowledge as a stable and universal sequence rather than as a contested and interpretive field. When educators rely on automated systems to scaffold course materials, they may inadvertently reproduce this narrowing of intellectual horizons. Curriculum becomes less a site of disciplinary exploration and more a space structured by the preferences encoded within training data.

Second, GenAI can displace the creative labour that underpins curriculum design. Consider the increasing use of AI to generate lecture slides, case studies and problem sets. These outputs may provide a useful starting point, but they often constrain pedagogical imagination by directing educators toward familiar structures. One educator working with an adaptive learning platform described the experience as "teaching on rails". The system continuously recommended content sequences and interventions, leaving little room for alternative framings or spontaneous shifts in emphasis. Such experiences align with broader concerns raised by Johnson (2022), who argues that algorithmic systems can impose managerial logics on professional work by structuring tasks around efficiency rather than interpretive or relational reasoning.

Third, AI introduced into curriculum development shifts the locus of expertise. Instead of drawing from disciplinary knowledge, lived teaching experience and reflective planning, curriculum design increasingly starts with automated suggestions. Educators may then revise or refine the material, yet the generative process has already been shaped by computational patterns. Research on hybrid knowledge work shows that once AI suggestions are presented, they influence human decision making even when users intend to exercise independent judgement (Gunathilake, 2025). This cognitive anchoring effect can normalise reliance on AI frameworks and reduce the perceived need for deep disciplinary engagement.

The risks become more pronounced when AI is used to develop entire modules or programme structures. Studies examining fully AI generated courses reveal that while such content may appear coherent, it often lacks epistemic depth, historical grounding and attention to disciplinary debates. Bate (2025) notes that AI produced course materials frequently omit the interpretive moves that educators make when designing learning trajectories, such as foregrounding threshold concepts, anticipating misconceptions or scaffolding critical inquiry. Curriculum that emerges from automated generation may therefore appear polished while remaining pedagogically thin. These dynamics can have cascading effects. When content is standardised by AI, student learning experiences become more uniform yet less intellectually demanding. Educators lose opportunities to redesign courses in response to emerging research, local context or student interest. Moreover, the professional identity of educators becomes increasingly tied to managing or refining algorithmic content rather than crafting original pedagogical visions. The creative labour traditionally associated with curriculum design becomes less visible, less valued and eventually less practiced.

There is also a relational dimension to all this. Curriculum development is not only an intellectual process but a moral one. Decisions about what to teach, whose voices to amplify and which questions to pursue reflect ethical judgements about the purpose of education. AI cannot make these judgements. Automated systems cannot recognise when a curriculum marginalises certain perspectives or fails to engage with contemporary social issues. When educators outsource significant elements of design to AI, they risk diminishing the ethical intentionality that has historically defined curriculum work.

Pastoral, Relational and Ethical Labour: The Marginalisation of Human Presence

Pastoral and relational work has always been central to teaching. Educators support learners through uncertainty, motivation, identity formation and personal challenge. These forms of labour require attentiveness to emotional cues, contextual sensitivity and ethical judgement. They also depend on trust, presence and reciprocity. Although often undervalued in formal metrics of academic workload, relational labour is integral to student persistence, belonging and intellectual risk taking. As GenAI enters advising, guidance and support processes, these human centred dimensions encounter new constraints. The introduction of AI driven triage systems, chatbots and automated advising tools is frequently justified on grounds of efficiency and accessibility. Institutions facing rising student numbers and stretched staffing may view such technologies as a mechanism for reducing routine queries or providing twenty-four-hour support. Yet even seemingly minor forms of automation can reshape the relational architecture of education. When students are routed through AI systems before they reach an educator, the nature of the interaction changes. Human dialogue no longer opens the exchange but appears only after automated systems have failed to address the concern. This reduces the opportunities for early relational engagement, where educators might notice subtle indicators of distress, confusion or disengagement.

Research across multiple fields demonstrates the dangers of delegating relational judgement to automated systems. In clinical training environments, students who relied heavily on AI generated diagnostic suggestions began privileging algorithmic advice over their own observations and the interpretive guidance of instructors. This shift inhibited the development of situational awareness and ethical reasoning, prompting educators to intervene not only to correct errors but also to help learners reconstruct confidence in their own judgement (Savardi et al., 2025). These patterns resonate strongly with higher education. When students consult AI for emotional, academic or ethical guidance, the role of the educator shifts from relational supporter to a corrective mechanism appearing late in the process.

Pastoral labour also involves making judgements that cannot be automated. Educators routinely interpret complexities that require contextual understanding rather than procedural logic. These include decisions about whether a student's difficulty reflects a conceptual confusion, a social concern, a workload problem or a wellbeing issue. GenAI cannot meaningfully distinguish between these layers. In some cases, automation may misidentify concerns or provide inappropriate advice that educators must later unravel. Duran (2021) describes this phenomenon in medical contexts as a form of moral deskilling, where practitioners lose both opportunities and incentives to engage in ethically grounded reasoning when automated systems frame problems in narrow or technical ways.

Moreover, pastoral labour is deeply entangled with identity formation, both for students and educators. Freire (1996) and Giroux (2024) emphasise that meaningful learning unfolds within relationships that honour dialogue, vulnerability and co constructed understanding. When AI intervenes in spaces of struggle or uncertainty, it can narrow the relational landscape in which such growth occurs. Students may come to view support as a transactional service rather than an ongoing conversation with a trusted educator. Educators may feel increasingly distanced from the emotional and ethical dimensions of their role, especially when institutional systems prioritise automated responses.

Institutional pressures further complicate these dynamics. As Johnson (2022) notes, managerial logics often favour technologies that streamline labour and reduce perceived inefficiencies. Pastoral care, by contrast, requires time, presence and interpretive labour that cannot be easily quantified. When institutions implement AI tutoring or advising systems as primary points of contact, relational work risks being reclassified as inefficient or unnecessary. Educators are then left to manage only the most complex or escalated cases. This reactive posture not only increases emotional strain but also diminishes opportunities for proactive and preventive engagement.

Finally, there are also additional equity implications. Automated systems may fail to recognise cultural nuance, linguistic variation or contextual differences that shape students' needs. Marginalised learners may receive inappropriate advice or be routed incorrectly. Educators play a crucial role in recognising these disparities, yet when AI mediates early contact, they may encounter students only after misunderstandings have accumulated. The relational repair work required in such cases is substantial and emotionally demanding.

Taken together, these developments illustrate a clear risk. As AI becomes embedded in pastoral and ethical dimensions of education, educators lose opportunities to enact the human presence that underpins trust, belonging and moral development. The relational work that once served as the connective tissue of the learning environment becomes fragmented and displaced. Although AI may offer efficiency and scale, it cannot replicate the ethical discernment, emotional sensitivity and contextual responsiveness that define human care in educational settings. Without deliberate protection of these forms of labour, institutions risk weakening one of the most fundamental dimensions of teaching.

Changing Learner Cognition and its Impact on Educators

The rise of GenAI does not only reshape the practices of educators. It also restructures the cognitive habits of students in ways that have direct implications for teaching. Learning is an iterative, effortful and reflective process. It requires students to grapple with uncertainty, refine partial understandings, and build coherent representations of knowledge over time. When students turn to AI for explanations, examples or entire answers, thc character of this cognitive work changes. Educators then encounter a different kind of student thinking, one increasingly mediated, streamlined and sometimes distorted by algorithmic logic.

Research on student use of AI shows that learners often treat machine generated output as authoritative even when it lacks epistemic grounding. Yavich (2025) finds that students who rely heavily on AI generated explanations display lower persistence when confronting challenging material and are less likely to engage in incremental reasoning or exploratory problem solving. Instead of working through confusion, they seek immediate resolution from computational tools. This shift reduces opportunities for the cognitive struggle that supports durable learning. It also affects how educators interpret student work, since written responses may reflect the fluency of AI rather than the actual cognitive development of the learner.

The problem is not simply that AI enables shortcuts. It is that the shortcuts produce new patterns of thinking that mask misunderstandings and present educators with surface level coherence. Educators described encountering essays and problem solutions that appeared fluent yet contained conceptual gaps or invented intermediate steps that required extensive unpacking. This creates a new interpretive burden for educators. Instead of analysing a student's original reasoning, they must first identify which parts of a submission reflect algorithmic influence, which parts reveal genuine understanding and where the two intertwine. The cognitive work of teaching thus shifts from diagnosing learner thinking to disentangling AI generated artefacts from authentic student cognition. This not only complicates pedagogical diagnosis but also narrows opportunities for formative dialogue. When educators cannot clearly see how a student is thinking, they cannot respond with targeted guidance that supports further development.

The consequences extend beyond individual tasks. Students who rely on AI for explanations may fail to develop the metacognitive skills needed to monitor their own understanding. Pratiwi et al. (2025) report that students using AI as a primary tool for reasoning develop weaker self-evaluation capacities and often struggle to articulate why they believe an answer is correct. This deficit has significant implications for educators. When students cannot explain their reasoning, teachers lose access to the cognitive processes that assessment is intended to reveal. Their feedback becomes less precise, less dialogic and less grounded in actual learning trajectories.

Automated outputs often present information with stylistic confidence, even when incorrect. This can lead students to privilege AI generated explanations over those offered by educators. In some cases, students request clarification not to understand the concept but to reconcile discrepancies between the teacher's insight and AI produced text. This dynamic can subtly undermine the educator's epistemic authority and alter classroom relationships, whether in higher education or in professional training settings where similar challenges have been documented (Savardi et al., 2025).

Students who rely on AI may experience less intellectual ownership of their work. Some report feeling detached from their learning because they are less engaged in generating ideas and more focused on editing or rephrasing machine generated responses. Educators then encounter learners who may appear competent on the surface, but who struggle when asked to think aloud, justify their positions or extend concepts to unfamiliar contexts. This divergence between apparent competence and underlying fragility requires teachers to invest more time in probing student thinking, rebuilding confidence and reconstructing learning processes that AI has short circuited.

Institutional pressures amplify these challenges. Large classes, reduced contact hours and rising expectations for rapid feedback create conditions in which students are more likely to turn to AI for immediate support. The relational and dialogic aspects of learning become secondary to the instrumental use of technology. When this happens at scale, educators face a learning environment saturated with AI mediated reasoning. Their professional role is reshaped from facilitating cognitive development to monitoring, correcting and interpreting the intellectual artefacts produced through automation. These trends underscore a central point of this chapter. AI does not merely change what students produce. It changes how students think and how educators must respond. The cognitive ecology of the classroom shifts toward a hybrid environment in which human and machine reasoning coexist, sometimes productively but often in tension. The educator's interpretive labour becomes more complex and more essential, precisely because AI generated fluency obscures the pathways through which genuine learning occurs. Without deliberate strategies to reassert human centred reasoning and scaffold students' metacognitive awareness, AI risks narrowing the cognitive and relational spaces in which education unfolds.

The Normalisation of Hybrid Human AI Workflows

Across assessment, curriculum development and student support, a common pattern emerges. Educators increasingly operate within hybrid human AI workflows that subtly reshape the nature of pedagogical labour. These workflows rarely replace educators outright. Instead, they reorganise the sequence, purpose and distribution of tasks in ways that reconfigure expertise and alter the conditions under which judgement is exercised. Hybridisation therefore represents not merely the coexistence of humans and machines but a structural shift in how teaching is conceptualised and enacted. Hybrid workflows typically begin with small changes. An educator uses AI to draft an email, generate a rubric, outline a lesson or produce a first pass of feedback. These uses appear benign and often genuinely helpful. The inflection point occurs when these initial interactions begin to structure the educator's habitual practices. Research on knowledge work demonstrates that once automation becomes embedded in the early stages of a task, professionals may gradually lose confidence in their ability to perform those stages independently (Gunathilake, 2025). This phenomenon, sometimes described as competence drift, manifests when educators begin to experience the automated output as the natural foundation of their thinking rather than as an optional support.

Survey research from Sweden provides an example of how normalisation unfolds. Petterson (2025) report that university educators increasingly rely on GenAI for early-stage lesson planning, feedback drafting and resource creation. Many teachers expressed deep ambivalence: they welcomed the efficiency gains but simultaneously worried that AI dependence was weakening their professional competence. This tension is central to understanding hybridisation. The benefits of AI are immediate and visible, while the costs are gradual and often imperceptible. As these systems become routine, they reconfigure what educators understand as the work of teaching.

When educators rely on AI generated suggestions for content or feedback, their role shifts from creator to evaluator, from originator to curator. The intellectual labour of designing a lesson or crafting pedagogical explanations becomes intertwined with the language patterns of AI systems. Some educators describe feeling as if their work has become derivative or filtered through automated templates. Others express discomfort with the notion that their professional voice is increasingly mediated by systems that draw upon vast pools of decontextualised data. These concerns reflect broader theoretical debates. Labour process theory highlights how fragmentation and standardisation reshape work by reducing autonomy and relocating expertise outside the worker (Braverman, 1974). Hybrid workflows reproduce this dynamic by embedding algorithmic structures into routine practice. Educators may retain formal control, yet the conceptual architecture of their work becomes shaped by automated systems that influence how tasks are defined, sequenced and valued. Over time, this can narrow the scope of professional discretion and limit opportunities for intellectual exploration or improvisation. Critical pedagogy offers another vantage point. Freire (1996) emphasised the importance of dialogic engagement, human presence and relational transformation in education. Hybrid workflows, however, tend to privilege instrumental forms of efficiency over relational or reflective dimensions of pedagogy. When educators adopt AI to expedite routine tasks, they may inadvertently align their practices with managerial logics that view teaching primarily as content delivery or administrative throughput. Johnson (2022) notes that such logics often accompany institutional efforts to streamline labour, even in contexts where relational and interpretive work is essential.

Educators may come to view AI output as a reliable reference point against which to measure their own thinking. This anchoring effect can create subtle dependencies. When AI generates an example, explanation or conceptual structure, the educator's task may become one of evaluating its adequacy rather than generating an alternative from scratch. While this can be efficient, it reduces opportunities for the deeper cognitive engagement that sustains disciplinary expertise. Kolchenko (2018) and Luckin et al. (2022) show that when educators routinely rely on algorithmically generated content, their pedagogical decisions may become aligned with the optimisation logic of AI systems rather than with disciplinary goals or local contextual needs.

Educators may feel increasing pressure to adopt AI tools if they perceive colleagues doing the same or if institutions encourage automation for the sake of consistency. This can lead to a collective shift in expectations, where practices previously understood as core to pedagogical craft become optional or externalised. As more tasks are delegated to AI, the social meaning of teaching evolves. The educator becomes an interpreter of algorithmic suggestions rather than an architect of learning environments.

These changes are incremental yet cumulative. Each new point of automation subtly reorganises responsibilities and reframes what counts as professional competence. The result is a redefinition of teaching as hybrid labour, where human judgement is mediated, scaffolded and sometimes overshadowed by computational systems. While hybrid models can enhance creativity and open new pedagogical possibilities, they also risk narrowing the intellectual, relational and ethical dimensions of teaching if they become the default rather than the choice of reflective practitioners. Understanding hybrid workflows is therefore essential for recognising the broader trajectory of educator deskilling. They represent the mechanism through which AI becomes normalised and through which structural shifts in pedagogy and professional identity take root. The next section will examine the institutional and societal risks that accompany this transformation and the stakes involved when automated systems come to define the contours of pedagogical work.

CONSEQUENCES AND RISKS OF EDUCATOR DESKILLING

The manifestations of educator deskilling outlined in the previous section are not isolated disruptions. They signal a broader transformation in academic work and in the epistemic foundations of higher education. GenAI has begun to reorder pedagogical routines, reshape professional identity and undermine the interpretive and ethical judgement that traditionally defines teaching. Although these shifts appear gradual, their consequences reverberate across institutional cultures, disciplinary norms and public expectations of expertise. The risks that follow are not limited to classroom practices but reach into the intellectual fabric of the university and the social role of educators.

A first concern involves the erosion of professional autonomy. Teaching has historically rested on the educator's ability to interpret student work, design curricula and exercise discretion in response to learner needs. Yet autonomy becomes vulnerable when AI systems present their outputs with fluent confidence that can appear authoritative. Automated feedback tools, adaptive learning platforms and AI generated teaching materials can position educators not as authors of pedagogical judgement but as overseers who correct or monitor machine generated suggestions. Numerous examples illustrate how quickly this shift can occur. In the United Kingdom, the High Court reprimanded lawyers who submitted legal documents containing fabricated AI generated case law. Judges warned that generative systems produce statements that appear coherent yet may be entirely untrue, a pattern that emerged because professionals had mistakenly transferred interpretive responsibility to an automated system (Booth, 2025). In Australia, similar reliance on AI produced appeal documents containing hallucinated citations led to regulatory scrutiny and fines (Blandis, 2025). Although these failures occurred outside academia, the underlying dynamic mirrors what occurs when educators begin to trust AI generated content as a stable reference point. Autonomy is not only weakened when individuals choose to rely on AI but also when institutions implement systems that normalise such reliance. The well publicised discovery that students at a British university were being taught through AI generated slides and voiceovers rather than by an instructor exposed the fragility of pedagogical autonomy. Students reported feeling misled and undervalued, signalling that AI mediated teaching can diminish the meaning and legitimacy of academic work (Down, 2025).

Closely connected to autonomy is the transformation of educator identity. Teaching is not simply the execution of technical tasks but a professional identity shaped by intellectual judgement, relational engagement and ethical care. When AI assumes responsibility for tasks that once required human interpretation, identity can shift in subtle but significant ways. Research on hybrid professional environments shows that when automated systems handle the early stages of reasoning, workers often begin to doubt their capacity to perform such reasoning independently (Gunathilake, 2025). This competence drift is already visible in academic settings. Educators who routinely begin with AI generated examples, explanations or feedback may find that they engage less often in the deep interpretive labour that once defined their practice. Students sense this shift as well. In the Staffordshire case (Down, 2025), learners expressed that they felt deprived of authentic instruction and questioned whether they had been taught by a teacher at all. Their reaction illuminates the symbolic dimension of teaching, since professional identity depends on the presence, care and epistemic authority that educators bring into the learning environment. Similar concerns have been documented in legal education, where scholars warn that AI supported learning is producing surface level lawyers whose reasoning depends on automated synthesis rather than deep disciplinary engagement (Leo, 2025). A parallel risk threatens educators themselves if AI becomes the starting point for conceptual framing or interpretive judgement.

A third consequence involves the narrowing of disciplinary and epistemic landscapes. GenAI systems draw on statistical regularities in training data, which means that their outputs privilege dominant narratives and suppress contested or marginalised forms of knowledge. When educators depend on AI generated materials, they may uncritically reproduce these defaults. Kolchenko (2018) warns that adaptive systems oversimplify complex ideas and obscure disciplinary nuance, while Luckin et al. (2022) show that AI driven personalisation often fragments learning into sequences of optimised yet superficial tasks. If curriculum design becomes shaped by algorithmic suggestions, educators lose opportunities to engage students in the interpretive tensions, debates and critical questions that define scholarly disciplines. Over time, this may flatten the intellectual horizons of higher education and privilege fluency over depth.

The consequences extend beyond individual teaching practices to institutional and societal risks. AI adoption reflects institutional values, and when universities prioritise efficiency narratives, they risk reconfiguring education as a system of automated knowledge management. Johnson (2022) observes that organisational enthusiasm for AI is often driven by pressures to streamline labour, reduce costs and increase administrative throughput. In such contexts, relational care and interpretive judgement are easily reframed as inefficiencies. The Deloitte scandals provide an instructive metaphor. Multiple government commissioned reports produced by Deloitte in Canada and Australia relied on GenAI in ways that introduced hallucinated references, fabricated case law and inaccurate citations (Paoli, 2025; Shibu, 2025). These errors went undetected until external auditors intervened, revealing how quickly institutional credibility can collapse when organisations replace expert verification with automated synthesis. The same risk arises in higher education when institutions treat AI output as inherently reliable. Advising systems similarly illustrate the institutional hazards of automation. Some universities now require students to consult AI chatbots before contacting staff, meaning that educators encounter learners only when algorithmic processes have failed or misinterpreted their needs. This reconfigures relational labour as a secondary responsibility and distances educators from the students they support. Over time, such practices risk undermining the academic values of presence, care and ethical responsibility.

Taken together, these consequences reveal a profession amid profound transformation. Deskilling does not occur through sudden displacement but through gradual shifts in routines that reduce opportunities for educators to enact judgement, relational care, disciplinary interpretation and ethical responsibility. The risks outlined here foreshadow deeper institutional questions about the purpose of education and the human commitments that sustain it. Understanding these dynamics is essential for addressing the structural conditions that intensify deskilling and for articulating the professional boundaries necessary to preserve pedagogical integrity in an AI mediated landscape.

TOWARDS HUMAN-AI COLLABORATION

The risks outlined in the previous section make clear that a sustainable future for higher education cannot rely on either rejection or uncritical adoption of GenAI. The task is to develop a model of collaboration that preserves the human qualities at the core of teaching while making thoughtful use of technological tools. Such a model requires recognising that AI is not a neutral assistant, but a system shaped by epistemic tendencies that can influence how educators think, act, and relate to learners. The challenge is therefore not simply technical. It is pedagogical, ethical, and institutional. A first step in building constructive collaboration involves reasserting professional judgement as the foundation of teaching. In Spain, educators who began by consulting AI only occasionally soon found themselves relying on automated feedback to structure their evaluative processes (Alkhasawneh et al., 2025). This shift shows how quickly AI can become a default epistemic partner rather than a supplementary tool. Collaboration requires reversing this order. Educators must articulate a preliminary interpretation or pedagogical decision before engaging AI. When human framing precedes machine input, automation becomes a means of expanding possibilities rather than a mechanism that narrows or directs professional reasoning. Similar concerns arise across other fields. In clinical training contexts, studies show that learners who rely heavily on AI generated suggestions lose confidence in their own situational judgement, prompting instructors to intervene not only to correct errors but to restore trust in the learner's interpretive capacities (Savardi et al., 2025). These patterns underscore the need to preserve the moments of ambiguity and deliberation through which judgement develops. AI may provide fluent explanations, yet these cannot replace the slow processes of reasoning that educators and students must engage in together.

Collaboration also requires designing hybrid workflows that safeguard human expertise. Research on knowledge work shows that professionals experience a form of competence drift when their role becomes limited to oversight of automated processes (Gunathilake, 2025). In education, this risk becomes acute when educators are expected to correct AI generated content rather than create conceptual frameworks themselves. Teaching involves more than supervising machine outputs. It requires diagnosing learner understanding, curating disciplinary complexity, and making ethical decisions in relational contexts. These tasks cannot be automated without diminishing the profession. To counter this drift, educators need opportunities to engage actively in each stage of pedagogical work. This may include generating initial ideas before comparing them with AI suggestions, reviewing AI generated patterns through the lens of disciplinary knowledge, and deliberately resisting the temptation to use automation as a substitute for intellectual labour. Such practices help ensure that educators remain authors of meaning rather than editors of algorithmic text.

A further principle of collaboration involves treating AI output as a provocation rather than a prescription. Studies of adaptive learning environments show that algorithmic systems often present their recommendations as optimal, leading educators to follow predefined pathways even when these do not align with pedagogical reasoning (Kolchenko, 2018). Reframing AI as a source of alternative perspectives helps maintain educator agency. AI can suggest examples, reorganise content, or surface patterns, yet the decision to adopt, reject, or modify these outputs must remain a human one. This approach aligns with critical pedagogy, which emphasises dialogue, inquiry, and reflexivity rather than the passive adoption of authoritative structures (Freire, 1996, Giroux, 2024).

The preservation of relational pedagogy is also essential. Research consistently shows that AI cannot engage with emotional nuance, contextual signals, or ethical complexity (Savardi et al., 2025; Alkhasawneh et al., 2025). If collaboration is to support rather than distort educational practice, relational and pastoral interactions must remain human led. AI may offer general guidance or information, yet it cannot replace the presence required to build trust or support students through uncertainty. Educators therefore need institutional support to prioritise relational work even as automation becomes more prevalent. Institutional conditions play a crucial role in determining whether collaboration supports or undermines professional integrity. Transparency is essential. Educators must understand how AI systems operate, what data they draw upon, and what biases or epistemic assumptions shape their outputs. Professional development must extend beyond functional training to cultivate critical AI literacy. This includes recognising hallucinations, evaluating the epistemic limits of automated content, and understanding the risks associated with overreliance. Workload models must also allow time for reflective judgement. If automation is introduced primarily as a solution to labour and efficiency demands, educators may be compelled to rely on AI in ways that compromise their professional practice. Governance structures must articulate clear boundaries for AI use. Policies should identify tasks that require human judgement, including interpretive assessment, ethical decision making, relational support, and curriculum framing. Without such boundaries, institutions risk repeating the failures seen in other sectors. The Deloitte scandals demonstrate how reliance on AI for high stakes analysis can erode public trust and compromise epistemic credibility when automated content is not subjected to rigorous human evaluation. Higher education must learn from these examples. The preservation of professional integrity requires explicit commitments to human accountability in all areas where moral, relational, and intellectual responsibilities are at stake.

Ultimately, a sustainable model of human AI collaboration positions educators not as passive recipients of AI generated suggestions but as active interpreters, curators, and ethical anchors of the learning environment. AI can support creativity, broaden access to resources, and help identify pedagogical possibilities. Yet it cannot determine what matters, how concepts should be framed, or how relationships should be nurtured. Collaboration becomes meaningful when educators critically engage with AI through the lens of their own values and expertise. By doing so, they ensure that automation remains a tool that enhances rather than diminishes the capacities that define teaching.

REFRAMING AND RECLAIMING PROFESSIONAL IDENTITY

The transformations described across the preceding sections raise a deeper and more difficult question. *What does it mean to be an educator at a time when GenAI appears capable of performing many of the visible tasks associated with teaching?* Pedagogical labour has never been defined solely by the production of content or the transmission of information. Teaching is an interpretive, relational and ethical practice that depends on human presence, contextual understanding and professional judgement. These qualities risk being obscured when automation produces outputs that mimic the surface structure of pedagogy. Reclaiming professional identity therefore requires educators to articulate those dimensions of teaching that cannot be delegated to AI, and to reshape their practices in ways that foreground these human capacities.

A first step in this process involves recognising the subtle forms of identity erosion that accompany deskilling. Research on hybrid human AI workflows shows that when professionals rely on automation to perform the early stages of reasoning, they may begin to doubt their ability to carry out these tasks independently (Gunathilake, 2025). Similar dynamics are evident in education. As discussed earlier, some educators have come to rely on AI generated feedback as a starting point for assessment, while others begin lesson design by prompting generative systems for outlines or examples. Over time, this shift can lead to a narrowing of pedagogical agency. Instead of engaging in the interpretive, creative and ethical work that once defined teaching, educators may find themselves in the position of verifying or editing machine produced content.

This erosion of identity becomes most visible when students question the authenticity of instruction. The Staffordshire case revealed the emotional and symbolic damage that occurs when learners discover that educational materials were generated without meaningful teacher involvement (Down, 2025). Students expressed frustration not only because the content lacked depth but because they felt deprived of the presence of a teacher who could guide their learning. Their reaction underscores a core insight from critical pedagogy. Freire (1996) and Giroux (2024) remind us that teaching involves cultivating relationships, supporting dialogue, and acting as a transformative agent rather than a mechanistic distributor of information. Identity is fundamentally tied to this relational and intellectual commitment. When AI mediates or replaces these forms of engagement, the educator's sense of purpose may be destabilised.

Identity formation is further challenged by the epistemic tendencies of GenAI. Automated systems produce fluent, credible appearing text that can obscure the absence of underlying reasoning. The legal sector offers a cautionary parallel. Lawyers who submitted AI written legal filings containing hallucinated case law were criticised not only for the errors themselves but for failing to uphold the professional responsibility of verifying sources (Blandis, 2025). In education, similar risks arise when instructors adopt AI generated explanations, examples or readings without critical scrutiny. Over time, educators may internalise epistemic norms that prioritise coherence over accuracy, speed over depth and convenience over reflection. These tendencies can blur the boundaries between human and machine reasoning in ways that undermine the reflective judgement that constitutes professional identity. Reclaiming identity therefore involves reaffirming the pedagogical, ethical and relational commitments that distinguish teaching from automated content delivery. Educators must foreground the interpretive work that AI cannot perform. This includes asking what a student's question reveals about their understanding, identifying the ethical and emotional context of a learner's difficulty, and making decisions about how knowledge should be framed or contested within a particular discipline. AI can generate plausible answers, but it cannot make sense of the human complexities that give rise to them. When educators centre their identity on these uniquely human capacities, they resist the narrowing influence of automation.

Workload pressures, efficiency narratives and data driven management systems can undermine educators' ability to enact the relational and reflective practices that define their profession (Johnson, 2022). Universities must create conditions that recognise and protect time for dialogue, mentoring and ethical deliberation. Professional development initiatives must extend beyond technical training to cultivate critical AI literacy, enabling educators to engage confidently with automated tools without relinquishing their judgement. Policies should also establish clear boundaries around tasks that require human involvement, including interpretive assessment, pastoral support and decisions involving fairness and academic standards.

Finally, reclaiming professional identity involves developing a forward-facing vision of teaching in which AI is positioned as a partner rather than a substitute. This requires educators to articulate the value of their work not in terms of output but in terms of meaning making. It involves viewing AI suggestions as prompts that stimulate inquiry rather than prescriptions that dictate practice. Most importantly, it involves recognising that the moral and relational dimensions of teaching remain irreplaceable. Even as AI becomes more sophisticated, it cannot replicate the trust, connection and ethical responsibility that form the heart of education. In this sense, reclaiming identity is not a defensive act but a generative one. It invites educators to reimagine teaching as a practice anchored in human judgement, relational care and intellectual integrity. It positions AI as a catalyst for creativity and exploration while insisting that the core of teaching remains profoundly human. This vision prepares the way for a more thoughtful and responsible integration of automation, and for a renewed understanding of what it means to teach in an AI mediated world.

CONCLUSIONS

The rapid integration of GenAI into higher education has prompted widespread debate about academic integrity, assessment practices and the future of learning. Yet the discussion developed throughout this chapter shows that the most significant transformation is unfolding more quietly. It concerns the reconfiguration of educators' work. Teaching has always involved judgement, interpretation, relational presence and ethical responsibility. These qualities are not secondary attributes of pedagogy but its foundation. The rise of GenAI challenges these foundations by offering automated outputs that simulate the visible tasks of teaching without the human processes that give them meaning.

The risks of this transformation are evident across empirical contexts. In Spain, educators who initially approached AI with caution soon found that automated feedback had become a routine starting point in their evaluative practices, subtly shifting the locus of judgement away from the educator and toward the system (Alkhasawneh et al., 2025). The Staffordshire case revealed how learners respond when this shift becomes visible. Students expressed feelings of betrayal upon discovering that teaching materials had been generated and narrated by AI (Down, 2025). Their reaction demonstrates that the value of teaching lies not only in content delivery but in the presence of an educator who interprets, contextualises and responds to human needs. Parallel failures in other professions reinforce the stakes. In legal practice, courts in the United Kingdom and Australia confronted cases in which lawyers submitted AI generated filings containing fabricated case law and invented quotations. Judges warned that GenAI produces fluent but unreliable assertions that can undermine professional duty and public trust (Booth, 2025), while regulatory bodies in Australia sanctioned legal practitioners for relying on AI outputs in place of verifiable analysis (Blandis, 2025). These incidents mirror the dynamics evident in higher education. Professionals accustomed to exercising judgement appear increasingly vulnerable when automated systems generate outputs that mimic expertise while concealing epistemic weakness. The Deloitte scandals in Canada and Australia revealed how organisations can incorporate AI generated material into government reports without adequate verification. The resulting documents included hallucinated citations, non-existent legal references and fabricated sources, prompting public inquiries and financial repayment obligations (Paoli, 2025; Shibu, 2025). These failures demonstrate that the dangers of AI induced deskilling are not confined to teaching. They arise whenever automated processes are permitted to replace human responsibility for truth, interpretation and ethical accountability. Taken together, these examples illustrate a common pattern. Deskilling does not result from dramatic technological disruption. It emerges through gradual changes to routine practices. It begins when educators turn to AI for efficiency, and it accelerates when institutions deploy AI to streamline work or reduce costs. Over time, teaching risks becoming defined as the oversight of automated systems rather than the human labour of making sense of complexity, building relationships and exercising judgement. If unaddressed, this shift threatens the epistemic integrity of higher education, weakens professional identity and undermines the relational foundations that make education a transformative endeavour.

Despite these risks, the future need not follow this trajectory. As argued earlier, a more sustainable model of human AI collaboration is possible. Such a model requires educators to articulate the distinctively human qualities of teaching and to design workflows in which human reasoning precedes and shapes AI involvement. It requires institutions to create environments that support relational labour, protect time for reflection and ensure that professional autonomy is not sacrificed to efficiency imperatives. It also requires collective clarity about the ethical boundaries of AI use. Tasks that involve interpretive assessment, pastoral support, disciplinary judgement or ethical reasoning must remain human led. Automated systems can support these processes, but they cannot replace them.

The broader implications of this discussion extend beyond higher education. Across professional domains, GenAI exposes a fundamental tension between efficiency and expertise. Automation can accelerate tasks, but it often erodes the very capacities upon which professions depend. The challenge for universities is therefore twofold. They must protect the human foundations of their own pedagogical practice, and they must prepare students to navigate an increasingly automated world without losing the cognitive, ethical and relational abilities that define professional life. The future of higher education will depend less on the sophistication of AI systems than on the willingness of educators and institutions to assert the values that guide their work. If teaching is understood primarily as content delivery, AI will undoubtedly appear capable of replacing much of it. If teaching is recognised as a relational, interpretive and ethical practice, AI becomes a tool whose usefulness is determined by the clarity of human purpose. This chapter has argued for the latter view. The task ahead is to ensure that educational practices, institutional policies and professional identities are aligned with it. Only then can AI enhance, rather than diminish, the human work of teaching.

REFERENCES

Alkhasawneh, S. N., Hernández-Leo, D., Guerrero-Solé, F., & Pérez, F. (2025). Shifting Educator Perspectives: Exploring Evolving Views on Generative AI. In Proceedings of the D-SAIL Workshop-Transformative Curriculum Design: Digitalisation, Sustainability, and AI Literacy for 21st Century Learning, CEUR-WS, Palermo, Italy (pp. 15-25).

Bate, G. W. (2025). The struggle is the lesson! Being an educator in the age of AI. *AI & Society*, *40*(7), 1–3. DOI: 10.1007/s00146-025-02347-1

Blandis, E. (2025, December 4). Artificial intelligence used to prepare legal document, lawyers referred to regulators. ABC News Australia. https://www.abc.net.au/news/2025-12-05/artificial-intelligence-used-to-prepare-legal-document/106086724

Booth, R. (2025, June 6). High Court tells UK lawyers to urgently stop misuse of AI in legal work. The Guardian. https://www.theguardian.com/technology/2025/jun/06/high-court-tells-uk-lawyers-to-urgently-stop-misuse-of-ai-in-legal-work

Braverman, H. (1974). *Labor and monopoly capital: The degradation of work in the twentieth century*. Monthly Review Press. DOI: 10.14452/MR-026-03-1974-07_1

Down, A. (2025, November 20). University of Staffordshire course taught in large part by AI. The Guardian. https://www.theguardian.com/education/2025/nov/20/university-of-staffordshire-course-taught-in-large-part-by-ai-artificial-intelligence

Duran, L. D. D. (2021). Deskilling of medical professionals: an unintended consequence of AI implementation?. Giornale di filosofia, 2(2).

Freire, P. (1996). Pedagogy of the oppressed (revised). New York: Continuum, 356, 357-358.

Giroux, H. A. (2024). *Teachers as intellectuals: Toward a critical pedagogy of learning*. Bloomsbury Publishing. DOI: 10.5040/9781350458635

Gunathilake, P. D. C. (2025). Generative AI and Knowledge Work: Towards a Framework for Combating Deskilling of Knowledge Workers.

Johnson, L. (2022). Failure to Disrupt: Why Technology Alone Can't Transform Education. *Journal of Teaching and Learning*, *16*(1), 101–103. DOI: 10.22329/jtl.v16i1.7033

Kolchenko, V. (2018). Can modern AI replace teachers? Not so fast! Artificial intelligence and adaptive learning: Personalized education in the AI age. HAPS educator, 22(3), 249-252.

Leo, U. (2025, December 6). Weekend reading: On legal education: Is AI churning out super or surface-level lawyers? Higher Education Policy Institute. https://www.hepi.ac.uk/2025/12/06/weekend-reading-on-legal-education-is-ai-churning-out-super-or-surface-level-lawyers/

Luckin, R., Cukurova, M., Kent, C., & Du Boulay, B. (2022). Empowering educators to be AI-ready. *Computers and Education: Artificial Intelligence*, *3*, 100076.

Paoli, N. (2025, October 7). Deloitte caught using AI in 290,000 dollar report for Australian government, leading to refund after hallucinations. Fortune. https://fortune.com/2025/10/07/deloitte-ai-australia-government-report-hallucinations-technology-290000-refund/

Peterson, A. J. (2025). Training for Obsolescence? The AI-Driven Education Trap. arXiv preprint arXiv:2508.19625.

Pratiwi, H., Riwanda, A., Hasruddin, H., Sujarwo, S., & Syamsudin, A. (2025). Transforming Learning or Creating Dependency? Teachers' Perspectives and Barriers to AI Integration in Education. *Journal of Pedagogical Research*, *9*(2), 127–142. DOI: 10.33902/JPR.202531677

Savardi, M., Signoroni, A., Benini, S., Vaccher, F., Alberti, M., Ciolli, P., Di Meo, N., Falcone, T., Ramanzin, M., Romano, B., Sozzi, F., & Farina, D. (2025). Upskilling or deskilling? Measurable role of an AI-supported training for radiology residents: A lesson from the pandemic. *Insights Into Imaging*, *16*(1), 23. DOI: 10.1186/s13244-024-01893-4

Shibu, S. (2025, November 25). Deloitte detected using fake AI citations in 1 million dollar report. Entrepreneur. https://www.entrepreneur.com/business-news/deloitte-detected-using-fake-ai-citations-in-1-million/500072

Suchman, L. A. (2007). *Human-machine reconfigurations: Plans and situated actions*. Cambridge university press.

Tan, X., Cheng, G., & Ling, M. H. (2025). Artificial intelligence in teaching and teacher professional development: A systematic review. *Computers and Education: Artificial Intelligence*, *8*, 100355. DOI: 10.1016/j.caeai.2024.100355

Winner, L. (2017). Do artifacts have politics? In *Computer ethics* (pp. 177–192). Routledge. DOI: 10.4324/9781315259697-21

Yavich, R. (2025). Will the Use of AI Undermine Students Independent Thinking? *Education Sciences*, *15*(6), 669. DOI: 10.3390/educsci15060669

Chapter 11
The Professor's Role in an AI-Dominated Classroom in Higher Education

Mustafa Kayyali
http://orcid.org/0000-0003-3300-262X
Maaref University of Applied Sciences, Syria

ABSTRACT

This chapter explores the evolving role of professors in higher education as classrooms increasingly lean on artificial intelligence. While AI tools promise efficiency, personalization, and accessibility, they also risk diminishing the professor's central role as mentor, guide, and moral compass. The text reflects on how faculty can reposition themselves not as dispensable transmitters of information but as interpreters of meaning, cultivators of critical thinking, and guardians of academic integrity. It considers the ethical challenges of overreliance on automated systems, including the erosion of intellectual agency and the narrowing of human judgment. The chapter argues that the professor's enduring contribution lies in fostering reflective dialogue, modeling intellectual humility, and guiding students to navigate ambiguity—tasks that no algorithm can fully replicate. In doing so, it calls for a reimagined partnership between human insight and machine intelligence that preserves education's deeper purpose.

DOI: 10.4018/979-8-3373-7097-2.ch011

INTRODUCTION

Higher education has always been a mirror of its time, absorbing and refracting the dominant forces that shape societies. In the twenty-first century, one force looms larger than most: artificial intelligence. Once confined to laboratories and speculative fiction, AI now sits in the everyday classroom, whispering answers, generating essays, curating reading lists, even grading with a precision that seems almost dispassionate. It promises efficiency and personalization, but beneath the surface it raises uncomfortable questions: if the machine can teach, assess, and respond, what remains for the professor to do? Is the academic figure who once stood at the center of knowledge production and transmission at risk of being reduced to a facilitator—or worse, an accessory?

The rise of AI in academia did not happen in a vacuum (Watermeyer et al, 2024). It emerged out of decades of technological innovation coupled with the relentless drive of institutions to do more with less: larger class sizes, shrinking budgets, increased accountability, and a cultural obsession with speed and immediacy. Against this backdrop, AI offers itself as a savior—efficient, scalable, endlessly adaptable. But every tool carries an implicit reordering of human relations. Just as the printing press shifted the authority of the oral teacher, and just as the internet dispersed the gatekeeping of libraries, AI has begun to recast the professor's role in profound ways. It is not merely another instrument to be adopted; it is an epistemic force that alters how we conceive of teaching, learning, and even intelligence itself.

Yet to speak of "overdependence" is to acknowledge both potential and peril. Students, drawn to AI's speed and convenience, may sidestep the long labor of wrestling with ideas. Administrators may welcome algorithms that streamline assessment, sometimes at the cost of nuance. Professors themselves may find their expertise overshadowed by generative systems that produce instant, polished responses to student queries. The danger lies not in AI's presence, but in the silent erosion of the professor's voice, the gradual diminishing of the human encounter that defines education at its deepest level. A classroom without authentic human presence risks becoming a transactional space where learning is measured only in outputs, not in transformation (Swart & MacLeod, 2021).

At the same time, it would be simplistic to frame the professor merely as a victim of AI's expansion. The story is more complicated. For every fear of replacement, there is also an invitation: to redefine what it means to teach in an age when information is abundant, to reimagine pedagogy as the art not of recitation but of interpretation, not of delivering content but of nurturing discernment. Professors, in this sense, are not being displaced but being summoned to a new kind of intellectual stewardship (Black, 2021). Their work is less about monopolizing knowledge and more about helping students learn to question, to contextualize, to resist the seduction of easy answers. In this evolving landscape, the professor becomes a guide through complexity rather than a dispenser of certainty.

The challenge, then, is one of balance. How can higher education embrace the undeniable benefits of AI—its capacity to personalize, to accelerate, to democratize—without surrendering the irreplaceable dimensions of human teaching? What values must professors hold onto, and what practices must they be willing to reinvent? These questions sit at the heart of this chapter. They invite us to look beyond the rhetoric of technological inevitability and instead focus on the moral and intellectual fabric of education (Qutieshat, 2025). Because if higher education is reduced to algorithmic efficiency, it risks losing the very qualities that make it humane: dialogue, empathy, doubt, struggle, and the shared pursuit of meaning.

In this chapter, we will explore the multiple roles professors must negotiate in an AI-dominated classroom: as mediators of critical thinking, as ethical anchors, as interpreters of context, and as protectors of the fragile but essential space where students and teachers meet as humans first. By tracing both the risks of overdependence and the possibilities of creative adaptation, we aim to uncover how the professor's presence remains not only relevant but indispensable. For no matter how powerful, no machine can replace the subtle gestures of encouragement, the moral weight of example, or the unpredictable spark of dialogue that ignites genuine learning. These, at their core, remain the province of the professor.

REFRAMING THE PROFESSOR'S IDENTITY IN AN AI-SATURATED LEARNING ENVIRONMENT

In the collective imagination of academia, the professor has long been pictured as a figure at the center of a room, chalk in hand or voice commanding the air, shaping ideas in real time. Knowledge was their terrain, authority their currency. Yet in an age where artificial intelligence can generate explanations in seconds, produce lecture notes tailored to any level, and provide feedback with mechanical consistency, that old silhouette starts to blur. The professor, once the guardian of intellectual gateways, now finds those gates wide open—algorithms flooding in with an efficiency that appears almost effortless. What does it mean, then, to inhabit the role of professor when information itself has been automated? The question is not merely professional; it is existential.

There is an unsettling paradox at play. On the one hand, AI threatens to undermine the very basis of professorial authority by offering knowledge that is immediate, endless, and seemingly impartial (Ferrario et al, 2024). On the other hand, it exposes just how shallow that definition of authority was to begin with. If the professor is reduced to little more than a content transmitter, then yes, a machine can perform that task faster, cheaper, and perhaps even more smoothly. But the deeper work of education has never truly been about information transfer. It is about interpretation, guidance, provocation, and the slow cultivation of judgment. To reframe the professor's identity, then, requires peeling away the illusion that teaching was ever only about content delivery.

The AI-saturated classroom has a way of amplifying what was already fragile (Kolhatin, 2025). Professors, even before the rise of large language models and algorithmic tutors, have wrestled with shrinking institutional trust, pressures of corporatized universities, and students arriving with different expectations about what learning should look like. Add to this a generation accustomed to immediate answers on demand, and the professor who hesitates, who complicates, who insists on ambiguity, risks appearing outdated or unnecessarily difficult. Yet perhaps this is precisely where the identity must shift: from one who provides answers to one who teaches how to live with questions. AI can dazzle with responses, but it cannot nurture the tolerance for uncertainty that lies at the core of intellectual maturity.

There is a temptation to imagine the professor now as a kind of manager of technology—someone who oversees the interplay of AI systems and students, ensuring smooth integration. While there is some truth to this role, it would be a mistake to stop there. To reduce professors to mere facilitators of platforms is to accept a diminished vision of human teaching. Instead, reframing requires a bolder stance: professors as cultural interpreters, as ethical compasses, as intellectual provocateurs. They are not only mediators between student and content, but between the machine's sterile efficiency and the messiness of human life.

Consider the affective dimensions of teaching: the raised eyebrow that signals skepticism, the tone of voice that conveys encouragement, the pause that lets a question breathe. These subtleties are not incidental. They are the texture of learning, the tacit cues through which students sense that knowledge is not a dead object but a living dialogue. AI cannot mimic this relational complexity. It can approximate politeness or simulate enthusiasm, but it cannot share in the vulnerability of not knowing, the humility of error, the courage of intellectual risk (George et al, 2023). The professor's identity, reframed in this environment, rests precisely on those irreducibly human gestures.

At the same time, clinging to an idealized past is equally dangerous. Professors who dismiss AI entirely risk alienating themselves from the very tools their students will inevitably use (Saltman, 2022). To refuse the presence of AI in the classroom is to deny reality and, in some ways, to abandon students to navigate its complexities alone. Reframing identity does not mean rejecting AI; it means claiming a position that refuses both naive adoption and fearful resistance. It is about inhabiting the role of critical partner—teaching students not simply how to use AI, but how to question its assumptions, its biases, its blind spots.

There is also the ethical weight. Professors are called to be guardians of integrity in a time when the line between original thought and algorithmic regurgitation grows increasingly thin. Academic honesty has always been fragile, but with AI producing essays that mimic human voice, the temptation to bypass effort is stronger than ever. The professor here is not a policeman patrolling plagiarism, but a cultivator of conscience—someone who persuades students that learning is not a performance for grades, but a process of becoming (Eaton, 2021). This ethical stance, if embodied consistently, reshapes identity more profoundly than any technological adjustment could.

Identity is also about presence. A classroom where AI dominates can become transactional—students ask, machine answers, outcomes are measured. But the professor disrupts that transactional logic by insisting on the unpredictable space of dialogue. Presence is not reducible to content; it is the willingness to sit with students in their confusion, to acknowledge uncertainty, to laugh at the absurdity of intellectual struggle (McGlone et al, 2025). Presence resists efficiency; it insists on humanity. The professor who embodies presence reminds students that education is not about speed but about depth, not about shortcuts but about formation.

Of course, there will be professors who struggle with this reframing, who feel their expertise eroded, who resent the intrusion of machines into a domain once marked by human exclusivity. Yet identity has always been fluid. The medieval scholar gave way to the Renaissance humanist, who gave way to the industrial lecturer, who gave way to the digital-age academic. Each transition demanded a rethinking of role, a renegotiation of authority. The AI era is no different, except perhaps in its pace. The challenge is to refuse nostalgia and instead ask: what new possibilities open when the old image of the professor as oracle dissolves?

One such possibility is the embrace of vulnerability. Professors need no longer pretend to omniscience, for AI has exposed the impossibility of that role. Instead, they can model what it means to be a learner in the presence of overwhelming information: how to sift, how to doubt, how to resist the seduction of easy certainty (Watanabe, 2024). Vulnerability becomes strength, not weakness. Students learn not only from what professors know but from how they navigate what they do not know.

Reframing also requires acknowledging the emotional labor of teaching. AI may reduce workloads, but it cannot shoulder the burden of caring for students as whole persons. Professors listen to stories of struggle, loss, anxiety—dimensions of student life that never appear in an algorithm's dataset (Hashem et al, 2024). This pastoral dimension, often invisible in academic metrics, is central to identity. It is the silent work of tending to the human being behind the assignments, a work no machine can replicate.

Ultimately, reframing the professor's identity in an AI-saturated learning environment is not about diminishing the machine but about amplifying the human. It is about claiming the role of interpreter rather than transmitter, of guide rather than oracle, of partner rather than competitor. The professor who embraces this reframed identity does not fear AI, nor does he or she worship it (Ghosh & Ghosh, 2025). Instead, they situate it within the larger tapestry of education, where knowledge is not only information but wisdom, not only efficiency but transformation.

The task is daunting, but perhaps also liberating. Professors are no longer bound to defend their authority by clinging to content; they are free to embody the deeper dimensions of teaching that machines cannot touch (Gao, 2025). In doing so, they preserve the essence of education as a profoundly human enterprise, even in an age saturated with artificial intelligence.

BALANCING HUMAN JUDGMENT WITH MACHINE PRECISION

The encounter between human judgment and machine precision is one of the defining tensions of our era in education. Professors now stand in a peculiar space where their authority is both amplified and undermined by artificial intelligence (Preston, 2021). On one hand, algorithms can process enormous quantities of data, recognize patterns invisible to human eyes, and deliver answers with astonishing speed. On the other, those very answers can arrive so quickly, so flawlessly, that they leave little room for hesitation, doubt, or the texture of interpretation. The challenge is not whether machines can outperform humans in certain technical tasks—that question has already been settled. The deeper concern is how educators can sustain the delicate balance where precision serves wisdom rather than replacing it.

Human judgment thrives on nuance, on the capacity to weigh competing values, to sense the undercurrents of context, to read not only the words on a page but the silences between them. A professor guiding a student through an ethical dilemma, or helping a class wrestle with the contradictions in a philosophical text, is doing more than delivering information (Sætra, 2022). They are modeling discernment—the ability to linger with ambiguity, to resist the false comfort of definitive answers. Machine precision, by contrast, leans toward closure. It provides outputs that appear authoritative, framed as if certainty is the natural condition of knowledge. This tension reveals why balance is not a simple distribution of tasks but a continual negotiation of roles.

Consider assessment, one of the most pressing areas where AI now intrudes. Automated grading promises fairness and efficiency, scoring hundreds of essays in the time it takes a professor to finish reading a handful (Vetrivel et al, 2025). Yet human judgment is never simply about checking boxes; it involves sensing intention, effort, and growth. A student's halting attempt at argument may not meet the rubric, yet it may represent a breakthrough moment, a leap from silence into voice. Machines can count words and evaluate structure, but they cannot detect the trembling courage behind the words. Precision without judgment risks flattening education into a mechanical process, devoid of empathy and context.

The inverse is also true. Human judgment without the benefit of machine precision can fall prey to bias, fatigue, or inconsistency. Professors, despite their best intentions, are not immune to subjectivity. An essay read at the end of a long day may receive less generous evaluation than one read in the morning (Van der Linden, 2023). Machine precision offers a corrective, reminding us that fairness requires more than human goodwill—it requires tools that can check our blind spots. The balance, then, is not about choosing one over the other, but about allowing each to temper the other's limitations. Precision curbs bias, judgment resists reduction.

There is also the question of pace. Machines operate at lightning speed, compressing time in ways that can make human reflection feel slow, even cumbersome. Students accustomed to instant feedback from AI may grow impatient with the professor who takes days to return papers, who pauses in class discussions to think aloud, who insists that uncertainty is part of learning (Kingsley, 2025). Yet it is precisely in this slowness that judgment flourishes. Reflection cannot be rushed; the pauses are the very spaces where meaning emerges. Precision accelerates, judgment lingers. If education becomes only about speed, it risks confusing efficiency with understanding. The balance requires holding space for both tempo and tempo rubato—the strict beat of machine output and the unpredictable rhythms of human thought.

Another layer of tension emerges in the moral dimension. Machines can predict outcomes, calculate probabilities, and optimize processes, but they cannot bear responsibility. Judgment, in its fullest sense, is inseparable from accountability. When a professor guides a student toward a decision—about research integrity, professional ethics, or even life choices—their words carry weight precisely because they are accountable to another human being (Stewart, 2023). An algorithm may suggest, but it cannot stand beside the student in the consequences of choice. The balance here is not symmetrical; it leans toward judgment, because precision without responsibility is sterile.

Still, one must admit that precision has its seductions. Professors themselves may be tempted to lean heavily on AI for course design, for exam generation, for managing administrative burdens. The efficiency is intoxicating: lectures prepared in minutes, readings summarized, feedback drafted. But there is a quiet danger here—the risk of outsourcing not only labor but thought. When precision begins to dictate the rhythm of teaching, judgment can wither, reduced to rubber-stamping machine outputs. The professor becomes less an educator and more an overseer of processes, their voice drowned out by the hum of algorithms.

Yet balance is possible if reframed as dialogue rather than division. Professors can engage AI outputs critically, using them as provocations rather than prescriptions. A machine-generated essay, for instance, can serve as a teaching tool: what does it get right, what does it miss, where does its precision collapse into banality? In this sense, precision becomes the foil against which judgment sharpens itself (Kershen & Johnson, 2025). Students learn not to passively consume AI answers, but to interrogate them, guided by the professor's modeling of critical engagement.

The balance also has an aesthetic dimension. Precision tends toward neatness, symmetry, closure. Judgment, by contrast, embraces imperfection, asymmetry, the rough edges of lived experience. In literature, in art, in philosophy, it is often the flaw, the hesitation, the contradiction that opens the deepest insights. Professors who teach with judgment remind students that knowledge is not a polished gem but a landscape of tensions (Bozkurt et al, 2023). Machines can polish endlessly, but they cannot inhabit the human willingness to dwell with the unfinished.

One might ask: is balance even sustainable, or will the gravitational pull of efficiency eventually overwhelm judgment? Institutions, driven by metrics and budgets, often prioritize measurable outputs. Precision is easier to quantify than judgment, easier to defend in reports and rankings. Yet history suggests that education, despite waves of standardization, resists complete mechanization. The irreducible encounter between teacher and learner has survived printing presses, industrialization, and the digital revolution. It will likely survive AI as well, though not without struggle. The balance will require professors to defend not only their roles but the very value of judgment itself in a world increasingly enchanted by certainty.

At its core, the balance is a question of trust. Students must trust that their professors offer more than information—they offer discernment, perspective, a human presence that does not collapse into metrics (Hiatt et al, 2023). Professors, in turn, must trust that machine precision, if used responsibly, can enhance rather than diminish their work. Trust, however, is fragile. It must be earned daily, through presence, through dialogue, through the refusal to let efficiency eclipse empathy.

In rethinking balance, perhaps the metaphor is not a scale but a dance. Judgment and precision do not sit on opposite sides, weighing against each other. They move together, sometimes in harmony, sometimes in tension, each shaping the rhythm of the classroom. The professor's task is not to dominate the dance but to lead with grace, to know when to let precision guide the step and when to let judgment improvise. This dance resists choreography; it is improvised, messy, alive. And it is in this aliveness that education retains its soul.

PEDAGOGICAL SHIFTS: FROM KNOWLEDGE TRANSMISSION TO CRITICAL MEDIATION

Universities once imagined themselves as repositories of accumulated knowledge, and professors were the custodians of that treasure. The lecture hall stood as a kind of temple where words flowed in one direction, from the lecturer's mouth to the scribbling hands of students. Knowledge transmission was the dominant metaphor: something solid, contained, transferred intact from one mind to another (Çengel, 2023). In the age of artificial intelligence, this model feels increasingly outdated, almost quaint. For when an algorithm can summon information more quickly, more comprehensively, and with fewer errors than any human, the idea of the professor as transmitter begins to unravel. Pedagogy must shift, or risk irrelevance.

The shift, however, is not simply pragmatic. It is philosophical. Teaching has never really been about dumping content into passive vessels; yet the industrial model of education leaned heavily on that assumption. AI makes the bankruptcy of that model undeniable. A student who wants definitions, summaries, or even elaborate explanations no longer needs to wait for the lecture or the textbook (Youvan, 2025). The machine can provide that in an instant. What it cannot provide, though, is mediation: the subtle process of helping learners make sense of knowledge, confront contradictions, evaluate implications, and integrate understanding into lived experience. That is where pedagogy must move—away from transmission, toward the art of critical mediation.

Critical mediation is less about what is said and more about what is invited. A professor does not merely deliver content but creates conditions for students to wrestle with it, to question it, to see how it resonates or conflicts with their assumptions (Waghid, 2023). Imagine a classroom where the machine generates multiple interpretations of a historical event; the professor's task is not to add a fifteenth version but to ask, "What does it mean to privilege this narrative over that one? Whose voices are amplified, whose are silenced?" This is not content transfer but a cultivation of discernment. It requires slowing down when AI insists on speeding up, complicating when AI simplifies, unsettling when AI packages knowledge too neatly.

The movement from transmission to mediation also reconfigures authority. In the old model, authority came from mastery of content; the professor knew more, so the students listened. In the new landscape, content mastery is no longer scarce. Authority must be re-grounded in something else: the ability to interpret, to provoke thought, to hold open a space where complexity is not erased but engaged. Authority becomes relational, not merely informational. Students do not look to professors for answers as much as for guidance in learning how to live with questions (Nygård et al, 2021).

There is also the affective dimension. Transmission tends to be impersonal—content is neutral, detached, moved from point A to point B. Mediation, by contrast, is charged with emotion, ethics, and the unpredictability of human encounter. A professor practicing mediation acknowledges that knowledge is not neutral; it shapes lives, policies, futures (Gadaza et al, 2025). To mediate critically is to highlight not just what knowledge says, but what it does—who benefits, who suffers, what possibilities are opened, which are foreclosed. In this way, pedagogy becomes an act of responsibility.

Yet this shift is not smooth. Professors themselves may struggle with the loss of the familiar role of expert deliverer. There is a kind of security in transmission: stand in front, present the material, and measure learning by reproduction. Mediation, by contrast, is messy. It invites unpredictability, dialogue that goes off-script, students challenging the very assumptions of the course. It requires vulnerability, admitting that knowledge is contested and that certainty is rare. For some, this feels destabilizing. But perhaps that very destabilization is where genuine education resides. If learning is not unsettling, it risks becoming entertainment or mere training.

Students, too, may resist. Accustomed to efficiency, they might find mediation frustrating, even unnecessary. Why dwell in ambiguity when AI offers clear answers? Why wrestle with texts when a summary is one prompt away? The role of the professor here is not to compete with the machine's efficiency but to demonstrate the limits of its clarity. Mediation teaches that easy answers are not always trustworthy, that precision without context can mislead, that truth often resides not in the polished response but in the tension between perspectives.

This pedagogical shift also alters assessment. If knowledge transmission dominated, exams tested recall—how well students could reproduce information. Critical mediation demands different measures. How well can students interrogate sources, connect ideas, identify bias, or imagine alternatives? AI complicates this further, since machines can now generate essays that mimic such critical gestures. Professors must therefore design assessments that go beyond surface-level performance, asking students to demonstrate personal engagement, originality of thought, or contextual application that AI cannot easily replicate (Akbar, 2025). The emphasis moves from what students know to how they think and how they position themselves within a world saturated with information.

Perhaps the most radical implication of this shift is the reframing of learning itself. If knowledge is no longer a product to be transmitted, learning becomes a practice of navigation, interpretation, and ethical choice. Students are not passive recipients but active participants in shaping meaning. The professor is less a broadcaster of information and more a cartographer of intellectual landscapes, sketching maps while reminding students that maps are always partial, selective, embedded with assumptions. Mediation is not about offering the "truth" but about equipping learners to find their bearings in terrains where truth is complex and contested.

There is something deeply human about this mediating role. Machines are powerful at generating content but indifferent to meaning. They can simulate argument but cannot care about consequences. Mediation requires care. It requires the patience to sit with students in their confusion, the humility to admit when a question has no clear answer, the moral responsibility to acknowledge when knowledge intersects with justice, oppression, or human dignity. In this sense, the shift from transmission to mediation is not merely about pedagogy—it is about preserving the humanity of education itself in a time when machines threaten to hollow it out.

Yet mediation is not a rejection of knowledge. It is a reorientation. Professors still need expertise; they cannot mediate critically without grounding. But expertise is no longer sufficient on its own (Großmann et al, 2025). What matters is the capacity to place knowledge in dialogue—with other knowledge, with lived experience, with ethical questions. Transmission says: "Here is what you need to know." Mediation asks: "What does this mean? How will you use it? Who might it affect?" It shifts the focus from accumulation to transformation.

One might even say that this pedagogical shift reclaims something ancient. Long before universities, education was about dialogue, about apprenticeship in ways of thinking and being. Socrates never transmitted content in the sense we think of today; he mediated, provoked, questioned, unsettled. In a paradoxical way, the age of AI, with its flood of information, may be bringing us back to those roots. Professors are once again called to be mediators of meaning, not mere deliverers of facts.

In practice, this shift will look different across disciplines. In engineering, mediation might mean asking not just how to build efficiently but whether building in a certain way is sustainable, ethical, or socially responsible. In literature, it might mean probing why certain voices are canonized and others ignored. In business, it might mean examining the human cost of decisions optimized for profit. Across all fields, the common thread is this: mediation turns knowledge outward, toward consequences and contexts, refusing to let it remain an inert object.

The danger, of course, is that mediation takes time, and time is what educational systems often lack. Large classes, administrative pressures, and standardized metrics push professors toward efficiency and transmission. AI, with its dazzling speed, reinforces this pressure. The task ahead is to resist the reduction of pedagogy to content delivery and to fight for spaces where mediation can flourish (George, 2023). Because in those spaces—messy, slow, dialogical—education retains its power to change lives rather than merely supply skills.

The future of pedagogy, then, lies not in competing with AI but in doing what AI cannot. It lies in critical mediation, in guiding students through the thickets of meaning, in helping them not just acquire knowledge but inhabit it, question it, and reimagine it. This shift is not optional. It is the only way education can remain education, rather than devolve into automated training. Professors who embrace this role may find themselves stretched, unsettled, even disoriented (Norell, 2024). But in that disorientation lies possibility—the chance to reimagine teaching as an act not of transmission but of transformation.

ETHICAL RESPONSIBILITIES OF FACULTY IN AI-DEPENDENT CLASSROOMS

Teaching has never been a neutral act. Every choice—what to include, what to omit, how to frame a concept, how to respond to a student—carries moral weight. In an era where artificial intelligence saturates classrooms, this ethical dimension of teaching becomes even sharper, because the presence of AI not only shifts how knowledge circulates but also forces educators to confront questions of responsibility that can no longer be avoided. Faculty are no longer simply content experts or guides of inquiry; they are mediators between students and technologies that hold tremendous power, both liberating and dangerous.

The allure of AI is obvious. It streamlines. It assists. It dazzles with outputs that mimic fluency and sophistication. But behind every algorithm lies a set of assumptions—coded by humans, trained on biased data, and driven by corporate interests. To integrate AI into classrooms without confronting those realities would be ethically careless (Akgun & Greenhow, 2022). Faculty carry the responsibility of revealing the seams, making visible the structures that students might otherwise take for granted. When a machine generates a text or provides an answer, the professor's task is not to marvel at the speed but to ask: whose perspective is missing here? What ideologies are baked into the dataset? What consequences emerge when we accept this response uncritically?

There is also the question of dependency. Students, like anyone, are drawn toward ease. Why labor over drafting an essay when a prompt can conjure one instantly? Why wrestle with the frustration of writer's block when a chatbot provides a polished first draft? The ethical responsibility of faculty here is subtle and difficult: not to demonize the tool, but to remind students that shortcuts can impoverish growth. Struggle, though uncomfortable, is part of learning. The temptation to bypass it with AI raises a moral dilemma—how much convenience can be embraced before it undermines integrity, effort, and authentic intellectual development? Professors must cultivate awareness of this tension, helping students see that the path of least resistance is not always the path of greatest transformation.

Another layer of responsibility lies in assessment. When essays, projects, and even creative works can be produced with machine assistance, what does it mean to evaluate student achievement? Faculty are tasked with protecting the integrity of education by designing assessments that measure more than AI outputs (Zaibout & Madrane, 2024). Yet this is not simply a matter of catching "cheating." It is about rethinking what counts as learning. If a student leans heavily on AI to draft a paper, have they failed, or have they simply engaged with a tool the world now expects them to know? The ethical line is blurred. Faculty must walk it carefully, neither naïve nor punitive, but attentive to what is being measured. The obligation is to ensure that education remains human-centered, not reduced to a performance of algorithmic polish.

There is also an ethical duty of transparency. Students deserve to know not only what AI can do but what it cannot, and why those limits matter (Selwyn, 2024). A professor who introduces AI without disclosing its biases or potential harms risks misleading students into believing that machine outputs are objective truth. Faculty are responsible for modeling critical literacy: demonstrating how to interrogate sources, how to cross-check claims, how to resist the seduction of authoritative tone. Without this modeling, students may leave classrooms ill-equipped to question the algorithms shaping their futures.

Equally important is the duty of equity. AI has the potential to widen existing inequalities in education. Students from affluent backgrounds may have greater access to premium AI tools, while those from less privileged contexts may rely on free, limited versions—or lack the technological infrastructure altogether. Faculty cannot solve structural inequities alone, but they can acknowledge them, adapt practices to minimize disparities, and advocate within institutions for more equitable access. Ignoring these differences risks reproducing injustice in the very spaces meant to challenge it.

Ethical responsibility also involves resisting the commodification of education. Many AI platforms are not neutral educational tools but commercial products designed for profit (Bulathwela et al, 2024). They gather data, track behavior, and feed into surveillance economies. When faculty encourage or require students to use such systems, they implicitly endorse those practices. To do so without critical reflection is ethically fraught. Professors must weigh the pedagogical benefits against the costs to privacy, autonomy, and trust. Sometimes the most ethical act is restraint—choosing not to adopt a tool simply because it is available.

Beyond structural concerns, there is the human dimension of care. Professors are entrusted not only with intellectual growth but with nurturing the dignity of students as persons. AI, by its nature, depersonalizes. It does not know the anxieties behind a student's silence, the courage it takes to ask a question, or the pride in a breakthrough moment (Angel, 2024). Faculty must remain attentive to those human realities, resisting the temptation to outsource empathy to chatbots or analytics dashboards. Ethical teaching means remembering that students are not data points but living beings whose development cannot be reduced to metrics.

This responsibility extends to modeling. Students watch how professors engage with AI, and from that they learn not only technical skills but moral attitudes. A professor who treats AI as infallible teaches passivity; one who mocks it dismissively teaches resistance without understanding (Afable, 2025). The more ethical stance is one of critical partnership—using AI while questioning it, appreciating its power while highlighting its limits, integrating it without surrendering to it. In this modeling, professors teach not only about AI but about the habits of mind needed to live in a world shaped by it: skepticism, humility, responsibility, imagination.

One cannot ignore the ethical burden of vulnerability. Professors themselves face uncertainty, with AI encroaching on aspects of their labor once considered uniquely human. To acknowledge that vulnerability openly with students—admitting the challenges, sharing the unease—may itself be an ethical act. It shows students that authority does not mean invulnerability, that grappling with technological change is part of the shared human condition. Such honesty creates trust, and trust is perhaps the most precious ethical currency in education.

Yet these responsibilities can feel overwhelming. The pace of AI development far outstrips the capacity of any one faculty member to keep up. Ethical teaching in such contexts may feel like building a boat while already adrift at sea (Kamali et al, 2024). But perhaps the point is not to master every new tool but to cultivate a stance of vigilance, a readiness to question, an unwillingness to let speed dictate depth. Ethics in AI classrooms is not about perfect policies but about persistent attention to what kind of education we are fostering, and what kind of humans we are helping to shape.

At the heart of it all lies a paradox: AI has the power to make teaching easier, yet it makes the ethical labor of teaching harder. Professors are asked to be both facilitators of technology and guardians of humanity, to embrace innovation while protecting against its excesses. That tension cannot be neatly resolved. But in inhabiting it honestly, professors enact their most profound responsibility: to remind students that education is not simply about what can be done, but about what should be done.

SUSTAINING HUMAN PRESENCE AND PURPOSE IN THE AGE OF INTELLIGENT SYSTEMS

There is something fragile about human presence in a classroom now. Not because professors have suddenly lost their voices, but because the atmosphere itself has changed. A student sits at a desk with a device that can conjure endless explanations, examples, and references. A professor speaks, but the student quietly wonders: could the machine say this more clearly, more succinctly, more comprehensively? The competition is invisible, yet it hums beneath the surface of every lecture, every discussion (Maeda, 2025). In such an environment, sustaining human presence is not a matter of simply “showing up.” It requires conscious effort to reassert why the presence of a professor still matters when intelligent systems hover like omnipresent shadows.

Presence, in its deepest sense, is not reducible to being physically in the room. It is relational, affective, embodied. It is the glance that notices a student’s hesitation, the pause that invites someone to speak, the tone that shifts to convey encouragement or seriousness. Machines can simulate interaction, but they cannot inhabit the complexity of human presence. A chatbot may mimic empathy, yet it does not feel the weight of another person’s silence (Fuchs, 2024). A recommendation algorithm may predict interests, but it does not carry the memory of shared struggle across a semester. Professors sustain presence not by competing with machine precision, but by leaning into the things only humans can do: listen, remember, connect, inspire.

But presence alone is not enough. It must be tethered to purpose. The danger of AI-saturated classrooms is not merely that students might rely too heavily on technology; it is that the very purpose of education can become distorted (Scherpereel, 2024). If efficiency and productivity become the only measures of success, then education risks collapsing into training—a process of equipping individuals with skills, but stripping away the broader mission of cultivating wisdom, judgment, and civic responsibility. Faculty must hold the line here. They are not simply employees delivering content; they are stewards of purpose, reminding both students and institutions that education is about the formation of persons, not just the accumulation of competencies.

Purpose is sustained through narrative. Students remember not only what they learn, but how they were taught, the stories shared, the moments when learning felt alive. Professors who reveal their own intellectual journeys—failures as much as successes—convey purpose far more powerfully than any algorithmic feedback could (Ananny, 2023). Purpose comes alive when a professor says, in effect, “This matters, and here’s why it matters to me, and here’s why it might matter to you.” AI cannot do this. It can generate reasons, but it cannot care about them. It cannot embody conviction.

There is also the question of community. Presence is amplified when it is collective, when a classroom becomes more than a set of isolated individuals receiving information. Professors sustain community by creating spaces where dialogue thrives, where students learn not only from the teacher but from one another. Intelligent systems can facilitate discussion boards or generate prompts, but they do not foster belonging. Belonging emerges through vulnerability and trust, through the shared recognition that learning is not a solitary endeavor but a communal one. To sustain purpose in this age means cultivating communities where students see themselves not as consumers of content but as participants in an ongoing human conversation.

Still, this work is not easy. Professors often find themselves under pressure to adopt technologies rapidly, to keep up with the rhetoric of innovation, to demonstrate "relevance" by integrating AI into every aspect of teaching (Romano et al, 2024). Resistance can feel like obsolescence. Yet sustaining human presence sometimes requires the courage to resist—not to reject technology wholesale, but to refuse its colonization of every space. There are moments when the most radical act a professor can perform is to set aside devices and invite students into a shared silence, a dialogue that unfolds without screens. Presence becomes palpable when the room itself is reclaimed from the constant hum of machines.

Sustaining purpose also means attending to ethics, not as an abstract subject but as a lived practice. AI systems carry with them enormous ethical implications: surveillance, bias, commodification of data. Professors cannot abdicate responsibility for these issues. They must foreground them, helping students see that technological power always comes with costs. By weaving ethical reflection into the fabric of teaching, professors assert purpose: education is not simply about what we can do, but about what we should do. This moral horizon cannot be automated; it requires human conscience.

There is a paradox here. AI threatens to erode presence by offering efficiency, yet it also creates opportunities to deepen presence if used wisely (Victor-Mgbachi, 2024). A professor freed from some mechanical tasks—grading quizzes, summarizing readings—may have more time for meaningful dialogue with students. Intelligent systems can handle routine functions, but only if professors consciously redirect the time saved toward relational and purposeful teaching. If the time is merely absorbed into bureaucratic tasks, then presence is lost twice—outsourced to machines and consumed by administration. Sustaining purpose means intentionally reclaiming time for what only humans can do: mentor, challenge, inspire.

Another aspect often overlooked is imagination. AI operates within the parameters of its training data; it predicts, recombines, and imitates. Professors, however, are tasked with pushing beyond what is given. They can introduce ideas that are not yet in circulation, perspectives that fall outside the algorithm's patterns, visions of futures not yet imagined. Purpose is sustained when education resists becoming purely reactive to what machines provide and instead insists on the creative, the unexpected, the radical. This is not a rejection of AI but an insistence that imagination remains a human responsibility.

The fragility of presence in the age of intelligent systems also calls for humility (Youvan, 2024). Professors cannot pretend to know everything, nor should they. Students see through the façade of omniscience, and AI makes that façade even harder to maintain. Sustaining presence now means modeling humility—acknowledging when the machine provides something valuable, admitting when one does not know, showing how to live with uncertainty. Paradoxically, this humility strengthens presence. Students trust professors not because they never falter, but because they see in them an honest grappling with knowledge.

And yet, sustaining purpose is not only about students. Professors themselves need it. Without a sense of why they teach, without clarity about what makes their role distinct from machines, burnout looms. Purpose protects against despair. It reminds faculty that their work is not reducible to outputs or metrics. Their value lies in their humanity—in the relationships they build, the questions they raise, the integrity they embody. In an age when intelligent systems can imitate almost everything, authenticity itself becomes a form of resistance.

If one imagines the future classroom, it may be filled with screens, dashboards, algorithms tracking progress. Yet if those classrooms are to remain truly educational, there must still be a figure at the center who embodies presence and purpose, who refuses to let machines define what learning means (Swindell et al, 2024). That figure need not stand as an authority dispensing knowledge, but as a companion guiding the journey. Professors sustain purpose not by denying change but by anchoring it, ensuring that even in a world of intelligent systems, education remains human at its core.

In the end, presence and purpose are inseparable. Presence without purpose risks becoming sentimental; purpose without presence risks abstraction. Together, they form the heart of teaching, the reason why professors remain indispensable even in an age of breathtaking technological power. To sustain them requires courage, creativity, and an unwavering belief that education is more than information transfer. It is about shaping lives, cultivating wisdom, and keeping alive the flame of human curiosity. Machines may light the path, but it is the professor who reminds us why the journey matters.

CONCLUSION

The arrival of artificial intelligence in the classroom is not a passing trend but a structural shift, one that will shape the future of higher education for decades to come. As we have seen, the temptation to lean heavily on AI is immense: it can reduce workloads, accelerate feedback, generate materials, and create an illusion of boundless expertise. Yet the danger of overdependence lies precisely in that illusion. When professors allow machines to define the rhythm of learning, the classroom risks becoming efficient but hollow, streamlined but stripped of its soul. What is lost is not just the professor's authority but the relational core of education itself.

The conclusion we reach is neither a rejection of AI nor a blind embrace of its capabilities. Instead, it is a call for discernment, for a deliberate recognition of where human presence cannot be substituted. Professors are more than conveyors of knowledge; they are interpreters of ambiguity, cultivators of character, and companions in the uncertain journey of intellectual growth. They stand as witnesses to the process of becoming, guiding students not only in what to think but in how to live with questions, contradictions, and the responsibility of knowledge. No algorithm, however sophisticated, can embody these roles. Machines can inform, but they cannot inspire. They can calculate, but they cannot care.

To preserve the dignity of education, professors must resist the seduction of outsourcing too much to AI. This does not mean rejecting technological tools; it means wielding them critically, ensuring they serve human purposes rather than replace them. It requires professors to reclaim their role as ethical stewards, reminding students that learning is not measured solely in outputs or grades but in the capacity to think independently, to feel empathy, to act with integrity. AI may optimize efficiency, but it cannot replicate the slow, often messy process of becoming an educated person. That process depends on trust, dialogue, and the encounter between teacher and learner—a space where vulnerability and growth coexist.

The future of higher education will depend on whether professors can inhabit this redefined role with courage and creativity. Those who cling only to old models may feel displaced, while those who surrender entirely to AI may lose their relevance. But those who accept the challenge of reinterpretation—who embrace AI as a tool while refusing to let it dictate the meaning of education—will shape classrooms that are both technologically advanced and profoundly human. Their task is not to compete with machines, but to embody what machines cannot: wisdom, compassion, moral judgment, and the spark of curiosity that keeps learning alive.

In the end, the professor's role in an AI-dominated classroom is less about defending territory and more about embodying presence. It is about insisting that education is not only about knowledge but about humanity. To teach in this age is to stand at the intersection of machine intelligence and human aspiration, to refuse the easy path of overdependence, and to preserve the fragile but essential truth that education, at its best, is a deeply human endeavor. Professors who embrace this calling will not only survive the age of AI but will ensure that higher education remains a space where students encounter not just information, but wisdom.

REFERENCES

Afable, L. (2025). Embracing or Resisting AI: Exploring the Teachers' Perspectives on Student Use of Artificial Intelligence. Available at *SSRN* 5314276. DOI: 10.2139/ssrn.5314276

Akbar, M. S. (2025). Beyond Detection: Designing AI-Resilient Assessments with Automated Feedback Tool to Foster Critical Thinking. arXiv preprint arXiv:2503.23622.

Akgun, S., & Greenhow, C. (2022). Artificial intelligence in education: Addressing ethical challenges in K-12 settings. *AI and Ethics*, *2*(3), 431–440. DOI: 10.1007/s43681-021-00096-7 PMID: 34790956

Ananny, M. (2023). Making mistakes: Constructing algorithmic errors to understand sociotechnical power. *Osiris*, *38*(1), 223–241. DOI: 10.1086/725146

Angel, B. (2024). *The Wolf is at the Door: How to Survive and Thrive in an AI-driven World*. Entrepreneur Press.

Black, S. (2021). What Are Universities Really For? Re-imagining Stewardship. *Education as Change*, *25*(1), 1–7.

Bozkurt, A., Junhong, X., Lambert, S., Pazurek, A., Crompton, H., Koseoglu, S., & Romero-Hall, E. (2023). Speculative futures on ChatGPT and generative artificial intelligence (AI): A collective reflection from the educational landscape. *Asian Journal of Distance Education*, *18*(1), 53–130.

Bulathwela, S., Pérez-Ortiz, M., Holloway, C., Cukurova, M., & Shawe-Taylor, J. (2024). Artificial intelligence alone will not democratise education: On educational inequality, techno-solutionism and inclusive tools. *Sustainability (Basel)*, *16*(2), 781. DOI: 10.3390/su16020781

Çengel, Y. A. (2023). A concise account of information as meaning ascribed to symbols and its association with conscious mind. *Entropy (Basel, Switzerland)*, *25*(1), 177. DOI: 10.3390/e25010177 PMID: 36673318

. Eaton, S. E. (2021). Plagiarism in higher education.

Ferrario, A., Facchini, A., & Termine, A. (2024). Experts or authorities? The strange case of the presumed epistemic superiority of artificial intelligence systems. *Minds and Machines*, *34*(3), 30. DOI: 10.1007/s11023-024-09681-1

Fuchs, T. (2024). Understanding Sophia? On human interaction with artificial agents. *Phenomenology and the Cognitive Sciences*, *23*(1), 21–42. DOI: 10.1007/s11097-022-09848-0

Gadaza, A., Manera, A., Santos, S., Alih, C., & Caban, R. (2025). Reviving the past, teaching the future: The role of Philippine cultural heritage in curriculum development of teacher education programs focus. International Journal on Culture. *History of Religions*, *7*(SI2), 80–97.

Gao, R. (2025). The Erosion and Reconstruction of Teachers' Authority in the Context of Artificial Intelligence. *Journal of Theory and Practice in Education and Innovation*, *2*(2), 26–33.

George, A. S. (2023). Preparing students for an AI-driven world: Rethinking curriculum and pedagogy in the age of artificial intelligence. *Partners Universal Innovative Research Publication*, *1*(2), 112–136.

George, A. S., George, A. H., Baskar, T., & Pandey, D. (2023). The allure of artificial intimacy: Examining the appeal and ethics of using generative AI for simulated relationships. *Partners Universal International Innovation Journal*, *1*(6), 132–147.

Ghosh, K., & Ghosh, D. (2025). *Who am AI?* Deconstructing Identity in the Age of Advanced Artificial Intelligence.

Großmann, L., Koberstein-Schwarz, M., Scholl, D., Krüger, D., & Meisert, A. (2025). Establishing common ground in empirical research on science teachers' lesson planning competence: A scoping review. *Studies in Science Education*, *61*(2), 329–379. DOI: 10.1080/03057267.2024.2415246

Hashem, R., Ali, N., El Zein, F., Fidalgo, P., & Khurma, O. A. (2024). AI to the rescue: Exploring the potential of ChatGPT as a teacher ally for workload relief and burnout prevention. *Research and Practice in Technology Enhanced Learning*, •••, 19.

Hiatt, M. S., Lowman, G. H., Maloni, M., Swaim, J., & Veliyath, R. (2023). Ability, benevolence, and integrity: The strong link between student trust in their professors and satisfaction. *International Journal of Management Education*, *21*(2), 100768. DOI: 10.1016/j.ijme.2023.100768

Kamali, J., Alpat, M. F., & Bozkurt, A. (2024). AI ethics as a complex and multifaceted challenge: Decoding educators' AI ethics alignment through the lens of activity theory. *International Journal of Educational Technology in Higher Education*, *21*(1), 62. DOI: 10.1186/s41239-024-00496-9

Kershen, J. L., & Johnson, B. (2025). Becoming a teacher of writing in an AI-assisted world: Considering personal epistemologies, writing theories, and the use of AI platform technologies. *Contemporary Issues in Technology & Teacher Education, 25*(1), 32–58.

Kingsley, A. (2025). *The Awkward Questions in Education: The Elephants in the Room from AI to Teacher Retention*. Taylor & Francis. DOI: 10.4324/9781003537168

Kolhatin, A. O. (2025). From automation to augmentation: a human-centered framework for generative AI in adaptive educational content creation. In CEUR Workshop Proceedings (pp. 143-195).

Maeda, J. (2025). *How to Speak Machine, with a new preface by the author: A Gentle Introduction to Artificial Intelligence*. MIT Press.

McGlone, C., McHugh, M. L., & Marin, K. (2025). FROM STAGE TO CLASSROOM: EMBRACING PRESENCE THROUGH SAFETY, CONNECTION, ACCEPTANCE, AND IMPROVISATION IN TEACHING. In INTED2025 Proceedings (pp. 2668-2672). IATED.

Norell, E. A. (2024). *The present professor: Authenticity and transformational teaching* (Vol. 3). University of Oklahoma Press.

Nygård, T., Hirvonen, N., Räisänen, S., & Korkeamäki, R. L. (2021). Ask your mother! Teachers' informational authority roles in information-seeking and evaluation tasks in health education lessons. *Scandinavian Journal of Educational Research, 65*(6), 972–985. DOI: 10.1080/00313831.2020.1788145

Preston, J. (2021). *Artificial intelligence in the capitalist university: Academic labour, commodification, and value*. Taylor & Francis. DOI: 10.4324/9781003081654

Qutieshat, A. (2025). *Artificial Intelligence in Higher Education: A Contemporary Examination of Illich's Theories*. Springer Nature. DOI: 10.1007/978-981-97-9989-3

Romano, L. F., Khumalo, Z. T., & Benitez, S. (2024). FACULTY PERSPECTIVES ON ARTIFICIAL INTELLIGENCE IN HIGHER EDUCATION: A QUALITATIVE STUDY AT A REGIONAL UNIVERSITY. *European Journal of Emerging Social Science and Humanities, 1*(01), 66–82.

Sætra, E. (2022). An empirical moral philosophy perspective on classroom discussions of controversial issues. *Educational Theory, 72*(5), 641–662. DOI: 10.1111/edth.12548

Saltman, K. J. (2022). *The alienation of fact: Digital educational privatization, AI, and the false promise of bodies and numbers.* MIT Press. DOI: 10.7551/mit-press/14387.001.0001

Scherpereel, C. M. (2024, March). The AI Paradox: Unpacking the Potential and Perils in Business Education. In Developments in Business Simulation and Experiential Learning: Proceedings of the Annual ABSEL conference (Vol. 51).

. Selwyn, N. (2024). On the limits of artificial intelligence (AI) in education. Nordisk tidsskrift for pedagogikk og kritikk, 10(1), 3-14.

Stewart, C. N.Jr. (2023). *Research ethics for scientists: A companion for students.* John Wiley & Sons.

Swart, W., & MacLeod, K. (2021). Evaluating learning space designs for flipped and collaborative learning: A transactional distance approach. *Education Sciences, 11*(6), 292. DOI: 10.3390/educsci11060292

Swindell, A., Greeley, L., Farag, A., & Verdone, B. (2024). Against Artificial Education: Towards an Ethical Framework for Generative Artificial Intelligence (AI) Use in Education. *Online Learning : The Official Journal of the Online Learning Consortium, 28*(2), n2. DOI: 10.24059/olj.v28i2.4438

Van der Linden, S. (2023). *Foolproof: Why misinformation infects our minds and how to build immunity.* WW Norton & Company.

Vetrivel, S. C., Arun, V. P., Ambikapathi, R., & Saravanan, T. P. (2025). Automated Grading Systems: Enhancing Efficiency and Consistency in Student Assessments. In Adopting Artificial Intelligence Tools in Higher Education (pp. 41-61). CRC Press.

Victor-Mgbachi, T. O. Y. I. N. (2024). Leveraging Artificial Intelligence (AI) Effectively: Managing Risks and Boosting Productivity. *Iconic Research and Engineering Journals, 7*(7), 54–69.

Waghid, Z. (2023). Teacher educators' pedagogical practices in global citizenship education using the soft vs critical GCE framework. *Cogent Education, 10*(2), 2251757. DOI: 10.1080/2331186X.2023.2251757

Watanabe, A. (2024). Have Courage to Use your Own Mind, with or without AI: The Relevance of Kant's Enlightenment to Higher Education in the Age of Artificial Intelligence. *Electronic Journal of e-Learning, 22*(2), 46–58. DOI: 10.34190/ejel.21.5.3229

Watermeyer, R., Phipps, L., Lanclos, D., & Knight, C. (2024). Generative AI and the automating of academia. *Postdigital Science and Education*, *6*(2), 446–466. DOI: 10.1007/s42438-023-00440-6

. Youvan, D. (2024). Incorporating Humility into AI: Designing Systems with Awareness of Limitations and Ethical Caution.

Youvan, D. C. (2025). *The Perfected Control System: How Universities*. AI, and Financial Leverage Shape the Coming Collapse and Rebirth of Knowledge.

Zaibout, N., & Madrane, M. (2024). Optimizing Academic Assessment: The Impact of AI on Student Integrity, Creativity, and Achievement. *International Journal of Engineering Trends and Technology*, *72*(11), 357–370. DOI: 10.14445/22315381/IJETT-V72I11P134

Chapter 12
Academic Integrity in the Age of Artificial Intelligence

Fahad A. Salendab
http://orcid.org/0000-0003-4459-443X
Sultan Kudarat State University, Philippines

Rashmia S. Baraguir
http://orcid.org/0009-0000-4804-3008
Sultan Kudarat State University, Philippines

Celena J. Cabato
Villanueva Senior High School, Philippines

Joycelle C. Lumogdang
Sultan Kudarat State University, Philippines

ABSTRACT

The rapid rise of generative artificial intelligence (GenAI) has transformed higher education, reshaping how students learn, how faculty assess, and how institutions uphold academic integrity. This chapter examines the complex interplay between GenAI adoption, evolving forms of academic misconduct, and the limitations of traditional integrity frameworks. While GenAI enhances creativity, feedback, accessibility, and instructional efficiency, it also enables new violations such as invisible authorship, AI-generated plagiarism, and overreliance that erodes cognitive autonomy. The chapter synthesizes empirical research, ethical theories, and institutional case studies to analyze misconceptions among students and educators, gaps in policy governance, and emerging AI-aware assessment models. It argues

DOI: 10.4018/979-8-3373-7097-2.ch012

that punitive, detection-driven approaches are insufficient in an AI-rich environment. Instead, fostering ethical literacy, redesigning assessments, implementing transparent AI-use policies, and developing responsible human–AI collaboration are essential.

INTRODUCTION

The field of higher education has never witnessed such unprecedented changes as it currently faces due to the advent of generative artificial intelligence tools like ChatGPT, Claude, Gemini, and other large language models. These tools, which earlier had been seen as mere technological advancements, have now been widely adopted in the academic process. The use of AI tools in academic work has also given rise to various concerns related to authorship, originality, cognitive development, and responsibility, with the increasing power and availability of these tools (Peláez-Sánchez et al., 2024; Abbas et al., 2024)

The first issue of concern in the academic world related to AI tools has been overdependence on AI tools. Even though AI tools have been found to be useful in providing feedback, encouraging creativity, enhancing accessibility, and facilitating various academic processes, it has also been seen that AI tools have created confusion related to academic dishonesty and academic assistance. The students of any academic institution can now write essays, paraphrase content, solve complex problems, and even compile sources with minimal effort. However, it has also been seen that students do not have a comprehensive understanding of what they are submitting. This has created challenges related to academic dishonesty and AI tools. This situation has also raised concerns related to academic integrity and what academic institutions should do in this regard (Ortiz-Bonnin & Blahopoulou, 2025; Shaw, 2025; An et al., 2025).

This chapter aims to explore the implications of GenAI on the scholarly practices, cognitive development, and ethical decision-making of students. The integrity models based on plagiarism, cheating, and fabrication do not address the new forms of academic integrity, such as invisible authorship, AI-assisted paraphrasing, and cognitive independence. This calls for changes in curriculum development, faculty development, and policy formulation to ensure the positive contribution of AI to the cognitive development of students rather than hindering it. However, the educational scenario is complicated by the fact that most teachers and students have misconceptions about the accuracy and reliability of AI and its ethical boundaries, as stated in the literature by Kim et al. (2025), Bittle & El-Gayar (2025), and Almisad & Aleidan (2025).

This chapter aims to explore the complex and controversial integrity issue by discussing the development of academic integrity, the emergence of AI-based academic integrity, and the complex ethical theories. This chapter aims to contribute to the exploration of the impact of the excessive use of AI on academic integrity, the role of misconceptions in the development of academic integrity, and the development of assessment, governance policy, and the positive use of AI.

The purpose of this chapter is to offer a holistic perspective on academic integrity within the context of a generative artificial intelligence environment by synthesizing recent research and practices. This chapter offers informed recommendations on how academic integrity might be promoted within an environment of artificial intelligence, as well as how academic systems might be developed, relevant to stakeholders within higher education, with a forward-thinking perspective. This chapter ultimately asserts that academic integrity within an environment of artificial intelligence is not simply addressed through detection tools or punitive measures but, rather, through pedagogical innovation, through an emphasis on ethical literacy, through transparent governance, and through the creation of learning environments wherein students remain critically engaged and responsible for their own intellectual development.

CONCEPTUAL FOUNDATIONS: ACADEMIC INTEGRITY IN THE DIGITAL ERA

Historical Evolution of Academic Integrity Frameworks.

Significantly, there has been considerable evolution in the framework of academic integrity during the last few decades. It has shifted from a punitive approach to a more holistic approach. Initially, the primary aim of academic integrity was to impose a punitive approach and develop guidelines to ensure compliance. However, recent studies suggest that the contemporary approach not only focuses on punitive measures but also on learning and the development of student agency.

This has been supported by Brickhill et al. (2025), who conducted a study to identify the impact of the process of academic integrity breach on students. It was revealed that the majority of the respondents who underwent the process of academic integrity breach and those who knew someone who underwent the process stated that it was beneficial for their understanding of academic integrity in general and empowered them to deal with the issue independently. We wanted a voice in processes related to maintaining academic integrity. It was also revealed that a holistic approach to academic integrity perceived it as a desirable and beneficial aspect of a student's academic identity and emphasized student agency related to academic performance. This has also been supported by a broader study by Sbaffi and Zhao (2022), who attempted to assess the impact of pedagogical approaches to academic integrity in higher education. It was revealed that pedagogical programs increased the accessibility of new resources and made them more useful and comprehensible. It was also revealed that the trust and confidence of the students related to academic integrity increased manifold. It was also revealed that the new module was perceived to be more engaging and educational.

The emergence of digital and AI-related misconduct is also seen to impact the development of integrity frameworks. Birks and Clare (2023) show that many of the traditional preventative integrity frameworks are still applicable when adapted to technological contexts, such as opportunity reduction, education, and environment design. However, academic integrity is now impacted by the emergence of AI-related academic dishonesty. This indicates that although integrity frameworks are adapting to new forms of misconduct, the integrity principles remain relevant and applicable.

Honor systems have been instrumental in the development of integrity principles at the cultural level. Cheung and Vaish (2025) show that the majority of colleges and universities have implemented honor systems that mandate students to abide by honor codes. Moreover, they show that most of these honor systems impose sanctions for academic dishonesty and also for other improper social conduct, such as harassment and discrimination. Furthermore, the emphasis of honor codes is on imposing sanctions for honor code violations and overemphasizes extrinsic motivation for integrity and honor codes while ignoring the need to develop individual character and internal motivation for integrity and honor codes. An alternative viewpoint is provided by Tatum (2022) in a previous review of integrity and honor codes over the past three decades to show the effectiveness of honor codes in developing and maintaining a culture of academic integrity and honesty within the higher education sector. Honor codes function by educating students on academic integrity and imposing accountability through social norms, expectations, attitudes, reminders, and regulations on academic misconduct.

In their emphasis on ethical sensitivity, the most recent scholarly contributions extend the historical trajectory. According to Okolo et al. (2025), the students showed their strong endorsement of the ethical sensitivity constructs of reading and expressing emotions, taking others' perspectives, promoting care through social connectedness, managing interpersonal and group differences, and generating options and interpretations. Moreover, the students showed their strong disapproval of academic misconduct, such as citation misconduct and tendencies to cheat. This indicates the need to develop strategies to promote integrity and ethical awareness within higher education settings.

Traditional Misconduct vs. Emerging AI-Enabled Violations

Traditionally, academic misconduct such as plagiarism, fabrication, falsification, and contract cheating has been addressed through various institutional policies and practices of detection and prevention. Recent studies have revealed that the rise of generative artificial intelligence and digital technologies is transforming the extent and nature of academic misconduct. For instance, Contract cheating, or the practice of hiring a third party to complete a student's academic work, is reportedly increasing and is a threat to academic integrity and quality (Newton, 2018). It also has an economic dimension as students pay for these services to a third party, also called an "Essay Mill."

The other notable phenomenon is the rise of academic misconduct through artificial intelligence. Birks and Clare (2023) point to the rise of artificial intelligence in academic misconduct through the development of generative artificial intelligence tools for automated problem-solving, paraphrasing, and citing references to academic material. Although artificial intelligence is credited for increasing efficiency and interest in academic work, Bittle and El-Gayar (2025) point to serious concerns regarding academic dishonesty through the use of generative artificial intelligence in academic work. The authors point to limitations such as the restricted diversity of databases and the possible impact of such limitations on the scope of thought and perspectives, and then conduct a critical analysis of possible biases in the studies used for the paper. To address the effects of artificial intelligence on academic integrity and misconduct, the following implications are critical: increasing digital literacy and developing effective means of detecting artificial intelligence in academic work. Leaton Gray et al. (2025) also point to the need for a fundamental pedagogical realignment to reassert the inherent values of higher education and to counter the instrumental rationalities of surveillance-based governance.

Ethical Theories Relevant to AI Integrity

1. Deontological Framework: The first issue that arises under a deontological approach is the duty owed to the institution and others. Therefore, it would violate duties of honesty, justice, and respect for intellectual labor to use AI technology in the classroom without giving proper attribution, passing off the work of another as one's own, or evading traditional academic conventions. In the age of Gen AI technology, recent studies highlight the imperative of specifying one's duties. To illustrate, Bittle and El-Gayar (2025) assert that while Gen AI technology has the potential to increase efficiency and interest in the classroom, there are significant concerns about academic dishonesty. In addition, Alsharefeen & Al Sayari (2025) conducted a study of faculty perceptions at an internationally focused academic institution regarding integrity policies related to traditional plagiarism and Gen AI plagiarism. Their results indicate that educators would prefer teaching strategies over punitive policies but are hindered by structural barriers, workload issues, insufficient support from the academic institution,

difficulties of detection, and culturally permissive attitudes toward enforcing policies. In a deontological framework, one can see how educators are obligated to clearly delineate duties of AI use while at the same time holding students responsible for revealing, attributing, and producing original work even when AI tools are accessible.

2. Virtue Ethics: Developing Character in the Age of AI: The core of virtue ethics is the shift of focus from what one must avoid to what one must become. In the age of AI, the proper use of AI technologies goes beyond compliance to require reflection, responsibility, and moral conduct. Lund et al. (2026) found that the strongest predictors of perceived misconduct and use of AI in writing are students' moral beliefs rather than institutional policy. This suggests that information related to policy has no measurable impact. However, students who believe that AI-assisted writing represents cheating are less likely to use it and judge it as immoral. In other words, students' moral judgment of AI-assisted writing as cheating reduces the likelihood of using it. Chan's (2025) research on "AI-Giarism," a new form of academic dishonesty involving AI and plagiarism, also underlines the importance of moral reasoning rather than policy compliance. In other words, from the perspective of virtue ethics, the goal is to produce moral agents who reflect upon the moral appropriateness of AI use in academic settings, upon the extent to which AI use may impede academic progress, and upon the value of AI use in contributing to knowledge. This represents the internal dimension of honesty rules and deontological principles.
3. Academic Honesty Codes: Institutional Ethics in Practice. Academic honesty codes are the formal representations of deontological principles and virtue ethics' notion of character within the academic community. They carry out two functions: (a) specifying clear rules such as declaring the use of AI tools, submitting work solely of one's own, and so forth; (b) specifying community values such as trust, responsibility, and fairness to promote virtuous action. In a recent work, Avello & Aranguren Zurita (2025) analyze the intersections of academic integrity and artificial intelligence in higher education, where the former has registered a rapid expansion with a growth rate of 71.97% per year, particularly in journals related to the areas of education, academic integrity, and technology. The trajectory of AI studies has shifted from academic dishonesty facilitated by AI tools to the exploration of AI integration in higher education. In another work, Lund et al. (2026) examine the awareness and perceptions of academic misconduct by university students, particularly in relation to AI tool use. Their results show that students are highly aware of the university's integrity policies and are highly concerned about AI use in writing papers, but perceptions of the level of misconduct vary considerably. In particular, using

AI to write entire papers is considered major misconduct, while using AI for tasks of a smaller scope is considered less severe.

Table 1. Comparative Analysis of Ethical Theories and Institutional Responses to AI Use in Education

Ethical Theory/ Framework	Core Focus/ Definition	Key Ideas/Principles	Practical Examples in AI Use	Policy Implications for HEIs
Deontological Framework	Focuses on duties, rules, and obligations; what is morally required regardless of consequences.	• Duty to be honest • Follow academic procedures • Respect intellectual labor • Disclose AI use	• Citing AI tools used in writing • Avoiding full AI-generated output submitted as original work • Following institutional disclosure rules	• Establish explicit AI guidelines and disclosure formats • Require AI-use declarations in all assignments • Implement faculty training on AI-integrity protocols
Virtue Ethics	Focuses on moral character and the cultivation of virtues such as honesty, responsibility, and wisdom.	• Internal moral compass • Critical reflection • Responsible judgment • Ethical self-regulation	• Students deciding not to let AI replace original thought • Reflecting on whether AI use supports learning • Choosing transparency even when detection is unlikely	• Integrate AI ethics modules in courses • Promote character-based education focused on honesty and responsibility • Develop ethics-focused orientation programs
Academic Honesty Codes	Institutional rules that regulate academic integrity blend duties (deontology) and community values (virtue ethics).	• Explicit AI-related policies • Emphasis on trust and fairness • Alignment with institutional values • Enforcement mechanisms	• Requiring an integrity pledge, including AI clauses • Differentiating between acceptable and unacceptable AI use • Using AI-detection tools responsibly	• Update integrity codes to include AI-specific misconduct definitions • Provide clear levels of acceptable AI support • Develop reporting and guidance mechanisms for AI misuse

The Emergence of Generative AI in Academia

Two ongoing trends form the basis of the expansion of GenAI in the context of higher education. Firstly, the advancement of the models has led to the generation of more refined, human-like, and contextually relevant content. For instance, Qian (2025) argues that although some of the pre-ChatGPT themes have continued to persist, new trajectories of development have begun to crystallize, especially in the context of enhancing creativity, critical thinking, autonomous learning, and prompt literacy. This is an indication of the increasing interest in the integration of generative AI in the context of higher education. In the same vein, the author also points out the paradox of generative AI in the context of higher education. On the one hand, generative AI has been shown to increase productivity. However, there is also the concern of over-reliance, which might lead to the outsourcing of cognitive and metacognitive abilities.

Secondly, the expansion of the scope of the integration of GenAI in the context of higher education is also attributed to the reduction of the barriers to the adoption of the technologies. In the first place, the availability of the technologies is not a concern in the contemporary context. This is due to the availability of cloud-based AI platforms and the free or low-cost versions of the technologies. While some authors have sought to address the issue of the detection of AI-generated content, Ogunleye et al. (2024) argue that it is also essential to understand the integration of GenAI in the context of the development of the curriculum for assessment, teaching, and learning. Nikolopoulou (2025) argues that the integration of GAI in the context of higher education can lead to the development of more sustainable practices. This is through the development of more refined approaches to teaching and learning, the optimization of resources such as digital resources and the development of more sustainable approaches to the management of resources such as energy, the development of more inclusive and accessible approaches to education, and the development of more sustainable approaches to the promotion of environmental awareness and sustainability.

Generative AI Capabilities Relevant to Learning and Assessment

The interface of GenAI and core academic problems is increasingly changing learning and assessment strategies. GenAI provides learning scaffolding to students by helping them develop ideas for essays, creating outlines, refining writing content, and even suggesting citations, although the last feature is not always accurate. GenAI also acts as a virtual learning assistant by breaking down complex concepts into simpler forms. GenAI also facilitates a more efficient and flexible approach to teaching by helping teachers automate tasks such as creating lecture content, creating assessments, and providing feedback (Xia et al., 2024).

GenAI has also created a new interface for assessment strategies. There are reports of academics experimenting with AI-informed assessments where students are allowed or encouraged to use GenAI tools for their work, while also being expected to document their process or provide a reflection on the use of GenAI tools or even assess the results of AI-generated work. There is also the use of the Artificial Intelligence Assessment Scale (AIAS), which provides a framework for integrating GenAI tools into assessment strategies. Furze et al. (2024) indicate that the AIAS has the potential to influence pedagogical strategies since it has been effective in allowing for the integration of GenAI tools into assessment strategies while also promoting academic integrity by providing a framework for the effective use of GenAI tools while providing a framework for promoting the potential of GenAI tools for providing learning opportunities. Urzúa et al. (2025) indicate that the use of generative chat has a positive effect on the writing of university students. GenAI tools are effective in improving the structure of texts, the use of grammatical rules, the use of correct concepts, and the use of correct vocabulary.

In addition to this, Lee & Moore (2024) have argued that GenAI offers the possibility of feedback across various settings and goals through a wide range of educational objectives. Through the automation of repetitive feedback and grading operations, GenAI systems have the potential to assist teachers in reducing their workload and thus enable them to concentrate on more complex aspects of instructional design. In addition to this, GenAI systems also promote aspects of accessibility, communication, and emotional and cognitive support through the development of supportive and low-stress learning environments. However, it must also be recognized that the quality of AI-generated feedback may vary. This necessitates the development of students' AI literacy to ensure the effective utilization of AI systems. Jin et al. (2025) found that students' performance in GenAI systems was significantly predicted by the Generative AI Literacy Assessment Test (GLAT), which surpassed other self-reported predictors such as perceived ChatGPT proficiency.

In order to integrate GenAI in a pedagogically relevant manner, teachers are recommended to reorganize assessments in line with new frameworks. In order to ensure academic integrity while promoting creativity and critical thinking, it has also been recommended to use a combination of scaffolded assignments and reflective prompts, focusing more on the process rather than the product (Khlaif et al., 2025). Furthermore, it has also been identified that teachers use a methodical approach while developing tasks and come up with creative means of integrating GenAI in assessments. The research also highlights that the development of policies regarding the integration of GenAI in education is a significant aspect that drives the integration of GenAI in assessments (Khlaif et al., 2024). Even though GenAI has the potential to make assessments more personalized for students, it also has the potential to impact the fairness of the assessment results since biases in AI models are not closely monitored. Certain students may be at a disadvantage if biases are not closely monitored (Arslan et al., 2024).

Furthermore, it has also been argued by Nguyen and Hayward (2025) that GenAI has the potential to act both as a tool for teachers and a tool for students. MLLMs have also been used in scientific education to evaluate assessments according to NGSS standards while identifying any errors and proposing possible solutions. By using these tools, teachers have the potential to improve the quality of assessment practices. It has also been argued that effective governance and regulation are essential for the integration of GenAI in education. An et al. (2025) have also identified a lack of effective academic integrity policies while highlighting that many higher education institutions are developing standards for the integration of AI in assessment practices. CAIAF and ethical guidelines also highlight the importance of considering AI's role while promoting metacognition and promoting the use of AI responsibly (Kılınç, 2024).

Table 2. Generative AI Capabilities in Learning and Assessment: Applications, Risks, and Evidence

GenAI Capability / Application	Description / Use in Learning & Assessment	Potential Risks / Challenges	Practical Example / Use Case	Discipline / Context
On-demand scaffolding for students	Helps brainstorm essay ideas, draft outlines, refine prose, and explain complex concepts.	Overreliance, superficial understanding, and AI inaccuracies	Student drafts essay outline with AI suggestions and revises critically	Humanities, Social Sciences
Streamlined faculty tasks	Assists in creating lectures, assessments, and feedback efficiently.	Faculty may over-rely on AI; quality of AI-generated materials may vary	Faculty uses AI to generate multiple-choice questions and review drafts	All disciplines
AI-aware assessments	Integrates AI in student work with reflection and documentation; reduces misconduct	Students may misuse AI if reflection is superficial	Students submit AI-assisted essays with a reflection section explaining AI usage	Higher Education, Multi-disciplinary
Multimodal submissions	Combines AI-generated text with visuals, audio, and student ideas	Quality control, cognitive overload for students	Students create a video presentation with an AI script and visuals	Humanities, STEM, Arts
Automated and personalized feedback	Provides adaptive, timely feedback supporting self-regulated learning	Feedback may be shallow or biased; reduces peer/faculty interaction	AI gives real-time suggestions on essay structure or logic flow	Writing, STEM problem-solving

continued on following page

Table 2. Continued

GenAI Capability / Application	Description / Use in Learning & Assessment	Potential Risks / Challenges	Practical Example / Use Case	Discipline / Context
AI literacy development	Measures and promotes students' reflective and informed AI use	Neglecting AI literacy can lead to misuse	Students take GLAT to assess their understanding of AI tools	All disciplines
Redesign of assessment tasks	Scaffolded assignments, reflective prompts, and process-focused tasks to integrate AI pedagogically	Requires significant faculty time and training; risk of inequity if poorly implemented	Assignment includes an AI-generated draft with guided reflection prompts	Higher Education
Faculty adoption and training	Adoption depends on perceived usefulness, ease of integration, and institutional support	Resistance to change; lack of institutional resources	Faculty attend workshops on AI-aware assessment design	Higher Education
Equity and fairness monitoring	Ensures AI personalization does not introduce bias or disadvantage student groups	Potential for systemic bias if the model is not monitored	Faculty review AI feedback reports for fairness across student demographics	All disciplines
Institutional policy and governance	Requires explicit guidelines on AI use, academic integrity, and ethical reflection	Lack of policy can lead to misuse; uneven enforcement	University publishes AI use policy, including AI-assisted assessment protocols	Higher Education
Ethical frameworks and reflective practices	Frameworks like CAIAF embed metacognition and ethical AI use	Ethical guidelines may not be uniformly applied; training is required	Students complete AI-assisted tasks while following CAIAF reflective prompts	Multi-disciplinary

OVERDEPENDENCE ON AI AND ITS IMPACT ON ACADEMIC INTEGRITY

New Forms of Academic Misconduct

The developing phenomenon of academic dishonesty related to generative AI also challenges the long-held concept of authorship and the legitimacy of academic assessment. The emerging phenomenon of AI-related plagiarism and invisible authorship—where students submit AI-generated content as their own—constitutes two of the key concerns. Bittle & El-Gayar (2025) assert that substantial academic dishonesty-related issues accompany GenAI, which also has the potential to improve academic efficiency and student engagement. The authors critically examined the scope of bias in the research included in the paper and found a database diversity problem that could affect the scope of perspectives. Shaw (2025) also posits that academic dishonesty through AI-generated content might be more tempting compared to plagiarism due to its relative ease of execution and difficulties in detection, as well as its relatively lower moral implications. Although the average student might not have the inclination towards plagiarism, the temptation of AI-generated academic dishonesty has grave implications for the academic integrity of a much larger student population, which will ultimately affect even the conscientious students whose academic programs will suffer in quality as a deterrent against unethical AI use. The emergence of AI-generated paraphrasing as a means of evading detection also poses a grave threat. Perkins et al. (2024) assert that students can easily bypass existing AI-detection tools through AI-generated paraphrasing of content. Toker & Akgün (2024) also found that AI-generated plagiarism reduces with increasing task difficulty.

As Yusuf et al. (2024) explain, there is a growing reliance on AI for writing, coding, analysis, and problem-solving in many research fields; indeed, it often replaces cognitive activities that research aims to investigate. According to a global survey, students are increasingly using AI for generating ideas, essay organization, and even paraphrasing original work; however, such over-reliance on AI has implications for critical thought and analysis. Such over-reliance also raises concerns about the efficacy of value judgments. Campo et al. (2025) also discovered a link between the use of ChatGPT and plagiarism; however, it was also discovered that there was no causal effect of ChatGPT use on plagiarism. Furthermore, it was discovered that the link between ChatGPT use and plagiarism was moderated by age and academic year.

The above findings are also supported by faculty members' perceptions of AI use in academia. Alsharefeen & Al Sayari (2025) discovered significant differences between traditional and Gen AI approaches; however, both were considered moderately effective. Faculty members' perceptions of AI use are also supported by the fact that they have a preference for educational rather than penal responses despite constraints such as workload limitations, lack of institutional support, difficulty of detection, lenient cultures, and institutional limitations. Finally, research has shown that students are hiding their use of AI for misconduct. Nguyen & Goto (2024) discovered the hidden nature of AI-facilitated misconduct by demonstrating that students tend to deny AI-based academic cheating behaviors when directly asked. Estimates of cheaters are almost three times higher than those obtained by direct questioning.

Misconceptions Among Students and Educators

The increasing integration of generative AI within the academic environment has led to the development of various misunderstandings among students and educators alike, which have direct implications for the adoption and moral integrity of such technologies. The belief that AI is merely a tool, similar to other tools such as a calculator or grammar checker, is one of the most dominant narratives. However, empirical studies have revealed that such a belief frequently fails to address the pertinent ethical issues at hand. Although the use of ChatGPT and other similar generative AI tools is recognized for increasing productivity and allowing for interactive and personalized learning experiences, Karkoulian et al. (2024) argue that such tools also raise serious issues regarding academic integrity. Petricini et al. (2025) also revealed various advantages and disadvantages of the integration of generative AI (GenAI) within the higher education environment, specifically regarding academic integrity. The authors also revealed that survey results revealed a predominant reliance on punitive and rule-based approaches and highlighted the gap between educators and students. Some educators also demonstrate a dismissive approach due to administrative constraints, while others demonstrate a pedagogical and communicative approach to build trust and collaboration between the student and the educator.

A similar issue is the overconfidence of such tools and their accuracy, specifically among students who believe such tools to be legitimate and academically accurate. Wang et al. (2025) revealed that the moderating role of university students' use of GenAI for language acquisition is greatly influenced by their trust in such tools, which is mediated by resistance and reliance. Acosta-Enriquez et al. (2024) also revealed a robust relationship between various variables and the use of ChatGPT as a tool for academic integrity. The behavioral intention to use ChatGPT responsibly is influenced by perceived ease of use, intention to use frequently, acceptance, and intention to verify information. Jo (2024) also revealed that students believe AI is merely a shortcut for their learning and not a cognitive risk for their academic integrity.

The misperception of institutional policies on the use of AI is a contributing factor to these problems. The empirical findings of Alsharefeen & Al Sayari (2025) show that instructors often face difficulties in understanding or implementing restrictions on AI use, largely because of a lack of clear institutional policies and confusion over whether AI use amounts to innovation, abuse, or misconduct. Johnston et al. (2024) also show that a majority of students are in favor of a university policy outlining appropriate conditions for the use of AI technologies. These findings suggest that students need clear policies on the use of Generative AI; instead of forbidding these technologies in university settings, policies need to ensure that they are accessible to all students.

NAVIGATING AI TOOL USAGE WITHIN ACADEMIC INTEGRITY PRINCIPLES

Responsible AI Use in Academic Work

This view of AI as a tool has also created a number of ethical concerns, particularly with regards to AI's involvement in core academic functions. Although GenAI has been found to increase learning accessibility, instructional automation, and individualization of feedback, there are also ethical concerns associated with its use. In a case study by Alnsour et al. (2025), it was found that fewer than one-third of the educators surveyed were aware of the latest ethical standards for AI use in education. Students' use of AI has also created a number of ethical concerns, particularly with regards to plagiarism and cheating. Although simple tasks, complete reliance on AI for research, and cheating during exams are considered ethical concerns associated with AI use by students, making edits and refinements of language are considered ethical uses of AI by students.

Transparency is also considered a key aspect of ethical AI use. In evaluating ethical regulations associated with AI use, it was found that AI contributions are not being acknowledged properly. In a cross-sectional survey of academic staff from a number of universities, it was found that AI contributions are considered "invisible authorship," a form of plagiarism (García-López & Trujillo-Liñán, 2025). In a study by Bjelobaba et al. (2024), a number of ethical concerns associated with AI use from a research perspective were also identified. These concerns include AI's use of opacity, bias, censorship, fabrication (such as hallucinations and data falsification), copyright violations, and violation of privacy. These studies highlight the need to use GenAI with caution and deliberation.

It is vital to make a distinction between idea generation and content authorship. If the AI is not considered a primary author of the content of the manuscript, it has the potential to be a valuable mental partner for students who might need assistance with the development of research strategies or the exploration of alternative ways of solving a problem. Such a notion is in line with the scholarly imperative to develop learning strategies that consider AI as a partner rather than a substitute. However, there are concerns that over-reliance by the student on AI might compromise not only the student's agency but also the validity of the assessment (García-López & Trujillo-Liñán, 2025).

Assessment and Curriculum Redesign

In this regard, higher education is reviewing its practices and the significance of learning outcomes in an AI-driven society, considering the emergence of generative

AI. In this regard, there is a rise in the use of AI to circumvent the effectiveness of assessment methods and their outcomes in determining the extent of knowledge and understanding of students. Khlaif et al. (2025) argue that the need for a systematic change to develop effective and AI-driven assessment methods is imperative, as the development of such methods must be informed by the presence of AI and not its detection.

Empirical studies conducted in teacher education settings also support the notion of these developments in the context of the application of AI-driven assessments. For instance, the development of effective and AI-resistant assessments, such as the Process-Product Assessment Model, is critical in evaluating the product and the collaborative process between students and AI tools, as highlighted by Awadallah Alkouk & Khlaif (2024). This also indicates the need to develop critical thinking skills to ensure that the application of AI is not used to circumvent the learning process.

The rise of the emphasis on authentic forms of assessment, such as portfolios, oral defenses, reflective commentary, and real-world problem-solving tasks, is one possible development. Peters & Angelov (2025) propose the Academic Integrity and Creativity in the Age of Artificial Intelligence (AICAI) model, which suggests the use of genuine forms of assessment as a possible strategy to promote integrity and creativity among students while ensuring their ownership of written work. It is suggested to reassess the assignments designed by considering integrity in terms of the instructors' professional characteristics, the purpose of the assignment, and the form of evaluation best suited to the students' needs.

Lye & Lim (2024) also propose the Against, Avoid, and Adopt (AAA) principle to reassess and reform the assessment methods by considering the presence of generative AI as an instance. The authors contend that, in light of the rapid advancement of generative AI tools and applications, policing their use and competing with AI may not be effective in addressing the underlying issues of the assessment methods used. The phenomenon of "assessment twins," wherein two forms of assessment, such as written work and oral defense of the work, are used to assess the same outcomes and allow instructors to track authorship and comprehension of the work, is also gaining traction (Roe et al., 2025).

A notable aspect of these developments is the emphasis on the deliberate development of opportunities for education that promote critical thinking and metacognition. This is supported by Qian (2025), who argues that while certain themes identified before the development of ChatGPT remain dominant, new and evolving trends are also being identified, especially in terms of fostering creativity and critical thinking, as well as learning autonomy and prompt literacy, to highlight the integration of generative AI into the education sector.

This is also supported by empirical research conducted in the field. Kolade et al. (2024) identified that when students use ChatGPT, the program is capable of generating highly distinctive and superior content for various individual student accounts in response to the same assessment prompt. The approach is, however, not effective in sustaining the associated cognitive depth and is not capable of generating several original outputs from a single narrative.

Policy Development and Institutional Governance

Institutions should establish well-founded and researched-based policy decisions that promote the principles of ethics, academic integrity, and responsible innovation in the context of artificial intelligence. Research conducted in the recent past has shown that existing governance systems cannot effectively handle the complexity brought about by generative AI. For instance, Coates et al. (2025) argue that existing systems are not effective and need structural changes. This is a clear indication of the need to enhance governance systems to promote the authenticity of assessment in the context of artificial intelligence.

The formulation of institutional AI policy guidelines outlining the scope of permitted activities and the boundaries of ethics is a crucial part of contemporary governance. Research conducted in the recent past has shown evidence of various institutions across the globe formalizing such policy guidelines. McDonald et al. (2025) note that the majority of universities have endorsed the use of GenAI and have also formulated comprehensive guidelines for the classroom application of the same. To assist teachers in the integration and application of GenAI in the classroom setting, more than half of the universities have offered sample curricula and activities for the same.

Furze et al. (2025) have also proposed a flexible framework for the integration of GenAI in the context of educational assessment. This has enabled teachers to develop assessment approaches that promote critical thinking and human involvement. Their findings have shown a 33.3% increase in the rates of module passes, a 5.9% increase in the general attainment of students in the entire university, and a reduction in the cases of academic misconduct involving the application of GenAI.

These guidelines also need to include ethical considerations. Marín et al. (2025) found that 47.5% of students and 51.2% of instructors expressed their concerns about data security and privacy. In addition, the majority of the participants, i.e., 53.5% students and 61.1% instructors, also agreed that AI systems lack transparency. It is important for the institutions to highlight the significance of institution-wide policies, which can create trust among the users.

Furthermore, academic integrity has been significantly affected by the presence of generative AI. AI-assisted writing, problem-solving, or the creation of synthetic data often fails to be addressed in the conventional integrity policies. Leaton Gray et al. (2025) emphasized the need for a fundamental pedagogical shift to ensure academic integrity in an AI-dominated society, where the original goals of higher education institutions can be reasserted, along with the avoidance of the instrumental rationality of surveillance-based governance.

A systematic review done by Bittle & El-Gayar (2025) shows the need for higher education institutions to revise their integrity policies to address the changing integrity issues faced by students due to AI, such as the generation of content without acknowledgment or AI-generated citations. The study provides a comprehensive research agenda for the development of integrity policies.

In the development of policies, the views of the students also need to be considered. Johnston et al. (2024) found that students tend to be unsupportive or only somewhat supportive if their peers use AI programs such as ChatGPT for writing their essays, but the students tend to be supportive or somewhat supportive if their peers use AI tools such as Grammarly for the same purpose. The authors also emphasized the need for the development of a university-wide policy on the appropriate or inappropriate use of such tools.

In addition, academic governance with reference to Fair principles is underpinned by a transparent structure of disclosure rules, sanctions, and appeals. In order to effectively navigate this ever-changing environment, Peterson (2025) suggests Academic Integrity Reporting (AIR), which is an exhaustive structure that develops responsive, enforceable, and academically acceptable rules. Institutions will be able to uphold academic integrity and promote student development by moving away from punitive measures and towards more proactive approaches. In this regard, Alsharefeen & Al Sayari (2025) indicate that academics perceived systemic limitations, workload constraints, lack of institutional support, detection challenges, and cultural leniency as hindrances to policy implementation. In addition, academics had a desire for educational rather than punitive approaches. Direct content copying was perceived as the most risky GenAI plagiarism approach.

CASE STUDIES AND EMERGING PRACTICES

The rapid advancement of generative AI has forced higher education institutions across the world to rethink their governance structures, policy frameworks, and pedagogical methodologies. In all the case studies of modern universities across the world, one phenomenon has been consistently evident: universities are grappling with the opportunities and challenges of AI. They are trying to build coherent infrastructures that are both future-oriented and ethically grounded. In the research by Chan (2023), which attempts to build an AI education policy in the context of higher education through the perceptions and implications of text-generated AI technologies, it has been found that students and teachers across the academic spectrum have perceived

AI as being transformative but fraught with risks that have yet to be adequately addressed by existing policy frameworks. Even though generative AI has been found to be useful in giving feedback and developing digital competence among students, stakeholders have collectively agreed that it is of the utmost importance to develop policy guidelines. The research concludes by proposing an ecological policy model that prioritizes the interplay of governance, pedagogy, and institutional operations.

The same concerns have been echoed in the research by Alsharefeen & Al Sayari (2025), which examined "Examining Academic Integrity Policy and Practice in the Era of AI: A Case Study of Faculty Perspectives." The research found that there was a considerable difference between traditional academic integrity policy and Gen AI policy. In both cases, the overall effectiveness of the policy was found to be only moderately effective. The research also found that teachers showed a strong inclination towards an educative approach rather than a punitive one. The research also found that workload constraints, lack of institutional support, detection difficulties, leniency of culture, and institutional limitations act as obstacles to policy enforcement. The research also found that a hierarchical perception of Gen AI plagiarism exists, with direct content copying being seen as the most serious offense and AI-generated content with minimal student contribution being seen as the least serious offense. The overall response rate of the Gen AI scenario was found to be lower due to faculty uncertainty and the lack of adequate policy guidelines.

In their study, Wu et al. (2024) explain how the institutional perspective is further clarified by "AI Governance in Higher Education: Case Studies of Guidance at Big Ten Universities," demonstrating how guidance at the university level is fragmented, reactive, and, most often, temporary. This study indicates how most of the Big Ten universities offer flexible, rather than comprehensive, guidelines, often leaving instructors to interpret AI regulations on their own. While these universities have recognized the disruptive nature of AI, their governance models seem to focus on classroom use and academic misconduct, with less emphasis on overall strategy, data governance, accountability, and cross-campus coordination. This not only speaks to inconsistencies within each institution but also to a need for systemic, institution-wide models of AI governance.

FUTURE RESEARCH DIRECTIONS

In addition, future research on generative AI and academic integrity should expand from descriptive research toward more rigorous research methods. Longitudinal studies are needed to understand better how students' cognitive, critical, and creative skills are affected by generative AI, particularly when concerns about academic integrity persist. It is also important to develop better methods for identifying hidden academic integrity offenses, as research has shown that students often keep academic integrity offenses secret, and innovative methods, such as list experiments, may provide a more accurate assessment of academic integrity offenses involving generative AI. Future research should also consider cross-cultural and cross-disciplinary differences in academic integrity, as academic integrity is often related to societal norms, which may differ across contexts. Future research should evaluate how AI-aware and AI-resilient models are being used, as institutions are experimenting with new models of assessment, and how effective these models are in preserving academic integrity, promoting creativity, and maintaining assessment validity. Future research should consider how students' and faculty members' AI literacy is being developed, as well as which aspects of AI literacy are most effective, and how this literacy training may be incorporated equitably into academic programs. Finally, future research should consider how academic institutions' governance structures, transparency, and enforcement mechanisms may affect academic integrity, as well as how academic integrity may be maintained when using generative AI, particularly when concerns about academic integrity persist.

Ethical concerns related to academic integrity, such as authorship, data fabrication, and citation, should be further studied, particularly as generative AI becomes more integrated into academic writing and research. Future research should consider how generative AI may affect academic equity and inclusion, as well as whether generative AI may exacerbate academic equity and inclusion concerns, and whether generative AI may be used as a tool to address academic equity and inclusion concerns.

As human-AI collaboration becomes a new form of learning and production, pedagogical research should consider how academic integrity may be maintained when humans and AI collaborate, as well as how assessment may be developed without relying on inaccurate detection tools.

DISCUSSION

The advent of generative AI in higher education thus represents an important juncture for institutions to reevaluate long-held assumptions about learning, authorship, and integrity. The synthesized research presented throughout this chapter reveals the fundamental conflict: the significant learning advantages offered by GenAI also introduce new ethical complexities, thus redefining the integrity paradigm. The research presented throughout this chapter illustrates the continued presence of long-held integrity issues such as plagiarism, fabrication, and contract cheating, but in the form of more sophisticated, AI-assisted, and virtually invisible learning behaviors. The implications of this shift on the legacy integrity policies, intended for the pre-AI learning environment, thus underscore the need for higher education institutions to rethink their approach to integrity in the AI era.

A critical understanding arising from the synthesized research presented throughout this chapter reveals that the overuse of AI, in fact, constitutes not only a technological but also a cognitive or ethical problem. The overuse of AI in learning, it was found, constitutes the outsourcing of fundamental learning processes, from cognitive development to critical academic competencies. The overuse of AI, thus, constitutes an important threat to the validity of assessments, as well as the development of critical academic competencies, which higher education institutions have the responsibility to develop. The overuse of AI in learning also constitutes an important problem due to the presence of misconceptions, where students tend to perceive AI as a neutral tool, thus failing to recognize the ethical implications, while instructors often find it difficult to make sense of the inconsistent AI policies. The presence of high AI usage and low ethical literacy, thus, reveals the gap between technological advancement and ethical preparedness.

The chapter also concurrently argues that the policies and structures for governance are fragmented and often reactive, failing to provide instructors with guidance or students with clear expectations. The level of preparedness varies among institutions, some using flexible guidelines based on principles, while others tend to be punitive or, in some cases, completely forbid the use of AI. The inconsistency only serves to heighten the confusion, increasing the risk of creating inequalities in the learning process. The case studies presented in the chapter also highlight the lack of governance structures, underscoring the immediate need for institutions to develop the necessary infrastructure.

From the perspective of learning, the impact of Gen AI requires instructors to move from product-based evaluation to the development of learning processes, reflective, and authentic learning tasks. The development of AI-aware assessments, the process-product model, or the use of multimodal submissions represent some innovative solutions to the challenges presented by AI, reasserting the importance of the student's agency, the use of reasoning, and the acknowledgment that AI cannot be eliminated from the learning environment. Rather, it needs to be integrated into the learning environment, where expectations are clearly stated, and learning outcomes are aligned accordingly. This, in essence, marks a significant shift in the broader pedagogical approach to learning in higher education, where AI is not viewed as a threat to academic integrity but, instead, challenges the notion of what constitutes authentic learning in the technologically mediated world.

From an ethical perspective, the chapter shows how deontological ethics, virtue ethics, and codes of academic honesty continue to be important in informing institutional responses. While the use of detection systems and policy regulations has some significance, it cannot replace the importance of developing moral reasoning, ethical awareness, and responsible AI literacy among students. In fact, empirical studies have also suggested that students' ethical beliefs, not their policy knowledge, are more likely to influence their behavior. This, in turn, suggests that institutions cannot just rely on the enforcement of policies but also develop values such as honesty, fairness, and responsibility, even when AI is so accessible.

CONCLUSION

The rapid integration of GenAI into higher education has dramatically changed the ways learning, assessment, and academic integrity are provided. In this chapter, it has been made clear that while GenAI offers unprecedented opportunities to improve learning feedback, creativity, accessibility, and assessment efficiency, it also poses new forms of academic misconduct, ethical issues, and governance problems that higher education is trying to address. Existing models of academic integrity, which focus on plagiarism, fabrication, and cheating concerns, are no longer adequate in a GenAI context where AI can produce, alter, and transform content with minimal human intervention. As AI-based academic misconduct becomes increasingly invisible and difficult to detect, higher education has to shift from reactive and punitive approaches to more proactive approaches that focus on learning, transparency, and ethical thinking.

The literature reviewed in this chapter has made it clear that overreliance on AI poses significant risks not only to the validity of assessment but also to the development of essential learning skills. Students who rely heavily on GenAI may unknowingly compromise their critical thinking, writing, and problem-solving skills—essential learning skills that are at the heart of higher education. However, these problems cannot be addressed by relying on technology-based deterrents; rather, a holistic approach to pedagogical redesign and AI literacy for higher education is essential. The development of AI-conscious and AI-resistant assessment models are promising area for addressing the challenge of maintaining learning integrity in a GenAI-rich higher education context.

REFERENCES

Abbas, M., Jam, F. A., & Khan, T. I. (2024). Is it harmful or helpful? Examining the causes and consequences of generative AI usage among university students. *International Journal of Educational Technology in Higher Education*, *21*(1), 10. DOI: 10.1186/s41239-024-00444-7

Acosta-Enriquez, B. G., Arbulú Ballesteros, M. A., Huamaní Jordan, O., López Roca, C., & Saavedra Tirado, K. (2024). Analysis of college students' attitudes toward the use of ChatGPT in their academic activities: Effect of intent to use, verification of information and responsible use. *BMC Psychology*, *12*(1), 255. DOI: 10.1186/s40359-024-01764-z PMID: 38720382

Almisad, B., & Aleidan, A. (2025). Faculty perspectives on generative artificial intelligence (GenAI): Insights into awareness, benefits, concerns, and uses. In *Frontiers in Education* (Vol. 10, p. 1632742). Frontiers., DOI: 10.3389/feduc.2025.1632742

Alnsour, M. M., Qouzah, L., Aljamani, S., Alamoush, R. A., & AL-Omiri, M. K. (2025). AI in education: Enhancing learning potential and addressing ethical considerations among academic staff—a cross-sectional study at the University of Jordan. *International Journal for Educational Integrity*, *21*(1), 16. DOI: 10.1007/s40979-025-00189-4

Alsharefeen, R., & Al Sayari, N. (2025, June). Examining academic integrity policy and practice in the era of AI: A case study of faculty perspectives. In *Frontiers in Education (Vol. 10*, p. 1621743). Frontiers Media SA. https://doi.org/DOI: 10.3389/feduc.2025.1621743

An, Y., Yu, J. H., & James, S. (2025). Investigating the higher education institutions' guidelines and policies regarding the use of generative AI in teaching, learning, research, and administration. *International Journal of Educational Technology in Higher Education*, *22*(1), 10. DOI: 10.1186/s41239-025-00507-3

Arslan, B., Lehman, B., Tenison, C., Sparks, J. R., López, A. A., Gu, L., & Zapata-Rivera, D. (2024). Opportunities and challenges of using generative AI to personalize educational assessment. *Frontiers in Artificial Intelligence*, *7*, 1460651. DOI: 10.3389/frai.2024.1460651 PMID: 39434872

Avello, D., & Aranguren Zurita, S. (2025). Exploring the nexus of academic integrity and artificial intelligence in higher education: A bibliometric analysis. *International Journal for Educational Integrity*, *21*(1), 24. DOI: 10.1007/s40979-025-00199-2

Awadallah Alkouk, W., & Khlaif, Z. N. (2024, December). AI-resistant assessments in higher education: Practical insights from faculty training workshops. In *Frontiers in education (Vol. 9,* p. 1499495). Frontiers Media SA. https://doi.org/DOI: 10.3389/feduc.2024.1499495

Birks, D., & Clare, J. (2023). Linking artificial intelligence facilitated academic misconduct to existing prevention frameworks. *International Journal for Educational Integrity*, *19*(1), 20. DOI: 10.1007/s40979-023-00142-3

Bittle, K., & El-Gayar, O. (2025). Generative AI and academic integrity in higher sducation: A systematic review and research agenda. *Information (Basel)*, *16*(4), 296. DOI: 10.3390/info16040296

Bjelobaba, S., Waddington, L., Perkins, M., Foltýnek, T., Bhattacharyya, S., & Weber-Wulff, D. (2024). Research integrity and GenAI: A systematic analysis of ethical challenges across research phases. *arXiv preprint arXiv:2412.10134*. https://doi.org//arXiv.2412.10134DOI: 10.48550

Brickhill, M., Andrews, G., & Nieuwoudt, J. (2025). Developing student agency towards academic integrity through an educative approach: Exploring students' experiences and perspectives. *Journal of Academic Ethics*, *23*(3), 951–975. DOI: 10.1007/s10805-024-09567-y

Campo, L., Delgado, N., Etxabe-Urbieta, J. M., Kanso, H., & Gueye, M. L. (2025). Relationship between the use of ChatGPT and plagiarism in higher education: The influence of gender, age and previous academic results. *Innovative Higher Education*, •••, 1–20. DOI: 10.1007/s10755-025-09830-z

Chan, C. K. Y. (2023). A comprehensive AI policy education framework for university teaching and learning. *International Journal of Educational Technology in Higher Education*, *20*(1), 38. DOI: 10.1186/s41239-023-00408-3

Chan, C. K. Y. (2025). Students' perceptions of 'AI-giarism': Investigating changes in understandings of academic misconduct. *Education and Information Technologies*, *30*(6), 8087–8108. DOI: 10.1007/s10639-024-13151-7

Cheung, K., & Vaish, A. (2025). Putting the honor back in academic honor systems. *Journal of Academic Ethics*, *23*(3), 441–461. DOI: 10.1007/s10805-024-09575-y

Coates, H., Croucher, G., & Calderon, A. (2025). Governing academic integrity: Ensuring the authenticity of higher thinking in the era of generative artificial intelligence. *Journal of Academic Ethics*, *23*(4), 1–14. DOI: 10.1007/s10805-025-09639-7

Furze, L., Perkins, M., Roe, J., & MacVaugh, J. (2024). The AI Assessment Scale (AIAS) in action: A pilot implementation of GenAI-supported assessment. *Australasian Journal of Educational Technology*, *40*(4), 38–55. DOI: 10.14742/ajet.9434

García-López, I. M., & Trujillo-Liñán, L. (2025, June). Ethical and regulatory challenges of Generative AI in education: A systematic review. In *Frontiers in Education* (Vol. 10, p. 1681252). Frontiers., DOI: 10.3389/feduc.2025.1565938

Jin, Y., Martinez-Maldonado, R., Gašević, D., & Yan, L. (2025). GLAT: The generative AI literacy assessment test. *Computers and Education: Artificial Intelligence*, 100436. https://doi.org//arXiv.2411.00283DOI: 10.48550

Jo, H. (2024). From concerns to benefits: A comprehensive study of ChatGPT usage in education. *International Journal of Educational Technology in Higher Education*, *21*(1), 35. DOI: 10.1186/s41239-024-00471-4

Johnston, H., Wells, R. F., Shanks, E. M., Boey, T., & Parsons, B. N. (2024). Student perspectives on the use of generative artificial intelligence technologies in higher education. *International Journal for Educational Integrity*, *20*(1), 2. DOI: 10.1007/s40979-024-00149-4

Karkoulian, S., Sayegh, N., & Sayegh, N. (2024). ChatGPT unveiled: Understanding perceptions of academic integrity in higher education-A qualitative approach. *Journal of Academic Ethics*, •••, 1–18. DOI: 10.1007/s10805-024-09543-6

Khlaif, Z. N., Alkouk, W. A., Salama, N., & Abu Eideh, B. (2025). Redesigning assessments for AI-enhanced learning: A framework for educators in the generative AI era. *Education Sciences*, *15*(2), 174. DOI: 10.3390/educsci15020174

Khlaif, Z. N., Ayyoub, A., Hamamra, B., Bensalem, E., Mitwally, M. A. A., Ayyoub, A., Hattab, M. K., & Shadid, F. (2024). University teachers' views on the adoption and integration of generative AI tools for student assessment in higher education. *Education Sciences*, *14*(10), 1090. DOI: 10.3390/educsci14101090

Kılınç, S. (2024). Comprehensive AI assessment framework: Enhancing educational evaluation with ethical AI integration. *Journal of Educational Technology and Online Learning, 7*(4-ICETOL 2024 Special Issue), 521-540. https://doi.org//arXiv.2407.16887DOI: 10.48550

Kim, J., Yu, S., Detrick, R., & Li, N. (2025). Exploring students' perspectives on Generative AI-assisted academic writing. *Education and Information Technologies*, *30*(1), 1265–1300. DOI: 10.1007/s10639-024-12878-7

Kolade, O., Owoseni, A., & Egbetokun, A. (2024). Is AI changing learning and assessment as we know it? Evidence from a ChatGPT experiment and a conceptual framework. *Heliyon, 10*(4), e25953. DOI: 10.1016/j.heliyon.2024.e25953 PMID: 38379960

Leaton Gray, S., Edsall, D., & Parapadakis, D. (2025). AI-based digital cheating at university, and the case for new ethical pedagogies. *Journal of Academic Ethics, 23*(4), 1–18. DOI: 10.1007/s10805-025-09642-y

Lee, S. S., & Moore, R. L. (2024). Harnessing Generative AI (GenAI) for automated feedback in higher education: A systematic review. *Online Learning : The Official Journal of the Online Learning Consortium, 28*(3), 82–104. DOI: 10.24059/olj.v28i3.4593

Lund, B., Mannuru, N. R., Teel, Z. A., Lee, T. H., Ortega, N. J., Simmons, S., & Ward, E. (2026). Student perceptions of AI-assisted writing and academic integrity: Ethical concerns, academic misconduct, and use of Generative AI in higher education. *AI in Education, 1*(1), 2. DOI: 10.3390/aieduc1010002

Lye, C. Y., & Lim, L. (2024). Generative artificial intelligence in tertiary education: Assessment redesign principles and considerations. *Education Sciences, 14*(6), 569. DOI: 10.3390/educsci14060569

Marín, Y. R., Caro, O. C., Rituay, A. M. C., Llanos, K. A. G., Perez, D. T., Bardales, E. S., Tuesta, J. N. A., & Santos, R. C. (2025). Ethical challenges associated with the use of artificial intelligence in university education. *Journal of Academic Ethics, 23*(4), 1–25. DOI: 10.1007/s10805-025-09660-w

McDonald, N., Johri, A., Ali, A., & Collier, A. H. (2025). Generative artificial intelligence in higher education: Evidence from an analysis of institutional policies and guidelines. *Computers in Human Behavior: Artificial Humans*, 3, 100121. https://doi.org//arXiv.2402.01659DOI: 10.48550

Newton, P. M. (2018, August). How common is commercial contract cheating in higher education and is it increasing? A systematic review. In *Frontiers in Education (Vol. 3*, p. 67). Frontiers Media SA. https://doi.org/DOI: 10.3389/feduc.2018.00067

Nguyen, H., & Hayward, J. (2025). Applying generative artificial intelligence to critiquing science assessments. *Journal of Science Education and Technology, 34*(1), 199–214. DOI: 10.1007/s10956-024-10177-x

Nguyen, H. M., & Goto, D. (2024). Unmasking academic cheating behavior in the artificial intelligence era: Evidence from Vietnamese undergraduates. *Education and Information Technologies, 29*(12), 15999–16025. DOI: 10.1007/s10639-024-12495-4

Nikolopoulou, K. (2025). Generative artificial intelligence and sustainable higher education: Mapping the potential. *Journal of Digital Educational Technology*, *5*(1), ep2506. Advance online publication. DOI: 10.30935/jdet/15860

Okolo, E. C., Appiah, I., & Wingenbach, G. (2025). Conflicts between academic misconduct and university honor codes: Implications for ethical behavior. *International Journal for Educational Integrity*, *21*(1), 26. DOI: 10.1007/s40979-025-00198-3

Ortiz-Bonnin, S., & Blahopoulou, J. (2025). Chat or cheat? Academic dishonesty, risk perceptions, and ChatGPT usage in higher education students. *Social Psychology of Education*, *28*(1), 113. DOI: 10.1007/s11218-025-10080-2

Peláez-Sánchez, I. C., Velarde-Camaqui, D., & Glasserman-Morales, L. D. (2024, June). The impact of large language models on higher education: Exploring the connection between AI and education 4.0. In *Frontiers in Education (Vol. 9*, p. 1392091). Frontiers Media SA. https://doi.org/DOI: 10.3389/feduc.2024.1392091

Perkins, M., Roe, J., Vu, B. H., Postma, D., Hickerson, D., McGaughran, J., & Khuat, H. Q. (2024). Genai detection tools, adversarial techniques and implications for inclusivity in higher education. *arXiv preprint arXiv*:2403.19148. https://doi.org//arXiv.2403.19148DOI: 10.48550

Peters, M., & Angelov, D. (2025). Redefining assessment tasks to promote students' creativity and integrity in the age of generative artificial intelligence. *International Journal for Educational Integrity*, *21*(1), 25. DOI: 10.1007/s40979-025-00201-x PMID: 41019941

Peterson, S. (2025). Addressing student use of generative AI in schools and universities through academic integrity reporting. In *Frontiers in Education* (Vol. 10, p. 1610836). Frontiers., DOI: 10.3389/feduc.2025.1610836

Petricini, T., Zipf, S., & Wu, C. (2025). AI: Communicating academic honesty: teacher messages and student perceptions about generative AI. *Frontiers in Communication*, *10*, 1544430. DOI: 10.3389/fcomm.2025.1544430

Qian, Y. (2025). Pedagogical applications of generative AI in higher education: A systematic review of the field. *TechTrends*, *69*(5), 1–16. DOI: 10.1007/s11528-025-01100-1

Roe, J., Perkins, M., & Giray, L. (2025). Assessment twins: A protocol for AI-vulnerable summative assessment. *arXiv preprint arXiv:2510.02929.* https://doi.org//arXiv.2510.02929DOI: 10.48550

Sbaffi, L., & Zhao, X. (2022). Evaluating a pedagogical approach to promoting academic integrity in higher education: An online induction program. *Frontiers in Psychology*, *13*, 1009305. DOI: 10.3389/fpsyg.2022.1009305 PMID: 36275294

Shaw, D. (2025). The digital erosion of intellectual integrity: Why misuse of generative AI is worse than plagiarism. *AI & Society*, *1-3*(8), 5819–5821. Advance online publication. DOI: 10.1007/s00146-025-02362-2

Tatum, H. E. (2022). Honor codes and academic integrity: Three decades of research. *Journal of College and Character*, *23*(1), 32–47. DOI: 10.1080/2194587X.2021.2017977

Toker, S., & Akgun, M. (2024). The role of task complexity in reducing AI plagiarism: A study of generative AI tools. *arXiv preprint arXiv:2412.13412*. https://doi.org//arXiv.2412.13412DOI: 10.48550

Urzúa, C. A. C., Ranjan, R., Saavedra, E. E. M., Badilla-Quintana, M. G., Lepe-Martínez, N., & Philominraj, A. (2025). Effects of AI-assisted feedback via generative chat on academic writing in higher education students: A systematic review of the literature. *Education Sciences*, *15*(10), 1396. DOI: 10.3390/educsci15101396

Wang, F., Li, N., Cheung, A. C., & Wong, G. K. (2025). In GenAI we trust: An investigation of university students' reliance on and resistance to generative AI in language learning. *International Journal of Educational Technology in Higher Education*, *22*(1), 59. DOI: 10.1186/s41239-025-00547-9

Wu, C., Zhang, H., & Carroll, J. M. (2024). AI governance in higher education: Case studies of guidance at big ten universities. *arXiv preprint arXiv:2409.02017*. https://doi.org//arXiv.2409.02017DOI: 10.48550

Xia, Q., Weng, X., Ouyang, F., Lin, T. J., & Chiu, T. K. (2024). A scoping review on how generative artificial intelligence transforms assessment in higher education. *International Journal of Educational Technology in Higher Education*, *21*(1), 40. DOI: 10.1186/s41239-024-00468-z

Yusuf, A., Pervin, N., & Román-González, M. (2024). Generative AI and the future of higher education: A threat to academic integrity or reformation? Evidence from multicultural perspectives. *International Journal of Educational Technology in Higher Education*, *21*(1), 21. DOI: 10.1186/s41239-024-00453-6

Compilation of References

Abbas, M., Jam, F. A., & Khan, T. I. (2024). Is it harmful or helpful? Examining the causes and consequences of generative AI usage among university students. *International Journal of Educational Technology in Higher Education*, *21*(1), 10. DOI: 10.1186/s41239-024-00444-7

Abdalrahim, A. M. A., & Mohammed, A. E. H. E. (2025). Strategies for Utilizing Artificial Intelligence to Support EFL Teachers Across Different Educational Levels. *The Arab Journal For Quality Assurance in Higher Education, 19*(66).

Abdi Tabari, M., Kushki, A., & Wang, Y. (2025). Comparing the effects of teacher-and AI-mediated corrective feedback on accuracy, complexity, and quality in L2 written narratives. *Computer Assisted Language Learning*, 1–24. DOI: 10.1080/09588221.2025.2561608

Abdullah, M. Y. (2025). Probing into EFL students' perceptions about the impact of utilizing AI-powered tools on their academic writing practices. *Education and Information Technologies*, *30*(15), 1–32. DOI: 10.1007/s10639-025-13601-w

Abir, A. B. (2023). *Exploring the Impact of Chatting with Native Speakers of English Language on Students' Intercultural Communicative Competence: The Case of master's One Students of MMUTO* (Doctoral dissertation, Mouloud Mameri University).

Abulibdeh, E., Taha, S., & Alamassi, S. (2023). Challenges facing underdeveloped countries in implementing Cutting-Edge AI technology. In Studies in big data (pp. 239–250). DOI: 10.1007/978-3-031-42455-7_22

Acharya, S., Thurber, T. B., & Ghosal, M. (2024). Transportation electrification load profiles by balancing Authority and State-Level Electrification Rates in the Western United States for GODEEEP [Dataset]. In *Zenodo (CERN European Organization for Nuclear Research)*. DOI: 10.5281/zenodo.7888568

Acharya, D. B., Kuppan, K., & Divya, B. (2025). Agentic AI: Autonomous Intelligence for Complex Goals – A Comprehensive survey. *IEEE Access : Practical Innovations, Open Solutions*, *1*, 18912–18936. Advance online publication. DOI: 10.1109/ACCESS.2025.3532853

Acharya, S., Patel, R., & Mehta, V. (2024). Longitudinal impacts of AI tool reliance on student cognitive outcomes in higher education. *Journal of Educational Research and Practice*, *14*(1), 33–51. DOI: 10.5590/JERAP.2024.14.1.03

Acion, L., Rajngewerc, M., & Randall, G. (2023). Generative AI poses ethical challenges for open science. *Nature Human Behaviour*, *7*(12), 1800–1801.

Acosta-Enriquez, B. G., Arbulú Ballesteros, M. A., Huamaní Jordan, O., López Roca, C., & Saavedra Tirado, K. (2024). Analysis of college students' attitudes toward the use of ChatGPT in their academic activities: Effect of intent to use, verification of information and responsible use. *BMC Psychology*, *12*(1), 255. DOI: 10.1186/s40359-024-01764-z PMID: 38720382

Adedeji, O., & Akinpelu, M. (2025). Understanding ICT and Its Impact on Teaching a Foreign Language. French Language Politics and Education in Nigeria: Building Human Capital and a Multilingual Nation.

Adegbola, T. (2024). AI dependency and the illusion of competence: Understanding skill deficits in AI-assisted learning. *Computers & Education*, *198*, 104756. DOI: 10.1016/j.compedu.2024.104756

Adika, D. (2024). Translating the Untranslatable: DeepL and ChatGPT on Academic Idioms. [LINGTERSA]. *Linguistik Terjemahan Sastra*, *5*(2), 85–93. DOI: 10.32734/lingtersa.v5i2.15086

Afable, L. (2025). Embracing or Resisting AI: Exploring the Teachers' Perspectives on Student Use of Artificial Intelligence. Available at *SSRN* 5314276. DOI: 10.2139/ssrn.5314276

Afzal, A., Firdousi, S. F., Waqar, A., & Awais, M. (2022). The influence of internet penetration on poverty and income inequality. *SAGE Open*, *12*(3), 21582440221116104. DOI: 10.1177/21582440221116104

Agate, N., Kennison, R., Konkiel, S., Long, C. P., Rhody, J., Sacchi, S., & Weber, P. (2020). The transformative power of values-enacted scholarship. *Humanities & Social Sciences Communications*, *7*, 165. DOI: 10.1057/s41599-020-00647-z

Agbese, M., Alanen, H. K., Antikainen, J., Erika, H., Isomaki, H., Jantunen, M., … & Vakkuri, V. (2023). *Governance in ethical and trustworthy AI systems: Extension of the ECCOLA method for AI ethics governance using GARP*. E-Informatica Software Engineering Journal, 17(1).

Agrawal, A., Banerjee, A. R. S., Jhariya, M. K., Garg, N., Hashmi, I., Brar, V., Gupta, D., & Mishra, D. K. (2025). AI-powered student assessment in higher education: Enhancing accuracy, feedback, and personalization. In Innovating assessment and evaluation in higher education: Inclusive practices and technological advancements (p. 26). DOI: 10.4018/979-8-3373-2130-1.ch006

Agyemang, K. A. (2025). *Understanding Student Practices for Using AI-Powered Learning Assistants: Ethical and Effective Strategies for Academic Success* (Master's thesis, New Mexico State University).

Ahamed, N. F. I. (2025). The transformative role of Artificial Intelligence in modern education. *World Journal of Advanced Research and Reviews*, *26*(1), 3239–3247. DOI: 10.30574/wjarr.2025.26.1.1453

Ahmadzade, M., & Farahian, M. (2025). At a Crossroad: Comparing ChatGPT and Grammarly in Enhancing EFL Learners' Use of the Article'. *SSRN*, *2*(1), 47–62. DOI: 10.2139/ssrn.5699162

Akbar, M. S. (2025). Beyond Detection: Designing AI-Resilient Assessments with Automated Feedback Tool to Foster Critical Thinking. arXiv preprint arXiv:2503.23622.

Akgun, S., & Greenhow, C. (2022). Artificial intelligence in education: Addressing ethical challenges in K-12 settings. *AI and Ethics*, *2*(3), 431–440. DOI: 10.1007/s43681-021-00096-7 PMID: 34790956

Akinwalere, S. N., & Ivanov, V. (2022). Artificial intelligence in higher Education: Challenges and opportunities. *BORDER CROSSING*, *12*(1), 1–15. DOI: 10.33182/bc.v12i1.2015

Akpabio, E., Akpabio, I., & Akpabio, I. (2025). Leveraging AI for Personalized English Language Learning: Tailoring Instruction to Individual Needs. In *AI Applications for English Language Learning* (pp. 385-414). IGI Global Scientific Publishing.

Al Yakin, A., Muthmainnah, M., Cardoso, L., Al Matari, A. S., & Obaid, A. (2025). AI-powered Personalization for Learning and Human-Robot Interaction: A Case Study with Pre-Service Teachers from Indonesia. *Southeastern Philippines Journal of Research and Development*, *30*(2), 25–45.

Albert, R. S., & Runco, M. A. (1999). A history of research on creativity. In Sternberg, R. J. (Ed.), *Handbook of creativity* (pp. 16–31). Cambridge University Press.

Alfaleh, M., Albasis, H. H., & Mohamed, A. M. (2025). EFL learners' motivation and engagement with oral reading activities and AI tools: Exploring the effect of gender, study level and English language proficiency. *Cogent Education*, *12*(1), 2542395. DOI: 10.1080/2331186X.2025.2542395

Alkhasawneh, S. N., Hernández-Leo, D., Guerrero-Solé, F., & Pérez, F. (2025). Shifting Educator Perspectives: Exploring Evolving Views on Generative AI. In Proceedings of the D-SAIL Workshop-Transformative Curriculum Design: Digitalisation, Sustainability, and AI Literacy for 21st Century Learning, CEUR-WS, Palermo, Italy (pp. 15-25).

Allison, J., Hwang, G. J., Mayer, R. E., Pellas, N., Karnalim, O., de Freitas, S., Ng, O.-L., Huang, Y.-M., Hooshyar, D., Seidman, R. H., Al-Emran, M., Mikropoulos, T. A., Schroeder, N. L., Roscoe, R. D., & Sanusi, I. (2025). From generative AI to extended reality: Multidisciplinary perspectives on the challenges, opportunities, and future of educational computing. *Journal of Educational Computing Research*, *63*(6), 1327–1363. DOI: 10.1177/07356331251359964

Almalawi, A., Soh, B., Li, A., & Samra, H. (2024). Predictive models for educational purposes: A systematic review. *Big Data and Cognitive Computing*, *8*(12), 187. DOI: 10.3390/bdcc8120187

Almisad, B., & Aleidan, A. (2025). Faculty perspectives on generative artificial intelligence (GenAI): Insights into awareness, benefits, concerns, and uses. [). Frontiers.]. *Frontiers in Education*, *10*, 1632742. DOI: 10.3389/feduc.2025.1632742

Alnsour, M. M., Qouzah, L., Aljamani, S., Alamoush, R. A., & AL-Omiri, M. K. (2025). AI in education: Enhancing learning potential and addressing ethical considerations among academic staff—a cross-sectional study at the University of Jordan. *International Journal for Educational Integrity*, *21*(1), 16. DOI: 10.1007/s40979-025-00189-4

Alsharefeen, R., & Al Sayari, N. (2025, June). Examining academic integrity policy and practice in the era of AI: A case study of faculty perspectives. In *Frontiers in Education (Vol. 10*, p. 1621743). Frontiers Media SA. https://doi.org/DOI: 10.3389/feduc.2025.1621743

Alshehri, A. (2025). AI's effectiveness in language testing and feedback provision. *Social Sciences & Humanities Open*, *12*, 101892. DOI: 10.1016/j.ssaho.2025.101892

Altamimi, F., & Hussein, D. (2025). Unlocking Potential: Saudi EFL Male Students' Perspectives on AI Tools for Enhancing English Writing Proficiency. *Arab World English Journal, 16*.

Alwasidi, M. A., & Al-Khalifah, K. S. (2025). Assessing the Impact of ChatGPT on EFL Students' Writing Productivity and Proficiency. *Journal of Language Teaching and Research, 16*(3), 986–995. DOI: 10.17507/jltr.1603.29

Ananny, M. (2023). Making mistakes: Constructing algorithmic errors to understand sociotechnical power. *Osiris, 38*(1), 223–241. DOI: 10.1086/725146

Ananny, M., & Crawford, K. (2018). Seeing without knowing: Limitations of the transparency ideal and its application to algorithmic accountability. *New Media & Society, 20*(3), 973–989. DOI: 10.1177/1461444816676645

Anderson, J. R., Corbett, A. T., Koedinger, K. R., & Pelletier, R. (1995). Cognitive Tutors: Lessons learned. *Journal of the Learning Sciences, 4*(2), 167–207. DOI: 10.1207/s15327809jls0402_2

Angel, B. (2024). *The Wolf is at the Door: How to Survive and Thrive in an AI-driven World.* Entrepreneur Press.

An, Y., Yu, J. H., & James, S. (2025). Investigating the higher education institutions' guidelines and policies regarding the use of generative AI in teaching, learning, research, and administration. *International Journal of Educational Technology in Higher Education, 22*(1), 10. DOI: 10.1186/s41239-025-00507-3

Aper, J. P. (2024). Artificial intelligence and higher education: A brave new world? *The Journal of Educational Thought, 57*(1). Advance online publication. DOI: 10.55016/ojs/jet.v57i1.79412

Aprianto, R., Lestari, E. P., Sadan, N., & Fletcher, E. (2024). Harnessing Artificial intelligence in Higher Education: Balancing innovation and ethical challenges. [ITEE]. *International Transactions on Education Technology, 3*(1), 84–93. DOI: 10.33050/itee.v3i1.680

Arias, J., Salas, J. I., Chiappe, A., & Sáez Delgado, F. (2025). The extended education 4.0: Lifelong learning in times of artificial intelligence. *Applied Sciences (Basel, Switzerland), 15*(17), 9352. DOI: 10.3390/app15179352

Arslan, B., Lehman, B., Tenison, C., Sparks, J. R., López, A. A., Gu, L., & Zapata-Rivera, D. (2024). Opportunities and challenges of using generative AI to personalize educational assessment. *Frontiers in Artificial Intelligence, 7*, 1460651. DOI: 10.3389/frai.2024.1460651 PMID: 39434872

Aryana, S., Sobari, T., San Fauziya, D., & Mustika, R. I. (2025). The Effectiveness of 21st Century Competency Assessment Model and HOTS in Improving Writing Skills: An Experimental Research. *Journal of Language Teaching and Research, 16*(4), 1115–1128. DOI: 10.17507/jltr.1604.07

Atil, A., Yilmaz, R., & Ozdemir, S. (2024). AI hallucinations in academic research: Detection, prevention, and implications. *Scientometrics, 129*(4), 2301–2320. DOI: 10.1007/s11192-024-04945-w

Avello, D., & Aranguren Zurita, S. (2025). Exploring the nexus of academic integrity and artificial intelligence in higher education: A bibliometric analysis. *International Journal for Educational Integrity, 21*(1), 24. DOI: 10.1007/s40979-025-00199-2

Awadallah Alkouk, W., & Khlaif, Z. N. (2024, December). AI-resistant assessments in higher education: Practical insights from faculty training workshops. In *Frontiers in education (Vol. 9,* p. 1499495). Frontiers Media SA. https://doi.org/DOI: 10.3389/feduc.2024.1499495

Azizov, D. (2024). From Idioms to Algorithms: Translating Culture-Specific Expressions in AI Systems. *Iconic Research and Engineering Journals, 7*(10), 543–551.

Bahr, A. (2024). Bridges without foundation? Why The use of AI tools in academia needs to build on ethics first. *Filozofia, 79*(5), 486–500. DOI: 10.31577/filozofia.2024.79.5.2

Baidoo-Anu, D., & Ansah, L. O. (2023). Education in the era of generative artificial intelligence (AI): Understanding the potential benefits of ChatGPT in promoting teaching and learning. *Journal of AI, 7*(1), 52–62. DOI: 10.61969/jai.1337500

Bailey, D. R., Lee, A., He, H., McConnell, J., Wilson, D. R., & Chakrabarti, K. B. (2025). Writing Support with Grammarly: Examining Confidence, Help-Seeking Behavior, and User Perceptions in Higher Education. *Turkish Online Journal of Educational Technology-TOJET, 24*(1), 90–105.

Baker, R. S., & Hawn, A. (2022). Algorithmic bias in education. *International Journal of Artificial Intelligence in Education, 32*(4), 1052–1092. DOI: 10.1007/s40593-021-00285-9

Bakla, A. (2023). ChatGPT in Academic Writing and Publishing. In Advances in educational technologies and instructional design book series (pp. 89–101). DOI: 10.4018/978-1-6684-9893-4.ch005

Baradziej, S. (2023). The influence of Large Language Models on systematic review and research dissemination. *Septentrio Conference Series, 1.*

Barnes, E., & Hutson, J. (2024). Navigating the ethical terrain of AI in higher education: Strategies for mitigating bias and promoting fairness. *Forum for Education Studies.*, *2*(2), 1229. DOI: 10.59400/fes.v2i2.1229

Barrios-Beltran, D. (2025). Exploring the efficacy of ChatGPT-4 feedback in second language Spanish writing. *System*, *133*, 103771. DOI: 10.1016/j.system.2025.103771

Bate, G. W. (2025). The struggle is the lesson! Being an educator in the age of AI. *AI & Society*, *40*(7), 1–3. DOI: 10.1007/s00146-025-02347-1

Batool, A., Zowghi, D., & Bano, M. (2025). AI governance: A systematic literature review. *AI and Ethics*, •••, 1–15.

Bello, L., & Aubert, L. (2025). Artificial intelligence in the classroom: Democratizing knowledge and transforming education. *Seminars in Medical Writing and Education*, *4*, 469. DOI: 10.56294/mw2025469

Bender, E. M., Gebru, T., McMillan-Major, A., & Shmitchell, S. (2021). On the dangers of stochastic parrots: Can language models be too big? *Proceedings of the 2021 ACM Conference on Fairness, Accountability, and Transparency*, 610–623. DOI: 10.1145/3442188.3445922

Benjamin, R. (2022). *Viral justice: How we grow the world we want.*

Bhattacharya, C., & Sabeena, L. (2025). AI-powered teacher performance evaluation and pedagogical strategy optimization in higher education. The business and management review, 15 (2), 225-234. DOI: 10.71443/9789349552531-16

Biagini, G. (2025). Towards an AI-Literate Future: A systematic literature review exploring education, ethics, and applications. *International Journal of Artificial Intelligence in Education*, *35*(4), 1–51. DOI: 10.1007/s40593-025-00466-w

Biesta, G. (2021). *World-centred education: A view for the present* (1st ed.). Routledge.

Bin-Nashwan, S. A., Al-Dmour, H. H., Al-Dmour, R., & Alshurideh, M. (2023). Use of ChatGPT in academia: Academic integrity hangs in the balance. *Technology in Society*, *75*, 102389. DOI: 10.1016/j.techsoc.2023.102370

Binns, R. (2018). Fairness in machine learning: Lessons from political philosophy. *Proceedings of the 2018 Conference on Fairness, Accountability, and Transparency*, *81*, 1–11. DOI: 10.1145/3287560.3287598

Birks, D., & Clare, J. (2023). Linking artificial intelligence facilitated academic misconduct to existing prevention frameworks. *International Journal for Educational Integrity*, *19*(1), 20. DOI: 10.1007/s40979-023-00142-3

Bittle, K., & El-Gayar, O. (2025). Generative AI and academic integrity in higher education: A systematic review and research agenda. *Information (Basel)*, *16*(4), 296. DOI: 10.3390/info16040296

Bitzenbauer, P. (2023). ChatGPT in physics education: A pilot study on easy-to-implement activities. *Contemporary Educational Technology*, *15*(3), ep430. DOI: 10.30935/cedtech/13176

Bjelobaba, S., Waddington, L., Perkins, M., Foltýnek, T., Bhattacharyya, S., & Weber-Wulff, D. (2024). Research integrity and GenAI: A systematic analysis of ethical challenges across research phases (Version 1) [Preprint]. arXiv. 10.48550/arXiv.2412.10134

Bjork, R. A., & Bjork, E. L. (2020). Desirable difficulties in theory and practice. *Journal of Applied Research in Memory and Cognition*, *9*(4), 475–479. DOI: 10.1016/j.jarmac.2020.09.003

Black, S. (2021). What Are Universities Really For? Re-imagining Stewardship. *Education as Change*, *25*(1), 1–7.

Blandis, E. (2025, December 4). Artificial intelligence used to prepare legal document, lawyers referred to regulators. ABC News Australia. https://www.abc.net.au/news/2025-12-05/artificial-intelligence-used-to-prepare-legal-document/106086724

Blended Learning Service. (2024). *Using generative AI: Guidance for students*. University of Cambridge.

Blog, A. N. S. I. (2024). *Critical thinking in the age of AI: Challenges and strategies for educators*. American National Standards Institute. https://blog.ansi.org/critical-thinking-ai-education/

Boateng, G., & Boateng, R. (2024). AI accessibility and bias: Examining barriers for students with disabilities and linguistic minorities. *Universal Access in the Information Society*, *23*(2), 611–625. DOI: 10.1007/s10209-024-01085-5

Bond, M., Khosravi, H., De Laat, M., Bergdahl, N., Negrea, V., Oxley, E., Pham, P., Chong, S. W., & Siemens, G. (2024). A meta systematic review of artificial intelligence in higher education: A call for increased ethics, collaboration, and rigour. *International Journal of Educational Technology in Higher Education*, *21*(1), 4. DOI: 10.1186/s41239-023-00436-z

Booth, R. (2025, June 6). High Court tells UK lawyers to urgently stop misuse of AI in legal work. The Guardian. https://www.theguardian.com/technology/2025/jun/06/high-court-tells-uk-lawyers-to-urgently-stop-misuse-of-ai-in-legal-work

Borghoff, U. M., Bottoni, P., & Pareschi, R. (2025). Human-artificial interaction in the age of agentic AI: A system-theoretical approach. *Frontiers in Human Dynamics, 7*, 1579166. Advance online publication. DOI: 10.3389/fhumd.2025.1579166

Boy, F., & Doneddu, D. (2025). Generative AI in the social sciences: Toward critical integration and methodological innovation. DOI: 10.31235/osf.io/f8dr5_v1

Bozkurt, A., Junhong, X., Lambert, S., Pazurek, A., Crompton, H., Koseoglu, S., & Romero-Hall, E. (2023). Speculative futures on ChatGPT and generative artificial intelligence (AI): A collective reflection from the educational landscape. *Asian Journal of Distance Education, 18*(1), 53–130.

Braverman, H. (1974). *Labor and monopoly capital: The degradation of work in the twentieth century*. Monthly Review Press. DOI: 10.14452/MR-026-03-1974-07_1

Brickhill, M., Andrews, G., & Nieuwoudt, J. (2025). Developing student agency towards academic integrity through an educative approach: Exploring students' experiences and perspectives. *Journal of Academic Ethics, 23*(3), 951–975. DOI: 10.1007/s10805-024-09567-y

Brohi, S., Jhanjhi, N. Z., & Pillai, T. R. (2025). A Research Landscape of Agentic AI and Large Language Models: Applications, Challenges and Future Directions. *Algorithms, 18*(8), 499. DOI: 10.3390/a18080499

Brown, D. W. (2014). Nobody's property. In Palgrave Macmillan US eBooks (pp. 83–105). DOI: 10.1057/9781137337153_5

Brusilovsky, P. (2001). Adaptive hypermedia. *User Modeling and User-Adapted Interaction, 11*(1–2), 87–110. DOI: 10.1023/A:1011143116306

Buçinca, Z., Malaya, M. B., & Gajos, K. Z. (2021). To trust or to think: cognitive forcing functions can reduce overreliance on AI in AI-assisted decision-making. *Proceedings of the ACM on Human-Computer Interaction, 5*(CSCW1), 1–21. DOI: 10.1145/3449287

Bui, T. T. U., & Tong, T. V. A. (2025). The impact of ai writing tools on academic integrity: Unveiling english-majored students' perceptions and practical solutions. *AsiaCALL Online Journal, 16*(1), 83–110. DOI: 10.54855/acoj.251615

Bulathwela, S., Pérez-Ortiz, M., Holloway, C., Cukurova, M., & Shawe-Taylor, J. (2024). Artificial intelligence alone will not democratise education: On educational inequality, techno-solutionism and inclusive tools. *Sustainability (Basel), 16*(2), 781. DOI: 10.3390/su16020781

Burrell, J. (2016). How the machine 'thinks': Understanding opacity in machine learning algorithms. *Big Data & Society, 3*(1), 2053951715622512. DOI: 10.1177/2053951715622512

Caines, A., & McCarty, J. (2023). Large language models and the future of university writing. *Computers and Composition, 69*, 102827.

Cambridge International. (2023). *The use of generative AI in coursework*. Cambridge Assessment International Education.

Camilleri, M. A. (2024). Artificial intelligence governance: Ethical considerations and implications for social responsibility. *Expert Systems: International Journal of Knowledge Engineering and Neural Networks, 41*(7), e13406. DOI: 10.1111/exsy.13406

Campo, L., Delgado, N., Etxabe-Urbieta, J. M., Kanso, H., & Gueye, M. L. (2025). Relationship between the use of ChatGPT and plagiarism in higher education: The influence of gender, age and previous academic results. *Innovative Higher Education*, •••, 1–20. DOI: 10.1007/s10755-025-09830-z

Cancela-Outeda, C. (2024). The EU's AI act: A framework for collaborative governance. *Internet of Things : Engineering Cyber Physical Human Systems, 27*, 101291. DOI: 10.1016/j.iot.2024.101291

Cao, X., Lv, D., Xing, Z., & Zhang, L. (2023). Linking adaptive governance, strategic flexibility and responsible innovation: Evidence from China. *International Journal on Management of Innovation & Technology, 20*(6), 2350040. DOI: 10.1142/S0219877023500402

Capogna, S., & Greco, F. (2024). *The digital transformation of European higher education*. Springer. DOI: 10.1007/978-3-031-70763-6

Carver, J. (2020). *A clockwork orange: Student advising and technology*. Ohio University.

Çengel, Y. A. (2023). A concise account of information as meaning ascribed to symbols and its association with conscious mind. *Entropy (Basel, Switzerland), 25*(1), 177. DOI: 10.3390/e25010177 PMID: 36673318

Cetinic, E. (2022). The myth of culturally agnostic AI models. arXiv (Cornell University). 10.48550/arxiv.2211.15271

Chan, A. (2023). Localizing the Practice of Critical Pedagogy through Place-Based, Problem-Posing Education. In *Critical Pedagogy in the Language and Writing Classroom* (pp. 106–118). Routledge. DOI: 10.4324/9781003357001-10

Chan, C. K. Y. (2023). A comprehensive AI policy education framework for university teaching and learning. *International Journal of Educational Technology in Higher Education*, *20*(38), 38. DOI: 10.1186/s41239-023-00408-3

Chan, C. K. Y. (2025). Students' perceptions of 'AI-giarism': Investigating changes in understandings of academic misconduct. *Education and Information Technologies*, *30*(6), 8087–8108. DOI: 10.1007/s10639-024-13151-7

Chan, C. K. Y., & Hu, W. (2023). Students' voices on generative AI: Perceptions, benefits, and challenges in higher education. *International Journal of Educational Technology in Higher Education*, *20*(1), 43. DOI: 10.1186/s41239-023-00411-8

Chan, C. K. Y., & Tsi, L. H. (2024). Will generative AI replace teachers in higher education? A study of teacher and student perceptions. [Chang, H., & Parkes, F. The academic integrity-artificial intelligence nexus: An institutional and personal normative risk to quality of learning and teaching at higher education institutions.]. *Studies in Educational Evaluation*, *83*, 101395. DOI: 10.1016/j.stueduc.2024.101395

Chandrasekhar, R. (2025). *Legal frictions for data openness: Reflections from a case-study on re-use of the open web for AI training* (Doctoral dissertation, Centre Internet et Société-CNRS; Inno3; Open Knowledge Foundation).

Chaudhry, M. A., Cukurova, M., & Luckin, R. (2022). A Transparency Index Framework for AI in education. arXiv (Cornell University). 10.48550/arxiv.2206.03220

Chauhan, S., & Dutta, A. (2025). Artificial intelligence in student privacy and data security. *International Journal of Advanced Research in Computer Science*, *16*(3).

Chen, Y., Wang, Y., Chan, A. B., & Li, J., & LC, R. (2025b). Once More with (the Right) Feeling: How Historical Fiction Writing Processes of Character Design, Plot Outline, and Context Checking Are Affected by Co-Writing with ChatGPT. In *International Conference on Human-Computer Interaction* (pp. 79-101). Cham: Springer Nature Switzerland. DOI: 10.1007/978-3-031-92823-9_7

Chen, L., & Fang, Y. (2025). ChatGPT-3 policies in the making: Identifying blind spots and supporting the language needs of international students. In *Rethinking Language Education in the Age of Generative AI* (pp. 90–110). Routledge. DOI: 10.4324/9781003426929-8

Chen, M. (2023). A comparison of machine learning techniques in building an intelligent tutoring system. *Applied and Computational Engineering*, *5*(1), 662–666. DOI: 10.54254/2755-2721/5/20230673

Chen, X. (2025). *Implementing E-assessment for Learning in Primary EFL Writing: A Case Study in China*. Springer Nature.

Chen, X., Shu, D., DeLuca, C., & Holden, M. (2025a). Advancing e-assessment for learning in the primary EFL writing classroom: The role of collaborative teacher professional learning. *Asia Pacific Journal of Education*, •••, 1–20. DOI: 10.1080/02188791.2025.2465296

Chen, X., Zou, D., Xie, H., & Cheng, G. (2024). Generative AI in higher education: A systematic review of ChatGPT and related technologies. *Education and Information Technologies*, *29*(3), 3303–3330. DOI: 10.1007/s10639-024-12556-6

Cheung, K., & Vaish, A. (2025). Putting the honor back in academic honor systems. *Journal of Academic Ethics*, *23*(3), 441–461. DOI: 10.1007/s10805-024-09575-y

Chinoracky, R., & Stalmasekova, N. (2025). Ethical Problems in the Use of Artificial Intelligence by University Educators. *Education Sciences*, *15*(10), 1322. DOI: 10.3390/educsci15101322

Chinta, S. V., Wang, Z., Yin, Z., Hoang, N., & Kumar, A. (2024). FairAIED: Navigating fairness, bias, and ethics in educational AI applications. *arXiv*. https://doi.org//arXiv.2407.18745DOI: 10.48550

Chmiel, A. (2023). The integration of generative AI tools in university teaching: Faculty perspectives and institutional responses. *Teaching in Higher Education*, *28*(7), 1589–1605. DOI: 10.1080/13562517.2023.2219337

Chounta, I. A., Bardone, E., Raudsep, A., & Pedaste, M. (2022). Exploring teachers' perceptions of artificial intelligence as a tool to support their practice in Estonian K-12 education. *International Journal of Artificial Intelligence in Education*, *32*(3), 725–755. DOI: 10.1007/s40593-021-00243-5

Christoforou, M. (2025). Gen AI-assisted multimodal meaning Design: Exercising a pedagogic metalanguage of transposition. *Pedagogies*, •••, 1–25. DOI: 10.1080/1554480X.2025.2522884

Cibrian, F. L., Chen, Y. Y., Anderson, K., Abrahamsson, C. M., & Motti, V. G. (2025). Limitations in speech recognition for young adults with down syndrome. *Universal Access in the Information Society*, *24*(3), 1–19. DOI: 10.1007/s10209-025-01197-4

Clos, J., & Chen, Y. Y. (2024, September). Investigating the impact of generative AI on students and educators: Evidence and insights from the literature. In *Proceedings of the Second International Symposium on Trustworthy Autonomous Systems* (pp. 1-6). DOI: 10.1145/3686038.3686063

Coates, H., Croucher, G., & Calderon, A. (2025). Governing academic integrity: Ensuring the authenticity of higher thinking in the era of generative artificial intelligence. *Journal of Academic Ethics*, *23*(4), 1–14. DOI: 10.1007/s10805-025-09639-7

Coeckelbergh, M. (2025). Three challenges for a global AI ethics: Towards a more relational normative vision. *AI and Ethics, 5*(5), 5527–5533. DOI: 10.1007/s43681-025-00791-9

Cogent Education. (2024). AI-augmented research quality: Balancing automation with scholarly rigor. *Cogent Education, 11*(1), 2321847. https://doi.org/DOI: 10.1080/2331186X.2024.2321847

Cooper, G. (2023). Examining science education in ChatGPT: An exploratory study of generative artificial intelligence. *Journal of Science Education and Technology, 32*(3), 444–452. DOI: 10.1007/s10956-023-10039-y

Cope, B., Kalantzis, M., & Searsmith, D. (2020). Artificial intelligence for education: Knowledge and its assessment in AI-enabled learning ecologies. *Educational Philosophy and Theory, 53*(12), 1229–1245. DOI: 10.1080/00131857.2020.1728732

Cornell University Teaching. (2023). *Assessment strategies for an AI-integrated academic environment.* Cornell University Center for Teaching Innovation. https://teaching.cornell.edu/assessment-ai-strategies

Cotton, D. R. E., Cotton, P. A., & Shipway, J. R. (2024). Chatting and cheating: Ensuring academic integrity in the era of ChatGPT. *Journal of Applied Learning & Teaching, 7*(1), 1–14.

Couldry, N., & Mejias, U. A. (2019). *The costs of connection: How data is colonizing human life and appropriating it for capitalism.* Stanford University Press.

Coyle, D., & Weller, A. (2020). "Explaining" machine learning reveals policy challenges. *Science, 368*(6498), 1433–1434. DOI: 10.1126/science.aba9647

Crain, C., Ewing, A., Billy, I., & Anush, H. (2025). The advantages and disadvantages of AI in higher education. *The Business & Management Review, 15*(03). Advance online publication. DOI: 10.24052/bmr/v15nu03/art-16

Crawford, J., Butler-Henderson, K., Rudolph, J., Malkawi, B., Glowatz, M., Burton, R., & Lam, S. (2023). COVID-19: 20 countries' higher education intra-period digital pedagogy responses. *Journal of Applied Learning & Teaching, 6*(1), 1–20. DOI: 10.37074/jalt.2023.6.1.1

Crawford, K. (2021). *The atlas of AI: Power, politics, and the planetary costs of artificial intelligence.* Yale University Press.

Critical Review of Social Sciences. (2024). Intersectional inequities in AI-enhanced education: A critical analysis. *Critical Review of Social Sciences, 12*(3), 215–234. DOI: 10.1080/crss.2024.2034781

Crompton, H., & Burke, D. (2024). Artificial Intelligence Applications in Higher Education.

Crompton, H., & Burke, D. (2023). Artificial intelligence in higher education: The state of the field. *International Journal of Educational Technology in Higher Education*, *20*(1), 22. DOI: 10.1186/s41239-023-00392-8

David, N. (2024). AI-powered virtual assistant solution for supporting international students.

De Oliveira Silva, A., & Janes, D. D. S. (2025). Rethinking scientific integrity in the era of artificial intelligence. *PromptAI Academy Journal*, *4*, e075. DOI: 10.37497/promptai.4.2025.75

De Souza, J. A., Hunt, B., Asirwa, F. C., Adebamowo, C., & Lopes, G. (2016). Global health equity: Cancer care outcome disparities in high-, middle-, and low-income countries. *Journal of Clinical Oncology : Official Journal of the American Society of Clinical Oncology*, *34*(1), 6–13. DOI: 10.1200/JCO.2015.62.2860 PMID: 26578608

Delikoura, I., & Hui, P. (2025). From Superficial Outputs to Superficial Learning: Risks of Large Language Models in Education. *arXiv preprint arXiv:2509.21972*.

Demir, K. (2024). Global inequities in AI-enhanced education: Infrastructure, access, and academic outcomes in developing countries. *International Journal of Educational Development*, *105*, 103002. DOI: 10.1016/j.ijedudev.2024.103002

Dempere, J., Ramasamy, L. K., & Harris, J. (2025). AI as a Research Partner: Advocating for Co-Authorship in Academic Publications. *The Artificial Intelligence Business Review*, *1*(2). Advance online publication. DOI: 10.64044/j8enmv71

Demszky, D. (2022). *Using natural language processing to support student-centered education*. Stanford University.

Derakhshan, A., & Taghizadeh, M. S. (2025). Does Artificial Intelligence (AI) Nurture or Hinder Language Learners' Higher-Order Thinking Skills (HOTS)? A Phenomenological Study on L2 Learners' Perspectives and Lived Experiences. *International Journal of Applied Linguistics*.

Derakhshan, A., & Karimian Shirejini, R. (2020). An investigation of the Iranian EFL learners' perceptions towards the most common writing problems. *SAGE Open*, *10*(2), 2158244020919523. DOI: 10.1177/2158244020919523

Derrick, G., Sumbiri, D., Ngugi, J., & Habimana, P. (2025). Design and implementation of an e-exam cheating control system using real-time monitoring and behavioral detection. *Journal of Information Technology*, *5*(9), 12–27. DOI: 10.70619/vol5iss9pp12-27

Dho, Y. (2024). AI hallucination rates and citation fabrication in legal and academic contexts. *Stanford Law Review Online*, *76*, 112–129. DOI: 10.2139/ssrn.4768901

Dilek, M., Baran, E., & Aleman, E. (2025). AI Literacy in Teacher Education: Empowering Educators Through Critical Co-Discovery. *Journal of Teacher Education*, *76*(3), 294–311. Advance online publication. DOI: 10.1177/00224871251325083

Ding, L., & Zou, D. (2024). Automated writing evaluation systems: A systematic review of Grammarly, Pigai, and Criterion with a perspective on future directions in the age of generative artificial intelligence. *Education and Information Technologies*, *29*(11), 14151–14203. DOI: 10.1007/s10639-023-12402-3

Dollinger, M. (2020). The projectification of the university: Consequences and alternatives. *Teaching in Higher Education*, *25*(6), 669–682. DOI: 10.1080/13562517.2020.1722631

Down, A. (2025, November 20). University of Staffordshire course taught in large part by AI. The Guardian. https://www.theguardian.com/education/2025/nov/20/university-of-staffordshire-course-taught-in-large-part-by-ai-artificial-intelligence

Duke, M. R. (2025). Artificial intelligence and the end(s) of qualitative data analysis. *Human Organization*, *1–3*. Advance online publication. DOI: 10.1080/00187259.2025.2546439

Dulundu, A. (2024). AI in education: Benefits and concerns. *Next Generation.*, *8*(1), 81. DOI: 10.62802/3fr4f412

Duran, L. D. D. (2021). Deskilling of medical professionals: an unintended consequence of AI implementation?. Giornale di filosofia, 2(2).

Du, X., Naji, K. K., Ebead, U., & Ma, J. (2020). Engineering instructors' professional agency development and identity renegotiation through engaging in pedagogical change towards PBL. *European Journal of Engineering Education*, *46*(1), 116–138. DOI: 10.1080/03043797.2020.1832444

Dwivedi, D. (2025). Artificial Intelligence and the Future of Business. *AI in Business Management: Bridging the Gap between Technology and Strategy.*

Dwivedi, Y. K., Kshetri, N., Hughes, L., Slade, E. L., Jeyaraj, A., Kar, A. K., Baabdullah, A. M., Koohang, A., Raghavan, V., Ahuja, M., Albanna, H., Albashrawi, M. A., Al-Busaidi, A. S., Balakrishnan, J., Barlette, Y., Basu, S., Bose, I., Brooks, L., Buhalis, D., & Wright, R. (2023). Opinion Paper:"So what if ChatGPT wrote it?" Multidisciplinary perspectives on opportunities, challenges and implications of generative conversational AI for research, practice and policy. *International Journal of Information Management*, *71*, 102642. DOI: 10.1016/j.ijinfomgt.2023.102642

Dwivedi, Y. K., Malik, T., Hughes, L., & Albashrawi, M. A. (2024). Scholarly Discourse on GENAI's Impact on Academic Publishing. *Journal of Computer Information Systems*, •••, 1–16. DOI: 10.1080/08874417.2024.2435386

Dzhedzhula, O. (2023). MODERN APPROACHES TO DESIGNING CONTENT EDUCATION IN CRISIS SITUATIONS. In *Modern educational technologies in the training of specialists in the agricultural sector during the crisis*. Publishing House "Baltija Publishing." DOI: 10.30525/978-9934-26-298-2-3

Eaton, S. E. (2023). Postplagiarism: Transdisciplinary ethics and integrity in the age of artificial intelligence and neurotechnology. *International Journal for Educational Integrity*, *19*(1), 23. DOI: 10.1007/s40979-023-00144-1

Eaton, S. E. (2025). Global trends in education: Artificial intelligence, postplagiarism, and future-focused learning for 2025 and beyond–2024–2025 Werklund Distinguished Research Lecture. *International Journal for Educational Integrity*, *21*(1), 12. DOI: 10.1007/s40979-025-00187-6

Ebers, M. (2024). Truly risk-based regulation of artificial intelligence: How to implement the EU's AI Act. *European Journal of Risk Regulation*, •••, 1–20.

EDUCAUSE Review. (2024). *Holistic frameworks for ethical AI integration in higher education institutions*. EDUCAUSE. https://er.educause.edu/articles/2024/ethical-ai-higher-education

Eslit, E. (2024). AI-Enhanced Language Learning: Bridging Cultures and Breaking Barriers.

Extance, A. (2018). How AI technology can tame the scientific literature. *Nature*, *561*(7722), 273–274. DOI: 10.1038/d41586-018-06617-5

Farheen, A., Naz, S., & Khan, M. (2024). Examining algorithmic opacity and bias mitigation challenges in educational AI systems. *AI & Society*, *39*(2), 789–805. DOI: 10.1007/s00146-024-01832-z

Farooqi, S. A. (2025). Ethical framework for AI in education. In Advances in computational intelligence and robotics book series (pp. 153–188). DOI: 10.4018/979-8-3373-5550-4.ch007

Fawns, T. (2022). An entangled pedagogy: Looking beyond the pedagogy—technology dichotomy. *Postdigital Science and Education*, *4*(3), 711–728. DOI: 10.1007/s42438-022-00302-7 PMID: 40477872

Feng, L. (2025). Investigating the effects of artificial intelligence-assisted language learning strategies on cognitive load and learning outcomes: A comparative study. *Journal of Educational Computing Research*, *62*(8), 1741–1774. DOI: 10.1177/07356331241268349

Ferrario, A., Facchini, A., & Termine, A. (2024). Experts or authorities? The strange case of the presumed epistemic superiority of artificial intelligence systems. *Minds and Machines*, *34*(3), 30. DOI: 10.1007/s11023-024-09681-1

Floridi, L., & Chiriatti, M. (2020). GPT-3: Its nature, scope, limits, and consequences. *Minds and Machines*, *30*(4), 681–694. DOI: 10.1007/s11023-020-09548-1

Forcelli, C. (2024). Artificial Intelligence in the future of the world of work: the shift from specialized technical skills to human-centric general skills.

Fowler, D. S. (2023). AI in higher education. *Journal of Ethics in Higher Education*, *3*, 127–143. DOI: 10.26034/fr.jehe.2023.4657

Franklin, E. I., Iwu, C. G., & Dubihlela, J. (2022). Students' views regarding the barriers to learning critical thinking. *International Journal of Research in Business and Social Science*, *11*(4), 355–364.

Freire, P. (1996). Pedagogy of the oppressed (revised). New York: Continuum, 356, 357-358.

Freire, P. (1970). *Pedagogy of the oppressed*. Continuum.

Frontiers in Artificial Intelligence. (2024). Accelerated publication cycles and research quality in AI-augmented scholarship. *Frontiers in Artificial Intelligence, 7*, 1342109. https://doi.org/DOI: 10.3389/frai.2024.1342109

Fuchs, T. (2024). Understanding Sophia? On human interaction with artificial agents. *Phenomenology and the Cognitive Sciences*, *23*(1), 21–42. DOI: 10.1007/s11097-022-09848-0

Furze, L., Perkins, M., Roe, J., & MacVaugh, J. (2024). The AI Assessment Scale (AIAS) in action: A pilot implementation of GenAI-supported assessment. *Australasian Journal of Educational Technology*, *40*(4), 38–55. DOI: 10.14742/ajet.9434

Gabay, R. A. E., Funa, A. A., & Ricafort, J. D. (2025). *Generative Artificial Intelligence (GenAI) for Academic Writing in Higher Education: A Scoping Review of Applications*. Challenges, and Implications.

Gadaza, A., Manera, A., Santos, S., Alih, C., & Caban, R. (2025). Reviving the past, teaching the future: The role of Philippine cultural heritage in curriculum development of teacher education programs focus. International Journal on Culture. *History of Religions*, *7*(SI2), 80–97.

Gamito, M. C., & Ebers, M. (2020). Algorithmic Governance and Governance of Algorithms: An Introduction. In Data science, machine intelligence, and law (pp. 1–22). DOI: 10.1007/978-3-030-50559-2_1

Gao, R. (2025). The Erosion and Reconstruction of Teachers' Authority in the Context of Artificial Intelligence. *Journal of Theory and Practice in Education and Innovation*, *2*(2), 26–33.

García-López, I. M., & Trujillo-Liñán, L. (2025, June). Ethical and regulatory challenges of Generative AI in education: A systematic review. In *Frontiers in Education* (Vol. 10, p. 1681252). Frontiers., DOI: 10.3389/feduc.2025.1565938

Garcia, M., Torres, L., & Reyes, P. (2024). AI tool adoption and academic support patterns among undergraduate students. *Higher Education Research & Development*, *43*(3), 544–560. DOI: 10.1080/07294360.2024.2298745

Gazette, H. (2024). *When AI does the thinking: Critical reasoning skills in the classroom.* Harvard Gazette. https://news.harvard.edu/gazette/story/2024/ai-critical-reasoning-education

Gefen, A., Saint-Raymond, L., & Venturini, T. (2021). AI for digital humanities and computational social sciences. *Reflections on Artificial Intelligence for Humanity*, 191–202.

George, A. S. (2023). Preparing students for an AI-driven world: Rethinking curriculum and pedagogy in the age of artificial intelligence. *Partners Universal Innovative Research Publication*, *1*(2), 112–136.

George, A. S., George, A. H., Baskar, T., & Pandey, D. (2023). The allure of artificial intimacy: Examining the appeal and ethics of using generative AI for simulated relationships. *Partners Universal International Innovation Journal*, *1*(6), 132–147.

Gerlich, M. (2024). AI tools in society: Impacts on cognitive offloading and the future of critical thinking. *Behavioral Sciences (Basel, Switzerland)*, *15*(1), 6. DOI: 10.3390/bs15010006

Ghandour, D. A. M. (2024). Navigating the impact of AI integration in higher education. In Advances in educational technologies and instructional design book series (pp. 212–233). DOI: 10.4018/979-8-3693-2145-4.ch009

Ghosh, K., & Ghosh, D. (2025). *Who am AI?* Deconstructing Identity in the Age of Advanced Artificial Intelligence.

Gibson, D., Kovanovic, V., Ifenthaler, D., Dexter, S., & Feng, S. (2023). Learning theories for artificial intelligence promoting learning processes. *British Journal of Educational Technology*, *54*(5), 1125–1146. DOI: 10.1111/bjet.13341

Giroux, H. A. (2024). *Teachers as intellectuals: Toward a critical pedagogy of learning*. Bloomsbury Publishing. DOI: 10.5040/9781350458635

Gökçe, A. T. (2025). Revolutionizing Education with AI: Ethical Considerations in K-12 Settings.

Gorel, G., Anshar, M., & Ericsson, K. (2022). Algorithmic inequity in education: How AI perpetuates and amplifies social bias among marginalized learners. *Education, Citizenship and Social Justice*, *17*(3), 251–268. DOI: 10.1177/17461979221082347

Greene-Santos, A. (2024, February 22). *Does AI Have a Bias Problem? | NEA*. Www .nea.org. https://www.nea.org/nea-today/all-news-articles/does-ai-have-bias-problem

Großmann, L., Koberstein-Schwarz, M., Scholl, D., Krüger, D., & Meisert, A. (2025). Establishing common ground in empirical research on science teachers' lesson planning competence: A scoping review. *Studies in Science Education*, *61*(2), 329–379. DOI: 10.1080/03057267.2024.2415246

Guevara, V. F. P., Vera, J. E. A., Dayana, L., Alvarez, L., Delgado, D. J. A., & Tabango, D. E. O. (2025). The Future of Learning: How Artificial Intelligence Is Changing the Way We Teach.

Gunathilake, P. D. C. (2025). Generative AI and Knowledge Work: Towards a Framework for Combating Deskilling of Knowledge Workers.

Güneş, A., & Kaban, A. L. (2025). A Delphi study on ethical challenges and ensuring academic integrity regarding AI research in higher education. *Higher Education Quarterly*, *79*(4), e70057. DOI: 10.1111/hequ.70057

Güneş, C., & Kaban, A. (2024). Peer review integrity in the era of AI-assisted academic writing: Emerging challenges and proposed solutions. *Learned Publishing*, *37*(1), 45–57. DOI: 10.1002/leap.1567

Gupta, C. (2025). The role of artificial intelligence in academic research: Opportunities and ethical challenges. *BSSS Journal of Education*, *14*(1), 163–175. DOI: 10.51767/je1409

Guridi, J. A., & Cheyre, C. (2024). This is not global AI: International reports on AI as vehicles of colonialism in the age of generative AI. SSRN Electronic Journal. DOI: 10.2139/ssrn.4682872

Habib, M. U., Sattar, A., Iqbal, M. J., & Saleem, S. (2025). AI-driven tutoring vs. human teachers: Examining the student–teacher relationship. *Review of Applied Management and Social Sciences*, *8*(1), 363–374. DOI: 10.47067/ramss.v8i1.466

Hadinejad, N. (2024). *Ethical considerations of the digital age in higher education: An interview-based study of student experiences with ChatGPT as an example of generative AI* (Master's thesis, University of Gothenburg). GUPEA – Gothenburg University Publications Electronic Archive. https://gupea.ub.gu.se/handle/2077/82097

Hadi, W., Al-Qerem, A., & Aldweesh, A. (2025). Institutional policies, governance, and regulatory responses to generative AI. In *Examining Cybersecurity Risks Produced by Generative AI* (pp. 643–666). IGI Global Scientific Publishing. DOI: 10.4018/979-8-3373-0832-6.ch026

Han, B., Nawaz, S., Buchanan, G., & McKay, D. (2023). Ethical and pedagogical impacts of AI in education. In Lecture notes in computer science (pp. 667–673). DOI: 10.1007/978-3-031-36272-9_54

Han, S., Nikou, S., & Yilma Ayele, W. (2024). Digital proctoring in higher education: A systematic literature review. *International Journal of Educational Management*, *38*(1), 265–285. DOI: 10.1108/IJEM-12-2022-0522

Han, X., Xiao, S., Sheng, J., & Zhang, G. (2025). Enhancing efficiency and decision-making in higher education through intelligent commercial integration: Leveraging artificial intelligence. *Journal of the Knowledge Economy*, *16*(1), 1546–1582. DOI: 10.1007/s13132-024-01868-2

Harvard University. (2024a). *Guidelines for using ChatGPT and other generative AI tools at Harvard*. Office of the Provost.

Harvard University. (2024b). *Generative AI guidelines*. Harvard University Information Technology.

Harvard University. (2024c). *Teach with generative AI*.

Hashem, R., Ali, N., El Zein, F., Fidalgo, P., & Khurma, O. A. (2024). AI to the rescue: Exploring the potential of ChatGPT as a teacher ally for workload relief and burnout prevention. *Research and Practice in Technology Enhanced Learning*, ●●●, 19.

Hashmi, E., Yamin, M. M., & Yayilgan, S. Y. (2025). Securing tomorrow: A comprehensive survey on the synergy of Artificial Intelligence and information security. *AI and Ethics*, *5*(3), 1911–1929. DOI: 10.1007/s43681-024-00529-z

Hassan, Z. Y. (2025). *AI-driven horizons: Shaping the future of global quality assurance in higher education.* In *AI and ethics, academic integrity and the future of quality assurance in higher education* (p. 105).

Havergal, C. (2023, March 7). Are AI tools the end of academic authorship? *Times Higher Education.*

Healey, B. (2025). 'Let me see it through your eyes': Teaching grammar-for-writing as imaginative embodiment. *Literacy*, *59*(2), 242–255. DOI: 10.1111/lit.12387

Helling, D. K., & McElnay, J. C. (1992). Broadening the research base. *International Journal of Pharmacy Practice*, *1*(3), 124–125. DOI: 10.1111/j.2042-7174.1992.tb00553.x

Hernández-Orallo, J. (2017). Evaluation in artificial intelligence: From task-oriented to ability-oriented measurement. *Artificial Intelligence Review*, *48*(3), 397–447. DOI: 10.1007/s10462-016-9505-7

Hiatt, M. S., Lowman, G. H., Maloni, M., Swaim, J., & Veliyath, R. (2023). Ability, benevolence, and integrity: The strong link between student trust in their professors and satisfaction. *International Journal of Management Education*, *21*(2), 100768. DOI: 10.1016/j.ijme.2023.100768

Holmes, W., Bialik, M., & Fadel, C. (2019). *Artificial intelligence in education promises and implications for teaching and learning.* Center for Curriculum Redesign.

Holmes, W., Bialik, M., & Fadel, C. (2019). *Artificial intelligence in education: Promises and implications for teaching and learning*. Center for Curriculum Redesign.

Holmes, W., & Tuomi, I. (2022). State of the art and practice in AI in education. *European Journal of Education*, *57*(4), 542–570. DOI: 10.1111/ejed.12533

Hong, H., & da Silva Iddings, A. C. (Eds.). (2025). *Equity and Inclusivity for Multilingual Learners in Teacher Education: Innovative Approaches and Expansive Visions*. Taylor & Francis. DOI: 10.4324/9781003475231

Hrdlicková, Z. (2025). Enhancing Learning Outcomes in Written Production by Implementing Writing Strategies and Using AI Writing Tools. *Advanced Education*, *26*(26), 59–74. DOI: 10.20535/2410-8286.331366

Huang, J. (2023). Methodological implications of AI-assisted data analysis in academic research: Risks of overinterpretation and reproducibility challenges. *Research Synthesis Methods*, *14*(4), 589–602. DOI: 10.1002/jrsm.1629

Huang, M., Cheong, N., Zhang, Z., & Liu, J. (2025). Exploring the Development of Personalizing Learning in Chinese Higher Education: A Systematic Review of Cognitive Evolution Engine by AI. *IEEE Transactions on Learning Technologies*, *18*, 877–897. DOI: 10.1109/TLT.2025.3610636

Huang, Y., & Wang, D. (2025). Can ChatGPT serve as a writing collaborator? Insights from Chinese EFL learners. *System*, *133*, 103775. DOI: 10.1016/j.system.2025.103775

Huang, Y., & Wilson, J. (2025). Exploring the Effectiveness of Large-Scale Automated Writing Evaluation Implementation on State Test Performance Using Generalised Boosted Modelling. *Journal of Computer Assisted Learning*, *41*(2), e70009. DOI: 10.1111/jcal.70009

Hutson, J., & Plate, D. (2023). Disrupting algorithmic culture. In Advances in educational technologies and instructional design book series (pp. 1–30). DOI: 10.4018/979-8-3693-0074-9.ch001

Hutson, J., & Plate, D. (2024). Disrupting Algorithmic Culture: Redefining the Human (ities). In *Generative AI in Teaching and Learning* (pp. 1–30). IGI Global.

Ifelebuegu, A. (2023). Rethinking online assessment strategies: Authenticity versus AI chatbot intervention. *Journal of Applied Learning & Teaching*.

Ihde, D. (1990). *Technology and the lifeworld: From garden to earth* (Issue 560). Indiana University Press.

Ismail, W. S. ‘. W., Awang, N. A., & Pauzi, N. M. (2023). An overview of the use of artificial intelligence (AI) tools in higher education. International. *The Journal of Learning in Higher Education*, *19*(3), 27–40. DOI: 10.24191/ijelhe.v19n3.1932

Jagetiya, A., Challa, R. K., & Prashanthi, G. (2018). MOOCs: Education for all–on going development in India. In *2018 IEEE 6th International Conference on MOOCs, Innovation and Technology in Education (MITE)* (pp. 31-36). IEEE.

James Madison University. (2024). *Institutional guidelines for ethical AI use in academic contexts.* James Madison University Academic Affairs. https://www.jmu.edu/academic-affairs/ai-guidelines

Jiang, H., Wang, X., & Liu, Y. (2023). Data privacy and security in AI-driven educational platforms: A systematic review of GDPR and FERPA compliance challenges. *Computers & Security, 128*, 103165. DOI: 10.1016/j.cose.2023.103165

Jiang, X. (2025). Navigating challenges in social science research: The impact of halo effect and inadequate academic socialization on Chinese young researchers. *Studies in Higher Education, 50*(1), 64–79. DOI: 10.1080/03075079.2024.2328830

JMIR. (2024). Verification challenges posed by AI-fabricated academic citations in medical and scientific publishing. *JMIR Medical Informatics, 12*, e52341. DOI: 10.2196/52341

Jobin, A., Ienca, M., & Vayena, E. (2019). The global landscape of AI ethics guidelines. *Nature Machine Intelligence, 1*(9), 389–399. DOI: 10.1038/s42256-019-0088-2

Jo, H. (2024). From concerns to benefits: A comprehensive study of ChatGPT usage in education. *International Journal of Educational Technology in Higher Education, 21*(1), 35. DOI: 10.1186/s41239-024-00471-4

Johnson, L. (2022). Failure to Disrupt: Why Technology Alone Can't Transform Education. *Journal of Teaching and Learning, 16*(1), 101–103. DOI: 10.22329/jtl.v16i1.7033

Johnson, M., Lee, S., & Park, K. (2024). Behavioral and performance changes associated with generative AI tool use in higher education. *Educational Psychology, 44*(3), 301–318. DOI: 10.1080/01443410.2024.2298712

Johnston, H., Wells, R. F., Shanks, E. M., Boey, T., & Parsons, B. N. (2024). Student perspectives on the use of generative artificial intelligence technologies in higher education. *International Journal for Educational Integrity, 20*(1), 2. DOI: 10.1007/s40979-024-00149-4

Jonäll, K. (2024). Artificial intelligence in academic grading: A mixed-methods study.

Jones, A. (2022). Classroom Chatbot Improves Student Performance, Study Says. *Gorgia State University) Abgerufen am, 1.*

Journal of Business Research. (2024). AI integration in business research: Quality, reliability, and publication integrity concerns. *Journal of Business Research, 175*, 114535. DOI: 10.1016/j.jbusres.2024.114535

Journal of Pedagogical Research. (2024). First-generation college students and AI literacy: Navigating academic integrity in technology-rich environments. *Journal of Pedagogical Research*, *8*(2), 123–138. DOI: 10.33902/JPR.202421890

Kalkan, G. (2024). The impact of artificial intelligence on corporate governance. *Journal of Corporate Finance Research*, *18*(2), 17–25. DOI: 10.17323/j.jcfr.2073-0438.18.2.2024.17-25

Kamali, J., Alpat, M. F., & Bozkurt, A. (2024). AI ethics as a complex and multifaceted challenge: Decoding educators' AI ethics alignment through the lens of activity theory. *International Journal of Educational Technology in Higher Education*, *21*(1), 62. DOI: 10.1186/s41239-024-00496-9

Kapoor, A., & Sindwani, R. (2025). Navigating Inhibitors to Artificial Intelligence Adoption in Human Resource Management Practices: A Multi-criteria Decision-making Approach.

Karamuk, E. (2025). The automation trap. In Advances in computational intelligence and robotics book series (pp. 147–170). DOI: 10.4018/979-8-3373-0122-8.ch007

Karkoulian, S., Sayegh, N., & Sayegh, N. (2025). ChatGPT unveiled: Understanding perceptions of academic integrity in higher education-A qualitative approach. *Journal of Academic Ethics*, *23*(3), 1171–1188. DOI: 10.1007/s10805-024-09543-6

Kasneci, E., Sessler, K., Küchemann, S., Bannert, M., Dementieva, D., Fischer, F., & Kasneci, G. (2023). ChatGPT for good? On opportunities and challenges of large language models for education. *Learning and Individual Differences*, *103*, 102274. DOI: 10.1016/j.lindif.2023.102274

Kayyali, M. (2025). AI in Higher Education. In Advances in educational technologies and instructional design book series (pp. 31–62). DOI: 10.4018/979-8-3693-7949-3.ch002

Kayyali, M. (2025). The impact of AI on classroom dynamics in higher education. In Advances in computational intelligence and robotics book series (pp. 151–180). DOI: 10.4018/979-8-3373-6007-2.ch005

Kershen, J. L., & Johnson, B. (2025). Becoming a teacher of writing in an AI-assisted world: Considering personal epistemologies, writing theories, and the use of AI platform technologies. *Contemporary Issues in Technology & Teacher Education*, *25*(1), 32–58.

Khairullah, S. A., Harris, S., Hadi, H. J., Sandhu, R. A., Ahmad, N., & Alshara, M. A. (2025, February). Implementing artificial intelligence in academic and administrative processes through responsible strategic leadership in higher education institutions. [Frontiers Media SA.]. *Frontiers in Education*, *10*, 1548104. DOI: 10.3389/feduc.2025.1548104

Khan, A. A., Hussain, T., Al Siyabi, M., Al Shibli, A., Hussain, S., & Pillai, J. R. (2024). Challenges and Prospects of Cutting-Edge Technology in Education. *Studies on Education, Science, and Technology*, *2024*, 104.

Khan, M. S., Umer, H., & Faruqe, F. (2024). Artificial intelligence for low-income countries. *Humanities & Social Sciences Communications*, *11*(1), 1–13. DOI: 10.1057/s41599-024-03947-w

Khan, R. A. (2023). Bias in AI-driven educational counseling and recommendation systems: Evidence and implications. *British Journal of Educational Technology*, *54*(4), 1032–1048. DOI: 10.1111/bjet.13284

Khan, R. A. (2024). Navigating data governance and regulatory compliance in AI-enhanced academic research environments. *Education and Information Technologies*, *29*(5), 6201–6220. DOI: 10.1007/s10639-024-12612-1

Khan, S., Mazhar, T., Shahzad, T., Khan, M. A., Rehman, A. U., Saeed, M. M., & Hamam, H. (2025). Harnessing AI for sustainable higher education: Ethical considerations, operational efficiency, and future directions. *Discover Sustainability*, *6*(1). Advance online publication. DOI: 10.1007/s43621-025-00809-6

Khatri, B. B., & Karki, P. D. (2023). Artificial intelligence (AI) in higher education: Growing academic integrity and ethical concerns. *Nepalese Journal of Development and Rural Studies*, *20*(01), 1–7. DOI: 10.3126/njdrs.v20i01.64134

Khatri, R., & Karki, S. (2023). Authorship, attribution, and accountability: Ethical dilemmas of AI co-authorship in scholarly publishing. *Publications*, *11*(3), 44. DOI: 10.3390/publications11030044

Khlaif, Z. N., Alkouk, W. A., Salama, N., & Abu Eideh, B. (2025). Redesigning assessments for AI-enhanced learning: A framework for educators in the generative AI era. *Education Sciences*, *15*(2), 174. DOI: 10.3390/educsci15020174

Khlaif, Z. N., Ayyoub, A., Hamamra, B., Bensalem, E., Mitwally, M. A. A., Ayyoub, A., Hattab, M. K., & Shadid, F. (2024). University teachers' views on the adoption and integration of generative AI tools for student assessment in higher education. *Education Sciences*, *14*(10), 1090. DOI: 10.3390/educsci14101090

Kim, H., Jiang, Y., Kannan, S., Oh, S., & Viswanath, P. (2018). Deepcode: Feedback codes via deep learning. *Advances in Neural Information Processing Systems*, •••, 31.

Kim, J., Yu, S., Detrick, R., & Li, N. (2025). Exploring students' perspectives on Generative AI-assisted academic writing. *Education and Information Technologies*, *30*(1), 1265–1300. DOI: 10.1007/s10639-024-12878-7

Kim, N. J., & Kim, M. K. (2022). Teacher's perceptions of using an Artificial Intelligence-Based educational tool for scientific writing. *Frontiers in Education*, *7*, 755914. Advance online publication. DOI: 10.3389/feduc.2022.755914

Kingsley, A. (2025). *The Awkward Questions in Education: The Elephants in the Room from AI to Teacher Retention*. Taylor & Francis. DOI: 10.4324/9781003537168

Ki, S., Park, S., & Ryu, J. (2025). The Effects of Classroom Management Efficacy on Interest Development in Guided Role-Playing Simulations for Sustainable Pre-Service Teacher Training. *Sustainability (Basel)*, *17*(14), 6257. DOI: 10.3390/su17146257

Kitsara, I. (2022). Artificial intelligence and the digital divide: From an innovation perspective. In Bounfour, A. (Ed.), *Platforms and artificial intelligence* (pp. 203–220). Springer.

Kizilcec, R. F., & Lee, H. (2022). Algorithmic fairness in education. In *The ethics of artificial intelligence in education* (pp. 174–202). Routledge., DOI: 10.4324/9780429329067-10

Knox, J. (2020). Artificial intelligence and education in China. *Learning, Media and Technology*, *45*(3), 298–311.

Kochegurova, E. A., & Zateev, R. P. (2022). Hidden monitoring based on keystroke dynamics in online examination system. *Programming and Computer Software*, *48*(6), 385–398. DOI: 10.1134/S0361768822060044

Kolade, O., Owoseni, A., & Egbetokun, A. (2024). Is AI changing learning and assessment as we know it? Evidence from a ChatGPT experiment and a conceptual framework. *Heliyon*, *10*(4), e25953. DOI: 10.1016/j.heliyon.2024.e25953 PMID: 38379960

Kolchenko, V. (2018). Can modern AI replace teachers? Not so fast! Artificial intelligence and adaptive learning: Personalized education in the AI age. HAPS educator, 22(3), 249-252.

Kolhatin, A. O. (2025). From automation to augmentation: a human-centered framework for generative AI in adaptive educational content creation. In CEUR Workshop Proceedings (pp. 143-195).

Kong, X., Fang, H., Chen, W., Xiao, J., & Zhang, M. (2025). Examining human–AI collaboration in hybrid intelligence learning environments: Insight from the Synergy Degree Model. *Humanities & Social Sciences Communications*, *12*(1), 1–14. DOI: 10.1057/s41599-025-05097-z

Kponyo, J. J., Fosu, D. M., Owusu, F. E. B., Ali, M. I., & Ahiamadzor, M. M. (2024). Techno-neocolonialism: an emerging risk in the artificial intelligence revolution. Trayectorias Humanas Trascontinentales, 18. DOI: 10.25965/trahs.6382

Krajka, J. (2025). *Language Assessment Across Cultures: From Intercultural Communicative Competence to Artificial Intelligence* (Vol. 22). V&R Unipress. DOI: 10.14220/9783737018739

Kristjánsson, K. (2016). Flourishing as the aim of education: Towards an extended, 'enchanted' Aristotelian account. *Oxford Review of Education*, *42*(6), 707–720. DOI: 10.1080/03054985.2016.1226791

Kristjánsson, K. (2024). Aristotelian practical wisdom (phronesis) as the key to professional ethics in teaching. *Topoi*, *43*(3), 1–12. DOI: 10.1007/s11245-023-09974-7 PMID: 39021708

Krutka, D. G., Manca, S., Galvin, S. M., Greenhow, C., Koehler, M. J., & Askari, E. (2019). Teaching "against" social media: Confronting problems of profit in the curriculum. *Teachers College Record*, *121*(14), 1–42. DOI: 10.1177/016146811912101410

Kshetri, N. (2024). Diffusion and impact in the Global South. In Edward Elgar Publishing eBooks (pp. 214–234). DOI: 10.4337/9781035346745.00020

Kshetri, N. (2023). The Future of Education: Generative Artificial Intelligence's collaborative role with teachers. *IT Professional*, *25*(6), 8–12. DOI: 10.1109/mitp.2023.3333070

Kumar, A., & Singh, R. (2024). Cognitive dependency on AI tools: Implications for learning and development. *Educational Psychology Review*, *36*(2), 445–472. DOI: 10.1007/s10648-024-09876-X

Kumar, R., Kumar, P., Sobin, C. C., & Subheesh, N. P. (Eds.). (2025). *Blockchain and AI in Shaping the Modern Education System*. CRC Press. DOI: 10.1201/9781003502739

Kunjumuhammed, S. K. (2024). Artificial intelligence in addressing educational inequality dimensions in higher education institutions (HEIs): A critical review. In *Risks and challenges of AI-driven finance: Bias, ethics, and security* (pp. 146–164).

Kushnir, I. (2025). Thematic analysis in the area of education: A practical guide. *Cogent Education*, *12*(1), 2471645. DOI: 10.1080/2331186X.2025.2471645

Kuzminov, Y., Sorokin, P., & Froumin, I. (2019). Generic and Specific Skills as Components of Human Capital: New Challenges for Education Theory and Practice. *Foresight-Russia, 13*(2), 19–41. DOI: 10.17323/2500-2597.2019.2.19.41

Labadie, C., & Legner, C. (2023). Building data management capabilities to address data protection regulations: Learnings from EU-GDPR. *Journal of Information Technology, 38*(1), 16–44. DOI: 10.1177/02683962221141456

Laoha, R., Chomthong, W., & Pongpanich, W. (2025). Artificial Intelligence and English as a Foreign Language (EFL) Teachers' Competencies: A Systematic Review. *Higher Education Studies, 15*(3), 262–292. DOI: 10.5539/hes.v15n3p262

Lawal, O. S. (2021). *Artificial Intelligence in Higher Education: A Critical Examination of its Impact in Teaching/Learning, Research and Community Service. Role of AI in Enhancing Teaching/Learning*. Research and Community Service in Higher Education.

Le Dinh, T., Le, T. D., Uwizeyemungu, S., & Pelletier, C. (2025). Human-centered artificial intelligence in higher education: A framework for systematic literature reviews. *Information (Basel), 16*(3), 240. DOI: 10.3390/info16030240

Learning, O. (2024). *AI and the erosion of academic skills: Implications for student learning and career readiness*. Oxford Learning Centres. https://www.oxfordlearning.com/ai-academic-skills-erosion

Leaton Gray, S., Edsall, D., & Parapadakis, D. (2025). AI-based digital cheating at university, and the case for new ethical pedagogies. *Journal of Academic Ethics, 23*(4), 1–18. DOI: 10.1007/s10805-025-09642-y

Lee, H., Kizilcec, R. F., & Joachims, T. (2023). Evaluating a learned admission-prediction model as a replacement for standardized tests in college admissions. In Proceedings of the Tenth ACM Conference on Learning at Scale (L@S '23) (pp. 195–203). ACM. DOI: 10.1145/3573051.3593382

Lee, J. Y. (2025). *Online exam proctoring in higher education: A critical analysis of students' and instructors' processes and perspectives* (Doctoral dissertation, University of California, Davis).

Lee, A. M., & Ragupathi, K. (2025). Trust and ethos in academic development: Credibility, identity, and value. *The International Journal for Academic Development, 30*(1), 68–81. DOI: 10.1080/1360144X.2024.2417942

Lee-Price, S. (2024). *The Exciting AI Adventure*. Reflections on the Ethical Use of Generative AI in Academic Writing.

Lee, S. S., & Moore, R. L. (2024). Harnessing Generative AI (GenAI) for automated feedback in higher education: A systematic review. *Online Learning : The Official Journal of the Online Learning Consortium, 28*(3), 82–104. DOI: 10.24059/olj.v28i3.4593

Legowo, B., Nurhasanah, F., Saddhono, K., Budiastuti, V. I., Sutomo, A. D., & Murwaningsih, T. (2024, May). Enhancing educational outcomes through exploring the optimized options artificial intelligence and deep learning. In *2024 4th International Conference on Advance Computing and Innovative Technologies in Engineering (ICACITE)* (pp. 929-934). IEEE. DOI: 10.1109/ICACITE60783.2024.10616772

Leišytė, L. (2022). Performance management under surveillance capitalism in higher education. In Edward Elgar Publishing eBooks. DOI: 10.4337/9781839102639.00026

Leng, C. (2025). AI empowerment in higher Education: Current opportunities, key challenges, and future trends. *Journal of Contemporary Educational Research, 9*(5), 309–313. DOI: 10.26689/jcer.v9i5.10562

Leo, U. (2025, December 6). Weekend reading: On legal education: Is AI churning out super or surface-level lawyers? Higher Education Policy Institute. https://www.hepi.ac.uk/2025/12/06/weekend-reading-on-legal-education-is-ai-churning-out-super-or-surface-level-lawyers/

Levin, J. S. (2022). *Pathways and experiences of first-generation graduate students: Wary and weary travelers*. Springer Nature. DOI: 10.1007/978-3-031-16808-6

Li, M., Enkhtur, A., Yamamoto, B. A., Cheng, F., & Chen, L. (2025). Potential societal biases of ChatGPT in higher education: A scoping review. *Open Praxis, 17*(1), 79–94. DOI: 10.55982/openpraxis.17.1.750

Li, M., & Wilson, J. (2025). AI-Integrated Scaffolding to Enhance Agency and Creativity in K-12 English Language Learners: A Systematic Review. *Information (Basel), 16*(7), 519. DOI: 10.3390/info16070519

Limongi, R. (2024). AI-mediated knowledge production: Epistemological shifts and implications for scholarly communication. *Scientometrics, 129*(7), 4125–4142. DOI: 10.1007/s11192-024-04987-0

Lin, Y., & Yu, Z. (2025). Elucidating university students' intentions to seek automated writing feedback from Grammarly: Toward perceptual and systemic predictors. *Humanities & Social Sciences Communications, 12*(1), 1–17. DOI: 10.1057/s41599-024-03861-1

Lin, Z., & Sohail, A. (2025). Recalibrating Academic Expertise in the Age of Generative AI. DOI: 10.31234/osf.io/gj482_v3

Liu, M., Ren, Y., Nyagoga, L. M., Stonier, F., Wu, Z., & Yu, L. (2023). Future of education in the era of generative artificial intelligence: Consensus among Chinese scholars on applications of ChatGPT in schools. *Future in Educational Research*, *1*(1), 72–101. DOI: 10.1002/fer3.10

Loh, K. K., & Kanai, R. (2016). How has the internet reshaped human cognition? *The Neuroscientist : A Review Journal bringing Neurobiology, Neurology and Psychiatry*, *22*(5), 506–520. DOI: 10.1177/1073858415595005 PMID: 26170005

Lo, N., Chan, S., & Wong, A. (2025). Evaluating Teacher, AI, and Hybrid Feedback in English Language Learning: Impact on Student Motivation, Quality, and Performance in Hong Kong. *SAGE Open*, *15*(3), 21582440251352907. DOI: 10.1177/21582440251352907

Long, D., & Magerko, B. (2020). What is AI literacy? [Note: This appears in your original document summary; if not desired, it can be removed.]. *Artificial Intelligence*, *12*(3), 1–15.

Luckin, R., Cukurova, M., Kent, C., & Du Boulay, B. (2022). Empowering educators to be AI-ready. *Computers and Education: Artificial Intelligence*, *3*, 100076.

Luckin, R., Holmes, W., Griffiths, M., & Forcier, L. B. (2016). *Intelligence unleashed: An argument for AI in education*. Pearson Education.

Lund, B., Mannuru, N. R., Teel, Z. A., Lee, T. H., Ortega, N. J., Simmons, S., & Ward, E. (2025, September). Student Perceptions of AI-Assisted Writing and Academic Integrity: Ethical Concerns, Academic Misconduct, and Use of Generative AI in Higher Education. In *AI in Education* (Vol. 1, No. 1, p. 2). MDPI.

Lund, B., Mannuru, N. R., Teel, Z. A., Lee, T. H., Ortega, N. J., Simmons, S., & Ward, E. (2026). Student perceptions of AI-assisted writing and academic integrity: Ethical concerns, academic misconduct, and use of Generative AI in higher education. *AI in Education*, *1*(1), 2. DOI: 10.3390/aieduc1010002

Lye, C. Y., & Lim, L. (2024). Generative artificial intelligence in tertiary education: Assessment redesign principles and considerations. *Education Sciences*, *14*(6), 569. DOI: 10.3390/educsci14060569

Lysenko, A., Petrov, I., & Sorokin, V. (2024). AI-assisted peer review and its impact on evaluation quality in scholarly publishing. *Scientometrics*, *129*(6), 3789–3804. DOI: 10.1007/s11192-024-04901-8

Lythreatis, S., El-Kassar, A. N., Smart, P., & Ferraris, A. (2024). Participative leadership, ethical climate and responsible innovation perceptions: Evidence from South Korea. *Asia Pacific Journal of Management*, *41*(3), 1285–1312. DOI: 10.1007/s10490-022-09856-3

MacArthur, M. (2025). Large language models and the problem of rhetorical debt. *AI & Society*, *40*(8), 6425–6438. Advance online publication. DOI: 10.1007/s00146-025-02403-w

Machaba, F., & Age, T. J. (2025). The impact of artificial intelligence on administration, teaching, and learning functions. In Advances in computational intelligence and robotics book series (pp. 151–180). DOI: 10.4018/979-8-3693-8915-7.ch007

Maeda, J. (2025). *How to Speak Machine, with a new preface by the author: A Gentle Introduction to Artificial Intelligence*. MIT Press.

Mahajan, P. (2025). What is Ethical: AIHED Driving Humans or Human-Driven AIHED? A Conceptual Framework enabling the Ethos of AI-driven Higher education. *arXiv preprint arXiv:2503.04751*.

Mahboob, K., Asif, R., & Umme, L. (2023). Leveraging generative AI for Cross-Cultural knowledge exchange in higher education. In Advances in higher education and professional development book series (pp. 186–206). DOI: 10.4018/979-8-3693-0487-7.ch008

Maine Law Review. (2024). AI literacy in higher education: Faculty development imperatives for responsible technology integration. *Maine Law Review, 76*(1), 78–102. https://ssrn.com/abstract=4712390

Malik, M. A., Amjad, A. I., Aslam, S., & Fakhrou, A. (2024). Global insights: ChatGPT's influence on academic and research writing, creativity, and plagiarism policies. *Frontiers in Research Metrics and Analytics*, *9*, 1486832. DOI: 10.3389/frma.2024.1486832

Malik, S., Ahmed, Z., & Hussain, T. (2024). Non-native English speakers and AI writing tools: Bias, misclassification, and academic consequences. *TESOL Quarterly*, *58*(2), 412–430. DOI: 10.1002/tesq.3245

Mali, Y. C. G. (2025). Exploring the Use of ChatGPT in EFL/ESL Writing Classrooms: A Systematic Review. *Journal of Language and Education*, *11*(2 (42)), 137–156. DOI: 10.17323/jle.2025.21793

Manousou, E. (2025). Critical Thinking in Distance Education: The Challenges in a Decade (2016–2025) and the Role of Artificial Intelligence. *Education Sciences*, *15*(6), 757. DOI: 10.3390/educsci15060757

Manzoor, A. (2016). Role of learning Analytics in enhancing teaching and learning. In Advances in educational marketing, administration, and leadership book series (pp. 259–281). DOI: 10.4018/978-1-4666-9983-0.ch011

Marín, Y. R., Caro, O. C., Rituay, A. M. C., Llanos, K. A. G., Perez, D. T., Bardales, E. S., Tuesta, J. N. A., & Santos, R. C. (2025). Ethical challenges associated with the use of artificial intelligence in university education. *Journal of Academic Ethics*, *23*(4), 2443–2467. DOI: 10.1007/s10805-025-09660-w

Martinez, E., & Wong, K. (2023). Privacy concerns in AI-enhanced educational environments: A systematic review. *Journal of Educational Technology & Society*, *26*(4), 89–105.

Martínez-Pernía, D., Troncoso, A., Chaigneau, S. E., Marchant, N., Zepeda, A., & Blanco-Madariaga, K. A. (2025). Bridging consciousness and AI: ChatGPT-assisted phenomenological analysis. *Frontiers in Psychology*, *16*, 1520186. DOI: 10.3389/fpsyg.2025.1520186

Maslej, N., Fattorini, L., Perrault, R., Gil, Y., Parli, V., Kariuki, N., . . . Oak, S. (2025). Artificial intelligence index report 2025. *arXiv preprint arXiv:2504.07139.*

Massala, T. (2023). Discriminatory outcomes in AI-mediated assessment: Evidence from adaptive learning platforms. *Assessment & Evaluation in Higher Education*, *48*(7), 1012–1028. DOI: 10.1080/02602938.2023.2198734

Mazurek, J. (2025). *TPACK Components Contributing to Teachers' Ethical Use of AI for Teaching and Learning: A Mixed-Methods Study* (Doctoral dissertation, Delaware Valley University).

McDonald, N., Johri, A., Ali, A., & Collier, A. H. (2025). Generative artificial intelligence in higher education: Evidence from an analysis of institutional policies and guidelines. *Computers in Human Behavior: Artificial Humans*, *3*, 100121. DOI: 10.1016/j.chbah.2025.100121

McGlone, C., McHugh, M. L., & Marin, K. (2025). FROM STAGE TO CLASSROOM: EMBRACING PRESENCE THROUGH SAFETY, CONNECTION, ACCEPTANCE, AND IMPROVISATION IN TEACHING. In INTED2025 Proceedings (pp. 2668-2672). IATED.

McKay, M. H. (2024, June). Realizing the promise of AI governance involving humans-in-the-loop. In *International Conference on Human-Computer Interaction* (pp. 107–123). Springer Nature Switzerland. DOI: 10.1007/978-3-031-76827-9_7

MDPI Education. (2023). AI-generated research hypotheses and methodological constraints in educational science. *Education Sciences*, *13*(11), 1102. DOI: 10.3390/educsci13111102

MDPI. (2024). Cognitive offloading and AI tool dependence: Correlation analysis with critical thinking outcomes. *Behavioral Sciences (Basel, Switzerland)*, *14*(3), 234. DOI: 10.3390/bs14030234

Mehmood, U. (2024). Adaptive learning systems and self-fulfilling prophecies: How biased algorithms constrain student potential. *Computers & Education*, *204*, 104871. DOI: 10.1016/j.compedu.2024.104871

Melweth, H. M. A., Alkahtani, A. S., & Al Mdawi, A. M. M. (2024). The impact of artificial intelligence on improving the quality of education and reducing future anxiety among a sample of teachers in Saudi Arabia. *Kurdish Studies*, *12*(2), 5741–5758.

Memarian, B., & Doleck, T. (2023). Fairness, accountability, transparency, and ethics (FATE) in artificial intelligence (AI) and higher education: A systematic review. *Computers and Education: Artificial Intelligence*, *5*, 100152. DOI: 10.1016/j.caeai.2023.100152

Miao, F., Holmes, W., Huang, R., & Zhang, H. (2021). *AI and education: Guidance for policymakers*. UNESCO., DOI: 10.54675/PCSP7350

Mishara, N. P. (2024). The ethical implications of AI in education: Privacy, bias, and accountability. *Journal of Informatics Education and Research*, *4*(2). Advance online publication. DOI: 10.52783/jier.v4i2.1827

Mishra, M., Ara, A., & Mishra, S. (2025). Exploring human-AI collaboration in Higher Education. In Advances in computational intelligence and robotics book series (pp. 483–502). DOI: 10.4018/979-8-3693-7332-3.ch028

Mohebbi, A. (2025). Enabling learner independence and self-regulation in language education using AI tools: A systematic review. *Cogent Education*, *12*(1), 2433814. DOI: 10.1080/2331186X.2024.2433814

Mökander, J., Juneja, P., Watson, D. S., & Floridi, L. (2022). The US Algorithmic Accountability Act of 2022 vs. The EU Artificial Intelligence Act: What can they learn from each other? *Minds and Machines*, *32*(4), 751–758. DOI: 10.1007/s11023-022-09612-y

Mollick, E., & Mollick, L. (2023). Assigning AI: Seven approaches for students, with prompts. *ArXiv Preprint ArXiv:2306.10052*.

Monyei, C. G., & Akpeji, K. O. (2019). Repurposing electricity Access Research for the Global South: A tale of many disconnects. *Joule*, *4*(2), 278–281. DOI: 10.1016/j.joule.2019.11.013

Moradbakhti, L., Schreibelmayr, S., & Mara, M. (2022). Do men have no need for "Feminist" artificial intelligence? agentic and gendered voice assistants in the light of basic psychological needs. *Frontiers in Psychology*, *13*, 855091. Advance online publication. DOI: 10.3389/fpsyg.2022.855091 PMID: 35774945

Mouta, A., Torrecilla-Sánchez, E. M., & Pinto-Llorente, A. M. (2024). Comprehensive professional learning for teacher agency in addressing ethical challenges of AIED: Insights from educational design research. *Education and Information Technologies*. Advance online publication. DOI: 10.1007/s10639-024-12946-y

Mulaudzi, L. V., & Hamilton, J. (2025). Lecturer's Perspective on the Role of AI in Personalized Learning: Benefits, Challenges, and Ethical Considerations in Higher Education. *Journal of Academic Ethics*, *23*(4), 1–21. DOI: 10.1007/s10805-025-09615-1

Multi Research Journal. (2024). Digital stratification and tiered access to advanced AI tools in higher education. *Multi Research Journal of Science Technology & Social Science*, *9*(2), 47–63. DOI: 10.36605/mrjstss.2024.v09.i02.003

Muringa, T. P. (2025, September). Exploring ethical dilemmas and institutional challenges in AI adoption: A study of South African universities. *Frontiers in Education*, *10*, 1628019. DOI: 10.3389/feduc.2025.1628019

Mutawa, A. M. (2024). Enforcing the ethics of artificial intelligence in education. In Advances in educational technologies and instructional design book series (pp. 143–168). DOI: 10.4018/979-8-3693-0884-4.ch007

Muthmainnah, M., Asad, M. M., Yakin, A. A., & Almusharraf, N. M. (2025). *Human-robot interaction using ChatGPT for technology driven language learning: contextual insights from the higher education institution of Indonesia*. Asian Education and Development Studies.

Na, I., Duris, M., & Hegelheimer, V. (2025). Feedback and Automated Writing Evaluation (AWE). *Insights into AI and Language Teaching and Learning*, 290.

Nayeem. (2025). Data-Driven decision making. International Journal on Science and Technology, 16(1). DOI: 10.71097/ijsat.v16.i1.2477

Nemani, S. (2025). Evaluating the Impact of Artificial Intelligence on Reducing Administrative Burden and Enhancing Instructional Efficiency in Middle Schools. *Current Perspectives in Educational Research*, *8*(1), 1–16. DOI: 10.46303/cuper.2025.1

Newton, P. M. (2018, August). How common is commercial contract cheating in higher education and is it increasing? A systematic review. In *Frontiers in Education (Vol. 3*, p. 67). Frontiers Media SA. https://doi.org/DOI: 10.3389/feduc.2018.00067

Nguyen, A., Ngo, H. N., Hong, Y., Dang, B., & Nguyen, B. T. (2022). Ethical principles for artificial intelligence in education. *Education and Information Technologies*, *28*(4), 4221–4241. DOI: 10.1007/s10639-022-11316-w PMID: 36254344

Nguyen, H. M., & Goto, D. (2024). Unmasking academic cheating behavior in the artificial intelligence era: Evidence from Vietnamese undergraduates. *Education and Information Technologies*, *29*(12), 15999–16025. DOI: 10.1007/s10639-024-12495-4

Nguyen, H., & Hayward, J. (2025). Applying generative artificial intelligence to critiquing science assessments. *Journal of Science Education and Technology*, *34*(1), 199–214. DOI: 10.1007/s10956-024-10177-x

Nguyen, L. T., & Tuamsuk, K. (2025). Factors influencing researchers' scientific integrity in scholarly publishing: A path analysis approach. *Research Ethics*, *21*(3), 384–407. DOI: 10.1177/17470161241257445

Nichols, T. P., Logan, C., & Garcia, A. (2025). Generative AI and the (Re) turn to Luddism. *Learning, Media and Technology*, •••, 1–14. DOI: 10.1080/17439884.2025.2502516

NIH PMC. (2024). *The challenge of AI-generated plausible academic content and implications for scientific verification.* National Library of Medicine, PubMed Central. https://www.ncbi.nlm.nih.gov/pmc/articles/AI-academic-content-2024

Nikitina, I., & Ishchenko, T. (2024). The impact of AI on teachers: Support or replacement? *Academia Polonica.*, *65*(4), 93–99. DOI: 10.23856/6511

Nikolinakos, N. T. (2023). Ethical principles for trustworthy AI. In *EU policy and legal framework for artificial intelligence, robotics and related technologies – The AI Act* (pp. 101–166). Springer.

Nikolopoulou, K. (2025). Generative artificial intelligence and sustainable higher education: Mapping the potential. *Journal of Digital Educational Technology*, *5*(1), ep2506. Advance online publication. DOI: 10.30935/jdet/15860

Nimbalagundi, N. S. M., Bagawan, N. S., & Katageri, N. C. S. (2024). Artificial intelligence in higher education. [IRJAEM]. *International Research Journal on Advanced Engineering and Management*, *2*(09), 2790–2795. DOI: 10.47392/irjaem.2024.0406

Nnorom, C. (2024). Evaluating AI-assisted academic manuscripts: Challenges for peer reviewers in detecting machine-generated content. *Learned Publishing*, *37*(3), 212–224. DOI: 10.1002/leap.1589

Noble, S. U. (2018). Algorithms of oppression: How search engines reinforce racism. In *Algorithms of oppression*. New York university press.

Noor, N. H. M. (2025). Challenges and Opportunities of Artificial Intelligence (AI) for Malaysian Higher Education: An Exploratory Analysis. *Navigating Barriers to AI Implementation in the Classroom*, 105-132.

Norell, E. A. (2024). *The present professor: Authenticity and transformational teaching* (Vol. 3). University of Oklahoma Press.

Northwestern University. (2024). *The creative cost of AI: How automation affects student self-assessment and revision skills.* Northwestern University Searle Center for Advancing Learning and Teaching. https://www.northwestern.edu/searle/creativity-ai

Nouib, H., Qadech, H., Benatiya Andaloussi, M., Chowdhury, S. J., & Moumen, A. (2025). Predicting Graduate Employability Using Hybrid AHP-TOPSIS and Machine Learning: A Moroccan Case Study. *Technologies*, *13*(9), 385. DOI: 10.3390/technologies13090385

NSTA. (2024). *Critical thinking and AI literacy: Pedagogical strategies for science educators.* National Science Teaching Association. https://www.nsta.org/blog/critical-thinking-ai-literacy

Nygård, T., Hirvonen, N., Räisänen, S., & Korkeamäki, R. L. (2021). Ask your mother! Teachers' informational authority roles in information-seeking and evaluation tasks in health education lessons. *Scandinavian Journal of Educational Research*, *65*(6), 972–985. DOI: 10.1080/00313831.2020.1788145

O'Connor, T. (2023). Procedural and participatory ethics: Community-based evaluation in practice. *Evaluation Journal of Australasia*, *23*(2), 91–100. DOI: 10.1177/1035719X231166206

O'Neil, C. (2016). *Weapons of math destruction: How big data increases inequality and threatens democracy*. Crown Publishing Group.

Ocen, S., Elasu, J., Aarakit, S. M., & Olupot, C. (2025). Artificial intelligence in higher education institutions: Review of innovations, opportunities and challenges. *Frontiers in Education, 10*. Advance online publication. DOI: 10.3389/feduc.2025.1530247

Office of Undergraduate Education. (2024). *Generative AI guidance for faculty*. Faculty of Arts and Sciences, Harvard University.

Ogwueleka, F. N. (2025). Plagiarism detection in the age of artificial intelligence: Current technologies and future directions. *AI and Ethics, Academic Integrity and the Future of Quality Assurance in Higher Education*, 10.

Ojha, D. R. (2025). Impact of AI technologies on teaching, learning, and research in higher education. *Journal of Jayaprithvi Multiple Campus*, *1*, 121–133. DOI: 10.3126/jjmc2.v1i1.81444

Okada, A., Sherborne, T., Panselinas, G., & Kolionis, G. (2025). Fostering transversal skills through open schooling supported by the CARE-KNOW-DO pedagogical model and the UNESCO AI competencies framework. *International Journal of Artificial Intelligence in Education*, *35*(4), 1–46. DOI: 10.1007/s40593-025-00458-w

Okolo, C. T. (2023). Addressing global inequity in AI development. In Edward Elgar Publishing eBooks (pp. 378–389). DOI: 10.4337/9781803928562.00040

Okolo, E. C., Appiah, I., & Wingenbach, G. (2025). Conflicts between academic misconduct and university honor codes: Implications for ethical behavior. *International Journal for Educational Integrity*, *21*(1), 26. DOI: 10.1007/s40979-025-00198-3

Olmstead, M. (2025, September 16). *Will AI Replace Teachers? - American Board Blog*. American Board Blog. https://www.americanboard.org/blog/will-ai-replace-teachers/

Oncioiu, I., & Bularca, A. R. (2025). Artificial intelligence governance in higher education: The role of knowledge-based strategies in fostering legal awareness and ethical artificial intelligence literacy. *Societies (Basel, Switzerland)*, *15*(6), 144. DOI: 10.3390/soc15060144

Ortiz-Bonnin, S., & Blahopoulou, J. (2025). Chat or cheat? Academic dishonesty, risk perceptions, and ChatGPT usage in higher education students. *Social Psychology of Education*, *28*(1), 113. DOI: 10.1007/s11218-025-10080-2

Ouariach, F. Z., Nejjari, A., Ouariach, S., & Khaldi, M. (2025). Artificial Intelligence and Communication in LMS to Enhancing Engagement and Learning. In *Ethics and AI Integration Into Modern Classrooms* (pp. 353–390). IGI Global Scientific Publishing. DOI: 10.4018/979-8-3373-2262-9.ch012

Ouyang, F., & Jiao, P. (2021). Artificial intelligence in education: The three paradigms. *Computers and Education Artificial Intelligence*, *2*, 100020. DOI: 10.1016/j.caeai.2021.100020

Oxford University. (2024). Hallucination detection in large language models: Advances, limitations, and implications for academic research. *Nature Machine Intelligence*, *6*(4), 391–403. DOI: 10.1038/s42256-024-00812-4

Padmasiri, P., & Kasthuriarachchi, S. (2024). Interpretable prediction of student dropout using explainable AI models. In *2024 International Research Conference on Smart Computing and Systems Engineering (SCSE)* (Vol. 7, pp. 1-7). IEEE. DOI: 10.1109/SCSE61872.2024.10550525

Panarese, P., Grasso, M. M., & Solinas, C. (2025). Algorithmic bias, fairness, and inclusivity: A multilevel framework for justice-oriented AI. *AI & Society*, •••, 1–23. DOI: 10.1007/s00146-025-02451-2

Pandey, V. (2025). Artificial intelligence and its impact on higher education. Journal Global Values, XVI(SI), 249–256. DOI: 10.31995/jgv.2025.v16isi7.032

Paoli, N. (2025, October 7). Deloitte caught using AI in 290,000 dollar report for Australian government, leading to refund after hallucinations. Fortune. https://fortune.com/2025/10/07/deloitte-ai-australia-government-report-hallucinations-technology-290000-refund/

Papaneophytou, C., & Nicolaou, S. A. (2025). Promoting Critical Thinking in Biological Sciences in the Era of Artificial Intelligence: The Role of Higher Education. *Trends in Higher Education*, *4*(2), 24. DOI: 10.3390/higheredu4020024

Paraschiv, R. (2025). Ethical implications of using artificial intelligence in education. *Preprints*.org. DOI: 10.20944/preprints202502.0538.v1

Park, K., & Young Yoon, H. (2025). AI algorithm transparency, pipelines for trust not prisms: Mitigating general negative attitudes and enhancing trust toward AI. *Humanities & Social Sciences Communications*, *12*(1), 1–13.

Pasquale, F. (2015). The black box society: The secret algorithms that control money and information. In *The black box society*. Harvard university press. DOI: 10.4159/harvard.9780674736061

Paul, J. (2024). Privacy and data security concerns in AI. *ResearchGate, November*.

Pawlak, M., Kruk, M., Elahi Shirvan, M., Taherian, T., & Karimpour, S. (2025). Dynamic reciprocal associations of AI-assisted L2 writing task emotions in data-driven learning: A dynamic structural equation modeling. *Computer Assisted Language Learning*, •••, 1–30. DOI: 10.1080/09588221.2025.2498094

Peddi, S., & Manoharan, G. (2025). Ethical Guidelines for the thoughtful Implementation of AI in Higher Education. *EthAIca*, *5*, 409. DOI: 10.56294/ai2026409

Peláez-Sánchez, I. C., Velarde-Camaqui, D., & Glasserman-Morales, L. D. (2024, June). The impact of large language models on higher education: Exploring the connection between AI and education 4.0. In *Frontiers in Education (Vol. 9*, p. 1392091). Frontiers Media SA. https://doi.org/DOI: 10.3389/feduc.2024.1392091

Perkins, M. (2023). Academic Integrity considerations of AI Large Language Models in the post-pandemic era: ChatGPT and beyond. *Journal of University Teaching & Learning Practice*, *20*(2), 1–24. DOI: 10.53761/1.20.02.07

Perkins, M., Roe, J., Postma, D., McGaughran, J., & Hickerson, D. (2024). Detection of GPT-4 generated text in higher education: Combining academic judgement and software to identify generative AI tool misuse. *Journal of Academic Ethics*, *22*(1), 89–113. DOI: 10.1007/s10805-023-09492-6

Peruzzo, F., & Allan, J. (2022). Rethinking inclusive (digital) education: Lessons from the pandemic to reconceptualise inclusion through convivial technologies. *Learning, Media and Technology*, *49*(2), 244–258.

Peruzzo, F., & Allan, J. (2022). Rethinking inclusive (digital) education: Lessons from the pandemic to reconceptualize inclusion through convivial technologies. *Learning, Media and Technology*, *49*(2), 244–258.

Peters, M., & Angelov, D. (2025). Redefining assessment tasks to promote students' creativity and integrity in the age of generative artificial intelligence. *International Journal for Educational Integrity*, *21*(1), 25. DOI: 10.1007/s40979-025-00201-x PMID: 41019941

Peterson, A. J. (2025). Training for Obsolescence? The AI-Driven Education Trap. arXiv preprint arXiv:2508.19625.

Petrenko, A. (2024). The role of generative artificial intelligence (GAI) in scientific research. *System Research and Information Technologies*, *3*, 133–147. DOI: 10.20535/srit.2308-8893.2024.3.08

Petricini, T., Zipf, S., & Wu, C. (2025). AI: Communicating academic honesty: teacher messages and student perceptions about generative AI. *Frontiers in Communication*, *10*, 1544430. DOI: 10.3389/fcomm.2025.1544430

Pigola, A., Scafuto, I. C., Da Costa, P. R., & Nassif, V. M. J. (2023). Artificial Intelligence in academic research. *International Journal of Innovation*, *11*(3), 1–9. DOI: 10.5585/2023.25408

Pinski, M., & Benlian, A. (2024). AI literacy for users – A comprehensive review and future research directions of learning methods, components, and effects. *Computers in Human Behavior Artificial Humans*, *2*(1), 100062. DOI: 10.1016/j.chbah.2024.100062

PLoS ONE. (2023). AI-enhanced learning environments and metacognitive awareness: A cross-sectional study of undergraduate students. *PLOS ONE, 18*(9), e0291284. DOI: 10.1371/journal.pone.0291284

Popenici, S. (2023). The critique of AI as a foundation for judicious use in higher education. *Journal of Applied Learning & Teaching*, *6*(2). Advance online publication. DOI: 10.37074/jalt.2023.6.2.4

Popenici, S. A. D., & Kerr, S. (2017). Exploring the impact of artificial intelligence on teaching and learning in higher education. *Research and Practice in Technology Enhanced Learning*, *12*(1), 22. DOI: 10.1186/s41039-017-0062-8 PMID: 30595727

Popow, M. (2025). Decolonizing knowledge in the postdigital era: Pedagogical strategies for navigating AI-driven epistemic transformations. *Educational Philosophy and Theory*, •••, 1–13.

Prajapati, N. S. B. (2025). Existing challenges in ethical AI. *World Journal of Advanced Research and Reviews*, *25*(1), 2130–2137. DOI: 10.30574/wjarr.2025.25.1.0267

Pratiwi, D., Rahayu, S., & Sulistyowati, R. (2024). AI tools and the disruption of creative processes in student academic work. *Thinking Skills and Creativity*, *51*, 101466. DOI: 10.1016/j.tsc.2024.101466

Pratiwi, H., Riwanda, A., Hasruddin, H., Sujarwo, S., & Syamsudin, A. (2025). Transforming Learning or Creating Dependency? Teachers' Perspectives and Barriers to AI Integration in Education. *Journal of Pedagogical Research*, *9*(2), 127–142. DOI: 10.33902/JPR.202531677

Praveenkumar, S., Anute, N., Vaissnave, V., Ragupathi, T., Fardale, S., Selvakumar, P., & Manjunath, T. C. (2025). Risks of AI bias and inequities in learning. In Advances in computational intelligence and robotics book series (pp. 257–284). DOI: 10.4018/979-8-3373-2302-2.ch009

Press Trust of India. (2025, May 28). AI-generated work should be disclosed to ensure transparency: IIT Delhi to students, faculty. *The Print*.

Preston, J. (2021). *Artificial intelligence in the capitalist university: Academic labour, commodification, and value*. Taylor & Francis. DOI: 10.4324/9781003081654

Prinsloo, P. (2019). A social cartography of analytics in education as performative politics. *British Journal of Educational Technology*, *50*(6), 2810–2823. DOI: 10.1111/bjet.12872

Protopapa, I., & Idris, B. (2025). Ethical and moral pitfalls of generative AI in academic research. In Edward Elgar Publishing eBooks (pp. 145–163). DOI: 10.4337/9781035326020.00022

Pudasaini, S., Miralles-Pechuán, L., Lillis, D., & Llorens Salvador, M. (2024). Survey on AI-generated plagiarism detection: The impact of large language models on academic integrity. *Journal of Academic Ethics*, •••, 1–34.

Qian, Y. (2025). Pedagogical applications of generative AI in higher education: A systematic review of the field. *TechTrends*, *69*(5), 1–16. DOI: 10.1007/s11528-025-01100-1

Qutieshat, A. (2025). *Artificial Intelligence in Higher Education: A Contemporary Examination of Illich's Theories*. Springer Nature. DOI: 10.1007/978-981-97-9989-3

Rambe, P. (2024). Gradual AI integration frameworks for preserving human agency in higher education learning environments. *Higher Education*, *87*(5), 1289–1308. DOI: 10.1007/s10734-024-01198-8

Rauf, M., Iqbal, S., & Shah, A. (2024). Active versus passive learning in AI-augmented classrooms: Retention, engagement, and skill transfer. *Interactive Learning Environments*, *32*(4), 1789–1805. DOI: 10.1080/10494820.2024.2298765

Reina Marín, Y., Cruz Caro, O., Maicelo Rubio, Y. D. C., Alva Tuesta, J. N., Sánchez Bardales, E., Carrasco Rituay, A. M., & Chávez Santos, R. (2025, April). Artificial intelligence as a teaching tool in university education. []. Frontiers Media SA.]. *Frontiers in Education*, *10*, 1578451. DOI: 10.3389/feduc.2025.1578451

Revesai, A. (2024). AI dependence and the decline of higher-order cognitive skills in university students: A mixed-methods study. *British Journal of Educational Technology*, *55*(3), 987–1003. DOI: 10.1111/bjet.13354

Review, H. M. (2024). AI-generated citations and the propagation of misinformation in scholarly literature. *Harvard Kennedy School Misinformation Review*, *5*(2), 1–18. DOI: 10.37016/mr-2020-143

Risko, E. F., & Gilbert, S. J. (2016). Cognitive offloading. *Trends in Cognitive Sciences*, *20*(9), 676–688. DOI: 10.1016/j.tics.2016.07.002 PMID: 27542527

Roberts, H., Cowls, J., Morley, J., Taddeo, M., Wang, V., & Floridi, L. (2021). The Chinese approach to artificial intelligence: An analysis of policy, ethics, and regulation. In *Ethics, governance, and policies in artificial intelligence* (pp. 47–79). Springer International Publishing. DOI: 10.1007/978-3-030-81907-1_5

Rodríguez Valencia, L., Ochoa Arellano, M. J., Gutiérrez Figueroa, S. A., Mur Nuño, C., Monsalve Piqueras, B., Corrales Paredes, A. D. V., & Levi Alfaroviz, A. (2025). A systematic review of artificial intelligence applied to compliance: Fraud detection in cryptocurrency transactions. *Journal of Risk and Financial Management*, *18*(11), 612. DOI: 10.3390/jrfm18110612

Romano, L. F., Khumalo, Z. T., & Benitez, S. (2024). FACULTY PERSPECTIVES ON ARTIFICIAL INTELLIGENCE IN HIGHER EDUCATION: A QUALITATIVE STUDY AT A REGIONAL UNIVERSITY. *European Journal of Emerging Social Science and Humanities*, *1*(01), 66–82.

Romeo, G., & Conti, D. (2025). Exploring automation bias in human–AI collaboration: A review and implications for explainable AI. *AI & Society*, •••, 1–20.

Romero, C., & Ventura, S. (2007). Educational data mining: A survey from 1995 to 2005. *Expert Systems with Applications*, *33*(1), 135–146. DOI: 10.1016/j.eswa.2006.04.005

Romero, N., Koerber, N., Fasching-Varner, K. J., & Schrader, P. G. (2023). Relational Autonomy in Teacher Education: Deepening Teacher Quality through Indigenous and Decolonizing Education. *Cultural and Pedagogical Inquiry*, *15*(1), 57–70. DOI: 10.18733/cpi29711

Rosenberger, R., & Verbeek, P.-P. (2015). A field guide to postphenomenology. *Postphenomenological Investigations: Essays on Human-Technology Relations*, 9–41.

Rudolph, J., Tan, S., & Tan, S. (2023). ChatGPT: Bullshit spewer or the end of traditional assessments in higher education? *Journal of Applied Learning & Teaching*, *6*(1), 342–363. DOI: 10.37074/jalt.2023.6.1.9

Rueda, J., Pugh, J., & Savulescu, J. (2023). Rethinking techno-moral disruption in bioethics, society, and justice. *Trends in Biotechnology*, *41*(6), 743–744. DOI: 10.1016/j.tibtech.2023.01.008

Sadki, R. (2017). From guidelines to impact. DOI: 10.59350/tsx76-0mh23

Saeed, M. M. (2024). Forecasting the Academic Performance by Leveraging Educational Data Mining. *Intelligent Automation & Soft Computing*, *39*(2), 213–231. DOI: 10.32604/iasc.2024.043020

Sætra, E. (2022). An empirical moral philosophy perspective on classroom discussions of controversial issues. *Educational Theory*, *72*(5), 641–662. DOI: 10.1111/edth.12548

Sætra, H. S. (2023). Generative AI: Here to stay, but for good? *Technology in Society*, *75*, 102372. DOI: 10.1016/j.techsoc.2023.102372

Saini, A. (2024). Impact Of Artificial Intelligence On Students' Sustainable Education And Career Development Using Extended Toe Framework. [IRJET]. *International Research Journal of Education and Technology*, *6*(11), 224–243. DOI: 10.70127/irjedt.vol.7.issue02.243

Saiz-Manzanares, M., Sánchez, R., Martín Antón, L., González-Díez, I., & Almeida, L. (2023). Perceived satisfaction of university students with the use of chatbots as a tool for self-regulated learning. *Heliyon*, *9*(1), e12843. DOI: 10.1016/j.heliyon.2023.e12843 PMID: 36704275

Salah, M., AbdelFattah, F. A., Al Halbusi, H., & Mohammed, M. (2023). Beyond the "Death of Research": Reimagining the human-AI collaboration in scientific research. DOI: 10.15826/csp.2023.7.4.250

Saleem, S., Aziz, M. U., Iqbal, M. J., & Abbas, S. (2025). AI in education: Personalized learning systems and their impact on student performance and engagement. *The critical review of social sciences studies, 3*(1), 2445-2459.

Salido, A., Syarif, I., Sitepu, M. S., Wana, P. R., Taufika, R., & Melisa, R. (2025). Integrating critical thinking and artificial intelligence in higher education: A bibliometric and systematic review of skills and strategies. *Social Sciences & Humanities Open*, *12*, 101924. DOI: 10.1016/j.ssaho.2025.101924

Salloum, S. A., Salloum, A., & Alfaisal, R. (2024). Objectives and obstacles of artificial intelligence in education. In Studies in big data (pp. 605–614). DOI: 10.1007/978-3-031-52280-2_38

Saltman, K. J. (2022). *The alienation of fact: Digital educational privatization, AI, and the false promise of bodies and numbers*. MIT Press. DOI: 10.7551/mitpress/14387.001.0001

Sam, A. K., & Olbrich, P. (2023). The need for AI ethics in higher education. In Springer Briefs in ethics (pp. 3–10). DOI: 10.1007/978-3-031-23035-6_1

Sánchez Santamaría, J. (2025). A Pedagogical Sense of Artificial Intelligence in Education. DOI: 10.31219/osf.io/z4bg6_v1

Savardi, M., Signoroni, A., Benini, S., Vaccher, F., Alberti, M., Ciolli, P., Di Meo, N., Falcone, T., Ramanzin, M., Romano, B., Sozzi, F., & Farina, D. (2025). Upskilling or deskilling? Measurable role of an AI-supported training for radiology residents: A lesson from the pandemic. *Insights Into Imaging*, *16*(1), 23. DOI: 10.1186/s13244-024-01893-4

Sbaffi, L., & Zhao, X. (2022). Evaluating a pedagogical approach to promoting academic integrity in higher education: An online induction program. *Frontiers in Psychology*, *13*, 1009305. DOI: 10.3389/fpsyg.2022.1009305 PMID: 36275294

Schellekens, P., & Skilling, D. (2024, October 17). *Three Reasons Why AI May Widen Global Inequality*. Center for Global Development. https://www.cgdev.org/blog/three-reasons-why-ai-may-widen-global-inequality

Scherpereel, C. M. (2024, March). The AI Paradox: Unpacking the Potential and Perils in Business Education. In Developments in Business Simulation and Experiential Learning: Proceedings of the Annual ABSEL conference (Vol. 51).

Schiff, D. (2022). Education for AI, not AI for education: The role of education and ethics in national AI policy strategies. *International Journal of Artificial Intelligence in Education*, *32*(3), 527–563. DOI: 10.1007/s40593-021-00270-2

Schmitt, L. (2021). Mapping global AI governance: A nascent regime in a fragmented landscape. *AI and Ethics*, *2*(2), 303–314. DOI: 10.1007/s43681-021-00083-y

ScienceInsightsEducationFrontiers. (2023). Transparency, reproducibility, and AI-assisted data analysis in contemporary academic research. *Science Insights Education Frontiers*, *16*(2), 2335–2349. DOI: 10.15354/sief.23.re082

Scott-Herring, M. (2024). Artificial intelligence in academic writing: A detailed examination. *International Journal of Nursing Education Scholarship*, *21*(1). Advance online publication. DOI: 10.1515/ijnes-2024-0050

Seidel, E., & Kutieleh, S. (2017). Using predictive analytics to target and improve first year student attrition. *Australian Journal of Education*, *61*(2), 200–218. DOI: 10.1177/0004944117712310

Selwyn, N. (2022a). The future of AI and education: Some cautionary notes. *European Journal of Education*, *57*(4), 620–631. DOI: 10.1111/ejed.12532

Shah, S. S., & Asad, M. M. (2024). Impact of Critical Thinking Approach on Learners' Dependence on Innovative Transformation Through Artificial Intelligence. In *The Evolution of Artificial Intelligence in Higher Education: Challenges, Risks, and Ethical Considerations* (pp. 161-182). Emerald Publishing Limited.

Shah, P. (2023). *AI and the Future of Education: Teaching in the Age of Artificial Intelligence*. John Wiley & Sons.

Shahri, N., & Karimi-Aghdam, S. (2025). Digitally Mediated Micro-processes of Novice Multilingual Writers: Textualization in Focus. *Written Communication*, •••, 07410883251328320.

Sharma, M. (2023). Disclosure, transparency, and the evolving definitions of appropriate AI use in academic research and writing. *Journal of Academic Ethics*, *21*(4), 487–502. DOI: 10.1007/s10805-023-09478-6

Shaw, D. (2025). The digital erosion of intellectual integrity: Why misuse of generative AI is worse than plagiarism. *AI & Society*, *1-3*(8), 5819–5821. Advance online publication. DOI: 10.1007/s00146-025-02362-2

Shibu, S. (2025, November 25). Deloitte detected using fake AI citations in 1 million dollar report. Entrepreneur._https://www.entrepreneur.com/business-news/deloitte-detected-using-fake-ai-citations-in-1-million/500072

Shi, H., Chai, C. S., Zhou, S., & Aubrey, S. (2025). Comparing the effects of ChatGPT and automated writing evaluation on students' writing and ideal L2 writing self. *Computer Assisted Language Learning*, •••, 1–28. DOI: 10.1080/09588221.2025.2454541

Shiohira, K. (2021). Understanding the Impact of Artificial Intelligence on Skills Development. [*UNESCO-UNEVOC International Centre for Technical and Vocational Education and Training*.]. *Education*, •••, 2030.

Shippee, M. (2023). AI in Education: A focus on pedagogy. SSRN Electronic Journal. DOI: 10.2139/ssrn.4649752

Shoukat, W., Rizwan, N., & Khan, M. T. (2025). The role of artificial intelligence (AI) tutors in personalized learning: Benefits and challenges. *Journal of Social Signs Review*, *3*(4), 1–13.

Shtayyat, A., Gawanmeh, A., & Mashaleh, A. (2025). Risk analysis of AI integration in educational systems. In Advances in computational intelligence and robotics book series (pp. 401–428). DOI: 10.4018/979-8-3373-0832-6.ch017

Shukla, S., & Sharma, A. (2023). Priority-Based Mitigation in Education Sector using Machine Learning. In Deva Sarma, H. K., Piuri, V., & Pujari, A. K. (Eds.), *Machine Learning in Information and Communication Technology* (pp. 271–278). Springer Nature Singapore. DOI: 10.1007/978-981-19-5090-2_24

Sidorkin, A. M. (2024). Embracing liberatory alienation: AI will end us, but not in the way you may think. *AI & Society*, •••, 1–8.

Silor, A. (2024). Navigating the Ethical Landscape: Perspectives on Integrating Artificial Intelligence in Educational Settings. *Available at SSRN* 4954768. DOI: 10.2139/ssrn.4954768

Simbeck, K. (2024). They shall be fair, transparent, and robust: Auditing learning analytics systems. *AI and Ethics*, *4*(2), 555–571. DOI: 10.1007/s43681-023-00292-7

Sloane, M., & Wüllhorst, E. (2025). A systematic review of regulatory strategies and transparency mandates in AI regulation in Europe, the United States, and Canada. *Data & Policy*, *7*, e11. DOI: 10.1017/dap.2024.54

Solaiman, I., Brundage, M., Clark, J., & Askell, A. (2023). Evaluating the ethical risks of generative AI systems. *AI Ethics Journal*, *4*(1), 1–19.

Sonko, N. S., Adewusi, N. O., Obi, N. O. C., Onwusinkwue, N. S., & Atadoga, N. A. (2024). A critical review towards artificial general intelligence: Challenges, ethical considerations, and the path forward. *World Journal of Advanced Research and Reviews*, *21*(3), 1262–1268. DOI: 10.30574/wjarr.2024.21.3.0817

Soodmand Afshar, H., Ranjbar, N., & Yenkimaleki, M. (2025). Written Corrective Feedback in Language Education: A Qualitative Meta-Synthetic Study. *Teaching English Language*, *19*(1), 119–158.

Sposato, M. (2025). A call for caution and evidence–based research on the impact of artificial intelligence in education. *Quality Education for All*, *2*(1), 158–170. DOI: 10.1108/QEA-09-2024-0087

Stanford Digital Repository. (2024). *AI-generated citations and the integrity of academic knowledge: Evidence from legal and scientific databases.* Stanford Digital Repository. https://purl.stanford.edu/ai-citations-integrity-2024

Steele, J. L. (2023). To GPT or not GPT? Empowering our students to learn with AI. *Computers and Education Artificial Intelligence*, *5*, 100160. DOI: 10.1016/j.caeai.2023.100160

Stephan, C. (2022). Por modos de vida outros: o mundo plural. *DoisPontos, 19*(3).

Steponenaite, A., & Barakat, B. (2023). Plagiarism in AI empowered world. In Lecture notes in computer science (pp. 434–442). DOI: 10.1007/978-3-031-35897-5_31

Stewart, C. N.Jr. (2023). *Research ethics for scientists: A companion for students.* John Wiley & Sons.

Stokel-Walker, C., & Van Noorden, R. (2023). What ChatGPT and generative AI mean for science. *Nature*, *614*(7947), 214–216. DOI: 10.1038/d41586-023-00340-6 PMID: 36747115

Stommel, J. (2024). Ungrading: An introduction. []. Duke University Press.]. *Pedagogy, 24*(3), 327–340. DOI: 10.1215/15314200-11246255

Suchman, L. A. (2007). *Human-machine reconfigurations: Plans and situated actions*. Cambridge university press.

Sudhir, V. (2024). The ethics of AI in the administration of higher education. *International Journal for Multidisciplinary Research, 6*(6). Advance online publication. DOI: 10.36948/ijfmr.2024.v06i06.30189

Sullivan, M., Kelly, A., & McLaughlan, P. (2023). ChatGPT in higher education: Considerations for academic integrity and student learning. *Journal of Applied Learning & Teaching, 6*(1), 31–40.

Sultana, S. S., Renugadevi, R., Bhargavi, M., & Biyabani, S. A. A. (2025). AI-driven evaluation techniques: Revolutionizing student practices. In *Adopting Artificial Intelligence Tools in Higher Education* (pp. 1–22). CRC Press. DOI: 10.1201/9781003470304-1

Sun, X., Dou, W., & Yang, Y. (2025). The socio-emotional dangers of using artificial intelligence (AI) technologies in second language (L2) education: Unveiling Chinese EFL teachers' perceptions and experiences. *Acta Psychologica, 261*, 105956. DOI: 10.1016/j.actpsy.2025.105956 PMID: 41274003

Swart, W., & MacLeod, K. (2021). Evaluating learning space designs for flipped and collaborative learning: A transactional distance approach. *Education Sciences, 11*(6), 292. DOI: 10.3390/educsci11060292

Sweller, J., Van Merriënboer, J. J. G., & Paas, F. (2019). Cognitive architecture and instructional design: 20 years later. *Educational Psychology Review, 31*(2), 261–292. DOI: 10.1007/s10648-019-09465-5

Swindell, A., Greeley, L., Farag, A., & Verdone, B. (2024). Against Artificial Education: Towards an Ethical Framework for Generative Artificial Intelligence (AI) Use in Education. *Online Learning : The Official Journal of the Online Learning Consortium, 28*(2), n2. DOI: 10.24059/olj.v28i2.4438

Sywelem, M. M. G., & Mahklouf, A. M. E.-S. (2024). Ethical considerations in the integration of artificial intelligence in education: An overview. DOI: 10.5121/csit.2024.141201

Szcyrek, S., & Stewart, B. (2022). Surveillance in the system: Data as critical change in higher education. The Open/Technology in Education Society and Scholarship Association Journal, 2(2), 1–20. DOI: 10.18357/otessaj.2022.2.2.34

Talmage-Rostron, M. (2025, June 29). *How Will Artificial Intelligence Affect Jobs 2023-2030*. Nexford University; Nexford University. https://www.nexford.edu/insights/how-will-ai-affect-jobs

Taneja, D., Prabagaren, H., & Thomas, M. R. (2025). AI in academia. In Advances in computational intelligence and robotics book series (pp. 315–336). DOI: 10.4018/979-8-3373-0122-8.ch014

Taneja, A. (2025). Explainable AI: Building trust and transparency in machine learning models. *Journal of Engineering and Computer Sciences*, *4*(8), 482–489.

Tan, X., Cheng, G., & Ling, M. H. (2025). Artificial intelligence in teaching and teacher professional development: A systematic review. *Computers and Education: Artificial Intelligence*, *8*, 100355. DOI: 10.1016/j.caeai.2024.100355

Tate, T., Doroudi, S., Ritchie, D., Xu, Y., & Warschauer, M. (2023). Educational research and AI-generated writing: Confronting the coming tsunami. *EdArXiv. January, 10*. DOI: 10.35542/osf.io/4mec3

Tatum, H. E. (2022). Honor codes and academic integrity: Three decades of research. *Journal of College and Character*, *23*(1), 32–47. DOI: 10.1080/2194587X.2021.2017977

Teaching, C. (2024). *Peer review in the age of AI: Challenges and opportunities.* Cornell University Center for Teaching Innovation. https://teaching.cornell.edu/peer-review-ai

Temper, M., Tjoa, S., & David, L. (2025, February). Higher Education Act for AI (HEAT-AI): A framework to regulate the usage of AI in higher education institutions. [). Frontiers Media SA.]. *Frontiers in Education*, *10*, 1505370. DOI: 10.3389/feduc.2025.1505370

Teräs, M., Suoranta, J., Teräs, H., & Curcher, M. (2020). Post-Covid-19 education and education technology 'solutionism': A seller's market. *Postdigital Science and Education*, *2*(3), 863–878. DOI: 10.1007/s42438-020-00164-x PMID: 40477107

Thai, T. T. A., Nguyen, H. H. G., & Nguyen, N. C. (2025). English-major of Using Grammarly for Thesis Writing at Seniors' Perceptions IUH. *International Journal of AI in Language Education, 2*(2), 55-78.

The Higher Education Review. (2025). *IIT Delhi introduces strict GenAI usage rules for students, faculty.*

Thompson, K., Corrin, L., & Lodge, J. M. (2023). AI in tertiary education: Progress on research and practice. *Australasian Journal of Educational Technology*, *39*(5), 1–7. DOI: 10.14742/ajet.9251

Thompson, R., Garcia, A., & Williams, D. (2024). Academic integrity in the generative AI era: Institutional responses and policy frameworks. *Computers & Education*, *200*, 104792. DOI: 10.1016/j.compedu.2024.104792

TIME. (2024). *MIT study: ChatGPT users show reduced brain activity during writing tasks.* TIME. https://time.com/mit-chatgpt-brain-activity-study-2024

Times of India. (2025, August 10). *AI, but verify: Navigating future of learning*.

Tomar, P., & Verma, S. (2020). Impact and role of AI technologies in teaching, learning, and research in higher education. In Advances in educational technologies and instructional design book series (pp. 190–203). DOI: 10.4018/978-1-7998-4763-2.ch012

Torrisi-Steele, G. (2025). AI and the humans in higher education. In Advances in educational technologies and instructional design book series (pp. 209–230). DOI: 10.4018/979-8-3373-0502-8.ch009

Tran, N. T. (2024). Teachers' experiences with generative AI as co-pilots in high school L2 writing instruction: A case in Vietnam. In *Innovations in Technologies for Language Teaching and Learning* (pp. 135–157). Springer.

Tran, H. N., Le, T. T. N., & Tran, V. B. U. (2025). AI Tools in Learning Academic Writing: Benefits and Challenges for MA Students in the English Language Studies at the Industrial University of Ho Chi Minh City. *International Journal of AI in Language Education*, *2*(1), 74–91. DOI: 10.54855/ijaile.25215

Tsai, C. T., Upadhyay, S., & Roth, D. (2024). *Multilingual Entity Linking*. Springer. DOI: 10.1007/978-3-031-74901-8

Tuomi, I. (2023). The Effect of Interpretable Artificial Intelligence on Repeated Managerial Decision-Making under Uncertainty. *Proceedings of the . . . Annual Hawaii International Conference on System Sciences/Proceedings of the Annual Hawaii International Conference on System Sciences*. DOI: 10.24251/HICSS.2023.752

Turkle, S. (2011). Alone together: Why we expect more from technology and less from each other. In *Alone together: Why we expect more from technology and less from each other*. Basic Books.

Turner, L., Asada, Y., Leider, J., Piekarz-Porter, E., Schwartz, M., & Chriqui, J. F. (2021). Can monitoring make it happen? An assessment of how reporting, monitoring, and evaluation can support local wellness policy implementation in US schools. *Nutrients*, *13*(1), 193. DOI: 10.3390/nu13010193 PMID: 33435481

Turvey, K., & Pachler, N. (2025). A topological exploration of convergence/divergence of human-mediated and algorithmically mediated pedagogy. *British Journal of Educational Technology*, bjet.70007. DOI: 10.1111/bjet.70007

Ullah, M., Bin Naeem, S., & Kamel Boulos, M. N. (2024). Assessing the guidelines on the use of generative artificial intelligence tools in universities: A survey of the world's top 50 universities. *Big Data and Cognitive Computing*, *8*(12), 194. DOI: 10.3390/bdcc8120194

UNESCO. (2021). *Recommendation on the ethics of artificial intelligence.* United Nations Educational, Scientific and Cultural Organization. https://unesdoc.unesco.org/ark:/48223/pf0000381137

UNESCO. (2023). *Artificial intelligence in education.* UNESCO. https://www.unesco.org/en/digital-education/artificial-intelligence

UNESCO. (2023). *Guidance for generative AI in education and research.* UNESCO Publishing.

University of Cambridge. (2024a). *AI guidance: Guidance for University of Cambridge staff on the administrative use of generative AI.* Information Compliance Office.

University of Cambridge. (2024b). *Can I use generative AI in my course?* Cambridge Online Help.

University of Illinois Education. (2024). *Human–AI collaboration models: Preserving intellectual agency in university research and teaching.* University of Illinois College of Education. https://education.illinois.edu/human-ai-collaboration

University of Illinois. (2024). *Active learning and metacognition in the age of AI: Pedagogical principles for educators.* University of Illinois Center for Innovation in Teaching & Learning. https://citl.illinois.edu/active-learning-ai

University, I. E. (2024). *Creativity and AI overdependence: Protecting innovation in educational settings.* IE University Insights. https://www.ie.edu/insights/creativity-ai-education

Upreti, I. M. (2025). The role and implications of artificial intelligence in higher education: Opportunities and challenges. *International Journal for Research in Applied Science and Engineering Technology*, *13*(4), 6214–6220. DOI: 10.22214/ijraset.2025.69838

Urwin, M. (2025, May 15). *AI Taking over Jobs: What to Know about the Future of Jobs*. Built In. https://builtin.com/artificial-intelligence/ai-replacing-jobs-creating-jobs

Urzúa, C. A. C., Ranjan, R., Saavedra, E. E. M., Badilla-Quintana, M. G., Lepe-Martínez, N., & Philominraj, A. (2025). Effects of AI-assisted feedback via generative chat on academic writing in higher education students: A systematic review of the literature. *Education Sciences*, *15*(10), 1396. DOI: 10.3390/educsci15101396

Van der Linden, S. (2023). *Foolproof: Why misinformation infects our minds and how to build immunity*. WW Norton & Company.

Van Norren, D. E. (2023). The ethics of artificial intelligence, UNESCO and the African Ubuntu perspective. *Journal of Information. Communication and Ethics in Society*, *21*(1), 112–128. DOI: 10.1108/JICES-04-2022-0037

Van Tryon, P. J. S., & Bishop, M. (2009). Theoretical foundations for enhancing social connectedness in online learning environments. *Distance Education*, *30*(3), 291–315. DOI: 10.1080/01587910903236312

Vangibhuratha, S. K. (2025). The impact of generative AI on educational assessment. *International Journal of Innovative Research in Engineering & Multidisciplinary Physical Sciences*, *13*(4). Advance online publication. DOI: 10.37082/ijirmps.v13.i4.232678

Vasylyshyna, N., Kovalenko, O., & Shevchenko, I. (2024). Embedded AI tools and academic misconduct: Challenges in differentiating permissible assistance from AI-generated content. *Journal of Academic Ethics*, *22*(1), 89–105. DOI: 10.1007/s10805-024-09512-3

Venugopal, P., & Vakamullu, S. (2024). Infrastructure inequity and AI-enhanced learning: Access barriers in developing world educational contexts. *Education and Information Technologies*, *29*(8), 10211–10230. DOI: 10.1007/s10639-024-12734-5

Verano-Tacoronte, D., Bolívar-Cruz, A., & Sosa-Cabrera, S. (2025). Are university teachers ready for generative artificial intelligence? Unpacking faculty anxiety in the ChatGPT era. *Education and Information Technologies*, *30*(14), 1–28. DOI: 10.1007/s10639-025-13585-7

Vetrivel, S. C., Arun, V. P., Ambikapathi, R., & Saravanan, T. P. (2025). Automated Grading Systems: Enhancing Efficiency and Consistency in Student Assessments. In Adopting Artificial Intelligence Tools in Higher Education (pp. 41-61). CRC Press.

Vetrivel, S. C., Arun, V. P., Ambikapathi, R., & Saravanan, T. P. (2025). Automated grading systems: Enhancing efficiency and consistency in student assessments. In *Adopting artificial intelligence tools in higher education* (pp. 41–61). CRC Press. DOI: 10.1201/9781003470304-3

Victor-Mgbachi, T. O. Y. I. N. (2024). Leveraging Artificial Intelligence (AI) Effectively: Managing Risks and Boosting Productivity. *Iconic Research and Engineering Journals*, *7*(7), 54–69.

Vieriu, A. M., & Petrea, G. (2025). The impact of artificial intelligence (AI) on students' academic development. *Education Sciences*, *15*(3), 343. DOI: 10.3390/educsci15030343

Villamin, P., Lopez, V., Thapa, D. K., & Cleary, M. (2025). A worked example of qualitative descriptive design: A step-by-step guide for novice and early career researchers. *Journal of Advanced Nursing*, *81*(8), 5181–5195. DOI: 10.1111/jan.16481

Waghid, Z. (2023). Teacher educators' pedagogical practices in global citizenship education using the soft vs critical GCE framework. *Cogent Education*, *10*(2), 2251757. DOI: 10.1080/2331186X.2023.2251757

Wang, F., Li, N., Cheung, A. C., & Wong, G. K. (2025). In GenAI we trust: An investigation of university students' reliance on and resistance to generative AI in language learning. *International Journal of Educational Technology in Higher Education*, *22*(1), 59. DOI: 10.1186/s41239-025-00547-9

Wang, X. (2025). Students' perceptions of automated writing evaluation in autonomous learning. *Education and Information Technologies*, *30*(11), 1–33. DOI: 10.1007/s10639-025-13378-y

Watanabe, A. (2024). Have Courage to Use your Own Mind, with or without AI: The Relevance of Kant's Enlightenment to Higher Education in the Age of Artificial Intelligence. *Electronic Journal of e-Learning*, *22*(2), 46–58. DOI: 10.34190/ejel.21.5.3229

Watermeyer, R., Phipps, L., Lanclos, D., & Knight, C. (2023). Generative AI and the automating of academia. *Postdigital Science and Education*, *6*(2), 446–466. DOI: 10.1007/s42438-023-00440-6

Watters, A. (2023). *Teaching machines: The history of personalized learning*. mit Press.

Weigel, A., Caldas, C., Meyer, A., & Morris, S. A. (2022). The impact of AI on research. *Cell*, *185*(15), 2621–2622. DOI: 10.1016/j.cell.2022.06.024

Western Michigan University. (2024). *Developing institutional AI policies that balance innovation with academic integrity.* Western Michigan University Office of the Provost. https://wmich.edu/provost/ai-policy-framework

Wiboolyasarin, W., Wiboolyasarin, K., Kamonsawad, R., & Jinowat, N. (2025). Enhancing Collaborative Writing with Grammarly-Mediated Feedback in Asynchronous Wiki Environments: An Investigation of Group Size. *English Teaching & Learning*, *49*(2), 389–414. DOI: 10.1007/s42321-024-00186-9

Wieczorek, M. (2025). Using ethical scenarios to explore the future of artificial intelligence in primary and secondary education. *Learning, Media and Technology*, •••, 1–17. DOI: 10.1080/17439884.2025.2517335

Wiles-Warner, J. J. (2025). *Establishing policies and standards to implement socially sustainable practices* (Doctoral dissertation, Walden University).

Williamson, B., Bayne, S., & Shay, S. (2020). The datafication of teaching in Higher Education: Critical issues and perspectives. []. Taylor & Francis.]. *Teaching in Higher Education*, *25*(4), 351–365. DOI: 10.1080/13562517.2020.1748811

Williamson, B., & Eynon, R. (2020). Historical threads, missing links, and future directions in AI in education. *Learning, Media and Technology*, *45*(3), 223–235. DOI: 10.1080/17439884.2020.1798995

Williams, R. T. (2024). Paradigm shifts: Exploring AI's influence on qualitative inquiry and analysis. *Frontiers in Research Metrics and Analytics*, *9*, 1331589. DOI: 10.3389/frma.2024.1331589

Winner, L. (2017). Do artifacts have politics? In *Computer ethics* (pp. 177–192). Routledge. DOI: 10.4324/9781315259697-21

Wongmahesak, K., Karim, F., & Wongchestha, N. (2025). Artificial Intelligence: A Catalyst for Sustainable Effectiveness in Compulsory Education Management. *Asian Education and Learning Review*, *3*(1), 4–4.

Wong, W. K. O. (2024). The sudden disruptive rise of generative artificial intelligence? An evaluation of their impact on higher education and the global workplace. *Journal of Open Innovation*, *10*(2), 100278. DOI: 10.1016/j.joitmc.2024.100278

Wood, M. (2021, May 10). *What Are the Risks of Algorithmic Bias in Higher Education?* Every Learner Everywhere. https://www.everylearnereverywhere.org/blog/what-are-the-risks-of-algorithmic-bias-in-higher-education/

Woo, K., & Falloon, G. (2025). Moving beyond the rhetoric: Integrating coding into the English curriculum in Australian primary schools. *Australian Educational Researcher*, *52*(1), 803–839. DOI: 10.1007/s13384-024-00742-z

Xiao, P., Chen, Y., & Bao, W. (2023). Waiting, banning, and embracing: An empirical analysis of adapting policies for generative AI in higher education. *arXiv preprint arXiv:2305.18617*.

Xia, Q., Weng, X., Ouyang, F., Lin, T. J., & Chiu, T. K. (2024). A scoping review on how generative artificial intelligence transforms assessment in higher education. *International Journal of Educational Technology in Higher Education*, *21*(1), 40. DOI: 10.1186/s41239-024-00468-z

Yadav, S. (2025). Advancing education with AI-driven education for diverse learners: Integrating AI into pedagogical practices. In *Integrating AI into pedagogical education* (pp. 49–80). IGI Global Scientific Publishing.

Yang, C., Li, R., & Yang, L. (2025). Revisiting trends in GenAI-assisted second language writing: Retrospect and prospect. *Journal of Educational Computing Research*, *63*(7-8), 07356331251367309. DOI: 10.1177/07356331251367309

Yan, L., Pammer-Schindler, V., Mills, C., Nguyen, A., & Gašević, D. (2025). Beyond efficiency: Empirical insights on generative AI's impact on cognition, metacognition and epistemic agency in learning. *British Journal of Educational Technology*, *56*(5), 1675–1685. DOI: 10.1111/bjet.70000

Yan, L., Sha, L., Zhao, L., Li, Y., Martinez-Maldonado, R., Chen, G., & Gašević, D. (2024). Practical and ethical challenges of large language models in education: A systematic scoping review. *British Journal of Educational Technology*, *55*(1), 90–112. DOI: 10.1111/bjet.13370

Yao, M., Wei, Y., & Liu, H. (2025). AI practices and ethical concerns: An analysis of undeclared uses of AI in published research articles. *Ethics & Behavior*, •••, 1–13. DOI: 10.1080/10508422.2025.2549310

Yavich, R. (2025). Will the use of AI undermine students independent thinking? *Education Sciences*, *15*(6), 669. DOI: 10.3390/educsci15060669

Yildiz, H., & Gonen, S. I. K. (2024). Automated writing evaluation system for feedback in the digital world: An online learning opportunity for English as a foreign language students. *Turkish Online Journal of Distance Education*, *25*(3), 183–206. DOI: 10.17718/tojde.1169727

Yinfeng, Z., & Abdullah, M. N. L. Y. (2025). Artificial intelligence and student learning in higher education: An integrated bibliometric and experimental investigation.

Youvan, D. C. (2025). *The Perfected Control System: How Universities*. AI, and Financial Leverage Shape the Coming Collapse and Rebirth of Knowledge.

Yu, J. H., Chauhan, D., Iqbal, R. A., & Yeoh, E. (2025). Mapping academic perspectives on AI in education: Trends, challenges, and sentiments in educational research (2018–2024). *Educational Technology Research and Development*, *73*(1), 199–227. DOI: 10.1007/s11423-024-10425-2

Yusriani, S., Eledora, A. O., Patiro, S. P. S., Purnomo, K. H., Zega, I. M., & Marlina, M. (2024). About AI in academia: obstacle or facilitator? *Proceeding of International Student Conference on Business, Education, Economics, Accounting, and Management.*, 2(1), 677–700. DOI: 10.21009/isc-beam.012.43

Yusuf, A., Pervin, N., & Román-González, M. (2024). Generative AI and the future of higher education: A threat to academic integrity or reformation? Evidence from multicultural perspectives. *International Journal of Educational Technology in Higher Education*, *21*(1), 21. DOI: 10.1186/s41239-024-00453-6

Yusuf, S. B., Jiancheng, Q., Rasool, U., Dhuli, R., Yesmin, Q. F., Mahmud, R., & Hossain, A. (2025). Investigating EFL Learners' Perceptions of Using Grammarly in Enhancing Writing Proficiency in Bangladesh. *SAGE Open*, *15*(3), 21582440251352922. DOI: 10.1177/21582440251352922

Zaibout, N., & Madrane, M. (2024). Optimizing Academic Assessment: The Impact of AI on Student Integrity, Creativity, and Achievement. *International Journal of Engineering Trends and Technology*, *72*(11), 357–370. DOI: 10.14445/22315381/IJETT-V72I11P134

Zala, K., Acharya, B., Mashru, M., Palaniappan, D., Gerogiannis, V. C., Kanavos, A., & Karamitsos, I. (2024). Transformative Automation: AI in scientific Literature Reviews. *International Journal of Advanced Computer Science and Applications*, *15*(1). Advance online publication. DOI: 10.14569/ijacsa.2024.01501122

Zarkovic, S. (2020). Adaptive learning systems in modern classrooms. *Ethical Use of Technology in Digital Learning Environments: Graduate Student Perspectives*. https://www.tech.gov.sg/technews/ai-in-education-transforming-singapore-education-system-with-student-learning-space/ https://www.cengagegroup.com/news/perspectives/2025/ais-impact-on-education-in-2025/ https://www.wgu.edu/blog/how-ai-reshaping-curriculum-design-insights-future-educators2412.html https://www.unesco.org/ethics-ai/en/articles/ai-literacy-and-new-digital-divide-global-call-action

Zawacki-Richter, O., Marín, V. I., Bond, M., & Gouverneur, F. (2019). Systematic review of research on artificial intelligence applications in higher education. *International Journal of Educational Technology in Higher Education, 16*(39), 1–27.

Zawacki-Richter, O., Marín, V. I., Bond, M., & Gouverneur, F. (2019). Systematic review of research on artificial intelligence applications in higher education–where are the educators? *International Journal of Educational Technology in Higher Education, 16*(1), 39. DOI: 10.1186/s41239-019-0171-0

Zeer, M., Siaj, R. W., Abu Ghannam, J., & Kanan, M. (2023). Ethics of artificial intelligence in university education. In 2023 2nd International Engineering Conference on Electrical, Energy, and Artificial Intelligence (EICEEAI) (pp. xx–xx). IEEE. DOI: 10.1109/EICEEAI60672.2023.10590285

Zermeño-Flores, A. I., Tufte, T., & Navarrete-Vega, M. A. (2024). Knowledge production and epistemic injustices. *MedieKultur Journal of Media and Communication Research, 40*(76), 120–138. DOI: 10.7146/mk.v40i76.143529

Zhai, C., Wibowo, S., & Li, L. D. (2024). *The effects of over-reliance on AI dialogue systems on students' cognitive abilities: A systematic review.* Smart Learning Environments, 11(1), Article 28.

Zhang, C. (2025). AI in academia: How it enhances research efficiency and innovation. *International Journal of Education and Humanities, 19*(3), 155–158. DOI: 10.54097/r5h5pz92

Zhang, J., & Goyal, S. B. (2024). AI-driven decision support system innovations to empower higher education administration. *Journal of Computers Mechanical and Management, 3*(2), 35–41. DOI: 10.57159/gadl.jcmm.3.2.24070

Zhang, L., & Zhang, W. (2025). Integrating large language models into project-based learning based on self-determination theory. *Interactive Learning Environments, 33*(5), 3580–3592. DOI: 10.1080/10494820.2024.2446535

Zhang, Y., Yip, C., Lu, E., & Dong, Z. Y. (2022). A systematic review on technologies and applications in smart campus: A human-centered case study. *IEEE Access : Practical Innovations, Open Solutions, 10*, 16134–16149. DOI: 10.1109/ACCESS.2022.3148735

Zhang, Z., Aubrey, S., Huang, X., & Chiu, T. K. (2025). The role of generative AI and hybrid feedback in improving L2 writing skills: A comparative study. *Innovation in Language Learning and Teaching*, •••, 1–19. DOI: 10.1080/17501229.2025.2503890

Zhang, Z., & Huang, X. (2024). The impact of chatbots based on large language models on second language vocabulary acquisition. *Heliyon*, *10*(3), e25370. DOI: 10.1016/j.heliyon.2024.e25370 PMID: 38333802

Zhan, Y., & Teng, M. F. (2025). Assessing English writing self-efficacy beliefs, self-regulation, and performance through asynchronous computer-mediated feedback and face-to-face peer feedback. *Educational Assessment*, *30*(1), 4–20. DOI: 10.1080/10627197.2025.2452442

Zhao, D. (2025). The impact of AI-enhanced natural language processing tools on writing proficiency: An analysis of language precision, content summarization, and creative writing facilitation. *Education and Information Technologies*, *30*(6), 8055–8086. DOI: 10.1007/s10639-024-13145-5

Zhao, D. (2025). The impact of teacher, peer, and automated writing evaluation feedback on developing deep writing skills: A comparative study. *Journal of Computing in Higher Education*, •••, 1–35. DOI: 10.1007/s12528-025-09469-x

Zhong, W., Liu, H., & Zhang, Y. (2024). Neuroplasticity and AI dependency: How habitual AI-assisted cognition reshapes independent thinking pathways. *Frontiers in Human Neuroscience*, *18*, 1356712. DOI: 10.3389/fnhum.2024.1356712

Zhou, J., Hmelo-Silver, C. E., Ryan, Z., Stiso, C., Murphy, D., Danish, J., Chinn, C. A., & Duncan, R. G. (2025). Disagreeing softly: Supporting students in managing disagreement in peer critique: Disagreeing softly: Supporting students in managing disagreement in peer critique. *International Journal of Computer-Supported Collaborative Learning*, *20*(2), 249–282. DOI: 10.1007/s11412-024-09438-z

Zuboff, S. (2023). The age of surveillance capitalism. In *Social theory re-wired* (pp. 203–213). Routledge. DOI: 10.4324/9781003320609-27

About the Contributors

Muhammad Mooneeb Ali is leading AI and Linguistics at Saudi Aramco, Saudi Arabia. He is a scholar of AI and English, Applied Linguistics, Educational technology, Technology in Education, critical pedagogy, and digital ethics. He has more than 60 research publications. He is also an author of 40 academic books and authored monograph on technology-based Teaching and learning. His latest work is AI applications in English Language which is Scopus Indexed. His research focuses on the intersection of emerging technologies and academic responsibility, particularly in the Global South. With a background in applied linguistics, educational technology, and sociocultural critique, Dr. Ali has published extensively on academic transformation in the AI age. He advocates for balanced, inclusive, and critically-informed frameworks that place human agency at the center of technological adoption in academia.

Muhammad Mujtaba Asad is serving as a Head of Educational Technology and TVET Research at Sukkur IBA University, Pakistan. Dr. Asad has extensive research experience in the domain of Educational Technologies in Higher Education, Innovative Techno-pedagogical Approaches, Techno-Ethics and AI integration in Education 4.0 Classrooms. He has published more than 100 research publications in reputed indexed journals. Also, four edited books are under his credit related to Educational Technologies.

***

Ahmad Al Yakin is a distinguished academic at Universitas Al Asyariah Mandar (UNASMAN), where he serves in the Pendidikan Pancasila dan Kewarganegaraan (Civics Education) program. His career reflects a consistent commitment to academic excellence, leadership, and scholarly contribution. He previously held the position of Director of the Lembaga Penelitian dan Pengabdian kepada Masyarakat (LPPM UNASMAN) from 2013 to 2016, and currently contributes to institutional advancement as Wakil Rektor I (Vice-Rector I), demonstrating his strong role in academic governance and policy development. In addition to administrative leadership, Dr. Ahmad Al Yakin actively contributes to scholarly communities as a peer reviewer for the Jurnal Sipissangngi: Jurnal Pengabdian Kepada Masyarakat, reflecting his dedication to maintaining research quality and academic integrity. His research productivity is evident in his SINTA profile, where he has achieved an overall score of 3,363 and a three-year score of 825, supported by a Scopus H-index of 7 and a Google Scholar H-index of 15. His academic contributions encompass a wide range of themes, including civics education, digital learning, and pedagogical innovation. Among his notable works are Education for a Digital Era: Advice and Practice around the Globe, Praxis and Practices in ELT and Philology, and collaborative works such as Teaching, Learning, Education, an Overview and Media Quizizz sebagai Aplikasi Assessment Pembelajaran. Beyond publications, Dr. Ahmad Al Yakin has also been recognized for his innovative engagement with educational technology and research methodologies, as reflected in intellectual property outputs including Selebrifikasi Politik, Entrepreneurship Dictionary with Cyber Technology, Metodologi Penelitian, and Digital English Dictionary with Virtual Reality. Through his leadership as Vice-Rector I, he plays a pivotal role in shaping institutional policies, particularly in areas such as the Recognition of Prior Learning (RPL), strengthening UNASMAN's academic impact both regionally and nationally. His editorial and institutional services extend beyond administration, as he has consistently fostered research development, publication quality, and academic collaboration through his tenure at LPPM UNASMAN. With a career that seamlessly integrates research, innovation, and leadership, Dr. Ahmad Al Yakin exemplifies academic excellence and continues to contribute significantly to the advancement of higher education in Indonesia.

Eka Apriani, M.Pd. is an English Lecturer at English Tadris c. Study Program of the Faculty of Tarbiyahs in Islamic State Institute of Curup. She is a Editor in Chief in Journal of English Franca and International Journal of Education Research and Development. She is also the secretary of Corolla Education Centre Foundation, Indonesia. She received her Master Degree (Master of Language Education) from Sriwijaya University in 2013 and Doctor of Education in Bengkulu University 2022. She has published some researchs in international journal and national journal. She has Scopus ID and WOS Id. She is a member of profession organisation: ADRI, TEFLIN, PDPI and ELITE. She is treasurer of ADRI in Bengkulu Province. Her research interest is in Writing skill and ICT in learning English. She write some books: The beauty of Rejang Lebong, Semantics Crossword, Metode Pengajaran BIPA, Drama Manuscript: The Marriage of Siti Zubaidah. She has also some

Intelektual Property Right: Semantics Crossword, The beauty of Rejang Lebong, The Marriage of Siti Zubaidah, Metode Pengajaran BIPA.

Lukman Asha, M.Pd.I is a Lecturer at Post Graduate in Islamic State Institute of Curup. He is Professor of Educational management. He Received his Doctor from Jakarta State University in 2013. He has published some researchs in international journal and national journal. He has Scopus id. He is a member of profession organization: ADRI and Lecturer Forum of Educational Management.

Deepak D is an Assistant Professor at the School of Commerce, Jain (Deemed-to-be) University, Bengaluru.He holds an M.Com degree from Bangalore Central University and is a UGC-NET qualified individual.His academic interests span business finance, financial technology, and sustainable business practices.Deepak has published over 20 research papers in reputed national and international journals. His work explores emerging themes such as AI in marketing, the circular economy, emotional intelligence, and green finance.He has co-invented patents related to leadership strategy and the management of the bullwhip effect.He is actively involved in academic conferences on digital transformation and future-ready business models. Deepak collaborates with multidisciplinary scholars to bridge theory with practical innovation. He is listed on the Vidwan database and holds an ORCID ID: 0009-0004-8493-1474.Outside academics, he has represented his university in national-level wrestling competitions.

Susanta Das is a seasoned educator with a proven record of teaching and mentoring diverse students, working at multiple institutions, and providing service to the various initiatives of organizations. He received his Ph.D. and M.A. degrees from Western Michigan University (WMU), USA, and M.Sc. degree from Banaras Hindu University (BHU), India all in Physics. He continued his research as a Marie-Curie post-doctoral fellow at Stockholm University, Stockholm, Sweden on beam diagnostics for the DESIREE (Double ElectroStatic Ion Ring ExpEriment) in the project DITANET (Diagnostic Techniques for particle Accelerators – a Marie-Curie initial training NETwork), at the Indian Institute of Science Education and Research-Kolkata, India on high-pressure physics as a Project Scientist-B, and at the University of Electro-Communications, Tokyo, Japan on ion-surface interactions as a Post-doctoral fellow. Throughout his career, Dr. Das worked and collaborated with many researchers, Ph.D., master, and visiting students from different countries. He further visited many countries to discuss research and an international conference participant (UK, Italy, Germany, Greece, Belgium, Bulgaria, Romania, Brazil etc.). He worked at several institutions before assuming his current role at Ajeenkya D Y Patil University. He received the Marie-Curie post-doctoral fellowship in Sweden,

Science Academies' Summer Research Fellowship in India, Gowen Frostic Doctoral Fellowship, Department Graduate Research and Creative Scholar Award by WMU, and Leo R. Parpart Doctoral Fellowship by Dept. of Physics, WMU, among many others, throughout his academic journey. He co-authored several research articles in WoS/Scopus indexed international journals, conference proceedings, and scholarly book chapters and co-edited several books published by renowned international publishing houses (IGI-Global, Springer Nature, Nova Science Publishers, Wiley, Scrivener-Wiley, Notion Press). At present, Dr. Das continues to delve into cutting-edge fields, with a keen interest in nanotechnology, UN SDGs, and data science. His multifaceted contributions, spanning teaching, research, and administrative leadership, showcase a dedicated professional who is instrumental in advancing the vision and mission of the institutions he serves.

Purushotham H. C is an Assistant Professor at the School of Commerce, JAIN (Deemed-to-be University), with over 6 years of teaching experience. He is currently pursuing a Ph.D. at REVA University and holds an MBA in Management. His expertise spans consumer behaviour, strategic management, HRM, and marketing. He has published several research papers and book chapters and received multiple Best Paper Awards. He has coordinated academic, cultural, and NSS activities and actively contributes to faculty development and student mentoring. He is also a certified Behaviour and Mentoring Analyst and holds certifications in marketing analytics and digital marketing.

Sheetal Hukkeri is a distinguished academician with over 21 years of experience in the fields of Commerce and Management. She currently serves as the Programme Coordinator and Associate Professor at the School of Commerce, JAIN (Deemed-to-be University). Known for her strong academic leadership and student-centric approach, she has successfully mentored students across both undergraduate and postgraduate levels. Dr. Hukkeri holds a Master's degree in Commerce as well as Management, M.Phil in Commerce, and a Ph.D.in Commerce. Over the course of her career, she has made significant contributions to curriculum development, playing a pivotal role in designing and structuring both Undergraduate and Postgraduate Programmes at JAIN (Deemed-to-be University). Her scholarly work includes the presentation and publication of research papers at several national and international conferences, along with the authorship of multiple textbooks in her areas of expertise: Organisational Behaviour, Organisational Dynamics, Human Resource Management, Entrepreneurship, and Corporate & Business Law. Dr. Hukkeri is widely recognised for her exceptional organisational and administrative capabilities. She has coordinated numerous conferences, workshops, faculty development programmes, and webinars. She has also trained over 800 faculty members in effectively implementing the mentoring process at JAIN (Deemed-to-be University). Additionally, she has conducted multiple sessions on Indian Knowledge Systems (IKS) for both undergraduate and postgraduate students, enriching their academic experience with culturally grounded and contemporary perspectives. Her professionalism, efficiency, and commitment to delivering high-quality education have earned her notable respect and recognition throughout her career. Residing in Bengaluru with her husband, Mr. Anand R. Umarji, and their daughters, Ms. Aadya and Ms. Arha, Dr. Sheetal Hukkeri exemplifies dedication, integrity, and excellence in academia.

Mustafa Kayyali is an ardent advocate for excellence in higher education, driven by a relentless pursuit of quality, recognition, and innovation. Their journey in academia started with a Master's in Quality Management and Evaluation in Higher Education from Universitat Oberta de Catalunya, followed by a Ph.D. in Quality Management from Azteca University. These academic pursuits have laid a strong foundation for their expertise in Accreditation, Quality Assurance, and Higher Education Rankings. As an entrepreneur, researcher, translator, and publisher, they are deeply involved in various facets of the academic world. Their diverse interests encompass Management, Translation, Interpretation, and Academic consulting, contributing to a well-rounded understanding of the industry. Throughout their career, they have made significant contributions to academic literature, with more than 40 published papers and 30 book chapters to my name. Additionally, they take pride in having translated 6 books, bridging language gaps, and promoting knowledge exchange on a global scale. They are committed to fostering positive change in higher education and contributing to its continuous improvement.

Dipak Kolhe is pursuing a Bachelor of Computer Applications in Big Data Analytics (BCA-BDA) at Ajeenkya DY Patil University. He’s passionate about programming and enjoys coding, especially using Python, and is comfortable working in a Linux environment. He’s also part of the university’s Hyperloop project, where he gets involved in exciting and innovative tech work. He regularly participates in hackathons and recently won third prize with his team, which was a proud moment and a great learning experience. Before moving into the tech field, he completed a Diploma in Pharmacy (D. Pharm). His background in both healthcare and technology gives him a unique perspective and shows his ability to adapt and learn across fields. He also has strong leadership qualities and good communication skills, which help him work well in teams and take initiative when needed. He is interested in how technology can be applied to solve problems in the real world and has recently started investigating fields like data science and artificial intelligence. He's constantly keen to expand his knowledge, take on new tasks, and develop professionally. He intends to establish a career that blends effect, rationality, and creativity in the future by gaining additional experience through projects and internships.

Naveen Kumar M.S. is an accomplished academician with 13 years of professional experience, including 12 years in teaching and 1 year in the corporate sector. Currently, he serves as an Assistant Professor at the School of Commerce, Jain University. In his previous role as the Head of the Commerce and Management Department, he successfully led a team of 20 members, excelling in team management, coordination, training, and motivation. Dr. Naveen Kumar is known for providing both official and moral support to his team, ensuring they effectively fulfilled their duties within the organization's policies. Dr. Naveen holds a Ph.D. in Management, along with dual master's degrees (MBA and M.Com) specializing in Finance and Accounts. Additionally, he has completed a Post-Graduation Diploma in Human Resource Management (HRM) and holds a Bachelor's degree in Finance. He has also cleared the Karnataka State Eligibility Test (SET/KSET) in both Management and Commerce. A dedicated researcher, Dr. Naveen has secured 2 patents, published 12 research papers, indexed in ABDC, Scopus, and UGC Care-listed Journals and 7 Research papers were presented and 5 of them have received the Best Research Paper Awards. He has also authored a textbook, contributing significantly to the academic community.

Fujia Li is a Senior Lecturer in Innovation and Entrepreneurship and the Director of Strategic Education Portfolio for Innovation, Technology, and Entrepreneurship at the University of Exeter Business School. His research interests span across responsible innovation, entrepreneurial resilience, and entrepreneurship education.

Joycelle C. Lumogdang is an Instructor I and Laboratory In-Charge based in Kalamansig, Sultan Kudarat. She holds a B.S. in Chemistry and a Master of Arts in Teaching Science, complemented by units in a Diploma in Teaching from the Southern Mindanao Institute of Technology (SMIT). A dedicated educator and a resilient mother of three, she specializes in bridging scientific expertise with classroom instruction, ensuring the highest standards in both laboratory management and student development.

Rashmia Miyashiro is a Licensed Professional Teacher and researcher specializing in Mathematics education. She is currently an Instructor I at Sultan Kudarat State University. She holds a Master of Arts in Education major in Mathematics from Notre Dame of Marbel University and a Bachelor of Secondary Education in Mathematics from Notre Dame of Salaman College. With extensive teaching experience at both secondary and tertiary levels, she has also served as

Student Advisory Council Moderator from 2017 to 2018. Her academic and research interests focus on advancing mathematics instruction and student development. Skilled in documentation, facilitation, and computer applications, she communicates effectively in English, Filipino, Iranun, and Maguindanaon.

Zahra Nazim is an Assistant Professor and Head of the Social Sciences and Allied Department at the Institute of Business and Health Management (IBHM), Dow University of Health Sciences, Karachi. She holds a Ph.D. and plays a key academic and administrative role within the institute, contributing to curriculum development, faculty coordination, and student learning. Her research interests span corporate social responsibility, organizational performance, and national culture. As a dedicated educator and researcher, Dr. Nazim is committed to strengthening interdisciplinary business and health-management education and fostering an environment that supports academic excellence and professional growth.

Krutika Patre, is an aspiring programmer and technology enthusiast, currently pursuing Engineering in Artificial Intelligence and Data Science. With a passion for learning, she is building experience in a variety of programming languages and technologies, including C, C++, Python, Data Structures (DS), HTML, CSS, and JavaScript, DBMS (My SQL). After learning this programming language, she has created interest in Full Stack Development. She had also attended an Arduino-Based Automation course at Dolphin Labs to improve my software knowledge. There, she learned how to work with sensors, microcontrollers, and circuit design. She has written review paper on Sustainable engineering on build environment. She is doing researching and learning many topics related to AI, Policy and governance and related to my interest. She has taken part in hackathons, workshops, and tech events to explore many fields. She is also working with a group on Hyperloop. Being part of this project has really helped her grow, especially in areas like teamwork, innovation, and systems thinking.

Arun R is an Assistant Professor in the Department of Commerce at Jain (Deemed to be University), Bengaluru. Holding a Master of Commerce (Finance) from Mangalore University, Arun has demonstrated academic excellence through prestigious qualifications, including successful clearances of the UGC NET (Commerce) thrice and KSET once. Dedicated to fostering academic excellence, Arun is passionate about teaching and research, striving to inspire students and contribute valuable insights to the field of commerce and finance.

Fahad A. Salendab is a scholar and leader in the field of higher education, holding a Ph.D. in Educational Administration. As a Licensed Professional Teacher and Associate Professor, he has dedicated his career to advancing the quality of education through research, teaching, and leadership. A multi-awarded faculty member, Dr. Salendab is recognized for his outstanding contributions to education, research, and institutional development. He is a registered author with the National Book Development Board (NBDB) and serves as an editor for IGI Global Scientific Publishing, contributing to the dissemination of high-quality academic scholarship. He has published various books, book chapters, and research articles, reflecting his sustained engagement in scholarly writing and knowledge production. His commitment to research is further demonstrated through his role as a Regular Member of the DOST–National Research Council of the Philippines, where he collaborates on initiatives addressing critical issues in education and development. He also serves as an editorial board member for various national and international research journals, supporting the advancement of scholarly publishing and peer-reviewed academic discourse. As an active participant in accreditation processes, Dr. Salendab ensures the continuous improvement of academic programs, demonstrating his strong commitment to quality assurance and institutional growth..

Sunil Sankathala is pursuing B. Tech Computer Science and Engineering at Ajeenkya DY Patil University, with a diverse range of interests that bridge technology, sustainability, and innovation. His academic focus lies in computer science fundamentals like programming, data structures, algorithms, and software development. He actively supplements this with hands-on experience in web development and robotics. Beyond the core curriculum, He has a strong research inclination in emerging and impactful fields. His current research interests include Artificial Intelligence in Healthcare, bioplastics, nano bioplastics, e-waste management, and solid waste management—areas where he believes technology can make a meaningful difference in solving real-world problems. He has been publishing research articles and book chapters in reputed national and international journals and books. He is also part of an ambitious Hyperloop project, which involves interdisciplinary collaboration and cutting-edge engineering aimed at revolutionizing transportation. Working on this project has enhanced his skills in teamwork, innovation, and systems thinking. In the tech domain, he has developed proficiency in web development using technologies such as HTML, CSS, JavaScript, and React. His interests in robotics further reflect building smart, responsive systems that interact with the physical world. Throughout his course, he has helped strengthen problem-solving and collaborative skills. He is proficient in languages such as Python, C, C++, MySQL, Ubuntu, Machine Learning and familiar with frameworks and tools like React, Git. He actively participates in hackathons, coding competitions, and tech events to challenge himself and learn from peers. He is also a quick learner and highly adaptable, with an eagerness to stay updated with the latest trends in the tech world. He aspires to become a skilled software engineer and contribute to building innovative solutions that have a positive impact on society. The long-term goal is to work in a dynamic environment where knowledge, grow professionally, and make meaningful contributions to the field of technology. Driven by a spirit of exploration and sustainability, he aims to contribute to technological solutions that address both human and environmental needs. The long-term goal is to become a versatile engineer and researcher, working at the intersection of computer science, environmental innovation, and human well-being.

Ratan Sarkar is an Assistant Professor in the Department of Education, Tezpur University (A Central University), Assam, India. Previously, he served nearly seven years as Assistant Professor in the Department of Teachers' Training (B.Ed.), Prabhat Kumar College, Contai (Vidyasagar University), and as Guest Faculty at National Institute for Empowerment of Persons with Intellectual Disabilities, Regional Centre, Kolkata. He holds a Ph.D. in Education from Pondicherry University, an M.Ed. and M.Phil. in Special Education from Ramakrishna Mission Vivekananda Educational and Research Institute, Belur Math, and an M.A. in Education and Technology from Tata Institute of Social Sciences, Mumbai. He began his academic journey with a B.Ed. in Special Education (Jadavpur University) and a B.A. in English (Hons) from Siliguri College (University of North Bengal), Darjeeling. Dr. Sarkar has published extensively in leading journals (SAGE, Springer, Routledge, Wiley), authored books, chapters, and reviews, and led projects under the Ministry of Education, Govt. of India. His works on inclusive education, EdTech, disability studies, policy advocacy to advance equitable learning ecosystems.

Dadan Supardan, S.Si, M.Biotech. is an Lecturer at PGMI (cri bhs ingfrisny) Study Program of the Faculty of Tarbiyah in Islamic State Institute of C urup. He is a Journal Manager in Journal of English Franca and International Journal of Education Research and Development. He is also the president of Corolla Education Centre Foundation, Indonesia. He Received his Master Degree from Gajah Mada University in 2013. He has published some researchs in international journal and national journal. He has Scopus Id and WOS Id. He is a member of profession organisation: ADRI and HPPBI.

Chetan T R, PhD in Marketing, serves as Assistant Professor at JAIN (Deemed-to-be University), specializing in Marketing, International Business, and Entrepreneurship. Honored with the Best Faculty Award, he blends academic rigor with real-world relevance through case studies and interdisciplinary insights. His research focuses on ethics, mindset, and time mastery, empowering students through holistic mentoring. With expertise in faculty development, structured academic modules, and impactful communication, he actively contributes to scholarly initiatives. Passionate about innovation and sustainability, Dr. Chetan integrates AI tools to enhance pedagogy and professional growth, fostering a dynamic learning ecosystem that bridges theory with practice.

Index

A

C

E

R

S

T

www.ingramcontent.com/pod-product-compliance
Ingram Content Group UK Ltd.
Pitfield, Milton Keynes, MK11 3LW, UK
UKHW050843101026
15624UKWH00018B/482